Autism
from the
Teacher's Perspective
Strategies for Classroom Instruction

Kathleen M. McCoy
Arizona State University

LOVE PUBLISHING COMPANY®
Denver • London • Singapore

Published by Love Publishing Company
P.O. Box 22353
Denver, Colorado 80222
www.lovepublishing.com

Library of Congress Catalog Card Number 2010924005

Copyright © 2011 by Love Publishing Company
Printed in the United States of America
ISBN 978-0-89108-348-1

Contents

TABLES

FIGURES

Preface

Autism from the Teacher's Perspective is a text written by and for general education and special education teachers targeting all individuals who provide services to children and youth with autism. This book is an introductory text focusing on children and youth with autism. *Autism from the Teacher's Perspective* introduces teachers, parents, and other caregivers to easily understood concepts that help them improve their instructional skills and gain appreciation for the complexity of autism spectrum disorders (ASDs). The text provides information on the characteristics of the disorder, learning styles associated with the disorder, communication challenges, and various assessment and intervention strategies that have proven to be successful when working with students with ASDs.

Autism from the Teacher's Perspective provides practical evidence-based suggestions designed to cultivate the understanding necessary to implement intervention strategies that enhance communication, learning, and teaching. Through a reader friendly style filled with many real-life examples, this text demonstrates how to account for core traits of children with autism when adapting classroom strategies for academics and social behaviors. The scope of the material covers content from preschool to postsecondary transitions. Content also addresses how to make sense of some of the current "hot topics" associated with ASD, such as, Applied Behavior Analysis (ABA), Theory of Mind (TOM), weak central coherence, biomedical issues, special diets, chelation, and other interventions.

Autism from the Teacher's Perspective would be appropriate for any introductory course in autism at either the graduate or undergraduate level. This text would be fitting for general and special educators, speech and language personnel, social workers, nurses, educational psychologists, or any service provider for individuals who fall on the autism spectrum. The reader friendly style of the text also makes the material appropriate for parents and other family members who are interested in any information regarding individuals with autism.

The authors of the chapters in this book have had extensive education and direct experience working with individuals who fall on the autism spectrum. The material in this text is reality based, reflecting real experiences with individuals with autism. The educational strategies and practices emphasize practical and efficient guidelines for how to meet the diverse needs of individuals classified as autistic. The premise of this text is that service providers for individuals on the spectrum want to present the best possible interventions in light of the core characteristics associated with this condition. *Autism from the Teacher's Perspective* describes simple yet powerful instructional activities which accommodate the specific needs of individuals on the autism spectrum.

The organization of this book focuses on three basic concepts: (1) the nature, extent, and history of the field and related conceptual approaches; (2) assessment; and (3) specific social and academic interventions from early childhood through postsecondary life.

Part One introduces major conceptual and historical background for contemporary issues surrounding children and youth who are categorized as being on the autism spectrum. Chapter 1 orients the reader to basic demographic information, such as definitions, prevalence characteristics, and central trends. Chapter 2 focuses on the development of communication and language, stressing the importance of communication to the overall development of a child as well as its significance to family members. Chapter 3 creates a general understanding of the ASD social characteristics and provides a framework to increase social interaction by teaching pragmatic language skills during everyday activities.

Part Two addresses the procedures and challenges in assessing children and youth suspected of and identified as falling on the spectrum. Chapter 4 targets the process used to formally diagnose and identify ASD and includes a thorough model case study. Chapter 5 focuses on the educational assessment of the individual learner's specific needs and assets, and Chapter 6 translates those assessments into targeted educational and behavioral interventions. Chapter 7 covers the diagnostic issues involved in the intersection of giftedness and ASD and how the correct identification of these individuals enables professionals to address educational and emotional needs with more precision. Chapter 8 views the collaborative partnerships between parents and professionals in the diagnostic process and in creating a bridge between their child's specific learning needs at home, at school, and in the community.

Part Three provides descriptions of interventions for the very young child through adulthood. Chapter 9 addresses the Early Intensive Behavioral Intervention (EIBI) , an empirically supported treatment for individuals with ASDs based on the principles of ABA. The purpose of this chapter is to provide an overview of the essential features of an EIBI program, including basic characteristics, composition of the treatment team, methods of instruction, format of service delivery, and curriculum. Chapters 10, 11, and 12 present information related to reading, writing, and mathematics instruction, respectively, with a focus on the interrelationship between core characteristics of autism and instructional content. The text concludes, fittingly, with Chapter 13, describing effective strategies and techniques to help individuals with ASD transition to adulthood, including an overview of the fundamentals of transition planning and implementation for students with ASD.

ACKNOWLEDGMENTS

The editor wishes to acknowledge the contributions of several important individuals. Special thanks go to Carrie Watterson for countless hours of editing and of course to Stan Love, a publisher without parallel, who has always supported my writing projects. I am grateful to the authors of the chapters for their contributions and for their expertise in providing services to children and youth who fall on the autism spectrum. I also wish to acknowledge all the dedicated service providers, parents, and friends who offer love and support to individuals with autism.

MEET THE EDITOR

Kathleen M. McCoy, PhD, serves as the Program Coordinator of the Master of Education in Special Education Consultation and Collaboration: Autism Emphasis Program in the College of Teacher Education and Leadership at Arizona State University. In more than 30 years of her professional life, Dr. McCoy has worked as a general educator, a special educator for children with extreme language disorders, and a teacher educator. Dr. McCoy has taught courses related to children with learning disabilities, emotional disorders, and mental retardation as well as autism spectrum disorders. She advises doctoral students who have special interests in the area of autism and learning disabilities. Dr. McCoy has published numerous books, chapters, and articles about inclusion practices for children with disabilities, including her latest text, *Strategies for Teaching Students with Special Needs: Methods and Techniques for Classroom Instruction.* Dr. McCoy currently serves as a board member for the Children's Center for Neurological Development, a school designed to provide services to children with severe disabilities. She is also heading a Transition Task Force designed to identify postsecondary needs and services for individuals who fall on the spectrum.

MEET THE CONTRIBUTORS

Michele R. Bishop, PhD, BCBA-D, has worked in the field of behavior analysis and developmental disabilities for more than 10 years. She teaches graduate courses in behavioral intervention, behavioral assessment, and applied behavior analysis in inclusive settings. She is also a member of the research and development faculty at the Center for Autism and Related Disorders, Inc.

M. Diane Bruening, MA, MEd, has been a general and special educator for 35 years and has spent the past 15 years as a Special Education Director. She has attended many hundreds of IEP and 504 accommodation plan meetings and implemented plans and adaptations for students aged preschool through college. Her professional and scholarly interests in the past three years at Arizona State University have been in the field of autism, mentoring teachers in new programs for ASDs and providing staff development. Currently, Ms. Bruening sits on the Special Education Advisory Panel to the Arizona State Board of Education and is affifliated with Council for Exceptional Children and the Council for Adminstrators of Special Education both in Arizona and nationally. She is a faculty member for Arizona State University, Northern Arizona University, and the University of Phoenix in Special Education, teaching now about inclusion, strategies for student success in general education, and collaboration.

Angela Caruso, MEd, has taught students with autism for more than 12 years. She received her graduate level certification for autism at Arizona State University in addition to masters degrees in Special Education and Bilingual Education from Northern Arizona University and Arizona State University, respectively. Ms. Caruso is an adjunct faculty member for Arizona State University and has presented several papers focusing on transition from secondary to postsecondary life for individuals with autism.

Linda Caterino, PhD, ABPP, is a Clinical Associate Professor and Coordinator of Clinical Placements at Arizona State University in the Division of Advanced Studies in Learning, Technology, and Psychology in Education. She is also a licensed psychologist and has been in practice for more than 33 years, specializing in the evaluation and therapy of children and adolescents with special needs. She has written eight book chapters and more than 30 journal articles and has presented more than 80 papers at professional conventions. She has also served on the editorial boards of seven journals. Dr. Caterino is a Fellow of the American Academy of School Psychology and has served as President and Secretary of this association. She has also served as Vice President of Professional Affairs of Division 16 of the American Psychological Association.

Martha A. Cocchiarella, PhD, is a Clinical Assistant Professor in the College of Teacher Education and Leadership at Arizona State University. She teaches courses in instructional planning, classroom management, and inclusion. Her focus of expertise is disability studies, collaborative practices, inclusion, and parent involvement. She has participated in funded projects emphasizing mentorship for first-year special education teachers and the preparation of teachers to service children with autism. She has certification as a special and general education teacher.

Simon Crawford, MEd, has been working in the field of special education for the last 10 years. He is currently pursuing his doctoral degree in Special Education at the Arizona State University, and his research interest is the transition process as it relates to special education students. Mr. Crawford currently works at a private high school as a classroom instructor and transition specialist.

Cindy Lee Herrick, MA, is the founder of Cindy Lee Studios, LLC, a music studio in Scottsdale that works with both typical students and students on the autism spectrum. Ms. Herrick, also a concert pianist, completed her classical music studies at the Colburn School of Performing Arts in Los Angeles and at the University of Southern California and is a member of the Music Teachers' National Association and a certified Suzuki educator. Ms. Herrick has presented her research on the use of music to develop advanced socioemotional skills for students with AS and HFA at the TECBD Conference on Severe Behavior Disorders of Children and Youth. Her current research focuses on the development of a college transitional program for students with AS and HFA, and she is part of a transitional program task force at Arizona State University. She currently serves as a board member of KiDS WiTH AUTiSM CAN, a nonprofit organization focused on promoting independence and successful transition into adulthood for kids with autism. Ms. Herrick volunteers as the music educator at Ethos School, a nonprofit school for students with learning challenges such as ADHD and ASD.

Juliane Hillock, MA, is a special education teacher for Mesa Public Schools in Mesa, AZ. She started a program for students with HFA or AS for the district at the elementary level. The program has now been established at the junior high level as well. Ms. Hillock has taught students with autism in the early intervention, elementary, and secondary levels. She is a regular contributor to the TECBD Conference as well as local workshops and enjoys assisting both aspiring and established teachers working with students with autism.

Amy L. Kenzer, PhD, BCBA-D, has worked in the field of behavior analysis and developmental disabilities for more than 10 years. She teaches graduate courses in behavioral assessment, principles and ethics of behavior analysis, and single-subject research design. She is also a member of the research and development faculty at the Center for Autism and Related Disorders, Inc.

Melanie Kelley, MEd, has worked with individuals with disabilities in both residential and classroom settings for nearly 20 years. Her area of focus has included teaching students with severe disabilities as well as students on the autism spectrum at the secondary level. She has presented on decreasing behavior by teaching social skills and communication at national conferences. Ms. Kelley is currently a content specialist in Mesa, AZ.

Jennifer Laurence, MEd, is a cross-categorical special education teacher in Tempe, AZ. She has 25 years of experience working with students with special needs in a variety of capacities, the last 13 being at Tempe High School. With the influx of students with ASD (HFA in her program), her areas of interest are in developing social skills and incorporating assistive technology to fully optimize each student's potential. She provides workshops and trainings to school staff, other teachers, and service providers. In addition to providing training at the local level, she has also presented nationally at Special Education and Autism conferences.

Joseph M. Mahoney, MA, is a doctoral student in the school psychology training program at Arizona State University. He has several years of work experience conducting behavioral interventions with school-age children, including students with autism and other developmental disabilities. Mr. Mahoney has conducted functional behavioral assessment in the school setting, trained students in adaptive behaviors and coping skills, and collaborated with school personnel on behalf of students with special needs.

Tiffany O'Neill, MEd in Cross-Categorical Special Education, is working on her PhD in Curriculum and Instruction. Ms. O'Neill has taught a variety of diverse learners, including students with learning disabilities, students with AS, gifted students, and twice exceptional students. She is the Gifted and Talented Education (GATE) coordinator for a high school district in Casa Grande, AZ. She sits on the boards of the Arizona Association for the Gifted and Talented and Arizona Future Problem Solving, Inc.

Catherine C. Orsak, MS, CCC-SLP, is a speech–language pathologist specializing in autism and related developmental disorders. Ms. Orsak's focus is on functional communication training and the implementation of augmentative and alternative communication systems in the educational setting. She provides direct educational and communication services to clients as well as ongoing consultation to educational programs serving individuals with ASD.

Renee Wozniak, MEd, has been teaching for more than 10 years in both special and general education and currently serves as a member of her school district's autism training team. She has also provided habilitation and respite services to children with autism for more than 12 years. Ms. Wozniak completed the Autism Certification Program through Arizona State University and is currently pursuing her PhD in Curriculum and Instruction for Special Education, as well as her BCBA certification. Her research interests include best practices for assisting parents and teachers in effectively working with children with autism.

PART ONE

Conceptual and Historical Background

Introduction to Autism

Kathleen M. McCoy

What condition, which is increasing exponentially, can have no known cause and no specific cure and yet receive banner headlines in newspapers, is featured in scientific journals as well as talk shows, and has over 18,300,000 references on Google? The answer to that question is the elusive condition known as autism, the fastest growing developmental disability in the United States.

DEFINITION

What is autism? Autism is a strange and increasingly more commonly diagnosed developmental condition that is one of a group of neurological disorders that compose the autism spectrum disorder. Autism can begin at birth or shortly after. Autism, however, is mysterious in that 20–30% children who appeared to be developing normal language, emotional responses and motor skills, lose these abilities somewhere between the ages of 18–36 months and are subsequently diagnosed as autistic.

Congenital and regressive autism

These two distinct courses are called *congenital autism* and *regressive autism* (Goin-Kochel & Myers, 2005). Children with congenital autism usually show developmental delays and abnormal behaviors from the beginning of life. Children with regressive autism appear to develop normally and then begin to lose previously acquired skills and no longer progress at their former rate. Regressive autism is found in children diagnosed with other developmental disorders (Molloy, Morrow, Meinzen-Derr, Dawson, et al., 2006).

Not all children fit easily into the congenital or regressive categories. Gino was not the classic case of autism. Although Gino exhibited numerous characteristics of autism, he was not officially diagnosed until he was 5 years old. Molly and her husband simply thought that they were dealing with a misbehaving child. Gino would often cry for hours on end and throw temper tantrums incessantly throughout the day to get the items that he sought. Gino would bite and kick when he did not get his way. He preferred sitting by himself playing with objects in the backyard rather than socially interacting with his family.

Gino's behavior in public was embarrassing, but that did not stop the family from being active in their community. Their trips to the mall often ended in a feeling of inadequacy and hopelessness. They received many disapproving looks from others who were surely questioning whether they were fit parents. Molly knew Gino did not follow the same developmental stages as her first son or show any interest in social interaction, but she figured that maybe Gino was just a late bloomer. When it became apparent that he was not learning to talk by the age of 4, Molly knew that she needed to seek help.

The terms congenital and regressive autism are not officially considered a part of a diagnosis because criteria from the *Diagnostic and Statistical Manual of Mental Disorders* (American Psychiatric Association [APA], 2000) only stipulates that the behaviors associated with ASD are present before age 3. In addition definitions of regression are not clear; that is, regression can entail deterioration and loss of language, loss of nonverbal actions children exhibit when they are interacting with others in social situations, or both (Goldberg et al.,2003).

PUZZLING BEHAVIORS

Most children seek nurturance from their parents and significant others. They want to interact. At a very young age they make eye contact, return smiles, and attempt to engage others. For many children with autism, these commonly expected behaviors do not appear. Some children with autism will become rigid when held and spend more time appearing to enjoy the sight of a whirling fan than the faces of their parents. Interaction seems minimal at best and at worse missing altogether. These behaviors are confusing to caregivers who often cannot understand why the child is not more responsive.

Peculiar interactions

Autism affects an individual's ability to communicate and interact with others in an expected manner. Many individuals with autism engage in puzzling behaviors, such as, suddenly becoming withdrawn or aggressive or losing language skills they have already acquired. Characteristic behaviors associated with autism are dysfunctional social interaction; verbal and nonverbal communication problems; and odd, repetitive, or severely restricted activities and interests. Because autism is on a spectrum, all or any of these traits can appear in varying degrees. Autism is a syndrome that manifests itself with a multitude of other conditions. Because autism is unique to the individual, a classroom teacher must create lessons that address the particular needs of each learner. In one class alone, a teacher could be designing similar lessons around specific themes for specific students, with each lesson tailored to the specific needs of each individual with autism.

Ms. Ventura designs lessons around her students' interests. Currently, many of her lessons with Marty have cowboys incorporated into them; her lessons with Steve and Lester have Star Wars included in them. Romero likes anything Disney, and Spenser loves learning if holidays are involved. Ms. Ventura almost never does the same lesson with one child that she does with another. However, Ms. Ventura often has to do the same lesson with the same child several times. She, along with other special education teachers, really do create "special" lessons for their students because she would not be able to reach her students if their interests were not incorporated. Adding to the special nature of lessons is that individuals with autism often demonstrate differential response to interventions. Anthony might learn very well when working on a computer, but if Bob were placed in front of a monitor, his mind would be as blank as the screen he would never turn on.

Sensory abnormalities

An additional common theme found in many of the current theories of autism suggests that sensory abnormalities are also core symptoms of autism (Happe´, 2005; Mottron & Burack, 2001). For example, some children and adults with autism can become easily distressed or preoccupied by harmless sights, sounds, odors, and textures and yet will not respond to more significant sensations such as the sound of their name (Talay-Ongan & Wood, 2000). Jackie demonstrates many of the traits associated with sensory abnormalities. Jackie is resistant to touch at times. He flaps his hands and has poor eye contact. His parents have spent a lot of money capping his teeth because he grinds his teeth so much. Jackie is very sensitive to noise and often covers up his ears when the sounds get too noisy. Jackie has developed a rather odd mouthing problem this year. He obsessively rolls his tongue around in his mouth from side to side, then he rolls it with his right hand around and around repetitively. Jackie has always been orally defensive and only eats soft textured foods. Abnormal sensory perceptual behaviors like Jackie's are often lifelong; vary from individual to individual; occur in the absence of visual, hearing or physical problems; and are found in approximately 30–100% of individuals with autism (Dawson & Watling, 2000).

CORE DEFICITS

Just as with typically developing children, each individual with autism will demonstrate a unique pattern of behavior, but also like typically developing children certain characteristics signal the condition. Within the wide range of effects autism is a syndrome characterized by three core deficits: disorders in social behavior, abnormal verbal and nonverbal communication, and limited interests. In addition repetitive behaviors are often considered another aspect of this syndrome.

Disorders in social behavior

Social behavior skills allow us to develop sensitivity to others and demonstrate appropriate responses to social situations. Disorders resulting in poor social skills can result in failure to make or keep friends, a lack of rapport with others, inappropriate conversations, and other behaviors which negatively impact daily living. Many individuals with autism exhibit poor social skills.

Social skill deficits

Humans by their very nature are social. For many individuals with autism, however, the awareness of intentions, desires, and beliefs of others that make human behavior predictable and comprehensible seem to be limited or lacking. Inferences and awareness of the feelings and thinking of others remain a mystery to many children found on the ASD, for others emotions simply do not appear to hold any meaning. Bernie is 4 years old and has autism. Bernie rarely speaks and even less frequently makes eye contact. Bernie makes lots of grunting gestures when he wants something, but even when Bernie was a baby he did not smile or try to grab his parents' faces when they would lean over and look at him. From a parent's perspective, Bernie was a great baby. He rarely made any noises with the exception of letting them know he was hungry or needed a diaper change.

Extensive testing suggests that individuals with social skill deficits do not understand the mental states of others. They experience difficulty processing emotion, including understanding the meaning of gestures and body language. Many individuals with social skill disorders have problems with imitation. Unlike normal babies who imitate their parents' smiles, children like Bernie are often nonresponsive to facial expressions and body language. They do not seem able to imitate or mimic people around them.

Individuals with autism are suspected of not being able to organize or integrate large bodies of information. These individuals, however, can show excellent performance on tasks that require perception of details and form because these low level tasks require no integration (Hamilton, 2008). Jose, for example, may process faces as collections of individual features rather than as unifying gestalts. Jose may not be able to recognize faces of people he commonly meets because he can only focus on the unconnected features.

A commonly held myth is that all individuals with autism are not affectionate. Not all children with autism withhold affection. Five-year-old Walter is affectionate with others. He will accept hugs and kisses from adults and babies, but children his own age seem to be invisible to him. Walter will ignore them and act as if they are not around. Walter has a hard time expressing emotion appropriately. He does not seem to know how to relate to those he loves. Walter, for example, is fascinated with dogs, but he will always hit them when they are near because he does not know how to express himself appropriately.

Abnormal verbal and nonverbal communication

The term language to most suggests the ability to talk with others to exchange ideas. Some are surprised to learn that language is more than words spoken aloud. Language also includes information provided through facial expressions, postures, and intonation patterns suggesting various states of emotion. Laughing, for example, depending on the tone, can convey joy or pleasure, but when paired with sarcasm can indicate a darker mood. Many individuals with autism do not use or recognize unspoken conventions of language. Some individuals with autism will display inappropriate or abnormal use of verbal, nonverbal or both aspects of language.

Language issues

Peculiar language or lack of language and strange intonation patterns are often found in individuals with autism. The timing and rhythm used by Jorge, for example, sound a lot like those of a robot. The rhythm of his speech and the tone of his voice simply do not hold the same kind of communicative intent as typical language expression. Other individuals may express themselves in inappropriately high-pitched tones. Syed, although 16 years old, speaks in a falsetto tone, reminiscent of a female cartoon character.

Language may often be limited to the literal level for many children with autism. To a greater or lesser degree many individuals with autism will have extreme difficulty with metaphors, irony, and jokes. Ghows was totally confused when his teacher called him a sharp cookie. He couldn't understand why she would say he was a cookie when he was really a boy.

Theory of mind

Social deficits seem to be correlated with damage to specific parts of the brain or networks of brain regions. The most prominent theoretical model for some of these communication and social skill deficits is called Theory of Mind (TOM; Baron-Cohen, Leslie, & Frith, 1985; Frith & Frith, 2003). TOM suggests an imbalance in higher level processing in the brain, which can result in a broad and wide-ranging assortment of impairments often associated with individuals with autism. Essentially TOM is a person's ability to relate to the verbal and nonverbal communication of others. Many individuals with autism have problems relating to the thoughts, feelings, and concepts of verbal and nonverbal language communicated by others. Issues with verbal and nonverbal behavior have been linked theoretically to TOM. The TOM brain network, for example, may be responsible for controlling mimicry or the ability to imitate (Brass, Derrfuss, & von Cramon, 2005). The ability to mimic is a double edged sword. Appropriate imitation can be seen as a sincere form of flattery, which can create positive bonds between individuals (Lakin & Chartrand,

2003). Excessive imitation, however, can be interpreted as ridicule. Amir possesses many language skills. He is a verbal child and engages in spontaneous speech, not just parroting. Amir has a problem developing good social skills because he habitually mimics what others say. He will often imitate what other people say and even repeat them in the person's exact voice.

Several theories have suggested that the ability to imitate is altered for children with autism. For some children with autism mimicry is excessive, as with echolalia, a parrot-like response to words. For other children or in other situations an atypical TOM brain network could result in an inability to imitate at all.

Limited interests

Many individuals with autism have been described as having intense, but limited, interests. Interests vary from person to person. Andre was fascinated with watching *Baby Einstein*. He would cry and become extremely upset if *Baby Einstein* was not on the television. Ken was obsessed with swinging the doors of the cabinets in the kitchen back and forth over and over again. Limited interests can take many forms and a person can have more than one interest. The interest could be so intense that a person could block out any unrelated or competing learning situations.

Victor at 9 years of age, for example, could recite the entire sports almanac. If asked which teams played in the Rose Bowl in 1989, 1979, and so forth, Victor would give the correct answer with 100% accuracy. However, Victor could not repeat his address or any other personal information such as phone number, date of birth, parents' names, and the like. Victor's interest in life was limited to sports, specifically Rose Bowl games. His personal information was not in the realm of the Rose Bowl, and thus not in the realm of Victor's interests.

To help Victor learn his address and other individual facts about his life, his teacher, Mr. Davis, created a book of personal information for Victor and put logos of sports teams on the pages, one date and team for each piece of personal information. By the end of the semester Victor was able to recite his address, phone number, and parents' names. By age 14, Victor had shifted from sports to Humphrey Bogart movies. New information now was paired with information about Humphrey Bogart.

Autism is complex in that the core conditions can emerge at different developmental stages. The core symptoms usually change over time and in different degrees, i.e., core social and cognitive deficits are not absolute (Levitt & Campbell, 2009).

Repetitive behaviors

Many individuals with autism will compulsively repeat behaviors such as hand flapping, lining up toys, counting, tapping, flicking, or repeatedly restating information, or display a preoccupation with household items, or a rigid adherence to routine and a marked resistance to change (Carcani-Rathwell, Rabe-Hasketh, & Santosh, 2006; Kanner 1943). To the onlooker these types of repetitions appear to have no real purpose. The behaviors that are repeated are unique to the individual. Some behaviors are obvious, although others are much more subtle and hardly noticeable. The repetitive behaviors, which interfere with everyday functioning, almost take on a ritualistic appearance and are thought to be compulsions used to relieve anxiety.

Peter was different from other babies. He loved to watch toys spinning for hours and hours. He would lie in bed and watch the toy mobile overhead without making a sound as long as the mobile kept spinning. Peter was absolutely fascinated with spinning objects, the tops of pots and pans, balls, and the like. Peter would focus on the spinning of tops. After getting the tops to spin as quickly as possible, Peter would put his face close to the top and stare until the spinning ended. Peter rarely blinked as he concentrated on the top. As Peter got older his top spinning repertoire expanded to the point where he could spin objects himself. At one point he was so good at spinning objects that he could spin up to 20 tops at the same time and keep them centered on the coffee table in the living room.

IMPLICATIONS OF THE TERM SPECTRUM

As the term spectrum would imply, severity and symptoms vary a great deal from person to person. Autism is the most well known member of Pervasive Developmental Disorders (PDDs), a group of neurological developmental conditions involving delays or impairments in communication and social skills. PDDs are also known as autism spectrum disorders (ASDs). Autism, as a member of the ASD, implies a continuum of behaviors that can range from profound to almost negligible involvement. Adam is nonverbal and appears to be severely mentally retarded. He spends his time rocking back and forth and will never engage in any social activity. He does not appear to be cognizant of the world around him. Individuals, like Adam, found at the lower functioning end of the spectrum appear to be living in a private world without the ability to receive or express ideas to others and are profoundly lacking in interpersonal skills. Individuals found at the low end of the spectrum are sometimes diagnosed with *Kanner's autism* or *classic autism.*

At the other end of the spectrum is Randy, who is captain of the debate team. Randy is a straight-A student but has very little patience with his team members. He gets visibly upset with them when they do not follow directions or make mistakes. He sometimes seems very sarcastic and often hurts the feelings of others. Randy is similar to many individuals found at the upper end of the spectrum. Such individuals are often labeled *High Functioning Autistic* (HFA) or as having *Asperger Syndrome* (AS).

Many individuals at the higher functioning end of the spectrum may be able to lead independent lives but still be out of their depth in social interactions. Lucas, for example, appears to understand what is asked of him or what he is told to do. The hard part for Lucas is to initiate these actions. Lucas also seems to have no desire for social interaction. When kids say hi to Lucas at school he does not even respond. Usually the teacher or paraeducator must prompt Lucas to respond to his peer. Even within more refined categories such as AS, a wide spectrum can be found. Lucas and Randy, both categorized as AS, have very different skills and need very different types of interventions.

Individuals with AS can lead relatively normal lives in a variety of professions. Just a few examples of people with autism who are independent and leading successful lives are:

➤ Christopher Knowles, American poet
➤ Richard Borcherds, mathematician specializing in group theory and Lie algebras
➤ Gary Numan, British singer and songwriter
➤ Dawn Prince-Hughes, PhD, primate anthropologist, ethologist, and author of *Songs for the Gorilla Nation*
➤ Temple Grandin, PhD, a designer of humane food animal handling systems
➤ John Elder Robison, author of *Look Me in the Eye*

Other, less common ASDs include *Rett Syndrome* (RS), which is most often found in females, and *Childhood Disintegrative Disorder* (CDD), which primarily is found in males. In both cases, a period of normal development precedes the onset of autistic symptoms. Pervasive Developmental Disorder–Not Otherwise Specified (PDD–NOS) may be diagnosed when an individual has autistic symptoms but does not fit into any other ASD diagnosis (Mauro, n.d.).

DIAGNOSIS

To recognize the signs or characteristics of conditions which fall on the autism spectrum has been a major goal of psychologists and educators. To provide a definitive explanation for autism has yet to be determined.

Factors to consider

Diagnosis of autism is no simple matter. Children as young as 24 months can be diagnosed accurately with autism, but inadequate screening practices, slow or no response to parental concerns, and lack of knowledge of early symptoms delays identification, with subsequent ramifications for intervention (Lord, Risi, DiLavore, Shulman, Thurm, & Pickles, 2006; Mandell, Novak, Zubritsky, 2005: Wiggins, Baio, Rice, 2006; Yeargin-Allsopp et al., 2003). Barney, for example, is 39 months old and received his diagnosis at 26 months. Had Barney not been a first child, he might have received an even earlier diagnosis. In retrospect Barney's parents believed that he had symptoms of autism since birth.

Barney was never a particularly "interesting" baby, requiring extra work to get to smile or giggle, and as he reached the age that he played with toys, he tended to sit among his toys and organize them rather than play with them. Because Barney was a first child, his parents assumed he was simply "different." Barney also appeared slow in mental development. Intellectual disability, measured as an intellectual quotient of 70 or less, occurs in approximately 50% to 60% of children with severe symptoms and can result in a primary diagnosis of developmental delay or mental retardation rather than autism (Fombonne, 2008).

Coexisting Conditions

Pinpointing who is autistic is elusive because of the coexistence of so many other conditions within and across individuals. Children with autism seem to have a greater probability for certain coexisting conditions, including fragile X syndrome (a cause of mental retardation), tuberous sclerosis (a condition in which tumors develop on the brain), epileptic seizures, Tourette syndrome, learning disabilities, and attention deficit disorder (ADD) (Hatton et al., 2002). John, who is 15 years old, has only recently been diagnosed with AS. At age 6, John was diagnosed by a pediatric neurologist with Tourette syndrome. At age 13, John's mother took him to see an occupational therapist who identified problems which assisted his neurologist in changing the diagnosis.

For unknown reasons, about 20% to 30% of children with autism develop epilepsy by adulthood (National Institute of Neurological Disorders and Stroke [NINDS], 2009). In addition, ASDs are often mistaken or hidden by other disorders, such as hyperactivity and behavioral problems, which can lead to a diagnosis of ADD instead of autism (Goldstein & Schwebach, 2004). Repetitive inappropriate behaviors and resistance to change may lead to a label of Oppositional Defiant Behaviors and Obsessive Compulsive Behaviors (OCD) (Remington, Sloman, Konstantareas, Parker, & Gow, 2001). For example, Sanford will perseverate on paper items. He focuses on stamps from different places, and he knows every stamp that he has and does not want a duplicate. If Sanford cannot get a new stamp, he will ask for a different stamp over and over again, and he will flap his hands in frustration. At school Sanford will perseverate on a question if he is not given a definitive answer. Sanford does not want to hear, "I don't know" or "maybe." He wants an answer. The answer does not need to be true but needs to be definite, or he will obsess over the question.

Medical conditions like sleep problems and gastrointestinal symptoms as well as psychiatric disturbances like anxiety and aggression are frequent and may emerge at different ages in children on the spectrum. Bedtime is problematic for Timmy. Timmy is very opposed to going to sleep. Even with a strict routine in place, sometimes a great deal of screaming and crying occur before Timmy will fall asleep. Timmy has difficulty in getting to sleep and wakes up very early in the morning. Very often Timmy wakes up four and five times during the night.

Sharing the ASD

In addition, other similar disorders which also fall on the ASD are grouped under the umbrella term Pervasive Developmental Disorder (PDD). PDD describes neurological developmental disorders that impact communication and social skills. Children with less severe social and behavioral problems may be diagnosed with AS, PDD, CDD, or PDD–NOS. Descriptions of the four conditions found under ASD are presented in Table 1.1.

RS is sometimes included as part of the ASD. Between the ages of 1 and 4, typical children begin to lose skills, for example, repetitive hand movements supplant fine motor hand skills. Other symptoms include slowed growth in brain and head, walking difficulties, seizures, problems in language and poor eye contact. RS, a progressive brain condition, occurs almost exclusively in girls.

INCREASING PREVALENCE OF AUTISM

Factors related to diagnosis

In the not so distant past, autism was considered to be a very rare condition. Times have changed along with perceptions and prevalence estimates. In spite of the myriad of issues surrounding the diagnosis of autism, the numbers continue to grow. Although autism is reported to be on the rise worldwide, controversy surrounds the statistics about the number of individuals who are considered autistic. Prevalence numbers vary, in part due to inclusion of the types of disorders allowed on the ASD; changes in diagnostic criteria; a broadening coexistence of other conditions with autism; and difficulty evaluating infants, toddlers, and very young children.

TABLE 1.1

Descriptions of Four Conditions found on the ASD

➤ **Autistic disorder (autism):** Classical autism sometimes known as Kanner's syndrome. A form of pervasive developmental disorder with an unknown cause which ranges from high functioning to severe in nature, manifested in communication, social interaction, and routine/repetitive behaviors.

➤ **Asperger Syndrome:** Severe and sustained problems with social skills, repetitive behaviors, and restricted interests and activities. Language skills tend to be good, although social communication may be affected.

➤ **Childhood disintegrative disorder:** A rare condition that occurs without a known medical cause which typically emerges after 2 years of normal social development, resulting in severe loss in language, social skills, or motor skills. Severe mental retardation is also a prognosis.

➤ **Pervasive developmental disorder – not otherwise specified (PDD-NOS):** An overall delay in development of communication and social skills that does not fit into another category and does not have a known cause.

Gender difference

Prevalence estimates vary from 3 to 6 children out of every 1,000 to 1% of the total population of children (Baird et al., 2006). The rates of autism and ASD have increased alarmingly in the U.S., tenfold, from fewer than 3 per 10,000 children in the 1970s to more that 30 per 10,000 children in the 1990s. Reported rates for the full spectrum of autistic disorders rose from the 5 to 10 per 10,000 range to the 50 to 80 per 10,000 range (Blaxill, 2004). When all neurodevelopmental conditions are counted, the most commonly quoted prevalence rate is 1 of every 150 individuals, with males being four times more likely than females to be diagnosed (Levitt & Campbell, 2009). The rising incidence of autism has become a topic of urgent public concern.

Race and ethnicity

Not only gender, but race and ethnicity also seem to be factors in determining the prevalence of autism. Until the last few years, research results were mixed. For example, black children were identified later in life (Mandell, Listerud, Levy, & Pinto-Martin, 2002), with a more likely misdiagnosis of conduct or adjustment disorder (Mandell, Ittenbach, Levy, & Pinto-Martin, 2007), than white children, but other studies found no such differences (Mandell, Novak, & Zubritsky, 2005).

In 2009, a study conducted over a multisite network identified 2,568 children aged 8 years who met criteria for ASD. The Centers for Disease Control and Prevention (CDC) sponsored Autism and Developmental Disabilities Monitoring (ADDM) network, which consists of multiple sites throughout the United States, collected population-based data on children who are at risk for ASD. Children who were black, Hispanic, or of other race or ethnicity were less likely than white children to have a documented ASD. This disproportion continued for black children, regardless of IQ, and when IQ was less than 70, the inequity was also found for children of other ethnicities (Mandell et al., 2009). Ethnic and racial disparities in diagnosis do seem to be real, but the reasons can only be speculative at this time. The relationship between autism and race is unconfirmed, conflicting, and, for the most part, missing (Dyches, Wilder, Sudweeks, Obiakor, & Algozzine, 2004).

Recent autism prevalence demands that health, education, and social care services recognize the needs of children who have some form of ASD. Programs must also be designed to target all ethnicities and races in order to provide better access to referrals, screenings, and education about milestones in development and ASD.

COMPLEXITY OF CAUSATION

Although the search for the cause of autism is a major goal, the reason or reasons remain obscure. Many theories abound, but the nature and complexity of the condition makes identification excruciatingly difficult. More than likely ASD will not have a single underlying cause.

The majority of research findings are correlational at best; that is, a relationship seems to exist, but not one that can be declared the reason for the development of autism. At this time, causation theories are polarized around three hypotheses: nature, nurture, or some combination of the two. Genetics and related stressors provide one major area of research for causation; however, the latest research is beginning to find that nutritional and environmental factors may also be major contributors to the development of autism (Curtis, & Patel, 2007).

Inheriting Autism

Unless a person has an identical twin, genes are unique. Both parents contribute half of the genes; each parent in turn received his or her genes from his or her parents, and so on, all the way back to a person's earliest ancestors. Inherited traits like eye color or height do not always appear in an obvious manner. Some traits may seem to skip a generation or affect only the females in a family. Common illnesses like asthma, diabetes, and heart disease, are partly influenced by genes and can be found in families. Some individuals inherit genetic conditions that may affect their mental or physical health. Debate surrounds the issue of whether or how genes influence the condition of autism.

Nature and genes

The nature camp is focused on the question, "Can autism be inherited?" At this time developing ASD appears to be decidedly heritable with certain types of gene mutations, that is, disruptions to the basic unit of heredity in human beings. (Abrahams & Geschwind, 2008; Veenstra-Vanderweele, Christian, & Cook, 2004). Researchers have identified genes that seem to be related to autism but do not cause the condition. Depending on the available research, the number of genes appears to vary from a few to over 100. Some genes may create a susceptibility to autism but not result in autism. Other genes may directly affect brain development. Based on the area of the brain affected different types of behaviors may occur, but all involvement of the brain, including the degree of severity, would also affect communication and language in some way.

Another consideration is whether multiple minor genetic abnormalities can have the same effect on the development of the neurological system as one or more major genetic abnormalities. Because ASD is a spectrum of disabilities that includes cooccurring physical conditions and mental health issues, many different kinds of autism have been recognized (Geschwind, & Levitt, 2007). The heterogeneity of ASD suggests that different genetic mechanisms may influence brain development in a variety of ways and at different levels of complexity (Hammock, & Levitt, 2006). Genetic research is therefore moving away from seeking a single cause related to a single behavioral dysfunction within specific populations. Instead genetic research is suggesting that no gene or genes directly regulate language or social behavior, but rather genes may be susceptible to disruption related to the formation and stabilization of synapses, those critical connections linking signals from one nerve cell to another (Levitt & Campbell, 2009).

Family studies

The credibility of the influence of genes as a contributing factor in ASD is found in studies of families. Typically traits of autism or conditions found on the ASD can be found in one or more family members. Correlational evidence that genes play a role is strong for many families. Support is mixed. Some studies show a higher rate of autism among identical than fraternal twins, and a higher rate among siblings than in the general population (Trottier, Srivastava, & Walker, 1999). Some cases, on the other hand, show one identical twin with autism and the other unaffected (Steffenburg, Gillberg, Hellgren, Jakobsson, & Bohman, 1989).

Observations, however, of family members showing subtle autism-like behaviors, such as peculiar communication styles and aloof personality traits suggest that the presence of some of the milder traits reflect genetic factors contributing to the development of autism (Murphy et al., 2000). Austin's family presents such a case. Austin, an eight year old, has been classified as high functioning and autistic. No other members of his family have been categorized as autistic. Mary, his mother, is a high strung overly organized mom of five children. Mary makes endless lists of what should be accomplished during the day and becomes very anxious when that list is not completed. Mary has facial tics when she is under undue stress. Mary has no classification other than soccer mom.

Just when the Nature Camp seems to be a comfortable area for explaining autism, results of other studies of families demonstrate absolutely no correlations. No other immediate or past generational members of the families have been identified with autism or autistic like behaviors. In some cases, genetic abnormalities appear to occur spontaneously. Even though proof of genetic causes is convincing, especially when considering research related to identical twins, evidence suggests that at least 40% of cases of autism probably have an environmental cause (Hertz-Picciotto et al., 2006).

Nurture and stressors

Enter the nurture or environmental causation theories. In the 1990s, collected databases revealed evidence of many risk factors for developing autism at the pre- and perinatal stages, that is, during gestation and the period immediately before and after birth. Drugs, such as thalidomide and cocaine, taken by mothers during the prenatal stage have been suggested as contributing factors to development of autism. Table 1.2 summarizes these risk factors.

Stressors include maternal smoking in early pregnancy as well as small size for gestational age, congenital malformations, and cesarean delivery. Prenatal stressors, such as problems during labor and delivery; damage to the amygdala, a portion of the brain that involves response to stress, fear, and social interactions; and the role of the immune system may play a role in causing autism (Beversdorf et al., 2005). The causation waters are muddied, however, because researchers cannot determine whether perinatal and prenatal stress is an independent risk factor or if perinatal or prenatal stress only affects the development of autism for those

TABLE 1.2

Possible Triggers of Autism

Perinatal Risk factors (Hultman, Sparen, & Cnattingius, 2002)	Prenatal Risk Factors
Maternal cigarette smoking in early pregnancy	Exposure to drugs, (e.g.,Thalidomide, Valproate, Cocaine) (Newschaffer et al., 2007; Stronland, Nordin, Miller, Akerstro, & Gillberg, 1994)
Small for gestational age	Stress during birth (e.g., face or foot presentation, asphyxia) (Beversdorf et al., 2008)
Congenital malformations	Season of birth (Lee et al., 2008)
Cesarean delivery	Maternal psychological stress during pregnancy (Claassen, Naude, Pretorius, & Bosman, 2008)
5-minute APGAR score below 7	

genetically at risk. The chicken or the egg dilemma applies to the nature or nurture issues related to autism.

CHARGE

The Childhood Autism Risk from Genetics and the Environment (CHARGE) Study, was funded in 2001 and began seeing participants around early 2003. It is addressing a wide spectrum of environmental exposures, factors rising from within the body, and the interaction between the two (CHARGE, 2006). The CHARGE study appears to be the first large-scale, population-based epidemiologic investigation focusing primarily on environmental exposures as well as their interactions with genes as underlying causes for autism. Preliminary results appear promising.

In an early study, CHARGE researchers discovered that the immune system of many children with autism was not the same as that of similar children without autism. Toxins, for example, might affect the child's immune system differently. Larry and Wendy, for example, both fall on the ASD. Larry becomes extremely agitated whenever he is in a room that has been cleaned with bleach or plays with toys that have been cleaned with bleach. Wendy, on the other hand, shows no stresses with bleach cleaned rooms or objects but will break out in hives and complain of stomach aches whenever she encounters aerosols used to cover normal household odors. At this time, the significance of the differences in the immune system is not known. Once again, however, caution must be taken with this finding. Is the difference in the immune system part of the cause or part of the effect of autism? Chicken or egg?

Hidden stressors

Clearly high levels of pollutants like those found in industrially contaminated ground water have been shown to have serious side effects, but other more hidden toxins may also put some children at risk for developing autism. One of the most ubiquitous and seemingly benign practices is found in putting flame retardants on furniture and clothing. An unexpected consequence may be the effect the chemicals have on the susceptibility of some individuals to develop autism or other central nervous system disorders. Pesticides, used in minute quantities, cause damage to the central nervous system of insects but could a cumulative effect of such small amounts coupled with genetic predisposition also contribute to developing autism in humans? No answer is yet forthcoming.

Many questions are yet to be explored including the identification of critical developmental periods when a stressor would or would not contribute to development of autism and what differences in tolerance levels exist at what times in an individual's development. When does the outside stressor or environmental influence reach a point when the individual can no longer adapt in a normal fashion? What is the level of interaction between the genetic makeup and environment, and why are some individuals more susceptible to stressors than others?

Viral infections and Thimerosal

Exploration of the role of environmental pollutants and viral infections, such as intrauterine rubella, have been investigated as possible triggers of autism (Burd, Severud, Kerbeshian, & Klug, 1999; Chess, 1971). One of the greatest controversies, some would say scandals, in autism centers on whether a link exists between autism and childhood vaccines which utilize Thimerosal.

Thimerosal is preservative containing mercury, which can eliminate or retard bacterial contamination. The practice of using Thimerosal was unquestioned until the 1970s, when public awareness was raised about the tragic effect upon human development of exposure to large amounts of methylmercury found in fish and industrial pollution. As a precaution, Thimerosal, which contained ethylmercury, a compound related to methylmercury, was reviewed and in 1976 was determined to be safe when used with vaccines.

Faulty logic

For about 20 years all was quiet on the Thimerosal front until two longitudinal studies evaluating the effect of diets composed of large quantities of fish on two island populations produced conflicting results. One suggested that low maternal methylmercury exposures could be dangerous to the fetus, and the other found no adverse effects (Baker, 2008). Never mind that ethylmercury in Thimerosal is very different than methylmercury; the names sound similar and public suspicion grew. Faulty logic created the belief that if the chemical names sound similar then their effects must also be similar. Once again, all food and drugs containing mercury were determined fit for human consumption (Ball, Ball, & Pratt, 2001), but just to be on the safe side of public opinion, the removal of any vaccines containing Thimerosal was recommended. By 2009 only the vaccine for diphtheria, tetanus, and pertussis (whooping cough) (DTaP) and three vaccines for the flu contain trace amounts of Thimerosal (CDC, 2008).

DTaP vaccines are routinely given to children. DTaP vaccines are typically scheduled at 2, 4, 6, and 15–18 months, and 4–6 years, and as fate would have it, one of the scheduled boosters occurs between 15–36 months, the same age at which regressive autism makes an entrance. Yet again, based on inferential and faulty logic, Thimerosal as found in the DTaP vaccine was labeled the causative agent for regressive autism. Even though no link has been found between autism and DTaP, old beliefs die hard, and regrettably some parents are no longer allowing their children to be inoculated against these highly contagious diseases (Weber, 2008).

NIDS

A relative newcomer to the causation field of autism is neuro-immune dysfunction syndromes (NIDS). NIDS raises the possibility that autoimmunity may be at the heart of many conditions currently found under ASD. Several studies have found an increased frequency of autoantibodies to the central nervous system for children with early onset autism when compared to children with regressive autism (Ashwood, Kwong, Hansen, Hertz-Picciotto, et al., 2008). More research is needed before legitimate conclusions can be drawn.

Autoimmunity and abnormal language and social development have been linked by several studies. Families with children with autism also appear to have a history of autoimmune disorders. Thus, problems with familial autoimmunity seem to be a significant risk factor (Molloy et al., 2006; Sweeten, Bowyer, Posey, Halberstadt, & McDougle, 2003). A group composed of researchers and parents has formed an institute to study NIDS. A primary goal of the NIDS Research Institute is to increase public awareness of the probable connection between neuro-immune and/or autoimmune disorders and conditions commonly found on the ASD (e.g. Autism, ADD, Alzheimer's, ALS, CFS/CFIDS, MS, PDD and other immune-mediated diseases). The NIDS Institute proposes that a dysfunctional immune system can result in reduction of blood flow to the temporal lobes of the brain. Decreased blood flow, especially in the early developmental years of life, can cause symptoms that have come to be associated with autism, namely, dysfunction in social skills, auditory processing, and language.

Diagnosis is conducted by examining blood work and also measuring blood flow to the temporal lobes using NeuroSpect brain imaging. If the scan finds a lower amount of blood flow to the temporal lobes than would be normally expected, then treatment should occur. According to the NIDS Institute, many children with NIDS can be treated in part through approved agents, many of which include diet modifications (Carson & Stoga, n.d.).

Complexity of research

If research in the area of autism were simple, many of the puzzles regarding cause, cure, and prevention would already be solved. Research, however, unlike speculation, takes time, careful planning, and execution. Research in the area of autism is complicated in that autism is rarely found without other comorbid conditions. The effect of these conditions cannot be separated from autism. Researching autism for school aged children who also have Down Syndrome would require a different study than investigating autism in school children who have also been categorized with ADD or bipolar disorders. Autism can involve an individual profoundly or almost negligibly, and the role of nature versus nurture are almost impossible to separate.

Matching researchers with target populations

Many health problems are caused by both genetic and environmental factors. More than likely future research findings will identify many different interactions between heredity and environment to pinpoint the hoped for cures for the many faces of autism. Given the large numbers of families with one of more members with autism, the research data pool is potentially huge and simultaneously complex to access. ASD studies are often delayed or not finished due to inability to access qualified participants.

Interactive Autism Network

In order to align researchers with appropriate participants, the Interactive Autism Network (IAN), an online project, brings together thousands of people affected by ASD and hundreds of researchers to search for the causes of autism. The IAN is the country's largest online autism research study designed to accelerate significant breakthroughs about causes, diagnosis, and treatments which could lead to the discovery of causes or of possible cures for autism and other related PDDs (IAN, 2009).

INTERVENTIONS

Given the heterogeneity of autism, the multitude of therapeutic treatments or intervention options available should not be surprising. Most interventions that appear somewhat beneficial for children with ASD and ADHD target pharmacotherapy (medications) and behavioral therapy (Daley, 2006; Filapek, Steinberg-Epstein, & Book, 2006; Howlin, 2005). Many other treatments, such as sensory integration, nutrition, chelation (the process of removing a heavy metal from the bloodstream as in treating lead or mercury poisoning), and environmental control are also widely held as treatments, however, many of these commonly practiced interventions and treatments lack hard data to support their use.

Despite the proliferation of testimonials and anecdotal information for and against various approaches, interventions for autism have surprisingly sparse objective supportive records. Most of the interventions lacking supportive data have been pop-ularized by word of mouth, which often results in fads, the most popular of which are often dietary (Levy and Hyman, 2005; Moran and Gibbons, 2001; Shattock and Whitely 2002). Even medications and behavioral therapies have had limited docu-mented success. Among the most commonly used treatments with empirical support are pharmacotherapy, behavior therapy, and the more recently emerging applied behavior analysis (ABA) (Matson & Dempsey, 2008).

Pharmacotherapy

Pharmacotherapy is the use of drugs to treat conditions, especially psychiatric disor-ders, which are primarily attributed to neurological issues. Many individuals with autism exhibit comorbid behaviors that fall under neurological, psychiatric, behav-ioral, and learning symptoms or disorders (e.g., epilepsy, self-injury, aggression and property destruction, acute distractibility, and anxiety disorder). An estimated 40%–80% of children with autism also display ADHD in combination with other disabilities (Biederman & Faraone, 2005). Lennie's parents have chosen to provide him with medication for his anxiety. They feel that his self-injurious and violent behaviors cannot be totally controlled through educational interventions. When Lennie's routine changes at all, he will get frustrated, and he will hit himself and become aggressive. Lennie takes medications to keep him calm, which is a major support for home because he is about 190 pounds and is too big for his mother to control physically. Finding the right dosage for Lennie continues to be a major chal-lenge.

Comorbid conditions

Pharmacotherapy often is not prescribed for autism, but rather as a treatment for comorbid conditions. The reason for medicating lies in the belief that by eliminating or reducing the impact of the comorbid condition, more effective interventions can be directed toward the core areas of autism. Just as frequently, however, in spite of claims that core symptoms of autism are not targeted, plentiful research with phar-macotherapy has been directed toward stereotypies like excessive repetition or lack of variation in movements, ideas, or patterns of speech, especially when viewed as a symptom of certain disorders typically found with individuals on the autism spec-trum (Matson & Dempsey, 2008). Six broad types of medications commonly used with individuals who fall on the autism spectrum are anticonvulsants, tranquilizers (antianxiety medications), stimulants, antidepressants, and antipsychotics (Aspy & Grossman, 2007; Simpson & Zionts, 2000). A brief overview of these medications is found in Table 1.3. Consult Matson & Dempsey (2008) for a more extensive review of medications.

Research support

Psychotropic medications appear to be effective in treating some significant associ-ated behaviors; however, evidence of major impact on the core features of autism

TABLE 1.3

Six Broad Types of Medications Commonly Used with Individuals Who Fall on the Autism Spectrum

Medication Categories	Behaviors Addressed	Common Side Effects	Selected Medications
Anticonvulsants	Seizure control	Behavioral and Cognitive	Phenobarbitol Dilantin Klonopin Zarontin
Tranquilizers or Antianxiety Drugs (Neuroleptics)	Hyperactivity Self-stimulation Tics Emotional outbursts Aggressive behavior Seizure control Depression	Marked drowsiness Blurred vision Impaired motor performance Anemia Tremors	Thorazine Mellaril Haldol Prolixin Xanax Librium Klonopin Valium Ativan Centrax
Stimulants	Unnecessary activity Attention deficits Overactivity Behavioral problems Hyperactivity	Loss of appetite Irritability Anxiousness Insomnia	Ritalin Cyclert Dexedrine
Antidepressants Subgroup 1 Tricyclics (TCAs)	Attention deficits Hyperactivity Enuresis School phobia Aggression Insomnia	Nausea Loss of appetite Dry mouth Irritability Fatigue Insomnia Heightened risk of suicide	Elavil Norpramin Pamelot Tofanil
Antidepressants Subgroup 2 Serotonin Reuptake Inhibitors (SSRIs)	Mood Anxiety Insomnia Obsessive compulsivity Communication deficits	Heightened risk of suicide	Luvox Prozac Zoloft Paxil Celexa
Antipsychotics	Psychosis Bi-polar disorder Tourette Syndrome Aggression Impulsivity Repetitive behaviors Communication deficits	Weight gain Fatigue Drowsiness Dizziness Drooling Tremors Constipation Loss of strength	Haldol Risperdal Zyprexa Abilify Seroquel

Note: This list is not meant to be comprehensive, but rather a broad introductory overview.

spectrum disorders is incomplete (Meyers, 2007). Despite the increasing trend of prescribing psychotropic medication, the short- and long-term safety and tolerance levels is not well documented. A disturbing trend seen in children, adolescents, and adults, is the increasing rate of unfavorable events associated with the major side effects of antipsychotics (McIntyre and Konarski, 2005; Vitiello, 2007). Glen, for example, was consumed with anxiety about going to school. Every morning he would perform the same 20 minute elaborate ritual to prepare for school. If this ritual could not be conducted, Glen would have a serious meltdown, and no level of persuasion could get him to go through his front door and out to school. As Glen's anxiety increased, so did the length of his ritual.

On the advice of his psychiatrist, Glen's parents began to give him a drug based on serotonin-reuptake inhibitors. Initially this treatment seemed to be effective, but within a week, Glen began to complain of headaches. He also became overly aggressive and agitated. New previously unseen behaviors began to emerge. Glen began to grimace, pucker, smack, and purse his lips. He made movements with his fingers as if he were playing an invisible guitar.

The "new" Glen now would go to school, but his new behaviors were much more disruptive than those before the SSRI. The solution, fortunately for Glen, was simple. The offending medication was replaced by another that seemed to help reduce the anxiety that Glen was feeling without the accompanying side effects. His rituals appeared less often and were shorter in duration.

Some medications appear to contribute to developing obesity, Type II diabetes, heart conditions, and digestive conditions. Neurological, nervous, or sensory conditions can also be found in higher than expected levels for individuals receiving psychotropic medications. Not surprising, results also suggest that children who take more than one antipsychotic medication consistently have a higher chance for developing undesirable physical and psychological complications (Jerrell & McIntyre, 2008).

The effect of medications also varies from person to person and can change over time. With children who are still developing, effects must be monitored and adjusted to fit the child's response to the medication or medications.

Wide-spread practice

Nonetheless, the use of stimulant medications with children is widely practiced in the United States. In fact 80% of stimulant prescriptions worldwide are written in the United States (Vitiello, 2008). In one study, for example, over half of 552 parents of children with autism reported that their children were using medications, another study of over 2500 parents reported similar findings, and in another study of 195 parents of children with autism between the ages of 2 and 8, over one fourth of the children were receiving medications (Green et al., 2006; Hume, Bellini, & Pratt, 2005).

At issue is a cost–benefit paradigm. Do the results of the medications outweigh their potential physical and psychological effects? Studies have not yet come forth in which drug effects have been operationalized in such a way as to be measured adequately to definitively support or reject particular interventions (Matson & Dempsey, 2008).

Educational Interventions

Instructing children with autism can often be a challenging task, especially when interventionists, therapists, or teachers assume that good principles of instruction employed with typically developing children will lead to learning. The very nature of the core issues in autism (i.e., disorders in social behavior, abnormal verbal and nonverbal communication and limited interests) call for an approach clearly directed toward the individual, where normal conventions of communication are few if existent at all. Commonly held assumptions regarding interactive and reciprocal communication between teachers and learners very often do not hold. Those teachers who need the warm feelings generated by adoring students may find themselves frustrated and unable to work with some children with autism.

By definition most individuals with autism lack or are atypical in awareness of basic understanding of others and have difficulty in developing specific skills or generalization. Teachers, therapists, and interventionists who believe that the child with autism thinks, feels, and acts like most other children may be as confused as the child they are trying to teach. Effective communication is the key to working with all learners, but with many children with autism what constitutes effective communication is unique to the teacher and learner. Finding the key to effective communication is one of the most challenging aspects of unlocking the minds of teacher and student.

Todd, for example, fits under the category of high functioning autism. He is semi-verbal. Todd loves rockets and anything having to do with space. Whenever Ms. Parker, his teacher, tries to work with Todd, he always goes into "his world" and begins to recite anything about space. Todd makes the perfect sounds of a rocket and then counts down to blast off. Refocusing Todd once he goes into his own world is very difficult. Ms. Parker decided that she was going to meet him in his own world, and maybe then he would work with her. So when Todd started the count down to blast off, Ms. Parker asked Todd where he was going. He replied, "to Mars." Ms. Parker then told Todd, "It's too bad I don't fit on that rocket and I have to stay on planet earth." Todd then looked at his teacher and said, "You don't fit on my rocket?" Ms. Parker said, "I don't think I do if it is just for one person."

Ms. Parker and Todd then proceeded to discuss how whenever Todd leaves planet earth, Ms. Parker gets left behind and cannot work with him. Todd loved this conversation. So now every time Ms. Parker goes to work with Todd, he says, "Ms. Parker, planet Earth." Then they both laugh and sit down to work. Communicating with Todd became easier once Ms. Parker used the style that her student wanted, and this style may have made Todd more willing to stay on "planet Earth" to work with her.

Children with autism, as noted earlier, are a heterogeneous group. An approach that works for one student may have no or even a deleterious effect on another. To instruct a child with autism is to throw out stereotypic notions of who fits the category and to be open to new and unique creative instructional opportunities.

Educational approaches to autism run the gamut from traditional behavioral approaches to developmental models. Many of the educational approaches incorporate the newer applied behavior analysis (ABA) approaches derived from learning theory and operant conditioning into developmentally based models founded in typical child development research.

Behavior Therapy

Behavior therapy utilizes basic learning techniques to alter or change inappropriate behavior patterns, replacing them with new, appropriate responses. Patrick, for example, throws tantrums whenever he must use soap to wash his hands. Tantrums are maladaptive behaviors. Using behavior therapy, his teacher can teach Patrick to replace his tantrums with more compliant and appropriate behavior when asked to wash his hands. Behavior therapy is also called behavioral therapy or behavior modification. In behavior therapy, maladaptive behavior patterns are modified by substituting new responses to those stimuli that previously evoked undesirable behavior. At least two different theoretical views form the basis of behavior therapy: operant conditioning and cognitive behavior therapy (Huber, & Zivalich, 2004).

Operant conditioning

In operant conditioning, learning is based on reinforced trials. Patrick would learn to wash his hands by being reinforced each time he engaged in the appropriate behavior for hand washing. Patrick loves chocolate chips. Each time Patrick exhibits appropriate hand washing behavior, he receives a chocolate chip. Under this behavioral system, Patrick is more likely to increase appropriate behavior each time he is given positive reinforcement. Patrick will come to associate the pleasure of obtaining a chocolate chip with appropriate hand washing behavior.

Cognitive behavior therapy

The other behavioral approach, cognitive behavior therapy (CBT), is based on the belief that humans guide themselves by cognitive expectancies directed toward some future goal. Humans psychologically direct their behaviors by the ways they anticipate events. Patrick, for reasons known only to himself, somehow seems to view hand washing as an event that would create serious negative outcomes. Patrick has taught himself that he must avoid hand washing at all costs and uses the tantrums to escape it.

Patrick's teacher must teach him that hand washing is not a dangerous or aversive situation. Patrick's teacher can teach Patrick to think that that hand washing is not a negative experience or that hand washing will lead to the much desired chocolate chip. This replaces Patrick's cognitive expectancy of negative experiences with hand washing with a cognitive expectancy which can motivate him to wash his hands, thus replacing tantrums with appropriate social behaviors.

External versus internal control

The theoretical underpinnings of these two behavioral approaches are quite different, although many of their interventions overlap. The key to behavioral therapy is that inappropriate behaviors are replaced with appropriate ones. In operant conditioning, the learner simply responds to a stimulus, as when Patrick responds to the reward of chocolate. His behavior is altered by his instructor. In contrast, the more constructivist approach focuses on how to help the learner create a new mind-set. Patrick's teacher helps him to create ways of thinking that will affect his expectations. The chocolate chip is clearly in evidence, but the goal is to have Patrick control his thinking about hand washing. In an oversimplification, under operant conditioning, Patrick's behavior is controlled externally. In the more constructivist approach, Patrick is controlling his behavior internally. Regardless of the theoretical construct behind the behavioral approach, practices like recording data and defining behaviors can be found to a greater or lesser degree in both developmental theories.

Developmental Theories

Most developmental theories look to normal child development or milestones to create maturationally appropriate interventions or instruction. Quite often developmental approaches will focus on the whole family as a unit rather than targeting only the child found on the autism spectrum.

Integration with ABA

Over the past two decades, developmental research has attempted to integrate with family centered practices and the teaching approaches associated with the ABA approach (Strain et al., 1992). Through the infusion of ABA practices (i.e., the need for consistency, intensity, and accountability) more developmental models have gained objective support for making instructional decisions. Integration of models is no easy feat. Some programs continue to use an either/or approach, that is, either behavioral or developmental.

Fragmentation of programs

At the other extreme are those all-encompassing programs that ultimately become programmatically fragmented (Prizant, Wetherby, Rubin, Laurent, 2003). For example, JaeWon may receive services at home that focus on compliance issues through a traditional ABA therapist but attend an elementary school that is focused on communication and peer interaction. To the degree that these two programs are coordinated, JaeWon will benefit. If the programs are not coordinated, JaeWon could become confused, his parent could become confused, and his teachers and therapists could find themselves in the center of a controversy regarding methods and approaches.

SELECTED COMMON MODEL PROGRAMS

Many educational programs have been developed for children with autism. They run the gamut from being almost entirely based on operant conditioning to more internally driven constructivist approaches to developmental models based on typical populations. No one program has been documented as being applicable to all children with autism; some programs have begun to have research support and other programs are based on faith and little else. Several common models used with individuals with autism are: Early Intensive Behavioral Intervention (EIBI), Treatment and Education of Autistic and related Communications handicapped Children (TEACCH), and SCERTS®.

Early Intensive Behavioral Intervention

The Young Autistic Program (YAP), one of the first studies to use operant conditioning with young autistic children, was housed at the University of California at Los Angeles about 30 years ago. This program, also known as the Early Intensive Behavioral Intervention (EIBI), was under the direction of Lovaas. EIBI has also been called behavior therapy, which has led to some confusion between EIBI, which uses behavioral techniques, and the much broader area of behavior therapy as a process.

EIBI is a highly structured intense intervention taught by therapists to children on an individual basis. Initial research results strongly suggested that early intervention and the approach used in EIBI resulted in normal development for almost half the children in the study. The language used to describe the results of the original study has been misinterpreted. Many have held out undue hope that children with autism can be cured using EIBI because they failed to take into account the small size of the subject pool. The language of the study has subsequently been clarified by the authors to make the reporting of the data less open to misinterpretation.

Misinterpretation of research

These results have been seriously questioned, as have two of the most well known aspects of the intervention, intensive time and negative corporal controls (Shea, 2004). EIBI requires 40 hours a week and encourages aversive techniques, such as shouting "no" and slapping the child's thigh whenever the child engaged in self-stimulating behaviors. The findings and techniques used in this study continue to be controversial, and many parents and therapists adhere to the original approach even though Lovaas has downplayed the length of time and aversive interventions (Lovaas, Smith, & McEachin, 1989).

EIBI continues to be used in home-based programs using a one to one ratio, more or less faithful to the original YAP. Results of the effectiveness of home-based EIBI vary, and adherence to an intense time based routine of 30–40 hours may not be as effective in gains as an approximately 20 hour approach (Reed, Osborne, & Corness, 2007).

Area Cooperative Educational Services (ACES)

ACES EIBI, a variation of the original EIBI, is also a highly structured technique, designed primarily for children ranging from 3 to 14 years of age whose clinical diagnoses falls along the autism spectrum or who present significant behavioral challenges. Like EIBI, ACES also uses a one-to-one ratio instructional delivery approach given by a team of instructors trained in Applied Behavior Analysis. A certified special education teacher and a nationally certified Behavior Analyst (BCBA) are assigned to a group of eight to 10 students.

TEACCH

TEACCH, which stands for the Treatment and Education of Autistic and related Communications handicapped CHildren, is a very structured teaching approach that was designed to provide individuals with ASD adaptations that would allow them to function within society at large. The approach originated at the University of North Carolina in 1966 (Schopler, Mesibov & Baker,1982).

TEACCH is also considered a behaviorist approach, but unlike the EIBI method, it recognizes that autism is a lifelong disorder and places a heavy emphasis on developing communication and independence, rather than mainly seeking to eliminate problem behaviors. Students in the TEACCH Model are encouraged to work together to develop social and communication skills.

Predictability and routine

TEACCH utilizes classrooms designed to promote a sense of routine, predictability, and organization. Through a variety of visual strategies, structured teaching is aligned with the special needs of each student to develop thinking, understanding, memory, and learning. Parents are considered partners with the teachers and therapists by extending practices learned in school to home situations. Because TEACCH is strongly rooted in behaviorist practice in specialized educational settings, concern about generalization to other situations beyond the classroom have been raised. Structured programs, like TEACCH, are considered by some to require such specific responses by trained therapists that application to the world beyond the classroom is unlikely (Tutt, Powell, & Thornton, 2006).

SCERTS®

SCERTS is a developmental and behavior model, which stands for Social Communication, Emotional Regulation, and Transactional Support.

➤ Social Communication: communicating spontaneously and establishing relationships
➤ Emotional Regulation: regulating emotional arousal to support learning and engagement
➤ Transactional Support: elements that aid an individual's progress as he or she works toward a goal

SCERTS incorporates educational and treatment strategies drawn from contemporary behavioral and developmental approaches. Much of the theory and practices used in the SCERTS model are based on child development.

In contrast to the very strict behavior models like EIBI, SCERTS exposes children with ASD to socially complex situations. In this sense SCERTS does not attempt to break down complex behaviors into simpler pieces, but rather uses a more natural learning environment. Family involvement is an integral aspect of this approach. SCERTS provides individualized instruction based on evidence-supported practice which is applicable to everyday events.

Eclectic approach

The eclectic approach is by far the most common model in public and private schools settings. The eclectic approach is an attempt to draw on the best practices found in fully developed models with long histories and research evidence. The manner and degree to which these practices are delivered in eclectic programs depends a great deal on the skill of the teachers and support staff as well as available financial resources.

Most public schools and many private schools are not designed to implement models such as the EIBI, TEACCH, and SCERTS® with the same level of intensity or expertise as found in centers specially designed for these programs. Many of the best practices from these three models, however, can be found to greater and lesser degrees in almost any configuration in most classrooms designed for children who fall on the autism spectrum. The degree of fidelity to the original formal models is influenced by multiple factors, including instructor training, socioeconomic level of the local education association, and partnerships with local universities.

The Ziggurat Model

The Ziggurat Model, designed specifically for children with high-functioning autism and Asperger Syndrome, is a good example of an eclectic model drawing upon best practices, and it is applicable in public school settings. The Ziggurat Model provides more of a comprehensive framework or process for evaluation and intervention than a specific step-by-step approach.

The system is comprehensive by drawing upon multiple solutions for solving the complex problems presented with the wide variety of differences seen in children who fall under the ASD umbrella. The Ziggurat Model guides teachers and therapists in designing an intervention based on the underlying deficits that may be unique to the child. The Ziggurat Model utilizes an interdisciplinary approach that relies heavily on the effective use of reinforcement and positive behavior supports by structuring situations to support the academic and social success of all students (Aspy & Grossman, 2007).

K-odles

The Ziggurat Model, more formalized than most eclectic models, could be called a K-odel. K-odel comes from the combination of the terms Kid and model. K-odles are kid-centered models in which the teacher selects aspects from formalized programs and best practices to create a model specific to each student.

Without data, however, no evidence exists to justify that a mixture of methods is more beneficial than one or another formal model (Tutt, Powell, & Thornton, 2006). Intuitively the K-odel is far more appealing than many formal models given the heterogeneity of the population within the autism spectrum, but until teachers begin reporting their experiences via applied research, the value of many K-odels and their more formal predecessors will remain unknown and unsubstantiated.

Applied Behavior Analysis (ABA)

ABA is systematic change of behavior based on observable and quantifiable behaviors. Techniques for recording changes in many ways can be considered the technology side of behavioral change. Autism cannot be addressed without consideration of ABA as a behavioral intervention. ABA has its foundation in behavioral therapy and utilizes strict recording systems used to make instructional management decisions about the value of an intervention for a child's behavior.

Discrete trial format

ABA has been defined as an intervention approach that follows a discrete trial format (DTT), breaking skills down into smaller components and teaching those smaller subskills individually. Students keep practicing, although prompting can be included, until the correct response is achieved. Reinforcement is used to facilitate learning. A discrete trial is one cycle of instruction that can be repeated as many times as needed until the targeted skill is mastered. DTT is just one of the many strategies using principles of ABA to facilitate learning. An example of a discrete trial used to teach Isaiah how to touch his mouth would consist of 5 basic steps:

1. An initial instruction: "Isaiah, touch your mouth."
2. A prompt or cue given by the teacher to help him respond correctly: Isaiah's teacher, Ms. Emily, points to Isaiah's mouth.
3. A response given by the child: Isaiah touches his mouth.
4. An appropriate consequence, such as a reward designed to motivate Isaiah to respond correctly again in the future: "Excellent job touching your mouth, Isaiah," and Ms. Emily gives Isaiah a dinosaur sticker.
5. A pause between successive trials, for example, waiting 1–5 seconds before beginning the next trial: Ms. Emily waits about 2 seconds before she asks Isaiah to touch his mouth again.

More than DTT

ABA, much more comprehensive than discrete trials, is the design, completion, and evaluation of environmental changes or modifications to produce socially significant improvements in academics; social skills; communication; and adaptive living skills, such as personal self-care, home and community orientation, and work skills. ABA focuses on explaining behavior in terms of external events that can be manipulated rather than internal constructs that are beyond our control.

ABA is an objective discipline, which focuses on the reliable measurement and objective evaluation of observable behavior. In order to ensure that the same behavior is being measured consistently, ABA requires an objective observable definition of the behavior.

Vague terms such as depression, tantrum, on task, and social skills are defined in countable and operational terms. Consider the term aggression. What is considered aggressive to one person may be thought of as forceful to another; it is a term open to interpretation. ABA transforms vague concepts by providing parameters. For a particular student, aggression might be defined as attempts to bite, pinch or pull hair. On a more positive note, interacting could be redefined as looking at a classmate and verbalizing an appropriate request to share a toy.

The growth of autism specific education programs using ABA methodologies has paralleled the increase in numbers of children identified as falling under ASD. Many school based ABA programs, however, seem to focus primarily on DTT, leaving out the full array of methodologies demonstrated to be effective with individuals on the autism spectrum (Steege, Mace, Perry & Longenecker, 2007). In addition, ABA can be very time intensive, requiring a recommended 25–40 hours of instruction per week (Howard, Sparkman, Cohen, Green, & Stanislaw, 2005), and may not lend itself to generalization in more natural settings than the classroom.

Complementary use of ABA with other interventions or treatments

One of the most significant and potentially valuable features found in ABA is the recording system. The system can lend itself to use with many other behavioral approaches, for example, cognitive behavioral therapy (CBT) or interventions not typically associated with behavioral therapies like medications.

The recording system is based on objective and well-defined ongoing measurement of behavior, which can be graphed to determine effectiveness. Interventions targeting specific operationalized behaviors in conjunction with ABA recording or graphing could shed light on the value of many of these approaches. Studies, for example, that combine ABA methodologies and programs in combination with drug trials virtually do not exist (Matson & Dempsey, 2008). By graphing the frequency, rate, duration, or any other significant aspect of the targeted behaviors, decisions about the value of an intervention on a specific behavior could be based on actual data.

Diminish ambiguity

Collaborative and complementary ventures between many of the popular but unsubstantiated therapies used as treatments or interventions with children with autism and ABA are also missing. By using the ABA methodologies in combination with many as yet objectively unsupported therapies, much of the ambiguity surrounding such therapies and methods could be dispelled. Lack of collaboration could be as simple as not having considered the possibility of linking the recording systems used in ABA with a treatment or as simple as the often found hubris associated with territoriality.

SPEECH, MUSIC, ART, DRAMA, AND SENSORY INTEGRATION THERAPIES

Very popular therapies or services used with children with autism are Speech, Music, Art, Drama, and Sensory Integration. Therapists have long traditions of assisting individuals through a particular medium among the arts-based tools of music, art and drama. Speech therapy focuses on language issues, and sensory integration centers more on organizing body sensations and the environment.

Interdisciplinary teams

Regardless of the medium used for therapy, most services are provided by professionals who combine educational and therapeutic approaches for evaluation, remediation, and case management on behalf of the children they serve. Therapists are usually members of an interdisciplinary team who support the goals and objectives for each child within the context of their particular area of expertise. Such therapies are generally considered part of a child's curriculum rather than an approach to that child's education.

Need for research support

Although many testimonials promote these popular therapies, for the most part only studies with small sample sizes usually in clinical settings have been reported. Without more scientific support, the value of therapies cannot be established. Without scientific support, in times of tight budgets, such programs may be the first to be cut and the last to be reinstated. Therapies and ABA collaborations might establish which services are the most effective for subgroups of children who are found on the autism spectrum.

Sensory Integration: Model or Therapy?

One therapy that has long been associated with autism is Sensory Integration (SI). SI was created to help individuals manage sensory input. SI Therapy is designed for children who respond inappropriately to sensory input (i.e., taste, touch, sight, hearing, and feeling). Sensory overresponsivity has been identified in children and adults with autism (Dunn Smith-Myles, & Orr, 2002; Pfeiffer, Kinnealey, Reed, & Herzberg, 2005).

A child could be overresponsive or underresponsive to some event and engage in behaviors like refusing from wearing clothing with certain of textures, covering their ears to typical sounds like dogs barking or the fire alarm ringing, or limiting the kinds of foods they eat because of oversensitivity to taste, smell, or texture

(Interdisciplinary Council on Developmental and Learning Disorders [ICDL] 2005; Lane 2002).

Children can also be insensitive or overly sensitive to pain. Charles, for example, developed a habit of standing behind a wooden rocking chair and laughing while the chair rocked and repeatedly hit his forehead. Charles did not appear to feel any pain and actually seemed to enjoy the thumping of the chair against his battered and bruised forehead.

When placed in situations in which they are forced to deal with perceived unpleasant sensory events, children with SI issues can easily become overwhelmed, resulting in disruptive behaviors (Parham & Mailloux, 2005). The purpose of SI therapy is to help the learner integrate the senses. In an SI intervention, a situation is created which stimulates all the senses. During SI therapy, the child interacts one-on-one with the occupational therapist and carries out an activity that merges sensory input with motion (Baranek, 2002; Dempsey & Foreman, 2001; Schaaf & Miller, 2005). Examples of SI activities include but are not limited to the following (Healing Thresholds, 2009):

➤ Swinging in a hammock (movement through space)
➤ Moving to music (sound)
➤ Playing in boxes filled with rice (touch)
➤ Crawling through tunnels (touch and movement through space)
➤ Swatting swinging balls (eye-hand coordination)
➤ Twirling on a chair (balance and vision)
➤ Balancing on a beam (balance)

Very few well-designed studies of SI and autism exist. The value of SI therapy is controversial because so many therapists and teachers have anecdotal and positive experiences with the activities. The jury is still out on its value. Of the available reports, about half show some type of change as a result of SI therapy, and the other half show no benefit at all (Dawson & Watling, 2000; Schaaf & Miller, 2005). These results once again must raise the question, "Is the cost in time and money worth the benefit received by the child?" The response must be, "Show me the data!"

CURRENT CHALLENGES AND FUTURE IMPLICATIONS

Autism, found on the spectrum of many interrelated and overlapping conditions, is a master of disguise. Camouflaged by comorbid disabilities, autism presents itself like the tip of an iceberg, with many of the fundamental issues hidden neatly out of sight. Many previously unsuspected issues concerning the care and provision of services to individuals who fall on the ASD are surfacing. Three of the many significant issues found in the world of autism are the influence and roles played by multiculturalism, medications, and program justification.

Multiculturalism

In the melting pot culture of the United States, a child with autism is challenged minimally on four factors: disorders in social behavior, abnormal verbal and nonverbal communication, limited interests, and culture. Abundant literature addresses the core issues associated with autism, but rarely is the multicultural factor thrown into the mix. At this time very little information is available that addresses the cultural expectations and needs of families of children with autism who are not from middle to upper middle class western culture (Dyches et al., 2004). Statistically, as defined with a normal distribution curve, a set of children found on the ASD must exist for any culture or socioeconomic group. A significant question to ask is, "What family characteristics affect the identification and intervention practices for individuals with autism?" Could programs that require extensive time and training on the part of the family be appropriate for all families? Do only a selected few types of families qualify in terms of time, money, and education for programs offered to individuals with autism?

At issue is the relationships among parenting styles, culture, and stresses related to raising a child with autism. Negative parenting styles and parental stress are predictors of the persistence of serious difficulties based in early childhood and continuing into adulthood (Campbell, 1995). Ample documentation shows that parent education programs positively impact preschoolers' behavior (Borr, Sanders, & Markie-Dadds, 2002; Sonuga-Barke, Daley, Thompson, Laver-Bradbury, & Weeks, 2001). Almost no studies have taken into account the ethnic, socioeconomic, or educational cultures of parents who are outside of a western European way of life.

Medication

How much medication is too much and when should medications be prescribed? Without a doubt one of the most highly medicated groups of children is found under ASD. Questions regarding the appropriate and safe utilization of medication with children and adults must be addressed, especially in light of the potential harm associated with psychotropic medications. The use of multiple psychotropic medications concurrently is widespread among preschool children, school-aged children, and adolescents (Rappley, 2006).

Guidelines need to be established for the use of medications for individuals who fall under ASD categories. For many individuals with autism, medication seems to be the first level of intervention. Research, however, has not yet revealed the most appropriate time or situation for the administration of medications, for which conditions, and at which ages. Although research literature persists in stating that medication in combination with behavioral therapy is more powerful than medication alone, the very premise must be challenged by the noteworthy absence of systematic investigation of various combinations of medications and behavioral therapies (Sonuga-Barke et al., 2001). With the exception of the most extreme circumstances, questions should be raised concerning the provision of psychotropic medications as the first treatment for individuals from preschool to adulthood who fall under ASD.

Program Justification

Most programs for individuals with autism are expensive in time and human resources. The cost of private programs can easily range from between $2,000 to $10,000 per month or more. Tuition does not always include the additional expense of a therapist, whose charge can easily run $100–$200 or greater per hour, with a child requiring many hours a week in therapy. Regardless of the funding source, parents, the government, or in some limited cases insurance companies, these pricey programs need to justify their existence from a cost–benefit perspective. Are the costs worth the advantages of the program? Are the individuals receiving services that actually benefit them in some tangible manner?

At this time a conservative estimate for taking care of a person with autism is about $3.2 million per year. True costs are probably higher when taking into account other services, like alternative therapies and personal family expenses (Ganz, 2007). Programs and related services of such financial magnitude cannot be warranted without some hard evidence that they have impact. Testimonials and anecdotes simply will not suffice in this age of accountability.

Until research evidence can provide answers to questions concerning the value of a program or intervention, the burden of responsibility will continue to fall on teachers, therapists or interventionists. Teachers and other service providers must demonstrate the effectiveness and efficiency of the intervention on the acquisition and maintenance of specified objectives within the program on the academic and social growth of the individual. Excuses for lack of progress cannot be acceptable and certainly will not be viewed favorably from a policy perspective related to the investment of public resources for services delivered.

The hue and cry of teachers and other interventionist who claim not to have time (or desire) for taking data needs to be reassessed if programs are going to be ethically and financially justifiable. The value of taking data for the purpose of making informed decisions related to the effectiveness of an intervention for an individual with autism cannot be overstated. How much longer can the autism community and the country at large continue to tolerate programs based on faith, hope, and genuine good will to meet the needs of individuals with autism?

SUMMARY

Autism, the sleeping giant of neurological disorders, has awakened with a vengeance. The most rapidly growing pervasive developmental disorder, autism is lifelong and characterized by three core behaviors: dysfunctional social interaction; verbal and nonverbal communication problems; and odd, repetitive, or severely restricted activities and interests. Many other conditions, for example, mental retardation or ADD, coexist with autism. Suspected causes of autism are many, but no one cause or cure has been discovered. More than likely multiple causes of autism will be revealed, but may be unique to individuals based on the interaction between their genes and environmental stressors. Autism as a category may eventually become known as "autisms" because of the heterogeneity of the condition. Commonly used treatments include medication, behavior modification, and models derived from normal child development. Most interventions have very little or no research support.

REFERENCES

Abrahams, B. S., & Geschwind, D. H. (2008). Advances in autism genetics: On the threshold of a new neurobiology. *Nature Reviews Genetics, 9,* 341–355.

American Psychiatric Association (APA). (2000). *Diagnostic and statistical manual of mental disorders* (4th ed., text rev.). Washington, DC: Author.

Ashwood, P., Kwong, C., Hansen, R., Hertz-Picciotto, I., Croen, L. I., Krakowiak, P., et al. (2008). Brief report: Plasma leptin levels are elevated in autism: Association with early onset phenotype? *Autism Developmental Disorders, 38,* 169–175.

Aspy, R., & Grossman, B. G. (2007). *The Ziggurat Model.* Shawnee Mission, KA: Autism Asperger.

Baird, G., Simonoff, E., Pickles, A., Chandler, S., Loucas, T., Meldrum, D., et al. (2006). Prevalence of disorders of the autism spectrum in a population cohort of children in South Thames: The Special Needs and Autism Project (SNAP). *Lancet, 368*(9531), 210–215.

Baker, J. P. (2008). Mercury, vaccines, and autism: One controversy, three histories. *American Journal of Public Health, 98*(2), 244–253.

Ball, L., Ball, R., &, Pratt, R. D. (2001). An assessment of thimerosal in childhood vaccines. *Pediatrics, 107,*1147–1154.

Baranek, G. T. (2002). Efficacy of sensory and motor interventions for children with autism. *Journal of Autism and Developmental Disorders, 32*(5), 397–422.

Baron-Cohen, S., Leslie, A. M., & Frith, U. (1985). Does the autistic child have a "theory of mind"? *Cognition, 21,* 37–46.

Biederman J., & Faraone, S. V. (2005). Attention-deficit hyperactivity disorder. *Lancet, 366,* 237–248.

Blaxill, M. F. (2004). What's going on? The question of time trends in autism. *Public Health Report, 119*(6), 536–51.

Beversdorf, D. Q., Manning, S. E., Hillier, A., Anderson, S. L., Nordgren, R. E., Walters, S. E., et al. (2005). Timing of prenatal stressors and autism. *Journal of Autism and Developmental Disorders, 35*(4), 471–478.

Borr, W., Sanders, M., & Markie-Dadds, C. (2002). The effects of the triple P-positive parenting program on preschool children with co-occurring disruptive behavior and attentional/hyperactive difficulties. *Journal of Abnormal Child Psychology, 30,* 571–587.

Brass, M., Derrfuss, J., & von Cramon, D. Y. (2005). The inhibition of imitative and overlearned responses: A functional double dissociation. *Neuropsychologia, 43,* 89–98.

Burd, L., Severud, R., Kerbeshian, J., & Klug, M. G. (1999). Prenatal and perinatal risk factors for autism. *Journal of Perinatal Medicine, 27,* 441–450.

Campbell, S. B. (1995). Behavior problems in preschool children: A review of recent research. *Psychology and Psychiatry and Allied Disciplines, 36,* 113–149.

Carcani-Rathwell, I., Rabe-Hasketh, S., & Santosh, P. J. (2006). Repetitive and stereotyped behaviors in pervasive developmental disorders. *Journal of Child Psychology and Psychiatry and Allied Disciplines, 47,* 573–581.

Carson, L. & Stoga, S. (n.d.). *Neuro-immune dysfunction syndromes.* Retrieved May 29, 2009, from http://www.nids.net/nidsfactsheet.pdf

Centers for Disease Control and Prevention (CDC). (2008). *History of Vaccine Safety.* Retrieved May 20, 2009, from http://www.cdc.gov/vaccinesafety/basic/history.htm

Chess, S. (1971). Autism in children with congenital rubella. *Journal of Autism and Childhood Schizophrenia, 1,* 33–47.

Childhood Autism Risk from Genetics and the Environment (CHARGE). (2006). *Childhood Autism Risk from Genetics and the Environment.* Retrieved May 26, 2009, from http://bencharge.ucdavis.edu/

Claassen, M., Naude, H., Pretorius, E., & Bosman, M. C. (2008). The contribution of prenatal stress to the pathogenesis of autism as a neurobiological developmental disorder: A dizygotic twin study. *Early Child Development & Care, 178,* 487–511.

Curtis, L. T., & Patel, K. (2007). Nutritional and Environmental Approaches to Preventing and Treating Autism and Attention Deficit Hyperactivity Disorder (ADHD): A Review. *The Journal of Alternative and Complementary Medicine, 14,* 79–85.

Daley, D. (2006). Attention deficit hyperactivity disorder: A review of the essential facts. *Child Care, Health and Development, 32,*193–204.

Dawson, G., & Watling, R. (2000). Interventions to facilitate auditory, visual, and motor integration in autism: A review of the evidence. *Journal of Autism & Developmental Disorders, 30*(5), 415–421.

Dempsey, I., & Foreman, P. (2001). A review of educational approaches for individuals with autism. *International Journal of Disability, Development and Education, 48,* 103–116.

Dunn, W., Smith-Myles, B., & Orr, S. (2002). Sensory processing issues associated with Asperger syndrome: A preliminary investigation. *The American Journal of Occupational Therapy, 56,* 97–102.

Dyches, T. T., Wilder, L. K., Sudweeks, R. R., Obiakor, F. E., & Algozzine, B. (2004). Multicultural Issues in Autism. *Journal of Autism and Developmental Disorders, 34*(2), 211–222.

Filapek, P. A., Steinberg-Epstein, R., & Book, T. M. (2006). Intervention for autistic spectrum disorders. *NeuroRx, 3,* 207–216.

Fombonne E. (2008). Epidemiology of autistic disorder and other pervasive developmental disorders. *Journal of Clinical Psychiatry, 66*(suppl 10), 3–8.

Frith, U., & Frith, C. D. (2003). Development and neurophysiology of mentalizing. *Philosophical Transactions of the Royal Society of London. Series B, 358,* 459–473.

Ganz, M. L. (2007). The lifetime distribution of the incremental societal costs of autism. *Archives of Pediatrics and Adolescent, 161,* 343–349.

Geschwind, D. H., & Levitt, P. (2007). Autism spectrum disorders: Developmental disconnection syndromes. *Current Opinion in Neurobiology, 17,* 103–111.

Goin-Kochel, R. P., & Myers, B. J. (2005). Congenital versus regressive onset of Autism Spectrum Disorders: Parent's beliefs about causes. *Focus on Autism and Other Developmental Disabilities, 20,* 169–179.

Goldberg, W., Osann, K., Filipek, P., Laulhere, T., Jarvis, K., Modahl, C., et al. (2003). Language and other regression: Assessment and timing. *Journal of Autism and Developmental Disorders, 33,* 607–616.

Goldstein S., & Schwebach, A. (2004). The co-morbidity of pervasive developmental disorder and attention deficit hyperactivity disorder: Results of a retrospective chart review. *Journal of Autism and Developmental Disorders, 34*(3), 329–339.

Green, V. A., Pituch, K. A., Itchon, J., Choi, A., O'Reilly, M., & Sigafoos, J. (2006). Internet survey of treatments used by parents of children with autism. *Research in Developmental Disabilities, 27,* 70–84.

Hamilton, A. F. de C. (2008). Emulation and mimicry for social interaction: A theoretical approach to imitation in autism. *The Quarterly Journal of Experimental Psychology, 61,* 101–115.

Hammock, E. A. D., & Levitt, P. (2006). The discipline of neurobehavioral development: The emerging interface of processes that build circuits and skills. *Human Development, 49,* 294–309.

Happé, F. (2005). The weak central coherence account of autism. In F. R. Volkmar, R. Paul, A. Klin, & D. J. Cohen (Eds.), *Handbook of autism and pervasive developmental disorders, Vol. 1: Diagnosis, development, neurobiology, and behavior* (3rd ed., pp. 640–649). New York: John Wiley & Sons.

Hatton, D. D., Hooper, S. R., Bailey, D. B., Skinner, M. L., Sullivan, K.M., & Wheeler, A. (2002). Problem behavior in boys with fragile X syndrome. *American Journal of Medical Genetics, 108*(2), 105–116.

Healing Thresholds (2009). *Sensory integration therapy for children with autism.* Retrieved June 2, 2009, from http://autism.healingthresholds.com/therapy/sensory-integration

Hertz-Picciotto, I., Croen, L. A., Hansen, R., Jones, C. R., van de Water, J., & Pessah, I. N. (2006). The CHARGE Study: An epidemiologic investigation of genetic and environmental factors contributing to autism. *Environmental Health Perspectives, 114*(7), 1119–1125.

Howard, J. S., Sparkman, C. R., Cohen, H. G., Green, G., & Stanislaw, H. (2005). A comparison of intensive behavior analytic and eclectic treatments for young children with autism. *Research in Developmental Disabilities, 26,* 359–383.

Howlin, P. (2005). The effectiveness of interventions for children with autism. *Journal of Neural Transmission (Supplement), 69,* 101–119.

Huber, R. J., & Zivalich, D. M. (2004). Lovaas's Behavioral Treatment of Autism Viewed from an Adierian Perspective. *Journal of Individual Psychology, 60,* 348–354.

Hultman, C., Sparen, P., Cnattingius, S. (2002). Perinatal risk factors for infantile autism. *Epidemiolog, 13,* 417–23.

Hume, K., Bellini, S., & Pratt, C. (2005). The usage and perceived outcomes of early intervention and early childhood programs for young children with autism spectrum disorder. *Topics in Early Childhood Special Education, 25,* 194–207.

Interactive Autism Network (IAN). (2009). Linking the Autism community and researchers. *Kennedy Kreiger Institute Autism Speaks.* Retrieved May 13, 2009, from http://www.ianproject.org/

Interdisciplinary Council on Developmental and Learning Disorders (ICDL). (2005). *Diagnostic manual for infancy and early childhood.* Bethesda: Author.

Jerrell, J. M., & McIntyre, R. S. (2008). Adverse events in children and adolescents treated with antipsychotic medications. *Human Psychopharmacological Clinical Expert, 23,* 283–290.

Kanner, L. (1943). Autistic disturbances of affective contact. *Nervous Child, 2,* 217–250.

Lakin, J. L., & Chartrand, T. L. (2003). Using nonconscious behavioral mimicry to create affiliation and rapport. *Psychological Science, 14,* 334–339.

Lane, S. J. (2002). Sensory modulation. In A. C. Bundy, S. J. Lane, & E. A. Murray (Eds.), *Sensory integration theory and practice* (2nd ed., pp. 101–122). Philadelphia, PA: F. A. Davis.

Lee, L.-C., Newschaffera, C. J., Lessler, J. T., Lee, B. K., Rashmi Shah, R., & Zimmerman, A. W. (2008). Variation in season of birth in singleton and multiple births concordant for autism spectrum disorders. *Paediatric and Perinatal Epidemiology, 22,* 172–179.

Levitt, P., & Campbell, D. B. (2009). The genetic and neurobiologic compass points toward common signaling dysfunctions in autism spectrum disorders. *Journal of Clinical Investigation, 119*(4), 747–754.

Levy, S. E., & Hyman, S. L. (2005). Novel treatments for autistic spectrum disorders. *Mental Retardation and Developmental Disabilities Research Reviews, 11,* 131–142.

Lord, C., Risi, S., DiLavore, P., Shulman, C., Thurm, A., & Pickles, A. (2006). Autism from 2 to 9 years of age. *Archives of General Psychiatry, 63*(6), 694–701.

Lovaas, O. I., Smith, T., & McEachin, J. J. (1989) Clarifying Comments on the Young Autism Study: Reply to Schopler, Short, and Mesibov. *Journal of Consulting and Clinical Psychology, 57,* 165–167.

Mandell, D. S., Ittenbach, R. F., Levy, S. E., & Pinto-Martin, J. A. (2007). Disparities in diagnoses received prior to a diagnosis of autism spectrum disorder. *Journal of Autism and Developmental Disorders, 37*(9), 1795–1802.

Mandell, D. S., Listerud, J., Levy, S. E., & Pinto-Martin, J. A. (2002). Race differences in the age at diagnosis among Medicaid-eligible children with autism. *Journal of the American Academy of Child Adolescent Psychiatry, 41*(12), 1447–1453.

Mandell, D. S., Novak, M. M., & Zubritsky, C. D. (2005). Factors associated with the age of diagnosis among children with autism spectrum disorders. *Pediatrics, 116*(6), 1480–1486.

Mandell, D. S., Wiggins, L. D., Yeargin-Allsopp, M., Carpenter, L. A., Daniels, J., & DiGuiseppi C. (2009). Racial/Ethnic disparities in the identification of children with autism spectrum disorders. *American Journal of Public Health, 99*(3), 493–498.

Matson, J. L., & Dempsey, T. (2008). Autism Spectrum Disorders: Pharmacotherapy for challenging behaviors. *Journal of Developmental & Physical Disabilities, 20,* 175–191.

Mauro, T. (n.d.) *Autism spectrum disorders*. Retrieved May 14, 2009, from http://specialchildren.about.com/od/gettingadiagnosis/g/Autism.htm

McIntyre, R. S., & Konarski, J. Z. (2005). Tolerability profiles of atypical antipsychotics in the treatment of bipolar disorder. *Journal of Clinical Psychiatry 66*(Suppl 3), 28–36.

Mesibov, G. B., & Howley, M. (2003). *Accessing the curriculum for pupils with autistic spectrum disorders*. London: David Fulton.

Molloy, C. A., Morrow, A. L., Meinzen-Derr, J., Dawson, G., et al. (2006). Familial autoimmune thyroid disease as a risk factor for regression in children with autism spectrum disorder: A CPEA study. *Journal of Autism and Developmental Disorders, 36*(3), 317–324.

Moran, R. W., & Gibbons, P. (2001). Intra-examiner and inter-examiner reliability for palpation of the cranial rhythmic impulse at the head and sacrum. *Journal of Manipulative Physiological Therapy, 24,* 183–190.

Mottron, L., & Burack, J. (2001). Enhanced perceptual functioning in the development of autism. In J. A. Burack, T. Charman, N. Yirmiya, & P. R. Zelazo (Eds.), *The development of autism: Perspectives from theory and research* (pp. 131–148). Mahwah, NJ: Erlbaum

Murphy, M., Bolton, P. F., Pickles, A., Fombonne E., Piven, J., & Rutter, M. (2000). Personality traits of the relatives of autistic probands. *Psychological Medicine, 30*(6) 1411–1424.

Myers, S. M. (2007). The status of pharmacotherapy for autism spectrum disorders. *Expert Opinion on Pharmacotherapy, 8,* 1579–1603.

National Institute of Neurological Disorders and Stroke (NINDS). (April, 2009). *Autism Fact Sheet*. Retrieved May 10, 2009, from http://www.ninds.nih.gov/disorders/autism/detail_autism.htm

Newschaffer, C. J., Croen, L. A., Daniels, J., Giarelli, E., Grether, J. K., et al. (2007). The epidemiology of autism spectrum disorders. Annual Review of Public Health, 28, 235–258.

Parham, L. D., & Mailloux, Z. (2005). Sensory Integration. In J. Case-Smith (Ed.) *Occupational therapy for children* (5th edition, pp. 356–411). St. Louis, MO: Elsevier.

Pfeiffer, B., Kinnealey, M., Reed, C., & Herzberg, G. (2005). Sensory modulation and affective disorders in children and adolescents with Asperger's disorder. *The American Journal of Occupational Therapy, 59,* 335–345.

Prizant, B. M., Wetherby, A. M., Rubin, E., & Laurent, A.C. (2003). The SCERTS Model: A transactional, family-centered approach to enhancing communication and socioemotional abilities of children with autism spectrum disorder. *Infants and Young Children, 16,* 296–316.

Rappley, M. D. (2006). Actual psychotropic medication use in preschool children. *Infants & Young Children, 19,* 154–163.

Reed, P., Osborne, L. A., & Corness, M. (2007). Brief report: Relative effectiveness of different home-based behavioral approaches to early teaching intervention. *Journal of Autism and Developmental Disorders, 37,* 1815–1821.

Remington, G., Sloman, L., Konstantareas, M., Parker, K., & Gow, R. (2001). Clomipramine versus haloperidol in the treatment of autistic disorder: A double-blind, placebo-controlled, crossover study. *Journal of Clinical Psychopharmacology, 21*(4), 440–444.

Schaaf, R. C., & Miller, L. J. (2005). Occupational therapy using a sensory integrative approach for children with developmental disabilities. *Mental Retardation and Developmental Disabilities Research Review, 11,* 143–148.

Schopler, E., Mesibov, G., & Baker, A. (1982). Evaluation of treatment for autistic children and their parents. *Journal of the American Academy of Child Psychiatry, 21,* 262–267.

Shattock, P., & Whitely, P. (2002). Biochemical aspects in autism spectrum disorders: Updating the opiodexcess theory and presenting new opportunities for biomedical intervention. *Expert Opinion Therapy Targets, 6,* 175–183.

Shea, V. (2004). A perspective on the research literature related to early intensive behavioral intervention (Lovaas) for young children with autism. *Autism: The International Journal of Research & Practice, 8,* 349–367.

Simpson, R. L., & Paul Zionts, P. (1999). *Autism: Information and Resources for Professionals and Parents* (2nd ed). Austin, TX : Pro-Ed.

Sonuga-Barke, E., Daley, D., Thompson, M., Laver-Bradbury, C, & Weeks, A. (2001). Parent-based therapies for preschool attention-deficit/hyperactivity disorder: A randomized, controlled trial with a community sample. *Journal of the American Academy of Child and Adolescent Psychiatry, 40*(4), 402–408.

Steege, M. W., Mace, F. C., Perry, L., & Longenecker, H. (2007). Applied behavior analysis: Beyond discrete trial teaching. *Psychology in the Schools, 44,* 91–99.

Steffenburg, S., Gillberg, C., Hellgren, L., Jakobsson, G., & Bohman, M. (1989). A twin study of autism in Denmark, Finland, Iceland, Norway and Sweden. *Journal of Child Psychology and Psychiatry and Allied Disciplines, 30,* 405–416.

Strain, P., McConnell, S., Carta, J., Fowler, S., Neisworth, & Wolery, M., (1992), Behaviorism in early intervention. *Topics in Early Childhood Education, 12,* 121–141,

Stromland, K., Nordin, V., Miller, M., Akerstrom, B. & Gillberg, C. (1994). Autism in thalidomide embryopathy: A population study. *Developmental. Medicine and Child Neurology., 36,* 351–356.

Sweeten, T. L., Bowyer, S. L., Posey, D. J., Halberstadt, G. M., & McDougle, C. J. (2003). Increased prevalence of familial autoimmunity in probands with pervasive developmental disorders. *Pediatrics, 112*(5), 420–424.

Talay-Ongan, A., & Wood, K. (2000). Unusual sensory sensitivities in autism: A possible crossroads. *International Journal of Disability, Development, and Education, 47,* 201–212.

Trottier, G., Srivastava, L., & Walker, C. D. (1999). Etiology of infantile autism: A review of recent advances in genetic and neurobiological research. *Journal of Psychiatry and Neuroscience, 24,* 103–115.

Tutt, R., Powell, S., & Thornton, M. (2006). Educational Approaches in Autism: What we know about what we do. *Educational Psychology in Practice, 22,* 69–81.

Veenstra-Vanderweele, J., Christian, S. L., & Cook, E. H., Jr. (2004). Autism as a paradigmatic complex genetic disorder. *Annual Review of Genomics and Human Genetics, 5,* 379–405.

Vitiello, B. (2007). Research in child and adolescent psychopharmacology: Recent accomplishments and new challenges. *Psychopharmacology, 191,* 5–13.

Vitiello, B. (2008). An international perspective on pediatric psychopharmacology. *International Review of Psychiatry, 20,* 121–126.

Weber, C. J. (2008). Update on Autism and Childhood Vaccines. *Urologic Nursing, 28,* 290–291.

Wiggins, L. D., Baio, J., & Rice, C. (2006). Examination of the time between first evaluation and first autism spectrum diagnosis in a population-based sample. *Journal of Developmental Behavioral Pediatrics, 27*(suppl 2), S79–S87.

Yeargin-Allsopp M., Rice, C., Karapurkar, T., Doernberg, N., Boyle, C., & Murphy, C. (2003). Prevalence of autism in a US metropolitan area. *Journal of the American Medical Association, 289*(1), 49–55.

Language Characteristics and Communication of Individuals with Autism

Catherine Orsak

hildren with autism often have significant difficulty acquiring and using communication skills. For many children, communication delays are the first sign of a potential problem reported by family members. Jamie, a mother of a child with autism, states her first concerns:

> I remember when Tyler was 14 months old, he always looked at my ear and not at my face when I talked to him. He didn't point at objects, babble, use any true words, or look at me when I called his name. He would lead me to objects around the house and cried all the time. I knew something wasn't right so I started with his pediatrician, and he was diagnosed with autism 4 months later.

Such delays in communication can affect children's ability to interact effectively as well as negatively influence other areas of development. The importance of communication to the overall development of a child, as well as its significance to family members, often makes communication deficits a priority for intervention (Schwartz & Garfinkle,1998). Some parents find it difficult to watch siblings want to play and interact with the sibling who has autism:

> Tyler's older brother did not understand why his brother was unresponsive when he called his name or why he did not know how to play with trucks or talk to him. As parents, we tried to explain autism and what it was, but it is hard for a 7-year-old to comprehend. Because Tyler made only a few sounds, I would talk for Tyler when his brother or any other family member wanted to interact with him.

41

The *DSM-IV-TR* (APA, 2000) definition of autism includes qualitative impairments in communication as manifested by at least one of the following:

(a) Delay in, or total lack of, the development of spoken language (not accompanied by an attempt to compensate through alternative modes of communication such as gesture or mime)
(b) In individuals with adequate speech, marked impairment in the ability to initiate or sustain a conversation with others
(c) Stereotyped and repetitive use of language or idiosyncratic language
(d) Lack of varied, spontaneous make-believe play or social imitative play appropriate to developmental level (p. 69).

Many individuals with autism display impairments in all these areas while some only demonstrate impairments in one. Alex is 10 years old. Alex demonstrates a total lack of spoken language and does not use gestures to compensate. After snack time, he hands his therapist his full soda can and just looks at her. His teacher knows from experience that if she does anything other than throw the can away, he will throw it across the room, but Alex cannot communicate this request on his own with words or gestures. Mary is 7 years old and is in a general education second grade class because academically she is at grade level. She is verbal and speaks in long multi-word phrases. Although grammar and syntax are affected, it is easy to understand the message she is trying to convey. She is unable to appropriately initiate or sustain a conversation with adults or peers. She does not answer questions consistently about daily events or activities and continues to talk over other people, interrupt, and only talk about what she is interested in.

Bryan is a 14-year-old who is verbal and communicates using short phrases. He is able to read and perform basic math skills such as simple addition and subtraction. However, he uses rote, memorized phrases to communicate his wants and needs. He demonstrates stereotyped and repetitive use of language and lacks varied, spontaneous use of social-imitative play appropriate for his developmental level. To indicate he is upset he uses the phrase, "It's OK" and repeats it until an adult says, "Yes, it is OK." When he does not want to do something he says, "Time to go home."

Children with autism have such varied communication and language characteristics that teaching these individuals with such different strengths and needs can be challenging. The purpose of this chapter is to describe the different language and communication impairments and discuss intervention strategies to assist in the remediation of these impairments.

COMMUNICATION, LANGUAGE, AND SPEECH

The terms *communication, language,* and *speech* are often interpreted as having similar meanings or as being identical. Actually, the terms are very different and denote different aspects of language development and use.

Communication is the most general term, encompassing any means, verbal or nonverbal, of transmitting a message from one person to another. Language is a set of symbols (spoken, written, sign language, pictures) and rules for combining those symbols to represent ideas for the purpose of communication (Watson, Lord, Schaffer, & Schopler, 1989). Speech is a verbal use of language to communicate or convey meaning (Owens, 1996). Speech is a process that requires very precise neuromuscular coordination and can be challenging for individuals with autism. Alex, who hands a soda can to someone to indicate "throw it away," is using preintentional communication, whereas Mary and Bryan, who use single words or multi-word phrases to convey a message, are using speech as a way to communicate through language.

COMMUNICATION

Communication is the transmission of all kinds of messages such as ideas, information, needs, perceptions, and feelings (Widerstrom, Mowder, & Sandall, 1997). All individuals communicate messages to others through preintentional or intentional communication.

Preintentional communication

Communication includes *preintentional communication,* which develops from birth to 8 months of age. Preintentional anticipatory behavior happens when children start to focus their attention and anticipate desired objects, people, and events. For example, a child may produce sucking movements, arm movements, and vocalizations in response to seeing a bottle. The response from the parent or caregiver needs to be sensitive (to recognize the communicative behavior), contingent (timely and contextually related to communicative or potential communicative behavior), and consistent (responding to the same behavior in the same way, over time) (Lloyd, Fuller, & Arvidson, 1997).

James, a typically developing 8-month-old, sees a cookie while he is sitting in his high chair and starts to babble. His mother immediately looks at him and sees he is looking at the cookie and then back at her. This is referred to as *joint attention* and results from her sensitivity to the communication act. She immediately gives him a cookie (contingent upon the communication act) and he eats it. So every time he subsequently sits in his highchair and vocalizes, his mother looks at him, follows his gaze to see what he wants, and bring it to him (consistency).

Intentional Communication

Responses that are sensitive, contingent, and consistent will help lead a child to the next level of communication, which is *intentional behavior.* Intentional behavior starts between 8 and 12 months of age and includes preintentional vocalizations and gestures (e.g., reaching), which become combined with more conventional behaviors (e.g., manipulating others' hands, using picture symbols, simple signs) (Lloyd, Fuller, & Arvidson, 1997) to intentionally communicate a message.

One day, when 10-month-old Tyler wanted to go outside, he walked to and stood by the back door (intentional communication act). His mother immediately thought he may want to go outside (sensitive), so she walked over to the door and opened it (contingent), and he went outside happy as can be. From that point on, every time he went to the door, his mother would open it for him (consistent).

When a child uses intentional behavior to communicate wants and needs, the message is easily understood by more people, therefore increasing the likelihood of the child using it again and continuing his or her development in the ability to communicate. If the intended message is difficult to understand, the response from the parent will be less consistent. In many children with autism, these early intentional communication behaviors are weak, infrequent, or absent and therefore may not elicit consistent responses. Thus, the progression to communicative competency is hindered, and an important link in communication development is missing. Ten-month-old Andre goes to the door and stands there. His mother walks over to the door and opens it. Andre just stands there. She is confused; he starts to get upset. She does not know what he wants, so she closes the door. He gets even more upset. She says to him, "I don't know what you want." Andre then goes and finds the dog and stands by the dog. "Do you want the dog to go outside?" Andre stops crying. She understood the message. In this instance, she did not feel successful in understanding what her son wanted because he became upset. When he gets upset when trying to communicate, she feels like she has failed.

The more consistent the response is to the communication behavior, the more the parent and child will interact, thereby increasing the probability of improved communication. If a child is unresponsive or inconsistent to a parent's attempts to interact or respond, the parent may feel ineffective at communicating with the child, decreasing parent–child interaction and negatively impacting the child's development of competent communication skills (Lloyd et al., 1997).

Sally is 6 years old and is nonverbal. Walking to the speech therapy room with the speech therapist, she turns to walk toward the playground. The therapists responds by taking her to the playground to show and tell her it is raining so we cannot play outside. Sally willfully walks inside, takes two steps, falls to the floor, starts to cry, and tries to take off her pants. When the therapist attempts to stop her from taking off her pants she starts to kick, scratch, and bite the therapist. At this point the therapist does not know what to do or understand what Sally wants, as her outburst appears separate from her initial interest in the playground. There may be other factors contributing to the "meltdown" that are not obvious. It is easy to assume and make judgments about intentional communication (the message of the individual communicating), yet without looking at the whole picture (i.e, the environment, what happened immediately prior to the behavior, and the consequences of the behavior) and analyzing the behavior over a period of time, your judgments may be inaccurate. When teaching students who are nonverbal and use limited gestures, it is important to consistently respond to any attempts to communicate. Responses can be following the child's lead (the child taking you to what they want), giving the child the toy or food item he or she is reaching for, or helping the child with an object he or she gives you.

Gestures

Any act of communication has a specific form (e.g., gestures, vocalizations, words, signs, etc.) and a specific function or intent (e.g., gaining attention, requesting, greetings, commenting, giving information, seeking information, expressing feelings, social routines). All individuals display behaviors that carry communicative intent, either inferred by the communication partner (Alex's teacher infers the meaning of his handing the soda can to the therapist) or intentionally based on the actions of the individual (Tyler goes to the door to indicate his desire to go outside), and all individuals use gestures either as their primary mode of communication or in conjunction with another mode of communication (Lloyd et al., 1997).

Gestures are the use of any part of the body to communicate. Gestures include body posture and pointing, and they can be used in conjunction with other nonverbal communicative behaviors such as eye gaze and facial expression. Pointing is a specific gesture that usually develops early on and is considered an essential part of early communication development (Owens, 1996). Gestures are a powerful communication modality and can be used in many ways, for example, tapping the floor to say sit down, using a head shake to indicate yes or no, and reaching to indicate up. Many children with ASD do not compensate for their lack of verbal skills with gestures but instead use gestures that are limited in both quantity and quality. Primitive motoric gestures (e.g., contact gestures of leading, pulling, or manipulating another's hand) are predominately used to communicate. Aaron, who is 4 years old, needs help placing a puzzle piece. He does not hand the puzzle piece to the teacher and point to the puzzle; he takes her hand and puts it on the puzzle. The use of many conventional gestures (e.g., showing, waving, pointing) and symbolic gestures (e.g., head nodding, imitation) are lacking in children with ASD (Woods & Wetherby, 2003).

Nonverbal social–communicative skills are also impaired in individuals with autism. They are characterized by significant difficulty with nonverbal joint attention skills (e.g., social orienting, establishing shared attention, monitoring emotional states, considering another's intentions). Mark, although 10 years old and verbal, sees another boy holding a toy he wants. He walks over to the boy, looks right at the object, and takes it, with no reference or acknowledgment to the boy holding the toy. Individuals with autism also demonstrate some difficulty with social turn-taking skills (e.g., initiating interactions, maintaining interactions by taking turns, providing contingent responses to interactions initiated by others) (Quill, 2000).

Nonverbal social communicative skills include sharing of attention. *Sharing of attention* is the ability to establish and maintain a common focus of attention with another person. This can be observed from birth when young children are able to orient to others and maintain face-to-face eye gaze. At approximately 4 to 6 months of age, children begin to look in the direction that their caregivers are looking. By 10 to 12 months of age, children are communicating intentionally to establish shared attention by showing objects and by pointing to objects and events they observe. This capacity is believed to underlie the later developing capacities of conversational ability and Theory of Mind (TOM). A limitation in shared or joint attention is a core deficit in individuals with ASD (Prizant, Wetherby, Rubin, & Laurent, 2003). Lisa is 3 years old and has a brother who is 7 years old and has autism. Lisa is always saying, "Watch this" or "Look at that." She comments on everything and wants to share it with her family. Her brother does not comment on things or activities he is engaged with and does not ever ask family members to share in anything he is doing. It is like they are not even there.

Sharing of intention is the ability to direct communicative acts to others to accomplish specific goals. Children begin to communicate intentionally at 8–10 months of age through gestures and vocalizations for a wide variety of purposes. In development, intentions are expressed through more conventional gestures and vocalizations allowing for greater *readability* (Prizant et al., 2003). If Alex would have given the therapist the soda can and pointed to a trash can, his communicative intent would have been more readable. As children acquire more sophisticated communicative means, functions or intentions initially expressed through preverbal means are replaced by more specific symbolic means (e.g., spoken words, sign language). A common pattern found in children with autism is that they express a limited range of functions with primarily unconventional means. Aaron takes people by the hand to indicate he needs help or wants something. Most of the time it is very difficult to determine what he wants before he becomes upset.

General Strategies for Enhancing Communication

The inability to communicate with others can be extremely frustrating. As teachers and individuals who work with those who have disordered communication, it is imperative that we use intervention strategies that enhance the communication abilities of our students.

➤ Follow and expand the child's attentional focus by imitating the child's behavior and commenting on his or her focus of attention.

➤ Present motivating materials and activities to the child to enhance sharing of attention and intention.

➤ Design the environment to create opportunities for communication. Put highly motivating objects and activities within sight yet out of reach or in clear containers that are too difficult for children to open without asking for assistance.

➤ When child is playing with a toy, turn the toy off so the child needs to request to turn it on, or find toys the child does not like so he or she can protest an undesired toy.

➤ Provide choices whenever possible.

➤ Stop a highly preferred activity (e.g., swinging) so the child needs to request to continue the activity.

LANGUAGE

Language or linguistic communication can be defined as a socially shared code or conventional system for representing concepts through the use of arbitrary symbols and rule-governed combinations of those symbols (Owens, 1996). Although most languages are transmitted via speech, speech is not an essential feature of language. American Sign Language (ASL) does not follow the same rule-governed system as spoken English but is a separate language with its own rules for symbol combinations. Following is the American Speech–Language–Hearing Association definition of language (Committee on Language, 1983; Owens, 1996):

> Language is a complex and dynamic system of conventional symbols that is used in various modes for thought and communication:
>
> ➤ Language evolves within specific historical, social, and cultural contexts.
>
> ➤ Language, as rule-governed behavior, is described by at least five parameters—phonologic, morphologic, syntactic, semantic, and pragmatic.
>
> ➤ Language learning and use are determined by the intervention of biological, cognitive, psychosocial, and environmental factors.
>
> ➤ Effective use of language for communication requires a broad understanding of human interaction, including such associated factors as nonverbal cues, motivation, and sociocultural roles.

Language is composed of two major systems: language comprehension and language production. *Language comprehension,* also referred as *receptive language,* refers to an individual's understanding of written language through reading or verbal language through listening. *Language production,* or *expressive language,* refers to an individual's ability to use speech, writing, or sign language to convey a message. Individuals with autism demonstrate disorders in both their ability to understand and use language effectively (Prizant et al., 2003).

Receptive Language

The receptive language system is also referred to as auditory comprehension. This language system involves understanding the meaning of words, either written or verbal. Alex hears what is being said yet does not understand when asked to get his shoes. He just stands there. When asked, "What is your name?" Mary replies, "Five years old?" The receptive language system or auditory comprehension of language includes skills such as concept and vocabulary development, responding to one's name, following directions, pointing to pictures or objects as they are named, and answering questions.

Many individuals with autism have difficulty processing auditory information and may respond to verbal directions and questions that are learned based on routine rather than genuine comprehension. Mark is able to hang up his backpack when asked as he arrives at school every morning, yet if asked to hang up his backpack in the middle of the day, he does not seem to understand what is being said. The act of hanging up his backpack is routine; he cannot process the verbal direction and follow the instruction independent of that routine.

Children with autism have problems comprehending information in meaningful and flexible ways. Children with autism tend to exhibit *overselective attention.* They tend to process one piece of information at a time, and information is often stored and remembered as a whole rather than reorganized and integrated in a flexible manner. Concept development, generalization, and social–communicative interaction are affected (Quill, 2000). Ben is 10 years old and has been reading a story about apple pie. All the apples in the story are red. Ben is able to point to all the red apples in the story, yet he cannot point to a green apple in a different story. This style of processing is known as *Gestalt processing:* information is processed and remembered as a whole, and the individual meanings of the parts of speech are missing. Information is stored as a whole and is unrelated to other similar experiences. Echolalic speech, or repeating what others say verbatim, and routinized conversations are examples of gestalt processing. Most children with autism have trouble understanding pronouns. Jeff does not understand when the teacher says, "It's your turn," but understands when the teacher says, "It's Jeff's turn."

Individuals with ASD are often limited to a concrete and literal understanding of language (Prizant et al., 2003). John does not respond when the teacher says, "Pay attention," but understands when she says, "Look at the book." Idioms and sarcasm are difficult to understand because they are abstract. George is 14, and after his mom says, "It is a piece of cake," when referring to work he is doing, he say, "No, it's paper."

Strategies to Improve Receptive Language Skills

The ability to listen and understand language is critical to being able to use language effectively and to learning. Some individuals present with delays in receptive language skills, while expressive language skills are intact.

➤ Be careful not to overestimate language comprehension, especially in individuals who are verbal. Receptive language development may lag behind expressive language. A child who is nonverbal may be able to understand more complex language than a child who uses two-word phrases.
➤ Adjust the complexity of your language to the language level of the child.
➤ Avoid excessive talking. Speak in clearly articulated sentences.

> ➤ Gain the child's attention using his or her name, a visual cue (e.g., turning lights on and off), or a gesture (e.g., touching the child's shoulder) before beginning to speak.
> ➤ Only give directions two times before assisting the child. Repeated directions only reinforce lack of attention to the speaker.
> ➤ Use gestures and visual aids (schedules, writing down directions) to supplement speech.

Expressive Language

The expressive language system is a complex system that can best be understood by breaking it down into its functional components. Language can be divided into three major although not equal components: *form, content,* and *use.* Form includes *syntax,* the form or structure of a sentence; *morphology,* the rules governing the changes in meaning; and *phonology,* the rules governing the structure, distribution, and sequencing of speech–sound patterns. Content encompasses meaning or *semantics,* and use is called *pragmatics.* These five components—syntax, morphology, phonology, semantics, and pragmatics—are the basic rule systems found in language (Owens, 1996).

Syntax

Syntax is the system of the rules that governs the form or structure of a sentence. These rules specify word order, sentence organization, and the relationships among words, word classes, and other sentence elements. In English, for example, adjectives precede nouns, and verbs agree with their subjects. Syntax specifies which word order combinations are acceptable, or grammatical (e.g., blue truck, she is), and which are not (e.g., truck blue, she are).

Individuals with autism who have developed language skills have difficulty with syntax. Gestalt processing affects the learning of the more abstract parts of speech such as articles (e.g., a, the), pronouns, verb forms (e.g., tense, irregular forms), and the like. These are only learned as whole units within a sentence. The flexibility to use these parts of speech in novel experiences is missing. Steven does not understand how to use past tense verbs when talking about events that happened earlier in the day. In response to the question, "What did you eat for lunch?" He responds, "I eat hamburger." The inability to use these more abstract parts of speech, the parts that are difficult to visualize, affects the ability to relay information, engage in conversations, and produce narratives that are clear and easy to understand. Matthew, a 6-year-old who is at grade level academically, has difficulty telling the class about what he did over the weekend. "I go park, play swings, go slide, go home."

Morphology

Morphology is concerned with the internal organization of words. Words consist of one or more smaller units called morphemes. A morpheme is the smallest grammatical unit that is indivisible without violating meaning or producing meaningless units. Therefore *dog* is a single morpheme because *d* and *g* are meaningless alone. Most words in English consist of one or two morphemes. The two types of morphemes are free morphemes and bound morphemes. *Free morphemes* can stand alone or in combination with other free or bound morphemes. Examples of free morphemes are *toy, big,* and *happy. Bound morphemes* are grammatical tags or markers that cannot function independently but denote meaning when they are attached to free morphemes. Examples include *-s, -est, un-,* and *-ly,* meaning plural, most, negative, and manner, respectively. By combining the free and bound morphemes we can create *toys, biggest,* and *unhappily.*

Preschool language development corresponds to increases in a child's average utterance length, measured in morphemes. The Mean Length of Utterance (MLU) is a numerical value determined by observing a child, writing down at least 50 utterances, counting the morphemes, and dividing by the total utterances taken. This value relates well to age for English speaking young children. For example a typically developing 4-year-old would have an MLU around 4.0 (Owens, 1996).

In typical language development, morphologic development proceeds in stages. The use of present progressive *-ing* emerges around 19 months of age and is usually mastered by 20 months of age. The use of prepositions *in* and *on,* and irregular past tense verbs such as *came, fell, broke* emerge around 27 months of age and are mastered by 46 months (Owens, 1996). Children with autism demonstrate difficulties using these morphemes when speaking and usually require speech and language therapy to learn how to use them. Steven is 6 and says, "ride car," instead of, "We are riding in the car."

The inability to understand that using the word *fell* instead of *fall* means something that happened in the past and saying, "She is running," means something happening right now will impact the ability to understand what is said and the ability to extract accurate meaning from written information. Disorders in morphologic development impact social communication and learning.

Phonology

Phonology is the aspect of language concerned with the rules governing the structure, distribution, and sequencing of speech sounds and the shape of syllables. Each language employs a variety of speech sounds or phonemes. A phoneme is the smallest linguistic unit of sound that can signal a difference in meaning. For example, the meaning of *dog* and *log* are very different, as are those of *dock* and *lock.* Phonological rules govern the distribution and sequencing of phonemes within the language. Most children with autism who are verbal do not demonstrate significant disorders of phonology. Occasionally, an individual may produce the /f/ sound for /th/ and may have difficulty with the production of /r/. These impairments do not typically affect their ability to communicate with others.

Semantics

Semantics is a system of rules governing the meaning or content of words or word relationships and distinguishing dissimilar words. Semantics is concerned with the relationship of language to our perceptions of objects, events, and relationships or to cognition and thought. It is the aspect of language function that relates to understanding the meanings of words, phrases, and sentences, as well as using words appropriately.

There is a difference between world knowledge and word knowledge. *World knowledge* refers to an individual's autobiographical and experiential understanding and memory of particular events. *Word knowledge* contains word and symbol definitions and is primarily verbal. Word knowledge forms each person's mental dictionary or thesaurus. These two types of knowledge are related because word knowledge is usually based on world knowledge. World knowledge is a generalized concept formed from several particular events. Therefore language meaning is based on what we, as individuals, know and experience. A child who has never experienced or read a book about horses may not be able to point to a picture of a horse when asked.

Gestalt processing present particular challenges for children with autism in learning semantics because these children learn by memorizing exact instances of experiences, including irrelevant information, rather than by analyzing information and relating it to previous experiences (Prizant et al., 2003). Events are remembered or retrieved with little analysis, and linguistic utterances may or may not be part of these events. In contrast, *analytic processing,* or *semantic memory,* requires the ability to attend to the most important information in an ongoing manner. It is important to be able to use language appropriately in different situations. For example, it is socially not acceptable for a child to ask adults how old they are even though it is appropriate to ask other children. The inability to make this distinction impacts the overall use of language for social purposes. Another example is teaching a child with autism what a dog is. If the child is only shown pictures and only experiences small dogs, when encountering a big dog, he or she will not know that it is also a dog. When teaching individuals with autism it is essential to help children move from purely rote memory strategies to more analytic based strategies which underlie the acquisition of flexible concepts and meanings. Introducing flexibility in all aspects of teaching, with an emphasis on conceptually based learning, rather than teaching to rote memory, fosters flexibility (Prizant et al., 2003).

Children with ASD also demonstrate a gestalt mode of language use or expressive language. Gestalt language forms are utterances that are learned as memorized forms or whole units. Jose had learned the phrase "I want to eat" as a whole unit so anytime he wanted something to drink he said, "I want to eat drink." Once these utterance are learned as whole units, it is difficult to reteach or change to add other words or phrases. Jose does not understand what the individual words *I* and *want* mean and is unable to use them in any other context. The use of echolalia is another example. Echolalia can be either delayed or immediate. Delayed echolalia is an exact or partial repetition of speech that is produced at a significantly later time after originally heard and may serve a variety of communicative and noncommunicative functions. For example, a child learns the phrase "See you tomorrow, sunshine" from a movie, he then uses this phrase every time he is leaving. Other individuals consistently engage in delayed echolalia. This communication is not directed at anyone and does not appear to serve a communicative function (i.e., requesting, commenting, asking a question). This type of language may not be contextually relevant (Quill, 2000). John is 5 and loves Dora. Throughout his day at school, he will repeat lines from the show, and most of the time they do not display communicative intent. Immediate echolalia is an exact repetition of speech that is produced immediately after it is heard and may also serve a variety of communicative or noncommunicative functions. For example, an individual with autism is asked "What do you want?" and immediately repeats "What do you want?" This serves no communicative function. However, if the student is asked to say "what do you want?" to another peer and immediately repeats it to the peer, then it has served the communicative function of asking a question.

Typical language development is a complex process that includes the ability to use what you know. Information that is integrated in flexible, meaningful ways can be accessed and used in the same manner for different situations. Individuals with autism learn and store information in fragmented, concrete associations (i.e., in situation A I do this, in situation B, I do this). The inability to learn new information and add the new information to an existing framework for future use is missing. The inability to learn and use language in flexible and meaningful ways is a core characteristic of autism (Prizant et al., 2003) and affects the social function of language called pragmatics.

Pragmatics

Pragmatics is a set of rules related to language use with communicative context. When we use language to affect others or relay information, we make use of pragmatics. Pragmatics is concerned with the way language is used to communicate rather than with the way language is structured. Core pragmatics include the knowledge of basic speech acts such as assertions (i.e., "I like that"), questions, requests, and commands. This type of knowledge is considered universally required in order to master one's own language. These rules also govern other acts that are done with words that are not speech acts. There is a specific set of rules and contexts as to when you say "congratulations" or "look at me" (Kasher & Meilijson, 2008). John's mother says to her son, "Say hello, John," and John echoes, "Say hello, John." John did not interpret the utterance or understand the context. John knows the words, knows how to imitate the grammatical sentence, but does not possess the pragmatic knowledge of rules that govern how to use words.

Every speech utterance is a speech act. In order to be valid, each speech act must meet certain conditions. It must involve the appropriate persons and circumstances, be complete and correctly executed by all participants, and contain the appropriate intentions of all participants. "May I have a donut, please?" is only valid when speaking to a person with access to donuts. Jared is 10 and is verbal and frequently when playing with cars he yells out the word "cookie" and then keeps playing. He is not looking at anyone and he does not gain anyone's attention. He is not communicating with intent, and therefore this is not considered a valid speech act.

Engaging in conversations is one component of pragmatics. In general, children learn language within conversational context. Conversation is governed by the "cooperation principle" (Owens,1996): Conversational participants cooperate with each other. The four maxims of the cooperation principle relate to quantity, quality, relation, and manner. *Quantity* is the informativeness of each participant's contribution: no participant should provide too much or too little information. The *quality* of each contribution should be governed by truthfulness and based on sufficient evidence. The maxim of *relation* states that a contribution should be relevant to the topic of conversation. Finally, each participant should be reasonably direct in *manner* and avoid vagueness, ambiguity, and wordiness.

Since language is transmitted primarily via the speech mode, pragmatic rules govern a number of conversational interactions: sequential organization and coherence of conversations, repair of errors, and role. *Organization and coherence* of conversations include turn-taking; opening, maintaining, and closing a conversation; establishing and maintaining a topic; making relevant comments and contributions to the conversation. *Repair* includes giving and receiving feedback and correcting conversational errors. Tommy is 14 years old and is talking about riding the bus. The person he is speaking to does not understand how he got hurt on the bus, but Tommy just keeps saying the same three sentences in the exact same way. He never adjusts what he is saying to repair the breakdown in conversation. During conversations you take on different *roles*; yet have to take the perspective of the other person, either as the listener or the speaker. Children with autism have difficulty using repair strategies when they do not understand the information or did not hear what was being said. They do not ask for clarification or make the distinction between how you act when you are in the listener role and what is expected when you are in the role of speaker.

Pragmatic knowledge governing the basic aspects of conversation is deficient in individuals with autism. Topic introduction, maintenance, and change can be inappropriate in many children with autism. Many highly verbal individuals use discourse markers (i.e., "by the way") when they are not introducing a new topic. Difficulties with preoccupation of specific topics and limited ability to shift topics are also prevalent in children with ASD. Alex, a 10-year-old with autism who is verbal, will only talk about Thomas the train. He can tell you everything about Thomas but cannot engage in a brief conversation about going to Disneyland or something that happened at school.

The multiple features of nonverbal communication in discourse include proximity, affect, and body language. *Proximity* is the ability to maintain appropriate distance and orient to the communication partner. The use of eye gaze, facial expression, and gesture are important ways to convey *affect*. Gestures and intonation comprise body language, which influences the meaning of the spoken message. These are critical skills that affect the ability to have a conversation.

Another skill that affects pragmatics is *sharing of affect*. Sharing of affect is the ability to experience and express emotional states by directing affective displays to others. Through affect sharing, a child demonstrates his or her social awareness of the presence of others and simultaneously experience empathy for the positive or negative emotion communicated. This capacity is believed to result in a child learning to both express emotions and read emotions expressed by others. Sharing of affect is an essential component of social-communicative interactions, and this component is impaired in individuals with autism, affecting their pragmatic language skills.

The complex, ongoing adjustments and modifications inherent in conversation challenge even the most able children with autism (Quill, 2000). The use of stereotypic, memorized scripts; interests in only a few topics; and difficulty attending to nonverbal cues affect communication for the purposes of social interaction. Because of impairments in taking others' perspectives, they show a limited awareness of speaker-listener roles and have difficulty maintaining topics and repairing conversational breakdowns. Receptive and expressive language skill deficits are core characteristics in autism and affect the ability to communicate for many different purposes. Most individuals with autism have disorders in both receptive and expressive language skills. However, there is variability to the severity and the overall impact on communication. The task of teaching these individuals these core language skills is a formidable responsibility.

Strategies for Enhancing Expressive Language Skills

Expressive language skills may also be delayed or disordered in individuals with ASD. Some may speak in only two word phrases and others may use long run-on sentences with disordered grammar. Some may use a speech generating device as their mode of expressive language. It is important to promote expressive language skills as a way for the individual to learn effective ways to communicate with others.

➤ Enhance comprehension of correct syntax and morphology with the use of visual aids (i.e., social stories, written words, picture symbols). Visual supports help to maintain attention, and visual information is processed and retrieved more effectively from memory.

➤ Keep a high degree of consistency and predictability for learning while fostering flexibility.

➤ During snack time, give children small amounts of food so they need to ask for more. Work on requesting help by putting food in small containers.

➤ Practice greetings when leaving and arriving. Teach within natural contexts.

➤ Use facilitative interaction to acknowledge the child's communicative intent and then expand on communicative behavior (i.e., the child wants and cracker and says "cracker." Model and provide visual aids for "I want a cracker.")

➤ Develop the individual's communication skills with peers. This should include topic management, the ability to expand and elaborate on a range of different topics initiated by others, shifting topics, and ending topics appropriately.

➤ Help the individual recognize and use a range of different means for communicating (i.e., social interacting, negotiating, persuading, discussing, and disagreeing through verbal means).

SPEECH

Speech is a verbal means of communicating or conveying meaning. It is the result of planning and executing specific motor sequences; speech is a process that requires very precise neuromuscular coordination. Each spoken language has specific sounds, or phonemes and sound combinations that are characteristic of that language (Owens, 1996). Articulation is the production of speech sounds. Speech is one way to communicate a message. However it is not the only means of human communication. Some individuals are capable of using speech as a way of communicating while others have to rely on gestures, speech generating devices, or picture symbols to communicate.

Autism is characterized by wide variability in the capacity to use vocal communication. Some children with autism have been found to use a limited consonant inventory and less complex syllable structures, while others show adequate complexity for vocalizations (McHale Simeonsson, Marcus, & Olley, 1980; National Research Council [NRC], 2001; Stone & Caro-Martinez, 1990; Wetherby & Prutting, 1984; Wetherby, Yonclas, & Bryan, 1989). Some children with autism display *apraxia,* a neurogenic impairment involving planning, executing and sequencing motor movements. *Verbal apraxia* affects the programming of the articulators and rapid sequences of muscle movements for speech sounds. *Oral apraxia* involves nonspeech movements (e.g., blowing, puckering, licking from the lips). Tyler is 6 years old and has autism and displays characteristics of oral and verbal apraxia. He makes good eye contact and primarily uses a speech generating device (described later in the chapter) to communicate. He is able to produce a few speech sounds. His mother has been trying for 3 months to get him to say "Mom." Tyler is able to produce a /b/ sound but is unable to hold his lips together long enough to produce /m/. He looks at his mother and attempts to imitate her mouth movement yet is unable.

Interventions for Individuals with Autism Who Are Nonverbal

The NRC (2001) reports a substantial portion of children with autism (20% to 40%) fail to make meaningful gains in speech production even with substantial intervention. Interventions for these children need to focus on teaching them to use Augmentative and Alternative Communication (AAC) systems such as speech generating devices (i.e., Vantage or Dynavox), the Picture Exchange Communication System (PECS), or sign language.

Being able to effectively communicate your wants and needs is something intrinsic to all individuals. All students with autism communicate their basic wants and needs in some form or another: some may use speech, some may use gestures, some may use picture symbols, and some may use speech generating devices. The goal is to help facilitate communication using modalities (sign, gestures, pictures) that are most effective for the individual, not to have them use a system that is too difficult for them. Some interventions such as PECS and speech generating devices have been more successful than others such as sign language in facilitating communication with a wide range of people. When communication intervention begins, the system that is going to best facilitate communication is unknown, and much of the intervention is trial and error using a total communication approach. The individual needs to choose what modality works best for him or her. Sam is 17 and is able to type and spell messages on his new speech generating device. His therapist wanted to teach him to use the picture symbols because she thought it would be a faster way to communicate his message. After 2 months of individual therapy, Sam made it very clear that he wanted to spell his messages by removing the picture symbol overlay from his device.

The goal of communication intervention for many individuals with autism who are primarily nonverbal is to improve functional communication skills. Functional communication requires that children be able to generalize communication skills from training sessions to other settings and situations and to the events experienced in daily living. To meet this functional criterion, communication skills need to be used not only across environments but spontaneously at contextually appropriate times and in a variety of settings (Carr & Kologinsky, 1983). John is able to use his speech generating device to request various objects at school during speech therapy time, however, he does not initiate using his device in the classroom.

Communication intervention should attempt to find whatever mode of communication works best for that individual. It may include gestures, vocalizations, picture symbols, speech, writing, and sign language (Lloyd et al., 1997). Jeremy is 10 years old and received a speech generating device a year ago. His goal is, when he wants something (i.e., to go outside), he independently finds his device and pushes the button "go." This has been addressed daily in the classroom with no progress. When Jeremy wants to go outside, he walks over to the door and stands there. It appears that he prefers to use gestures as his way of communicating.

Communication needs to be easy, effective, and individualized. The communication partner (person being communicated to) is critical to the development of an individual's communication abilities (Gutstein & Sheely, 2002). The communication partner needs to create opportunities to practice and needs to respond contingently and consistently to any communication attempts made with an AAC system.

Many individuals with autism display positive and negative behaviors. Negative behaviors such as aggression may be more prevalent in those who are nonverbal and for whom communication is challenging. It is believed by some people who specialize in the area of communication that all individuals display behaviors that carry communicative intent and that all excessive or problem behaviors that occur in the presence of others may be thought of as attempts to communicate (Lloyd et al., 1997). Many times behavioral interventions focus on punishment instead of reinforcement. Punishment leads to negative outcomes and does not teach a replacement behavior or new skill. Individuals who are nonverbal use these problem behaviors as a way to communicate. Jacob is 10 and is nonverbal. He does not have a consistent AAC system that he uses. He is sitting at the table working with the teacher and starts to scream and pound his fists on the table. The teacher tells him he needs to do one more and he hits her. At that moment she stops because she is hurt, and he is allowed to leave the table. An assessment of this behavior revealed that he was screaming as a way to communicate he was done. Teaching an appropriate way to communicate "All Done" using an AAC system (pictures, sign language) will decrease the problem behavior. When Jacob appropriately communicates "All Done," he is allowed to leave the table. This is the concept behind *Functional Communication Training* (FCT).

FCT is a communication- or language-based program for addressing problem behaviors of individuals with and without language disabilities. FCT involves assessing the function that a problem behavior serves for the individual, then teaching a new response that serves the same function using the most effective communication system for that individual (McCauley & Fey, 2006). Research has demonstrated the efficacy of FCT at decreasing the range of problem behaviors including aggression toward peers and adults, property destruction, self-injurious behavior, and tantrums. In a study on FCT, Carr and Durand (1985) used functional analysis for determining the function of the challenging behaviors, then investigated the effects of an FCT intervention for teaching a communication replacement identified through analysis. The results demonstrated that the replacement behavior (communication) increased and the problem behavior decreased only when the replacement matched the function (escape, attention, access to a tangible, or sensory stimulation). The results of these studies exemplified the connection between behavior and communication (Diehl, 2003).

Augmentative and Alternative Communication Systems

Augmentative and Alternative Communication (AAC) is the supplementation or replacement of natural speech or writing using aided or unaided symbols or both. Aided symbols are Picture Communication Symbols or high- and low-tech devices. Unaided symbols are sign language, gestures, and finger spelling (Lloyd et al., 1997). As stated before, between 20 and 40% of individuals with autism will not make meaningful gains in speech (NRC, 2001). For those individuals who do not acquire functional speech or have difficulty processing or comprehending spoken language, augmentative and alternative communication system needs to be considered so the individual has a consistent way to communicate (NRC, 2001).

Vocalizations can imply various physical states by their different intonations. The way an individual responds to the different vocalizations is a valuable part of intervention. Many individuals with autism vocalize, and some of those vocalizations are intentional forms of communication. When students vocalize, it is important to respond by going over to them or acknowledging them by name and asking them what they need.

The use of sign language has advantages and limitations. Some of the advantages of using sign language are that it is fast, portable, and motorically easier than speech (Lloyd et al., 1997). It is limited, however, because it requires other people to understand sign, it requires a fair degree of hand and finger control, and the individual has to be able to imitate. Most of the research in regards to autism and sign language has focused on the acquisition of labeling, not on the spontaneous use of sign language as a mode of communication. The results of Layton (1988) indicate that even after intensive training with sign, the majority of children had gained only a small repertoire of functional signs. Other studies indicate signs that were acquired were not generalized unless systematic instruction was in place for generalization, and many individuals did not generalize the use of learned signs to untrained situations (Schwartz & Garfinkle, 1998). The NRC (2001) reports that the size of the sign vocabulary and accuracy of sign formation were highly correlated with measures of fine motor abilities and tests of apraxia, executing, and sequencing movements. This supports the role of a motor impairment in the level of competence attained in sign language and speech acquisition for individuals with autism.

Picture symbols or real photos used with the Picture Exchange Communication System (PECS) are a good place to begin teaching communication skills for many individuals who are nonverbal. PECS is popular because it does not require any prerequisite behaviors, is relatively simple and inexpensive, and may facilitate speech (Bondy & Frost, 1994). Although used to remediate the same deficits as verbal training and sign language, PECS differs from these training protocols in two significant ways. First, PECS training is based on child initiation. Throughout every stage of PECS training, children request preferred items and receive the requested item as a result of the communicative act. Second, generalization strategies are embedded in the teaching protocol. Individuals with autism have difficulty initiating interactions, so this system facilitates development in spontaneous communication, which is a requirement of functional communication skills.

PECS begins with highly motivating toys, food, and activities to build requesting and expands into labeling. Bondy and Frost (1994) reported impressive outcomes when PECS was used with 85 nonverbal preschool children with autism. In that study, 95% of the children learned to use picture symbols for communication, and 76% used a combination of speech and picture symbols to make requests and label after 6 months of training. PECS was also an effective method for teaching nonverbal ways of gaining attention prior to conveying a message (Quill, 2000). Martha is 6 and nonverbal, and she has been using PECS for 2 weeks. She goes to her communication notebook, a notebook with picture symbols for her preferred activities and foods, chooses a picture symbol of juice, brings it to her mother, and her mother gets her juice.

Speech generating devices, also known as Voice Output Communication Aids (VOCAs) or High-Tech Augmentative Communication Devices, are other forms of communication that students with autism may be able to use. The advantage of speech output devices is that they give children a "voice" (Quill, 2000). A wide variety of high-technology communication devices are available. The individual needs and skill level will assist in determining what kind of device is appropriate. Some devices are more concrete, they have real photos or picture symbols with set pages and contain only a few choices. Israel uses a speech generating device that has real photos of preferred objects on one page. He does not navigate through the device to create messages. He pushes the eat button when he wants to eat and the button that has a picture of a chair when he wants to sit in his favorite chair.

Other speech generating devices use a language based system. A language based system is a system that allows the user to generate their own messages using a set of core vocabulary in stable key locations. This core vocabulary (e.g., I, want, eat, drink, go) is combined with other parts of speech such as nouns that represent preferred objects, foods, feelings, and so forth. An example of this type of program is the Language Acquisition through Motor Planning (LAMP).

LAMP is a strategy that uses a speech generating device as a tool to develop communication systematically with children with ASD. The desired outcome of this strategy is that the individual will become a more proficient communicator utilizing a variety of communication modes which may include a Voice Output Communication Aid, speech production, or a combination of the two; that language comprehension and expression will develop so that the individual can communicate beyond the one word level; and that an increased understanding of the power of communication will develop (Halloran & Emerson, 2006). This program was implemented with 13 children under the age of 9 who are nonverbal and diagnosed with ASD in two beta test sites for 6 months. A year and a half after the beta test, 10 of the 13 children who participated in the study continued to use AAC as part of their communication repertoire, and during the study all participants learned to spontaneously and independently use the words *go, eat, more, help, more +noun, stop, want,* and *go+ verb* on their AAC device (Halloran & Emerson, 2006).

Assessment of an individual's desire to communicate is extremely important. Individual differences in intrinsic motivation are strongly associated with effective and efficient learning, and this intrinsic motivation is largely shaped by past experiences. Motivation, demands or expectations put on the individual, and opportunities to communicate all play an important role in the ability to communicate and the level of communication (Watson et al., 1989). Individuals who have something to say, a reason to say it, and have consistent expectations are more likely to communicate. People with autism are motivated to communicate their basic wants, and these needs are often met by caregivers without the needs being first communicated by the individual. These factors impact those with autism in that they communicate only their basic needs. Many times they are able to get their needs met independently and do not have consistent expectations on how they are supposed to communicate. In order to teach an individual with autism to communicate using an AAC system, expectations need to be consistent and opportunities to communicate need to created.

Strategies for Enhancing Intentional Communication:

Intentional Communication is using whatever modality (i.e., gestures, sign language, speech) necessary to convey a message to another person so that the person understands.

One intervention strategy that can be implemented to teach intentional communication is to capitalize on the student's natural inclination to use gestures. This can be effective regardless of impairment and severity. Gestures can be used to fulfill a variety of communication functions. These include gaining attention, requesting, indicating pain or hunger, rejecting, and protesting. Using nonlinguistic communication helps build a foundation for the eventual use of intentional behaviors or linguistic forms. Expand on initiated behaviors and focus on interests, subjects that are interesting and make sense to the student. Motivation of the individual and having a reason to communicate are critical to teaching individuals with autism to be successful and independent in communicating with others.

Another intervention strategy is to distinguish between intentional communication behaviors and other behaviors and recognize how the other behaviors can be shaped by the responses from the communication partner to make them communicative and more functional. Jared is 6 and uses a speech generating device. He likes to push the button that says "Hello" in a silly intonation, so he pushes this button a lot. Every time he pushes the button a staff member walks over to him and says, "Hello." It is important to increase responses to the child's communication and to be sensitive, contingent, and consistent. John has a new speech generating device and uses it to say "I want a tissue" frequently throughout the day. Every time he does this, the teacher brings him a tissue, so he can make the connection between his words being said and the meaning of those words.

SUMMARY

All individuals are born with the desire to communicate, and as professionals who work with these individuals it is our responsibility to facilitate all communication attempts and teach effective communication strategies using whatever modality is most successful in generating spontaneous and independent communication. If we think of autism as a culture and understand the differences between their culture and ours, we are better prepared to assist and teach any skill to them.

Speech, language, and communication characteristics of children with ASD are exceedingly heterogeneous. Language impairments range from the failure to develop any functional speech to the development of functional but idiosyncratic use of spontaneous speech and language. One third to one half of children and adults with autism do not use speech functionally. For both verbal and nonverbal individuals, impairments in social or pragmatic aspects of language and related cognitive skills are the most salient (NRC, 2001).

It is clear that making decisions regarding autism and AAC for those who do not acquire verbal language are complex and challenging. Selection of one or more types of AAC requires careful assessment and individualization, and at this time, because of the lack of current research, it is more of an art than a science (Miranda, 2003). Although there are arguments for and against the use of aided symbols, manual signing, PECS, and Voice Output Communication Aids, the fact is that very little comparative research currently exists to inform intervention in this area; therefore, decisions concerning appropriate AAC need to be specific to the needs of the individual. The ultimate measure of a successful intervention is the extent to which it results in functional, unprompted communication across environments and people, and interventions with such outcomes deserve both respect and support, regardless of the modality.

REFERENCES

American Psychiatric Association (APA). (2000). *Diagnostic and statistical manual of mental disorders* (4th ed., text rev.). Washington, DC: Author.

Bondy, A., & Frost, L. (1994). The picture exchange communication system. *Focus on autistic behavior, 9,* 1–19.

Carr, E. G., & Durand, V. M. (1985). Reducing problem behaviors through functional communication training. *Journal of Applied Behavior Analysis, 18,* 111–126.

Carr, E. G., & Kologinsky, E. (1983). Acquisition of sign language by autistic children II: spontaneity and generalization effects. *Journal of Applied Behavior Analysis, 16,* 297–314.

Committee on Language, American Speech-Language-Hearing Association. (1983). Definition of language, *ASHA, 25,* 44.

Diehl, S. (2003). Autism spectrum disorder: the context of speech-language pathologist intervention. *Language, Speech, and Hearing in Schools, 34,* 253–254.

Gutstein, S. E., & Sheely, R. K. (2002). *Relationship development intervention with young children.* United Kingdom: Jessica Kingsley.

Halloran, J., & Emerson, M. (2006). *Language acquisition through motor planning.* Wooster, OH: Prentke-Romich.

Kasher, A., & Meilijson, S. (2008). *Autism and pragmatics of language.* Retrieved July 7, 2009, from www.math.tau.ac.il/isaco/autism_english

Layton, T. (1988). Language training with autistic children using four modes of presentation. *Journal of Communication Disorders, 21,* 333–350.

Lloyd, L. L., Fuller, D. R., Arvidson, H. H. (1997). *Augmentative and Alternative Communication: A Handbook of Principles and Practices.* Boston: Allyn and Bacon.

McCauley, R., & Fey, M. (2006). *Treatment of Language Disorders in Children.* Baltimore, MD: Brookes.

McHale, S. R., Simeonsson, L., Marcus, & Olley, J. (1980). The social and symbolic quality of autistic children's communication. *Journal of Autism and Developmental Disabilities, 10,* 299–310.

Mirenda, P. (2003). Toward functional augmentative and alternative communication for students with autism: Manual sign, graphic symbols, and voice output communication aids. *Language, Speech, and Hearing Services in Schools, 34,* 203–216.

National Research Council (NRC). (2001). *Educating Individuals with Autism.* Washington, DC: National Academy Press.

Owens, R. E. (1996). *Language Development.* New York: Allyn and Bacon.

Prizant, B. M., Wetherby, A., Rubin, E., and Laurent, A. (2003). The SCERTS model: A transactional, family-centered approach to enhancing communication and socioemotional abilities in children with autism spectrum disorder. *Infants and Young Children, 16,* 296–316.

Quill, K. (2000). *Do-Watch-Listen-Say: Social and communication intervention for children with autism.* Baltimore, MD: Brookes.

Schwartz, I., & Garfinkle, A. N., (1998). The picture exchange communication system: communication outcomes for young children with disabilities. *Topics in Early Childhood Special Education, 18,* 111–120.

Stone, W. L., & Caro-Martinez, L. M. (1990) Naturalistic observations of spontaneous communication in autistic children. *Journal of Autism and Related Disorders, 20,* 437–453.

Watson, L. R., Lord, C., Schaffer, B., & Schopler, E. (1989). *Teaching spontaneous to autistic and developmentally handicapped children.* Texas: Pro-Ed.

Wetherby, A., & Prutting, C. (1984). Profiles of communicative and cognitivesocial abilities in autistic children. *Journal of Speech and Hearing Research, 27,* 364–377.

Wetherby, A., Yonclas, D., & Bryan, A. (1989). Communicative profiles of handicapped preschool children: Implications for early identification. *Journal of Speech and Hearing Research, 54,* 148–158.

Widerstrom, A. H., Mowder, B., & Sandall, S. R. (1997). *Infant development and risk.* Baltimore, MD: Brooks.

Woods, J., & Wetherby, A. (2003). Early identification of and intervention for infants and toddlers who are at risk for autism spectrum disorder. *Language, Speech, and Hearing Services in Schools, 34,* 180–193.

Bridging the Social Disconnect: Social Characteristics of ASD

Melanie Kelley & Cindy Lee Herrick

ncreasing the development of social characteristics and pragmatic language among children with autism continues to pose challenges for educators, parents, and support providers alike. Acquisition of these essential skills is required to assist in bridging the social disconnect experienced by individuals on the autism spectrum during daily situations. Each and every day is filled with social opportunities which are governed by social norms, rules, and acceptance. When difficult social situations revolve into teachable moments for students on the AS, they will be better equipped to generalize the skills learned to other settings. This chapter describes strategies and examples of how to increase social skills in children with ASD.

Social and communication deficits are among the hallmarks associated with ASD. The *DSM-IV-TR* (APA, 2000) criteria explain that people with autism display a qualitative impairment in social interaction as manifested at by at least two of the following:

a)   Marked impairment in the use of multiple nonverbal behaviors such as eye to eye gaze, facial expression, body postures, and gestures to regulate social interaction
b)   Failure to develop peer relationships appropriate to developmental level
c)   Lack of spontaneous seeking to share enjoyment, interests, or achievements with other people
d)   Lack of social or emotional reciprocity

Since autism is a spectrum disorder, a myriad of atypical social characteristics can be observed in children with ASD (Centers for Disease Control and Prevention

[CDC], n.d.). The purpose of this chapter is to create a general understanding of the ASD social characteristics and to provide a framework to increase social interaction by teaching pragmatic language skills during everyday activities.

According to *The Ziggurat Model* (Aspy & Grossman, 2007) common social differences include (but are not limited to) the following:

➤ Difficulty recognizing the feelings and thoughts of others (mindblindness)
➤ Poor eye contact
➤ Difficulty maintaining personal space; physical intrusions on others
➤ Appearing rude or tactless
➤ Difficulty making or keeping friends
➤ Difficulty joining an activity
➤ Naïveté; being easily taken advantage of or bullied
➤ Tendency to be less involved in group activities than most same-age individuals
➤ Difficulty understanding others' nonverbal communication (e.g., facial expressions, body language, tone of voice)
➤ Difficulty understanding jokes

EARLY SOCIAL DEVELOPMENT AND ASD

To understand social differences seen in students with AS and ASD, it is important to first comprehend childhood social skill development. In the 1950s, early childhood development studies indicated that children did not develop peer relations until they were at least 2 years of age. The prevailing theory was that babies were not interested in other babies and perceived each other as objects rather than people. However, countless studies conducted over the last several decades have altered this theory and created a deeper comprehension of the stages of early childhood social development. Research has shown that babies become interested in one another as early as 2 months of age. By 6 months, the babies have instinctively developed basic eye contact skills and will attempt communication through body language and facial expression. By 9 to 12 months of age, babies begin developing imitation skills and "play" through reciprocal imitating actions (Shonkoff, 2000). This ability to imitate is a crucial part of early childhood social development, as it becomes the foundation upon which more complex social skills are built.

Another factor in early social development is that most children are naturally encouraged to acquire social skills when they are positively reinforced with verbal or emotional praise from teachers or parents. However, children with AS/ASD may not perceive any positive encouragement from typical praise. These children also lack the natural comprehension and inherent drive to observe and imitate the social interactions and behaviors of others. This research reveals that the onset of complex social development in children is surprisingly early, which further emphasizes the importance of early social intervention in children with ASD (Shonkoff, 2000).

While typically developing children often learn basic social rules through observation of peer behavior and specific instruction from parents, children with ASD often require further instruction on these social skills.

ASD AND MIXED SOCIAL SIGNALS

A common and widespread misconception regarding children with AD/ASD is that they do not want to socialize (Quill, 2000). In reality, while children with autism may not socialize in a mainstream fashion, they do communicate. As educators, it is our job to familiarize ourselves with these social attempts so that we are able to recognize and further develop these social skills. Much like translating one language to another, we must attempt to understand each method of socialization of the child with ASD and help the child learn to translate his or her message into a universal social language. It is important to understand that the child with ASD or AS does not consciously make a decision to ignore social cues; rather, the child is simply unaware that social rules exist.

It is also a common myth that children with autism do not have the capacity and ability to understand what is going around them. Many of them have extreme potential for understanding their environment; however, they may be unaware or unsure of how they can tap into their potential. In fact, most of these students are not even aware that they can benefit from understanding their environment. In fact, it is ironic that sometimes children with autism comprehend and feel *too much* because they are so sensitive to their surroundings and are so overwhelmed by the bombardment of stimuli that they are unable to process everything fast enough for them to thoroughly comprehend (Quill, 2000).

Often, students with ASD are taught to see the world from our perspective without our understanding of how the child with autism sees the world. It is important to attempt to see the world from the ASD perspective in order to better help these children understand the world around them. It is important to stress that a *different* perspective does not mean *no* perspective.

Researchers have found that friendships are developed through mutual empathy and understanding. In other words, the ability to see something from a different perspective and reason out another person's feelings is crucial to developing a relationship (Stewart, 2007). It helps people relate to each other and ultimately develop feelings of closeness and intimacy. Thus, while children with AS/ASD do crave social interaction, their lack of social skills causes them to exhibit social behaviors and body language that can be classified by others as uncaring, odd, and disengaged—all factors that make it very difficult to develop friendships and other relationships.

Many children with AS/ASD seem to prefer playing by themselves to playing with peers. While most children derive pleasure from the act of social and interactive play, this is not the case for children with AS/ASD. Most children with AS/ASD derive satisfaction from restrictive and repetitive personal interests and/or behaviors

(Quill, 2000). Often, these interests may seem odd, obsessive, and may not be age or developmentally appropriate. The interest level and satisfaction experienced by the child overshadows and detracts from the need for social interaction. Thus, a student with AS/ASD will often engage in repetitive solitary play and seemingly ignore classmates and peers. However, the preference of the child with ASD or AS for solitary play should not be confused with the desire for perpetual solitude. Chris, an 8-year-old with AS, would sit at the same table each day for lunch. As he glanced toward his peers, they would say, "Hello," to him each day. Chris would ignore the greetings and look away, continuing to eat his lunch and turn the pages of his comic book. When the teacher told the students at the tables to ask about his comic book, Chris began interacting with the peers at his table.

SOCIAL PRAGMATICS

Since social and communication skills encompass virtually every aspect of daily life, efforts to build these skills in children with autism can be an overwhelming task for educators and parents (Quill, 2000). Thus, it is important to tackle each skill in smaller, more manageable steps. Almost every social skill taught to a child with ASD is done through task analysis, a process in which each step of a specific social skill is simplified into individual steps and taught in a structured fashion. Task analysis, paired with behavioral repetition and consistent reinforcement, is often one of the most effective methods of helping a child with ASD develop appropriate social skills (Cress, 2004). Research shows that while teaching new skills to children with autism, we learn new skills best if the new information is the only new "hard thing" in that situation. More aspects of tasks and situations constitute "hard things" for children with ASD than expected for other children (Cress, 2004).

Task analysis plays a major role when teaching a student social pragmatics. *Social pragmatics* is the study of social language within social context. It goes beyond verbal utterances; rather, it focuses on subtle social language such as tone, body language, situation, sequence, and the like. The instruction of pragmatic language is an effective way to help students with ASD bridge the social disconnect and increase social interaction skills (American Speech Language Hearing Association [ASHA], 1997–2009). An individual may say words clearly and use long, complex sentences with correct grammar but still have a communication problem if he or she has not mastered pragmatics, the rules for social language (ASHA, 1997–2009).

According to ASHA (1997–2009) pragmatics involves three major communication skills:

1. Using language for different purposes, such as
   - ➤ greeting (e.g., hello, goodbye),
   - ➤ informing (e.g., I'm going to get a cookie),
   - ➤ demanding (e.g., give me a cookie),

> promising (e.g., I'm going to get you a cookie), and
> requesting (e.g., I would like a cookie, please).

2. Changing language according to the needs of a listener or situation, such as

> talking differently to a baby than to an adult,
> giving background information to an unfamiliar listener, and
> speaking differently in a classroom than on a playground.

3. Following rules for conversations and storytelling, such as

> taking turns in conversation,
> introducing topics of conversation,
> staying on topic,
> rephrasing when misunderstood,
> using verbal and nonverbal signals,
> knowing how close to stand to someone when speaking, and
> using facial expressions and eye contact.

These rules may vary across cultures and within cultures. It is important to understand the rules of your communication partner.

An individual with pragmatic problems may (ASHA, 1997–2009):

> say inappropriate or unrelated things during conversations,
> tell stories in a disorganized way, or
> have little variety in language use.

The skills addressed must be imbedded into daily routines throughout the home and in the school environment. In order to set up a successful environment to increase social interactions among students with autism, it is important to provide organizational supports and systematic routines to provide a security and trust for the students to begin to express themselves communicatively. These supports prove to be effective with all students (Quill, 2000), especially those with disabilities, to transition from classroom to classroom throughout their educational pathway. From the words of Hans Asperger, "The teacher who does not understand that it is necessary to teach autistic children seemingly obvious things will feel impatient and irritated" (1944, p. 57). This quotation reflects the importance in teaching some of the minute often hidden rules for conversation and socialization.

Virtually every social situation requires the ability to watch, listen to, or communicate with others while engaged in an activity (Quill 2000). Many theories exist as to why people with autism have difficulty developing social awareness.

Social skills are generally required in every context, and every moment is an opportunity to build social competence (Quill, 2000). Social competence must be embedded within our school curriculum and into daily routines for children with autism, and a focus on teaching skills in the natural context in structured settings is suggested (Quill 2000). Continuous practice of new skills throughout the school, home, and community environment greatly assists children with ASD to generalize skills across settings.

As discussed above, it is important for students on the autism spectrum to acquire seemingly obvious skills. Social skills—such as responding to adult direction, independently participating in the routines of the classroom, expressing needs to adults, and requesting the assistance of adults—all become important functional skills necessary for children to be successful in classroom settings (National Research Council [NRC], 2001). For example, a student was observed sitting at his desk, with his head down, appearing frustrated. If this student were in an inclusive environment, this behavior could be perceived as noncompliant. When the teacher approached him, he pointed at the problem on his sheet. The teacher said, "Do you need help?" The student said, "Yes!" The teacher gave the student the needed help and told the student it is all right to ask for help. If this is difficult for the student to initiate, teachers can include "students will ask for help when needed" in the class rules or place written or visual cues to prompt the student to ask for help on the desk or wall.

Teaching the skill to ask for help can be set up in structured situations as well. For example, give the student directions to find an item stored in a classroom cabinet. Often students will continue to search for the item without asking for help. At this time one person is providing the direction while the other person provides the prompts. When it is clear that the student is having difficulty finding the item, prompt the student to ask for help finding the item. For example, a teacher could give a direction to the student: "Please get the folder out of the cabinet." While the student is looking for the item and it is obvious that he or she cannot locate the folder, the paraprofessional could use a visual cue card indicating a picture of (I need help) or could gently and quietly say, "Remember, you can ask for help if you need it." The student asks the teacher for help, and the teacher reinforces the student right away for asking. After several sessions the student will be able to ask for help independently. Once this skill can be accomplished in the classroom, is it important to teach it in other settings such as the community, out on campus, and at home.

Sophie, an 11-year-old with ASD, was taken with her class on a field trip to the grocery store, where each student had a specific list of the items to locate and purchase. When she could not find an item, she was observed cautiously approaching a store worker and asking for help to find the dog food. This was a success, as she was able to generalize the skill to ask for help, in an unstructured unfamiliar setting. Mason was in his math class. He was was observed looking at another student's math paper in class. He then began to copy the other student's answers onto his paper. When the teacher quietly asked him if he was cheating on his assignment, he said, "No, I am only looking at his paper." The teacher asked, "Why are you looking at his paper?" Mason said, "because I don't know how to do the problems." This student could have asked for help, but he was not taught this seemingly obvious skill that it is acceptable to ask for help in this situation. Had this happened during a testing situation, Mason could have been given a zero on his test.

CREATIVE SOCIALIZATION

Teachers as well as parents can set up situations to require students to ask for items they need such as pencils, paper, or the game they want to play rather than getting out of their desk to retrieve the items on their own. It is important to make situations motivating and meaningful when requiring students to socially participate. If the student is not enjoying a specific game, it is going to be more difficult to elicit social expressions. On the other hand, playing a favorite game or with a favorite toy may provide more opportunities for social interaction. Once the student is familiar with the context of the interaction, then a new game or toy can be introduced.

Often, too much emphasis is placed on the deficits of children with autism and not enough attention on the abilities of these children. Understanding student interests is a huge asset for increasing social dialogue and building trust with the student. Sometimes it is much more beneficial and effective to use a child's interest in a particular subject or object to help him or her develop other skills and abilities. While this is something that should be used to help all children learn, it becomes an invaluable tool in helping children with ASD develop specific abilities (Quill, 2000). Finding a way to incorporate the student's interests into social skill development often motivates the child to become more socially engaged.

Interest Inventories

Interest inventories can be a valuable tool that can be completed with the student and the parents. For example, many children with autism show an interest in the alphabet, numbers, books, computers, and maps (Quill, 2000). Any of these interests can be used as conversation starters and set the stage for the development of more complex social skills. Not only is the child more likely to stay focused on and interested in what he or she is learning because it is fun and engaging, it also helps the teacher build a certain bond and rapport with the child. This bond is especially important between a teacher and a child with autism because the child often requires a higher level of comfort and trust before becoming willing to actively work with a new teacher. Eventually, the interest-specific social development can be guided towards discussions outside of the student's restricted interests.

Peer Modeling

One approach that can teach and develop pragmatic language skills for children with autism is *peer modeling*. In peer modeling, typical age peers model appropriate communication or social pragmatic interactions to demonstrate the desired communicative intent using the correct body language and rules for conversation. Students then participate with the general education students to practice these interactions. Students tend to respond well to working with peers their age. It appears to be very motivating to them (Quill 2000). The peer models need to be trained on how to use the visual aides and methods beforehand.

Generally the peer helper begins the conversation or request during structured activities such as games, during structured conversational routines set up by the teacher, or during lessons. The peer is pretaught what is expected during the lesson. For example, during a cooking lesson in the foods lab, all the students have a copy of a recipe. The teacher asks the students to name an ingredient needed for the recipe. The peer model names the first ingredient, which prompts the other students to name all the other ingredients of the recipe.

Peer models can be trained and used during all lessons and activities in the self-contained or inclusive setting. Using peer models as a tool to increase pragmatic language is often effective for students with pragmatic language difficulties. Research has found increased reading fluency and comprehension for children who received peer tutoring, as compared with those received traditional reading instruction (NRC, 2001). The concept of using peers could be applied to increasing pragmatic language acquisition and social interaction among students with autism. Typical peers can be trained on specific rules for social language routines, such as greetings, like "Hi, how are you?" "I'm fine, How are you?" "Great!" or "Not so good!" "What have you been up to?" Once the peer models are trained, they can be used as a tool to motivate and teach students on the autism spectrum to interact. Students on the autism spectrum are then given supports such as premade scripts, social stories, and activity schedules.

When students on the autism spectrum are given supports such as scripts, social stories, and activity schedules, they are better equipped to interact with their environment (Quill, 2000). The students are taught the rules for communicating greetings and all the nonverbal cues associated with the interaction by utilizing premade scripts to which they can refer. Each student has responses listed to answer the question, "What have you been up to?" The script also assists students in maintaining the topic of conversation, rather than discussing their own conversational agenda. The answers are taken from the student inventory of interests, described previously. Using peers can be motivating to students with disabilities in exercises like these. Once the students master this skill within a structured environment, it can be generalized to other contexts, such as the lunch room, hallway, or community. The use of the scripting card is gradually reduced as the student requires less prompting to participate in the communicative routine. Research shows that students with autism learn routines if they are practiced prior to the actual event occurring (Jones, Feeley, & Takacs, 2007).

Role Play/Priming

Role-playing is a method where the appropriate communicative routine is demonstrated by setting up mock situations to practice skills before the actual event occurs. This method is effective in preparing students for introductions, mock job interviews, purchases in class, phone conversations, campus errands, and the like (Aspy & Grossman, 2007). The possibilities for using this strategy are endless. For example, the trainer practices with a peer or other staff member modeling conversational turns, while incorporating the nonverbal communicative language into the structured routine. The students have premade scripting cards, using pictures if needed for students who are nonreaders. The teacher sets up the scenario by saying, "We are going to practice introducing ourselves to new people." It is important that each part of the routine is sequentially consistent: "Hi, my name is _____" (shake hands, eye contact). "My name is _____. Nice to meet you." Have each of the students practice with the familiar people. Then set up random visits to your class from unfamiliar people. Each time an unfamiliar person visits the classroom, it is important to allow students the opportunity to introduce themselves to this new person, even though it may interrupt the academic session. These natural opportunities in a familiar setting will lead to generalization to other areas on campus (Jones, Feeley, & Takacs, 2007).

Another way to teach pragmatic and social skills is through the use of games, either store bought or teacher made. Introduce games or activities of interest for the child to encourage an increase in communication. The teacher directed game that follows is structured to promote turn-taking skills, make age appropriate comments about the game, and set up natural opportunities to teach how to appropriately win or lose a game. Winning and losing gracefully are skills that need to be taught systematically, considering the emotions of the individual student. In general, students with autism demonstrate lack of emotional understanding when they are faced with a loss in a game or activity. On the other hand, winning can also be difficult for a student to express. The student may not be able to recognize the feelings of others; he or she may often perseverate on the win and unintentionally hurt the feelings of others by rubbing in the win of the game. A loss of a game can often result in stress for the remainder of the school day for the student, if he or she has not been provided with relevant coping strategies.

Tom is a bright seventh grader. He is above grade level in reading, math, and writing. He is very concrete while making comments to describe others. He may say things he is thinking about people out loud, such as, "You look like an old grandma," or "Your haircut is ugly." He enjoys playing games such as Uno,™ Scrabble,™ and Yahtzee™ with others. He has been having difficulty finding a peer who is willing to play a game with him because of the behavior he displays while interacting in a game, specifically winning or losing. When he loses a game, he begins to tantrum by arguing with peers and staff. If he does not receive the reinforcement he is seeking, he begins to cry and pout. When he wins, he makes comments such as, "I am the winner! You lost!" The family reports that this social behavior is evident at home with siblings. The effect of this behavior is that his siblings and peers avoid playing games with him. The teacher recognized that this social deficit was inhibiting his ability to interact with peers during games on a regular basis. One of the challenges in identifying which social skills to teach is recognizing that most people on the spectrum require lessons on skills that others are never discretely taught or on skills that are usually taught and mastered at a much younger age (Aspy & Grossman 2007). It appropriate to teach play skills in an isolated setting in order to increase success in real play situations such as on the playground (Aspy & Grossman, 2007).

The teacher uses a game to teach turn taking and winning and losing skills. She prepares prescripted visuals of appropriate verbal responses for the students to utilize during the game. Pictures with words are appropriate as visuals for any students who are nonreaders or need the extra visual support. The teacher also makes a power point that discusses winning and losing a game. This is shown prior to the start of the game (preteaching). She also discusses the feelings that one might experience associated with winning and losing prior to the start of the game. During the game, she prompts Tom to make comments relevant to the game and to look at his visual aid to say "bummer" rather than arguing with peer. The game keeps going until the end, when one student must lose, and one is the winner. The teacher then refers back to the power point to discuss ways to cope with winning and losing the game.

REVIEW/RETEACHING OF SKILLS

When a student demonstrates difficulty with social communication skills, it can be of benefit to review or reteach the skill. This is done in a nonthreatening, calm way to discuss possible alternatives to the situation, not to point blame at the student. Listen to the student's perspective to gain an understanding of why he or she handled the situation in a particiular way. Discuss what events occurred, and determine ways that the situation could be handled differently the next time. Be sure to point out some of the positive interactions the student performed as well.

THEORY OF MIND: LEARNING TO READ BETWEEN THE LINES

Theory of Mind (TOM) refers to the ability to understand the thoughts and feelings of others and apply this understanding to predict their actions (Aspy & Grossman 2007). Because of deficits in this area, children with autism have difficulty understanding figurative language or recognize when they are being deceptive or others are being deceptive to them. The inability to show empathy also falls under the category of TOM. Children with ASD/AS often have a self-focused perspective—that is, they are initially only able to see things from their own perspective (Aspy & Grossman, 2007). In other words, they are unable to see a situation from another person's point of view. This lack of variable perspective is often one of the main social obstacles, because empathy and perspective plays a major role in any social relationship. The ability to perceive different points of view is essential in helping people connect with others in various parts of their lives: work, family, friends, school, group activities, and so forth. During a class session, one of the paraprofessionals received a message that her uncle had passed away. Death is an abstract concept difficult for children with ASD to understand, especially the emotions tied to a death. As she entered the classroom, Isabel, a 7-year-old students with AS, observed that she was crying and asked, "What's wrong?" As the paraprofesional explained that her uncle had died, Isabel began to laugh. The student lacked the empathy to understand that the paraprofessional's feelings about the sad news of the death.

When real life situations like this occur during the school day, they can become teachable moments for students on the autism spectrum. It is difficult to recreate this type of emotion. Use moments such as this to teach student responses to death or other unexpected situations. It would be of benefit to have the discussion regarding the situation and brainstorm possible responses that would be relevant to the current situation, teaching statements such as, "I am sorry for your loss" or "How sad!" Another student showed up to his class and announced proudly with a huge smile, "My dog died!" This provided another opportunity to teach new skills. The teacher immediately pulled the student aside and asked whether he was happy or sad that his dog had died, and he was able to verbalize that he was sad. However, he lacked the empathy and facial expression that are typically paired with the emotion sadness. The teacher showed him what a sad face looked like. Later that day he was telling a friend on campus about his dog, and he was able to say it with the appropriate facial expression, body language, and tone of voice.

It is also difficult for students with autism to recognize the intent of the others, whether actions are accidental or intentional. This can often be seen in crowded hallways or in the cafeteria when another student may accidentally bump into a student with autism while they are waiting in line. This action may be perceived as intentional and could cause a confrontation between the two students. It is important to teach students how to cope during unstructured situations such as this. One teacher reports that her student with autism was having difficulty in his PE class. This was a high school class where the students were very competitive while playing the game of basketball. Although this student enjoyed basketball, he was unable to recognize the intention of others (accidental/intentional) during the game. The situation began to escalate, to the point where he began hiding in the restroom during PE class.

Once the teacher realized the student was avoiding the PE class, she created picture cards that had scenarios such as bumping into a table or a child pouring his milk on the floor. She worked with student to understand accidental behavior versus intentional actions, and the student was able to return to the class with success.

TOM also pertains to the student being able to maintain the topic of conversation. This is often difficult for students with autism, as they prefer to talk about their specific interests and lose interest in what others are concerned about. Friendships can often be difficult for students with autism because of skill deficits in TOM. We can teach preferences for friends based on concrete characteristics. It is often easier to teach students characteristics of what not to look for in a friend rather than teaching them what to look for in a friend. As students with autism become more familiar with the particular characteristics and can indicate their preferences, they are more apt to truly begin to build friendships.One way to increase and work on skills under TOM is to create a campus club. Students can work on pragmatic language skills, learn to understand the feelings of others, and create friendships. The club can incorporate social skill activities or social videos to teach all the students how to interact in social settings.

TOM deficits can create unique problems for students with ASD. Cody was a 17-year-old young man with autism who had a specific interest in sports. He befriended one of the female athletes on campus. Jennifer was a very nice teenager who always said "hi" to Cody in the halls. She would reach out and shake his hand and answer his many questions about the games that she was playing in. Cody misinterpreted her friendliness as an indication that she wanted to have a relationship with him. Cody began meeting Jennifer after class, walking her to classes, sending notes, and showing up to her soccer practices unexpectedly. It got to the point where Jennifer was feeling as if Cody was stalking her.

When dealing with relationships between young adults, it is important to consult with the students' parents, to take into consideration their specific morals and values relevant to the situation. The teacher scheduled a meeting with the parents. During the meeting they discussed strategies to teach Cody that Jennifer was not interested in him as more than a friend. Jennifer then wrote Cody a note indicating that they were just friends and that she did not like him as a boyfriend.

The classroom teacher as well as his parents had conversations with Cody regarding their friendship. He kept saying, "How do you know she doesn't like me? She talks to me!" Even after Cody received the note, he still had difficulty understanding they were just friends as he wanted there to be something more. He could not understand Jennifer's perspective.

The teacher set up biweekly meetings with Cody so he could discuss his feelings. He was also taught to write his feelings in a journal rather than writing notes to Jennifer. This took an extensive amount of time for him to understand. The teacher used social skill lessons for self-reflection that displayed a specific story related to peer relationships. Cody was able to reflect how he would respond to the scenario, then his teacher discussed his answers and taught alternative choices to the situation. It may take continuous teaching, reinforcement, and discussion to teach students on the autism spectrum how to handle situations like this and to help them understand feelings from another person's perspective.

During the school day, time should be given to address pragmatic language concerns. Teaching these skills, especially in the context of a social situation that arises during the course of the day, may need to take priority over academic instruction. It is helpful to embed these teaching subsets into academic lessons when possible. This is why it is important to begin teaching these skills at a young age and embed the skills into the daily routines.

APPLIED BEHAVIOR ANALYSIS

Throughout history, researchers and philosophers have investigated human behavior in hopes of finding a way to understand, predict, and change it. As educators, this research is crucial in helping us teach and educate in an efficient manner. Inevitably, each educator will encounter this series of questions at some point in his or her career: Why do my students behave in such a manner? Is there a specific cause for their behavior? If so, are similar possible behaviors predictable? What can be done to change undesirable behavior—and most importantly, how do we know when a method is effective in changing behavior?

Today, these questions regarding human behavior are categorically answered through a scientific method called applied behavior analysis (ABA). ABA is defined as "the science in which tactics derived from the principles of behavior are applied to improve socially significant behavior and experimentation is used to identify the variables responsible for the improvement in behavior" (Cooper, Heron, & Heward, 2007).

ABA is a science that focuses on the study of human behavior, with the ultimate goal of improving human behavior. ABA is also unique in the specificity of its goals, methods, and focus. The main goal of ABA is to scientifically discover the influence that environmental variables may have on socially significant behavior. This goal is achieved through a general three-step process:

1. Definition of target behavior
2. Quantification
3. Controlled experimentation

How can ABA help me?

Thomas is an 11-year-old boy diagnosed with AS and ADHD. He often has difficulty completing class assignments and frequently disrupts the class by talking out of turn or leaving his seat. Whenever he is disruptive, he is given a time-out and is asked to sit outside. While the time-outs seemed to be effective initially, Thomas seems to have reverted to his disruptive ways over time. Exasperated, the teacher assumes that Thomas may just be a "difficult" student, and Thomas's parents attribute his behavior in school to his diagnosis of ADHD and AS.

ABA is an important tool for an educator because it offers some structured explanations for certain ASD behaviors (Cooper, Heron, & Heward, 2007). While many people may agree with Thomas's teacher and parents, the key point in this example is that the teacher and parents based their explanations for Thomas's behavior on *assumptions* and not on fact. ABA requires us to look more closely at the student, their problem behavior, *and* surrounding variables such as motivation and reinforcement.

ABA provides instructors and researchers a structured method to measure and document any relationship between a specific intervention and its target behavior. ABA requires the educator to find an objective method of documenting the problem behavior and subsequent modifications in the behavior. For example, Thomas's teacher could not properly evaluate and compare the effectiveness of either the time-outs or office visits on Thomas's behavior because she did not establish a method to document the behavior. She merely relied on her subjective perception of how effective the methods are. How would the outcome be different if Thomas's teacher had implemented ABA?

Since Thomas was still disrupting the class and not completely his assignments, Thomas's teacher decided to start keeping a log of Thomas's problem behavior and their respective "punishments." To get a benchmark of Thomas's "natural" behavior, Thomas's teacher found out that without time-outs, Thomas disrupted the class at least 4 times a day. Since Thomas's disruptions were usually a daily occurrence, she defined a time-out as "effective" if Thomas managed not to be disruptive for the remainder of the day and the next full school day. After 3 weeks of keeping detailed records, the teacher is surprised to discover that Thomas's disruptive behavior actually *increased* to an average of 5 times a day when sent on time-outs.

By using ABA methods, Thomas's teacher was able to collect objective data on the effect of each consequence on Thomas's behavior, respectively. These data provided her with these unexpected, yet crucial revelations: Sending Thomas to the office is effective in slightly lowering his disruptive behavior, and sending Thomas on a time-out actually increased his disruptive behavior. How can ABA explain this seemingly contradictory data?

Thomas's teacher could not figure out why time-outs increased Thomas's disruptive behavior and office visits only slightly decreased his disruptive behavior. She got her answer one day during science class when she discovered that Thomas had an intense interest in rocks. During the next time-out she gave Thomas, she observed that he actually *enjoyed* his time-outs because he could collect and examine rocks.

While ABA is useful for all educators, it is especially importantly for educators who work with students with ASD. The behavioral dilemmas instructors encounter while working with students with ASD or AS may be very perplexing because common societal constructs are often not applicable when working with students with autism. What this means is that teachers often have to start from scratch with each student with ASD and figure out teaching methods through tedious trial and error.

In the case of Thomas, ABA allowed his teacher to discover that behavioral interventions do not have a uniform impact on all students. While time-outs may work with other students, ABA indicated that time-outs did not decrease Thomas's disruptive behavior. Through trial and error, she was able to figure out that Thomas's interest in rocks was a variable that affected the outcome of the behavior intervention (time-outs).

ABA plays a major role in the area of ASD social skills development. It is crucial to have quantifiable data regarding social behavior in the form of controlled experiments, detailed target behavior definition, and procedural validity so that social interventions can be scientifically documented and used. Often, social interventions are measured through subjective means. For example, parents may think that their children are progressing socially because they *seem* to be more outgoing— but the truth is that the parent has no objective way to prove measurable progress.

ABA is also important in helping to develop a dependable database and technology for behavioral intervention. Often, social interventions vary depending on the administrator and his or her background. The objective data collection and documentation used in ABA is crucial in helping to keep everyone on the same page and is an important tool that holds administrations and their interventions accountable. The detailed objective definitions help minimize subjective assumptions that can influence the outcome of any intervention. While ABA is a complex science of quantifying human behavior, it is beneficial for educators to have a basic understanding of ABA. Even if educators do not personally implement ABA methods, the knowledge of ABA will undoubtedly have a positive affect on their teaching.

THE SENSORY–SOCIAL CONNECTION

Imagine that you woke up with the flu one day—with all of the classical flu symptoms. You body aches, everything sound seems too loud, the light hurts your eyes, and every smell makes you nauseated. How would you feel? Would you be irritable or agreeable? Would you like to be visited by a talkative friend, or would you rather be left alone? Would you be more comfortable in your own home, or in a different environment?

It is not difficult to understand that physical discomfort seldom brings out the best in people. This is a crucial insight into social behaviors of children with ASD. It is easy to understand how those on the autism spectrum can overlook the nuances of empathy and other emotions when they are simply struggling to cope with the bright lights, loud sounds, and funny smells in their daily environment. Often, what are perceived as "social meltdowns" or tantrums is simply the child's way of signaling sensory overload and physical discomfort. While the sensory and physical discomforts brought on by the flu usually disappear after a few days, the sensory discomfort experience by many children with ASD is something they must be taught to tolerate in order to further their social–emotional development.

This connection between socioemotional development and physical comfort has been explored in depth by Temple Grandin in her book *Thinking in Pictures: My Life with Autism* (2006). Grandin reveals an interesting insight that sparked her initial comprehension of human empathy: In order for a person to feel compassionate and gentle, he or she must first experience bodily comfort. While most children experience physical comfort from hugs and kisses, a myriad of sensory sensitivities make it quite difficult for a child with ASD to feel comfortable.

Social development in children with autism is ultimately a piece of the ASD puzzle. It is important to look at the big picture of ASDs and understand that many external factors can affect social development. For example, difficulties in social relationships and interactions may stem from other sources such as biological, cognitive, and sensory differences (Grandin, 2006). We tend to gravitate towards interventions for the *visible* signs of autism because those are clearly evident to us on a more frequent basis. However, we often overlook the fact that autism is very much a biological and medical condition. It is helpful to recognize that various medical issues are associated, or comorbid, with autism that can affect the student's social behavior (Ashley, 2007).

It is easy to get so caught up with the actions and behaviors of children with autism that we sometimes forget that many of these behaviors are partially rooted in physical, medical, and biological issues. While each area may independently make sense, piecing everything together may give us an entirely different perspective of the complex causes of social difficulties in children with ASD.

SOCIAL DEVELOPMENT AND COMMUNICATION

Understanding the myriad of unconventional reasons for a child with ASD to exhibit problem behaviors helps teachers figure out more appropriate methods of intervention. Since children with autism have limited avenues of communicating clearly, their actions and behavior often should not be taken literally. Rather, assessing the communication and social skills of a child with ASD often requires the observer to look beyond the surface and dig deeper to interpret the child's true message (Quill, 2000). Even if the child has some verbal skills, the assessor will have to test out various interpretations of the child's actions and behaviors to decipher the true intention and meaning of the child's communication. Ultimately, the hope is to work with the child to the point where he or she is able and comfortable enough to communicate confusion or anxiety in a more controlled and understandable manner.

Universal Languages

While students with ASD may not socialize and communicate through typical channels, they often excel through other social avenues. Art, music, and animal interaction are common channels through which students with ASD can work on creative expression and socioemotional development. In fact, some researchers believe that artistic expression can be effective in sorting out confused identities that often arise from their socioemotional difficulties. Artistic expression often allows students who have difficulty verbally expressing themselves to find an alternate method of emotional release. Expression through creative works can be a form of self-therapy through which people with ASD can sort out any "perceptual puzzlement" they may experience and help them make sense of the world (Fitzgerald, 2005). Many children with ASD are able to pick up indirect socioemotional cues in music or art that they cannot pick up in typical social situations (Heaton, Hermelin, & Pring, 1999). It is often beneficial to use these abilities to help the student further develop skills to empathize and relate to others (Fitzgerald, 2005). Having creative and nontraditional outlets offers students perceptual versatility and gives them a different venue to communicate. Since students with ASD may perceive the world differently (Ashley, 2007), alternative forms of expression through art can help them nonverbally articulate their emotions. Often, students who are unable to verbally articulate their sentiments may find emotional and social release through nonverbal forms of expression. Students with ASD, just like any other student, should be encouraged to think "out of the box" in order to develop creative concepts.

Jon is 7 years old and was diagnosed with AS at a young age. While he has a wide vocabulary, he has trouble expressing his feelings and understanding social situations. When he is frustrated, he often barks like a dog and grunts. He also interrupts others when they are speaking to talk about his favorite movies (his favorite topic)—even if it has nothing to do with this topic at hand, and then he becomes confused when his peers are mad at him. Jon looks forward to music class and often calms down during music lessons. While he may have difficulty understanding what other people are feeling, he has no problem relating to the music and writes music with complex storylines. He will listen to music and say, "This song sounds like a little girl is happy because she is playing with her friend," or, "This song sounds like Beethoven is angry that he cannot hear his own music!" When he is able to relate to the music, the instructor will encourage Jon to understand his perceptions by asking follow-up questions like, "Don't you think that you would be mad like Beethoven if you couldn't do something you wanted to? How do you think your friends feel when they can't do something they would like to?"

Developing social skills through social interaction with animals is another effective nontraditional method. Since animals do not share the same verbal language as humans, they are very adept at communicating via body language. When interacting with humans, animals respond according to the treatment they are given. If a child with ASD grips a cat or dog too hard, the cat or dog will growl, hiss, or run away. If the child does not give his or her horse stern guidance, the horse will not follow direction. There is a strong "action and reaction" connection between the student's actions and the elicited response from the animal. This helps the child gradually grasp that actions have consequences, either positive or negative. This understanding can later be generalized to improve the child's social interactions with friends and peers.

SUMMARY

"People who look through keyholes are apt to get the idea that most things in the world are keyhole shaped." ~Author Unknown

As the quotation above suggests, we cannot begin to understand children with ASD until we attempt to see the world through their eyes. Ultimately, the social development of students with ASD relies on the ability and willingness of people around them to attempt to see things from their point of view. Since people with ASD are unable to put themselves in our shoes, it is up to us to be open to alternative perspectives. Perhaps by demonstrating the empathy we strive to teach, we will gain another key in the quest to decode the autism puzzle.

This chapter delineated the many social characteristics of students with ASD and the various methods, tips, and skills that can be incorporated into personal routines and academic schedules. Social pragmatics, applied behavior analysis, peer modeling, and artistic expression are examples of the myriad ways to help students "bridge the gap." Perhaps the most important point in this chapter is the realization that there is no "right" way for all students; there is only what is right for *each individual* student.

REFERENCES

American Psychiatric Association (APA). (2000). *Diagnostic and statistical manual of mental disorders* (4th ed., text rev.). Washington, DC: Author.

American Speech Language Hearing Association (ASHA). (1997–2009). *Social Language Use (Pragmatics)*. Retrieved March 15, 2009, from http://www.asha.org/public/speech/development/Pragmatics.htm

Asperger, H. (1944). Autistic psychopathy' in childhood. In U. Frith (1991) *Autism and Asperger syndrome*. Cambridge University Press.

Aspy, R., & Grossman, B.G. (2007). *The Ziggurat Model*. Shawnee Mission, KA: Autism Asperger.

Ashley, S. (2007). *Asperger's Answer Book*. Naperville, IL: Sourcebooks.

Centers for Disease Control and Prevention (CDC). (n.d.). *Autism Information Center*. Retrieved March 15, 2009, from www.cdc.gov

Cress, C. J. (2004). *Strategies to Improve Pragmatic/Social Skills and Executive Functioning in Students with Autism*. Retrieved April 19, 2009, from http://www.unl.edu/barkley/present/cress/LPSAutism04.pdf

Cooper, Heron, & Heward (2007). *Applied Behavior Analysis* (2nd ed.). Upper Saddle River, NJ: Pearson, Merrill, Prentice Hall.

Fitzgerald, M. (2005). *The Genesis of Artistic Creativity: Asperger's Syndrome and the Arts*. London & Philadelphia: Jessica Kingsley.

Grandin, T. (2006). *Thinking in Pictures*. New York: Vintage Books.

Heaton, P., Hermelin, B., & Pring, L. (1999). Can children with autistic spectrum disorders perceive affect in music? An experimental investigation. *Psychological Medicine, 29*, 1405–1410 doi:10.1017/S0033291799001221.

Jones, E. A., Feeley, K. M., & Takacs, J. (2007). Teaching spontaneous responses to young children with autism. *Journal of Applied Behavior Analysis, 40*, 565–570. Retrieved March 15, 2009, from PubMed Central Database.

National Research Council (NRC). (2001). *Educating Children with Autism*. Washington, DC: National Academy Press.

Quill, K. A. (2000). *Do-Watch-Listen Say: Social and Communication Intervention for Children with Autism*. Baltimore: Brookes.

Shonkoff, J. P. (2000) *From Neurons to Neighborhoods: The Science of Early Childhood Development*. Washington, DC: National Academies Press.

Stewart, K. (2007). *Helping a Child with Nonverbal Learning Disorder of Asperger's Disorder* (2nd ed.). Oakland, CA: New Harbinger.

PART TWO

Procedures and Challenges in Assessment

Evidence-Based Procedures for the Assessment of Children with Autism

Linda C. Caterino and Joseph M. Mahoney

Assessment processes for children with autism require not only a determination of whether the child has autism but also a deeper understanding of the child's cognitive processes, language skills, academic achievement, and adaptive behavior, as well as socioemotional and behavioral skills. It is imperative that the psychologists and clinical teams engaged in these evaluations be aware of the research support for the assessment instruments they use, particularly in regard to this population. This chapter will present an overview of the assessment process, including information on the assessment instruments available and a review of research using these instruments. The evaluation process is comprehensive and should integrate information obtained from a variety of procedures, including record review, parent and teacher interviews, and observations, as well as structured standardized assessment measures.

In the initial stages of the evaluation, the psychologist should gain parent involvement. Parents, of course, have the longest and most consistent involvement with their children, and while they may not always be able to present an objective view of their child or be aware of norms for typical children, they provide invaluable information that the clinical team can use in making their diagnosis and subsequent treatment plan. In addition, the parent interview provides the opportunity for the psychologist to gain parent support, which may lead to a more harmonious collaborative experience for the child and his or her family.

During the first interview the psychologist should gather as much information as possible regarding the child's early history and current functioning. The parents can also grant the psychologist permission to contact other adults who have worked with the child, such as caregivers, habilitators, pediatricians, preschool teachers, therapists, and other professionals. Here the emphasis will be on comparing the child's behavior to that of typical children and making note of any behaviors or symptoms that may be present that are consistent with the criteria for autistic disorder presented in the *DSM-IV-TR* (American Psychiatric Association [APA], 2000). The *DSM-IV-TR* lists three major criteria for autistic disorder (299.00):

1. Qualitative impairment in social interaction
2. Qualitative impairment in communication
3. Restricted, repetitive, and stereotyped patterns of behavior, interests, and activities

The psychologist should determine whether the child has displayed typical developmental patterns in communication, both verbal and nonverbal behaviors, and in socialization, and whether or not atypical behaviors such as stereotypies or repetitive behaviors are present. In typical children, nonverbal communication begins quite early. By 3 months of age, a typical child may attempt to communicate through facial expressions and body movements and may even imitate adults. By 8 to 12 months of age, typical children may indicate their understanding of others' words, point, shake their head to signal "no," and wave good-bye (Menyuk, Liebergott, & Schultz, 1995). Werner, Dawson, Osterling, and Dinno (2000) found that infants with autism from 8 to 10 months of age display a diminished response to their name in comparison to typical children; however, other behaviors, such as looking at others, looking at the face while smiling, and orienting to name were not significantly different from other children of this age. Colgan et al. (2006) looked at social interaction gestures in 9- to 12-month-old infants with autism using video analysis. They found that decreased variety in type of gestures was significantly associated with a diagnosis of autism; however, neither number of total gestures nor initiation of gestures was significantly associated with autism status. Children with autism also show relative strengths in the use of gestures to regulate others' behaviors (Mundy, Sigman, & Kasari, 1990; Wetherby & Prutting, 1984).

Verbal development in typical children progresses at a rapid rate. For example, a typical child will babble by about 6 months of age and by 8 to 10 months will vocalize using vowel and vowel–consonant combinations (Werner et al., 2000). First words are usually spoken around 10 to 15 months, with 13 months being the average (Berko Gleason, 2000), and by 18 months most children have a vocabulary of 50 words and are using two-word phrases. By 2 years of age, children's vocabulary is about 200 words (Bloom, Lifter, & Broughton, 1985), and by 3 years of age, children understand pronouns and plurals, can use four- to five-word sentences, and have a vocabulary of up to 1000 words. Children at 4 years of age are able to tell stories using four- and five-word sentences, and by 5 years of age, they are telling much longer stories with complex sentences (Bloom, 1998). See Chapter 2 for a comprehensive treatment of language characteristics in children with autism.

A child with autism may not develop speech at all or may show significant delays after 3 years of age (Charman, Drew, Baird, & Baird, 2003; Chiang & Lin,

2008). If speech is acquired, children with autism may not be able to sustain a conversation or may use repetitive, echolalic, and/or stereotypic words or phrases (Fay, 1969). They may have difficulty understanding multiple meanings of words and have problems with sarcasm (Papp, 2006). They may seem to understand language in a very concrete manner, having problems with slang and metaphors. They may also have difficulty with pragmatic language or the use of language in social situations (Young, Diehl, Morris, Hyman, & Bennetto, 2005). In addition, their speech may be characterized by an odd tonal pattern lacking the emotional emphasis most typical children use to get their point across (Shriberg et al., 2001).

In order to assess a child's social abilities, the evaluator must obtain information regarding the child's play patterns, preferably through observation. Bergen (1988) described various categories of play. *Sensori-motor play* is practiced by infants and involves the use of senses such as hearing and touch. Around 12 months, children begin enjoying toys with a cause-and-effect relationship. The next step, *practice play,* begins during the preschool years and involves the repetition of new skills, in particular, physical skills such as running, jumping, and throwing. *Constructive play*, which consists of the manipulation of physical objects such as blocks in order to build something, occurs in older infants and preschoolers. Between 18 to 24 months of age, children begin *pretense* or *symbolic play,* which involves the use of make-believe or socio-dramatic role playing. This type of play typically reaches a peak at 4 or 5 years of age and then gradually declines in frequency.

Social interaction is evident even in infancy in typical children. By 3 months of age, children can recognize their parents and have developed a social smile. They can engage with others and even cry when their play is discontinued. By 7 months they can respond to others' emotional expressions, and by 12 months they can express intense feelings for their caretakers. At 11 months, children may engage in social play such as patty-cake and peek-a-boo. By 12 months of age, children show a preference and affection for certain people. They can cry when parents or caregivers leave and can be shy or anxious with strangers. They seem to enjoy imitating people and demonstrate joint attention. By 2 years of age, typical children play pretend games and seem excited about the company of other children. They also show awareness of their own feelings and those of others. By 3 years of age, typical children may engage in parallel play and may join into play situations. They also use objects symbolically in play. By 4, children show a wide range of emotions and can participate appropriately in games by taking turns and sharing. Their dramatic play becomes more elaborate and inventive. By 5 years of age, they show an ability to understand others' feelings and are able to negotiate solutions to conflicts, which typically lead to the development of strong friendships (Centers for Disease Control and Prevention [CDC], n.d.).

Children with autism may show social interaction difficulties from the earliest ages. Abundant evidence suggests that children with autism show less joint attention than typical peers (e.g., Dawson et al., 2004; Jones & Carr, 2004; Leekam, Lopez, & Moore, 2000; Loveland & Landry, 1986; Stahl & Pry, 2002). Osterling and

Dawson (1994) reviewed videotapes of first birthday parties of 11 typical children and 22 children with autism and found that the children with autism exhibited fewer social and joint attention behaviors such as pointing, showing objects, looking at others, and orienting in response to name. In a later study, Osterling, Dawson, and Munson (2002) extended this same study to another group of 20 children with autism, 20 typical children, and 14 children with mental retardation. They replicated the results from their 1994 article and also showed that children with autism showed fewer social behaviors than the children with mental retardation.

It is also important to determine the type of play in which the child engages. Young children with autism may show very repetitive types of play (Sherman, Shapiro, & Glassman, 1983). They may not develop play patterns at the same rate as typical children or may never develop certain types of play (Doussard-Roosevelt, Joe, Bazhenova, & Porges, 2003; Libby, Powell, Messer, & Jordan, 1998). For example, Charman et al. (1997) noted that none of the 20-month-old children with autism in their study used representational or symbolic play. Stone and Lemanek (1990) found that preschool children with autism showed more differences in imaginative play, peer play, and imitation skills as compared to children with mental retardation. Hobson, Lee, and Hobson (2009) observed a group of children with autism and a typical group and found that the children with autism showed less "playful pretend involving self-conscious awareness of pretending, [less] investment in the symbolic meanings given to play materials, [less] creativity and [less] fun" (p. 12).

Children with autism also demonstrate patterns of behavior and interests that are rigid and persistent in nature. They may show stereotypic and repetitive motor movements such as hand flapping (Kanner, 1971; Ward, 1970), although such movements may not be present at all times, depending on the situation (Dadds, Schwartz, Adams, & Rose, 1988). They may also become preoccupied with certain restricted interests or parts of objects and become upset if their routine is changed (APA, 2000).

INTERVIEW

Commercial interview procedures are available to assist the psychologist in the interview process. The most widely used is the Autism Diagnostic Interview–Revised (ADI–R; Rutter, Le Couteur, & Lord, 2008), which is specifically designed for children with autism. Using the ADI–R, a trained interviewer will interview a parent or caregiver to obtain information regarding three primary domains of autism: language/communication; reciprocal social interactions; and restricted, repetitive, and stereotype behaviors. Interviewees are asked questions regarding the child's behavior between 4 years, 0 months and 5 years, 0 months of age; the last 3 months; and his or her entire lifetime. Questions also involve time frames for the completion of developmental milestones. They are asked about the child's communication skills including language acquisition and the presence of any autistic symptoms (e.g., echolalia, stereotyped utterances, etc.). Parents are further questioned regarding the child's social interactions, including the presence of imaginative play, imitations, social smiling, showing and directing attention, sharing enjoyment with others, prosocial behaviors such as offering comfort, use of appropriate facial expressions, interest in other children, friendships, and social disinhibition. Parents are queried about any unusual preoccupations, circumscribed interests, the presence of compulsions or rituals, unusual sensory interests or sensitivity, unusual attachment to objects, and hand and finger mannerisms.

Although the interview is lengthy, at times lasting from 2 to 3 hours, the interview process allows parents the opportunity to gain insight into their child's functioning. The ADI–R test manual reports very good psychometric properties for the instrument (Rutter et al., 2008, p. 41). A study of inter-rater reliability conducted by Cicchetti, Lord, Koenig, Klin, and Volkmar (2008) involved the ratings of seven different examiners in the case of a 3½-year-old girl. This study showed 100% agreement on 74% of the ADI–R items. A study examining the stability of clinical diagnosis using the ADI–R found that all children diagnosed as autistic at 20 months of age received a diagnosis of autism or PDD at 42 months of age (Cox et al., 1999). The ADI–R has demonstrated strong agreement with team clinical diagnoses for children with mental ages above 24 months (Le Couteur, Haden, Hammal, & McConachie, 2008; Mazefsky & Oswald, 2006). However, the instrument may not be as accurate for children with lower mental ages (Cox et al., 1999; Lord, 1995; Lord, Storoschuk, Rutter, & Pickles, 1993). It may overdiagnose children with severe cognitive delays at age 2 but underdiagnose those of this age who do not show restricted patterns of interests and behaviors (Lord & Risi, 2000). While the ADI–R may show good validity for the diagnosis of autism, it may not discriminate well among the different PDD diagnoses (Klin, Lang, Cicchetti, & Volkmar, 2000). A principal components analysis by Tadevosyan-Leyfer et al. (2003) provided further support for the validity of the ADI–R for children over 24 months. The ADI–R has also been translated into Spanish.

OBSERVATIONS

Any child who is being evaluated should be carefully observed in several environments, including the classroom, the playground, and, if possible, the home. They should be observed in both structured and nonstructured situations and with different individuals. Observational measures specifically designed for the assessment of autism include the Autism Diagnostic Observation Schedule–Generic (ADOS–G: Lord, Rutter, DiLavore, & Risi, 1999). The ADOS–G is an outgrowth of the original Autism Diagnostic Observation Schedule (ADOS) and the Pre-Linguistic Autism Diagnostic Observation Schedule (PL–ADOS; see Lord et al., 2000). The ADOS–G is described as a "semi structured standardized assessment of communication, social interaction, and play or imaginative use of materials for individuals who have been referred because of possible autism or other pervasive developmental disorders" (Lord et al., 1999, p. 1). The ADOS–G, which is available in both English and

Spanish, consists of various structured activities that allow the examiner to observe the child's social and communication behaviors. The instrument measures nonverbal behaviors such as eye contact, gaze, facial expression, gesture, affect communication, and shared attention and enjoyment, as well as understanding of others' emotions and language skills. It assesses the presence of target behaviors, including asking for help, symbolic play, reciprocal play, giving help to the interviewer, taking turns in a structured task, use of descriptive gesture and mime, description of agents and actions, the ability to tell a sequential story, use of reciprocal communication, and the ability to use language to discuss socioemotional topics. The ADOS–G contains four different modules that can take about 30–45 minutes each. In each module, the examiner sets up specific vignettes and observes and records the child's behavior in each situation. Typically, one module is selected for the subject based on his or her age and expressive language skills.

The ADOS–G is reported to be a reliable and valid tool for measuring autism symptoms. It demonstrates very good inter-rater reliability and good validity. One recent study showed 77% agreement between ADOS classification and a clinical multidisciplinary team diagnosis (Mazefsky & Oswald, 2006). Tomanik, Pearson, Loveland, Lane, and Shaw (2007) also found that the ADOS resulted in 75% correct diagnosis of autism in their sample of 129 children and adolescents. In a study examining the validity of both the ADOS and the ADI–R, Gray, Tonge, and Sweeney (2008) found that children with a clinical diagnosis of autism scored significantly higher on all algorithm domains of the two instruments as compared to nonautistic children. In addition, the ADOS has certain benefits over ADI–R. While the ADI–R only attempts to distinguish between autism and typically developing children, the ADOS provides diagnostic cut-offs for both autism and PDD-NOS. Also, for very young children, the ADOS may be more predictive of autism than the ADI–R (Lord & Risi, 2000). A recent revision to the algorithm of ADOS–G (Gotham, Risi, Pickles, & Lord, 2007) should result in improvements to the instrument's already strong diagnostic validity.

COGNITIVE ASSESSMENT

A cognitive evaluation can be useful in determining the child's potential and possible learning rate. In addition to an IQ score, cognitive assessments can yield information regarding visual perception, language, and attention, as well as working memory, processing speed, and abstract reasoning processes. It can also provide useful information regarding whether the child's communication skills are discrepant from his or her developmental level (Klinger, O'Kelley, & Mussey, 2009). Koegel, Koegel, and Smith (1997) suggested that standardized cognitive assessment instruments may not be valid or appropriate for the assessment of children with autism. Magiati and Howlin (2001) also acknowledged the problems in cognitive assessment and suggested that using more than one measure may provide a more valid measure of cognitive ability. According to Klin, Saulnier, Tsatsanis, and Volkmar

(2005), it is very important to gain some understanding of the child's intellectual ability since "the level of cognitive functioning has been shown to be possibly the most important factor mediating a wide range of clinical phenomena, such as severity of symptomatology in the social, language, and communication domains, as well as in terms of stereotypic behaviors and self-injury, and level of self-sufficiency eventual outcome and medical complications such as seizures" (p. 783). While an intellectual score or profile may not be considered as the defining factor in a diagnosis of autism, it does provide a framework for further assessment, such as neuropsychological assessment and may form the basis for treatment planning.

At one time it was thought that all children with autism had mental retardation, but this is no longer the case (Baron-Cohen & Belmonte, 2005). Recent research has indicated that only 55% of children with ASD (Baird et al., 2006) and only 70.4% of those specifically diagnosed with autism (Frombonne, 2005) have IQ scores in the mentally retarded range. Several tests of cognitive ability may be used with children with autism, including the Bayley Scales of Infant and Toddler Development III (Bayley, 2005), the Mullen Scales of Early Learning (Mullen, 1995), the Kaufman Assessment Battery for Children–2nd Edition (KABC-2; Kaufman & Kaufman, 2004), the Woodcock–Johnson Tests of Cognitive Ability (Woodcock, McGrew, & Mather, 2001a), the Differential Ability Scales–II (DAS-II; Elliott, 2007), the Stanford-Binet–V (SB–V; Roid, 2003), the Wechsler Preschool and Primary Scales of Intelligence–3rd Edition (WPPSI–III: Wechsler, 2002), the Wechsler Intelligence Scale for Children–IV (WISC–IV: Wechsler, 2003), and nonverbal assessments such as the Leiter International Performance Scale–Revised (Roid & Miller, 1997), the Universal Non-Verbal Intelligence Test (UNIT: Bracken & McCallum, 1998), and the Naglieri Nonverbal Ability Test (NNAT: Naglieri, 1997).

The Bayley Scales of Infant and Toddler Development–3rd Edition (Bayley, 2005) assesses cognitive ability in children from 1 month to 42 months of age. In a 2001 survey of autism service centers across the United States, Luiselli et al. (2001) found that the Bayley Scales were the most frequently used measure of cognitive ability in young children. The Bayley takes about one hour to administer. The test includes three main components: the Mental Development Index, which assesses problem-solving and language skills, the Psychomotor Development Index, which measures fine and gross motor skills, and the Behavior Rating Scale, which is used to rate the child's behavior during the evaluation, including attention, social engagement, and affect. It provides scores in four domains including Cognitive, Language, Social, and Motor. Seventy children with a diagnosis of PDD including autistic disorder were included in the standardization sample and their scores on all scales (Cognitive, Receptive Communication, Expressive Communication, Fine Motor, Gross Motor, and Social–Emotional) and composite measures (Language and Motor) were found to be lower than for typical children, with higher level nonverbal problem-solving skills than expressive language skills. Klin, Jones, Schultz, and Volkmar (2005) argued that the child's subtest profile may be more informative than the summary scores since the summary scores average highly discrepant skills.

The Mullen Scales of Early Learning (Mullen, 1995) measures both verbal and nonverbal abilities. It provides an overall Early Learning Composite score and five scale scores: Gross Motor, Visual Reception, Fine Motor, Receptive, and Expressive Language. It yields T scores in all five domains and a Composite Score based on the first four domains. The Mullen takes between 15 and 60 minutes to administer and can be used for children from birth to 68 months of age. While no children with autism were included in the standardization sample, some studies have been conducted using the Mullen with young children with autism spectrum disorder. Landa and Garrett-Mayer (2006) found that children with ASD demonstrated delays in all areas except Visual Reception. In addition, their Visual Reception scores were higher than their Receptive Language scores. Similar findings were noted by Akshoomoff (2006) in a study with children with ASD between 16 and 43 months of age. The children received lower scores on all scales, with a relative strength on the Fine Motor scale and a weakness on the Receptive Language scale. In terms of behaviors noted during the administration, Akshoomoff found that children in the ASD group required less time to complete the assessment but spent proportionately more time off task (e.g., out of position, whining, crying, looking away) and less time engaged with the assessment.

The Cognitive Assessment System (CAS; Naglieri & Das, 1997) is intended for children from 5 to 17 years of age and takes about 1 hour to administer. The test was developed according to Naglieri's PASS model, and it assesses planning, attention, simultaneous, and successive processes. Children with autism were included in the standardization sample. A dissertation by Gutwirth (1996) looked at CAS functioning among three groups of children: typical children, learning disabled, and emotionally disturbed children including children with autism. Results indicated that children with autism were represented in the low-functioning group and that they showed particular difficulty on successive tasks. Further research using the CAS with children with autism is planned (J. Naglieri, personal communication, March, 2010).

The Kaufman Assessment Battery for Children–2nd Edition (KABC–II: Kaufman & Kaufman, 2004) is designed for children from 3 to 18 years of age. The test yields three different IQ scores: the Mental Processing Index (MPI), the Fluid-Crystallized Index (FCI), and the Nonverbal Index (NVI). The KABC–II includes five scales: Sequential Processing, Simultaneous Processing, Learning Ability, Planning Ability, and Knowledge. The authors reported that a small sample of 38 children (32 males and 6 females) diagnosed with autism were included in the standardization sample. The children with autism scored significantly lower on all IQ measures (mean MPI score = 68.1, mean FCI score = 66.9, mean NVI score = 68.6), but the NVI score was not significantly discrepant from the other obtained IQ scores. Mean scores on all scales were significantly discrepant from the norm group as well (Sequential = 72.3, Simultaneous = 68.3, Learning = 76.1, Planning = 70.7, Knowledge = 66.1; Kaufman & Kaufman, 2004, p. 128). The highest subtest scores were on the visual tests of Gestalt Closure, Triangles, and Atlantis, and the lowest subtest scores were Riddles, Verbal Knowledge, and Rover, which requires a high level of executive functioning and deductive reasoning (Kaufman, Lichtenberger, Fletcher-Janzen, & Kaufman, 2005). While the KABC–II does not include a specific assessment of the child's ability to understand social situations, it does include a subtest that assesses the child's ability to remember faces which has demonstrated some ability to distinguish between children with autism and typical children (Klin et al., 1999).

The Stanford-Binet–5th Edition (SB–V; Roid, 2003) can be used with individuals from 2 to 85+ years of age. The SB–V yields a full scale IQ score, a Nonverbal IQ (NVIQ), and a Verbal IQ (VIQ) score and includes five factor scales: Fluid Reasoning (the ability to solve verbal and nonverbal problems using inductive or deductive reasoning), Knowledge (accumulated fund of acquired information), Quantitative Reasoning (facility with numbers and numerical problems), Visual–Spatial Processing (ability to see visual patterns and relationships), and Working Memory (ability to store and transform information). Eighty-three children with autistic disorder were included in the standardization sample. In a study by Harris, Handelman, and Burton (1990), the SB–IV was administered to 24 children with autism, and results indicated that these children scored lowest on the Absurdities subtest and highest on the Pattern Analysis subtest. Carpentieri and Morgan (1994) found that the verbal scores of children with autism were significantly lower than those of retarded children with the same IQ score. In their study, the Comprehension and Absurdities subtest were the weakest subtests, and the Quantitative Reasoning subtest was the highest. In a study of young children 3 to 7 years of age, Mayes and Calhoun (2003) also found that nonverbal IQ scores were greater than verbal IQ. Roid and Pomplun (2005) compared children with ADHD to children with autism with average intelligence and found that the Fluid Reasoning and Quantitative Reasoning factor index scores were the best predictor scores. These scales correctly classified 61% of the students, while for a mentally retarded vs. lower-IQ autism group, the Working Memory factor index score was the best predictor and this equation correctly classified 58% of the students.

Most of the research regarding the cognitive abilities of children with autism has been conducted with the Wechsler scales. The Wechsler Preschool and Primary Scale of Intelligence–3rd Edition (WPPSI–III: Wechsler, 2002) can be used with children 2 years, 6 months to 7 years, 3 months. A Full Scale IQ score is derived, as well as composite scores for Verbal, Performance, Processing Speed, and General Language. Only 21 children with a diagnosis of autism were included in the standardization sample. The WPPSI–III technical manual indicates that the autistic sample obtained a significantly lower Full Scale IQ (76.6) and that they scored significantly lower than a matched control group on all composite scores, with a Performance IQ Score higher than a Verbal (88.2 vs. 70.6).

The Wechsler Intelligence Scale for Children–IV (WISC–IV: Wechsler, 2003) can be administered to children from 6 years, 0 months to 16 years, 11 months. The WISC–IV yields a Full Scale IQ score, as well as scaled scores in Verbal Comprehension, Perceptual Reasoning, Working Memory, and Processing Speed. Only 19 children diagnosed with autism were included in the standardization sample, with the mean Full Scale IQ score being 76.4. The children with autism scored significantly lower on all composites and on all required subtests except Block Design (Wechsler, 2003). Children with autism scored highest on the Block Design, Matrix Reasoning, and Picture Concepts subtests and lowest on Coding, Symbol Search, and Comprehension subtests (Wechsler, 2003). Thus, while the sample size was quite small, this study suggests that children with autism generally perform better on nonverbal tasks than on subtests that measure verbal or processing speed skills.

Early research using previous revisions of the WISC also found that individuals with ASD demonstrated higher nonverbal skills than verbal skills (Allen, Lincoln, & Kaufman, 1991; Ameli, Couchesne, Lincoln, Kaufman, & Grillon, 1988; Asarnow, Tanguay, Bott, & Freeman, 1987; Lincoln, Courchesne, Kilman, Elmasian, & Allen, 1988), especially for individuals with lower cognitive scores (i.e., IQ < 85; Rumsey, 1992). However, research using the WISC–III (Mayes & Calhoun, 2003) found that while preschool children with autism did show greater strength in nonverbal skills, this pattern did not hold across the lifespan, and by elementary school age, this non-verbal to verbal discrepancy was not evident, especially for children with IQ scores above 80. In a more recent study using the WISC–IV, Mayes and Calhoun (2008) found that children (mean age 8.2 years) with HFA earned above normal scores on the Perceptual Reasoning and Verbal Comprehension indexes and below normal scores on the Working Memory and Processing Speed indexes. The untimed, motor-free visual reasoning subtests of Matrix Reasoning and Picture Concepts, both new to the WISC–IV, were found to be the highest of the nonverbal subtests, and Coding was the lowest mean subtest score. They suggested that the use of the WISC–IV may be more advantageous to children with autism, who may have a strength in visual reasoning but may have more difficulty with visual motor skills and with working under a time constraint. They also found that children with HFA performed significantly lower on the WISC–IV Comprehension subtest than they did on the Similarities and Vocabulary subtests, suggesting a weakness in social reasoning as well as language comprehension.

In the Mayes and Calhoun study (2008), the General Ability index (GAI) of 113 was significantly higher than the Full Scale IQ (FSIQ) of 101 for the autistic group; however, they found that the FSIQ was a better predictor of academic achievement in reading, math, and written expression. Miller and Ozonoff (2000) found no significant difference between Verbal and Performance IQ scores using the WISC–III. It now appears that about half to three quarters of individuals with autism have non-significant verbal–nonverbal discrepancies (Gilchrist et al., 2001; Manjiviona & Prior, 1995; Siegel, Minshew, & Goldstein, 1996). This effect could be influenced by differences in diagnostic criteria (e.g., inclusion of children with AS in the autistic sample). It may also be attributed to differences in versions of the WISC, since a newer study using the WISC–IV by Lincoln, Hansel, and Quirmbach (2007) found a significant discrepancy between the Perceptual Reasoning index and the Verbal Comprehension Index (18.5 points). Most studies of subtest analysis, however, support the pattern of lower Comprehension scores (Barnhill, Hagiwars, Myles, & Simpson, 2000; Lincoln et al., 2007), as well as lower Symbol Search and Coding scores (Lichtenberger, 2004) and relatively higher scores on Block Design (Lincoln et al.,

2007; Siegel et al., 1996). The Wechsler scales were found to have a four-factor structure for both individuals with autism and normative samples (Goldstein et al., 2008). However, the authors suggest that despite a similar organization of cognitive abilities in children with HFA, a lower intercorrelation between scales indicated the possibility of reduced communication between brain regions in this population.

Two other comprehensive cognitive assessments are The Differential Ability Scales–II (DAS–II; Elliott, 2007) and the Woodcock–Johnson III Tests of Cognitive Abilities (WJ III; Woodcock et al., 2001a), both of which are based on the CHC view of intelligence. The DAS can be administered to children from 2 years, 6 months to 17 years, 11 months. It has excellent internal consistency reliability and validity (Sattler, 2001). The test contains seven cognitive subscales and three achievement tests which yield General Conceptual Ability scores, as well as four cluster scores, Verbal Ability, Nonverbal Ability, Nonverbal Reasoning Ability, and Spatial Ability. In addition, a Special Nonverbal Composite can be computed for the lower preschool level, which may be useful in the autistic population. However, no research regarding the DAS with the autistic population was discovered.

The WJ III can be administered to individuals from 2 to 90 years of age. The test is divided into seven clusters: Comprehension-Knowledge, Long-Term Retrieval, Visual–Spatial Thinking, Auditory Processing, Fluid Reasoning, Processing Speed, and Short Term Memory. The test can take from 40 minutes to 2 hours to administer, depending on the number of subtests administered. The test has excellent internal consistency reliability and validity, but it has not been used extensively with the autistic population. No research regarding the use of these instruments with children with autism has been published. However, a new book describing clinical patterns on the WJ III is scheduled for publication soon and specific factor patterns for children with autism will be discussed (F. Schrank, personal communication, March, 2010).

Since many children with autism have significant language difficulties, it may be necessary to also use ability tests that focus on visual perceptual skills. These tests include the Leiter–R (Roid & Miller, 1997), the Test of Non-Verbal Intelligence–3rd Edition (TONI–3; Brown, Sherbenou, & Johnsen, 1997), the Universal Nonverbal Intelligence Test (UNIT; Bracken & McCallum, 1998), the Naglieri Test of Nonverbal Abilities (NNAT; Naglieri, 1997), and the Comprehensive Test of Nonverbal Intelligence (CTONI; Hammill, Pearson, & Wiederholt, 1997).

The Leiter–R (Roid & Miller, 1997) is a nonverbal cognitive assessment measure designed for individuals from 2 years, 0 months to 20 years, 11 months of age. The Leiter–R contains two batteries, Visualization and Reasoning, and Attention and Memory, with 10 different subtests included in each battery. The internal consistency reliability and validity of the instrument are acceptable (Sattler, 2001). While no children with autism were included in the standardization sample, a study by Tsatsanis et al. (2003) found that, in general, children with autism performed better on the Fundamental Visualization composite than on the Fluid Reasoning Composite.

The TONI–3 (Brown et al., 1997) is another language-free test that can be administered to individuals from 6 years of age to adulthood. The TONI–3 is designed to measure problem solving and abstract reasoning abilities. It has been shown to be moderately positively correlated with the WISC–IV Matrix Reasoning subtest (Banks & Franzen, 2000). The TONI has a high floor and may not be appropriate for children with severe cognitive delays. A study by Edelson, Schubert, and Edelson (1998) using the TONI–2 found that in their sample of almost 400 children with autism, only about 66% were able to complete the test due to problems with attention. Three other nonverbal tests are the UNIT (Bracken & McCallum, 1998) which can be administered to children and adolescents from 5 years, 0 months to 17 years, 11 months of age, the NNAT (Naglieri, 1997), which was normed on children from 5 to 18 years of age, and the CTONI, which can be used with individuals from 6 to 89 years of age. No studies of children with autism and the UNIT, the NNAT, or the CTONI were found.

During the cognitive assessment, the psychologist also has an opportunity to observe the child's approach to the evaluation, his or her attention span, language abilities, cooperation, and other behaviors, which should be useful in designing treatment plans.

NEUROPSYCHOLOGICAL ASSESSMENT

Specific neuropsychological assessments can extend the depth of a typical cognitive assessment by looking at specific skills such as attention, memory, and executive functioning. Various researchers have shown that children with autism perform poorly on measures of attention and executive functioning (Calhoun & Mayes, 2005; Hughes, Russell, & Robbins, 1994; Mayes & Calhoun, 2003, 2004; Nyden, Gillberg, Hjelmquist, & Heiiman, 1999). Williams, Goldstein, and Minshew (2006a) found that the neuropsychological skills that best discriminated between children with autism and typical children were sensory perceptual, motor, complex language, and complex memory. In their study, attention did not discriminate between the autistic and typical groups. They concluded that problems for children with autism are most evident when they are confronted with complex information or higher order tasks that require integration of information, yet they can perform simple skills as well as or even better than peers.

Attention

Attention is the ability to concentrate on a particular stimulus. *Selective attention* involves inhibiting responses to distracting stimuli, and *sustained attention* involves the ability to attend over time (Naglieri, 2005). Mayes and Calhoun (1999), using a sample of 143 children with autism, found that 93% had significant attention problems but could also hyperfocus for long periods of time on activities of their own choosing. Children with ASD exhibit difficulties in both visual and auditory attention (Corbett & Constantine, 2006), as well as selective attention (Ciesielski, Courchesne, & Elmasian, 1990). Continuous performance tests such as the Integrated

Visual and Auditory Continuous Performance Test + Plus (IVA+ Plus; Sandford & Turner, 2000), the Gordon's Diagnostic System (Gordon, McClure, & Aylward, 1996), the Conners' Continuous Performance Test–II (CPT–II; Conners & MHS Staff, 2000), or the Test of Variables of Attention (TOVA; Greenberg & Waldman, 1993; Leark, Greenberg, Kindschi, Dupuy, & Hughes, 2007) may be used to obtain a measure of the child's ability to attend to auditory or visual stimuli. They assess sustained attention over time, as well as response inhibition and impulsivity.

Corbett and Constantine (2006), in a study using the older version of the IVA, demonstrated that children with autism exhibited significant deficits in visual and auditory attention and even greater deficits in impulsivity as compared to typical children and those with ADHD. In their sample, they found that the majority of the children with autism demonstrated symptoms consistent with a diagnosis of ADHD–combined type. Mayes and Calhoun (2007), in a study using a large clinical sample (n = 866) and 149 typical children from ages 6 to 16, found that children with autism scored significantly more poorly on the Gordon's than did control children, but that their performance was not significantly different from children with ADHD.

Memory

Since memory is complex and includes many specific types, research in this area has been inconsistent. Some studies have shown that for individuals with autism, verbal memory may be impaired (Pennington et al., 1997; Toichi & Kamio, 1998), while visual–spatial memory skills may be intact. Ameli et al. (1988) did not find any impairment in visual recognition memory for children with autism, and de Gelder, Vroomen, and Van der Heide (1991) found that children with autism could appropriately recall pictures of everyday scenes, pictures of buildings (Boucher & Lewis, 1992), and even shoes (Gepner, de Gelder, & de Schonen, 1996). However, children with autism have been shown to have deficits in social memory. Memory for faces has been found to be difficult for children with autism as compared to both typical children and children with mental retardation (Boucher & Lewis, 1992; Boucher, Lewis, & Collis, 1998; Klin et al., 1999). Hauck, Fein, Maltby, Waterhouse, and Feinstein (1998) found that children with autism had difficulty in facial memory and that scores on the Face Memory task correlated significantly with scores of social ability, including the Vineland Communication, Daily Living, and Socialization domain scores. Children with autism may also have difficulty remembering visual sequences (Boucher & Warrington, 1976; Minshew, Goldstein, & Seigel, 1997). Other researchers have not found deficits in verbal memory for noncomplex information (Ozonoff & Strayer, 2001), but have found deficiencies in spatial working memory tasks (Williams, Goldstein, Carpenter, & Minshew, 2005). Williams, Goldstein, and Minshew (2006b) provided insight into these contradictory findings by stating that children with autism have difficulty with complex memory tasks in both visual and verbal domains because "children with autism do not use organizational strategies or context to support memory. For example, children with autism remember randomly organized words as well as mentally retarded controls but do not demonstrate the expected benefit of semantic or syntactic organization" (p. 21).

The Wide Range Assessment of Memory and Learning–2nd Edition (WRAML–2: Sheslow & Adams, 2003) is a well-respected assessment for memory functioning. Williams, Goldstein, and Minshew (2006b) administered the first edition of the WRAML to 38 children with autism and 38 matched controls from 8 to 16 years of age. They found that children with autism showed deficits in memory for complex visual and verbal information and spatial working memory, with relatively intact associative learning ability, verbal working memory, and recognition memory. Significant differences were found between groups for the Sentence Memory, Story Memory, Design Memory, and Picture Memory subtests, with the Finger Windows subtest, a measure of spatial working memory, discriminating most accurately between the autism group and typical controls. Delayed recall for children with autism was not significantly different from the matched controls, with the exception of recall for sentences and stories, which may be attributed to language development.

Another test of verbal memory is the California Verbal Learning Test–Children's Version (CVLT–C; Delis, Kramer, Kaplan & Ober, 1994). This test, which is designed for children from 5 to 16 years of age, requires the youth to remember two word lists. Minshew and Goldstein (1993) compared 21 children with autism to 21 typical children on the CVLT and found that children with autism scored worse than controls on 30 of the 33 variables, but only 6 variables, including free recalls, intrusion errors, and semantic cluster and global cluster ratios, reached significance. Minshew and Goldstein concluded that children with autism may not be able to formulate efficient organizational strategies for recall.

Another memory test, the Children's Memory Scale (CMS; Cohen, 1997) measures auditory/verbal learning and memory, visual/nonverbal learning and memory, and attention and concentration. It is appropriate for children from 5 to 16 years of age. No children with autism were included in the norm group, and no specific studies using the CMS for children with autism were found.

Executive Functioning

Executive functioning refers to impulse control, response inhibition, planning, goal selection, and utilization of feedback. Executive functions are "responsible for guiding, directing, and managing cognitive, emotional, and behavioral functions, particularly during novel problem solving" (Gioia, Espy, & Isquith, 2003 p. 1). Hill (2004) characterized the executive dysfunction in autism as being primarily caused by rigidity and perseveration that can affect both cognitive and social functioning. Ciesielski and Harris (1997) compared children with autism to typical children on various neuropsychological measures, including the Wisconsin Card Sorting Test (WCST; Heaton, Chelune, Talley, Kay, & Curtis, 1993), the Halstead-Reitan's Category Test and Trail Making Test–Part B (TMT–B; Reitan & Wolfson, 1993) and found that youth with autism scored significantly more poorly than controls on all executive tasks. Children with autism took much longer to complete the TMT–B, and their error rate was higher. Performance on the WCST was uneven in the autism group, and the HCT produced high levels of perseverative errors. Ciesielski and Harris stated that children with autism may have difficulty in "disengaging cognitive operations from an earlier mental set and, therefore, in the governing of selective inhibition resources" (p. 10). Other researchers have also found problems for children with autism in perseveration and planning (Ozonoff & Jensen, 1999). A recent study by Kenworthy, Black, Harrison, della Rosa, and Wallace (2009) found a significant relationship between laboratory tasks and behavior rating scales of executive functions in children with autism. Auditory attention and behavioral regulation were significantly correlated with symptoms of autism. They concluded that executive dysfunction is related to all three of the clusters of behavioral symptoms in autism.

Various neuropsychological measures, including the Wisconsin Card Sorting Test (WCST; Heaton et al., 1993), the Delis–Kaplan Executive Functioning System (D–KEFS: Delis, Kaplan, & Kramer, 2001) and the Developmental Neuropsychological Assessment–2nd Edition (NEPSY–II; Korkman, Kirk, & Kemp, 2007), can be used to assess aspects of executive functioning in children with autism. The WCST measures perseveration and cognitive flexibility. It is designed for individuals from 6½ to 89 years of age. Ozonoff (1994) found the original WCST to be highly reliable for use with autistic children. She also noted that children with autism performed better on the computer-administered test than on the traditional administration. Ozonoff, Pennington, and Rogers (1991) discovered that children with autism with average intelligence perseverated on the WCST significantly more than a matched group of children with learning disabilities. Ozonoff (1995) also found significant differences between an autistic group of children and adolescents and normal controls on the WCST. A study by Kaland, Smith, and Mortensen (2008) compared 13 typical to 13 youth with autism (mean age = 15.6 years). While the youth with autism scored less well on all categories, the only statistical difference found was for the failure to maintain set category

The D–KEFS (Delis et al., 2001) can be administered to individuals from 8 through 89 years of age. It measures such skills as problem solving, verbal and spatial concept formation, flexibility of thinking, fluent productivity in both verbal and spatial domains, verbal inhibition, planning and reasoning, deductive reasoning, verbal abstract thinking, and metaphorical thinking. Kleinhans, Akshoomoff, and Delis (2005) administered several subtests from the D–KEFS (i.e., the Color–Word Interference Test, the Trail Making Test, the Verbal Fluency Test, and the Design Fluency Test) to a group of adolescents and adults with HFA, as well as a group of typical individuals and found that the affected group scored significantly below average on the composite measure of executive functioning. They noted that complex verbal tasks that require cognitive switching and efficient lexical retrieval strategies were the most difficult for the individuals with HFA, but that cognitive inhibition was intact.

The NEPSY–II (Korkman et al., 2007) measures several neuropsychological abilities. It was normed on children 3 to 16 years, 11 months of age. The NEPSY–II assesses six domains: Attention and Executive Functioning, Language, Memory and

Learning, Sensorimotor, Social Perception, and Visuospatial processing. Aside from tests of memory and executive functioning, it also includes tests on TOM (which assesses the ability to recognize the feelings and thoughts of others) and Affect Recognition (which measures the student's ability to recognize feelings expressed on faces). The clinical studies in the NEPSY–II manual include small groups of individuals with autism (23) and AS (19). The authors reported that the autistic group scored significantly lower than the control group on the Animal Sorting subtest. Research using the first edition of the NEPSY has shown that children with autism have demonstrated difficulty on tasks of attention and memory, especially memory for faces (Korkman et al., 2007). A study by Hooper, Poon, Marcus, and Fine (2006) using the first version of the NEPSY with 23 children with HFA from 5 to almost 13 years of age and a typical group selected from the standardization sample showed significant differences for Phonological Processing, Auditory Attention and Response Set, Speeded Naming, and Comprehension of Instruction and Narrative Memory; however, these differences were not significant after controlling for IQ. The HFA group also showed significantly lower scores on the Arrows subtest.

The Behavior Rating Inventory of Executive Functioning (BRIEF; Gioia, Isquith, Guy, & Kenworth, 2000) is a parent rating scale that yields scores for initiation, working memory, planning/organizing, inhibition, emotional control, behavior regulation, and shifting. It is designed for children from 5 to 18 years of age. The BRIEF yields a global measure of executive functioning (Global Executive Composite) and two indexes: Behavior Regulation and Metacognition. Eight clinical scales are also derived: Inhibit, Shift, Emotional Control, Initiate, Working Memory, Plan/Organize, Organization of Materials, and Monitor, as well as two validity scales. The authors reported that children with autism score most poorly on the initiation and working memory scales.

There is also a BRIEF scale for younger children from 2 years to 5 years, 11 months: the Behavior Rating Inventory of Executive Function–Preschool Version (BRIEF–P; Gioia et al., 2003). The standardization of the BRIEF–P included individuals with various developmental delays, a study by Rogers, Wallace, and Happe (2002) (cited by Gioia et al., 2003), using an earlier version of the BRIEF–P, found that parents of children with autism rated their children significantly higher on all of the BRIEF– P scale and index scores in comparison to controls.

Cognitive and neuropsychological assessments provide important information regarding the child's verbal and nonverbal problem-solving ability, concept formation, reasoning, learning style, and memory skills (Klin, Saulnier, Tsatsanis, & Volkmar 2005), which can be very helpful in determining the child's ability to benefit from formal academic instruction.

LANGUAGE AND COMMUNICATION

Language and communication difficulties are frequently observed in children with autism. Wetherby, Prizant, and Huchinson (1998) reported difficulties in preverbal communication and a potentially delayed development of pointing gestures (Dawson, Meltzoff, Osterling, Rinaldi, & Brown, 1998) and a reduced rate of responsiveness to speech, such as responding to their name (Osterling & Dawson, 1994). Mesibov, Adams, and Klinger (1997) reported that 35% to 40% of individuals with autism fail to develop functional language abilities. Those who do may display difficulties in both receptive and expressive language (Tager-Flusberg, 2001; Whitehouse, Barry, & Bishop, 2008), lexical–semantic and grammatical development (Kjelgaard & Tager-Flusberg, 2001), as well as oromotor impairments (Page & Boucher, 1998; Whitehouse et al., 2008). Echolalia is evident in 85% of children with autism who eventually do develop speech. Children with autism may also display pronoun reversal, and their comprehension skills may be concrete (Mesibov et al., 1997). Children with autism typically have difficulty in pragmatic language skills such as the ability to use language in a conversation (Young et al., 2005). They may include inappropriate detail, perseverate on topics, make unusual shifts to new topics, and ignore others' initiations (Mesibov et al., 1997). They typically display difficulty in prosody (rhythm, pitch, tone, phrasing, etc.), repetitive use of language and metalinguistics (understanding and use of nonliteral speech such as metaphors, humor, and sarcasm), and the ability to express feelings but do not usually have articulation problems (Kjelgaard & Tager-Flusberg, 2001). According to Deisinger, Wahlberg, Obiakor, Burkhardt, and Rotatori (2001), the evaluation of language abilities is a critical part of assessment for autism. Rapin and Dunn (2003) found that language comprehension was particularly weak for young children with autism. In their sample of 491 children (229 with autism and 262 with developmental language disorder), none of the children with autism had normal or near normal comprehension as compared to 35% of the children with language disorder who did. They also found that a mixed receptive/depressive disorder in which both syntax and phonology are affected was the most common diagnosis for the children with autism.

The Clinical Evaluation of Language Fundamentals–4th Edition (CELF–4; Wiig, Semel, & Secord, 2003) is a comprehensive language assessment that measures both receptive and expressive language skills. It yields the following core language scores: Receptive Language Index, Expressive Language Index, Language Structure Index, Language Context Index, Language Memory Index, as well as the supplemental Working Memory Index. It also includes a Pragmatic Language Checklist. The CELF–4 can be administered to children and young adults from 5 to 21 years of age, and it is also available in a preschool version (CELF–P: Wiig, Semel, & Secord, 2004) that can be used with younger children from 3 years, 0 months to 6 years, 11 months. An earlier version of the CELF–4, the CELF–3, has been shown to be effective in classifying verbal individuals with autism into language groups based on receptive and expressive ability (Tager-Flusberg & Joseph, 2003). Lloyd, Paintin and Botting (2006), using a British version of the CELF (CELF UK 3) or the CELF–P with children from 5 to 10 years of age, showed that children with specific language impairment, those with ASD, and those with both characteristics all demonstrated the least difficulty with the Listening to Paragraphs subtest of the CELF (which involves abstracting and remembering information from two texts) and that all three groups had the most difficulty with the Recalling Sentences subtest (which involves repeating sentences of increasing length and difficulty). Interestingly, they found that the group with specific language impairment (SLI) scored significantly more poorly than the group with ASD and significantly more poorly than the group with shared symptoms on both expressive and receptive language. The SLI group showed nonsignificantly higher receptive language scores than expressive language scores, and the other two groups showed nonsignificantly higher scores on expressive than on receptive language. They also found that Word Associations was a relative weakness for the ASD and shared groups but not for the SLI group, suggesting that the CELF may be useful in treatment planning. In a study by Condouris, Meyer, and Tager-Flusberg (2003), the CELF was found to be significantly correlated with natural language samples for children with autism. The Comprehensive Assessment of Spoken Language (CASL; Carrow-Woolfolk, 1999) has scales for both pragmatic judgment and supralinguistic forms, which includes nonliteral uses of language, inferences, and understanding of idioms. The Test of Language Competence (Wiig & Secord, 1989) also examines pragmatic language, including the comprehension of multiple meanings, figurative usage, and inferences.

Two other tests for the assessment of pragmatic language skills are the Test of Pragmatic Language–2nd Edition (TOPL–2; Phelps-Teraski & Phelps-Gunn, 1992) and the Strong Narrative Assessment Procedure (SNAP; Strong, 1998). The TOPL was normed on children from 5 years, 0 months to 13 years, 11 months, but no children with autism were reported to be in the norm group. The TOPL–2 elicits functional communication by using familiar situations. In the SNAP, the child is required to retell a story to the examiner using picture storybooks and to answer 10 comprehension questions (5 factual and 5 inferential). In a study comparing the TOPL and the SNAP, Young et al. (2005) found that the TOPL was more effective in differentiating pragmatic language disorders in children with autism spectrum disorders than the SNAP. The SNAP did not differentiate between the two groups on narrative length, semantics and syntax, cohesion, clause development, story grammar, or number of complete episodes. However, the study found a significant difference in the ability to answer inferential questions.

Other tests that may be used to measure language ability but for which no specific studies regarding children with autism were found include the Test of Language Development–Primary, 3rd Edition (TOLD–3; Newcomer & Hammill, 1997), The Peabody Picture Vocabulary Test–4th Edition (PPVT-4; Dunn & Dunn, 2007), the Expressive Vocabulary Test–2nd Edition (EVT–2; Williams, 2007), the Expressive One Word Picture Vocabulary Test (EOWPVT; Brownell, 2000a), and the Receptive One-Word Picture Vocabulary (ROWPT; Brownell, 2000b).

ACADEMIC ASSESSMENT

Children with autism are reported to have a relatively high rate of learning difficulties. A study by Mayes and Calhoun (2006), using a large sample of 949 children, found that 67% of children with autism with normal intelligence had a learning disability. Children with autism may have a varied academic profile. In general, decoding has been found to be a relative strength for children with autism, but reading comprehension has been shown to be weaker (Goldberg, 1987; Minshew, Goldstein, Taylor, & Siegel, 1994; O'Connor & Hermelin, 1994; Patti & Lupinetti, 1993). Writing also has been shown to be a relative weakness (Gross, 1994; Mayes & Calhoun, 2003). Math performance appears to be related to general cognitive development (Mayes & Calhoun, 2003), and high-functioning children with autism may score at an average level in math computation (Minshew et al., 1994).

Standardized measures of academic assessment include the Psychoeducational Profile: TEACCH Individualized Psychoeducational Assessment for Children with Autistic Spectrum Disorders–3rd Edition (PEP–3; Schopler, Lansing, Reichter, & Marcus, 2005), the Autism Screening Instrument for Educational Planning, Second Edition (ASIEP; Krug, Arick, & Almond, 2008), the Woodcock–Johnson Tests of Achievement–III (Woodcock et al., 2001a) and the Wechsler Individual Achievement Test–III (Wechsler, 2009).

The PEP–3 (Schopler et al., 2005) is made up of 10 subtests, 6 of which measure developmental abilities in communication (Cognitive Verbal-Preverbal, Expressive Language, Receptive Language) and motor skills (Fine Motor, Gross Motor, and Visual-Motor Imitation) and four of which assess maladaptive behaviors (Affective Expression, Social Reciprocity, Characteristic Motor Behaviors, Characteristic Verbal Behaviors). There are three composite scores: Communication; Motor and Maladaptive Behaviors; and the Caregiver Report, which has three subtests including Problem Behaviors, Personal Self-Care Skills, and Adaptive Abilities. The test can be used for children 2 years, 7 months to 6 years of age and for older children who are functioning within this age range. In the revision for the PEP–3, 407 individuals with autism or other PDD as well as 146 children were added to the standardization sample. Brassard and Boehm (2007) reported that the PEP–3 has a number of features that make it a good choice to use in the assessment of children with autism, including "administrative flexibility, untimed items, limited dependence on language … and the items' developmental range (allowing every child to have some success)" (p. 482). Children may enjoy the assessment because the test has many manipulatives, the tasks are varied, and it starts with playful and fairly easy items that most students will attempt. This instrument is designed to be useful for basic curricular planning.

Another instrument that can be used for academic planning is the Autism Screening Instrument for Educational Planning—2nd Edition (Krug et al., 2008). It is best used for those students whose language and social age are between 3 months and 49 months. It consists of five subtests, including the Autism Behavior Checklist (which will be discussed in a later section), the Educational Assessment measure, the Interaction Assessment measure, the Sample of Vocal Behavior, and the Prognosis of Learning rate subtest. The Educational Assessment measures the child's readiness to learn (e.g., the child's ability to stay seated and follows directions). It is designed to assess the child's ability in five areas: Staying in Seat, Receptive Language,

Expressive Language, Body Concept, and Speech Imitation. The Interaction Assessment measures the child's social responses in a 12-minute play session.

The Woodcock–Johnson–III (Woodcock et al., 2001a) is a comprehensive achievement test, which is designed for individuals aged 2 to 90. It assesses reading (basic reading skills, reading comprehension, and reading fluency), math (calculations, reasoning, and fluency), and written expression (spelling, sentence construction, and writing fluency) as well as general knowledge. While the WJ–III is commonly used, no studies regarding the WJ–III with children with autism were found in the literature.

Most studies of academic achievement in children with autism have used the Wechsler Individual Achievement test. While the Wechsler Individual Achievement Test–III (WIAT–III; Wechsler, 2009) is the most current test in this series, most of the research has been conducted with previous editions of the battery. Mayes and Calhoun (2008) found that mean standard scores for children with autism on the WIAT–II for Word Reading, Reading Comprehension, and Math subtests (99, 100, and 99, respectively) were not significantly different from the norm or from each other, but they were significantly different from the mean score on Written Expression (87). Children with HFA showed problems with both handwriting and expressing their thoughts in writing. In a more recent study by the same authors (Mayes & Calhoun, 2006), learning disabilities in written expression were found in 60% of their sample of autistic children, but the learning disabilities rates for other areas were much lower (i.e., reading, 6%; math, 23%; spelling, 9%). They again found that the mean WIAT–II scores for their sample of autistic children with average intelligence was average in all areas except written expression (Basic Reading = 103, Reading Comprehension = 103, Numerical Operations = 97, Spelling = 100, and Written Expression = 87).

The academic performance of the child with autism can be assessed using Response to Intervention (RtI) techniques as well as standardized tests of achievement; however, the latter seem to be more favored by evaluators. A recent survey by Allen, Robins, and Decker (2008) found that only 18.8% of the school psychologists surveyed reported that their school districts used RtI in determining eligibility for ASD special education services. When the school psychologist participants were directly asked whether RtI is an appropriate model for determining special education eligibility under the ASD category, 53.0% answered "no," 28.2% responded "yes," and the remaining 18.8% selected "other." This may be because RtI is more often used in the assessment of learning disabilities.

BEHAVIOR RATING SCALES

The assessment process should also include a measure of the child's socio–emotional and behavioral functioning. This is especially relevant since children with autism have been found to exhibit greater rates of anxiety and depression than typical peers (Kim, Szatmari, Bryson, Streiner, & Wilson, 2000). Muris, Steerneman,

Merckelbach, Holdrinet, and Meesters (1998) found that severe anxiety symptoms are very prevalent in children with PDD and that more than 84% of their sample met the full criteria for at least one anxiety disorder. Gillott, Furniss, and Walter (2001), in a study of children 8 to 12 years of age with HFA, found that these children were more anxious than children with speech and language impairments and typical children and showed particular difficulty with separation anxiety and obsessive compulsive disorder. Bellini (2004, 2006) also found that adolescents with autism exhibit higher rates of anxiety than typical youth.

Ghaziuddin, Ghaziuddin, and Greden (2002) reported that depression appears to be very common in individuals with autism, and Stewart, Barnard, Pearson, Hasan, and O'Brien (2006) commented that the presence of depression in children and adolescents with autism can be difficult to assess due to the impaired verbal abilities of children in this population. Broad spectrum rating scales can be used to assess for various emotional and behavioral symptoms. These rating scales can be useful in detecting any comorbid behavioral or psychiatric disorders in children with autism, as well as the previously discussed attentional problems. They can provide information on various behaviors from different informants, usually parents and teachers and, at times, the children themselves. Several commonly used behavior rating scales include the Behavior Assessment Scale for Children–2nd Edition (BASC–2: Reynolds & Kamphaus, 2004), the Achenbach System of Empirically Based Assessments (ASEBA; Achenbach & Rescorla, 2001) and the Conners Rating Scales–3rd Edition (Conners, 2008).

The BASC–2 (Reynolds & Kamphaus, 2004) can be used with children and young adults from 2 through 25 years of age. It offers self-rating scales for youth and young adults, as well as rating scales for teacher and parents. The BASC–2 includes a developmental history form and a structured observational system. The following scales are included on the BASC–2 Teacher and Parent Rating Scales: Adaptive Skills, Behavioral Symptoms Index, Externalizing Problems, Internalizing Problems, and School Problems. It also includes 16 primary scales including Attention, Hyperactivity, Functional Communication, Activities of Daily Living, Withdrawal, Adaptability, Social Skills, and Atypicality. While no information was included in the test manual specifically for children with autism, profiles for children with PDD show elevations on Atypicality, Withdrawal, Adaptability, Social Skills, and Functional Communication (p. 192). A dissertation by Knoll (2008) using the BASC–2 found that all composite scales, adaptive scales, and content scales, along with the Hyperactivity, Anxiety, Atypicality, Withdrawal, and Attention Problems clinical scales, were useful in discriminating between typically developing children and those with ASDs.

The ASEBA (Achenbach & Rescorla, 2001) is a multi-rater system used to assess the personality and behavior of youth from 1½ years of age to young adulthood. It includes the Child Behavior Checklist (CBCL), the Teacher (TRF) and Caregiver Report Forms (CRF), and the Youth Self Report Form (YSR), as well as a semi-structured clinical interview (SCICA). It also includes a Pervasive Developmental Disorders Scale as one of the *DSM*-oriented scales. A study by Holtmann, Bolte, and Poustka (2007) found that children with ASD demonstrated a high rate of attentional problems on the ASEBA. Hurtig et al. (2009) administered the YSR, the CBCL, and the TRF to a group of adolescents with HFA or AS and found that the target group exhibited significantly more psychiatric symptoms, especially withdrawn, anxious/depressed, and social and attention problems, than typical adolescents. The parents of the affected adolescents reported significantly more problems on most of the CBCL scales. For boys they reported more withdrawal and social problems but less delinquency than controls, and for girls more withdrawal, social, thought, and attention problems than girls in the control group. The adolescents with autism rated themselves higher than controls on internalizing problems, as well as withdrawn, anxious/depressed, social, thought, and attention problems. In addition, adolescents with autism tended to report more problems with anxiety and depression than their parents. Teachers reported a high rate of attentional problems.

Another commonly used rating scale is the Conners Rating Scale–3rd Edition (Conners, 2008), which can also be administered to parents, teachers, and the youth themselves. The Conners–3 is appropriate for children 6 to 18 years of age for the teacher and parent reports and 8 through 18 years of age for the self-report. The Conners–3 provides scores on Inattention, Hyperactivity/Impulsivity, Learning Problems, and Executive Functioning, as well as Aggression and Peer Relations. Corbett and Constantine (2006) compared an earlier version of the Conners' parent rating scale to the IVA in a group of 15 children with HFA, 15 children with ADHD, and 15 typical children and found a moderate correlation between Conners' attention and the IVA attention variables.

The use of broad rating scales can alert the evaluator to the possibility of comorbid behavioral or psychiatric difficulties that the child with autism may be experiencing and lead to further assessment in these areas.

ADAPTIVE FUNCTIONING

Adaptive functioning involves daily living skills including communication, self-care, socialization, independent living skills, and community functioning. In addition to gathering information regarding the child's cognitive and executive functioning abilities, it is critical that the psychologist evaluate the child's day-to-day functioning in his or her own environment. Adaptive behavior scales have been found to be routinely administered in autism evaluations 87% of the time (Allen et al., 2008). Tomanik et al. (2007) found that the use of an adaptive behavior measure (i.e., the Vineland Adaptive Behavior Scales) significantly improved the diagnostic accuracy of the ADI–R and the ADOS. Studies have shown that autism severity negatively correlates with adaptive behavior (Perry, Flanagan, Geier, & Freeman, 2009).

The Vineland Adaptive Behavior Scales–2nd Edition (VABS–II; Sparrow, Cicchetti, & Balla, 2005) includes two survey forms (a Survey Interview Form administered by the examiner and a Parent/Caregiver Rating Form or checklist) as well as a Teacher Rating Form. The Vineland–II may be used with individuals from

0 to 90 years of age. It yields scores in the following domains: Communication, Daily Living, Socialization (including Interpersonal Relationships, Play and Leisure Time, and Coping Skills), Motor Skills, and Maladaptive Behavior, as well as 11 subdomains. Seventy-seven individuals with autism were included in the standardization sample. Significant differences were obtained between this group and age-matched typical peers in the Adaptive Behavior Composite scores, Interpersonal Relationships, Play and Leisure Time, and Expressive Language. On the Maladaptive Domain, the Internalizing scale was elevated. The Vineland–II may be helpful in discriminating between children with autism and those with mental retardation without autism, since research using the first Vineland scale indicated that individuals with autism demonstrated a more uneven profile than did children with mental retardation. Children with autism scored more poorly on interpersonal skills than did individuals with Down Syndrome (Rodrigue, Morgan, & Geffken, 1991) or those with other developmental delays (Volkmar et al., 1987). They showed relative strengths in Daily Living and Motor Skills and relative deficits in Socialization and, to a lesser extent, in Communication (Volkmar, Szatmari, & Sparrow, 1993). Carter et al. (1998) reported special population norms for the Vineland for individuals with autism, including mute children under 10 years of age, children with at least some verbal skills under 10 years of age, mute individuals 10 years of age or older, and individuals 10 years or older with some verbal skills. They found that young children with autism had higher standard scores than older individuals with autism across all Vineland domains. In the Communication domain, younger verbal autistic children were least impaired, and older mute individuals with autism were most impaired. Verbal individuals achieved higher scores in Daily Living Skills than mute individuals.

In a recent study by Perry et al. (2009), the Vineland–II was used in a large sample of young children (mean age = 51.7 months) with varying cognitive levels. Perry et al. found that IQ scores were higher than the VABS–II composite score among high-functioning children, but the opposite pattern was found for children with lower IQ scores. In a comparison of children with autism and mental retardation, children with autism were found to have lower scores in Socialization and Communication. Akshoomoff (2006), in a study with preschoolers, found that Communication and Socialization scores on the Vineland–II strongly correlated with Expressive Language scores on the Mullen, and VABS–II Communication scores were also significantly correlated with the Mullen Receptive Language score. In a study with older children with autism (aged 7–18 years), Klin et al. (2007) found that their sample scored 1 to 2 standard deviations below the norm for communicative adaptive skills and 2 to 3 standard deviations below the norm on interpersonal skills. While they did not find a strong negative correlation between autism symptoms as measured by ADOS scores and the Vineland–II, they did find a negative relationship between age and Vineland–II scores, suggesting that these youth become increasingly more impaired relative to their same age peers as they age.

A study by McGovern and Sigman (2005), however, found that parents described improvements in adaptive behavior as their children aged from middle school to adolescence and young adulthood in daily living skills and socialization. Communication skills, however, did not significantly improve. Youth with higher IQs showed greater improvement than lower functioning children. Similar findings were noted by Freeman, Del'Homme, Guthrie, and Zhang (1999) who, using the first Vineland, found that children with autism improved in all areas of adaptive behavior (Communication, Daily Living Skills, and Social) as a function of age and IQ. It is interesting to note that improvement in social skills was found to be independent of initial IQ. Thus, the Vineland–II should be quite useful in assessing gains in adaptive skills over time.

Another measure of adaptive behavior is the Adaptive Behavior Assessment System–2nd Edition (ABAS–II: Harrison & Oakland, 2003). This instrument can be used with adults as well as children and is normed for individuals from 0–89 years of age. It includes a form for the parent and teacher as well as an adult self-rating form. Scores are given for Communication, Community Use (depending on the individual's age), Home/School Living (depending on the rater), Functional Academics, Motor (depending on the individual's age), Health and Safety, Leisure, Self-Care, Self-Direction, Social Functioning, and Work Aptitude. It produces three separate Adaptive Domain scores: Conceptual (communication and academic skills), Social (interpersonal and social competence skills), and Practical (independent living and daily living skills), as well as an Adaptive Composite (GAC). Individuals with ASD were included in the standardization group. This group showed significant deficits in the GAC as well as the adaptive domains and each skill area as compared to age-matched controls, with the greatest discrepancy being in Communication, Health and Safety, Leisure, and Social. Functional Pre-Academics, although significantly below the control group, was still a relative strength for young (under 6 years of age) children with autism.

The Scales of Independent Behavior–Revised (SIB–R; Bruininks, Woodcock, Weatherman, & Hill, 1996) is a third standardized and comprehensive assessment for adaptive behavior. It yields a Broad Independence score, which is a measure of overall adaptive behavior. It is composed of four main domains, Motor Skills, Social and Communication, Personal Living, and Community Living, and includes a Problem Behavior Scale. No specific studies using the SIB–R with children with autism were located.

SPECIFIC AUTISM SCALES

Various instruments have been developed to assess symptoms of autism and the likelihood of an autism diagnosis. These include screening instruments, such as the Checklist for Autism in Toddlers (CHAT; Baron-Cohen, Allen, & Gillberg, 1992), the Modified Checklist for Autism in Toddlers (M-CHAT; Robbins, Fein, Barton, & Green, 2001), the Screening Tool for Autism in Two-Year-Olds (STAT; Stone, Coonrod, & Ousley, 2000), and the Social Communication Questionnaire (SCQ; Rutter, Bailey, & Lord, 2003); and diagnostic instruments such as the Autism

Behavior Checklist (ABC; Krug, Arick, & Almond, 2008), the Childhood Autism Rating Scale (CARS; Schopler, Reichler, & Renner, 2008), the Gilliam Autism Rating Scale–2nd Edition (GARS–2; Gilliam, 2005), and the Autism Spectrum Rating Scale (ASRS; Goldstein & Naglieri, 2009). Information about social interaction in general may be useful as well. Scales such as the Social Responsiveness Scale (SRS; Constantino & Gruber, 2005) can be used to assess interpersonal relationships and use of social skills.

The Checklist for Autism in Toddlers (CHAT; Baron-Cohen et al., 1992) is a brief screening instrument consisting of only nine questions, which is typically administered to parents during the child's 18-month check-up. A longitudinal study using the CHAT showed poor sensitivity (ability to discern autism) of only 20% and predictive validity of only 26.3% (Baird et al., 2000). However, others contend that the CHAT can accurately discriminate between young children with autism and children with other developmental disabilities (Scambler, Rogers, & Wehner, 2001).

The Modified Checklist for Autism in Toddlers (M–CHAT; Robbins, Fein, Barton, & Green, 2001), an adaptation of the CHAT, is a 23-item yes–no parent report questionnaire. It can be used with children from 16 to 30 months of age and focuses on the following areas: pointing, gaze, monitoring, and pretend play. The test appears to have greater sensitivity (.95) and better predictive validity (64%) than the CHAT (Robbins et al., 2001). Empirical research suggests that the M–CHAT can be a useful screening instrument for young children in its specified age range (e.g., Kleinman et al., 2008). One recent study suggested that the M–CHAT is accurate for very young children (16 to 23 months) whose parents have expressed developmental concerns. However, the instrument is not as accurate when a parent has not expressed such concerns (Pandey et al., 2008). Recent evidence shows that the M-CHAT can accurately screen for ASDs in the primary care setting (Robbins, 2008).

The Screening Tool for Autism in Two-Year-Olds (STAT; Stone et al., 2000) is a brief screening instrument that can be administered to children 24 to 35 months of age. It consists of only 12 items and assesses the child's play, imitation skills, directing attention, and response to requests (although the latter is not scored). One preliminary study found the STAT to demonstrate acceptable inter-rater agreement and test–retest reliability (Stone, Coonrod, Turner, & Pozdol, 2004). Another preliminary study suggested that a high rate of false positives may occur when children are under 24 months old (Stone, McMahon, & Henderson, 2008).

The Social Communication Questionnaire (SCQ; Rutter et al., 2003), previously known as the Autism Screening Questionnaire (ASQ), is a 40-item yes–no parent questionnaire. It is a screening instrument with items taken from the ADI–R. It also provides subscores that parallel the ADI–R, including Qualitative Abnormalities in Communication; and Restricted, Repetitive, and Stereotyped Patterns of Behavior. The SCQ consists of two versions: Lifetime, which is completed with reference to the individual's complete developmental history; and Current, which only assesses the child's behavior during the last 3 months. There is empirical support for the usefulness of the SCQ as a screening instrument for autism spectrum disorders.

A study by Witwer and Lecavalier (2007) found the SCQ to be effective in distinguishing children with a PDD from children with intellectual disabilities. The SCQ may also effectively discriminate between older children with autism and children with other PDDs or typical development (Chandler et al., 2007). The instrument may not be as useful for children between 2 and 4 years of age (Allen, Silove, Williams, & Hutchins, 2007). For example, a study by Eaves, Wingert, Ho, and Mickelson (2006) compared the Modified Checklist for Autism in Toddlers (M–CHAT) and the SCQ. On both measures false negatives were higher than true positives. Eaves, Wingert, Ho, and Mickelson (2006) concluded that both the SCQ and the M–CHAT "were not as robust as the developers reported" (p. 238) but that these checklists might be useful in focusing discussions with parents.

The Autism Behavior Checklist (ABC; Krug et al., 2008), which is part of the ASIEP, can be used by teachers to identify autistic behaviors in a severely handicapped population. It consists of five scales: Sensory, Relating, Body and Object Use, Language and Social, and Self-Help. Research has generally failed to support the usefulness of the Autism Behavior Checklist. A study by Eaves and Williams (2006) indicated that the reliability of ABC subscale scores may be questionable. The validity of the ABC appears to be problematic as well. Several authors have reported that the cut-off scores for autism are too high and result in a high rate of false negatives (Krug, Arick, & Almond, 1993; Miranda-Linne, Fredrika, & Melin, 1997; Volkmar, Cicchetti, Dykens, Sparrow, Leckman, & Cohen, 1988; Wadden, Bryson, & Rodger, 1991). Sevin, Matson, Coe, and Fee (1991) found that by using the ABC suggested cut-off scores, 50% of their sample of autistic children were misclassified as compared to only 8% when using the CARS. Agreement between ABC classification and a clinical diagnosis was found to be low in another study, with the ABC generating a relatively high number of false negatives (Rellini, Tortolani, Trillo, Carbone, & Montecchi, 2004). Finally, factor analysis has failed to provide evidence for the validity of the subscales proposed by the developers (e.g., Miranda-Linne & Melin, 2002).

The Childhood Autism Rating Scale (CARS; Schopler, Reichter, & Renner, 1988, 2008) is designed for children 24 months and older. It measures the presence and severity of autistic symptoms based on the examiner's observation and parental report. The 15 subscales include: Relating to People; Imitation; Emotional Response; Body Use; Object Use; Adaptation to Change; Visual Response; Listening Response; Taste, Smell, and Touch Response and Use; Fear or Nervousness; Verbal Communication; Nonverbal Communication; Activity Level; Level and Consistency of Intellectual Response; and General Impressions. The CARS shows good psychometric properties in terms of reliability and validity. In a recent study, Mayes et al. (2009) found that for children with low-functioning autism, classification accuracy for the CARS was 98%. There appears to be strong agreement between a CARS categorical diagnosis and a clinical diagnosis of autistic disorder based on *DSM–IV* criteria (Perry, Condillac, Freeman, Dunn-Geier, & Belair, 2005; Rellini et al., 2004). Moreover, the CARS shows a positive correlation with both the ADI–R (Pilowsky, Yirmiya, Shulman, & Dover, 1998; Saemundsen,

Magnusson, Smari, & Sigurdardottir, 2003) and the ADOS–G (Ventola et al., 2006). The CARS has been shown to discriminate children with autism from those without autism and those with some mental handicap (Schopler et al., 1988; Teal & Wiebe, 1986) and those with PDD–NOS (Perry et al., 2005). A factor structure evaluation by Magyar and Pandolfi (2007) supported the notion that the CARS measures autism-related constructs. Not surprisingly, then, the CARS is considered to have the best psychometric support for children with low-functioning autism (e.g., Eaves & Milner, 1993; Rellini et al., 2004). The CARS is used at a relatively high rate by professionals at autism service centers across the country (Luiselli et al., 2001). According to a recent study by Allen et al. (2008) the CARS was the most commonly used assessment instrument for the assessment of autism in the schools. More than half of the school psychologists in their survey reported including the CARS in more than 75% of their ASD evaluations and only 13.7% had never included the CARS in evaluations. Lord and Corsello (2005) contended that the CARS may be overinclusive in that it may classify children with poor verbal skills and moderate to severe cognitive delays as autistic when they are not; thus it should not be used as the sole diagnostic measure for autism.

The Gilliam Autism Rating Scale–2nd Edition (GARS–2; Gilliam, 2005) can be used with individuals from 3 to 22 years of age. It is divided into three subscales related to the *DSM–IV* criteria: Stereotyped Behaviors, Communication, and Social Interaction and also includes a Developmental Disturbance scale. However, some researchers have expressed concern regarding the use of the GARS. Mazefsky and Oswald (2006) found that the GARS consistently underestimated the likelihood of autism, compared to clinical diagnosis by a multidisciplinary team. Similar findings were noted by South et al. (2002), who found that the GARS underestimated the presence of autism as compared to the ADI–R and the ADOS–G. No significant correlations were noted for the GARS and the ADOS subscales and only very low correlations (.21 to .26) were found among the ADI–R social domain and the GARS total score and Social Interaction and Repetitive Behaviors subscales. A factor analysis by Lecavalier (2005) with 284 subjects (mean age 9.3 years) also raised questions about the validity of diagnostic classification by GARS. He found that almost half of all items loaded on a Repetitive and Steretyped Behavior factor and that the three-factor solution only explained 38% of the variance. Lecavalier reported that the Developmental Disturbance subscale did not contribute to the total Autism Quotient and was poorly related to the other subscales. In addition, the internal consistency of the Developmental Disturbance subscale was low. Moreover, Lecavalier also obtained much lower inter-rater reliability than that originally reported by the instrument's developer (.31 to .48). Lecavalier suggested "caution when using the GARS as a screening or diagnostic tool" (p. 804). However, Montgomery, Newton, and Smith (2008), in a review of the newer GARS–2, reported that the GARS–2 showed some improvement over the original GARS and stated that "the GARS–2 can be a useful screening tool for autism when used as part of a comprehensive assessment or for use in evaluating treatment" (p. 401).

The Autism Spectrum Rating Scale (ASRS; Goldstein & Naglieri, 2009) has just recently been made available to the public. It consists of parent and teacher rating forms and is available in an Early Childhood Version (for children ages 2–6 years) and a School Age Version (for children 7–18 years). It contains three scales: Self-regulation (for 6–18 year olds only), Social/Communication, and Stereotypical Behaviors, as well as a Total Scale. The ASRS is based on *DSM–IV* criteria and offers diagnostic classifications for autism, AS, and PDD–NOS (Goldstein, Naglieri, & Ozonoff, 2009). The ASRS was compared to the CARS and the GARS and was found to moderately correlate with the GARS Autism Index, but correlations with the CARS were lower and especially weak for the parent preschool ratings. The authors suggested, however, that this may result from the fact that the CARS's ratings were completed by clinicians and the ASRS ratings were completed by parents and teachers.

The Social Responsiveness Scale (SRS; Constantino & Gruber, 2005) is administered to caregivers to assess the child's interpersonal behavior, communication, and repetitive/stereotypic behaviors. The SRS can be used with youth from 4 to 18 years of age and takes only 15 to 20 minutes to complete. It yields a total score as well as scores for five treatment subscales: Social Awareness, Social Cognition, Social Communication, Social Motivation, and Autistic Mannerisms. The SRS differs from many of the other autistic checklists in that it does not provide a dichotomized diagnosis but rather conceptualizes the symptoms as a spectrum condition. The manual reports that scores on the SRS were significantly higher for children with autism as compared to typical children. Although the SRS has received limited research attention to date, one study found a moderate correlation between the SRS and all domains of the ADI–R (Constantino et al., 2003).

While specific autism rating scales can be very useful in a comprehensive evaluation, as they provide information as to how the child is performing in regard to autistic criteria, they should never be used as the only method of assessment.

SUMMARY

The assessment of children with autism is certainly complex. Evaluation should be comprehensive and move beyond just a dichotomous classification regarding the presence or absence of autism to a description of the child's functioning in all areas—cognitive, neuropsychological, academic, adaptive, linguistic, and socio-emotional. The evaluation may be completed by an individual psychologist, but a team approach may provide information from experts in specific disciplines, as well as additional observations. Any information discovered through the evaluation should be looked at in relationship to the child's daily functioning. A comprehensive evaluation is essential for the development of appropriate treatment goals. This chapter has outlined the assessment areas, provided a brief description of standardized measures that can be used in the evaluation process, and has reviewed pertinent literature related to standardized assessment of children with autism.

REFERENCES

Achenbach, T. M., & Rescorla, L.A. (2001). *Manual for ASEBA: School-age form profiles.* Burlington: University of Vermont, Research Center for Children, Youth, and Families.

Akshoomoff, N. (2006). Use of the Mullen Scales of Early Learning for the assessment of young children with autism spectrum disorders. *Child Neuropsychology, 12,* 269–277.

Allen, C. W., Silove, N., Williams, K., & Hutchins, P. (2007). Validity of the Social Communication Questionnaire in assessing risk of autism in preschool children with developmental problems. *Journal of Autism and Developmental Disorders, 37,* 1272–1278.

Allen, M. H., Lincoln, A. J., & Kaufman, A. S. (1991). Sequential and simultaneous processing abilities of high functioning and language impaired children. *Journal of Autism and Developmental Disorders, 21,* 483–502.

Allen, R. A., Robins, D., & Decker, S. L. (2008). Autism spectrum disorders: Neurobiology and current assessment practices. *Psychology in the Schools, 45,* 905–917.

Ameli, R., Couchesne, D., Lincoln, A., Kaufman, A., & Grillon, C. (1988). Visual memory processes in high-functioning individuals with autism. *Journal of Autism and Developmental Disorders, 18,* 601–615.

American Psychiatric Association (APA). (2000). *Diagnostic and statistical manual of mental disorders* (4th ed., text rev.). Washington, DC: Author.

Asarnow, R. F., Tanguay, P. E., Bott, L., & Freeman, B. J. (1987). Patterns of IQ in nonretarded autistic and schizophrenic children. *Journal of Child Psychology and Psychiatry, 28,* 273–280.

Baird, G., Charman, T., Baron-Cohen, S., Cox, A., Swettenham, J., Wheelwright, S., et al.. (2000). A screening instrument for autism at 18 months of age: A 6-year follow-up study. *Journal of the American Academy of Child & Adolescent Psychiatry, 39,* 694–702.

Baird, G., Simonoff, E., Pickles, A., Chandler, S., Loucas, T., Meldrum, D., et al. (2006). Prevalence of disorders of the autism spectrum in a population cohort of children in South Thames: The Special Needs and Autism Project (SNAP). *Lancet, 368,* 210–215.

Banks, S. H., & Franzen, M. D. (2000). Concurrent validity of the TONI–3. *Journal of Psychoeducational Assessment, 28,* 70–79.

Barnhill, G., Hagiwars, T., Myles, B. S., & Simpson, R. L. (2000). Asperger's syndrome: A study of 37 children and adolescents. *Focus on Autism and Other Developmental Disorders, 15,* 146–153.

Baron-Cohen, S., Allen, J., & Gillberg, C. (1992). Can autism be detected at 18 months: The needle, the haystack and the CHAT. *British Journal of Psychiatry, 168,* 158–163.

Baron-Cohen, S., & Belmonte, M. K. (2005). Autism: A window onto the development of the social and the analytic brain. *Annual Review of Neuroscience, 28,* 109–126.

Bayley, N. (2005). *Bayley Scales of Infant and Toddler Development* (3rd ed.) San Antonio, TX: Harcourt Assessment.

Bellini, S. (2004). Social skill deficits in anxiety in high-functioning adolescents with autism spectrum disorders. *Focus on Autism and Other Developmental Disabilities, 19,* 78–86.

Bellini, S. (2006). The development of social anxiety in adolescents with autism spectrum disorders. *Focus on Autism and Other developmental Disabilities, 21,* 138–145.

Bergen, D. (1988). Stages of play development. In D. Bergen (Ed.), *Play as a medium for learning and development.* Portsmouth, NH: Heinemann.

Berko Gleason, J. (2000). Language: An overview. In A. Kazdin (Ed.), *Encyclopedia of psychology.* Washington, DC: American Psychological Association.

Bloom, L. (1998). Language acquisition in its developmental context. In W. Damon (Ed.), *Handbook of child psychology* (5th ed., Vol. 2). New York: Wiley.

Bloom, L., Lifter, K., & Broughton, J. (1985). The convergence of early cognition and language in the second year of life: Problems in conceptualization and measurement. In M. Barrett (Ed.), *Single word speech*. London: Wiley.

Bolte, S., Poustka, F., & Constantino, J. N. (2008). Assessing autistic traits: Cross-cultural validation of the Social Responsiveness Scale (SRS). *Autism Research, 1,* 354–363.

Boucher, J., & Lewis, V. (1992). Unfamiliar face recognition in relatively able autistic children. *Journal of Child Psychology and Psychiatry, 33,* 843–859.

Boucher, J., Lewis, V., & Collis, G. (1998). Familiar face and voice matching and recognition in children with autism. *Journal of Child Psychology and Psychiatry, 39,* 171–181.

Boucher, J., & Warrington, E. K. (1976). Memory deficits in early infantile autism: Some similarities to the amnesic syndrome. *British Journal of Psychology, 67,* 73–87.

Bracken, B. A., & McCallum, S. (1998). *Universal Non-verbal Intelligence Test.* Odessa, FL: Psychological Assessment Resources.

Brassard, M., & Boehm, A. (2007). *Preschool assessment: Principles and practices.* New York: Guilford Press.

Brown, L., Sherbenou, R. J., & Johnsen, S. K. (1997). *Test of Non-Verbal Intelligence* (3rd ed.). Wood Dale, IL: Stoelting.

Brownell, R. (2000a). *Expressive One-Word Picture Vocabulary Test.* Novato, CA: Academic Therapy.

Brownell, R. (2000b). *Receptive One-Word Picture Vocabulary Test.* Novato, CA: Academic Therapy.

Bruinicks, R. H., Woodcock, R.W., Weatherman, R. F., & Hill, B. K. (1996). *Scales of Independent Behavior- Revised.* Rolling Meadows, IL: Riverside.

Calhoun, S., & Mayes, S. D. (2005). Processing speed in children with clinical disorders. *Psychology in the Schools, 42,* 333–343.

Carpentieri, S. C., & Morgan, S. B. (1994). Brief report: A comparison of patterns of cognitive functioning of autistic and nonautistic retarded children on the Stanford-Binet–Fourth Edition. *Journal of Autism and Developmental Disorders, 24,* 215–223.

Carrow-Woolfolk, E. (1999). *Comprehensive assessment of spoken language.* Circle Pines, MN: American Guidance Service.

Carter, A. S., Volkmar, F. R., Sparrow, S. S., Wang, J., Lord, C., Dawson, G., et al. (1998). The Vineland Adaptive Behavior Scales: Supplementary norms for individuals with autism. *Journal of Autism and Developmental Disorders, 28,* 287–302.

Centers for Disease Control and Prevention (CDC). (n.d.). *Developmental milestones.* Retrieved January 26, 2010, from http://www.cdc.gov/ncbddd/actearly/milestones

Chandler, S., Charman, T., Baird, G., Simonoff, E., Loucas, T., Meldrum, D., et al. (2007). Validation of the Social Communication Questionnaire in a population cohort of children with autism spectrum disorders. *Journal of the American Academy of Child & Adolescent Psychiatry, 46,* 1324–1332.

Charman, T., Drew, A., Baird, C., & Baird, G. (2003). Measuring early language development in preschool children with autism spectrum disorder using the MacArthur Communicative Development Inventory (Infant Form). *Journal of Child Language, 30,* 213–236.

Charman, T., Swettenham, J., Baron-Cohen, S., Cox, A., Baird, G., & Drew, A. (1997). Infants with autism: An investigation of empathy, pretend play, joint attention, and imitation. *Developmental Psychology, 33,* 781–789.

Chiang, H. M., & Lin, Y. H. (2008). Expressive communication of children with autism. *Journal of Autism and Developmental Disorders, 38,* 538–545.

Child Development Institute. (n.d.). *Language development in children.* Retrieved January 26, 2010, from http://www.childdevelopmentinfo.com/development/language_develop ment.shtml

Cicchetti, D. V., Lord, C., Koenig, K., Klin, A., & Volkmar, F. R. (2008). Reliability of the ADI–R: Multiple examiners evaluate a single case. *Journal of Autism and Developmental Disorders, 38,* 764–770.

Ciesielski, K. T., Courchesne, E., & Elmasian, R. (1990). Effects of focused selective attention tasks on event-related potentials in autistic and normal individuals. *Electroencephalography & Clinical Neurophysiology, 75,* 207–220.

Ciesielski, K. T., & Harris, R. J. (1997). Factors related to performance failure on executive tasks in autism. *Child Neuropsychology, 3,* 1–12.

Cohen, M. (1997). *Children's Memory Scale.* San Antonio, TX: Psychological Corporation.

Colgan, S. E., Lanter, E., McComish, C., Watson, L. R., Crais, E. R., & Baranek, G. T. (2006). Analysis of social interaction gestures in infants with autism. *Child Neuropsychology, 12,* 307–319.

Condouris, K., Meyer, E., & Tager-Flusberg, H. (2003). Spontaneous speech in children with autism. *American Journal of Speech-Language Pathology, 12,* 349–358.

Conners, C. K., & MHS Staff (Eds.). (2000). *Conners' Continuous Performance Test II: Computer Program for Windows Technical Guide and Software Manual.* North Tonwanda, NY: MultiHealth Systems.

Conners, C. K. (2001). *Conners' Kiddie Continuous Performance Test.* North Tonawanda, NY: MultiHealth Systems.

Conners, C. K. (2008). *Conners Rating Scales* (3rd ed.). New York and Toronto: Multi-Health Systems.

Constantino, J. N., Davis, S. A., Todd, R. D., Schindler, M. K., Gross, M. M., Brophy, S. L., et al. (2003). Validation of a brief quantitative measure of autistic traits: Comparison of the Social Responsiveness Scale with the Autism Diagnostic Interview–Revised. *Journal of Autism and Developmental Disorders, 33,* 427–433

Constantino, J. N., & Gruber, C. P. (2005). *Social Responsiveness Scale.* Los Angeles, CA: Western Psychological Services.

Corbett, B. A., & Constantine, L. J. (2006). Autism and Attention Deficit Hyperactivity Disorder: Assessing attention and response control with the Integrated Visual and Auditory Continuous Performance Test. *Child Neuropsychology, 12,* 335–348.

Cox, A., Klein, K., Charman, T., Baird, G., Baron-Cohen, S., Swettenham, J., et al. (1999). Autism spectrum disorders at 20 and 42 months of age: Stability of clinical and ADI-R diagnosis. *Journal of Child Psychology and Psychiatry, 40,* 719–732.

Dadds, M., Schwartz, S., Adams, T., & Rose, S. (1988). The effects of social context and verbal skill on the stereotypic and task-involved behaviour of autistic children. *Journal of Child Psychology & Psychiatry, 29,* 669–676.

Dawson, G., Meltzoff, A., Osterling, J., Rinaldi, J., & Brown, E. (1998). Children with autism fail to orient to naturally occurring stimuli. *Journal of Autism and Developmental Disorders, 28,* 479–485.

Dawson, G., Toth, K., Abbott, R., Osterling, J., Munson, J., Estes, A., et al. (2004). Early social attention impairments in autism: Social orienting, joint attention, and attention to distress. *Developmental Psychology, 40,* 271–283.

de Gelder, B., Vroomen, J., & Van der Heide, L. (1991). Face recognition and lip-reading in autism. *European Journal of Cognitive Psychology, 3,* 69–86.

Deisinger, J. A., Wahlberg, T., Obiakor, F., Burkhardt, S., & Rotatori, A. (2001). Autistic spectrum disorders: Educational and clinical interventions. *Advances in Special Education, 14,* 181–209.

Delis, D. C., Kaplan, E., & Kramer, J. H. (2001). *Delis Kaplan Executive Functioning System.* San Antonio, TX: Psychological Corporation.

Delis, D. C., Kramer, J. H., Kaplan, E., & Ober, B. A. (1994). *California Verbal Learning Test–Children's Version.* San Antonio, TX: Psychological Corporation.

Doussard-Roosevelt, J. A., Joe, C. M., Bazhenova, O. V., & Porges, S. W. (2003). Mother-child interaction in autistic and nonautistic children: Characteristics of maternal approach behaviors and child social responses. *Development and Psychopathology, 15,* 277–295.

Dunn, L. M., & Dunn, D. M. (2007). *Peabody Picture Vocabulary Test,* (4th ed.). Bloomington, MN: Pearson Assessments.

Eaves, R. C., & Milner, B. (1993). The criterion-related validity of the Childhood Autism Rating Scale and the Autism Behavior Checklist. *Journal of Abnormal Child Psychology, 21,* 481–491.

Eaves, R. C., & Williams, T. O. (2006). The reliability and construct validity of ratings for the Autism Behavior Checklist. *Psychology in the Schools, 43,* 129–142.

Eaves, L. C., Wingert, H.D., & Ho, H. H. (2006). Screening for autism: Agreement with diagnosis. *Autism, 10,* 229–242.

Eaves, L. C., Wingert, H. D., Ho, H. H., & Mickelson, E. C. (2006). Screening for autism spectrum disorders with the Social Communication Questionnaire. *Journal of Development & Behavioral Pediatrics, 27,* S95–S103.

Edelson, M. G. (2006). Are the majority of children with autism mentally retarded? *Focus on Autism and Other Developmental Disabilities, 21,* 66–83.

Edelson, M. G., Schubert, R. T., & Edelson, S. (1998). Factors predicting intelligence scores on the TONI with individuals with autism. *Focus on Autism and Other Developmental Disabilities, 13,* 17–27.

Elliott, C. (2007). *Differential Ability Scales* (2nd ed.) San Antonio, TX: Harcourt Assessment.

Fay, W. H. (1969). On the basis of autistic echolalia. *Journal of Communication Disorders, 2,* 38–47.

Flanagan, D., & Kaufman, A. (2004). *Essentials of WISC-IV Assessment.* New York: John Wiley & Sons.

Freeman, B. J., Del'Homme, M., Guthrie, D., & Zhang, F. (1999). Vineland Adaptive Behavior Scale scores as a function of age and initial IQ in 210 autistic children. *Journal of Autism and Developmental Disorders, 29,* 379–384.

Frombonne, E. (2005). Epidemiological studies of pervasive developmental disorders. In F. R. Volkmar, R. Paul, A. Klin, & D. Cohen (Eds.). *Handbook of autism and pervasive developmental disorders. Vol. 1. Diagnosis, development, neurobiology, and behavior* (3rd ed., pp. 42–69). Hoboken, NJ: John Wiley & Sons.

Gepner, B., de Gelder, B., & de Schonen, S. (1996). Face processing in autistics: Evidence for a generalised deficit? *Child Neuropsychology, 2,* 123–139.

Ghaziuddin, M., Ghaziuddin, N., & Greden, J. (2002). Depression in persons with autism: Implications for research and clinical care. *Journal of Autism and Developmental Disorders, 32,* 299–306.

Gilchrist, A., Green, J., Cox, A., Burton, D., Rutter, M., & LeCouteur, A. (2001). Development and current functioning in adolescents with Asperger Syndrome: A comparative study. *Journal of Child Psychology and Psychiatry, 42,* 227–240.

Gilliam, J. E. (2005). *Gilliam Autism Rating Scale* (2nd ed.). Austin, TX: Pro-Ed.

Gillott, A., Furniss, F., & Walter, A. (2001). Anxiety in high-functioning children with autism. *Autism, 5,* 277–286.

Gioia, G., Espy, K., & Isquith, P. (2003) *Behavior Rating Inventory of Executive Function–Preschool Version,* Odessa, FL: Psychological Assessment Resources.

Gioia, G., Isquith, P., Guy, S., & Kenworthy, L. E., (2000). *Behavior Rating Inventory of Executive Function.* Odessa, FL: Psychological Assessment Resources.

Goldberg, T. E. (1987). On hermetic reading abilities. *Journal of Autism and Developmental Disorders, 17,* 29–44.

Goldstein, G., Allen, D. N., Minshew, N. J., Williams, D. L., Volkmar, F., Klin, A.H., et al. (2008). The structure of intelligence in children and adults with high functioning autism. *Neuropsychology, 22,* 301–312.

Goldstein, S., & Naglieri, J. A. (2009). *Autism Spectrum Rating Scale.* Toronto: MultiHealth Systems.

Goldstein, S., Naglieri, J. A., & Ozonoff, S. (2009). *Assessment of autism spectrum disorders.* New York: Guilford Press.

Gordon, M., McClure, F. D., & Aylward, G. P. (1996). *The Gordon Diagnostic System* (3rd ed.). DeWitt, NY: Gordon Systems.

Gotham, K., Risi, S., Pickles, A., & Lord, C. (2007). The Autism Diagnostic Observation Schedule: Revised algorithms for improved diagnostic validity. *Journal of Autism and Developmental Disorders, 37,* 613–627.

Gray, K. M., Tonge, B. J., & Sweeney, D. J. (2008). Using the Autism Diagnostic Interview–Revised and the Autism Diagnostic Observation Schedule with young children with developmental delay: Evaluating diagnostic validity. *Journal of Autism and Developmental Disorders, 38,* 657–667.

Greenberg, L. M., Corman, C. L., & Kindschi, C. L. (1988–1996). *Test of Variables of Attention.* Los Alamitos, CA: Universal Attention Disorders, Inc.

Greenberg, L. M., & Waldman, I. D. (1993). Developmental normative data on the Test of Variables of Attention. *Journal of Child Psychology and Psychiatry, 34,* 1019–1030.

Gross, J. (1994). Asperger's syndrome: A label worth having? *Educational Psychology, 10,* 104–110.

Gutwirth, B. L. (1996). The relationship between cognitive processing profiles according to the PASS model: Planning, Attention, Simultaneous and Successive processes, and childhood psychopathology. Psy.D. dissertation, Pace University, NY. Retrieved January 28, 2010, from Dissertations & Theses: Full Test. (Publication No. AAT 9709089).

Hammill, D., Pearson, N., & Wiederholt, J. (1997). *Comprehensive Test of Nonverbal Intelligence.* Austin, TX: Pro-Ed.

Harris, S. L., Handelman, J. S., & Burton, J. L. (1990). The Stanford Binet Profiles of Young Children with Autism. *Special Services in the Schools, 6,* 135–143.

Harrison, P. L., & Oakland, T. (2003). *Adaptive Behavior Assessment System* (2nd ed.). San Antonio, TX: Psychological Corporation.

Hauck, M., Fein, D., Maltby, N., Waterhouse, L., & Feinstein, C. (1998). Memory for faces in children with autism. *Child Neuropsychology, 4,* 187–198.

Heaton, R. K., Chelune, G. J., Talley, J. L., Kay, G. G., & Curtis, G. (1993). *Wisconsin Card Sorting Test (WCST) manual: Revised and expanded.* Lutz, FL: Psychological Assessment Resources.

Hill, E. L. (2004). Evaluating the theory of executive dysfunction in autism. *Developmental Review, 24,* 189–233.

Hobson, R. P., Lee, A., & Hobson, J. A. (2009). Qualities of symbolic play among children with autism: A social–developmental perspective. *Journal of Autism and Developmental Disabilities, 39,* 12–22.

Holtmann, M., Bolte, S., & Poustka, F. (2007). Attention Deficit Hyperactivity Disorder symptoms in Pervasive Developmental Disorders: Association with autistic behavior domains and coexisting psychopathology. *Psychopathology, 40,* 172–177.

Hooper, S. R., Poon, K. K., Marcus, L., & Fine, C. (2006). Neuropsychological characteristics of school-age children with high functioning autism: Performance on the NEPSY. *Child Neuropsychology, 12,* 299–305.

Hughes, C., Russell, J., & Robbins, T. W. (1994). Evidence for executive dysfunction in autism. *Neuropsychologia, 32,* 477–492.

Hurtig, T., Kuusikko, S., Mattila, M., Haapsamo, H., Ebeling, H., Jussila, K., et al. (2009). Multi-informant reports of psychiatric symptoms among high-functioning adolescents with Asperger syndrome or autism. *Autism, 13,* 583–598.

Jones, E. A., & Carr, E. G. (2004). Joint attention in children with autism: Theory and intervention. *Focus on Autism and Other Developmental Disabilities, 19,* 13–26.

Kaland, N., Smith, L., & Mortensen, E. L. (2008). Brief report: Cognitive flexibility and focused attention in children and adolescents with Asperger syndrome or high-functioning autism as measured on the computerized version of the Wisconsin Card Sorting Test. *Journal of Autism and Developmental Disorders, 38,* 1161–1165.

Kanner, L. (1971). Follow-up study of eleven autistic children originally reported in 1943. *Journal of Autism & Childhood Schizophrenia, 1,* 119–145.

Kaufman, A. S., & Kaufman, N. L. (2004). *Kaufman Assessment Battery for Children* (2nd ed.). Circle Pines, MN: American Guidance Service.

Kaufman, A. S., Lichtenberger, E. O., Fletcher-Janzen, E., & Kaufman, N. (2005). *Essentials of KABC–II Assessment.* New York: John Wiley & Sons.

Kenworthy, L., Black, D. O., Harrison, B., della Rosa, A., & Wallace, G. L. (2009). Are executive control functions related to autism symptoms in high-functioning children? *Child Neuropsychology, 15,* 425–440.

Kim, J. A., Szatmari, P., Bryson, S. E., Streiner, D. L., & Wilson, F. J. (2000). The prevalence of anxiety and mood problems among children with autism and Asperger Syndrome. *Autism, 4,* 117–132.

Kjelgaard, M. M., & Tager-Flusberg, H. (2001). An investigation of language impairment in autism: Implications for genetic subgoups. *Language and Cognitive Processes, 16,* 287–308.

Kleinhans, N., Akshoomoff, N., & Delis, D. C. (2005). Executive functions in autism and Asperger's Disorder: Flexibility, fluency, and inhibition. *Developmental Neuropsychology, 27,* 379–401.

Kleinman, J. M., Robins, D. L., Ventola, P. E., Pandey, J., Boorstein, H. C., Esser, E. L., et al. (2008). The Modified Checklist for Autism in Toddlers: A follow-up study investigating the early detection of autism spectrum disorders. *Journal of Autism & Developmental Disorders, 38,* 827–839.

Klin, A., Jones, W., Schultz, R. T., & Volkmar, F. R. (2005). The executive mind—from actions to cognition: Lessons from autism (pp. 682–703).) In F. Volkmar, R. Paul, A. Klin, & D. Cohen (Eds.), *Handbook of autism and pervasive developmental disorders* (3rd Edition). Hoboken, NJ: John Wiley & Sons.

Klin, A., Lang, J., Cicchetti, D., & Volkmar, F. (2000). Interrater reliability of clinical diagnosis and DSM-IV criteria for autistic disorder: Results of the DSM-IV autism field trial. *Journal of Autism and Developmental Disorders, 30,* 163–167.

Klin, A., Saulnier, C., Sparrow, S., Cicchetti, D., Volkmar, F. R., & Lord, C. (2007). Social and communication abilities and disabilities in higher functioning individuals with autism spectrum disorders: The Vineland and the ADOS. *Journal of Autism and Developmental Disabilities, 37,* 748–759.

Klin, A., Saulnier, C., Tsatsanis, K., & Volkmar, F. R. (2005). Clinical evaluation in autism spectrum disorders: Psychological assessment within a transdisciplinary framework. In F. Volkmar, R. Paul, A. Klin, & D. J. Cohen (Eds.). *Handbook of autism and pervasive developmental disorders,* (3rd ed., Vol. 2, pp. 772–798). New York: Wiley.

Klin, A., Sparrow, S. S., de Bildt, A., Cicchetti, D. V., Cohen, D. J., & Volkmar, F. R. (1999). A normed study of face recognition in autism and related disorders. *Journal of Autism and Developmental Disorders, 29,* 499–508.

Klinger, L. G., O'Kelley, S. E., & Mussey, J. L. (2009). Assessment of intellectual functioning in autism spectrum disorders. In S. Goldstein, J. Naglieri, & S. Ozonoff (Eds.), *Assessment of autism spectrum disorders.* New York: Guilford Press.

Knoll, V. (2008). Clinical and adaptive skill characteristics of children with autistic spectrum disorders using the Behavior Assessment System for Children, Second Edition. *Dissertation Abstracts International, Section B: The Sciences and Engineering, 69,* 2654.

Koegel, L. K., Koegel, R. L., & Smith, A. (1997). Variables related to differences in standardized test outcomes for children with ASD. *Journal of Autism and Developmental Disorders, 27,* 233–243.

Korkman, M., Kirk, U., & Kemp, S. (2007). *NEPSY* (2nd ed.). San Antonio, TX: Harcourt Assessment.

Krug, D. A., Arick, J. R., & Almond, P. (1993). *Autism Screening Instrument for Educational Planning.* Portland, OR: ASIEP Educational.

Krug, D. A., Arick, J. R., & Almond, P. (2008). *Autism Screening Instrument for Educational Planning* (3rd ed.). Austin, TX: Pro-Ed.

Landa, R., & Garrett-Mayer, E. (2006). Development of infants with autism spectrum disorders: A prospective study. *Journal of Child Psychology and Psychiatry, 47,* 629–638.

Leark, R. A., Greenberg, L. K., Kindschi, C. L., Dupuy, T. R., & Hughes, S. J. (2007). *Test of Variables of Attention: Professional Manual.* Los Alamitos, CA: The TOVA Company.

Le Couteur, A., Haden, G., Hammal, D., & McConachie, H. (2008). Diagnosing autism spectrum disorders in pre-school children using two standardized assessment instruments: The ADI-R and the ADOS. *Journal of Autism and Developmental Disorders, 38,* 362–372.

Lecavalier, L. (2005). An evaluation of the Gilliam Autism Rating Scale. *Journal of Autism and Developmental Disorders, 35,* 795–805.

Leekam, S. R., Lopez, B., & Moore, C. (2000). Attention and joint attention in preschool children with autism. *Developmental Psychology, 36,* 261–273.

Libby, S., Powell, S., Messer, D., & Jordan, R. (1998). Spontaneous play in children with autism: A reappraisal. *Journal of Autism and Developmental Disorders, 28,* 487–497.

Lichtenberger, E. A. (2004). Autism-spectrum disorders. In D. P. Flanagan & A. S. Kaufman (Eds.), *Essentials of WISC-IV assessment* (pp. 183–199). New York: John Wiley & Sons.

Lincoln, A. J., Courchesne, E., Kilman, A., Elmasian, R., & Allen, M. H. (1988). A study of intellectual abilities in high-functioning people with autism. *Journal of Autism and Developmental Disorders, 18,* 505–524.

Lincoln, A. J., Hansel, E., & Quirmbach, L. (2007). Assessing intellectual abilities of children and adolescents with autism and related disorders. In S. R. Smith & L. Handler (Eds.),

The clinical assessment of children and adolescents: A practitioner's handbook (pp. 527–544). Mahawah, NJ: Erlbaum.

Lloyd, H., Paintin, K., & Botting, N. (2006). Performance of children with different types of communication impairment on the Clinical Evaluation of Language Fundamentals (CELF). *Child Language Teaching & Therapy, 22,* 47–67.

Lord, C. (1995). Follow-up of two-year-olds referred for possible autism. *Journal of Child Psychology and Psychiatry, 36,* 1365–1382.

Lord, C., & Corsello, C. (2005). Diagnostic instruments in autistic spectrum disorders. In F. Volkmar, R. Paul, A. Klin & D. Cohen. (Eds.) *Handbook of Autism and Pervasive Developmental Disorders,* (3rd ed., pp. 730–771) New York: Wiley.

Lord, C., & Risi, S. (2000). Diagnosis of autism spectrum disorders in young children. In A. M. Wetherby & B. M. Prizant (Eds.), *Autism spectrum disorders: A transactional developmental perspective* (pp. 11–30). Baltimore: Brooks.

Lord, C., Risi, S., Lambrecht, L., Cook, E. H., Jr., Leventhal, B. L., DiLavore, P. C., et al. (2000). The Autism Diagnostic Observation Schedule–Generic: A standard measure of social and communication deficits associated with the spectrum of autism. *Journal of Autism and Developmental Disorders, 30,* 205–223.

Lord, C., Rutter, M., DiLavore, P. C., & Risi, S. (1999). *Autism Diagnostic Observation Schedule–WPS Edition (ADOS–WPS).* Los Angeles: Western Psychological Services.

Lord, C., Rutter, M., & Le Couteur, A. (1994). Autism Diagnostic Interview–Revised: A revised version of a diagnostic interview for caregivers of individuals with possible pervasive developmental disorders. *Journal of Autism and Developmental Disorders, 24,* 659–685.

Lord, C., Storoschuk, S., Rutter, M., & Pickles, A. (1993). Using the ADI-R to diagnose autism in preschool children. *Infant Mental Health Journal, 14,* 234–252.

Loveland, K. A., & Landry, S. H. (1986). Joint attention and language in autism and developmental language delay. *Journal of Autism and Developmental Disorders, 16,* 335–349.

Luiselli, J. K., Campbell, S., Cannon, B., DiPietro, E., Ellis, J. T., Taras, M., & Lifter, K. (2001). Assessment instruments used in the education and treatment of persons with autism: Brief report of a survey of national service centers. *Research in Developmental Disabilities, 22,* 389–398.

Magiati, I., & Howlin, P. (2001). Monitoring the progress of preschool children with autism enrolled in early intervention programmes: Problems in cognitive assessment. *Autism, 5,* 407–429.

Magyar, C. I., & Pandolfi, V. (2007). Factor structure evaluation of the Childhood Autism Rating Scale. *Journal of Autism and Developmental Disorders, 37,* 1787–1794.

Manjiviona, J., & Prior, M. (1995). Comparison of Asperger syndrome and high-functioning autistic children on a test of motor impairment. *Journal of Autism and Developmental Disorders, 25,* 23–39.

Mayes, S., & Calhoun, S. (1999). Symptoms of autism in young children and correspondence with the DSM. *Infants and Young Children, 12,* 90–97.

Mayes, S., & Calhoun, S. (2003). Analysis of WISC–III, Stanford-Binet-IV, and academic achievement test scores in children with autism. *Journal of Autism and Developmental Disorders, 33,* 328–341.

Mayes, S., & Calhoun, S. (2004). Similarities and differences in Wechsler Intelligence Scale for Children–Third Edition (WISC–III) profiles: Support for subtest analysis in clinical referrals. *The Clinical Neuropsychologist, 18,* 559–572.

Mayes, S., & Calhoun, S. (2006). Frequency of reading, math, and writing disabilities in children with clinical disorders. *Learning and Individual Differences, 16,* 145–157.

Mayes, S., & Calhoun, S. (2007). Learning, attention, writing, and processing speed in typical children and children with ADHD, autism, anxiety, depression and oppositional defiant disorder. *Child Neuropsychology, 13,* 469–493.

Mayes, S., & Calhoun, S. (2008). WISC-IV and WIAT-II profiles in children with high-functioning autism. *Journal of Autism and Developmental Disorders, 38,* 428–439.

Mayes, S., Calhoun, S., Murray, M., Morrow, J., Yurich, K., Mahr, F., et al. (2009). Comparison of scores on the Checklist for Autism Spectrum Disorder, Childhood Autism Rating Scale, and Gilliam Asperger's Disorder Scale for children with low functioning autism, high functioning autism, Asperger's disorder, ADHD, and typical development. *Journal of Autism and Developmental Disabilities, 39,* 1682–1693.

Mazefsky, C. A., & Oswald, D. P. (2006). The discriminative ability and diagnostic utility of the ADOS–G, ADI–R, and GARS for children in a clinical setting. *Autism, 10,* 533–549.

McGovern, C. W., & Sigman, M. (2005). Continuity and change from early childhood to adolescence in autism. *Journal of Child Psychology and Psychiatry, 46,* 401–408.

Menyuk, P., Liebergott, J., & Schultz, M. (1995). *Early language development in full-term and premature infants.* Hillsdale, NJ: Erlbaum.

Mesibov, G. B., Adams, L. W., & Klinger, L. G. (1997). Autism: Understanding the disorder. New York: Kluwer Academic/Plenum.

Miller, J., & Ozonoff, S. (2000). The external validity of Asperger disorder: Lack of evidence from the domain of neuropsychology. *Journal of Abnormal Psychology, 109,* 227–238.

Minshew, N. J., & Goldstein, G. (1993). Is autism an amnesic disorder? Evidence from the California Verbal Learning Test. *Neuropsychology, 7,* 209–216.

Minshew, N. J., Goldstein, G., & Siegel, D. J. (1997). Neuropsychologic functioning in autism: Profile of a complex information processing disorder. *Journal of the International Neuropsychological Society, 3,* 303–316.

Minshew, N. J., Goldstein, G., Taylor, H. G., & Siegel, D. J. (1994). Academic achievement in high functioning autistic individuals. *Journal of Clinical and Experimental Neuropsychology, 16,* 261–270.

Miranda-Linne, F. M., Fredrika, M., & Melin, L. (1997). A comparison of speaking and mute individuals with autism and autistic-like conditions on the Autism Behavior Checklist. *Journal of Autism and Developmental Disorders, 27,* 245–264.

Miranda-Linne, F. M., & Melin, L. (2002). A factor analytic study of the Autism Behavior Checklist. *Journal of Autism and Developmental Disorders, 32,* 181–188.

Montgomery, J. M., Newton, B., & Smith, C. (2008). Review of GARS-2: Gilliam Autism Rating Scale–Second Edition. *Psychoeducational Assessment, 26,* 395–401.

Mullen, E. M. (1995). *Mullen Scales of Early Learning.* Minneapolis: NCS Pearson.

Mundy, P., Sigman, M., & Kasari, C. (1990). A longitudinal study of joint attention and language development in autistic children. *Journal of Autism and Developmental Disorders, 20,* 115–128.

Muris, P., Steerneman, P., Merckelbach, H., Holdrinet, I., & Meesters, C. (1998). Comorbid anxiety symptoms in children with pervasive developmental disorders. *Journal of Anxiety Disorders, 12,* 387–393.

Naglieri, J. A. (1997). *Naglieri Nonverbal Ability Test.* San Antonio, TX: Psychological Corporation.

Naglieri, J. A. (2005). The cognitive assessment system (pp. 441–460). In D. Flanagan & P. Harrison (Eds.), *Contemporary intellectual assessment—Second Edition: Theories, tests and issues.* New York: Guilford Press.

Naglieri, J. A., & Das, J. P. (1997). *Cognitive assessment system.* Itasca, IL: Riverside.

Nyden, A., Billstedt, E., Hjelmquist, E., & Gillberg, C. (2001). Neurocognitive stability in Asperger syndrome, ADHD, and reading and writing disorder: A pilot study. *Developmental Medicine and Child Neurology, 43,* 165–171.

Nyden, A., Gillberg, C., Hjelmquist, E., & Heiiman, M. (1999). Executive function/attention deficits in boys with Asperger syndrome, attention disorder, and reading/writing disorder. *Autism, 3,* 213–228.

O'Connor, N., & Hermelin, B. (1994). Two autistic savant readers. *Journal of Autism and Developmental Disorders, 37,* 760–774.

Osterling, J., & Dawson, G. (1994). Early recognition of children with autism: A study of first birthday home videotapes. *Journal of Autism and Developmental Disorders, 24,* 247–257.

Osterling, J., Dawson, G., & Munson, J. (2002). Early recognition of 1-year-old infants with autism spectrum disorder versus mental retardation. *Development and Psychopathology, 14,* 239–251.

Ozonoff, S. (1995). Reliability and validity of the Wisconsin Card Sorting Test in studies of autism. *Neuropsychology, 9,* 491–500.

Ozonoff, S., & Jensen, J. (1999). Specific executive function profiles in three neurodevelopmental disorders. *Journal of Autism and Developmental Disorders, 29,* 171–177.

Ozonoff, S., Pennington, B. F., & Rogers, S. J. (1991). Executive function deficits in high-functioning autistic individuals: Relationship to theory of mind. *Journal of Child Psychology and Psychiatry, 32,* 1081–1105.

Ozonoff, S., & Strayer, D. L. (2001). Further evidence of intact working memory in autism. *Journal of Autism and Developmental Disorders, 31,* 257–263.

Page, J., & Boucher, J. (1998). Motor impairments in children with autistic disorder. *Child Language Teaching and Therapy, 14,* 233–259.

Pandey, J., Verbalis, A., Robins, D. L., Boorstein, H., Klin, A. M., Babitz, T., et al. (2008). Screening for autism in older and younger toddlers with the Modified Checklist for Autism in Toddlers. *Autism, 12,* 513–535.

Papp, S. (2006). A relevance-theoretic account of the development and deficits of Theory of Mind in normally developing children and individuals with autism. *Theory & Psychology, 16,* 141–161.

Patti, P. J., & Lupinetti, L. (1993). Brief report: Implications of hyperlexia in an autistic savant. *Journal of Autism and Developmental Disorders, 23,* 397–405.

Pennington, B. F., Rogers, S. J., Bennetto, L., Griffith, E. M., Reed, D. T., & Shyu, V. (1997). Validity tests of the executive dysfunction hypothesis of autism (pp. 143–178). In J. Russell (Ed.), *Autism as an executive disorder.* New York: Oxford University Press.

Perry, A., Condillac, R. A., Freeman, N. L., Dunn-Geier, J., & Belair, J. (2005). Multi-site study of the Childhood Autism Rating Scale (CARS) in five clinical groups of young children. *Journal of Autism and Developmental Disorders, 35,* 625–634.

Perry, A., Flanagan, H., Geier, J., & Freeman, N. (2009). Brief report: The Vineland Adaptive Behavior Scales in young children with autism spectrum disorders at different cognitive levels. *Journal of Autism and Developmental Disabilities, 39,* 1066–1078.

Pilowsky, T., Yirmiya, N., Shulman, C., & Dover, R. (1998). The Autism Diagnostic Interview–Revised and the Childhood Autism Rating Scale: Differences between diagnostic systems and comparison between genders. *Journal of Autism and Developmental Disorders, 28,* 143–151.

Rapin, I., & Dunn, M. (2003). Update on the language disorders of individuals on the autistic spectrum. *Brain and Development, 25,* 166–172.

Reitan, R. M., & Wolfson, D. (1993). *The Halstead-Reitan Neuropsychological Test Battery: Theory and clinical interpretation* (2nd ed.). Tucson, AZ: Neuropsychology Press.

Rellini, E., Tortolani, D., Trillo, S., Carbone, S., & Montecchi, F. (2004). Childhood Autism Ratings Scale (CARS) and Autism Behavior Checklist (ABC) correspondence and conflicts with DSM-IV criteria in diagnosis of autism. *Journal of Autism and Developmental Disorders, 34,* 703–708.

Reynolds, C., & Kamphaus, R. (2004). *Behavior Assessment System for Children* (2nd ed.). San Antonio, TX: Pearson.

Robbins, D. L. (2008). Screening for autism spectrum disorders in primary care settings. *Autism, 12,* 537–556.

Robbins, D. L., Fein, D., Barton, M., & Green, J. (2001). The Modified Checklist for Autism in Toddlers: An initial study investigating the early detection of autism and pervasive developmental disorders. *Journal of Autism and Developmental Disorders, 31,* 131–144.

Rodrigue, J. R., Morgan, S. B., & Geffken, G. R. (1991). A comparative evaluation of adaptive behavior in children and adolescents with autism, Down syndrome, and normal development. *Journal of Autism and Developmental Disorders, 21,* 187–196.

Rogers, J., Wallace, G., & Happe, F. (2002). Behavior Rating Inventory of Executive Function–preschool ratings in children with autism spectrum disorders. Unpublished raw data as cited in G. Gioa, K. Espy & P. Isquith, *Behavior Rating Inventory of Executive Function–Preschool Version.* Lutz, FL: PAR.

Roid, G. H. (2003). *Stanford-Binet Intelligence Scales* (5th ed.). Itasca, IL: Riverside Publishing.

Roid, G. H., & Miller, L. J. (1997). *Leiter International Performance Scale* (rev.). Wood Dale, IL: Stoelting.

Roid, G. H., & Pomplun, M. (2005). Interpreting the Stanford-Binet Intelligence Scales Fifth Edition. In D. Flanagan & P. Harrison (Eds.), *Contemporary intellectual assessment* (2nd ed., pp. 325–343). New York: Guilford Press.

Rumsey, J. (1992). Neuropsychological studies of high functioning autism. In E. Schopler & G. Mesibov (Eds.), *High functioning individuals with autism.* (pp. 41–64). New York: Plenum.

Rutter, M., Bailey, A., & Lord, C. (2003). *Social Communication Questionnaire (SCQ).* Los Angeles: Western Psychological Services.

Rutter, M., Le Couteur, A., & Lord, C. (2008). *Autism Diagnostic Interview* (rev.). Los Angeles: Western Psychological Services.

Scambler, D., Rogers, S. J., & Wehner, E. A. (2001). Can the Checklist for Autism in Toddlers differentiate young children with autism from those with developmental delays? *Journal of the American Academy of Child & Adolescent Psychiatry, 40,* 1457–1463.

Saemundsen, E., Magnusson, P., Smari, J., & Sigurdardottir, S. (2003). Autism Diagnostic Interview-Revised and the Childhood Autism Rating Scale: Convergence and discrepancy in diagnosing autism. *Journal of Autism and Developmental Disorders, 33,* 319–328.

Sandford, J. A., & Turner, A. (2000). *Integrated Visual and Auditory Continuous Performance Test.* Richmond, VA: Braintrain.

Sattler, J. (2001). *Assessment of children: Cognitive applications* (4th ed.). San Diego, CA: Sattler.

Schopler, E., Lansing, M., Reichler, R., & Marcus, L. (2005). *Psychoeducational Profile: TEACCH Individualized Psychoeducational Assessment for Children with Autistic Spectrum Disorders* (3rd ed.). Austin, TX: Pro-Ed.

Schopler, E. M., Reichler, R. J., & Renner, B. R. (1988). *The Childhood Autism Rating Scale.* Los Angeles, CA: Psychological Services.

Schopler, E., Reichler, R. J., & Renner, B. R. (2008). *The Childhood Autism Rating Scale.* Los Angeles, CA: Western Psychological Services.

Sevin, J.A., Matson, J. L., Coe, D. A., & Fee, V. E. (1991). A comparison and evaluation of three commonly used autism scales. *Journal of Autism and Developmental Disorders. 21,* 417–432.

Sherman, M., Shapiro, T., & Glassman, M. (1983). Play and language in developmentally disordered preschoolers: A new approach to classification. *Journal of American Academy of Child and Adolescent Psychiatry, 22,* 511–596.

Sheslow, D., & Adams, W. (2003). *Wide Range Assessment of Memory and Learning* (2nd ed.). Lutz, FL: Psychological Assessment Resources.

Shriberg, L. D., Paul, R., McSweeny, J. L., Klin, A. M., Cohen, D. J., & Volkmar, F. R. (2001). Speech and prosody characteristics of adolescents and adults with high-functioning autism and Asperger syndrome. *Journal of Speech, Language, and Hearing Research, 44,* 1097–1115.

Siegel, D. J., Minshew, N. J., & Goldstein, G. (1996). Wechsler IQ profiles in diagnosis of high-functioning autism. *Journal of Autism and Developmental Disabilities, 26,* 398–406.

South, M., Williams, B. J., McMahon, W. M., Owley, T., Filipek, P. A., Shernoff, E., et al. (2002). Utility of the Gilliam Autism Rating Scale in research and clinical populations. *Journal of Autism and Developmental Disorders, 32,* 593–599.

Sparrow, S. S., Cicchetti, D. V., & Balla, D.A. (2005). *Vineland Adaptive Behavior Scales* (2nd ed.). Circle Pines, MN: American Guidance Service.

Stahl, L., & Pry, R. (2002). Joint attention and set-shifting in young children with autism. *Autism, 6,* 383–396.

Stewart, M. E., Barnard, L., Pearson, J., Hasan, R., & O'Brien, G. (2006). Presentation of depression in autism and Asperger syndrome. *Autism, 10,* 103–116.

Stone, W. L., Coonrod, E. E., & Ousley, O. Y. (2000). Brief report: Screening tool for autism in two-year olds (STAT). *Journal of Autism and Developmental Disorders, 30,* 607–612.

Stone, W. L., Coonrod, E. E., Turner, L. M., & Pozdol, S. L. (2004). Psychometric properties of the STAT for early autism screening. *Journal of Autism and Developmental Disorders, 34,* 691–701.

Stone, W. L., & Lemanek, K. L. (1990). Parental report of social behaviors in autistic preschoolers. *Journal of Autism and Developmental Disorders, 20,* 513–522.

Stone, W. L., McMahon, C. R., & Henderson, L. M. (2008). Use of the Screening Tool for Autism in Two-Year-Olds (STAT) for children under 24 months: An exploratory study. *Autism, 12,* 557–573.

Strong, C. (1998). *The Strong Narrative Assessment Procedure.* Eau Claire, WI: Thinking Publications.

Tadevosyan-Leyfer, O., Dowd, M., Mankoski, R., Winklosky, B., Putnam, S., McGrath, L., et al. (2003). A principal components analysis of the Autism Diagnostic Interview–Revised. *Journal of the American Academy of Child & Adolescent Psychiatry, 42,* 864–872.

Tager-Flusberg, H. (2001). Understanding the language and communicative impairments in autism (pp. 185–205). In L. M. Glidden (Ed.), *International review of research in mental retardation: Autism.* San Diego, CA: Academic Press.

Tager-Flusberg, H. & Joseph, R. M. (2003). Identifying neurocognitive phenotypes in autism (pp. 43–66). In U. Frith & E. Hill (Eds.), *Autism: Mind and brain.* New York, NY: Oxford Press.

Teal, M. B., & Wiebe, M. J. (1986). A validity analysis of selected instruments used to assess autism. *Journal of Autism and Developmental Disorders, 16,* 485–494.

Toichi, M., & Kamio, Y. (1998). Verbal memory in autistic adolescents. *Japanese Journal of Child and Adolescent Psychiatry, 39,* 364–373.

Tomanik, S. S., Pearson, D. A., Loveland, K. A., Lane, D. M., & Shaw, J. B. (2007). Improving the reliability of autism diagnoses: Examining the utility of adaptive behavior. *Journal of Autism and Developmental Disorders, 37,* 921–928.

Tsatsanis, K. D., Dartnall, N., Cicchetti, D., Sparrow, S. S., Klin, A., & Volkmar, F. R. (2003). Concurrent validity and classification accuracy of the Leiter and Leiter-R in low-functioning children with autism. *Journal of Autism and Developmental Disorders, 33,* 23–30.

Ventola, P. E., Kleinman, J., Pandey, J., Barton, M., Allen, S., Green, J., et al. (2006). Agreement among four diagnostic instruments for autism spectrum disorders in toddlers. *Journal of Autism and Developmental Disorders, 36,* 839–847.

Volkmar, F. R., Cicchetti, D. V., Dykens, E., Sparrow, S. Leckman, J., & Cohen, D (1988). An evaluation of the Autism Behavior Checklist. *Journal of Autism and Developmental Disorders, 8,* 8–97.

Volkmar, F. R., Sparrow, S. S., Goudreau, D., Cicchetti, D. V., et al. (1987). Social deficits in autism: An operational approach using the Vineland Adaptive Behavior Scales. *Journal of the American Academy of Child & Adolescent Psychiatry, 26,* 156–161.

Volkmar, F. R., Szatmari, P., & Sparrow, S. (1993). Sex difference in pervasive developmental disorders. *Journal of Autism and Developmental Disorders, 23,* 579–591.

Wadden, N., Bryson, S., & Rodger, R. (1991). A closer look at the Autism Behavior Checklist: Discriminant validity and factor structure. *Journal of Autism and Developmental Disorders, 21,* 529–542.

Ward, A. J. (1970). Early infantile autism: Diagnosis, etiology, and treatment. *Psychological Bulletin, 73,* 350–362.

Wechsler, D. (2001). *Wechsler Individual Achievement Test* (2nd ed.). San Antonio, TX: Psychological Corporation.

Wechsler, D. (2002). *Wechsler Preschool and Primary Scale of Intelligence* (3rd ed.). San Antonio, TX: Psychological Corporation.

Wechsler, D. (2003). *Wechsler Intelligence Scale for Children* (4th ed.). San Antonio, TX: Psychological Corporation.

Wechsler, D. (2009). *Wechsler Individual Achievement Test* (3rd ed.). San Antonio, TX: Pearson.

Werner, E., Dawson, G., Osterling, J., & Dinno, H. (2000). Recognition of autism spectrum disorder before one year of age: A retrospective study based on home videotapes. *Journal of Autism and Developmental Disorders, 30,* 157–162.

Wetherby, A., Prizant, B., & Hutchinson, T. (1998). Communicative, social–affective, and symbolic profiles of young children with autism and pervasive developmental disorder. *American Journal of Speech-Language Pathology, 7,* 79–91.

Wetherby, A. M., & Prutting, C. A. (1984). Profiles of communicative and cognitive-social abilities in autistic children. *Journal of Speech & Hearing Research, 27,* 364–377.

Whitehouse, A. J., Barry, J. G., & Bishop, D. V. (2008). Further defining the language impairment of autism: Is there a specific language impairment subtype? *Journal of Communication Disorders, 41,* 319–336.

Wiig, E. H., & Secord, W. (1989). Test of language competence. San Antonio, TX: Psychological Corporation.

Wiig, E. H., Semel, E., & Secord, W. (2003), *Clinical Evaluation of Language Fundamentals* (4th ed.). San Antonio, TX: Harcourt Brace Jovanovich.

Wiig, E. H., Semel, E., & Secord, W. (2004). *Clinical Evaluation of Language Fundamentals–Preschool.* San Antonio, TX: Harcourt Brace Jovanovich.

Williams, D. L., Goldstein, G., Carpenter, P. A., & Minshew, N. J. (2005).Verbal and spatial working memory in autism. *Journal of Autism and Developmental Disorders, 35,* 747–756.

Williams, D. L., Goldstein, G., & Minshew, N. J. (2006a). Neuropsychological functioning in children with autism: Further evidence for disordered complex information-processing. *Child Neuropsychology, 12,* 279–298.

Williams, D. L., Goldstein, G., & Minshew, N. J. (2006b). The profile of memory function in children with autism. *Neuropsychology, 20,* 21–29.

Williams, K. T. (2007). *Expressive Vocabulary Test* (2nd ed.). Circle Pines, MN: American Guidance Service.

Witwer, A. N., & Lecavalier, L. (2007). Autism screening tools: An evaluation of the Social Communication Questionnaire and the Developmental Behaviour Checklist–Autism Screening Algorithm. *Journal of Intellectual & Developmental Disability, 32,* 179–187.

Woodcock, R., McGrew, K., & Mather, N. (2001a). *Woodcock-Johnson Tests of Cognitive Abilities* (3rd ed.). Itasca, IL: Riverside.

Woodcock, R., McGrew, K., & Mather, N. (2001b). *Woodcock-Johnson Tests of Achievement* (3rd ed.). Itasca, IL: Riverside.

Young, E. C., Diehl, J. J., Morris, D., Hyman, S. L., & Bennetto, L. (2005). The use of two language tests to identify pragmatic language problems in children with autism spectrum disorders. *Language, Speech, and Hearing Services in Schools, 36,* 62–72.

Psychological Evaluation

Child's Name: Jimmy S.
Date of Birth: 12/9/03
Chronological Age: 3 years, 10 months
Gender: Male
Primary Language: English
Ethnicity: White
Evaluation Dates: 10/30/07 and 11/5/07

REASON FOR REFERRAL

Jimmy S., a 3-year, 10-month-old male was referred for a psychological evaluation to provide diagnostic clarity and further information about the presence and severity of any symptoms related to the diagnosis of autism. The chief concerns of Ms. S., Jimmy's mother, are: no reciprocal communication, lack of eye contact, poor receptive communication, inability to break routines, and lack of socially appropriate interactions. Jimmy was recently evaluated by the school district and found eligible for preschool services under the category Preschool Moderate Delay in the areas of communication and social–emotional development. An ADOS performed by the school district indicated behavior presentation consistent with a diagnosis of autism. He will begin the special needs preschool program in November.

BACKGROUND INFORMATION

Background information was gathered from Ms. S.'s completion of the Initial Care Planning packet and parent interview.

125

Medical/Developmental History:

Prenatal history was without significance. Jimmy weighed 10 pounds at birth following an unremarkable full term pregnancy, 12-hour labor, and repeat Caesarean section delivery. He had difficulty breathing at birth, as the umbilical cord was wrapped around his neck, and he required a very brief stay in the NICU. He was mildly jaundiced in the neonatal period, which resolved with sunlight treatment. Motor milestones were met on time, with Jimmy walking independently at 14 months of age. Language milestones were met late with first words spoken at 3 years and two word phrases around 38 months. Mother reported Jimmy now has a large vocabulary; however, he does not use language to communicate with others.

Relevant medical history includes chronic ear infections treated with antibiotics and PE tubes at 1½ years of age. A second set of tubes is scheduled, as ear infections have not resolved. Relevant medical concerns include difficulty falling asleep unless mother is with him. Snoring is excessive. He has seasonal allergies. Jimmy does not take any medications currently. A hearing evaluation in September was within normal limits. Vision was also screened in September; Jimmy is slightly far-sighted but not in need of corrective lenses.

Social History:

Jimmy resides with his mother, Suzanne S., and his 7-year-old brother Matt. Ms. S.'s mother also lives in the home. Ms. S. is a single parent who is a special education teacher. English is the language spoken in the home and Jimmy's language of instruction. There is a family history of autism, as Jimmy's older brother was recently diagnosed with autism.

Jimmy's temperament was described as "slow to warm up." Mother reported that Jimmy prefers to be alone, bullies others, and prefers adults over peers. He does not make friends easily or play well with his peers. He is very intelligent and has learned letters, letter sounds, some basic sight words and numbers. He enjoys gross motor activities such as running, swinging, and jumping.

Educational History/Previous Evaluations:

Jimmy has attended preschool since January. Mother believes Jimmy's learning potential is above average. Jimmy has never received developmental therapy services. Comprehensive assessment was completed in October by the School District. On the Developmental Assessment of Young Children, Jimmy attained a Cognitive standard score of 77 and an Adaptive Behavior standard score of 84. On the Preschool Language Scale–4, Jimmy's auditory comprehension was delayed, with a standard score of 77, Expressive Language score of 82 resulting in a Total Language Standard score of 77. Pragmatic language challenges were noted. Behavior concerns were reported by mother with clinically significant scores on the Hyperactivity and Atypicality scales. The Autism Diagnostic Observation Schedule Module 2 was administered. Jimmy's score was above the cutoff score, indicating his current presentation is consistent with a diagnosis of autism. Sensory processing differences were noted and consultative occupational therapy was recommended. Jimmy was considered a candidate for special education preschool services as a child with Preschool Moderate Delay (PMD). An IEP was written with goals in the areas of social skills and communication.

ASSESSMENT PROCEDURES:

Wechsler Preschool and Primary Scale of Intelligence–III
Autism Diagnostic Observation Schedule (ADOS) Module 2
Vineland Adaptive Behavior Scales–II, Survey Interview Form
Child Behavior Checklist for ages 1½ to 5
Parent Interview
Records Review
Behavioral Observations

BEHAVIORAL OBSERVATIONS

Jimmy was accompanied by his mother to the appointment. They were not separated during testing. Jimmy is tall and appears slightly older than his chronological age. He presented as a pleasant boy whose cooperation varied with the time and nature of the task. Jimmy's verbalizations were usually understandable; however, most of his spontaneous verbalizations consisted of self-talk where he named objects. Jimmy's activity level was moderate to high, as he was active and had a short attention span for directed activity. Eye contact was poorly modulated, as Jimmy demonstrated fleeting eye contact unless he was interested in a particular toy. He did not usually pair eye contact with vocalization. He did not point out objects of interest to his mother or the examiner. Test results are considered to be representative of Jimmy's current functioning levels.

INTERPRETATION OF TEST RESULTS

Intellectual Ability:

Jimmy was administered 5 subtests of the Wechsler Preschool and Primary Scale of Intelligence–3rd Edition (WPPSI–III) from which his composite scores are derived. The Full Scale IQ (FSIQ) is derived from the combination of four subtest scores and is considered to be the most representative measure of global intellectual functioning. Jimmy's general cognitive ability is in the Average range of intellectual functioning, as measured by the FSIQ. His overall thinking and reasoning abilities exceed those of approximately 50% of children his age (FSIQ = 100; 90% confidence interval = 95–105). His FSIQ score is comparable to that of his peers.

Although Jimmy performed better on nonverbal than on verbal reasoning tasks, these differences in performance are not unusual among children his age. Those who know him may notice a preference for nonverbal activities, but the difference is not excessive.

The Verbal IQ (VIQ) is derived from the combination of two subtest scores and is an estimate of verbal reasoning and comprehension, acquired knowledge, and attention to verbal stimuli. Jimmy's verbal abilities, as measured by the VIQ, are in the Average range and exceed those of 32% of his peers (VIQ = 93; 90% confidence interval = 88–99). His VIQ score is comparable to that of his peers. Jimmy performed comparably on tasks measuring his general fund of information (Information = 8) and tasks measuring the ability to process and comprehend verbal information (Receptive Vocabulary = 10). These scores suggest that these verbal cognitive abilities are similarly developed. Jimmy performed significantly better on tasks measuring the ability to identify and name pictured stimuli (Picture Naming = 11) than on tasks measuring his general fund of information (Information = 8). Such a difference is unusual for a child his age and is likely to be observable in his daily activities. Jimmy had difficulty understanding what the questions were asking and often responded with a tangential thought to one of the key words in the question.

The General Language Composite (GLC) is derived from scores on the Picture Naming and Receptive Vocabulary subtests and provides a measure of basic expressive and receptive language development. Jimmy's GLC falls in the Average range and is higher than that of 55% of children his age. His GLC score is comparable to that of most of his peers. Jimmy performed about equally well on tasks that allowed him to point to pictures named by the examiner and tasks requiring him to name pictured objects aloud. These scores suggest that his expressive and receptive language abilities are similarly developed.

The Performance IQ (PIQ) is derived from the combination of two subtest scores and is an estimate of fluid reasoning, spatial processing, attentiveness to detail, and visual–motor integration. Jimmy's perceptual–organizational and nonverbal reasoning abilities, as measured by the PIQ, are in the Average range and exceed those of 63% of his peers (PIQ = 105; 90% confidence interval = 97–112). His PIQ score is comparable to that of his peers. Jimmy performed similarly on tasks requiring him to reproduce abstract block arrangements (Block Design = 11) and tasks requiring him to assemble puzzles depicting common objects (Object Assembly = 11). These scores suggest that these perceptual–organizational abilities are similarly developed.

Autism Diagnostic Observation Schedule:

The Autism Diagnostic Observation Schedule (ADOS) Module 2 was administered to assess the presence of symptoms related to a diagnosis of autism. The ADOS is a semistructured play observation task designed to assess a child's communication and social relatedness. The child is exposed to a series of "presses," or play tasks, and his behavior is observed. Afterwards, the examiner rates specific behavior patterns on a scale from 0 (no impairment) to 3 (severe impairment). Scores are combined and the following total scores are calculated: Communication, Qualitative Impairments in Reciprocal Social Interaction, Imagination/Creativity, and Stereotyped Behaviors and Restricted Interests. Scores at or above 5 on Communication, 6 on Social Interaction, and 12 on the combined Communication + Social Interaction score are indicative of autism.

Jimmy received a Communication total score of 7, falling above the autism cutoff score of 5. Verbalizations consisted of phrases with some grammatical markings. Some vocalizations were directed at the examiner to direct her behavior. Intonation, pitch, and rate of speech were judged to be normal. His voice volume was unusually loud throughout and not well modulated. Some of Jimmy's verbalizations were immediate echolalia. He used words and phrases that tended to be repetitive. He was not able to engage in reciprocal conversation despite the number of verbalizations produced. Pointing when in close proximity with a vocalization was observed. Limited use of spontaneous descriptive, conventional, or instrumental gestures was noted. Conventional gestures included a head nod for "yes."

Jimmy also demonstrated abnormal reciprocal social interaction, as indicated by a Social Interaction score of 12, falling above the autism cutoff of 6. Eye contact was poorly modulated to regulate social interaction. Some direction of facial expressions was observed, as he has a wonderful smile. He showed pleasure in his play with various toys but did not show pleasure in interaction with the examiner during the same activities. Jimmy preferred to play with the toys by himself. Jimmy responded to his name called by the examiner in the first press. He responded to the examiner's use of eye gaze to acquire joint attention. Jimmy never spontaneously referenced an object to initiate joint attention. He did not show toys during the session. The quality of social overtures was inappropriate, as they lacked integration into context. He was responsive to most social situations but was negative at times, as he refused some tasks. Rapport was difficult to establish, and the order of presentation was modified.

Jimmy played with most toys in a conventional manner. He preferred cause–effect toys. Little spontaneous creative or make-believe play was observed, and he was unable to engage in imaginative play with the examiner. Play was restricted to labeling objects and manipulating them. Jimmy preferred certain toys and repeatedly wanted to play with them. No hand flapping, sensory interest in materials, or self-injurious behaviors was noted. Repetitive interest in certain toys and topics was noted.

Jimmy's combined Communication + Social Interaction Total score of 19 falls above the autism cutoff of 12. Based on behaviors observed during the ADOS administration, Jimmy's behavior presentation is consistent with an ADOS diagnosis of autism. Developmental history and today's results find Jimmy's current behavioral presentation consistent with a *DSM-IV* diagnosis of autistic disorder.

Adaptive Behavior:

The Vineland Adaptive Behavior Scales–II, Survey Interview Form was administered to assess Jimmy's level of personal and social self-sufficiency. Adaptive behavior is defined on the basis of day-to-day activities necessary to take care of oneself and get along with others. It is age-based as defined by the expectation and standards of others. Adaptive behavior represents the typical performance rather than the potential ability of the individual—what the person actually does as opposed to what a person is capable of doing. Ms. S. was interviewed, and Jimmy's communication, daily living skills, socialization, and motor skills were discussed. According the mother's report, an Adaptive Behavior Composite standard score of 86 +/-5 (at the 90% level of confidence) was attained. This falls in the low average range of adaptive ability and indicates Jimmy's level of independence is somewhat compromised.

Communication ability was rated within normal limits with a standard score of 97 +/-7. However, this score may be unduly inflated by Jimmy's interest in the alphabet. Jimmy's receptive understanding of language was estimated to be at the 1 year, 11 month level. He does not always listen to instructions. He is able to follow single-step instructions and instructions with two actions, but he is not able to follow instructions given in if–then form. He can listen to a story for at least 30 minutes while a parent reads a book to him. Jimmy knows most body parts but does not point to them on request. Expressively, Jimmy has a spontaneous vocabulary of well over 100 words. He speaks in phrases and uses prepositions within his utterances. Jimmy will say his first and last name when asked his name. He asks "wh" questions such as what, where, and why. Jimmy does not use pronouns in his phrases. He is able to name all colors on request. Pronunciation of sounds is considered good. Expressive language skills are at an approximate 2 year, 11 month level. Written communication skills are Jimmy's relative area of strength. He is able to recognize all upper and lower case letters of the alphabet and recognize his name in print form. He is able to read at least 10 simple words.

Daily living skills were rated in the lower end of the Average range with a standard score of 91 +/-8. Personal self-help skills include the ability to feed himself using a spoon and fork sometimes held correctly. He can also use a knife. Jimmy drinks from an open cup and a straw. He became daytime toilet trained at age 3½, but he is not yet night trained. He dresses with parent assistance. He cannot button or snap. He can zip zippers that are fastened at the bottom. He needs assistance for grooming and bathing tasks. With regard to domestic daily living skills, Jimmy has poor danger awareness and is not aware that hot things are dangerous. He clears his own unbreakable items from the table after eating. Jimmy will help with cooking by mixing and stirring, and he can use a toaster. He helps with simple household chores and puts his toys away when asked. Community daily living skills include awareness of the telephone, clock, and money. He does not follow household rules unless cued. Jimmy is able to count with one to one correspondence to 25.

Socialization skills are in the Mildly Impaired range with a standard score of 68 +/-6. Mother reports that Jimmy imitates simple movements and repeats phrases heard spoken before by an adult. He does not initiate play with other children and can be aggressive on the playground. The only feeling he is able to describe is anger, saying, "I'm mad." Jimmy's play is functional and simple make-believe play is not observed. He will play in a parallel fashion with peers. Jimmy prefers playing with cars, trucks, trains, and blocks. He does not share even when specifically cued to do so. He sometimes uses "manner" words such as "thank you" and "please." He chews with his mouth open and wipes his face and hands after eating.

Motor skills are also in the Average range, as Jimmy attained a standard score of 100 +/-8. Gross motor skills include the ability to walk downstairs alternative feet, ride a bicycle with training wheels, climb on high play equipment, run smoothly, and catch a beach ball–sized ball thrown from 2–3 feet away. In the fine motor area, Jimmy can color inside lines. He makes some recognizable numbers and letters. Jimmy uses glue to hold things together. He is not able to open and close scissors with one hand.

Behavior Rating Scales:

Ms. S. completed the Child Behavior Checklist regarding Jimmy's behavior at home. Clinically significant scores were found on the Withdrawn, Emotionally Reactive, and Aggressive Behavior syndrome scales. Identified concerns include "acts young for age," "avoids eye contact," "does not answer when people talk to him," "unresponsive to affection," "little affect," "little interest in things around him," and "withdrawn." The Pervasive Developmental Problems scale was clinically significant on the *DSM* Oriented Scales for boys. The Oppositional Defiant Problems scale was in the borderline clinical range.

DIAGNOSTIC IMPRESSION

Jimmy's behavioral presentation is consistent with autism. Jimmy's cognitive intellectual ability is in the Average range. Visual motor skills are above average at this time. Overall adaptive functioning falls in the Low Average range, with lowest subdomain scores in Receptive Communication, Personal Daily Living Skills, Interpersonal Relationships, Play and Leisure Skills, and Social Coping Skills. With regard to a diagnosis of autistic disorder (299.00), Jimmy meets the following *DSM-IV* criteria:

> The following qualitative impairments in reciprocal social interaction are noted:
>
> ➤ Failure to use nonverbal behaviors to regulate social interaction, as evidenced by poorly modulated eye contact, minimal use of descriptive gestures, and limited range of facial expression

➤ Failure to develop peer relationships, as evidenced by lack of imaginative play alone and with peers and lack of interest in what other children are doing
➤ Lack of spontaneous seeking to share enjoyment, interest, or achievement with other people, as evidenced by lack of showing to share and lack of initiation of joint attention

The following qualitative impairments in communication are noted:

➤ Flexible speech; a marked impairment in the ability to sustain a conversation with others
➤ Lack of varied spontaneous make-believe play or social imitative play appropriate to developmental level, as evidenced inability to play interactively with make-believe materials

The following repetitive behaviors and stereotyped patterns of behavior are noted:

➤ Encompassing preoccupation with one or more stereotyped and restricted patterns of interest as evidenced by repetitive play with toys
➤ Preoccupations with parts of objects or nonfunctional elements of material as evidenced by sensory interests

Abnormality of development was evident before 36 months, as he has delays in expressive language, symbolic play, and social interaction.

Jimmy does not have Rett's Disorder or Childhood Disintegrative Disorder.

RECOMMENDATIONS

1. Apply for developmental disabilities services as well as long term care.
2. Continue in the special needs preschool program to provide Jimmy with opportunities for social interactive play.
3. Apply for medically based developmental therapies including occupational therapy, music therapy, and speech/language therapy.
4. Reciprocal social activities are recommended to enhance joint attention. The family was referred to Steve Gutstein's website, www.rdiconnect.com. The book *Relationship Development Intervention in Young Children* contains activities to enhance reciprocal social interaction.
5. Use a picture schedule at home to help ease transitions and provide Jimmy with an idea of what will occur next in his day.
6. The family is referred to the Autism Resource Center for support group information as well as possible social language programs for Jimmy and his brother.
7. Social stories are also suggested as a means to reduce meltdowns when transitions occur or something unexpected happens. Carol Grey's books in this area are recommended.
8. Follow-up with physical regarding hearing status, ear infections, and allergies.

PSYCHOMETRIC SUMMARY

Wechsler Preschool and Primary Scale of Intelligence–3rd Edition

Verbal Subtests	Scaled Score	Performance Subtests	Scaled Score
Receptive Vocabulary	10	Block Design	11
Information	8	Object Assembly	11
(Picture Naming)	11		

Scale	IQ Composite	%ile Rank
Verbal	93	32
Performance	105	63
Full Scale	100	50
General Language	102	55

Vineland Adaptive Behavior Scales–II

Domain	Standard Score	%ile Rank	Age Equivalent
Receptive			1 y, 11 m
Expressive			2 y, 11 m
Written			5 y, 2 m
Communication	97 +/-7	42	———
Personal			2 y, 9 m
Domestic			4 y, 7 m
Community			3 y, 6 m
Daily Living Skills	91 +/-8	27	———
Interpersonal Relationships			1 y, 4 m
Play and Leisure Time			0 y, 10 m
Coping Skills			1 y, 10m
Socialization	68 +/-6	2	———
Gross Motor			4 y, 5 m
Fine Motor			3 y, 7 m
Motor Skills	100 +/-8	50	———
Adaptive Behavior Composite	**86 +/-5**	**18**	———

A sincere note of appreciation to Janet Chao, EdD for providing a clinical example for this chapter and to Birgit Lurie, EdS, for comments on an earlier version of the chapter.

Using Behavioral Assessments to Guide Intervention

Amy L. Kenzer and Michele R. Bishop

The previous chapter provided information on the use of standardized assessments to identify a student's diagnostic category, skill deficits, and learning barriers. While this information is very important and useful in determining the types of special education services a student needs, standardized assessments typically fail to provide the individualized information necessary to develop a teaching procedure or response-reduction intervention for a particular student (Lerman, Vorndran, Addison, & Kuhn, 2004). For example, the results of a standardized language assessment allow the educational team to identify whether a child's language skills are impaired and intervention is necessary. However, knowing that a child's standard score is in the impaired range does not provide information about specific skill deficits, the type of intervention that is most likely to be effective, or how to increase the child's motivation. When Billy's teacher received a report indicating that Billy's standard score on his language assessment was 65, she knew that this score is significantly low and within the impaired range. What she did not know is whether Billy can say "hi" to his friends, ask for a toy when he wants it, or point to and name animals that he sees in a book. The standard score also failed to provide Billy's teacher with any information about how well he can imitate what other people say and whether modeling the correct response will be an effective way to teach Billy what to say and how to say it. Finally, when given the standard score, Billy's teacher still does not know how to motivate Billy to practice new skills that may be difficult for him.

The development of effective interventions is a critical component in the treatment and education of individuals with autism and other developmental disabilities. Effective interventions need to be individualized to meet the needs of each student.

When interventions are not individualized and a cookie cutter approach to intervention is taken, the intervention delivered is likely to be effective for some, ineffective for others, and potentially harmful to a few students. As a result, it is imperative that interventions are guided by assessment of the individual student's specific needs and assets. This chapter will present an overview of several behavioral assessments, basic parameters of behavioral assessments, and a description of the basic assessment methods.

BEHAVIORAL ASSESSMENTS

Behavioral assessment involves a full range of inquiry methods to identify probable antecedent and consequent controlling variables for behavior. *Antecedent* variables are those events that precede the target behavior, while *consequent* variables follow the target behavior. Assessment is a critical component to both skill building and response reduction interventions (Cooper, Heron, & Heward, 2007). *Skill-building interventions* are designed to teach a child new skills where as *response-reduction interventions* are designed to reduce or eliminate problem behaviors. In both cases, the interventions need to be tailored to the student's needs, utilize the student's strengths, and maximize the child's motivation. Thorough and accurate assessment will ensure that these requirements are met.

Functional Behavior Assessments

Interventions aimed at reducing problem behaviors are often necessary for students with autism spectrum disorders. As discussed in previous chapters, these students frequently exhibit social and communication deficits. As a result, they will often communicate their wants and needs in ways that are effective but inappropriate, such as by crying. Additionally, students with ASD commonly engage in restricted, repetitive, and ritualistic patterns of behavior that can be disruptive in the classroom and impede the student's ability to learn or socialize with peers.

When developing a response reduction intervention, it is critical to identify the function of the behavior through the use of a functional behavior assessment (FBA). An FBA is the process of identifying the conditions under which a problem behavior is likely to occur and what environmental events are maintaining it (Cooper et al., 2007). In other words, an FBA reveals why and when a problem behavior happens in order to guide the development of an effective intervention. Identifying these variables allows for the manipulation of these conditions to reduce the likelihood that problem behavior will occur. By conducting an FBA, the response-reduction intervention is much more likely to be effective, less likely to involve punitive procedures, and more likely to include a skill-building component (Hanley, Iwata, & McCord, 2003).

In the absence of an FBA, the cause of problem behavior is commonly attributed to emotional states or internal factors that are difficult to intervene in and thus treat. For example, when asked why Johnny hits his teacher, it is not uncommon to hear responses like "he hits when he is angry or frustrated" or "he always hits every-one" or even "he's just an aggressive child." These reasons for hitting focus on the student's feelings (angry or frustrated), the behavior itself (hitting), or the general temperament of the child (aggressive). Unfortunately, these reasons lend very little useful information for developing an intervention. We still do not know why Johnny is hitting his teacher because we do not know why he is an "aggressive child," why he "hits everyone," or even why he is "angry or frustrated." An FBA helps identify why Johnny is hitting so that a function-based intervention can be implemented. For example, after conducting an FBA on Johnny's hitting behavior, it is clear that Johnny hits his teacher because hitting results in a brief break from difficult class-work when he is put into time-out. This reason for hitting focuses on the function of the behavior and allows the teacher to identify several effective alternative means of intervening to reduce the hitting behavior. For example, the teacher can modify the difficulty of the class work to make it less likely that Johnny will be motivated to hit, stop putting Johnny in time-out when he hits, and teach Johnny to ask for help when he is given work that is difficult for him.

Skill Assessment

The education of students with ASD will always include skill-building interventions to address language, play, social, academic, adaptive, and cognitive deficits. While some of these skill deficits are obvious, others are not. Any time it is uncertain whether or not a student can perform a skill, it is important to assess the student's ability to perform the skill to avoid spending valuable time teaching an already known skill. When selecting specific targets to teach a student, several variables will come into play including decisions based on curricular sequence, function of the skill and need within the student's daily life, baseline level of skills, and identifica-tion of skills that the child already knows and skills the child needs to learn, all the while ensuring that the skills targeted for intervention are age-appropriate and include behaviors that are socially valid (Taylor & McDonough, 1996).

One important step in selecting a particular skill for intervention is to assess the student's performance on tasks drawn from the educational curricula. A skill assess-ment is the process of identifying the behaviors in which a student engages, given particular antecedent conditions, and whether those behaviors match skills taught in the student's curriculum. In other words, a skill assessment determines whether and when a child can perform a given task, in order to develop an effective skill-build-ing intervention (Noell, Freeland, Witt, & Gansle, 2001). By evaluating a student's performance on curricular tasks, the teacher is able to determine which tasks need to be taught, maintained, and generalized.

Those skills the student is unable to demonstrate in the natural environment need to be targeted for intervention. These are the skills that need to be taught. In order to develop an effective intervention to teach these skills, it is important to determine whether the lack of skills is the result of a performance deficit or a skill deficit (Duhon et al., 2004). A *performance deficit* refers to the failure to perform a skill as a result of insufficient motivation. In this case, the student may have the ability to perform the skill but lacks the motivation to do so. A performance deficit may also be the result of problematic behavior such that compliance with instructions tends to decrease with higher levels of inappropriate behavior (Parish, Cataldo, Kolko, Neef, & Egel, 1986). In this situation, the goal of intervention is not to teach a new skill but to focus on treating the interfering problem behavior or to address the student's motivation to perform in the classroom. FBAs are useful when the performance deficit is a result of problem behavior, while preference assessments are useful when the performance deficit is to the result of insufficient motivation.

A *skill deficit* refers to a student's inability to perform a given task because of a lack of knowledge or training in that skill area. In this case, the skill needs to be targeted for intervention and effective prompting strategies need to be identified and implemented. Effective prompting strategies can be drawn from the results of the skill assessment wherein those skills at which the child is particularly good can be used to help teach the child new or more difficult tasks. For example, a child may be particularly good at reading but have difficulty learning to discriminate between pictures of objects. A textual prompt, in which the name of the object is written on the picture, may be an effective prompt to help teach the child the discrimination task.

When a skill assessment reveals that a child is able to perform a given skill, it is important to conduct further assessments to ensure that the child can perform that skill in all of the necessary contexts—with teachers and peers, in the classroom and on the playground, with a variety of materials—and will persist over time. The maintenance and generalization of skills can be assessed through repeated skill assessments across a variety of antecedent conditions and a number of observation periods. When a skill is consistently performed during the skill assessments, then the skill has maintained and generalized—the student knows it. When a skill is inconsistently performed, it should be targeted for continuing intervention to ensure that the student can maintain and generalize those tasks being taught.

In the absence of a skill assessment, the skills being taught to a student may be determined by variables other than the student's need to learn that skill. As a result, students may have interventions in place to teach skills that the child can already perform simply because it was the next target in the curriculum. As a result, students may spend precious time "learning" a skill that they already know how to perform. For example, Johnny has just learned to label the color red and now the teacher is beginning to teach him to label the color blue. In order to minimize errors, the teacher utilizes a prompt procedure that involves providing very obvious prompts and then gradually reducing those prompts as the student demonstrates correct responding. The teacher begins by modeling the behavior for Johnny, saying "blue" as she shows him the color blue. Johnny is very successful with this prompt so the teacher eliminates part of the prompt and just says "bl" as she shows him the color blue. Again, Johnny is successful, so the teacher finally eliminates the prompt and simply shows Johnny the color blue. Johnny is able to say "blue." After several teaching episodes, the teacher is confident that Johnny is able to label the color blue and begins to teach Johnny the color green.

However, the teacher did not perform a skill assessment prior to teaching Johnny to label the color blue, so it is not clear whether Johnny was already able to label the color blue or if his success was due to the effective teaching procedures. Going back to our example, before teaching Johnny to label the color blue, the teacher conducts a skill assessment. The teacher presents Johnny with several different blue objects and pictures and asks Johnny "what color" they are. Johnny is able to accurately perform this skill with a variety of materials. Now the teacher knows that Johnny is able to label the color blue and she does not spend time trying to teach him that skill. Instead, the teacher evaluates whether Johnny can label the color green. Following the assessment, it is clear that Johnny may not know the color green, and the teacher begins teaching him this skill. By evaluating Johnny's ability to perform skills before teaching them, the teacher is able to ensure that precious time was spent only teaching those skills that Johnny needs to learn.

Preference Assessment

Reinforcement is defined as the process in which a behavior is followed by a particular consequence, and as a result that behavior is more likely to occur again in the future (Cooper et al., 2007). In other words, the probability of a behavior increases because of the consequences that followed it. For example, when Tyler waits patiently in line at the cafeteria, rather than pushing other kids out of the way as he usually does, we know that we should reinforce his calm, quiet, waiting behavior if we want him to wait patiently the next time. The same thing is true for teaching a child to share nicely. For example, when Mayah asks her classmate for the toy car instead of yanking it out of his hand, reinforcing that behavior will encourage Mayah to start sharing nicely more often with her classmates.

The consequence that produces the increase in behavior is called the *reinforcer* (Cooper et al., 2007). While reinforcers can be either positive (giving a child something preferred) or negative (removing something aversive), positive reinforcers are frequently used in the classroom to strengthen students' desirable behavior. Positive reinforcers can include

> ➤ attention, such as praise;
> ➤ toys, such as a prize from the treasure box;
> ➤ access to activities, such as computer time;
> ➤ tokens, such as stickers; and
> ➤ anything else a child may enjoy.

Negative reinforcers can include removal of aversive objects, such as worksheets, and breaks from aversive activities, such as circle time.

Many of the naturally occurring consequences for good behavior in the classroom will function as reinforcers for most students. Most students like to be told they are doing well, enjoy access to classroom activities or supplies that are typically limited (e.g., computer, class pet, special toys), and welcome the occasional class party or chance to choose from the treasure box. However the specific consequence that will function as a reinforcer for a given student will vary based on that child's unique experiences and preferences. For example, Tyler may like it when his teacher tells him he did a "good job," but his classmate Sally may not like this type of public recognition.

This poses a particular concern for students with ASD. Since two of the core deficits are social and communication skills, many consequences for good behavior, such as praise, may not function as reinforcers for these students. These students may not understand the difference between praise and corrective feedback, social praise may not be meaningful for them, and social interactions may be very difficult, making them aversive rather than enjoyable for the student. Additionally, students with ASD often need more frequent and salient reinforcers for smaller steps and greater repetitions when learning new skills. As a result, the identification of effective reinforcers is a critical component to any skill-building intervention. Furthermore, the identification of effective reinforcers is fundamental to response reduction interventions designed to teach replacement behaviors, such as asking for help instead of crying when difficult tasks are presented.

Effective positive reinforcers can be identified through the use of preference assessments. A *preference assessment* is the process of identifying those objects, activities, and events that the individual likes and the relative value of each. (Cooper et al., 2007). In other words, a preference assessment identifies consequences that will likely function as effective reinforcers when provided contingently on behavior. By evaluating a student's preference for particular items and events, the teacher can identify those that will motivate the student to behave in particular ways and increase the efficacy of his or her skill-building and response-reduction interventions (Carr, Nicolson, & Higbee, 2000; Vollmer, Marcus & Leblanc, 1994).

In the absence of preference assessments, the consequences for good behavior in the classroom tend to be the same for all students regardless of a student's particular preference. As a result, students may make very little or no progress in learning new skills because the consequences provided for doing so are not reinforcing. Furthermore, this lack of progress can result in unnecessary and ineffective modifications to the teaching procedures in an attempt to increase the student's success. Such modifications are unlikely to be effective given the lack of functional reinforcers. For example, Johnny's IEP includes a goal to respond to greetings from his classmates in 8 out of 10 opportunities without assistance. Occasionally, Johnny will respond to greetings, and when he does the teacher gives Johnny a high five and a sticker. However, Johnny has been working on this goal for most of the school year and has made very little progress. The teacher has tried several different strategies to try to teach Johnny to respond to peers including role playing, video modeling, and visual modifications, none of which have been successful. Johnny continually needs to be reminded to respond to greetings, and the teacher starts to believe that this goal is just too difficult for Johnny, given his general lack of social skills. Unfortunately, the lack of a preference assessment resulted in ongoing failure. The teacher did not know whether the student's lack of progress was due to a skill deficit or a lack of motivation and erroneously assumed that the child's failure was a result of skill deficits. However, in our example, the student was able to perform the skill, at least occasionally, but was not motivated to engage in this task because the consequence for doing so was not reinforcing for this student. After conducting a preference assessment, the teacher learned that Johnny really enjoys a particular book in his classroom. Now, each time Johnny responds to greetings from his peers, the teacher gives him a few minutes to look at this book. Soon, Johnny is returning greetings from his peers on a regular basis, meets his IEP goal, and the teacher can introduce a new goal in the area of social skills. By identifying an effective reinforcer, the teacher was able to ensure that the intervention was successful.

BASIC PARAMETERS OF BEHAVIORAL ASSESSMENTS

Behavioral assessments are dynamic, in that procedures vary in accordance with the purpose and type of assessment conducted. However, all behavioral assessments share some basic parameters of timing, setting, and administration that increase the accuracy and reliability of information obtained. These general guidelines include when and where assessments are conducted as well as guidelines regarding who should develop and implement behavioral assessments.

When to Conduct Assessments

Assessment is an ongoing process that should occur before, during, and after intervention. First, assessment should precede the development of an intervention. By conducting assessments before developing an intervention, you can be sure that you create an intervention that actually targets the right behavior, whether it is building a new skill or reducing a problem behavior. Pretreatment assessment also helps ensure that the treatment plan will be effective, because it can help identify the reason why the behavior is or is not occurring, and that information will help point to ways to remedy the situation. Additionally, assessment before intervention will identify motivational variables that will enhance the efficacy of the intervention.

Once an intervention has been developed, the assessment process continues throughout the implementation of that intervention. Frequent assessment during intervention is important, because it helps ensure that the intervention is truly effective. Ongoing assessment to monitor the intervention is necessary to make sure that the student is actually learning and engaging in new skills and that the problem behavior is being reduced. Without ongoing assessment it is possible that effective interventions will be discontinued prematurely. When assessment information is available and someone says the plan is not working, the team can review the assessment data and objectively determine whether the child is making progress. Similarly, in the absence of ongoing assessment, ineffective interventions may continue to be implemented for much too long. Ongoing assessment allows the teacher to identify when the intervention has been successful and the child has mastered a new skill or a problem behavior has been effectively treated.

Lastly, assessment should not cease upon completion or termination of the intervention procedures. Rather, the results of the intervention should continue to be monitored and assessment conducted to ensure that the treatment effect endures once the intervention is removed or modified. In other words, once the student learns a new skill, it is important to make sure that the student continues to perform that skill over time and in all appropriate contexts. So once Billy learns how to say "hi" to several children in his class, the teacher can assess whether Billy continues to say "hi" to his friends throughout the remainder of the school year and to new children he encounters on the playground. Likewise, after treating a student's problem behavior, it is good practice to assess whether the reduction in problem behavior persists after the student is out of school for a week on spring break or when a substitute teacher is leading the class.

Where to Conduct Assessments

Assessments should be conducted in a setting that will provide the most accurate, reliable, and useful information to guide effective interventions. If assessments are inaccurate or unreliable, the assessor will have very little confidence in the results, and the assessment does not provide much help in developing an effective intervention for the student. The greater the number of uncontrolled variables introduced to the assessment process, the less accurate and reliable the results are. As a result, it is often desirable to conduct assessments in a contrived setting, where the assessor is able to control most of the environmental variables to evaluate their effect on the child's behavior (Repp, 1994).

One of the drawbacks of using controlled assessment settings is the lack of naturally occurring antecedents and consequences. It is possible that variables assessed in a contrived setting do not have the same effect on the student's behavior as naturally occurring variables. If assessments are conducted in a setting that does not provide information relevant to the child's daily performance and needs, then the assessment results will not be helpful.

When determining the most appropriate setting to conduct an assessment, the decision must take into account the accuracy, reliability, and validity of the results. Often a blend of natural and contrived settings will lend very useful information in guiding the assessment. This can be done by controlling for as many variables as possible within the natural environment and measuring and accounting for any uncontrolled variables in the analysis of assessment results. The decision of where to conduct the assessment will be also be influenced by the student's individual needs as well as the needs of the classroom and school in which the assessment is conducted. For example, it may not be feasible to conduct an assessment on a child's severe aggression towards peers in the natural classroom environment if it puts other students at risk. In this case, it may be necessary to conduct the assessment in a resource room when other students are not present.

Who Conducts Assessments

As with any educational procedure, assessments should only be conducted by individuals trained in that assessment procedure. The level of training necessary for each type and level of assessment will vary, but as a general rule, the training requirements will increase as the complexity, severity, and importance of the behavior being assessed increases. It is likely that many assessments will need to be conducted by individuals who are extensively trained, while other assessments can and should be implemented by the student's teacher or aide after minimal training (Iwata et al., 2000). It is also possible that in some situations, the student's behavior is of such complexity or severity that external consultation with a specialist is necessary to adequately assess the student's behavior and develop an effective intervention. However, even in this situation, the school personnel, teacher, and classroom aide will likely participate in the assessment process by providing background information, assistance in implementation of the assessment procedure, and feedback on the social validity of the assessment results.

ASSESSMENT METHODS

While the exact format and nature of each assessment will vary based on the student's needs, teacher's needs, and goal of the assessment, there are three basic assessment methods:

1. Indirect
2. Direct
3. Experimental

Each method of assessment has several advantages and disadvantages that must be considered when deciding which assessment or combination of assessment methods will be used in the development of an effective intervention for a particular student.

Indirect Assessment

Indirect assessments involve gathering information through informant assessments. Informant assessments involve written or verbal reports or both from the student or others familiar with the student and behavior being evaluated. Informant assessments can (Wallace, Kenzer, & Penrod, 2004):

➤ be structured, semistructured, or unstructured;
➤ include questions about setting events, antecedents, consequences, and topography of behavior;
➤ involve questionnaires, checklists, rating scales, or interviews; and
➤ gather information about potential functions of behavior, skill performance, student motivation, as well as other variables that may influence the occurrence of behavior, such as daily schedules and physiological factors.

The purpose of indirect assessments is to gather sufficient information to develop a hypothesis about the student's behavior and motivation in order to develop an effective intervention.

Indirect assessments are particularly useful in the preliminary stages of assessment. Information gathered through student, parent, and teacher report can help identify potential functions of behavior, sources of motivation, and skills to be taught. Indirect assessments can help identify appropriate observation periods for further assessment, refine the definition of the behavior being assessed, and establish buy-in for assessment-based treatment.

While indirect assessments can be useful in the development of a hypothesis regarding a student's behavior, it does not allow for a cause–effect, behavior–environment relationship to be determined. Assessors are only able to make educated guesses about a student's behavior and motivation when indirect assessments are used. Furthermore, the indirect method of assessment is the method most likely to produce inaccurate and unreliable results (Sigafoos, Kerr, Roberts, & Couzens, 1993). Indirect assessments rely on the report and memory of people who may be unfamiliar with assessing behavior. As a result, informants may fail to recall, recognize, and report important information. Information obtained is likely to be restricted in nature, based on a very small sample (i.e., the most recent instance of a problem behavior), and include irrelevant, subjective information.

Functional Behavior Assessment

Indirect FBAs are common in the educational setting, because they allow the assessor to gather information from a variety of sources to ensure that further assessments and interventions are guided in the right direction. An example of an indirect assessment method is a teacher interview. The assessor conducts an interview with the teacher regarding her student's problem behavior. During the interview the teacher reports that the student engages in silly, disruptive behavior when he is bored, and the last time this happened, the teacher redirected the student to begin the next activity on his schedule. However, the teacher forgot to report that the other students in the class also laughed when this behavior occurred. As a result, the interviewer is provided with some very useful information about the consequences of the student's behavior involving teacher attention. However, the interview did not produce an objective, specific description of the antecedent conditions that precede the disruptive behavior, because it failed to provide information about other potentially relevant variables influencing the behavior such as other children laughing.

Skill Assessment

Indirect skill assessments can be particularly useful because of the vast number of different skills that need to be evaluated for any given student. The speed and ease of informant assessments makes them ideal for simultaneously assessing multiple skills. By asking teachers and parents about the student's abilities, the assessor can get a good sense of the child's skills within a variety of domains within a matter of minutes. For many students, this type of informant assessment will reveal several skills the student is definitely able to perform as well as those the child definitely cannot. However, for many students, the indirect assessment will also reveal uncertainty about a number of the skills assessed. The teacher or parent may not know whether a student can perform a given skill because they have not had opportunity to observe it. For example, when asked if the student can read the word "their," the teacher says, "I don't know, I have never asked him to read that word." Uncertainty about a student's ability may also occur when the child performs the skill inconsistently or the child partially performs the skill.

Preference Assessment

One of the simplest means of assessing preference is by asking the student and others familiar with the student what he or she likes. This type of informant assessment can be very quick and easy to conduct and can provide some valuable information. For some students, this is a fairly easy way to get a long list of items and activities that they like. However, for many students with ASD, simply asking them what they want is not possible or very accurate because of a lack of functional language skills. The student may not be able to recall more than a few toys or games he or she likes. The student may like items but not know the names of them to be able to tell anyone. Furthermore, students may report they like something when, in actuality, they do not.

Other informants, such as teachers, parents, caregivers, siblings, and classmates, can provide additional information about potential reinforcers as well. However, it is important to evaluate the accuracy and reliability of informant reports. Research has indicated that, while informants may be able to identify some potential reinforcers, they are not always very good at predicting what another person likes or what will work as a reinforcer to increase someone else's behavior (Green et al., 1988; Resetor & Noell, 2008). For example, Sam's teacher reports that he likes to play on the computer, color, and play cards, but she does not know whether those activities would motivate Sam to do his math homework. Similar to asking the students themselves, other informants may not be able to recall many potential reinforcers, may identify items that the student does not like, or may be unaware of items and activities the student likes. As a result, indirect assessments frequently need to be supplemented with other strategies for identifying positive reinforcers.

Direct Assessment

A direct assessment involves directly observing and recording the student's behavior, antecedents, consequences, and other relevant stimuli as they occur (Thompson, & Iwata, 2001). The observation of behavior typically occurs in the natural environment, such as the classroom, school playground, or cafeteria. Observations are typically conducted at a time and location in which the behavior is most likely to occur, as identified through informant assessments. Observations can be structured in the form of checklists, in which observed events are checked off as they occur, or narrative in nature, in which the observer writes details of the observation in an open-ended format. The purpose of the direct assessment is to observe and record these events and stimuli in order to identify the variables associated with the behavior in the natural environment (Fox, Gunter, Davis, & Ball, 2000).

Direct assessments gain an advantage over the indirect assessment method because they do not rely on memory of past events. Rather, the events are observed and recorded as they occur. Additionally, direct assessments are conducted by trained observers who know how, what, and when to record behavior, so it is much more likely that specific, objective, and relevant information is gathered. The accuracy of the information is also increased with direct observation of the behavior. These advantages are not without cost, however. Direct assessments take more time and effort to conduct, and the act of observing may interfere with the typical occurrence of behavior in the natural environment. For instance, the teacher, student, and classmates may behave differently when an observer is present and recording data, or the behavior may not occur during the observation period. While efforts can be made to reduce the effects of reactivity to an observer, this is always a possibility and can affect the accuracy of the information collected.

Functional Behavior Assessment

Direct FBAs involve observing and recording the antecedents and consequences for problem behaviors. Direct assessments can provide strong support for a hypothesized function, particularly when behavioral observations match reports provided in the indirect assessment. Using information gathered through an indirect FBA, the assessor can develop a checklist with the antecedents and consequences thought to be associated with the problem behavior listed. While observing the student, the assessor is able to check off which antecedents and consequences actually occurred and evaluate which of those events are contributing to the student's problem behavior. For example, when observing Cal, each time he is given spelling worksheets he bangs his desk. The teacher reminds Cal to keep his hands calm and to ask for a break if the work is too hard. As a result of the observation, it becomes clear that Cal bangs his hand on the desk when he is given spelling work and the consequences for doing so include teacher attention and escape from the task for a short time.

While very clear antecedents and consequences for problem behavior can be identified, a functional relationship is still not possible to determine based on the results of a direct assessment. Direct assessments allow for the identification only of correlations among behavior, stimuli, and environmental events. In other words, direct assessments establish a relationship between behavior and the environment, but cannot verify that one causes the other. In order to determine a functional relationship, experimental methods must be used.

Skill Assessment

Direct skill assessments involve observing the student and recording if and when a student performs a particular skill, given the opportunity to do so. By conducting a direct assessment, the assessor is able to follow up on those skills that informants were uncertain about. Direct skill assessments are typically conducted in a structured format with a predetermined set of skills to be assessed. The assessor observes the child in the natural environment when opportunities to perform that skill are likely to occur. For example, when observing the student reading, the child comes to the word "their," and the assessor records whether the student read the word correctly or not.

While this direct assessment of the student's skills can reveal accurate and useful information, the opportunity to perform the skill is not always present during direct observations, and, as a result, the assessor is unable to gather useful information. Likewise, the student may behave differently with the assessor present, and this may alter the probability that the student will perform the skill, making the validity of the assessment results questionable.

Preference Assessment

Direct preference assessments involve observing the student in the natural environment and recording current reinforcers maintaining other behaviors as well as items and activities that the child engages in frequently and seems to enjoy (Hanley, Cammilleri, Tiger, & Ingvarsson, 2007). Direct preference assessments involve recording the consequences for behavior that occurs frequently and noting the frequency and duration of interaction with items or activities that the child requests and has access to during the day. The purpose of the direct assessment is to observe and record the events that the student enjoys in order to identify those items and activities currently functioning as reinforcers in the natural environment.

Returning to the example of Tyler learning to wait patiently in line in the cafeteria, the assessor notes that when Tyler pushes students out of the way, he typically ends up near the front of the line and waits less time to get his lunch. As a result of the direct observation, the assessor has learned that Tyler prefers to wait a short duration to get his food. This consequence can now be used to teach Tyler to wait patiently in line. Now the teacher allows Tyler to move to the front of the line if he waits patiently in line for several minutes. Gradually, the teacher increases the amount of time Tyler has to wait in line patiently before he can move to the front of the line, and soon Tyler is waiting patiently in line every day.

Identifying the current reinforcers for problem behaviors will often reveal a powerful reinforcer that can then be used to increase the frequency of a more appropriate alternative behavior. However, it is not always easy to identify a current reinforcer for a current behavior and use it to reinforce a new one. Furthermore, identifying a student's current reinforcers does not always provide a very large list or a wide enough variety of reinforcers to use throughout a person's day, week, month, and so on to increase a variety of behaviors.

In addition to observing and identifying current reinforcers, a direct preference assessment involves watching the student and identifying activities the student engages in often and seems to enjoy. In this way, the assessor is able to identify high-rate behaviors that are likely to be things the person finds enjoyable, fun, pleasant, and entertaining. For example, if you can usually find Jack swinging at recess, then swinging is probably on Jack's list of preferred items and will likely function as a positive reinforcer. Likewise, if Adam is always selecting blocks and coloring during free play, the assessor can be fairly confident that both blocks and coloring are on Adam's list of potential reinforcers, and that giving Adam access to these items contingent on some behavior is going to increase the probability of that behavior occurring again in the future. By simply watching and noting what a student likes to do, the assessor can develop a useful list of potential reinforcers.

An advantage of the direct assessment is the reliance on observation rather than memory to identify current and potential reinforcers. By observing the student, the assessor is able to see what consequences are commonly used in the student's classroom, which of those consequences seem effective in strengthening the students behavior, and which activities the child requests and selects when given an opportunity to choose among available options. As a result, it is much more likely that a greater array of potential reinforcers will be identified, that those items will readily be available in the students natural environment, and that more specific information about the potential reinforcer's effectiveness will be gathered.

Direct preference assessments are not without disadvantage. While direct assessment allows the assessor to identify a variety of potential reinforcers, it does not provide specific information about the student's relative preference for those items and activities. In other words, a direct assessment provides a list of preferred items for a given student but does not indicate what items a student likes the most, the least, or somewhere in between. By identifying those items that are more preferred than others, the teacher can reserve these potential reinforcers for teaching skills that are particularly difficult for the student when greater motivation is necessary.

Experimental Assessment

Experimental assessments involve the systematic manipulation of environmental events in order to evaluate the student's behavior. In other words, the assessor introduces specific antecedent events, provides particular consequences for student behavior, or both in order to determine the conditions under which a student is likely to behave in particular ways. Experimental analyses are extremely helpful when developing skill-building and response-reduction interventions. By conducting experimental analyses, the assessor can be very confident about the assessment results and gather useful information.

However, one major disadvantage to experimental assessments is the time and effort required to conduct in comparison to indirect and direct assessment methods. Additionally, experimental assessments often require substantially more training, and most educators are unfamiliar with this type of behavioral assessment method. As a result, experimental assessments are more likely to be conducted by consultants.

Another disadvantage of the experimental assessment method is the fact that they are frequently conducted in very controlled settings, such as a resource room or an empty classroom that can be quite different from the child's natural environment. However, research has demonstrated the efficacy of experimental assessments conducted in the child's natural environment with experimental conditions that mimic and coincide with the child's daily schedule and naturally occurring activities (Hanley et al., 2007).

Even given these disadvantages, the experimental functional analysis has a major advantage over the indirect and direct assessment methods. While the indirect and direct assessment methods allow the assessor to make an educated guess about the student's behavior, the experimental assessment is the only method that allows assessors to identify cause–effect relationships between the environment and behavior.

Functional Behavior Assessment

An experimental FBA is referred to as a functional analysis (FA). The FA involves systematic manipulation of the antecedents, consequences, or both associated with problem behavior to identify those stimulus conditions maintaining the problem behavior (Cooper et al., 2007). The standard FA procedures include four basic conditions, presented in a rotating format:

1. Alone or no interaction
2. Attention
3. Play
4. Demand

A fifth condition, tangible, may be included when necessary. Each condition involves the presentation of various antecedents and consequences in order to test for a particular function of behavior (Iwata, Dorsey, Slifer, Bauman, & Richman, 1982/1994). For example, Johnny has been hitting other children in the class. A behavioral consultant is conducting an FA on Johnny's hitting with the teacher's assistance. During the alone or no interaction condition, the teacher is instructed to ignore any instances of hitting in order to determine whether Johnny will continue to hit even when people do not react to it. During the attention condition, the teacher is instructed to ignore Johnny until he hits, at which time the teacher provides brief vocal and physical attention such as touching his shoulder while saying, "Johnny, remember the rules." The attention condition is designed to determine whether Johnny will hit when it produces attention from the teacher. In the demand condition, the teacher is instructed to present Johnny with several consecutive instructions that are typically associated with hitting. Each time Johnny hits, the teacher will give Johnny a brief break from the demands in order to determine whether Johnny will hit under these conditions. In the tangible condition, the teacher is instructed to give Johnny a preferred toy, food, or activity for a few minutes before taking them away. The teacher then gives the preferred item(s) back to Johnny each time he hits in order to determine whether Johnny will hit when things are taken from him. Finally, the play condition is considered the control condition against which each of the test conditions are compared. In the play condition, the teacher is instructed to give Johnny brief attention every few seconds, allow Johnny to play with preferred toys, and not present any instructions. Additionally, the teacher is instructed to ignore any instances of hitting. The results of the FA indicate that Johnny does not hit very often during the play, alone, attention, or tangible conditions. Johnny does hit frequently, though, during the demand condition, indicating Johnny hits to escape doing difficult work.

As you can see in the above example, the experimental functional analysis involves a greater amount of time, effort, and training to implement than the indirect or direct functional assessments. Often, it is necessary to have a consultant design the FA conditions, evaluate the necessary methodological and procedural variations, train the teachers or aides who may participate in the assessment, and ensure everyone's safety. However, it is possible to train teachers and parents to implement the functional analysis conditions with relatively brief training (Wallace, Doney, Mintz-Resudek, & Tarbox, 2004). Also, FAs can often be conducted in a relatively short period of time with the use of the brief FA, in which experimental conditions are implemented for only a few minutes at a time (Wallace & Iwata, 1999). Additionally, in those situations where the child's problem behavior is particularly severe or dangerous, experimental FAs can be conducted on precursor behaviors. By conducting the FA on less intense problem behaviors (e.g., screaming) that typically precede more severe problem behaviors (e.g., hitting), the probability of severe problem behavior occuring during the assessment is reduced, thereby reducing the risk of injury or property destruction. (Borrero & Borrero, 2008; Langdon, Carr, & Owen-DeShryver, 2008; Najdowski, Wallace, Ellsworth, MacAleese, & Cleveland, 2008; Smith & Churchill, 2002).

Skill Assessment

Experimental skill assessments include presenting the student with particular antecedent stimuli associated with the skill being assessed in order to determine whether the child will consistently perform the skill with accuracy. The experimental skill assessment is advantageous because it eliminates the uncertainty of indirect assessments and avoids some of the problems of the direct assessment. With an experimental skill assessment, the assessor can present antecedent events rather than watch and hope those opportunities present themselves in order to assess the student's response to them.

The experimental assessment also allows the assessor to evaluate the student's response to a variety of antecedent events to ensure that known skills have generalized to all appropriate contexts. For example, when determining whether Sam is able to recognize his name in print, the assessor presents Sam with several cards with different names written on them such as Sam, Sally, and Scott. The assessor then asks Sam to point to or show the card with his name on it. If Sam touches the card with his name on it, the assessor records the response as correct. If Sam touches another card, the assessor scores the response as incorrect. The assessor will repeat this assessment several times using a variety of materials including names on desks, folders, and worksheets in order to determine whether Sam consistently identifies his own name when given an array of similar names to select from. Sam inconsistently selects items with his name on it and frequently selects items with other names beginning with the letter S. As a result of the assessment, Sam's teacher knows that she needs to teach Sam to recognize his name in print.

Preference Assessment

Experimental preference assessments involve the systematic manipulation of antecedent and consequent events to determine which items and activities an individual will select and engage with when given the opportunity to do so. An experimental preference assessment involves a comparison of the frequency with which items are selected and the duration of engagement with those items for a variety of potential reinforcers. Those items selected most often or engaged in for the longest duration are considered most preferred while those items that are rarely or never selected and result in the shortest duration of interaction are considered least preferred. High-preference items are more likely to function as reinforcers than low-preference items.

Experimental preference assessments allow the assessor to develop a larger number and variety of potential reinforcers as well as to create a hierarchy of preference. Identifying a hierarchy of preference is important to match reinforcers to the skills being taught. When teaching a behavior that is difficult for the student, requires a lot of effort to complete, takes a long time to finish, or is simply unpleasant, it is necessary to provide a reinforcer that is of greater value than one that may be used to increase the frequency of an easier, less effortful, or more pleasant task. For example, to increase the probability that Jack is going to participate in social group, a very powerful reinforcer will be necessary, since the social group is so difficult for Jack. Jack may like swinging, but he might not like it enough to talk during social group. With experimental assessments, the assessor can determine how much Jack likes swinging relative to other preferred items. Then the teacher can make sure to give Jack a higher value item or activity when he talks during social group and let him swing contingent on some other easier, more pleasant behavior. An experimental FA is necessary to determine a student's relative preference for a variety of potential reinforcers.

Experimental methods can be used to identify preferred foods, leisure and play activities, or sensory stimuli that a student enjoys watching, feeling, tasting, hearing, and smelling (Deleon, Iwata, & Roscoe, 1997; Green et al., 1988; Parsons & Reid, 1990; Rincover & Newsom, 1985). Preference assessments have been used to identify the type of social interactions a student enjoys, the type of work assignments and academic tasks a student prefers, and even what residential options a person wants (Bambara, Ager, & Koger, 1994; Dunlap et al., 1994; Faw, Davis, & Peck, 1996; Fisher et al., 1992; Pace, Ivancic, Edwards, Iwata, & Page, 1985).

When conducting an experimental preference assessment, a variety of items and activities are selected to use in the assessment. These items and activities include

➤ those identified through previous indirect or direct preference assessments,
➤ those items that other students their age typically enjoy,
➤ items that are readily available in the classroom, as well as
➤ novel items that share some similarity with those items the child is known to like.

For example, through a direct assessment, the assessor knows Anna likes to play with a spinning top that plays music, so the assessor includes a new toy that also plays music in the experimental preference assessment. It is important to note that when novel items or activities are included in the experimental preference assessment, the student should have an adequate opportunity to explore new items and engage in new activities before assessing preference for them.

There are three basic experimental preference assessment formats:

1. Single stimulus presentation
2. Paired stimulus presentation
3. Group presentation

Each assessment provides different information, and therefore the appropriateness of each depends on the needs of the student. In the *single stimulus* preference assessment, the assessor presents the student with a variety of items and activities, one at a time, to see whether the student approaches each one (Pace et al., 1985). Those items that are approached are considered preferred. In addition to measuring approach, the duration of engagement with the item can be measured. Measuring the duration of engagement allows for a comparison of relative preference. If the goal of the preference assessment is to increase the number or variety of positive reinforcers, then a single stimulus presentation is the most appropriate preference assessment method.

If the goal of a formal assessment is to identify fewer, but perhaps more potent or powerful reinforcers, the paired presentation is more appropriate, because it provides distinct rankings from most to least preferred. In the *paired stimulus* preference assessment, the assessor presents the student with a variety of items and activities, two at a time, to see which, if any, the student likes the most (Fisher et al., 1992). Preference is measured by noting what the student selects during each of the pairings, and those items selected most frequently are considered most preferred.

If efficiency is a priority and preference among a small number of stimuli is acceptable, then the grouped procedure is most appropriate. The *group presentation* format is also known as the *multiple stimulus* preference assessment. In the group presentation format, the student is presented with a variety of items and activities, several at a time, to see which, if any, he or she likes the most (Windsor, Piche, & Locke, 1994; DeLeon & Iwata, 1996). Many aspects of group presentation preference assessments are similar to those for the single and paired stimulus presentation methods. The primary difference is that rather than present items one or two at a time, several items are presented simultaneously.

This preference assessment can be done in one of two ways: with or without replacement of the selected items. In the multiple stimulus with replacement format, after an item is selected from the group of options, that item is returned to the group and the student is allowed to select again. For example, when assessing Johnny's preference for a music player, bouncy ball, dinosaur, and car, Johnny is presented with all of the items at the same time, making sure that Johnny can see and reach all items. Once Johnny makes a selection, the car, he gets to play with the car briefly and all the other toys are removed from his reach. Once Johnny has played with the car for a short time, the car is removed, and in the multiple stimulus with replacement method, the car is placed back with the group of items, and Johnny is presented with the music player, bouncy ball, dinosaur, and car and allowed to select an item again.

In the multiple stimulus without replacement format, after an item is selected, it is removed from the group and the student is allowed to select from only the remaining items that have not yet been selected. Returning to the example with Johnny, after he selects the car, in the multiple stimulus without replacement method, the car is NOT placed back into the group of items that are re-presented to Johnny. Instead Johnny is only presented with the music player, bouncy ball, and dinosaur from which to select. This process is repeated until Johnny is presented with the single remaining item. Preference is measured in the same manner as the paired stimulus preference assessment—by noting which items are selected most frequently.

As with all experimental assessment methods, the experimental preference assessment gains an advantage over the indirect and direct assessments in providing objective, clear, and specific information about the student. Likewise, the major disadvantage is that it requires more time and effort to complete, particularly when assessing preference for activities. However, it is possible to conduct experimental preference assessments in relatively brief periods of time (Carr et al., 2000). In many cases, a small sample of the item or activity is sufficient to assess preference, such that the student gets a small bite of cookie rather than a whole cookie, plays the computer for 30 seconds rather than 15 minutes, or places one piece in the puzzle rather than completes the entire puzzle during the assessment.

While preference does contribute to a reinforcer's efficacy, it does not guarantee it, and preference can vary from hour to hour, day to day, and week to week (Carr et al., 2000). As a result, it is important to frequently assess preference, diligently update the list of potential reinforcers for a student, and check to make sure that these consequences are actually functioning to change a student's behavior.

UNDERSTANDING ASSESSMENT RESULTS

Each of the assessments described in this chapter has specific rules for scoring and interpreting data obtained during the assessment. As such, individual training on the specific types and methods of assessment is necessary to accurately implement as well as interpret assessment results. A clear understanding of assessment results is necessary before an intervention can be developed. The results of any assessment are stronger when multiple types of assessments are conducted and the results of each coincide with the others. In this case, it is much more likely that a successful intervention will be developed.

When assessment results provide insufficient information, only a single assessment type is used, or the results of multiple assessments are conflicting, it is necessary to conduct further assessments. For example, the interview with Johnny's teacher identifies attention and escape from demands as potential functions. However, the interview results from his aide indicate the behavior is maintained by attention and access to toys. The results are very unclear because of disagreement between these two sources. The assessor is not confident that the single assessment method with conflicting results has provided sufficient information to develop an adequate intervention. The assessor then conducts a direct observation and records the actual antecedent and consequent events that occur in the classroom to find that the behavior is frequently followed by attention. Based on the results of the indirect assessment in which both respondents identified an attention function and the direct assessment that identified an attention function, the assessor can be much more confident when developing an intervention to reduce Johnny's problem behavior.

When an assessment produces insufficient information to develop an intervention, it may also be necessary to modify the assessment methods. Many procedural and methodological variations exist for each type of assessment including the experimental assessments. It may also be necessary to bring in a consultant to conduct and interpret assessment results to obtain the most objective, accurate, reliable, clear, and useful information.

SUMMARY

This chapter provides an overview of three types of behavioral assessments that can be used to guide the development of interventions. Through FBAs, the cause or function of behavior can be identified and effective response reduction interventions developed. Skill assessments distinguish between performance and skill deficits, resulting in the selection of appropriate skill building interventions aimed at motivation, instructional strategies, or a combination of the two. Preference assessments aid in the development of response reduction and skill-building interventions by identifying potential reinforcers to strengthen desirable behavior.

The basic parameters of behavioral assessments were also presented in this chapter. In particular, guidelines regarding the frequency and timing of behavioral assessments, assessment settings, and assessor training requirements were reviewed. Behavioral assessments should be conducted prior to, during, and following the development and implementation of interventions. Assessments should be conducted in a setting that balances the advantages and disadvantages of contrived and natural settings while meeting the needs of the students and staff involved. Behavioral assessments should only be conducted by individuals trained in that assessment procedure, and the level of training necessary will vary in accordance with the complexity, severity, and importance of the behavior being assessed.

This chapter also presented three assessment methods in order of increasing accuracy, complexity, effort, and training required to conduct. Indirect assessments are faster and easier to conduct but have limited reliability; direct assessments gain accuracy and reliability as well as effort, time, and training requirements; and experimental assessments are the most complex yet valid and reliable method of assessment. Additionally, a description of how FBAs, skill assessments, and preference assessments are conducted with each of these methods was provided.

In summary, behavioral assessments should be used to guide the development of effective skill-building and response-reduction interventions. Assessments should be conducted frequently, in appropriate settings, by trained assessors, and they should include indirect, direct, and experimental methods as necessary. Finally, interpretation of assessment results will suggest effective teaching strategies, intervention methods, the need for further assessment, or a combination of these outcomes.

REFERENCES

Bambara, L., Ager, C., & Koger, F. (1994). The effects of choice and task preference on the work performance of adults with severe disabilities. *Journal of Applied Behavior Analysis, 27,* 555–556.

Borrero, C. S. W., & Borrero, J. C. (2008). Descriptive and experimental analyses of potential precursors to problem behavior. *Journal of Applied Behavior Analysis, 41,* 83–96.

Carr, J. E., Nicolson, A. C., & Higbee, T. S. (2000). Evaluation of a brief multiple-stimulus preference assessment in a naturalistic context. *Journal of Applied Behavior Analysis, 33,* 353–357.

Cooper, J. O., Heron, T. E., & Heward, W. L. (2007). *Applied Behavior Analysis* (2nd ed.). Upper Saddle River, NJ: Pearson.

DeLeon, I. G., & Iwata, B., A. (1996). Evaluation of a multiple-stimulus presentation format for assessing reinforcer preferences. *Journal of Applied Behavior Analysis, 29,* 519–533.

Deleon, I. G., Iwata, B. A., & Roscoe, E. M. (1997). Displacement of leisure reinforcers by food during preference assessments. *Journal of Applied Behavior Analysis, 30,* 475–484.

Duhon, G. J., Noell, G. H., Witt, J. C., Freeland, J. G., Dufrene, B. A., & Gilbertson, D. N. (2004). Identifying academic skill and performance deficits: The experimental analysis of brief assessments of academic skills. *School Psychology Review, 33,* 429–441.

Dunlap, G., dePercazel, M., Clarke, S., Wilson, D., Wright, S., White, R., et al. (1994). Choice making to promote adaptive behavior for students with emotional and behavioral challenges. *Journal of Applied Behavior Analysis, 27,* 505–518.

Faw, G. D., Davis, P. K., & Peck, C. (1996). Increasing self-determination: Teaching people with mental retardation to evaluate residential options. *Journal of Applied Behavior Analysis, 29,* 173–188.

Fisher, W., Piazza, C. C., Bowman, L. G., Hagopian, L. P., Owens, J. C., & Slevin, I. (1992). A comparison of two approaches for identifying reinforcers for persons with severe and profound disabilities. *Journal of Applied Behavior Analysis, 25,* 491–498.

Fox, J., Gunter, P., Davis, C. A., & Ball, S. (2000). Observational methods in functional behavioral assessment: Practical techniques for practitioners. *Preventing School Failure, 44,* 152–157.

Green, C. W., Reid, D. H., White, L.K., Halford, R. C., Britain, D. P., & Gardner, S. M. (1988). Identifying reinforcers for persons with profound handicaps: Staff opinion versus systematic assessment of preferences. *Journal of Applied Behavior Analysis, 21,* 31–43.

Hanley, G. P., Cammilleri, A. P., Tiger, J. H., & Ingvarsson, E. T. (2007). A method for describing preschooler's activity preference. *Journal of Applied Behavior Analysis, 40,* 603–816.

Hanley, G. P., Iwata, B. A., & McCord, B. E. (2003). Functional analysis of problem behavior. *Journal of Applied Behavior Analysis, 36,* 147–185.

Iwata, B. A., Dorsey, M. F., Slifer, K. J., Bauman, K. E., & Richman, G. S. (1994). Toward a functional analysis of self-injury. *Journal of Applied Behavior Analysis, 27,* 197–209. Reprinted from *Analysis and Intervention in Developmental Disabilities, 2,* 3–20, 1982.

Iwata, B. A., Wallace, M. D., Kahng, S. W., Lindberg, J. S., Roscoe, E. M., Conners, J., et al. (2000). Skill acquisition in the implementation of functional analysis methodology. *Journal of Applied Behavior Analysis, 33,* 181–194.

Langdon, N. A., Carr, E. G., & Owen-DeShryver, J. S. (2008). Functional analysis of precursors for serious problem behavior and related intervention. *Behavior Modification, 32,* 804–827.

Lerman, D. C., Vorndran, C., Addison, L., & Kuhn, S. A. C. (2004). A rapid assessment of skills in young children with autism. *Journal of Applied Behavior Analysis, 37,* 11–26.

Najdowski, A. C., Wallace, M. D., Ellsworth, C. L., MacAleese, A. N., & Cleveland, J. M. (2008). Functional analyses and treatment of precursor behavior. *Journal of Applied Behavior Analysis, 41,* 97–105.

Noell, G. H., Freeland, J. T., Witt, J. C., & Gansle, K. A. (2001). Using brief assessments to identify effective interventions for individual students. *Journal of School Psychology, 39,* 335–355.

Pace, G. M., Ivancic, M. T., Edwards, G. L., Iwata, B. A., & Page, T. J. (1985). Assessment of stimulus preference and reinforcer value with profoundly retarded individuals. *Journal of Applied Behavior Analysis, 18,* 249–255.

Parrish, J. M., Cataldo, M. F., Kolko, D. J., Neef, N. A., & Egel, A. L. (1986). Experimental analysis of response covariation among compliant and inappropriate behaviors. *Journal of Applied Behavior Analysis, 19,* 241–254.

Parsons, M. B., & Reid, D. H. (1990). Assessing food preferences among persons with profound mental retardation: Providing opportunities to make choices. *Journal of Applied Behavior Analysis, 23,* 183–195.

Repp, A. (1994). Comments on functional analysis procedures for school-based behavior problems. *Journal of Applied Behavior Analysis, 27,* 409–411.

Resetor, J. L., & Noell, G. H. (2008). Evaluating preference assessments for use in the general education population. *Journal of Applied Behavior Analysis, 41,* 447–451.

Rincover, A., & Newsom, C. D. (1985). The relative motivational properties of sensory and edible reinforcers in teaching autistic children. *Journal of Applied Behavior Analysis, 18,* 237–248.

Sigafoos, J., Kerr, M., Roberts, D., & Couzens, D. (1993). Reliability of structured interviews for the assessment of challenging behaviour. *Behaviour Change, 10,* 47–50.

Smith, R. G., & Churchill, R. M. (2002). Identification of environmental determinants of behavior disorders through functional analysis of precursor behaviors. *Journal of Applied Behavior Analysis, 35,* 125–136.

Taylor, B. A., & McDonough, K. A. (1996). Selecting teaching programs. In C. Maurice, G. Green, & S. Luce (Eds), *Behavioral intervention for young children with autism: A manual for parents and professionals* (pp. 63–177). Austin, TX: Pro-Ed.

Thompson, R. H., & Iwata, B. A. (2001). A descriptive analysis of social consequences following problem behavior. *Journal of Applied Behavior Analysis, 34,* 169–178.

Vollmer, T. R., Marcus, B. A., & Leblanc, L. (1994). Treatment of self-injury and hand mouthing following inconclusive functional analyses. *Journal of Applied Behavior Analysis, 27,* 331–334.

Wallace, M. D., Doney, J. K., Mintz-Resudek, C. M., & Tarbox. R. S. F. (2004). Training educators to implement functional analyses. *Journal of Applied Behavior Analysis, 37,* 89–92.

Wallace, M. D., & Iwata, B. A. (1999). Effects of session duration on functional analysis out-comes. *Journal of Applied Behavior Analysis, 32,* 175–183.

Wallace, M. D., Kenzer, A. L., & Penrod, B. (2004). Innovation in functional behavioral assessment. In W. L. Williams (Ed.) *Developmental disabilities: Etiology, assessment, intervention, and integration.* Reno, NV: Context Press.

Windsor, J., Piche, L. M., & Locke, P. L. (1994). Preference testing: A comparison of two presentation methods. *Research in Developmental Disabilities, 15,* 439–455.

Translating Assessment Results into Intervention Plans

M. Diane Bruening

Educational evaluations of students take significant time for the school personnel or outside providers that perform them. They utilize significant resources of the school and public education agency that pay for them and require significant time and effort on behalf of students and their families. All this work results in substantial information that, when well blended and sorted, becomes a plan of action for teachers and specialists working with a student with ASD. We now have the "who, why, what, how" for initial consideration of the individual for special education. We have educationally relevant medical, historical, and developmental information to apply in our plans and strategies. We have diagnostic results that give a realistic place to start with goals in a variety of areas—academic, speech, motor, social–emotional and behavior. Parents and possibly other providers have given input. Recommendations are written. With eligibility for special education comes services and supports packaged in intervention plans. The intervention plans start when individuals with ASD are very young and continue through the years to adulthood and beyond.

Percy has always been impossible to fully or accurately assess at least in the traditional sense. We don't know what he knows. He was diagnosed medically with ASD before age 3. While his parents have done extensive intervention on his behalf, he remains nonverbal and requires full aide assist in general education where he spends most of his school day. He is now in 6th grade. Even though the assessment results for him may be limited, his teachers, parents, and others have teased out important information, developed ideas for his services and school day, and implemented his intervention plans for him these past 9 years. Even with this quite limited information, his teachers were able to move forward with the next appropriate

—the interventions, adaptations and supports Percy needs to be successful in
ol.

DEVELOPING INTERVENTION PLANS

*Individualized education plans have been discussed for students of
all types in the political news in recent years. However, they are
required for and generally associated with students with disabilities
since 1975. Individual education programs (IEPs) have been
expanded and refined since that time into what they are today. They
have been described as a product, a written plan, but also as a
process, involving a multi-member team working together (Lee-Tarver,
2006).*

The IFSP: Birth to 3 Years

School provided services for children birth to 3 years of age first became available
through Part H of the Individuals with Disabilities Education Act (IDEA)
Amendments of 1986 (Murray et al., 2007). Children birth to age 3 born with or at
risk for disabilities in the United States are able to receive educational or public
school services through federal and state supported programs at no cost through
local public education agencies. Early intervention and services are important as
they make a major difference in outcome for children with disabilities like ASD
(National Research Council, Lord, & McGee, 2001).

Empirically based or research-based practices for early intervention have been
identified. Such programs (Stahmer, 2007)

- start early,
- are of high intensity,
- are derived from on-going assessment,
- are individualized, and
- focus on key characteristics like communication, behavior, and the like.

An Individual Family Service Plan (IFSP) is a written plan for providing early intervention supports and services. They are developed in many "birth to two" programs
and incorporate the present levels of the child, goals and specific services, and locations for invention that will be given in that time period noted in the plan. Additional
interventions often provided on an IFSP include speech, occupational, and physical
therapies; behavior management services; sensory integration; and transportation
(Stahmer, 2007). Parent education is another aspect of early intervention and may
frequently take place in the home, the most natural environment for infants and toddlers. Goals for an IFSP are often derived after informal assessment or observation
of the child and are efforts to improve the child's performance in the goal areas.
Common goals on IFSPs for infants and toddler with ASD include social and play

skills, self-help skills, behavior management, motor skills, sensory ii
readiness to learn (Stahmer, 2007).

Services given in the IFSP are usually delivered by professio.
directly with the child or with the parent or caregiver. In early interven..ug services,
increased attention is given to "identifying families, not just children, as the recipi-
ents of services" (Murray et. al, 2007, p. 112). Partnering with the family is supported by IDEA 2004 and professional and advocacy organizations such as Council
for Exceptional Children (CEC). Young children are often served on IFSPs in the
context of their family. Observing the child, giving tips on strategies, offering information on support groups, participating in meetings or appointments for the child,
and communicating with parents and agencies are frequent activities of the IFSP
providers. Some services are provided in a one provider–to–one child ratio.
Strategies suggested for the preschool setting, however, must be useful and possible
where the child–adult ratio is higher than the home setting and includes children
with many variations in functioning and other types of disabilities (Stahmer, 2007).
Services on an IFSP in preschool may be implemented in groups, large and small.

We know what elements contribute to results for children with ASD but quality
and sufficient depth are highly variable (Stahmer, 2007). Challenges for parents and
caregivers seeking early childhood programs are particularly acute in the area of
ASD. High demand, the often pervasive needs of young children with ASD, financial constraints on the part of families and agencies, and limitations in trained
providers for ASD intervention are common (Stahmer, 2007). Intensity and frequency of services provided have often been found to be less than recommended
(NRC, 2001). Few programssupport 20 to 30 hours per week that is research-based
(NRC, 2001), and nearly all parents must look for additional needed services
through health care providers covered by their insurance, government agency support, or private pay.

Supporting families in decision making in the development of IFSPs is a recommended practice in early intervention service (Murray et al., 2007), and professionals associated with services should serve as a guide, supporting family decision making (Murray et al., 2007). When those who develop IFSPs recognize family expertise
about their child, utilize family strengths, and research and identify options, families
are informed and supported (Murray et al., 2007). Considering the abilities, talents,
and preferences that family and caregivers bring to the table will result in better
IFSPs. Professionals should recognize appropriate interventions, share the pros and
cons of service options, and discuss needed resources and their availability (Murray
et al., 2007). As families and professionals make informed choices early on, families
of children with ASD can achieve their vision and goals. When family choice conflicts with professionals' views or research-based practice, challenges result.
Therefore, the partnership of professional and family is critical to successful early
intervention.

Percy first received early intervention services at about 2.8 years. A specialist
from the birth to two agency in his state made about five visits per month to his
home, one of them devoted to coordinating with all the providers involved and

informing everyone on the team about all the services Percy received and his progress. Percy was seen by speech, occupational, and physical therapists, and he was recommended for a community based social group with other toddlers. The specialist, in her visits, worked on structured play, building the child's interests as a bridge to new skills, and served as a resource to Percy's parents, all goals on his IFSP. By the time Percy was ready to transition to the school district's preschool at age 3, he displayed widely scattered skills, from about 15 months level in cognitive ability, social skills ranging from 12–22 months, and remaining nonverbal even though several methods were tried, including sign language.

The Individualized Education Program

The Individualized Education Program (IEP) is central to the educational provision of services to children in school years from kindergarten through graduation from high school, age5 up through age 22, with educational disabilities including ASD. Assessment has provided guidance to teams that participate in IEPs and helps families and educators to recognize the student's strengths and weaknesses, which helps in the development of appropriate services in the school setting that support learning. IEPs help teachers and families to focus on achievable goals in deficiency areas and focus teaching and related services for student performance improvements during the year the IEP is being implemented.

IEPs are federally required to include specific components:

➤ Present levels of academic achievement and functional performance (the student's current performance and needs in areas like social–behavioral, strengths, academics, progress on previous goals if appropriate)
➤ Who contributed to this information
➤ How the disability specifically affects the student's involvement and progress in the general curriculum

IEP teams must consider special factors and supports, devices, strategies, or plans needed in appropriate areas of communication, behavior, assistive technology, limited English, braille, and direct communication for students who are deaf or hard of hearing. Measurable goals and objectives or benchmarks to reach them if the student is in functional or modified curriculum are meant to lead toward additional and successful participation in general curriculum.

For transition at age 16, goals must be based on assessments related to training or further education, employment, and independent living skills when appropriate. Instructional adaptations are listed in the IEP for the student. Program supports are incorporated for any staff members and parents needing training, information, or assistanceto effectively work with the student. The IEP delineates participation in extracurricular and nonacademic activities as well as extent of participation with nondisabled peers; explanations are required for students not in general curriculum with typical peers. The IEP records participation in district and state assessments and specifies their nature and adaptations, particularly for testing The IEP specifies how goals are measured and how often progress is reported to parents. Students at age 16 must have transition services outlined in the IEP; at age 17, more information is added about expected rights and responsibilities of the student at age of majority. All services in special education or by therapist and the district are listed with a projected date of initiation, frequency, location, and the date the program will again be reviewed. The IEP asserts that the placement is based on the program, least restrictive environment (LRE) provisions, proximity to the student's home, and consideration of harmful effects on the student or on the quality of services. Extended school year services are designated for the student when appropriate, and this year's IEP goals are targeted for review and services the next year. IEPs are comprehensive!

Children with ASD exhibit neuro-developmental deficits in domains of communication, social skills, and behavior that must be addressed in school programs. Other comorbid conditions such as cognitive deficits, emotional problems, and adaptive deficits recognized in assessment often confound the process of developing service programs like IEPs (Kanne, Randolph, & Farmer, 2008). Evaluations of children with ASD assist educators in providing appropriate interventions in the classroom. Ideally, IEP services minimize symptoms of ASD and increase independence (Myers, Johnson, & Council on Children With Disabilities, 2007). School settings are perfect for many interventions for ASD as the focus is on learning, language, sensory and life skills, all core deficits in ASD. IEPs by their intent address improvement in deficit areas. IEPs for students with ASD must include attention to goals, adaptations and services in communication, social, and behavior areas in order to accomplish progress in these critical areas of school success (Wilczynski, Menousek, Hunter, & Mudgal, 2007).

By the mid fourth grade, Percy is in an inclusion setting with a full-time paraprofessional. Placing Percy in the general education setting was controversial for his previous classroom teacher and some others on the IEP team, but his parents were very sure it was best. The general education teacher this year seems more at ease with his presence in the classroom. Percy needs redirecting and assistance with academics, escorts around campus, and help or cues for communicating with staff and peers. He is able to handle transitions and changes in daily classroom routine. He follows routine classroom directions and safety commands such as "stop" or "wait."

While he will engage in play with classmates, he does not initiate conversations with peers, even in the small group special education environment. He smiles and sustains eye contact with very familiar people at school and demonstrates a sense of humor by laughing loudly when he is especially amused. The staff experimented with how Percy would demonstrate reading comprehension (i.e., multiple choice, matching, matching manipulatives), writing (i.e., cutting samples in three pieces for Percy to assemble in order, selecting and combining a connecting word and two sentences all on cards, using color stickers for correctly placing capitals and punctuation) and math (i.e., using number charts for facts, noting calendar and time through pictures, counting actual coins, using a measurement line). Most of these activities require an adult prompt to attend to the task.

Percy has an augmentative communication device provided by a state agency in collaboration with health insurance, but it is not yet ready with software and a trained staff member to program it daily with responses for the academic tasks that week. The district will have to find someone to assist with that job, up to one hour daily, because the speech therapist who might usually attend to this has an unusually busy caseload daily already. The speech therapist reports that Percy's communication skills are emerging and not generalized, requiring much prompting and manipulation of the environment, and she believes his receptive language seems more advanced than his ability to express language.

His parents requested a daily communication log from school so they can more closely monitor Percy's activities in school. They have outwardly expressed that they do not want their child relegated to a classroom corner, lacking instruction. The school team is baffled and wonders why a special education classroom full time would not be the preferred setting for Percy's learning. They talk about how much more time could be dedicated to Percy's particular instructional needs in a specialized classroom—they have personally seen how other students with ASD have progressed in such a classroom. Everyone seems on different pages. What Percy knows and can do and what is appropriate for IEP services is still debated.

Measurable Goals

Goals; modifications of curriculum, instruction, products, or environments; and behavioral supports are key components for IEPs for students with ASD (Kanne et al., 2008). Focusing on targeted areas like verbal and nonverbal communication, social competence, and adaptive behavior skills encourages growth in independence and responsibility—the intended outcome of school (Kanne et al., 2008). Because children with ASD may not speak, nonverbally communicate with success, understand social language, or engage in pretend play (Wilczynski et al., 2007), many school activities will require speech and language or communication support. Working on the acquisition of skills in communication areas likely requires work during the school years to generalize or to be successful under varying conditions (Wilczynski et al., 2007). "Give and take" and typical social interactions are continuous in school settings. Goals in communication around requesting, labeling, receptive language, conversation, spontaneous communication skills, greetings, nonverbal communication, and pragmatic language are important aspects of an IEP for students with ASD (Wilczynski et al.., 2007).

Maladaptive, restricted, and repetitive patterns of behavior are another hallmark of ASD that are often addressed in IEP goals for students. Stereotypic behaviors that may require attention include hand flapping, unusually postured fingers, or rocking back and forth (Wilczynski et al., 2007). Some children may use objects in restricted or inappropriate ways, such as staring continuously at clocks or rubbing endlessly in eraser crumbs. Repetitive behaviors are thought to interfere with acquisition of academic skills if not redirected or in social development because typical peers might shy away (Wilczynski et al., 2007). Interruptions of the restricted behaviors or unusual rituals by the day-to-day demands of classroom teachers and peers may cause the student with ASD to "meltdown," or tantrum or outburst inappropriately. Appropriate IEP goals in this area might include "identifies 'safe' and/or 'private' location to perform stereotypies" (Wilczynski et al., 2007, p. 660) and "uses thought-stopping strategies" (Wilczynski et al., 2007, p. 660).

IEP-listed adaptations and work with specialists can build student skill in the flexibility required for everyday school and classroom activities (Wilczynski et al., 2007). IEP teams should know that ritualistic and repetitive behaviors in ASD do not improve much with age (Attwood, 1998). Sometimes special interest areas of students with ASD, especially in those with HFA/AS (i.e., passionate and narrow interests) can be utilized as a strength. Instead of viewing special interest areas as quirky, solitary, ritualistic, or idiosyncratic behavior, teachers and specialists have the opportunity for very responsive adaptations to their usual and customary assignment or activity during instruction (Winter-Messiers, 2007) by allowing the student with ASD to study the instructional objectives of the day around their interest. Limited interests or restricted topics of their choice, however, can interfere in peer interactions. Working on IEP goals like "quickly assimilates new information into a conversation" (Wilczynski et al., 2007, p. 656) helps to expand interests and decrease repetitive behaviors which are critical to student learning and interaction in the classroom environment (Wilczynski et al., 2007).

Associated features of ASD may also require IEP goals and adaptations. Students may have diagnoses such as ADHD; a broad range of behaviors that are aggressive or self-injurious; learning difficulties; sleep, eating, or digestive difficulties; depression; anxiety; and safety concerns due to fearfulness or lack thereof (Wilczynski et al., 2007). Services from the special educator or related services from therapists designated in the IEP can support or address attention and distractions from learning. Covering the clocks in Percy's classroom so he does not stress out, getting additional individual or specific learning help during Resource sessions for reading and writing daily, allowing time outs for a walk outside when Percy gets overly anxious or starts noise-making, and providing incentive systems that highlight small-increment achievements are simple and easy for teachers to increase Percy's attention to instruction and to avert removals from class.

Sometimes academic skills are overlooked in the IEP for students with ASD, as considerable school time and resources are dedicated to services around the core characteristics of communication and social behavior. However, attention to academic skill development is necessary through the school years in order to avoid more restrictive school environments where peers are less likely to assist with social skill acquisition (Wilczynski et al., 2007). Balancing the IEP for services in academics can ensure that students with ASD are keeping up in the 3 Rs (reading, writing, and arithmetic) and, therefore, spending more time in the general education environment. More time in inclusion settings allows for correct models and reinforcement by age-appropriate peers for the communication and social deficits of ASD. Percy learns from all the others in his classroom, not just adults.

Identifying the conditions under which the target behavior is demonstrated is equally important for planning the IEP, since students with ASD have great difficulty transferring from one situation to the next (Wilczynski et al., 2007). Goals should not be considered mastered until they are generalized to new settings, when different people are present, and when different materials are used. IEP teams must write goals that encourage generalization and that represent age appropriate proficiency in navigating the school day, like"uses problem-solving solutions in context to avoid aggression," "deals with teasing appropriately," and "negotiates with peers" (Wilczynski et al., 2007, p. 659). At the same time, not all deficiency areas for a student with ASD can or should result in goals to be addressed each IEP. IEP teams must consider individual needs and prioritize goals that can be met in the nine or ten months of each school year. On the other side, IEP teams must be careful to avoid the temptation of focusing on limited domains of successful goal areas. Because school success is achieved across a broad range of skills, IEP attention should not be disproportionately narrow in focus (Wilczynski et al., 2007) but should be balanced for a student's more even development across the years.

At times in Percy's school years, the staff thought too much attention was given to speech acquisition. By the end of Percy's sixth-grade year, his lack of any speech is obvious. Percy can make a few sounds, say his name to the trained ear, and use his augmentative communication or aug com device with prompting. Teachers think they should now shift gears and attend to other goal areas like writing for communicating. Percy can use assistive technology, like his laptop, to indicate wants and needs and to express content knowledge in writing. Staff say that maybe lots of time on IEP goals in past years for teaching Percy to speak took away from time on learning more achievable skills. No one on an IEP team has a crystal ball.

IEPs are developed and implemented for 1 year, at which time it is federally required that the team involved with the student must review the plan. IEP goal attainment during the year should be tracked via data collection, hence the need for the IEP target goals and behaviors to be clearly objective and measurable (Wilczynski et al., 2007). IEPs are the outcome of a meeting each year, but they are also a guide to teachers and parents—to show improvements in specific areas, indicate student levels of performance in various need areas, and note what additional services and supports are necessary for access to general education or functional curriculum in school (Lee-Tarver, 2006. The IEP process is dynamic and always evolving with development, implementation, review, refinement, repeated at the successive IEP meetings.

Over the years, Percy's goals have always broadly addressed the core characteristics of ASD, communication and social defecits, plus academic areas. But each IEP year, Percy's team of school and district staff and his parents tweaked those goals and the conditions under which he was to demonstrate them for mastery. Some years, Percy's oral expression was a major focus, and his IEP was extensive with many goals and benchmark increments for fulfilling the communication area. Other years, demonstrating what Percy knows for reading and comprehending text and using his parent-provided laptop with voice software had the IEP team's attention.

Keeping the effective and reasonable in an IEP

Many students with ASD from age 3 to 22 (or beyond 22 in some states) receive the bulk, if not all, of their intervention in the school setting. "The best programs for children and youth with ASD appear to be those that plan for the unique styles and individualized needs of students by using a variety of objectively verified practices" (Simpson, McKee, Teeter, & Beytien, 2007, p. 216). Keep in mind that the isolated abilities and complex splinter skills associated with ASD (Simpson et al., 2007) make teaching such students challenging (Hessler & Konrad, 2008). A good place for teachers and specialists to begin would be focusing on the IEP's set of meaningful goals (Hessler & Konrad, 2008) and utilizing evidence-based instruction (Tincani, 2007) tailored on the explicit needs of students with ASD. However, the ever-dynamic schools and staff may be overburdened with demands and may lack resources or be unable to implement them with fidelity to support interventions (Tincani, 2007). Few practices for students with ASD are agreed as evidence-based, and few practical guidelines are used in implementing the practices when they are known (Simpson et al., 2007). "More curricula are available today but most of these resources are dedicated to one major area of deficit (e.g., social skills)" (Wilczynski et al., 2007, p. 664). Conditions that may coexist with ASD, like depression, anxiety, and high IQ, may be out of the teacher and specialist realm of expertise to address (Wilczynski et al., 2007). Practitioners must be aware, however, that the challenges associated with developing and implementing IEPs for students with ASD cannot excuse the team of teachers and specialists working with a student with ASD. All are accountable under the No Child Left Behind Act (NCLB) of 2001 to let no child get behind in learning, neglect exposure to general curriculum, or limit participation with their (neuro-) typical peers (Lee-Tarver, 2006). Qualified professionals, using effective methods in an approved fashion will achieve optimal student outcomes (Simpson et al., 2007).

Clearly written and appropriate goals "guide instruction most effectively" (Kanne et. al, 2008, p. 370). Additionally, understanding the function of behaviors and their role in daily routines will help IEP teams to select effective strategies. IEP work should not disrupt the schedules and routines of school, for if they do, they are not functional, natural, or likely to bring school success (Jung, Gomez, Baird, & Galyon Keramidas, 2008, p. 29). Also, the student likely will not be considered for placement in the general classroom if IEP work is too intensive to take place in that setting. Alienation or segregation of the student within the general classroom can result.

When addressing selected IEP goals, the educational team can discuss strategies to use for achieving desired results, though these are not required to be incorporated in IEPs themselves or required to be discussed at the IEP meeting. However, teachers and specialists can go a long way to developing parent and staff trust by sharing their knowledge about a variety of methods and research on effective practices to be used for reaching student IEP goals. As the IEP year begins, concrete examples and modeling of the instructional, communication, or behavioral strategy to be used with the student can ensure that all parties (i.e., parents, students, and general education teachers) are comfortable with and utilize the strategy themselves when appropriate and with fidelity (Jung et al., 2008). Using research-based interventions has been a focus since accountability emphases in NCLB and IDEA 2004. Use of strategies that are not working and have not been replicated in research is a waste of everyone's effort and time during IEP year. Students with any type disabilities have no time to waste with ineffective strategies or practices.

Teachers can and should actually use the IEP as a guide for producing student progress and achievement (Heward, 2008). Although teachers may find IEPs locked away elsewhere and not useful in day-to-day instructional planning and delivery (Lee-Tarver, 2006), our IEPs should be dog-eared and coffee-stained from frequent use (Baird, 2005). Quick notations of progress, attached to a portfolio folder of example work, all clipped to the IEP in a confidential but convenient location on a teacher desk or clipboard make the IEP a "working" document.

How do teachers know whether an IEP strategy or instructional practice does work? "Data collection is a vital part of the intervention design process and should be a tool with which teachers facilitate conversation with the family about their child's progress as well as used for subsequent evaluation and revision to the intervention plan and/or the IEP" (Jung et al., 2008, p. 32). Continuously assessing instruction pro- vides the data to determine impact on the student's performance and need for revi- sions in strategies and instruction and should be included in the next IEP meeting. Immediate and quick curriculum-based measurements implemented by teachers in their classrooms every day can be very responsive to shifts or changes in academic learning. Monitoring student progress can be straightforward for classrooms or home through the use of simple frequency charts or communication logs between home and school. Checklists with key words, dates, and setting are almost effortless to mark even every day, once collaboratively developed, and can serve as a valuable tool in instruction (Jung et al., 2008). Seeing student progress in the data collection tells teachers, specialists, and parents that learning across any dimension is occurring.

Evaluating the IEP at the end of the year is a team effort, too. Reviewing data collected as a team, including parents, therapists, general and special educators, and any outside personnel the district or parents choose, helps determine whether IEP change is in order for the new year. If slow or no progress on IEP goals is evidenced for the services and supports that service year, then adjustments are necessary in the new IEP. Goals, strategies, and supports must be reviewed for continuous, and no less than annual, progress. Changes in routine, concerns, and priorities can cause need for amendments to an IEP (Jung et al., 2008), even before one year is over.

Supports for personnel and family should be considered for an IEP and its adjustment. Training for all professionals and family can be important value added to an IEP any year. Teacher actions or lack thereof are critical to student success and learning. "Student access was affected more by instructional decisions or actions of the teacher than anything the student did, and the curriculum modifications and accommodations provided were both few and limited in scope and potential impact" (Lee, Wehmeyer, Palmer, Soukup & Little, 2008, p. 105). Teachers, specialists, therapists, school administrators, and paraprofessionals need extensive training on curriculum modifications and classroom accommodations in order to increase student access to curriculum and learning (Lee et al., 2008).

Services

Teachers find IEPs time-consuming to prepare (Lee-Tarver, 2006). IEPs should be developed not only to fit the student and his or her characteristics, but also with a sense of the variables of staff and environment for IEP implantation (Tincani, 2007). Three or four ways of serving a student may be possible and appropriate. No IEP needs to reflect "the" perfect service or services, nor is that usually possible. Congress likely was wise in writing into IDEA a directive for multidisciplinary IEP team membership, taking advantage of the various backgrounds, knowledge, and skills of each member. Multidisciplinary teamwork, ideas, and approach ensure balance and practicality in the IEP.

Inclusion may be an environment where students with ASD are unsuccessful, so care must be taken to plan inclusion thoroughly. Symptoms or characteristics of the student with ASD can preclude student and staff comfort in settings with others. Routine and consistency and help for the many transitions from activity and place during the school day will help students with ASD function more fully and avoid upheaval, meltdowns, and frustration for everyone (Lock & Layton, 2008). Considering the use of peers for tutoring increases opportunities for learning and student engagement (Van Norman, 2007). Well-selected and structured extracurricular activities and clubs with sensitive and accepting advisors can be meaningful for students with ASD who have social deficiencies and poor responses in competitive academic environments (Safran & Safran, 2001). Teacher attitudes about inclusion of students with a high number of needs, such as in disabilities like ASD, are little known (Cook, Tankersley, Cook, & Landrum, 2002). However, many teachers may worry about a high level of resources required to have the student with ASD in their classroom (Lee-Tarver, 2006). "The personality of the teacher may ultimately determine the child's success in school. The ideal teacher is patient, predictable, flexible, genuinely accepting of differences, calm, kind, and concerned with social, as well as academic development" (Safran & Safran, 2001, p. 390).

The teachers working with Percy would have welcomed some answers. Training was limited to 1 or 2 days a year for a specific provider or two and most often was done "on the fly" in the classroom while school was going on. If the teacher agreed, parent-provided training might occur, in the form of parent "volunteering" in the classroom to work with the teacher or aide, or observing the first few days of school and later offering ideas that could work better. The school staff working with Percy, however, often felt this was much less than optimal and were not always able to take advantage of suggestions when they were offered. Information on ASD was limited at the time Percy began at their school, and many discussions ensued about why Percy was in general education and not in a special classroom learning functional or life skill–type standards. Some years the speech therapist was a very primary provider of services to Percy and saw him extensively through the week. Other school years, the resource teacher had the hefty load of special education services, working with the nonverbal Percy on his reading, while the occupational therapist was at the side teaching him to type and write his thoughts and answers on paper.

Sometimes it seemed to the school team that IEP review meetings occurred too often for thorough efforts on the goals. . The school team felt tugged in competing directions with the constant ebb and flow of priorities, interests, and attention on the IEP—feeling pushed and pulled, trying many (and sometimes strange) activities, seeing limited continuity and agreement in direction. Progress was hard to see during the school year when new goals became the focus of several IEPs in a year. Now, though, Percy is moving to the secondary level of schooling. What to do and what works for him are now much more clear. The decision for services, goals, and environment in secondary school is more quickly accomplished. The IEP team, which has worked together for almost 10 years, knows Percy well and confidently sends him off to gain skills for independence, finding his preferences and interests for his future as a new focus of work, and increasing functional and adaptive skills in communication and social areas.

Percy was part of his IEP meeting and sat at the table with his parents and teaching team at the end of sixth-grade year. Percy was asked to provide input on his present levels of performance and interests to pursue at the secondary level. His parents seemed so pleased that he was asked. The deficits of ASD are still part of Percy's profile. Yet, many basic skills and individualized adaptations now give the next IEP team a direction for the older Percy that will take him beyond the school years to what is envisioned for him—a satisfying adulthood.

Transition: Anticipating the Changes from School to Adulthood

Planning transitions for students with special needs is expected under IDEA 2004. Beginning at age 16 and continuing through high schoolgraduation or aging out, the IEP emphasizes a focus on activities that will lead to long-term success for the individual with ASD (Peck and Scarpati, 2007). Transition also includes preparation for employment, extracurricular or recreational activities, and living in the community either independently or with supports.

Individuals with ASD, particularly those in the mild end of the autism spectrum with HFA/AS, are increasingly participating in postsecondary programs like community college, university, and similar training settings. This may be attributed to the increase in the incidence in ASD (Centers for Disease Control and Prevention [CDC], 2008) but also to overall increase in the number of higher functioning individuals with autism (Cavignaro, 2007) or the increase in individuals with autism who were early identified, had early intervention services, and had improved outcomes (Adreon & Durocher, 2007). Getting to the post–high school settings is one milestone. Succeeding there might be less achievable without significant attention to the skills needed at that level and stage of life. Individuals with HFA/AS are "likely to experience significant and unique challenges in adjusting to postsecondary educational settings" (Adreon & Durocher, 2007, p. 271). Explicit instruction in needed postsecondary skills becomes important.

For the student to be successful as an adult, IEP teams in the high school years should provide additional or new emphases for goal work, including different directions and practices. In the early school years, skill development is specific to academic content, language and speech development, and learning pro-social behaviors. Now, for an older student readying for after high school, IEP goals should include instructional activities for the development of self-advocacy. Since pragmatic and most communication skills are still difficult yet more expected for older students, those with ASD or HFA/AS likely need very specific special instruction in self-advocacy. At a minimum, students should be taught about their ASD and how it affects their participation in school, work, community activities, and relationships. "To self-advocate effectively, students with disabilities must have an accurate and realistic understanding of themselves and use that knowledge appropriately" (Schreiner, 2007, p. 300). Speaking up for individual wants and needs is an expectation for college and life success. Students with ASD who are approaching the end of their K–12 school years should have a basic understanding of their skills, strengths, areas of learning needs, and appropriate and successful adaptations in a variety of their life settings (Schreiner, 2007). Knowing how to access appropriate help and resources for their challenges is also essential (Schreiner, 2007, p. 302). When individuals with ASD are not good self-advocates, opportunities for independent and satisfying adulthood narrow. Studies have shown that individuals who must live or work in more restrictive, communal settings experience fewer choice opportunities and lower self-determination. "Higher self-determination is correlated with high quality of life and predicts desired outcomes like employment or independent living" (Chambers et al., 2007, p. 12). Curriculum, such as the Self-Determined Learning Model of Instruction from the University of Kansas Department of Special Education (Chambers et al., 2007), supports enhancement of self-determination. Choice-making, articulating needs and wants, and cultivating self-awareness are now activities for success in adult years and must be demonstrated in new settings with different people, a wrinkle for many individuals with ASD. However, success in occupational and adult life settings will depend on this.

In the world of work, Percy will need to rely less on others and more on himself. Particularly for communication, Percy will probably rely on writing skills, such as email, texting, or the internet to get his point across. Problem solving, self-prompting, and self-regulation (Renzaglia, Karvonen, Dragsow, & Stoxen, 2003) must become part of Percy's skill sets since he may no longer have another adult nearby to anticipate for him or assist. P Preferences are no longer the reward for sustaining or completing activities as in school years. Preferences in the later school years become Percy's avenue to perfect and polish effective communication and interaction skills necessary in his work, recreation and leisure, and family or personal relationships. We all end up as adults, hopefully, with our preferred ways to live, work, and relate. With preparation, so will Percy.

In the work setting during adulthood, Section 504 of the Rehabilitation Act is the federal regulation protecting covered individuals against disability discrimination. Section 504 plans are simple—as the law calls it, "reasonable"—accommodations or adaptations that the individual with ASD requires to perform the basic functions of the job. Ideas for adapting job tasks will need to be shared with the key staff working with or supervising the individual with ASD. An uncomplicated strategy for employee support could be organizing and training a coworker to briefly prompt or model the task at hand. Working collaboratively and complementing one another's abilities may be all that is needed for everyone, with and without disabilities, to complete jobs successfully (Renzaglia et al., 2003).

At work, a visual schedule is probably all that Percy will need to complete tasks given to him in the correct steps or sequence required. A visual schedule has pictures or symbols of what Percy must do, broken down for each key step of the task, like an assembly diagram for a new home appliance. Percy is shown the picture and the task is demonstrated. Percy does not need a lot of words. In fact, he might get lost on what to do if the task at hand has too much verbal explanation. Percy is already, at the early secondary level, always compliant with picture or simple verbal directions from familiar people. When he has a visual to review, all he needs is a quick point from that familiar person near him to get working and stay working. Percy can be fast with the right task and a little reminding. These next IEP meetings will now include all the adaptive skill work that the elementary level staff had been so wanting to start with him. Now everyone on the IEP team is feeling more on the same page about what to do next with and for Percy.

Person-centered planning is a concept that is driven by the individual's desires, strengths, needs, and dislikes (Renzaglia et al., 2003). Establishing specific priorities for an individual with disabilities can facilitate success with future planning (Renzaglia et al., 2003). The old saying "if you don't know where you are and where you want to go, how can you possibly get there" is particularly true in the case of individuals with disabilities like ASD. When measuring progress toward achieving life goals, the cyclical process of data collection, periodic review, goal reassessment remains critical.

At Percy's last IEP meeting, before he was to transition to the secondary level, one person asked, "Can we get some input from Percy about his interests, goals, and what he would like to work on for this year?" It was a touching moment in a long line of annual IEP meetings it seemed his mother might cry. And not because she was worried, distrustful, or in denial—she seemed so happy that Percy's opinion would count. It takes so little to make a difference on an IEP team.

Parents and IEPs

According to one recent study (Fish, 2008), the majority of parent participants in IEP meetings reported positive overall IEP meeting experiences and had positive perceptions of the meetings. Valued parental input, respectful treatment and a welcoming and comfortable atmosphere contributed to this positive parent perception (Fish, 2008). Most of the parents in the study agreed they had an understanding of the IEP process and special education law. However, another study reports the "majority of parents believed that they were moderately to highly knowledgeable and involved in their child's IEP process but reported that schools were not doing enough to address their child's most pressing needs" (Spann, Kohler, & Soenksen, 2003, p. 236).

Parent involvement in the development and implementation of IEPs and their services requires communication on a regular basis between school and home and back. "Because many young people with ASD (and those without disabilities) experience difficulty in expressing their strengths, weaknesses, and needs for support, parents are often the primary source of information about their child's needs" (Dymond, Gilson, & Myran, 2007, p. 134). The whole special education process, procedures, and service provision can be confusing and daunting to parents new to the system (Stoner & Angell ., 2005; Thompson, Meadan, Fansler, Alber, & Balogh, 2007). Professional staff in IEP meetings should do a lot of listening to parents (Thompson et al., 2007). After all, parents know their children better than anyone at an IEP meeting. Effective communication with parents is "vital to enhancing parental involvement, partnerships, and family-centered approaches to service delivery" (Stoner & Angell, 2006, p. 178). At times, communication on the school team may be lacking. General education must dialogue with special educators. Paraprofessionals must speak to the respective teachers of the students with whom they work. School staff must find out what agency and other home supports are doing to coordinate and leverage services and results (Dymond et al., 2007).

Parents experience difficulties finding services outside the school setting, implementing IEP services when they move (Worchester, Nesman, Raffaele Mendez & Keller, 2008, p. 518), and coordinating care and outside or home services with school schedules. "An overriding frustration among parents in this category was the time and energy they exerted 'fighting' to obtain services for their child. Parents are exhausted from working with 'the system' and do not want to have to fight to obtain services" (Dymond et al., 2007, p. 140). Parents may question accountability for student progress and distrust staff who repeatedly state their lack of knowledge or training on ASD. Parents of children with ASD have reported little IFSP/IEP involvement, lack of choice in services, and lack of effective services (Stoner & Angell, 2006). It is as crucial to be aware and be inclusive of parents as it is to be so aware and diligent with students.

Consider the roles parents play as they work together with the professionals in school and agencies, as discussed in Chapter 8 (Stoner & Angell, 2006). Parent roles include negotiator for desired outcomes, monitor of content and quality (especially when dissatisfied), supporter and encourager of teachers, and advocate in outside activities related to ASD. Parents often express appreciation for the professionals and teachers whom they perceive as going above and beyond the routine level of service when providing support to their children (Worcester et al. 2008). Professionals build trust when they act with competence, display individual interest, focus on their students , and do what they say they will do (Stoner & Angell, 2006). "Establishing effective family/professional partnerships is not an episodic event, but rather a process requiring good faith efforts over time" (Thompson et al., 2007, p. 19). Repeated negative interactions with professionals lower parent trust in them (Stoner & Angell, 2006). If professionals fail to build this trust in the schools, parents can hardly be blamed for turning to the internet as the primary source for information to support their child and the disability (Worcester et al., 2008). "An ASD diagnosis forges a relationship between education professionals and families that is necessary, interdependent, and similar to an arranged marriage with no possibility of divorce. This relationship can be tenuous and fraught with conflict or it can be supportive, mutually beneficial, and extremely rewarding" (Stoner & Angell, 2006, p. 177). IEP meetings are a common meeting ground for parents and school staff each year. Respecting opinions, incorporating what can be done, and learning from each other's unique perspective and expertise helps parents and everyone on the IEP team.

Improving IEPs

Incorporating a consistent and continuous review process ensures that IEPs are good for students. "Seven steps to intervention planning are to (1) refine IEP goals, (2) analyze baseline functional skills, (3) identify natural learning opportunities, (4) select empirically based strategies to facilitate learning, (5) ensure fidelity of instruction, (6) design a data collection and analysis system, and (7) evaluate the plan" (Jung, Gomez, Baird, & Galyon Keramidas, 2008, p. 27). Looking at intervention plan development as an evolving process with the preceding components is preferred. Perfunctory IEP meetings, full of educational jargon and disgruntled or clueless participants must be avoided.

Sometimes IEPs and the services in them for students with ASD are a subject of much debate and disagreement. What one set of parents advocate for their children is "at times the complete opposite of what other parents requested" (Dymond et al., 2007, p. 143). No consensus exists for one method, program, or environment for students with ASD, and what one IEP team member might think inappropriate may be endorsed by another (Dymond et al., 2007). Valuing the expertise and recommendations of various outside providers, like neuropsychologists, that parents may bring to the school IEP meeting is beneficial (Kanne et al., 2008).

Thinking in person-centered rather than system-centered terms can result in individual and new services when existing ones are insufficient (Dymond et al., 2007). "Parents felt they often were more knowledgeable than school personnel about autism and various instructional strategies and treatments. They frequently found themselves in the position of needing to train teachers about the needs of their child and how best to educate the child" (Dymond et al., 2007, p. 141). Well-meaning teachers may lack the expertise needed to be effective or may be fearful or leery when they are unprepared to teach students with special needs (Dymond et al., 2007). Professionals working with students with ASD cannot be inflexible and resistant to learning new techniques (Dymond et al., 2007). Parents can never be too informed of school and community services, approaches, treatments, locations, and provider information, yet this is all too often found lacking (Dymond et al., 2007). If special educators concentrate so much on the document writing for IFSP/IEP/504 plans, the general education teacher, parents, and student may feel alienated or left out the process (Burstein, Sears, Wilcoxen, Cabello, & Spagna, 2004).

Special educators likely need to take the lead and connect IEP services, stated accommodations, goals, and strategies with general education classroom routines in order for their students to have successful inclusion with peers. General educators can engender discouragement in their special education colleagues if they do not incorporate specially created supports like picture schedules in the everyday classroom activities (Jung et al., 2008). Practical support from paraprofessionals in classrooms is often mentioned by general education teachers as important to student success (Jung et al., 2008). School and district administration can provide welcoming atmosphere, ensure parents have a relationship with at least one other member of the IEP team, ensure that predetermined decision-making is avoided, and allow time for parents and staff to communicate and share information well in advance of meetings (Fish, 2008). Remembering that *I* stands for *individual* in IDEA and IEP is essential to creating and delivering appropriate programs for students with ASD during preschool through adulthood.

COLLABORATION AND TEAMING

Intervention plans and services, at least good ones, happen when many elements and people work together. The term collaboration has many definitions like teamwork, group effort, alliance, relationship, and cooperation, even working with one's enemy.

Working cooperatively in partnership to achieve important outcomes for students with ASD with participants with varying views, values, information, experience, and skills is not an easy feat. Collaboration is like doing inclusion on our own team.

What is a Collaboration Team?

Collaboration teams create intervention plans like special education or accommodation plans. Educators in general and special education often use the words "team" and "collaborating" as they describe working together for a student. Teachers working together likely defines collaboration in the most general sense. However, many others working for the individual with ASD—parents, therapists, outside medical or consulting professionals, general education teachers, special education teachers, and, later on, the individual with ASD—are included in the collaborative effort to develop and deliver appropriate plans for intervention. The saying "two (or more) heads are better than one" applies in developing good intervention plans for those with ASD.

Special Education Teachers

Special educators bring specific information about the student with ASD to the collaborative team, gleaned from individual evaluation and observations of their students. They also bring expertise in adaptations and differentiated strategies to use

with learners who have not achieved school skills through traditional teaching methods in the general classroom. Their role may be considered the "special" in a student's education.

Historically, special educators have spent more time in their own rooms, but
they did (in the best practice) align their work with other specialists who would also
spend time with their students and might even, sometimes with an invitation, come
into the special classrooms. Staff who might team with special education teachers
for students with ASD include speech, occupational, and physical therapists (Lamar-
Dukes & Dukes, 2005). Special education teachers might have the proximity for collaboration and teaming with the specialists, but they come from various fields with
slightly different training, methods and views on what helps. With all these different
professionals though, coming and going in and out of the same special or resource
classroom, collaboration and teaming may be hard to enact. In inclusion settings,
special educators must additionally step out and work with more content area specialists such as the general education teachers in Social Studies, Science, Language
Arts, and Math. Who is responsible for what with the student and how everyone
works together so as not to fragment the student's learning should be reviewed.
Teacher roles, otherwise, maybe fuzzy and mixed (Lamar-Dukes & Dukes, 2005).
Coteacher and collaborators' distinct skills in the various content and support areas
contribute to success in all types of classes and particularly at the secondary level
(Peck & Scarpati, 2007, p. 4). The work required to do collaboration well is worth
the extra effort.

General Education Teachers

Many students with disabilities spend most of the school day in the general education classroom with their nondisabled peers. Students with ASD are no different. For
collaboration, general educators are very important members of the team. They bring
knowledge of the grade level or content curriculum, State Standards or expectations
for students at that level or in that content, and a general knowledge of age- and
grade-level abilities. When diverse learners like students with ASD are included in
general education, their teachers may need help gauging appropriate academic and
behavioral standards or expectations. Collaboration with special educators remains
important for general educators' "temperature check" on where the student with
ASD falls in the general curriculum, in communication, and in behavioral skills.
When schools are inclusive and the school system is unified, general educators and
special educators do work collaboratively, providing integrated and comprehensive
services to students (Lee-Tarver, 2006).

Sometimes general educators are not empowered to problem-solve about their
included student. Sometimes the student with disabilities may not be "owned" at all
by the general classroom teacher. Outlining agreed-upon roles and duties for each
educator working with a student facilitates effective collaboration and can be relatively easy to develop. The roles and duties laid out in Tables 6.1–6.4 were originally developed by the author with collaborating general education and special education team members at a Midwestern junior high school with seventh through

ninth grade students, including students with ASD. The information in the tables was extended in recent years to all types of students with disabilities by the author and a new group of southwestern school district group team members representing counselors, special educators, and related service personnel. Creating a responsibilities chart like these can assist all teachers to know who is and should be doing what and are particularly effective when collaboratively developed and agreed upon. Table 6.1 defines the responsibilities of all teachers in the school for all students. Table 6.2 represents the responsibilities of the special education and general education teachers for the student with disabilities who is fully mainstreamed and needs little to no extra assistance in academics or behavior. Table 6.3 delegates responsibilities for students with disabilities who need adaptations or modifications in the general education setting. Finally, Table 6.4 addresses the needs of students with disabilities in the most segregated setting, which applies to only a small percentage of students.

Successful general educator and special educator collaboration should also include preplanning exactly which students (including some without special education labels) will be assisted and by whom and defining tasks for the special educator while in the classroom. General and special educators must determine how each

TABLE 6.1

Responsibilities Working With all Students

Student	Special Education Teacher	General Education Teacher
A. General Education- All	A. Consult with general education teacher on students at risk of failing B. Perform observations and make suggestions for problem areas reported by general education teacher C. Allow general education students access to special education group work or tutoring as appropriate while in general education classroom for inclusion D. Provide specialized prereferral interventions for appropriate students when required	A. Provide grade or content level instruction B. Monitor student progress routinely and often C. Adapt instruction & assessment for students who struggle D. Consult with others on staff regarding students at risk of failing E. Participate with special education staff for referral and evaluation of appropriate students

TABLE 6.2

Responsibilities Working With Fully Mainstreamed Students Who Require no Adaptation

Student	Special Education Teacher	General Education Teacher
B. Special Education student, fully mainstreamed No adaptation needed in the content area(s) or behavior	A. Monitor progress B. Follow-up with parents C. Consult with general education teacher when needed D. Collaborate on an ongoing basis E. Collect data	A. Provide core content instruction B. Consult with special education teacher in curricular content areas, student expectations, behavior, etc. C. Provide normal curriculum/behavior management D. Maintain parent contact E. Seek special education assistance when needed F. Collect data

and both will adjust the learning process, core content, and allow for varying student interests, or learning styles for the student with ASD (Lamar-Dukes & Dukes, 2005). Defining the time of school day and for what part of a lesson each is responsible takes preplanning and agreement (Lamar-Dukes & Dukes, 2005). Collaboration must be woven into teacher routines (Myers, Vergason, & Whelan, 1996). If staff members have various prep times, uncommon lunch times, or other duties which obligate them before and after school, only classroom time and email remains for daily discussing what is next. Using teacher work days or intersessions (summer, spring, holiday) can require dedication above and beyond the other demands for these time periods in teacher contract days. The special educator's interpersonal skills, Like sensitivity, nonjudgmentalism, supportiveness, adaptability, and flexibility, are important characteristics for collaboration (Klinger & Vaughn, 2002).

Teacher perceptions

The latest reauthorization of the IDEA in 2004 requires that IEP teams of teachers and parents consider appropriate services and supports to students, including supports to the personnel who work with them. Knowledge and use of appropriate research-based supports are critical factors in providing appropriate educational

TABLE 6.3

Responsibilities Working With Mainstreamed Students Who Require Adaptations

Student	Special Education Teacher	General Education Teacher
B. Special education student, mainstreamed Able to meet adjusted general curriculum and/or behavioral expectations with adaptations for special needs	A. Consult with general education teacher in curriculum, instruction, environmental, and behavioral adaptations B. Provide supplementary material C. Follow-up on general classroom instruction (tutoring/strategies/ monitoring) D. Complement IEP goals E. Observe in/out of classroom regularly F. Contact parents related to IEP G. Pull out as necessary for extended time, testing, adaptations, etc. H. Coteach when appropriate I. Provide adaptive equipment and materials as needed J. Collaborate with outside agencies or providers as appropriate K. Collect data	A. Provide core content instruction B. Consult with special education teacher in curricular content area, student expectations, behavior, etc. C. Adapt curriculum requirements, instructional presentation, and/or environment D. Collect data E. Maintain parent contact – areas of concern not related to special needs F. Seek special education assistance when needed G. Contact parents re: grades/behavior or as requested H. Provide instructional materials for adaptation to special education staff in a timely manner

services to students with ASD/HFA/AS. Lack of knowledge about ASD/HFA/AS and lack of appropriate strategies with students labeled with autism presents a significant problem for school staff. Teachers are well-meaning and accepting of students with ASD/HFA/AS but may be daunted by the task of teaching such students effectively (McCoy, Gehrke & Bruening, 2009). General and special educators may have issues with parents if undertrained in HFA/AS (Scheuermann, Webber, Boutot, & Goodwin, 2003). Teachers need and want training to assist their students with ASD and HFA/AS to be successful in general education classrooms.

TABLE 6.4

Responsibilities Working With Students in the Special Education Classroom

Student	Special Education Teacher	General Education Teacher
D. Special Education student placed in Special Education classroom for some or all subject area(s) Unable to meet mainstream general curriculum requirements and/or behavioral expectations because of special needs even with adaptations	A. Provide direct intervention for disability area B. Provide core content instruction C. Follow state standards for teaching content. D. Provide instructional/behavioral management E. Implement IEP goals F. Adapt grade level material as needed G. Collect data H. Provide instruction in other settings when students are able to be included with general education peers I. Monitor progress to determine readiness to return to general education J. Maintain parent contact K. Seek general education teacher assistance when needed; collaborate with general education staff L. Provide in-school/out of school resources to parents M. Acquire and provide adaptive equipment and materials as needed N. Collaborate with outside agencies or providers as appropriate	A. Consult with special education teacher in curricular content area, student expectations, etc. B. Assist special education teacher in providing instruction in areas where student is excluded from general grade level instruction (e.g. lab work, instructional groups, whole group teaching) through joint participation or teacher exchange

To develop a stronger knowledge base for teachers of students with ASD and to develop a teacher education delivery system that provides timely, specific, and easily accessible interventions, data was collected in a suburban Southwestern U.S. school district in late 2008 and 2010; it is still being analyzed. Teachers in general education, itinerant special education resource teachers, and self-contained teachers in autism were surveyed, interviewed and asked for written input. See Table 6.5 below.

TABLE 6.5

Teacher Survey for Special and General Educators

With whom they work	Each other most commonly Paraeducators almost as commonly
What they know	50% had training in ASD "mentioned in one or two classes in BA program." 25% said "no real information was provided" on ASD. Special educators had "at least one school level meeting, presentation on the topic" and "attended at least one training session in the district and one outside/paid by the district" About 75% read books/articles/used the internet on ASD 50% learned about ASD on TV and radio
What teachers need to know	75% said the following are critical: characteristics of ASD, adaptations for communication, social interaction, social-emotional deficits, sensory over/under sensitivity, what the IEP says about the student, how to collaborate with special andgeneral educators andparas assigned in the classroom. One teacher who is also a parent wrote, "What is being done at home,"
What training helps to work with students with ASD in general education classrooms	75% thought it "critical" to attend a special seminar outside the district or one provided by staff in-district. 66% said it was "unnecessary" for an online class on the topic. One teacher noted, "Any would be good."
What the district can do to help	75% said "pay for attendance at an outside workshop on autism"; One noted particularly, "Provide research-based materials and training for in-class use for behavior and social development."
Their confidence	30% or fewer strongly agreed they were confident to determine appropriate interventions, counsel family members of students with ASD, and deliver effective strategies to students with ASD.
What they would commit to for professional development	75% were positive about having assistance and direction from another professional when developing appropriate programs for students with ASD. Nearly all in the study would commit to training if it were available in the district or outside the district if supported financially.
What they think for professional development	Nearly all in the study thought strongly that faculty could benefit from more training in ASD for their particular school setting. 75% saw need for more postgraduate learning opportunities in autism to benefit the field.

Other personnel within and outside school

Other staff members can be valuable on the team for students with ASD. Some of them have specialized training and skills. Others are found typically in schools and may be overlooked for their contributions.School counselors are helpful on the collaboration team (Gibbons & Goins, 2008), and most schools have them available part or full time. School counselors are trained in methods of assisting student's social and emotional development and can provide services such as classroom, small group, or individual lessons. Language development and pragmatic speech may be in their background of study and expertise with children. They know how to consult with parents and other agency personnel for planning. Counselors by their training understand the intricacies, challenges, and frustrations of working with special populations like students with ASD and can help others to develop understanding and positive working relationships.

Collaboration with administrators should not be overlooked. School and district administrators can set high standards (Simpson et al., 2007, p. 207) and establish or request the infrastructure to deliver on them. Administrators provide leadership in identifying and selecting effective and evidence-based practices. They set aside the resources required by students with ASD. Teachers, on their own, may not be able to gather special or extra materials and supplies, nor can they direct others and their time. Principals oversee the activities of support staff such as paraprofessionals, assistants, and aides who frequently work with students in both general and special classrooms. Oversight of support staff is important as evidence suggests that paraprofessionals might be inappropriately used if unsupervised, if general or special education teachers' caseloads are overloaded, if classes are large, or if too little teacher supervision is provided by the administrator (Giangreco Smith, & Pinckney, 2006). The school principal can help with comprehensive professional and teacher development needed to work effectively with students with ASD (Simpson et al., 2007). Keep in mind that administrators may be called when student conduct expectations or school rules have been broached. Understanding how students with ASD must be approached verbally and nonverbally during a behavior incident and subsequent discipline actions can prevent further disruptions or misbehaviors. A principal, trying to help and intervene in a typical disciplinary fashion, was bitten by a student with HFA/AS during a meltdown, which caused further discipline measures to be levied against the student. Such a situation is unfortunate for everyone involved—principal, student, parent who was beside herself—and preventable when everyone who has contact with the child works together. Overall, administrators have system accountability to all their students, including those with ASD, their families, school staff, and the community.

Paraprofessionals or teacher assistants or aides are part of good collaboration teams. "Many schools have increased their use of paraprofessionals as a primary mechanism to include more students with various disabilities in general education classes" (Giangraco et al., 2006). Paraprofessionals are used in most special classrooms as well. Overreliance on them to deliver special education services is problematic. Lack of training in ASD or in appropriate intervention techniques can frustrate the student and the paraprofessional who may, like the unfortunate principal, have unexpected or poor results for his or her efforts or, in the worst case, sustain injuries. Supporting multiple goals for multiple staff, working with the student and with parents (Giangreco et al., 2006, p. 215) can overload paraprofessionals. Nearly three fourths of paraprofessionals in one study reported making instructional or curriculum decisions without always having teacher oversight (Giangreco & Broer, 2005). Undesirable outcomes for students result if paraprofessionals are not aligning their activities with other team member expectations. Paraprofessionals should be included in discussions about how much assistance to give for their students with ASD, such as how to avoid student overdependence on assistance, how to make and record observations about peer interactions, the best ways and times to intervene for their students while navigating the school day, and how to overall appropriately sharing ownership of the student with all teachers (Giangreco et al., 2006). Including support staff like paraprofessionals in collaboration team discussions, communication, and planning is very important for their proper and full utilization.

Collaboration teams should not be restricted in membership to only to teachers (Peck & Scarpati, 2007) or those hired by the school. Teaming with agencies is overlooked as much as half the time (Stahmer, 2007,). With all the resource limitations today, partners in and outside of schools should feel compelled to work together to efficiently, effectively, and economically provide the consistent services of increased intensity recommended for individuals with ASD (Stahmer, 2007). Consultants who have expertise in ASD may be able to "translate" common behaviors or characteristics exhibited by the student with ASD to school personnel, since the condition is still little known or understood (Safran & Safran, 2001). Consultants, whether provided by the school or family, can prepare the student, family, or staff with what to expect; explain how best to approach the child or situation; and give ASD-specific interventions such as redirecting obsessive comments, preparing for transitions that are difficult, or widening student interests (Safran & Safran, 2001).

Be aware, though, that not all consultants are welcomed openly and warmly at IEP meetings or parent–teacher conferences, and especially if they are not invited by the school. Consultants would improve their team relationships and find their recommendations more enthusiastically received and applied when they develop them in close collaboration with those implementing them (Hunt, Soto, Maier, Liboriron, & Bae, 2004) or when the consultants step forward to teach school staff how to develop further interventions on their own (Hunt et al., 2004). In the best practice, teachers learn how to independently develop additional interventions from the consultants, rather than relying on the consultant's next visit. Good consultation helps teachers at the school to adapt or develop further strategies for other settings like inclusion or for use in other program or content areas (Hundert, 2007). Teachers then will know what to do to fit the needs of that child or another similar child and to add an extra twist to interventions, extending them to their many additional classroom and school routines (Hundert, 2007, p. 171).

Parents

IDEA has many supports in place to encourage parental involvement in special education planning (Turnbull, Turnbull, Erwin, & Soodak, 2006) on all steps of the way
"from assessment to goal development to progress monitoring" (Whitbread, Bruder,
Fleming, & Park, 2007, p. 6). This process begins again each year with new intervention plans and the new or old staff delivering them. Parents may be the ones to
start the partnership needed for intervention plan development by their initial contact with the school system. However, early intervention or therapy professionals,
previous schools or preschools, outside agencies, or the community may begin the
relationship with parents and reach out first.

For collaboration to be at its best, someone must take the lead to coordinate, focus
interventions, share goals, and plan for skill reinforcement across settings (Safran &
Safran, 2001). The workplaces, intervention team, and student and family are constantly changing—no wonder successful collaboration is so hard to do! This dynamic
characteristic of schools and families means that communication is essential and fore-
most. Communication does not have to be complicated to be comprehensive. After initial face-to-face enrollments and introductions, communication can take many forms.
Special education is famous for their extensive and frequent meetings, but communication can take simple and time-efficient forms—email, voicemail, and written reports
(Lamar-Dukes & Dukes, 2005)—which can enhance collaboration team member
"availability" and communicate much of what is needed by other team members.

Respecting parents for what they bring to the partnership develops trust in the
collaboration team. School staff must understand the dedication of time and energy
by parents for the additional, yet ordinarily expected, tasks related to school: homework help, extra skill practice, and support for behavioral expectations. Parents can
be good partners for improving intervention and goal attainment. School staff should
recognize, however, that adding to home tasks can be taxing or complex for parents,
as discussed in Chapter 6. Parents of children with disabilities like ASD are often
beleaguered by many requirements and demands on their time. School staff should
consider and respect this. Strategies, such as making appointments for weekly phone
conversations or ascertaining parent interest in specific skills, performances, or services to be included on a chart or daily checklist, are simple to implement, very infor-
mational and timely, yet efficient of everyone's time. Another way to boost parent
involvement and participation in meetings is to make times (during workday breaks
or lunch times) and methods (alternate participation like phone or computer confer-
encing) convenient for parents.

Barriers exist to collaboration even though a great deal of research supports better outcomes for students when the family participates in schooling (Turnbull et al.,
2006). Professionals in the schools must avoid the view that families and parents are
resistant or in denial about their child with disabilities like ASD. This is simply not
the case (Harry, 2008). Parents are children's first and most important teachers
(Lucyshyn, Dunlap, Horner, Albin, & Ben, 2002) and "experts in their children's
lives" (Roberts, Keane, & Clark, 2008, p. 509). Teachers may resent burdens of

taking care of parents and their needs, such as extensive communication, requests for information or resources, or ideas that are not necessarily approved or possible in the school environment (Whitbread et al., 2007). Teachers may think of parents are unappreciative or difficult (Lytle & Bordin, 2001). Parents often view their job as getting useful and accurate information and obtaining services, and some feel better informed than even their pediatrician (Worcester et al., 2008). On the other side, parents also report feeling financial stress, stress in the family, and isolation from the community (Worcester et al., 2008). Parents may lack knowledge or understanding of special education procedures and processes and limitations of the school, and they may be reluctant to ask questions about services and supports (Whitbread et al., 2007). Parents may be skilled collaboration team members, unskilled, or something in between, just like others working with their child. Flexibly using ideas from everyone on a collaboration team can maximize effects and save costs for time, effort, equipment, and otherwise expensive training.

Percy's parents were very informed and very involved at home with instructing their son. They were upfront about their priorities and each had specific notions about how their child should be approached. In some annual IEP meetings during the elementary grade years, and especially in the beginning, their suggestions were met with extensive questioning or need for explanation to school personnel, , occasionally disputed as impractical or unavailable, and sometimes flat-out rejected for other ideas already in place at the school. In retrospect, not all the ideas for their son were developed collaboratively with the school team. Such suggestions had only a 50% chance of hitting the target. Over the years and after working longer as a team, parent suggestions were more often perceived by the school staff as doable. Moreover, as the parent suggestions became more familiar, and as school staff had more training to implement the ideas, then the parents' ideas often got tried. Percy's parents had good ideas, particularly regarding helpful assistive technology, and they were often very hands on with helping the school staff with training and implementation. This parent practice of going above and beyond as participating members of the collaboration team—rather than just idea people—guaranteed implementation and utilization of their ideas for Percy.

Research on evidence-based practices in ASD includes strong support for parent involvement if generalization and maintenance of skill, particularly behavior, is to be achieved (Stahmer, 2007). Parent involvement takes many forms (Stahmer, 2007). Intensive parent training on very specific techniques including parent practice and feedback is among the most involved methods. Simple communication logs between home and school, as described in Chapter 6; home based therapies that allow for parent observation and participation; home visits by professionals to report, share, and problem-solve are less complex ways to involve parents. Some school districts might offer parent classes on related topics for ASD. The importance of parent involvement as equal and collaborating team members to student progress cannot be overemphasized.

Cooperation, communication, knowledge, and experience are all required for everyone interested in a student's welfare and success to perform as a smoothly functioning and effective team. In reality, the techniques of teaming and collaboration are not natural to everyone who must do it. In fact, school professionals, parents, and outside agencies might have something to learn from business management in this regard (Peck & Scarpati, 2007). District and site administrators can help with supporting training in collaboration models and methods when teams are not functioning successfully. Teams can learn how to successfully work together and then come to consensus on what works for this child with ASD, with this team, at this time.

For long-term success of students with ASD and for the school personnel and parent teams, collaboration and teaming is the insurance that many good things happen. Collaboration benefits others and not just students: less redundancy, less work, everyone on the same track pulling together, and, best of all, "no biting the dogs in your own yard" when everyone gets along. The job is hard enough. Collaboration is not work but insurance for smooth, easy, effective work.

INTERVENTION DELIVERY IN THE LEAST RESTRICTIVE ENVIRONMENT

Placements or environments where students spend their school day vary as much on a continuum of locations as the students themselves vary along the spectrum of autism disorders. Intervention plan placements for services can range from very segregated and intensive in goal work to inclusion in the general classroom with little support or specialized help. IEP teams of professionals and parents determine placement or environment for a student with ASD to receive the various services listed on that IEP. In fact, the decision about how much time the student spends in and out of special education settings and how much time the student with ASD is with his or her nondisabled peers is directly determined by the goals or objectives with the collaboration team member most appropriate to work on these goals.

The concept of LRE is foundational in special education law and was a cornerstone for the 1975 federal legislation Public Law 94-142 at its beginnings. LRE, or normalization, means that, with the appropriate supports and skill development, any individual with disabilities of any nature can be successful in more inclusive environments (Renzaglia et al., 2003). The whole point of inclusion is to "create a life that is both satisfying and successful for a person with a disability" (Renzaglia et al., 2003p. 141). Simply stated, LRE decisions by IEP teams should consider that individuals with ASD belong, at least sometimes or at some point, in all places with everyone else.

Inclusion is a term that actually has a couple of "names" that might be used interchangeably and can have different meanings depending upon the person using it. For consistency, this chapter adopts the ideas below:

> "*Inclusion* is a philosophy that urges schools, neighborhoods, and communities to welcome and value everyone, regardless of differences.

Central to the philosophy of inclusion are the beliefs that everyone belongs, diversity is valued, and we can all learn from each other. This is different from the educational practice of mainstreaming. *Mainstreaming* implies that individuals with disabilities have a separate placement and enter the mainstream only for the activities that they can perform at the level needed to succeed. Inclusion is also different from integration. *Integration* implies bringing an individual back into a unified system; the physical act of bringing people back does not necessarily create an inclusive environment An inclusive environment is created by building a system that meets everyone's needs from the onset, and inclusion extends beyond the K-12 school boundaries to people of all ages with disabilities. Inclusion is a lifelong goal that crosses all environments and social settings where people without disabilities learn, work, live, and play" (Renzaglia et al., 2003, p. 140).

"Inclusion should be activities or environments that embrace differences and accommodate varying abilities, as opposed to those that fit individuals into the existing environments or activities" (Renzaglia et al., 2003, p. 141). Students with ASD require a variety of environments that change with needs, preferences, goals, and IEP team decisions. No one "best" environment or placement exists for students with disabilities, and that goes, too, for ASD. Placement decisions for students should be flexible and "fluid, as opposed to static" (White, Scahill, Klin, Koenig, & Volkmar, 2007, p. 1411) and based on the student's 's characteristics and those of the setting where the student is schooled. What the student needs to work on and what resources, supports, and staff are available in the setting must be considered (White et al., 2007). IEP team members must weigh, ultimately, where the individual with ASD will benefit and progress appropriately.. For students with ASD, that means considering where success academically, emotionally, and socially can be accomplished (White et al.). Watching for inclusion readiness might include the following questions (Roberts. Keane, & Clark, 2008):

➤ Has the student increased communication skills?
➤ Participation with others?
➤ Independent functioning?

"Perhaps the strongest argument in favor of inclusion is that the mainstream social milieu promotes social development in children with ASD" (Dahle, 2003). Children can learn from the adults around them, but they will eventually grow up to live with those in their own age group—their classmate peers. Friendships and socialization groups with other same-age students is more than just nice or a time filler for the student with ASD. "Positive social relationships with peers are an essential ingredient to a good quality of life, both for children and adults" (Boutot, 2007). Working on social relationships can help students with ASD to fit in. Children with ASD can improve social interactions skills with intervention (Bauminger, 2002). "Given that children with autism can advance in this domain, placement in a classroom with typically developing children may be an ideal setting" (White et al., p. 1404). Research has found that students with ASD in the milder form and with less social impairment were more likely to be in general education settings (White et al.) although "degree of social deficit is not predictive of special education placement" (White et al., p. 1410). Keep in mind that students with ASD who cannot benefit from modeling appropriate peers might require another placement than inclusion (White et al.). Few accepting peers or peer friendships for students with ASD may be the norm in general education classrooms (Chamberlain, 2002), though not always (Ochs, Kremer-Sadlik, Solomon, & Sirota, 2001). Somewhat comforting to think about in this regard is that children with autism have been noted in studies as "not accurately perceiving the degree of isolation, which may serve a protective function (i.e., to not view themselves as lonely or rejected)" (White et al., 2007, p. 1404–1405).

While few educators now debate the inclusion of students with disabilities and those with ASD in classrooms, significant challenges remain in planning student involvement so that progress in the general education setting is attained with maximum benefit for all students there (Hundert, 2007). Students with ASD, without appropriate intervention plans, might play or stay by themselves or only with adults, use immature or no methods to interact with others, or be isolated during partner activities (Hundert, 2007, p. 159-160; Koegel, Keogel, Frea, & Fredeen, 2001; McGrath, Bosch, Sullivan, & Fuqua, 2003; Pierce-Jordan & Lifter, 2005). Many transitions, changing daily schedules of activities, and keeping up with the curriculum might be too challenging for some students with ASD (White et al., 2007). Overreliance on adults for classroom support becomes an unintended and undesirable result (White et al., 2007). "With few exceptions, teachers have not been trained to develop interventions for use in the inclusive setting to accommodate children with disabilities" (Hundert, 2007, p. 160). Students with ASD in the classroom might overextend the general education teacher, and then all students in the room could be negatively affected for learning (Fisher & Meyer, 2002).

Students with ASD and lower cognitive ability and communication skill are more often found in special education placements (White et al., 2007) while high functioning individuals with average or above average intelligence and fewer social deficiencies remain in general education (Safran & Safran, 2001).

> Based on parent-report, most students stayed in the same placement (regular or special education) in which they began first grade and the majority of students received special services in their schools (most often speech/ language intervention). Findings highlight the emphasis placed on certain child characteristics (e.g., cognitive ability), with far less emphasis on other areas (e.g., degree of social deficit), in educational placement and service provision. (White et al., 2007, p. 1403)

Consideration of all deficiency areas and all proficient skills of individuals with ASD must be weighed in deciding inclusion in general classrooms. Each student brings unique skills and levels, so their environments for services and support should vary accordingly. "Inclusion does not change an individual's needs but should provide a wider range of instructional environments in which to teach" (Renzaglia et al., 2003, p. 144). "One size fits all" approaches are ineffective in selecting environments for students with ASD. Competing issues are at work: Very specialized needs and approaches are required, but general or more typical placements are an emphasis.

IEP team members may need to take extra efforts to think, act, and plan for students with ASD in the general classroom. Preparation of the student with ASD and a proactive flexible approach, moving students along a continuum of inclusive environments, is recommended (Roberts et al., 2008). "The essential element of inclusion is shared responsibility on the part of all educators in the school toward the student with disabilities" (Vaughn, Bos, & Schumm, 2003). Special educators are key to jump-starting inclusion efforts, either through consulting or working directly in the general education inclusion classroom of the student, ensuring appropriate activities and meaningful student engagement (Lamar-Dukes & Dukes, 2005). All teachers of the student meeting early and proactively to know the characteristics of a student's ASD and to go over appropriate classroom strategies can mean more positive teacher attitudes for inclusion and derail problems (Safran & Safran, 2001).

Inclusion of students with ASD will not likely be natural or quickly and simply accomplished. The transition to general education settings and inclusion must be planned, to put students with ASD in inclusion at the right times and for the right reasons. Renzaglia et al. (2003) mention relevant considerations for promoting inclusion such as environmental accommodations to include a range of participants, flexible strategies and adaptations in place for instruction, positive behavior supports that are comprehensive and individualized and prevent problem behavior, and curriculum options that best meet the student's needs. We needto put students with ASD in inclusion at the right places at the right times and for the right reasons.

What is needed to enhance LRE

Data was collected on this topic in a suburban Southwestern U.S. school district and is still being analyzed (McCoy, Gehrke & Bruening, 2009). Teachers in general education, itinerant special education resource teachers, and self-contained teachers in autism participated in a survey and then a focus group interview on the topic of what teachers need to work with students with ASD and HFA/AS in general classrooms.

What teachers felt they needed to know in order for them and their students with ASD to be successful revolved around four themes. They needed:

1. information about characteristics of autism;
2. adaptations that were appropriate and easy to understand (as in a checklist format) for communication, social emotional, and social interaction, and sensory areas;
3. critical elements of an IEP for improving student performance in classrooms; and
4. collaboration.

Teachers talked about needing adaptation ideas and information (such as student triggers) before the student arrived at the classroom door and not "on the fly." Teachers said they had a hard time telling what to push and what to let go (academics or behavior?). From the IEP, teachers thought that student performance levels, goals for the year, and accommodations needed to be plainly stated and summarized at a glance. Regarding collaboration, they wanted "to be met at the classroom door the first day" and wondered what previous teachers had tried successfully and unsuccessfully. They did not want a monthly "how's it going?" from their collaborating partners. One teacher noted, "We had to start comprehensively and at the very beginning—at our high school ASD meant after school detention!"

To help teachers work with and improve student outcomes, training and assistance from others was regarded as very needed. Learning about specific techniques, resources like websites with templates to use, and advance information was important to them. Learning with other teachers having the same needs or students or connecting with them was desirable. Hearing others' stories in personal interaction was a preference for this group's learning about ASD. "No offense to all the specialists but we like to hear about the teacher piece," Noted another teacher. Broad school-based training that was extended beyond one session and given when it was needed—pronto—was on the teacher wishlist.

SUMMARY

Plans of action or intervention plans like IFSPs and IEPs for students with ASD are specific, complex, and comprehensive. IFSPs detail services for little ones before kindergarten in natural settings and with parents as primary in helping their children to progress in development. IEPs for the preschool through high school years contain services to support learning, remediate deficiency areas particular to the core characteristics of ASD, and focus on instructional goals to improve student academic, behavioral, and functional or adaptive performance. Teachers, specialists, various school staff, parents, other outside providers, and older students themselves are involved—ideally in good team working relationships—to make the best IEPs for students. The "who, why, what, how" of special education is in place through these written plans. They are the framework for specific and timely activities, lessons, and tasks daily and through the year for the individual with ASD. School work in core areas advance the academic, speech/language, motor, social–emotional and behavior skill development of students with ASD.

Intervention plans like IFSPs and IEPs must be reasonable but also effective. Unfortunately, evidence-based practices and teachers with training in ASD are few and far between. This means well-written intervention plans that are collaboratively developed are a must. Challenges exist for services that are sufficiently intense and frequent. Inclusion is not yet fully or properly implemented and supported. Research and additional efforts remain to be done in those areas. In spite of a host of challenges and obstacles to inclusion, defined roles and responsibilities for all the participants in intervention plans assist students to communicate, learn, achieve needed skills, and relate with their life-long partners—peers.

The goal for special education services is, in the end, getting students to their future. Transition beyond the school years and 504 adaptation plans reaching into adult lives for individuals with ASD must be thoughtfully approached with preplanning and attention to the communication, social and interaction skills necessary in the workplace, postsecondary training or college settings, and for adult life in general. Self-awareness becomes self-advocacy for the older student with ASD who now can relay to others what adaptations or supports are necessary for success.

Parents are along for the full span of school years and are significant partners with school personnel and their older child. While many potholes exist on the journey, parents generally find the special education planning process a positive experience, particularly when they have trust in the school and the professionals working with their child.

IEPs result in improved student outcomes with a consistent and timely review process, decisions based on data, individualized and empirically based strategies, and the valued expertise of all development team members. General and special education staff take the lead to connect the services, accommodations, strategies and supports for the student with ASD to have satisfying and achievement-rich school years. Services and supports are reviewed and repackaged annually when the intervention plan reviews take place. Schools have more to learn about what is needed to work with and improve performance of students with ASD educated in the general classroom. Teacher input in this area will be beneficial.

All these efforts by all these people interested in the student with ASD culminate in instructional goals, services and adaptations written in one neat, yearly intervention plan. Whether an IFSP, an IEP, or a 504 accommodation plan, the interventions necessary to begin the intensive and specialized content instruction needed by the student with ASD are written and in place. Now work begins on appropriate teaching and learning. The intervention plans represented by IFSPs, IEPs and 504 accommodation plans are solid starting points for what teachers need to do next.

REFERENCES

Adreon, D., & Durocher, J. S. (2007). Evaluating College and Transition Needs. *Intervention in School and Clinic, 42*(5), 271–279.

Attwood, T. (1998). *Asperger syndrome: A guide for parents and professionals*. Philadelphia, Pennsylvania: Kingsley.

Baird, M. (Presenter). (2005). *Regular Educator's Compliance* [Video]. (Available from LRP Publications, Palm Beach Gardens, FL)

Bauminger, N. (2002). The facilitation of social–emotional understanding and social interaction in high-functioning children with autism: Intervention outcomes. *Journal of Autism and Developmental Disorders, 32*, 283–298.

Boutot, E. A. (2007). Fitting In: Tops for Promoting Acceptance and Friendships for Studnets with Autism Spectrum Disorder in Inclusive Classrooms. *Intervention in School and Clinic, 42*(3), 156–161.

Burstein, N., Sears, S., Wilcoxen, A., Cabello, B., & Spagna, M. (2004). Moving Toward Inclusive Practices. *Remedial and Special Education, 25*(2), 104–116.

California Health & Human Services Agency. (2007). In A. T. Cavignaro (Ed.), *Autism spectrum disorders - Changes in the California caseload. An update: June 1987–June 2007.* Retrieved June 14, 2009, from http://www.dds.ca.gov/autism

Cavignaro, A. T. (Ed.). (2007). *Autism spectrum disorders – Changes in the California caseload. An update: June 1987-June 2007.* California Health and Human Services Agency (pp. 1-31). Retrieved June 14, 2009, from http://www.dds.ca.gov/autism

Centers for Disease Control and Prevention (CDC). (January 30, 2008). FAQ's - Prevalence of ASD. In *Autism Information Center.* Retrieved June 14, 2009, from http://www.cdc.gov/ncbddd/autism/faq_prevalence.htm

Chamberlain, B. O. (2002). Isolation or involvement? The social networks of children with autism in regular education classes. *Dissertation Abstracts International, 62*, 8-A.

Chambers, C. R., Wehmeyer, M. L., Saito, Y., Lisa, K. M., Lee, Y., & Singh, V. (2007). Self Determination: What Do We Know? Where Do We Go? *Exceptionality, 15*(1), 3–15.

Cook, B. G., Tankersley, M., Cook, L., & Landrum, T. J. (2002). Teachers' attitudes toward their included students with disabiities. *Exceptional Children, 67*, 115–135.

Dahle, K. B. (2003). Services to include young children with autism in the general classroom. *Early Childhood Education Journal, 31*, 65–70.

Dymond, S. K., Gilson, C. L., & Myran, S. P. (2007). Services for Children with Autism Spectrum Disorders — What Needs to Change? *Journal of Disability Policy Studies, 18*(3), 133–147.

Fish, W. W. (2008). The IEP Meeing: Perception of Parents of Students Who Receive Special Education Services. *Preventing School Failure, 53*(1), 8–14.

Fisher, M., & Meyer, L. H. (2002). Development and social competence after two years for students enrolled in inclusive and self-contained educational programs. *Research and Practice for Persons with Severe Disabilities, 27*, 165–174.

Giangreco, M. F., & Broer, S. M. (2005). Questionable utilization of paraprofessionals in inclusive schools: Are we addressing symptoms or causes? *Focus on Autism and Other Developmental Disabillities, 20*, 10–26.

Giangreco, M. F., Smith, C. S., & Pinckney, E. (2006). Addressing the Paraprofessional Dilemma in an Inclusive School: A Program Description. *Research & Practice for Persons with Severe Disabilities, 31*(3), 215–229.

Gibbons, M., & Goins, S. (2008). Getting to Know the Child with Asperger Syndrome. *Professional School Counseling, 11*(5), 347–352.

Harry, B. (2008). Collaboration with Culturally and Linguistically Diverse Families: Ideal versus Reality. *Exceptional Children, 74*(3), 372–388.

Hessler, T., & Konrad, M. (2008). Using Curriculum-Based Measurement to Drive IEPs and Instruction in Written Expression. *Teaching Exceptional Children, 41*(2), 28–37.

Heward, W. L. (2008). *Exceptional Children: An Introduction to Special Education.* Upper Saddle River, New Jersey: Pearson/Prentice-Hall.

Hundert, J. P. (2007). Training Classroom and Resource Preschool Teachers to Develop Inclusive Class Interventions for Children with Disabilities. *Journal of Positive Behavior Interventions, 9*(3), 159–173.

Hunt, P., Soto, G., Maier, J., Liboriron, N., & Bae, S. (2004). Collaborative teaming to support preschoolers with severe disabilities who are placed in general education early childhood programs. *Topics in Early Childhood Special Education, 24*, 123–142.

Jung, L. A., Gomez, C., Baird, S. M., & Galyon Keramidas, C. L. (2008). Designing Intervention Plans: Bridging the Gap Between Individualized Education Programs and Implementation. *Teaching Exceptional Children, 41*(1), 26–33.

Kanne, S. M., Randolph, J. K., & Farmer, J. E. (2008). Diagnostic and Assessment Findings: A Bridge to Academic Planning for Children with Autism Spectrum Disorders. *Neuropsychology Review, 18*, 367–384.

Klinger, J. K., & Vaughn, S. (2002). The changing roles and responsibilities of an LD specialist. *Learning Disability Quarterly, 25*(1), 19–31.

Koegel, L. K., Keogel, R. L., Frea, W. D., & Fredeen, R. M. (2001). Identifying early intervention targets for children with autism in inclusive school settings. *Behavior Modification, 25*, 745–761.

Lamar-Dukes, P., & Dukes, C. (2005). Consider the Roles and Responsibilities of the Inclusion Support Teacher. *Intervention in School and Clinic, 41*(1), 55–61.

Lee, Wehmeyer, M. L., Palmer, S. B., Soukup, J. H., & Little, T. D. (2008). Self-Determination and Access to the General Education Curriculum. *The Journal of Special Education, 42*(2), 91–107.

Lee-Tarver, A. L. (2006). Are Individualized Education Plans a Good Thing? A Survey of Teachers' Perceptions of the Utility of IEPs in Regular Education Settings. *Journal of Instructional Psychology, 33*(4), 263–272.

Lock, R., & Layton, C. (2008). Creating Introductory Portfolios for Students with Autism Spectrum Disorders. *The Delta Kappa Gamma Bulletin, Winter*, 15–24.

Lucyshyn, J. M., Dunlap, G., Horner, R. H., Albin, R. W., & Ben, K. R. (2002). *Families and positive behavior support: Addressing problem behavior in family contexts.* Baltimore: - Brookes.

Lytle, R. K., & Bordin, J. (2001). Enhancing the IEP team: Strategies for parents and professionals. *Teaching Exceptional Children, 33*, 40–44.

McCoy, K. M., Gerhke, R., & Bruening, M. D. (2009). *Interventions for students with autism spectrum disorders and high functioning autism/Asperger Syndrome in general education classrooms.* (Unpublished Manuscript).

McGrath, A. M., Bosch, S., Sullivan, C. L., & Fuqua, W. (2003). Training reciprocal social interactions between preschoolers and a child with autism. *Journal of Positive Behavioral Interventions, 5*, 47–54.

Murray, M. M., Christensoen, K. A., Umbarger, G. T., Rade, K. C., Aldridge, K., & Niemeyer, J. A., 2007). Supporting Family Choice. *Early Childhood Education Journal, 35*, 111–117.

Myers, E. L., Vergason., G. A., & Whelan, R. J. (Eds.). (1996). *Strategies for teaching exceptional children in inclusive settings.* Denver, Colorado: Love Publishing.

Myers, S. M., Johnson, C. P., & Council on Children With Disabilities, U. S. (2007). Management of children with autism. *Pediatrics, 120*(5), 1162–1182.

National Research Council, Lord, C., & McGee, J. P. (Eds.). (2001). *Educating Children with Autism.* Washington, D.C., USA: National Academy Press.

Ochs, E., Kremer-Sadlik, T., Solomon, O., & Sirota, K. G. (2001). Inclusion as social practice: Views of children with autism. *Social Development, 10*, 399–419.

Peck, A., & Scarpati, S. (Eds.). (2007). Collaboration and Transition: Important Strategies for Teacher and Student Success [Special issue]. *Teaching Exceptional Children, 39*(6).

Pierce-Jordan, S., & Lifter, K. (2005). Interaction of social and play behaviors in preschoolers with and without pervasive developmental disorder. *Early Childhood Special Education, 25*, 34–47.

Renzaglia, A., Karvonen, M., Drasgow, E., & Stoxen C. C. (2003). Promoting a Lifetime of Inclusion. *Focus on Autism and Other Developmental Disabilities, 18*(3), 140–149.

Roberts, J. M. A., Keane, E., & Clark, T. (2008). Making Inclusion Work: Autism Spectrum Australia's Satellite Class Project. *Teaching Exceptional Children, 41*(2), 22–27.

Safran, J. S., & Safran, S. P. (2001). School-Based Consultation for Asperger Syndrome. *Journal of Educational and Psychological Consultation, 12*(4), 385–395.

Scheuermann, B., Webber, J., Boutot, E.A., & Goodwin, M. (2003). Problems with Personnel Preparation in Autism Spectrum Disorders. *Focus on Autism & Other Developmental Disabilities, 18*(3), 197–206.

Schreiner, M. B. (2007). Effective Self-Advocacy: What Students and Special Educators Need to Know. *Intervention in School and Clinic, 42*(5), 300–304.

Simpson, R. L., McKee, M., Teeter, D., & Beytien, A. (2007). Evidence-Based Methods for Children and Youth with Autism Spectrum Disorders: Stakeholder Issues and Perspectives. *Exceptionality, 15*(4), 203–217.

Spann, S. J., Kohler, F. W., & Soenksen, D. (2003). Examining Parents' Involvement in and Perceptions of Special Education Services: An Interview with Families in a Parent Support Group. *Focus on Autism and Other Developmental Disabilities, 18*(4), 228–237.

Stahmer, A. C. (2007). The Basic Structure of Community Early Intervention Programs for Children with Autism: Provider Descriptions. *Journal of Autism and Developmental Disorders, 37*, 1344–1354.

Stoner, J. B., & Angell, M. E. (2006). Parent Perspectives on Role Engagement: An Investigation of Parents of Children with ASD and Their Self-Reported Roles with Education Professionals. *Focus on Autism and Other Developmental Disabillities, 21*(3), 177–189.

Thompson, J. R., Meadan, H., Fansler, K. W., Alber, S. B., & Balogh, P. A. (2007). Family Assessment Portfolios—A New Way to Jumpstart Family/School Collaboration. *Teaching Exceptional Children, 39*(6), 19–25.

Tincani, M. (2007). Beyond Consumer Advocacy: Autism Spectrum Disorders, Effective Instruction and Public Schools. *Intervention in School and Clinic, 43*(1), 47–51.

Turnbull, A., Turnbull, R., Erwin, E. J., & Soodak, L. C. (2006). *Families, professionals, and exceptionality* (5th ed.). Upper Saddle River, New Jersey: Merrill Prentice Hall.

Van Norman, R. K. (2007). "Who's on First?": Using Sports Trivia Peer Tutoring to Increase Conversational Language. *Intervention in School and Clinic, 43*(2), 88–100.

Van Norman, R. K. (2007). Using Sports Trivia Peer Tutoring to Increase Conversational Language. *Intervention in School and Clinic, 43*(2), 88–100.

Vaughn, S., Bos, C., & Schumm, J. S. (2003). *Teaching exceptional, diverse, and at-risk students in the general education classroom* (3rd ed.). Boston: Allyn & Bacon.

Whitbread, K. M., Bruder, M. B., Fleming, G., & Park, H. J. (2007). Collaboration in Special Education: Parent-Professional Training. *Teaching Exceptional Children, 39*(4), 6–14.

White, S. W., Scahill, L., Klin, A., Koenig, K., & Volkmar, F. R. (2007). Educational Placements and Service Use Patterns of Individuals with Autism Spectrum Disorders. *Journal of Autism and Developmental Disorders, 37*, 1403–1412.

Wilczynski, S. M., Menousek, K., Hunter, M., & Mudgal, D. (2007). Individualized Education Programs for Youth with Autism Spectrum Disorders. *Psychology in the Schools, 44*(7), 653–666.

Winter-Messiers, M. (2007). From Tarantulas to Toilet Brushes. *Remedial and Special Education, 28*(3), 140–152.

Worcester, J. A., Nesman, T. M., Raffaele Mendez, L. M., & Keller, H. R. (2008). Giving Voice to Parents of Young Children with Challenging Behaviors. *Exceptional Children, 74*(4), 509–525.

Giftedness and ASD

Tiffany O'Neill

Ms. Morris looked at the hunched, red-hooded figure at the back of the classroom with a mixture of confusion, awe, and consternation. John, never without his red sweatshirt, had again disengaged from classroom activity after an interaction with his group that could only be described as bizarre. Every time that John showed her a piece of the writing he was posting under his avatar on the website he frequented, she was impressed by both his advanced technique as well as the symbolism and raw emotion in his writing. John's skills were far beyond the writing Ms. Morris saw among the college students in her adjunct faculty position at a local university, not to mention among his peers in her ninth grade English class. In spite of this irrefutable gift, John rarely engaged in lecture or class discussion, preferring to bury himself in the heaping volumes of fantasy fiction he carried with him everywhere. Today had been strange, even by John's standards. After being placed in a group to answer questions about the novel assigned in class, *Pride and Prejudice,* John had shifted his desk just outside his group's circle, pulled his hood further down against his forehead, and began reading again in his novel, unmoved by the assignment she had given. Todd, a student in John's group began asking pointed questions, pressuring John to interact. Just as Ms. Morris was crossing the room to address the increasingly tense situation, Todd stood up and pushed the hood of the red sweatshirt off of John's brow. With what could only be described as a wail, John jumped from his seat, clutched the hood tightly around his face and began pacing agitatedly at the back of the classroom. Along with the other students, Todd stared openmouthed, too surprised to react. It had taken Ms. Morris over 15 minutes of class time to calm John down. Now she wondered whether she really knew the real reasons behind John's disengaged behavior.

One might question the necessity of a chapter on giftedness in a text about students with autism. Certainly, societal perceptions, even teacher perceptions, place people with disabilities and individuals who are gifted on opposite poles from one another both in the academic community and arguably in society itself. It may surprise many to find out how often giftedness and disability coincide, particularly in the case of individuals whose disability lies on the autism spectrum. A myriad of educational concerns surround giftedness and ASD and their intersection. As we will learn later in the chapter, both giftedness and AS come with their own sets of educational, societal, and affective challenges. It is interesting that many of the challenging characteristics of both giftedness and AS are so similar that they are not correctly distinguished by diagnosticians, including pediatricians, psychiatrists, and school psychologists. This confusion can result in both misdiagnosis or missed diagnosis. The labels that diagnosticians place on students largely determine the nature of the services provided, and if they are assigned incorrectly, they could have disastrous results for the student both academically and socially. School psychologists, pediatricians, psychiatrists, and teachers must have information to help them distinguish giftedness from AS, identify a student who is displaying characteristics of both, and finally offer academic interventions based on the multipotentiality of the student. The goal of this chapter is to give the reader a working knowledge of giftedness, AS, twice exceptionality, and the issues that surround them, along with strategies for planning and providing appropriate interventions.

DEFINING GIFTEDNESS

Many definitions of giftedness exist, each having its own specific characteristics; however, the multiple definitions do share some commonalities. The National Association for Gifted Children (NAGC), an advocacy group for gifted individuals and education, identifies a child as being gifted if he or she "shows or has the potential for showing, an exceptional level of performance in one or more areas of expression" (NAGC, 2008, ¶ 4). Included in these areas would be intellectual ability, academic aptitude, creative thinking, leadership ability, and the visual or performing arts (Webb et al., 2005). The Javits Grant, a federal program that funds gifted student education defines giftedness as:

> children and youths who give evidence of higher performance capability in such areas as intellectual, creative, artistic, or leadership capacity, or in specific academic fields, and who require services or activities not ordinarily provided by the schools in order to develop such capabilities fully. (U.S. Department of Education, 1988, ¶ 7)

Both of these definitions embrace a wide-ranging view of giftedness that spans well beyond the clear cut boundaries of academics and into the grey areas of less measurable abilities such as leadership, creativity, and artistic talent. Giftedness should not be looked at as a label depending strictly on IQ scores, but rather it should be flexible and fluid, taking into account cognitive function, academic ability, special talents, leadership ability, and the presence of the affective traits of giftedness. To add even more variability to the mix, giftedness can take many forms and can be manifested to different degrees. Individuals can range from the category of "gifted" with an IQ of 130 to 155 to "profoundly gifted" with IQ scores above 155 (Webb et al., 2005). In some cases, gifted individuals are even found with IQ scores above 200 (Lovecky, 2005). Rarely is an individual equally gifted in all the aforementioned areas, rather even the most holistically gifted demonstrate strengths and weaknesses. Gifted people can be very different from one another both in the manifestation of their giftedness and their affective needs.

COMMON BEHAVIORAL CHARACTERISTICS

Specific behavioral characteristics are associated with giftedness. However, not all gifted children will display the majority of the characteristics, and in rare circumstances, a child may exhibit none of the typical characteristics of giftedness. However, in most cases, the behavioral characteristics that gifted children exhibit will carry on into adulthood. Webb et al. (2005) maintain that although a number of research studies have been conducted on the topic of gifted behavioral characteristics, most of them focus on the academic and intellectual realms of giftedness, while very few examine the social–emotional aspects of gifted behaviors. The authors go on to synthesize the research on the behavioral traits of gifted children to include the following characteristics (Webb, et al., pp. 4–5):

➤ Unusually large vocabularies and complex sentence structure for their age
➤ Greater comprehension of the subtleties of language
➤ Longer attention span; persistence
➤ Intensity and sensitivity
➤ Wide range of interests
➤ Highly developed curiosity and limitless questions
➤ Interest in experimenting and doing things differently
➤ Tendency to put ideas or things together in ways that are unusual, not obvious, and creative (divergent thinking)
➤ Ability to learn basic skills more quickly with less practice
➤ Predisposition to largely teach themselves to read and write as preschoolers
➤ Ability to retain much information; unusual memory
➤ Tendency to have imaginary playmates
➤ Unusual sense of humor
➤ Desire to organize people and things primarily through devising complex games

INSTRUCTIONAL NEEDS

Individuals who are gifted often have the ability to pace rapidly through their area or areas of giftedness or to achieve great depth in areas of study. While most students need 7–9 repetitions to grasp a concept, many gifted individuals can gain understanding in 1–3 repetitions. The ability to learn quickly coupled with an intense curiosity can make gifted people fantastic students, earning the proverbial "gold star" from teachers as they progress through school. Unfortunately however, these unique abilities can also make gifted students challenging in a variety of ways.

Gifted students need specialized instruction that allows them to progress through material at their own pace or to explore areas of interest in depth. In a heterogenous classroom where teachers encounter ability ranges that include students with disabilities, English language learners, average students, bright students, and gifted learners, there is little time and in many cases little know-how to appropriately differentiate instruction. Well-meaning teachers will simply assign more work to gifted students, offering them little additional depth or complexity in assignments.

Another common fate of the gifted individual in school is to become the perpetual teacher's helper. Since these students usually grasp ideas more quickly than the rest of the class, they are often called upon by the teacher to help others with homework, rotate from group to group, or perform special duties. A favorite strategy is to identify the brightest students in the classroom and form groups around each of these individuals. For example, in a common classroom grouping, one student completely understands the material (gifted), another student has a good basic level of understanding but has still more information to acquire (average student), and another student has not mastered the objective and needs a great deal of practice (below average student). The groups are formed this way with the best intentions: The teacher believes that the student with the highest degree of mastery can guide the other two students (Davidson, Davidson, & Vanderkam, 2005; Winebrenner, 2001).

Sylvia is a good-natured, charming fifth grader with a lot of spunk. As he watches her draw a diagram for the other students in her group to demonstrate the life cycle of a butterfly, Mr. Jones, her teacher, reflects that he is lucky to have her in class. Sylvia masters the material she doesn't already know with lightning speed and asks for more. She is always willing to help other students and seems pleased that Mr. Jones often asks her to do so. He can, and often does, put the students with the most fragile understanding of objectives into her group, and she often has a way of reteaching the concepts in a way that kids really understand. Although Mr. Jones really appreciates Sylvia's nimble mind and charismatic behavior, he can't help but feel a little twinge of guilt. "She could be learning so much more," he thinks to himself. "If she only spent all the time she is teaching others on material that is challenging to her, imagine how far beyond she'd be." With a wistful sigh, Mr. Jones pushes the thought to the side as the constrictions of time, appropriate differentiation materials, and, for that matter, expertise come rushing in. He walks over to the group to see how they are progressing. As expected, Sylvia is working her magic on the other two students. He wonders if she even knows what she is missing.

Although these roles may boost the self-esteem of gifted students to some degree, little new learning takes place for the gifted student. Often, gifted students already know the concepts they are being taught in their age-level classroom, so in essence, these students could go through days of school learning very few new concepts or even possibly no new information. In fact, gifted children are waiting for their age peers to catch up to what they already know for one fourth to one half of regular class time (Webb, Meckstroth, & Tolan, 1982). I once had a student say to me with an earnest wistfulness about her: "Ms. O'Neill, if I could only learn one new thing each day in school, I would be happy." Imagine the tragedy of that situation! An adult taking a class that is too easy or otherwise inappropriate can drop the class and trade it for another more suitable one. Most students in grades K–12 do not have that option. Essentially, these students are trapped in a school system that relies upon age rather than ability to form most groupings.

PROBLEMATIC BEHAVIORS

Although many of the characteristics giftedness are viewed as positive behaviors, the unique affective characteristics of gifted individuals can cause the parents and teachers concern. Webb et al. (2005) cited frequent referral problems for gifted children surrounding the following social–emotional behaviors:

➤ High activity level coupled with poor impulse control (e.g., interrupting, incessant questioning)
➤ Seriousness beyond age level peers, frequently asking deep or philosophical questions
➤ Impractical behaviors
➤ Perfectionistic tendencies
➤ Sleep problems (e.g., insomnia, nightmares or terrors, extremely vivid dreams, sleepwalking, bedwetting)
➤ Sensory overexcitability (i.e., unusual sensitivity to light, sound, odor, and textures)
➤ Emotional oversensitivity (e.g., intense reactions to injustice, unusual empathy toward sadness or unfortunate situations of others, angry tantrums when frustrated or impatient, mood swings)
➤ Lack of social skills, inability to socialize with age peers, difficulty finding common interests with age peers
➤ Asynchronous development (i.e., advanced ability in some areas, below average ability in others)
➤ Disorganized behavior

"Being gifted is not all it's cracked up to be," Jessica, a ninth grade student told me during one of our conferences together to address some of the unique challenges she was experiencing her freshman year in high school. The label of giftedness has a societal perception attached that includes a bit of mystery, bookishness, perfection, teacher's pet, and geek all rolled into one categorization. Gifted students often encounter serious social challenges as they navigate their differences throughout life stages. Finding friends can present a huge hurdle for gifted individuals. A gifted child can have difficulty relating to age peers who do not share the same interests or who are not at the same intellectual level.

Mark looked around at his classroom with regret. Not one of the other kids knew what he was talking about when he tried, again, to talk to them at lunch. No one in his class even knew what the Large Hadron Collider was! How could he explain how worried he was that the atomic particle splitter would inadvertently create a black hole, sucking the universe into oblivion? Wow, he thought, third graders really need to get a clue!

A lack of intellectual peers can isolate gifted students within their own classrooms. This is not to say that a gifted students cannot have nongifted friends; however, they often mention that the difference in intellectual capacity and interests acts as a barrier to friendship forming and peer acceptance. It is common for gifted children to seek older individuals to form friendships because of shared interests and abilities. Classroom age groupings are not conducive to these types of pairings, however, and socializing with older individuals is often discouraged by adults. It is easy for isolated gifted students to become introverted, seeking out activities that can be accomplished alone, like reading, research, fantasy play, or video games, further cutting themselves off from the unaccepting, unrelatable world around them. These difficulties relating to peers often continue into adulthood and can cause major difficulty in finding mates and being successful in the workplace (Davidson et al., 2005; Kerr & Cohn, 2001; Webb et al., 2005).

Over-Excitabilities (OE)

Polish psychiatrist Kazimierz Dabrowski's Theory of Positive Disintegration (Dabrowski, 1964) identified gifted individuals as being more likely to have overexcitabilities (OE) or, more aptly translated from the Polish, "super-stimulibilities" than age peers. What this means is that a gifted individual's stimulus response is different from the norm because of the intensity, duration of the response, or a variance in the significance of the response trigger (Tolan, 1999). Dabrowski categorized these over-excitabilities into five arenas: intellectual, sensual, emotional, imaginational, and psychomotor. Not all gifted individuals exhibit characteristics of overexcitability; however, the behavioral characteristics that accompany overexcitiability often account for misunderstood, bizarre, or eccentric behaviors often associated with giftedness.

Intellectual OE

Intellectual OE is the most common OE associated with gifted individuals and is exhibited as an intense curiosity or drive to know, a love of brain teasers and puzzles, heightened logical reasoning ability or adherence to logic, or an extreme focus on an area of interest. These individuals also love academics, enjoy complex cognitive reasoning, and search out new information with a heightened degree of frequency and vigor.

Sensual OE

Sensual OE refers to both a heightened pleasure and, conversely, discomfort at sensory stimuli. Individuals with Sensual OE often react intensely to music and art, taking joy from the pleasurable sensory input. They also revel in pleasant tastes, textures, and smells. Sensual OE also causes unusually negative reactions to sensory input that is displeasing, for example, scratchy clothing labels, bright lights, loud noises, and touch (like hair washing). A child can be moved to tears at a Chopin prelude or stare at a Monet for hours, while also being limited by his or her tolerance for light, sound, and other elements in the environment.

Psychomotor OE

Individuals with Psychomotor OE have a heightened ability to be active and energetic. This boundless energy results in the constant need to move, poor impulse control, rapid speech or movement, or tics or other nervous gestures. Many of the behaviors associated with ADHD are common to individuals with psychomotor OE, leading to frequent misdiagnosis. These children may talk constantly, fidget, move at inappropriate times, become excessively competitive, or misbehave. All of this seemingly boundless verve gets these students into trouble both at home and in the classroom.

Imaginational OE

Individuals with Imaginational OE have a love of fantasy, dreaming, and imagery that may be expressed through creative media like art, poetry and writing, music, and drama. In young children, this often emerges through the belief in an intricate imaginary friend and sometimes in imaginary worlds. Imaginational OE also leads to a belief in the magical, and individuals may have vivid dreams both during the day and night as well as nightmares or night terrors. People with Imaginational OE can have intense daydreams and at times are unable to focus on the reality around them because of the poignancy of these fantasies.

Emotional OE

Emotional OE refers to an intensity of emotion (happier when happy, sadder when sad) and a broader range of emotion when compared to others. A heightened sense of justice and the seeking of fairness in all situations can make individuals with Emotional OE extreme idealists. Additionally, Emotional OE contributes to a deep sense of empathy with others, sensitivity to suffering, and intense descriptions of feelings both in verbal and written expression. People with Emotional OE look for deep friendship, valuing a depth of connection beyond typical relationships and, when unable to find it, will often revert to creating imaginary friends and immersing themselves in imaginational dreaming. These individuals are often criticized for being overly sensitive and too emotional and are often misunderstood by their peers. This lack of connection can lead in the most severe of cases to extreme depression and suicidal ideation. Emotional OE presents unique struggles for boys who are often overtly and covertly discouraged from showing their feelings. Dabrowski believed that Emotional OE was the nexus from which all the other OE areas sprung (Tolan, 1999).

Tears slipped down Daniel's slightly reddened face. He didn't want to be crying in front of Ms. Zinnia, but he couldn't help himself. How could he have been so rude, so stupid in his math class? Ugh, he was just so angry. That teacher didn't understand him at all, let alone know all the trouble he was having getting used to this crazy new school. He knew that he had crossed the line, calling that teacher on her "bullshit" assignment of after school detention. He had only been one minute late! Couldn't she see how out of breath he was after running across the sprawling campus? He knew he was in for it when the math teacher had called Ms. Zinnia, his gifted case manager. He had been surprised when Ms. Z. hadn't looked mad, and, when she started asking him questions about how he was really feeling, he just couldn't keep it in anymore. All the worries about his dad's lost job and the new city had come pouring out. He had been safe from tears though until she had asked about friends. He missed his old best friend Stuart so much. Stu got his jokes, was into *Battlestar Galactica,* watched the history channel, and was on the debate team with him. They played every sport together—they had been inseparable since the age of 5. Now at 15 he had to start over. He knew he would never find a friend like Stu again. None of the kids he had met so far were even close. Daniel had never felt so alone in his life. He had wanted to talk to someone about his feelings, but he didn't trust any of the new kids he had met. Most were on the football team and talked about parties, girls, and more football. His parents were worried enough with money stuff, so all of the anger, loneliness, and disappointment had been building up inside him. To be honest, it was a good thing that his outburst had been as small as it was. The last time he had bottled feelings up like this, the explosion had gotten him sent to the principal's office.

ASYNCHRONOUS DEVELOPMENT

Asynchronous development is a term used to describe the sometimes drastically varying levels of ability within gifted individuals themselves (Delisle, Galbraith, & Espeland, 2002; Lovecky, 2005; Rogers, 2002; Silverman, 1993; Webb, et al., 2005). For example, a gifted individual may have very advanced skills in mathematics and spatial reasoning, while her verbal abilities are just average. Alternatively, social skills may lag behind intellectual capacity. It would not be unusual to find a gifted child whose skills are all over the board. For example, a sixth grade student may be reading at the twelfth grade level, performing mathematically at the seventh grade level, with the social skills of a fifth grader. Over time, the skill levels of most gifted individuals catch up to one another and level out, however, some will remain out of synch into adulthood. What differentiates this challenge from other social struggles is that the battle is occurring within the individual. These differences in ability can lead to confusion and frustration on the part of the student and his or her teachers and parents. On one hand, the individual mentioned above can read and comprehend *Go Ask Alice,* a memoir about drug addiction; however, the content level and theme of the book may be inappropriate for the child's maturity level. Additionally, teachers and parents can be easily exasperated by social behavior or judgment that is far behind intellect. "How can he be so smart and be so immature?" The most unfortunate part of asynchronous development is the acute frustration that is felt by the individuals themselves. Gifted people are often keenly aware of their uneven skills and many times are baffled by them. Societal expectations of well rounded intelligence coupled with the perfectionistic tendencies already found in most gifted individuals further exacerbate the negative feelings that may already be building inside.

Judgments and Impulses

Perhaps the greatest challenge asynchronous development presents is the disparity that can occur between intellectual reasoning and social awareness. Social competence, or fitting in to accepted societal norms, is developed over time. While academic information can be acquired through reading, experimentation, research, and so forth, social adeptness is gained through experience and time spent with others. The most significant reason for this lies within the development of the brain itself. Since social adeptness and maturity can really only be learned over time and with experience, it is unreasonable to expect a person, even one with heightened intellectual ability, to have a greater maturity than their age. Additionally, judgment, or executive functioning, finds its home in the frontal lobes of the brain. These areas do not fully develop until an individual's early 20s, while the areas that enable academic knowledge develop much sooner. Most intellectually gifted students will have a maturity level that matches their age or that is slightly behind. By the time that gifted students reach their late 20s, skills have usually leveled out (Webb et al., 2005); however, in the interim these individuals make what seem like ridiculous social mistakes, which are somewhat exacerbated by the tendency to socialize with older children and adults.

Chandler wondered if Ms. Smith was in her office. He liked the cramped space, with the chaos of books and papers spread about, and he knew he could count on Ms. Smith to listen to his latest confusing experience in class. Although he secretly wondered if he spent too much time in her office, knowing she was busy, today couldn't wait. It had been a disaster. His English teacher, Mr. Brazil, had decided to engage the students in a debate. They often talked about current events in Mr. Brazil's class, and Chandler loved the mental exercise these discussions presented. To be honest, he really hadn't learned much new information in an English class since the seventh grade, so he appreciated his tenth grade teacher for spicing it up a bit. He entered, ready for the ensuing fight, pretty sure that he probably knew more about the topic than anyone else. He could impress her today; get her to notice him. Sophia was so beautiful, with auburn ringlets framing her petite face, and smart. Most of the guys that she dated were popular, but they never really were at the same level as she was. Chandler could see this and hoped that she would see past his geeky exterior and realize they were intellectual peers.

To his delight, Mr. Brazil selected him as a debate team leader and Sophia as the leader for the other side. After preparing arguments with their respective teams, they both took the floor and the debate began. Chandler enjoyed the opportunity for a challenge, and Sophia did not disappoint as an opponent. She was quick, feisty, and had a great deal of factual knowledge behind her arguments. But he was a step ahead. He was a skilled debater, and although he was ambivalent about the topic itself, he loved to win, to make his point so resolutely, to support it so completely that there would be no room for further questions or argument. He almost had his rival ensnared in his trap. After briefly wondering whether he might need to "calm down" as his mother often told him and dismissing the idea, it was all over. Even the rest of the class knew it was finished when his adversary had directly contradicted herself. He had won, hands down. He broke character and looked at Sophia, beaming. Now she knew what he could do with words, how well his arguments were structured, how logical! He was startled to see tears brimming in her eyes. Her face was flushed, she looked down at her desk as she slid in, covertly trying to erase the streaks on her cheeks with the back of her hand. Oh no … what had gone so wrong? He looked askance at his lone friend in the room, Marcos, who sat behind him: "You made her look like a fool, dude," he said. Chandler groaned inwardly. He had let his brain take over when he should have been thinking with his heart. Another day of doing the wrong thing.

It is important for adults to remember that being smart is not the same as being mature, but rather, being smart can get in the way of social adeptness. Often, the desire to acquire and use knowledge overrides judgment, or that judgment may not be developed in the first place. Sometimes the search for knowledge, or as Winner (1996) described the "rage to learn," can lead to bizarre or obsessive interests that further serve to ostracize gifted people from their peers.

Unusual or Obsessive Interests

Profoundly gifted individuals have an emotional need for intellectual stimulation that is similar to the physical need for food and water. Without the proper stimulus, these individuals can encounter extreme emotional consequences ranging from socially unacceptable behaviors to depression. The "rage to learn" that Winner (1996) describes fuels the fire of giftedness. This desire to pick up any and all possible knowledge on one single topic or a variety of them can appear strange to others. As has been discussed in this chapter so far, gifted people are very different from their age peers and are also a diverse group themselves.

Some gifted individuals are so passionate about learning that they have a desire to know about everything. They are fascinated equally with zoology, history, literature, art, culture, and the like, progressively gathering more and more information about the topics of their choice, often jumping from one interest to another. Many of the parents of these children cannot keep up with the flow. "One day he was working on insect models in his room, the next reading Edgar Allen Poe, and later that week I found him trying to build a hovercraft in the garage!" This variance in interest presents challenges not only for parents and teachers of gifted students, but for the students themselves. Often they have a difficult time identifying a career that they want to pursue or an interest in which to focus their time. The idea of so many options available at which the student could actually be successful causes some gifted people to flit between interests even into adulthood. This can cause strain both at home and at school, with parents trying to support ever-changing interests with both time and money and teachers attempting to provide interest based enrichment to a child whose interests change frequently. Parents of these children are often concerned about their child's ability to follow through with projects and how that will translate in college and beyond. As adults they may have difficulty with selecting long-term careers, and others may interpret them to be shallow, flighty, or noncommittal.

The broad range of interests that gifted children experience may also serve to further differentiate them from their peers, because they more frequently cross gender lines (Kerr, 1994; Kerr & Cohn, 2001). Girls may be interested in the traditional female pursuits but also learn chess, go to science and math camps, and play sports, while boys' interest may include dance, drama, and art in addition to traditional sports, scouting, and so on. Although these experiences serve only to further enrich both children and adults, gifted students' gender identities may be called into question by their peers, and they may have difficulty as the minority in a certain pursuit.

Conversely, gifted students may have an intense single-minded interest in one specific area. This "obsessive" interest may be in a relatively broad subject such as dinosaurs or in a very specific one like fruit fly mating (Lovecky, 2005; Webb et al., 1982; Webb et al., 2005). Parents and teachers are often confused about whether to support these pursuits or to discourage them, because even the most socially well-adjusted gifted person may be differentiated from his or her peers by an obsessive interest. On the other hand, this kind of specific, focused interest leads to breakthroughs in research, invention, entrepreneurship, and other endeavors in life that create tangible improvements to society. Gifted people who are changing the way that we view the world, like Steve Jobs, Bill Gates, John Nash, and Oprah Winfrey, all pursue their individual passions with fervor. Nevertheless, all of the other challenges that giftedness brings with it compound the social consequences of obsessive interests. Not only might a child have a single-minded interest in penguins, he or she may talk about it incessantly, become bored in the classroom if the lesson is not about or related to penguins, become such an expert in penguin science that he or she inadvertently corrects the teacher on a fact in front of the class, or take over classroom discussion during the penguin unit in science. This person may have trouble finding a friend who shares his or her interest in penguins or even someone with the same passion for any subject at all.

Friendship

It is easy to see how all the challenges that have been discussed so far in the chapter can make it very difficult for gifted children and adults to form valuable, enriching friendships. The prospect of finding another person who not only shares the same interests but is also understanding of all the eccentricities that can accompany giftedness without assistance is daunting. Lovecky (2005) refers to these unique pairings as true peers, as opposed to age peers (children at the same age) or mental peers (individuals who can keep up intellectually with the gifted person, or another who shares the same interest regardless of age). True peers are other gifted children who have the same need for intellectual nourishment, are understanding of the passions and interests of their friend even if they do not share them, and who have a deep and meaningful connection with each other. Lovecky maintains that although friendships with true peers are difficult to find, they are vital to the social and emotional stability of a gifted individual, and these friendships often last over many years and even great distances. By giving gifted children opportunities to find each other through purposeful classroom grouping, schools can offer significant possibilities for gifted students to find their true peers.

With all the challenges that gifted people face, it is easy to see how brilliance comes with a price. Gifted individuals struggle to find their place within the family, classroom, and society. Strikingly, many of the characteristics of giftedness are shared by individuals on the autism spectrum. How do teachers and other educational professionals tell the difference?

TWICE EXCEPTIONALITY

Gifted? Disabled? Both? Twice exceptional is the term used to describe a person who is both gifted and has a disability. Gifted people can have physical disabilities, sensory disabilities, AS, emotional and behavioral disorders, learning disabilities, and ADD/ADHD. *Twice exceptionality* is the existence of heightened academic abilities or talents in a specific area coupled with significantly below average or problematic functioning in another (Baum & Owen, 2004). Distinguishing the subtleties that separate giftedness, AS, and the coexistence of these two exceptionalities within the same individual is paramount in providing targeted holistic interventions in the school setting. Examining side by side the characteristics of giftedness, AS, and twice exceptionality with AS will illuminate similarities and differences so that educational practitioners can best serve these unique students.

Asperger Syndrome

Both AS and giftedness are regarded with a certain mystique. Finding both of these exceptionalities in the same person presents a paradox of sorts. As is the case with asynchronous development among gifted children in general, it is counterintuitive to many people for a disability and a talent to exist in the same person. For twice exceptional children, this wide span from ability to disability presents many challenges for parents, teachers, and education support personnel. To add more confusion to the mix, many of the eccentricities typically found in gifted individuals are behaviors identified with AS (Asperger, 1944; Cash, 1999; Lovecky, 2005; Neihart, 2000). Three current issues in the field are the significant problem of the misdiagnosis of AS within gifted individuals; the issue of masking, or the ability of gifted individuals with AS to use their gifts to compensate for their disability (Neihart, 2000; Webb et al., 2005); and the lack of teaching strategies to address these unique students.

Asperger Syndrome, also referred to as Asperger Disorder, is characterized by significant, pervasive problems with social relationships and limited interests. (Attwood, 2007, Lovecky, 2005). This, coupled with extreme difficulty relating to others, is the impetus for many scholars to believe that AS lies on the autism spectrum as a "mild" form or as "high functioning autism" (HFA) (Lovecky, 2005). The American Psychiatric Association's *Diagnostic and Statistical Manual, Fourth Edition, Text Revised* (*DSM-IV-TR;* APA, 2000) lists the indicators of AS as the following:

➤ Impairment significantly impairs the ability to maintain social relationships both at work and in an individual's personal life.
➤ Social skills impairment shown in at least two of the following ways:
    ➤ Impaired ability to pick up on nonverbal social cues such as eye contact, facial expressions, and body language
    ➤ Inability to develop appropriate relationships with developmental peers
➤ Lack of interest in sharing enjoyment with others; lack of understanding of the interests of others
➤ Impaired ability to share emotionally and socially with others
➤ Repetitive or stereotyped behaviors, interests, and activities shown in at least one of the following ways:
    ➤ Abnormal preoccupation with specific behaviors or interests
    ➤ Rigid routines or ritual that serve no practical purpose
    ➤ Repetitive physical movements (e.g., finger snapping, hand flapping)
➤ No evidence of significant language delay
➤ No evidence of cognitive impairment

Inconsistencies in diagnosis of AS are common, in part because of the controversy surrounding whether AS is an ASD or a disability in its own right. Disagreements arise over whether AS is HFA or a diagnosis separate and distinct from autism. After their own review of the literature, Ozonoff and Griffith (2000) could find no clear evidence for differentiating the two disorders, and we will use the terms, AS and HFA, interchangeably in this chapter. What distinguishes AS/HFA from classic autism is the individual's level of cognitive development and language skills. According to the *DSM-IV-TR* (APA, 2000), individuals with AS have normal cognitive ability, language development, and language acquisition, although the effective use of this language in social situations is impaired. People with AS may have a broad range of verbal ability but may have difficulty integrating these skills with nonverbal cues like facial expression and body language.

When Hans Asperger, a Austrian pediatrician, began his work at the University Pediatrics Clinic in Vienna, he began work on remedial pedagogy which at that time was the way the society attempted to medically treat children with difficult or odd behavior. When Asperger arrived, the children at the clinic where he worked were treated as though they were ill. They lay in bed in a hospital ward and were seen on rounds. Asperger believed that many of the children in these wards were not ill but rather had a persistent lifelong handicap for which the treatment was routine, education, and behavior modification. Asperger was fascinated by a group of students who exhibited many of the same challenging characteristics. These patient were socially odd, with difficult behaviors. Asperger began work on his doctoral thesis on autistic psychopathy, observing the behavior of these children within the clinical setting. Soon Asperger had implemented changes to the hospital routine. Children were out of bed participating in daily activities in and around the hospital and were being taught by a local nun, Sister Viktorine Zak, whom Asperger revered for her ability to both calm and teach the children. As his interventions progressed, Asperger chose four children to focus on in his doctoral dissertation, even following one into adulthood. All of the patients that Asperger observed were socially odd, exhibiting some of same difficulties in communication as the children described in Leo Kanner's (1943) study of children with the more classic symptoms of autism (Frith, 1991). Those in Asperger's study however, did not have some of the overt behaviors that Kanner observed, had language skills, and also had IQs ranging from very low to very gifted. Although through a great coincidence, Kanner and Asperger published some of the seminal information about autism at about the same time, they never met. Kanner's work was immediately met with acclaim; however, Asperger's work, *Die Autistischen Psychopathen Im Kindesalter* (1944), was largely unknown until it was translated from the German and reviewed by Lorna Wing in 1981 in her article "Asperger's Syndrome, a Clinical Account." After her article's publication, diagnostic criteria for AS were added to the *DSM-IV,* and the idea of a spectrum of autistic behaviors was adopted to include both low and high functioning individuals.

The discrepancy in diagnosis of AS occurs because psychologists may not strictly adhere to multiple indicators when diagnosing the syndrome. Since this loose interpretation exists, diagnosticians may both overdiagnose, when too few indicators are followed, and underdiagnose, when symptoms are not perceived as severe enough to warrant identification. Another factor adding to the underdiagnosis is the difference between the severity of behaviors associated with autism and those that indicate AS. Lovecky (2005) maintains that the label itself is a significant influence on how individuals with AS are perceived. She believes that HFA is a difficult term for individuals to understand because autism is commonly associated with mental retardation. With this perception already in place, it may be difficult for parents and teachers to identify children with AS because children with this condition have an above average IQ.

According to Aspy and Grossman (2007), people with AS and HFA have impairments in three general categories: perseverative or repetitive behaviors, social functioning and appropriateness, and communication. They refer to these categories as a triad.

Mindblindness and Theory of Mind

Aspy and Grossman (2007) note that many of the behavioral characteristics related to AS are shared by other disabilities and disorders, making social differences the hallmark characteristics of the disorder. In the past, people thought that individuals with AS were incapable of feeling emotion or did not want to interact with others, but this is simply not true. People with AS do have feelings and often express the desire to make friends with others. Their ability to correctly interpret social situations and act upon that interpretation is impaired.

One of the most significant social impairments is *mindblindness*. The expression was coined by psychologist Simon Baron-Cohen and is used to describe the inability of people with AS to imagine or predict the thoughts of others. In his essay "Mindblindness: An Essay on Autism and the Theory of Mind" (1995), Baron-Cohen describes most people as *mindreaders*. Most people observe the behavior of another and make predictions about the motivation behind those behaviors. For example, if we see someone cross the street, look closely at the ground, and then cross back, we can imagine that perhaps the person is looking for something. Maybe the person thought the bus stop was on the other side of the street but then realized he was wrong, or perhaps he just felt like crossing the street and then reconsidered and crossed back. Baron-Cohen maintains that, as mindreaders, we could come up with many different "maybe" scenarios. People with mindblindness are unable to come up with a normal variety of "maybe" scenarios. People with AS are often unable to recognize the motivation for the actions of others or simply equate the actions only with what their own behavior in such a situation would be.

The ability to understand the thoughts, perceptions, and emotions of others and the use of this understanding to surmise about the behavior of other people is called the Theory of Mind (TOM). TOM begins to develop in infancy. By the age of 14 months, infants will use gestures and read facial expressions to direct the attention of other people to an object they want. An example of this would be pointing at a cookie. This simple action, called joint attention, discussed in Chapter 2, shows that the infant is aware that the people surrounding him or her have their own thoughts and awareness (Aspy & Grossman, 2007). Individuals with AS/HFA are described as having an impaired TOM. Baron-Cohen and Swettanham (1996) believe that infants with AS have difficulty reading and interpreting the faces of those around them, causing a delay in initiating joint attention and thus an impaired TOM. The mindblindness associated with impaired TOM development can explain many of the social differences of people with HFA, including making friends, understanding jokes, interpreting nonverbal cues, developing social adroitness, and overcoming naïveté. Many of the communicative differences people with HFA experience can also be attributed to degrees to mindblindness. These include difficulties with the conversational etiquette, like interrupting; monopolizing conversation or talking constantly; using advanced, too formal, or too specific language at inappropriate times or with inappropriate social groups; and difficulty listening to or discussing the interests of other people.

Sameness, Behavioral Differences and Special Interest Areas

Individuals with AS usually have a need for routine and may have a difficult time reacting to change and unpredictability. Transitions, surprises, or changes from routine, even pleasant ones, may be difficult for people with AS and could initiate behaviors such as repetitive questioning, meltdowns, or withdrawal. When individuals with AS are unable to maintain routine, they may begin to feel overwhelmed and become distressed.

People with AS may also have repetitive behaviors or narrow interests and activities. These are usually not physical behaviors like flapping, clapping, rocking, and spinning that one may observe in classically functioning people with autism, but rather they display themselves as obsessive interests, atypical fascinations (e.g., washing machines, road signs, train station maps), or interests that are unusual for the individual's age group (e.g., interest in Thomas the Tank Engine at the age of 12). These areas of preoccupation are described by Winter-Messiers (2007) as Special Interest Areas or SIAs. Individuals can spend countless hours attending to the SIA, and preoccupation with this interest area can lead to social withdrawal and obsessive behaviors. (Aspy & Grossman, 2007). Both Asperger (1944) and Attwood (2007) noted that individuals with AS are able to acquire an amazing depth of information and skill in their SIA, with Asperger noting that certain students acted like "little professors" (Frith, 1991, p. 137) giving informative lectures on their SIA to whomever would listen. According to Winter-Messiers (2007) the special interest area is a vital part of functioning for an individual with AS and even went on to say, "Students with AS do not consider their SIAs to be mere hobbies or leisure activities, but regard them as integral to themselves. They do not see a separation between the SIA and their core being" (Winter-Messiers, 2007, p. 73).

Communication, Sensory and Motor Differences, and Emotional Challenges

Arguably, communication is what most differentiates people with AS from their peers. These challenges affect individuals with AS in all stages of life, from infancy to adulthood, inhibiting the ability to connect with family, make friends, and succeed both in school and in the working world. Many of the communicative differences could be a result of mindblindness: failure to identify, interpret, or use nonverbal cues such as facial expression and body language; difficulty with social and conversational etiquette; difficulty with figurative language, humor, sarcasm, and the multiple meanings of language (Baron-Cohen, 1995). Additionally, people with AS often have difficulty asking for help and following instructions and may also exhibit echolalia (i.e., recitation or repetition of phrases, words, or sounds).

Sensory hypersensitivity is also a common characteristic of AS, with individuals having negative or unusual reactions to particular sights, sounds, temperatures, tastes, and textures (Atwood, 2007). People with AS may have negative reactions to environments that are overstimulating (e.g., too much noise, sound, smell) and have tantrums or melt-downs when the antagonizing source may be as commonplace as the swish of the dishwasher, a teacher's perfume, or the texture of a polyester sock inside a shoe. Failure to recognize smells, textures, and feelings may also occur. This too can prove troublesome, in particular if the individual is not sensitive to pain, prolonging diagnosis and treatment of various maladies or injuries (Attwood, 2007).

According to Aspy and Grossman (2007), almost all individuals with AS have motor differences, and the identification of these differences is playing a greater role in the diagnosis of HFA. Some suggest that motor differences among individuals with ASD can be seen during the first year of life, before communicative discrepancies are noticed. This idea also calls into question the existence of rapid onset autism.

Finally, individuals with ASD are also more emotionally vulnerable than their peers. This vulnerability results from both the challenges they face understanding the emotions of others and controlling emotions within themselves. Stress is difficult for people with ASD to regulate and can result in rage and tantrums. In addition, depression is the most commonly diagnosed psychiatric disorder among individuals with ASD, resulting in sadness, irritability, aggravation of repetitive or maladaptive behaviors associated with AS, and finally suicide (Aspy & Grossman, 2007). People with AS may operate in emotional extremes: they often have difficulty controlling emotions; may be anxious, perfectionistic, have low self-esteem; and may have difficulty understanding both their own emotions and those of others.

"Oh my God, oh my God! Help!" Mr. Bradbury could hear the panicked shrieks of a young woman echoing down the hall from his office. The frantic note in the girl's voice could not be mistaken, so he set off at a run down the short hallway connecting the science lab to his office. Chrissy was at the door flushed and wide eyed. "It's Gabriel," she said. He cracked the door, frightened at what he might see. Ever since Gabriel had found out that he was moving at the end of the semester, he had been inconsolable, fixating on the topic unwaveringly. Mr. Bradbury had found him crying outside the lab door that day mumbling incoherently about moving to Washington state. "All my friends are here. I don't want to go to a new place. It rains 209 days on average there," Gabriel had sobbed over and over again. After referring him to the school counselor and having a meeting with his IEP team, Mr. Bradbury had a list of strategies to use to redirect Gabriel, but he still was feeling overwhelmed. The first crying episode had occurred 3 weeks ago with a replay happening almost every day. He had talked with administrators and Gabriel's parents about his concerns; however, the only response he had received was a directive to follow the intervention plan.

Last Friday, Gabriel had taken off his belt and put it around his neck saying, "I'm going to kill myself if I have to go there." Although Mr. Bradbury had referred him once again to the counselor, Gabriel had not been placed under a crisis team's care. His parents and counselor all thought that he was simply engaging in attention seeking behavior and had discouraged Mr. Bradbury from listening to his complaints, referring to his long talks with Gabriel as "encouraging his outbursts." He could hear Chrissy breathing in small gasps as he opened the office door, increasing the sense of foreboding he already felt. On the floor, in a crooked heap was Gabriel, a brown woven belt around his neck. The beginning of a bruise outlined the belt as Mr. Bradbury loosened it. Shallow breaths escaped Gabriel's slightly parted lips and his eyes began to flutter. He was just unconscious. Maybe this would finally convince the team that Gabriel was serious about hurting himself. Mr. Bradbury felt tears pricking at his eyes. "Call 9-1-1," he said.

Connections, Confusion, and Misdiagnosis

It is interesting and frequently highlighted in the literature on the misdiagnosis of AS in gifted individuals that the traits of giftedness bear striking similarities to characteristics associated with AS (Asperger, 1944; Cash, 1999; Lovecky, 2005; Neihart, 2000). In particular, the challenges with social skills, perfectionism, impracticality, and oversensitivity to outside stimuli cause both psychologists and families to suspect that their gifted child has AS or lies somewhere on the continuum of ASD. To add additional confusion, the issue of masking presents a significant challenge in correct identification (Neihart, 2000; Webb et al., 2005). The ability of gifted children to compensate for their disability hinders correct diagnosis and can result in legitimately twice exceptional individuals not receiving proper interventions.

In their book, *Misdiagnosis and Dual Diagnosis of Gifted Children and Adults*, Webb et al. (2005) extensively discuss the "modern tragedy" (p. xix) occurring in the realm of gifted education. The text details the many similarities between giftedness and various psychological disorders and laments that many well-respected and knowledgeable clinicians are mistaking gifted eccentricities for disability. This misdiagnosis has grave consequences for gifted individuals. The assignment of an incorrect label may have harmful effects on an individual's self-esteem and may result in incorrect educational placement. In addition, individuals are often medicated or counseled to change behavior that is typical for gifted people. After examining the traits inherent to giftedness and AS, it is easy to see how the two can become confused. Many of the behaviors, both positive and negative, that are associated with giftedness are also found with a high prevalence in those with AS. Figure 7.1 shows their shared characteristics.

How do we tell these groups of people apart? What is the value of such a differentiation? The first step to differentiating between gifted eccentricity and AS (or any other disability) is to consider behaviors of the individual and the environment in which they occur. The characteristic that is most distinguishing is an impaired TOM, in other words, mindblindness. Gifted children are often engrossed in projects, reading, or their own inner world, making them seemingly unaware of others around them. However, when gifted individuals are with true peers, exploring areas of interest together, they show empathy, are able to predict the actions of others, and seek engagement (Lovecky, 2005; Webb et al., 2005). Additionally, gifted individuals are aware of how their behavior affects others (although they may continue the

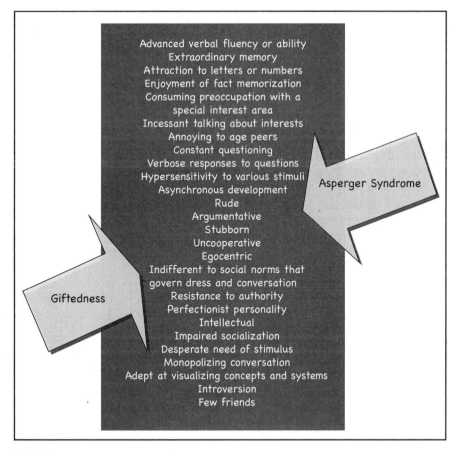

Advanced verbal fluency or ability
Extraordinary memory
Attraction to letters or numbers
Enjoyment of fact memorization
Consuming preoccupation with a
special interest area
Incessant talking about interests
Annoying to age peers
Constant questioning
Verbose responses to questions
Hypersensitivity to various stimuli
Asynchronous development
Rude
Argumentative
Stubborn
Uncooperative
Egocentric
Indifferent to social norms that
govern dress and conversation
Resistance to authority
Perfectionist personality
Intellectual
Impaired socialization
Desperate need of stimulus
Monopolizing conversation
Adept at visualizing concepts and systems
Introversion
Few friends

Asperger Syndrome

Giftedness

FIGURE 7.1

Shared Characteristics of Giftedness and Asperger Syndrome

behavior in spite of the realization) and are aware of the emotions of others and the unique dynamics of interpersonal relationships. A gifted individual's sense of humor is often advanced or adult-like. Distinguishing them from individuals with AS, gifted people will use and understand humor that incorporates social give and take. In sum, individuals who are solely gifted are, as Baron-Cohen would describe, mindreaders. They aware of the differing thoughts and selves of others, are able to predict their actions, can infer meaning from those around them, and are aware of how other people perceive them. Other characteristics which distinguish gifted individuals from those with AS include: their need for routine is less acute and they exhibit better adaptability to change; strange motor movements (if any exist) are related to stress, anxiety, or an overabundance of energy; they understand and uses figurative language; and their distractibility is related to outside stimuli rather than from own ideas or inner world (Lovecky, 2005; Neiheart, 2000; Webb et al., 2005).

Individuals who are gifted and have AS will exhibit the mindblindness discussed earlier, however, some characteristics these twice exceptional individuals possess differentiate them from people with the singular diagnosis of HFA/AS. Gifted people with AS are more likely to relate their SIAs to the world around them. Cash (1999) believes that the giftedness in individuals with AS could be developed into careers or vocations that may both be productive and also improve societal perceptions of twice exceptional people. Gifted people with AS are also more likely to use complex language at an earlier age than nongifted age peers with AS and learn and use complex words from their SIA at a quicker rate.

Given the striking similarities among gifted individuals, those with AS, and people with both, what is the purpose of differentiating the categories? In a perfect world, where schools cater exclusively to the needs of each individual child, there would be no need. In the real world however, labels often are the sole determinants of service and to some degree define the individual for the rest of their lives. It is important for teachers, school psychologists, and other education personnel to be aware of the similarities, differences, and comingled characteristics of giftedness and AS so that students can receive the proper interventions and future planning. A student who is gifted and does not have access to a challenging curriculum that includes both depth and complexity will suffer greatly in school. The boredom, ostracism, and underachievement that can result from the misplacement of a gifted child, the misunderstanding of the characteristics of giftedness, and the lack of appropriate curriculum is well-documented in the literature (Baum & Owen, 2004; Davidson et al., 2005; Delisle et al., 2002; Kerr, 1994; Kerr & Cohn, 2001; Lovecky, 2005; Webb et al., 2005; Winebrenner, 2001). This disconnection both from peers and the curriculum can leave a gifted student feeling alone and strange in a sea of age peers. Often, the feelings of loneliness associated with unrecognized giftedness can be remedied by identifying the student and placing him or her in a classroom with other gifted children. This opportunity for intellectual peer recognition helps students understand that there are others like themselves.

Alternately, students who are masking symptoms of AS through use of their giftedness may also experience adversity. In addition to hiding a daily struggle with specific academic skills, the individual will be misunderstood by a very confusing world. Behaviors that seem rational and logical to those with AS can be viewed by others as bizarre and out of place within the typical societal framework. People with AS need direct, purposeful instruction to develop and hone their social behavior. Without proper interventions, people with AS may not develop social skills, workplace skills, and other vital behaviors necessary for successful independent living.

I read through Collin's file with increasing dismay. It had all started with a phone call from his mother. Collin was a recent transfer from a tiny place in the state of Maine. Our high school has more students than there were residents in his last hometown, and Collin's mother was nervous about the transition for her son. Collin had been diagnosed at a young age with Sensory Processing Dysfunction, ADD, and AS, and his IEP had crossed my desk about 2 weeks before. My boss had asked me to take a look at his file because all of his previous teachers, psychologists, and counselors had made anecdotal remarks about his brightness. Additionally, she asked that we place Collin in my class of gifted students until placement could be determined.

So, Collin joined us. Strangely, I saw no evidence that the quirky behaviors Collin exhibited were adversely affecting his ability to function in the classroom. In fact, with regard to the diagnosis of AS, I was baffled. Collin was one of the most empathetic students I had ever encountered. I decided to observe Collin for a while before I voiced my concerns about his identification. When Collin's mother called and talked about the progress he had made since his initial diagnosis 8 years ago, some of my suspicions were confirmed.

As I leafed through the voluminous file, I read time after time how educational personnel had mentioned his brightness, motivation, and complex sense of humor. They also noted that Collin seemed to often be daydreaming about books he was reading or other imaginative scenarios. Teachers reported that although very bright, Collin was very introverted, preferring to read or take solitary walks during recess. He had only one friend in school and clung to the other child with ferocity.

Collin's mother had initially referred him to a pediatrician because of the tantrums that he threw when she tried to wash his hair. She also reported Collin having tantrums at school when any water spilled in the classroom or the lunch area, with complete meltdowns when the water spilled on him. All of the instances of violent behaviors had ceased by the time that Collin was finishing second grade, however, his introversion and subsequent isolation continued throughout elementary school.

When Collin entered the middle grades, he participated in school sports, performing very well in football, track, and baseball. Along with inclusion in these sporting activities came more friends, although none would be as close as his initial friend from the early days of school. It struck me as unfortunate that despite repeated mention of his brightness and psychological evaluations that consistently placed his IQ in the 140 range, Collin was never offered gifted services. All of the behaviors he had exhibited as a child could be explained by his giftedness, and the sharp decline of these behaviors over time reminded me of what I had learned about asynchronous development.

After talking to Collin's mother, I learned that he was on the medication Concerta to help him focus, but that he did not take it in the summer. "Why?" I asked. "Oh, well, he never gets bored in the summer. He is always reading or playing sports or researching about WWII. He can just do his own thing then. He's really focused when he can learn at his own pace—fast," she said. As I put down the phone, I knew it was time to reevaluate Collin. Thank goodness I was lucky. The psychologist at my school had taken courses about gifted individuals. With her wealth of information both about giftedness and disabilities, I was sure that we would get the appropriate services designated for Collin.

It's 3 weeks later, and I have Collin in my office. After two evaluations, one by the school psychologist and another with both a pediatrician and a psychiatrist, all of the diagnoses have come into question. Both evaluations are in agreement that Collin fails to meet the *DSM-IV-TR* characteristics for either ADD or AS. As I explain the characteristics of giftedness to Collin, I see a change come over his face. He sits and listens intently, staring at the Powerpoint I am showing him. I'm concerned when I see tears forming in his eyes. "What's the matter?" I ask. "I always thought there was something wrong with me," he says with amazement. "There's nothing wrong with you," I reply, "you're just gifted."

Ms. Webb experienced the opposite problem in her classroom. "The information we are learning in this class is juvenile. The material is so substandard, I am completely dismayed. Last year I was mating fruit flies, recording mutations, and attempting to create a new species in independent study with Mr. Bass. Now I am learning about what each letter in DNA stands for?! This is ridiculous. I want to see your teaching certification. Are you highly qualified in Biology? Did you take upper level science classes in college? Do you even have a masters degree? I strongly suspect that you are not qualified to teach me." Ms. Webb stood and looked at Kara unbelievingly. The rest of the seventh grade class just stared.

"Get out! Go to the office!" Kara turned her head quizzically and asked, "Which office?" "Are you mocking me? Just get out!" Ms. Webb's voice reached a high pitched shrill. As Kara left, she called the principal's office to let them know that Kara would be on her way down with a discipline referral. Fifteen minutes later, the phone in the classroom rang. Kara had never arrived. School personnel and the school resource officer began to search the grounds. They found Kara standing in front of the athletic office. "It was the first one I came to," she later explained.

Twenty minutes later, the principal watched the mess unfold in her office. After listening to a frustrated Ms. Webb give an impassioned recitation of the incident, she called in Kara to give her version of the events in the classroom. At first she thought Kara was being glib when she explained her desire to become a geneticist in the future. "It is really important that I have excellent instructors who can guide my research. I just wanted to ascertain whether Ms. Webb was prepared to instruct me. Degrees in biology and genetics would be best." When Kara seemed genuinely confused about how upset Ms. Webb was, the principal was sure of her sincerity and was also pretty sure that she wasn't seeing the full picture of the child.

Everything began to become clear when Kara's mother arrived. She told the principal that Kara had been diagnosed 2 years ago with AS. She and her husband hadn't wanted to tell the school because they were afraid that Kara would be removed from the gifted classes or placed in a self-contained program for people with autism. Kara was so bright that they could barely handle her demands for information at home. She had been getting by in school quite well because of her precocity. Most teachers just tried to keep up with her requests for material. Over the years some had expressed concern over her intense focus on life sciences, specifically reproduction and genetics, however, most had chalked it up to the quirkiness of a "dorky" (as one teacher had put it) kid. Kara's mother and her husband had suspicions that Kara was not developing normally, however, and so had taken her to visit a psychiatrist. "Since her diagnosis, Kara has been in therapy once a week, and we implement the strategies at home. She has had outbursts like this at home, but this is the first in school." Kara's mother relayed nervously.

The principal sighed. If only the school had been aware, appropriate interventions and strategies could have been developed to educate both Kara and her teachers about the unique academic and affective needs of a gifted student with AS.

WHAT TEACHERS CAN DO

Given the confusing and volatile nature of both giftedness and AS, what can teachers do to best serve these twice exceptional students in the classroom? The literature is surprisingly sparse on best practice interventions, and this is an area that requires further study. This being said, however, teachers can take information and resources both from the literature on giftedness and AS and use it flexibly to enhance the strengths and bolster the weaknesses of these unique students. Much of the available literature does have one thing in common, and that is to focus on a strengths-based approach for learning.

Addressing the Gift and Special Interest Areas

When teaching gifted students with AS, it is critical to address the student's giftedness. In many educational settings, remediation takes precedence over enrichment and acceleration. This results from a focus on creating a well-rounded individual with relatively equal strengths in all areas. The gifts of twice exceptional students are often ignored, put to the side to focus on weaknesses, seen as bizarre or obsessive, or simply not accommodated in a traditional school setting. To ignore the giftedness in an individual is tantamount to educational neglect. If anything, the giftedness in a child should be the focus of all education. Many gifted individuals with HFA have the potential to masters in the field associated with their special interest area (Asperger, 1944; Grandin, 2001). By ignoring the gifts of these twice exceptional individuals in an effort to completely focus on areas of weakness, we are depriving the world of the next potential paleontologists, geneticists, authors, and professors. In his book, *The Complete Guide to Asperger's Syndrome* (2007), Attwood devotes a chapter to the special interests of individuals with AS. He discusses the main functions of the SIA in the life of an individual with AS (pp. 182–188):

➤ A way to overcome anxiety
➤ A source of pleasure
➤ A means of relaxation
➤ An attempt to achieve coherence
➤ The creation of an alternate world
➤ A sense of identity
➤ A way to occupy time, facilitate conversation, and indicate intelligence

It is easy to see how integral the SIA is to a person with AS. In the case of gifted students with AS, the special interest may be one of the few venues to tap the child's true potential for learning. Temple Grandin, a gifted woman with HFA, advocates nurturing twice exceptional students' expertise in their area of interest to enhance their career opportunities (2004). The specificity or unusual nature of the SIAs of gifted people with AS coupled with advanced intellectual capacity and the drive to know sets these twice exceptional people on the road to becoming experts in their field. Grandin (2004) suggests that if gifted people with AS work on becoming specialists within their SIA, they will be so desirable in their field that employers may overlook certain social challenges, or that twice-exceptional individuals may have more power to mold a work environment to suit their own unique needs. Grandin bases these assertions on her own life experience as a sought-after expert in animal behavior and humane slaughter techniques.

There are also indicators that instruction in the SIA may decrease negative or challenging behaviors associated with AS. Winter-Messiers et al. (2007) found that when questioned about their SIA, individuals with AS had a decrease in impairments. All students involved in the study showed improved functioning in one or more areas when discussing their SIA. Students became more animated when speaking; used more appropriate social interaction (the authors theorize to encourage others to listen), verbal language, and body language; and had improved communication skills. Students also used SIAs to attempt social interactions with others by finding a common interest, using socially sophisticated strategies like being a "good friend" first and then introducing the SIA, if the other child does not seem initially interested in the interest area. SIAs also help students deal with their own emotions and the emotions of others. Students reported feeling calmer, less stressed, and happier when engaging in their SIA. The authors also observed improvement in fine motor tasks when engaged in SIA activities such as "drawing, sculpting, cartooning, building airplane models, building things with Legos and playing musical instruments [which] often required exceptional fine motor skills." Parents reported that students who otherwise had deficits in executive functioning were able to organize information pertaining to their interest. Interviews about the SIA showed more organized sequential speech and the use of sophisticated, professional words to inform the listener. Winter-Messiers et al. (2007) also cited the emotional expression of individuals with AS in music performance and composition, even though this ability is directly at odds with the difficulties people with AS have in empathizing. The passion that individuals with AS feel about their SIA motivates them to practice these difficult activities to improve their skills.

Teachers can bank upon this interest area and use it both to further encourage the building of strengths in the student and to address areas of challenge. Teachers of the gifted use areas of special interests or passions to develop individualized or small group curriculum frequently, and although this individual differentiation does require extra planning, teachers can create interdisciplinary thematic units that offer many days and weeks of activities surrounding the interest area. The thematic unit can relate the interest area to Language Arts, Math, History, Science, Social/Cultural Studies, Music, and Art. Bianco, Carothers, and Smiley (2009) suggested that teachers begin this process by creating a concept map with their student that will encompass all of the possible areas of study regarding the SIA that are of interest to the student. Figure 7.2 offers an example of how concept mapping can lead to activities that support both content and the student's SIA. In some cases, students can even design their own activities that display mastery of a concept to the teacher. Often, students will create more complex, higher level thinking assignments than the teacher, specifically because they have more information on hand about the subject and a deep passion that leads to intricate questioning.

Mentoring

Finding an expert to mentor a twice exceptional individual has never been easier. With the advent of the internet and networking devices like Skype, Facebook, Twitter, Microsoft Live Chat, and others, students have easy and virtually limitless access to professionals from all over the world. These mentors may include doctors, engineers, university professors, professional artists, writers, and so on—any individual who can offer expertise in the SIA and is willing to communicate with a student. Mentoring is frequently mentioned in literature as a productive strategy to link gifted students with specific, professional expertise and instruction in an area of interest and passion (Attwood, 2007; Baum & Owen, 2004; Bianco et al., 2009)

Compacting

Compacting is an instructional strategy in which students are preassessed over concepts to be taught, to see what they already know and which areas need additional instruction. Students are then given instruction in only those areas in which they have not shown mastery of objectives. The student is then offered accelerated curriculum, assigned projects or research that increase the depth of knowledge of a particular subject, or both. Instead of wasting time learning concepts they already know,

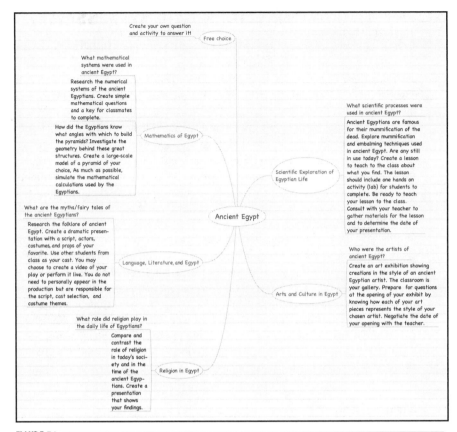

FIGURE 7.2

Concept Map and Example Activities—Ancient Egypt

gifted students and their teachers can spend time more judiciously, both instructing concepts yet to be learned and exploring new information in depth.

In her book, *Teaching Gifted Kids in the Regular Classroom,* Winebrenner (2001) offers many practical strategies for the implementation of curriculum compacting within a heterogenous regular classroom. The key to compacting is the preassessment of objectives to be taught within small units of the curriculum, measured perhaps in weeks, days, or units (although the amount and time span of objectives is completely up to the implementing teacher), coupled with activities that either accelerate or offer depth and complexity of knowledge. Curriculum compacting couples perfectly with the use of SIAs in instruction, because it confirms that students are acquiring the objectives the teacher has set while also pursuing areas of interest in depth. Including the student in the development of these explorational activities and incorporating elements of student choice can further increase interest and motivation.

AUTHENTIC EXPERIENCES AND ASSESSMENT

Authentic experiences and assessment take learning into the real world by showing how knowledge is applied and assessing a student's ability to apply it in contextual settings. Through the vehicles of field trips, internships, investigations, community service, and outside experiences, teachers expose students to the practical application of the knowledge they are acquiring in the classroom. Authentic assessment is successfully used with twice exceptional students because it is performance based and allows students to develop products, flexibly and with variety (Baum, 2001; Bianco et al. 2009; Winter-Messiers et al., 2007).

Flexibility, Creative Teaching, and Showing Interest

Winter-Messiers (2007) suggested that teachers make a significant effort to discover a student's SIA along with information about it and resources with which to research the topic. Not only will this investigation give teachers information they can use when incorporating information into instruction, but it also will show interest to the student and perhaps help form a better connection between teacher and student. By showing interest in a student's SIA, the teacher is getting to know an integral part of the student's personality and motivation. Teachers should also examine their curriculum and think about how to incorporate the SIA daily, even if it is in the form of a reward. Although the use of rewards to motivate students may be undesirable to some teachers, the challenge that gifted students with AS can present in the classroom (in terms of student effort, behavior, or acquisition of skills) may necessitate this practice, at least until the teacher becomes more comfortable integrating the SIA into the curriculum itself. Additionally, the SIA may not fit the curriculum in every instance. Even the best teachers may have difficulty integrating the topics. Creative teaching, reaching out beyond the box to help students connect to learning through the vehicle of their SIA, will stretch both the student and instructor. Finally, teachers should be flexible, both with modes of learning and product choices. Permit students to create their own assignments and research and create products in preferred modalities, such as videos, photographic essays, compositions, artwork, or presentations.

SUMMARY

Gifted people have special academic and affective needs. Not addressing these gifts as an integral part of a student's educational setting can have long-ranging negative effects, including boredom, ostracism, loneliness, underachievement, and depression. Gifted people need to have a rigorous academic curriculum that provides a challenge and excites interest areas in addition to exposing them to other gifted individuals.

Giftedness and disability can coexist within the same person and is referred to as twice exceptionality. Twice exceptional students require an even greater degree of intervention than gifted students, because their needs are so specialized and unique. Teachers must address the giftedness of the student while also providing remediation in areas of weakness.

To add even more to confuse teachers, twice exceptional individuals are often unidentified for two reasons. These individuals can use their gifts to mask a disability, implementing enough coping strategies and adaptations to skate under the radar of a special education qualification. Twice exceptional students also are often mislabeled because the identified disability acts as a barrier against gifted identification, either because school personnel only see the student in the context of the disability or the student is enrolled only in classes that focus on areas of weakness rather than strength and is never placed in a situation where the individual's gifts are allowed to shine.

Twice exceptional students with AS are in particular need of accurate labeling and appropriate intervention. Shared characteristics that are common in both giftedness and in AS make these diagnoses particularly difficult. Diagnosticians and school personnel are often unaware of these similarities and do not how to distinguish among an individual who is gifted, one who has AS, and one who is both gifted and who has AS. The differentiation of these is integral to the correct labeling and subsequent appropriate interventions for students.

When teaching a student who is gifted with AS, educators should focus on addressing the student's gift or talent before attempting to offer interventions to address academic or affective needs. Teachers should pay special attention to the SIAs of gifted students with AS and attempt to integrate them into daily instruction. Individuals with AS have the potential to be experts in the field pertaining to the SIA. By giving twice exceptional students access to subject matter that inspires and excites them, teachers can ensure that content objectives are mastered through integration in the SIA, while also allowing students the opportunity to gather even more knowledge and expertise in the SIA.

Students who are gifted and have AS are fascinating, puzzling, complex, and endearing. Through increased awareness of the unique traits of giftedness and AS and how they are interrelated, educational professionals will be better able to serve these individuals in the classroom and help them step into both a well fitted role in society and the fulfillment of their potential.

> Failure to help the gifted child reach his potential is a societal tragedy, the extent of which is difficult to measure but which is surely great. How can we measure the sonata unwritten, the curative drug undiscovered, the absence of political insight? They are the difference between what we are and what we could be as a society.
>
> —James J. Gallagher

REFERENCES

American Psychiatric Association (APA). (2000). *Diagnostic and statistical manual of mental disorders* (4th ed., text rev.). Washington, DC: Author.

Asperger, H. (1944). Die autistischen psychopathen im kindesalter. *European Archives of Psychiatry and Clinical Neuroscience, 117*(1), 76–136.

Aspy, R., & Grossman, B. (2007). *The Ziggurat model.* Shawnee Mission, KS: Autism Asperger.

Attwood, T. (2007). *The Complete Guide to Asperger's Syndrome.* London: Jessica Kingsley.

Baron-Cohen, S. (1995). *Mindblindness: An essay on autism and the theory of mind.* Cambridge: Massachusetts Institute of Technology Press.

Baron-Cohen, S., & Swettenham, J. (1996). The theory of mind hypothesis and alternative accounts. In D. J. Cohen, and F. R. Volkmar (Eds.) *Handbook of Autism and Developmental Disorders* (pp. 880–893). New York: Wiley.

Baum, S., & Owen, S. (2004). *To be gifted and learning disabled: Strategies for helping bright students with LD, ADHD, and more.* Mansfield Center: Creative Learning Press.

Bianco, M., Carothers, D. E., & Smiley, L. R. (2009). Gifted students with Asperger syndrome: Strategies for strength-based programming. *Intervention in School and Clinic, 44*(4), 206–215.

Cash, A. (1999). A profile of gifted individuals with autism: The twice-exceptional learner. *Roeper Review, 22,* 22–29.

Dabrowski, K. (1964). *Positive disintegration.* Boston: Little Brown.

Davidson, J., Davidson, B., & Vanderkam, L. (2005). *Genius denied.* New York: Simon and Schuster.

Delisle, J., Galbraith, J., & Espeland, P. (2002). *When gifted kids don't have all the answers: How to meet their social and emotional needs.* Minneapolis, MN: Free Spirit.

Frith, U. (Ed.). (1991). *Autism and Asperger syndrome.* Cambridge: Cambridge University Press.

Grandin, T. (1995). *Thinking in pictures and other reports from my life with autism.* New York: First Vintage Books.

Grandin, T. (2001). Genius may be abnormality: Educating students with Asperger's Syndrome, or high functioning autism. *Autism Research Institute,* Retrieved June 13, 2008, from http://www.autism.com/individuals/genius.htm

Grandin, T. (2004). Label of 'autism' could hold back gifted children. *Nature, 430,* 399.

Kanner, L. (1943). Autistic disturbances of affective contact. *Nervous Child, 2,* 217–250.

Kerr, B. (1994). *Smart girls: A new psychology of girls, women and giftedness.* Scottsdale, AZ: Gifted Psychology Press.

Kerr, B., & Cohn, S. (2001) *Smart Boys: Giftedness, manhood, and the search for meaning.* Scottsdale, AZ: Great Potential Press.

Lovecky, D. (2005). *Different minds: Gifted children with AD/HD, Asperger Syndrome, and other learning deficits.* Philadelphia, PA: Jessica Kingsley.

National Association for Gifted Children (NAGC). (2008) *What is Gifted?* Retrieved June 15, 2008, from http://www.nagc.org/index.aspx?id=574

Neihart, M. (2000). Gifted children with Asperger's Syndrome. *Gifted Child Quarterly, 44,* 222–230.

Ozonoff, S., & Griffith, E. M. (2000). Neuropsychological function and the external validity of Asperger syndrome. In A. Klin, F. R. Volkmar, & S. S. Sparrow (Eds.), *Asperger Syndrome* (pp. 72–96). New York: Guilford Press.

Rogers, K. (2002*). Reforming gifted education: How parents and teachers can match the program to the child.* Scottsdale, AZ: Great Potential Press.

Silverman, L. (1993) *Counseling the gifted and talented*. Denver, CO: Love.

Tolan, S. (1999, February). *Dabrowski's over-excitablities, a layman's explanation*. Retrieved March 22, 2010, from http://www.stephanietolan.com/dabrowskis.htm

U.S. Department of Education, Academic Improvement and Teacher Quality Programs. (1988). *Jacob K. Javits Gifted and Talented Students Education Act* (Elementary and Secondary Education Act of 1965, as amended, Title V, Part D, Subpart 6; 20 U.S.C. 7253 et seq.). Washington, DC: Author.

Webb, J., Meckstroth, E. A., & Tolan, S. S. (1982). *Guiding the gifted child: A practical source for parents and teachers*. Scottsdale, AZ: Great Potential Press.

Webb, J., Amend, E., Webb, N., Goerss, J., Beljan, P., & Olenchack, F (2005). *Misdiagnosis and dual diagnosis of gifted children and adults: ADHD, Bipolar, OCD, Asperger's, Depression, and other disorders*. Scottsdale: Great Potential Press.

Winebrenner, S. (2001). *Teaching gifted kids in the regular classroom*. Minneapolis, MN: Free Spirit.

Wing, L. (1981). Asperger's syndrome: A clinical account. *Psychological Medicine, 11*(1), 115–129.

Winner, E. (1996) *Gifted Children: Myths and realities*. New York, NY. Basic Books.

Winter-Messiers, M. A., (2007). From tarantulas to toilet brushes: Understanding the special interest areas of children and youth with Asperger Syndrome. *Remedial and Special Education, 28,* 140–152.

Winter-Messiers, M. A., Herr, C. M., Wood, C. E., Brooks, A. P., Gates, M. M., Tingstad, K. I., et al. (2007). How far can Brian ride the Daylight 4449 Express? A strength based model of Asperger Syndrome based on special interest areas. *Focus on Autism and Other Developmental Disabilities, 22,* 69–79.

Families and Parents: Involvement, Support and Management

Martha Cocchiarella and Renee Wozniak

Our children are impulsive, forgetful, extremely active and sometimes downright difficult. They are also exuberant, fun, witty, loving, spontaneous, imaginative, creative and overall wonderful children. With our love, support, understanding and guidance they can and will become all they dream to become and more. (Author Unknown)

I worry about whether my child understands that I love her. I'm afraid she will never understand how much her family loves her. She can't say mom but I would rather wait for the day when she comes to understand the concept of love. (Author Unknown)

Epstein (2001) identified six types of parent involvement, including parenting, communicating, volunteering, learning at home, decision-making, and collaborating with the community. Each type of involvement presents its own unique challenges for both parents and schools. However, each component is ultimately crucial when formulating an effective, comprehensive plan for initiating and maintaining parent involvement. In this section, we explore various techniques professionals can employ to enhance parent and family involvement in the education of their child with autism.

FAMILY EDUCATION—CREATING A SUCCESSFUL HOME ENVIRONMENT

The home environments of children with autism can vary significantly from the home environments of their nondisabled peers. Often, home programs are in place, whether formal or informal. Depending on the severity of autism, structures may also be in place, such as schedules, visible boundaries, or items that are not likely found in a typical household (e.g., sensory equipment, assistive technology). It is imperative that teachers and other professionals recognize this distinct difference when attempting to assist families in developing a supportive home environment. The family of a child with autism is already encountering a plethora of challenges at home, so structuring their environment or activities any differently could prove to be a daunting task. Jeremy, for example, has claimed most rooms in his house as "his territory," by lining up several of his toy cars in each room and hanging signs that say "do not touch" near these and any other possessions that are his. Attempting to create new structures in the home for educational purposes, which would likely mean the restructuring of these items, could cause a great deal of stress on Jeremy and the rest of the family, as Jeremy gets physically aggressive toward himself and others when any of his items are moved. Knowledge of the home environment in conjunction with careful collaboration and planning is necessary whenever restructuring the environment of a child with autism. Equally important for the student is the teacher's willingness to learn how to help him or her generalize home programs in the school environment. Learning how to carry over curriculum from one environment to the other is a two-way street when a child with autism is involved. Additionally, it is important that professionals realize that the home environment and needs of the child and family change as the child ages (National Research Council [NRC], 2001).

Parents of children with autism may feel inundated with information coming from a variety of sources including teachers, habilitation or respite providers, speech–language therapists, occupational therapists, music therapists, and more. Conversely, some parents may not have enough information in relation to helping their child at home. If parents are to be able to effectively carry over programming and learning into the home setting, they need to be informed of the distinct characteristics and expectations of their child's school setting. School programs usually involve homework, studying, assessment, socializing, field trips, and instruction in various subject areas. For a child with autism, any of these elements can go awry if not tackled properly by both parent and teacher.

The academic skills and needs of a child with autism may vary greatly from those of nondisabled peers and even from other peers on the autism spectrum. For example, though a child with autism may be able to answer multiplication facts as accurately as same-age peers, he or she may need additional time to process the multiplication facts, and in turn additional time to complete in-class assignments and homework. Student-specific curricular needs must be communicated to the parent, so the parent knows how to work with the child at home in a manner consistent with that of the school setting. A parent of a child with autism cannot simply peruse a textbook or search the internet to discover what his or her child should be learning in any given grade level. The distinct needs of each child on the autism spectrum create the need for a much more individualized curriculum. Parents who are well-informed of activities that will benefit their child at home may be better able to foster learning environments through everyday activities, creating a bridge between their child's specific learning needs at home and at school. This link between learning at home and at school facilitates consistency and repetition, both of which can be beneficial for students on the autism spectrum. Table 8.1 outlines the ways in which professionals can collaborate with families and assist them in gaining knowledge about the best practices in the home environment to benefit their child.

TABLE 8.1

Family Education – Creating a Successful Home Environment

Suggestions for Helping Families	• Provide families with methods to structure the home in such a way that supports structures in place at school (e.g., schedule, visual cues, etc.) • Provide families with information about and instruction in specific skills their child is working on in all subject areas, areas of need, and methods for promoting skill acquisition, maintenance, and generalization at home (including information about homework) • Provide families with materials (or suggestions to create materials) necessary to implement any instructional programs at home • Provide families with a regular schedule of activities they may have the opportunity to implement in the areas of communication, social skills, adaptive behavior, and academics (for both the school year and summer months) • Provide families with tangible instructional materials including DVDs, media clips, and newsletters on parenting a child with autism at various ages and transitional periods • Provide families with information about or opportunities for classes, workshops, educational opportunities, support groups, or trainings specific to autism, special education, and parenting

(continued)

TABLE 8.1 *(continued)*

Suggestions for Helping Families *(continued)*	• Provide families with information about or opportunities for learning more about therapies, interventions, diets, medications, financial planning, government funding, etc.
Meeting the Needs of All Families	• Suggestions should not be too overwhelming in time or content for the family to implement • Consider families' access to media players if media is provided • All information exchanged to and from school must be clearly communicated, practical, and conducive to child's success in home, school, and community • For students who have difficulty communicating, teachers must be responsible for keeping parents aware of homework assignments and what students are working on in school • Consider time constraints of the home environment (e.g., parents working, therapies, or other home programs in the evening or on weekends, etc.) • Consider the possibility of behavioral challenges in the home environment when doing schoolwork or in general • Consider that parenting styles and expectations may vary from culture to culture • Present all information in primary language of families • Consider the possibility of differences in home versus school activities depending on language, customs, and traditions • Consider parents' views on disability and their role as parents and in the educational process • Consider the primary home language of students and families and its effect on completing work at home • Consider the evening and weekend commitments of families (e.g., Temple, Greek School, taking care of extended family members, etc.) • Consider the family's beliefs about techniques and methods being used to implement instruction (e.g., making eye contact, sitting down in a chair during instruction, etc.) • Be sensitive to the knowledge base of families (e.g., limit and/or explain special education or autism jargon)

FAMILY PARTICIPATION AND EMPOWERMENT

School-based involvement for parents should incorporate activities that allow parents to be involved in a welcoming school environment while including specific opportunities for parent involvement in their child's school setting (Hoover-Dempsey et al., 2005). All teachers know parents they can rely on to consistently volunteer and parents that they have not even met. The question that remains is that of willingness. Are the parents who consistently volunteer really that much more willing to do so than other parents, or are the rarely seen parents just unaware of volunteer opportunities that fit their schedules and talents? Perhaps they do not think their child wants them at school or chaperoning a field trip. For a child with autism, a parent might think being involved at school will somehow cause their child to be "thrown off," and it is highly possible that they are correct in that assumption. For teachers, the task then becomes keeping parents informed of every volunteer opportunity, even if it means creating new opportunities and making parents feel more than welcome by both the way they treat the parents and in the structures they put in place that keep their child involved in the normal routine, so as not to allow him or her to be "thrown off."

The availability of both parent volunteers and opportunities to volunteer may be more prevalent in a special education classroom setting than in a general education setting. Regardless of the setting, for children with autism, parents' involvement helps them to remain cognizant of what is happening at school in order to promote generalization of skills learned in school to the home environment. Therefore, developing creative participation opportunities bolsters success in the classroom.

Participation in the educational process does not have to include only volunteering in the classroom or school. In addition to participating in the activities and events of the class and school, parents should also be decision-makers when it comes to activities and curriculum at the levels of the classroom, school, district, and even higher levels of programming and planning. Examples of decision-making practices include active participation in parent-teacher organizations, involvement in advocacy groups working toward school improvement, membership in district-level committees, awareness and involvement in school and local elections, and networking with parent representatives (Epstein, 2001). Inherently, parents of children with autism should be involved in educational decision-making and planning processes as members of the IEP team. Even so, what matters most is the *degree* to which parents are involved in planning and decision-making. A parent might physically attend an IEP meeting, nodding his or her head in agreement with everything the teachers and service providers suggest. This type of situation can be deceiving. Teachers must analyze the true involvement of parents in the decision-making and planning processes. Parents may be informed of curriculum and decisions, but are they truly involved in the planning process? Moreover, are they involved in the planning process at levels that both directly and indirectly affect their child?

In an effective collaboration, responsibility and decision-making power should be shared between parents and professionals (Murray et al., 2007). Furthermore, parents do not have to be involved in decision making solely for their children; they can also be involved in decision-making processes of the school or the school district. This can include joining the parent–teacher association; being a board member or site council member; or helping to plan and organize fine arts, sports, or other school events. For parents of a child with autism, being involved at higher levels can be the key to improving their child's education, as administrators and other highly involved community members work in conjunction with the parent of a child with special needs. A parent who is a member of the school board, for example, may have more opportunities to bring up concerns regarding special education programs in the school district than a parent who never makes contact with key district decision-makers. Some school districts even offer parent advisory councils solely for decision making in special education. Teachers, schools, and school districts must develop ways of recruiting parents, especially parents who likely have very limited time, as is the case for many parents of children with autism. Table 8.2 outlines the ways in which families can be encouraged to participate as well as empowered to assist in decision-making.

TABLE 8.2

Family Participation and Empowerment

Suggestions for Helping Families	• Provide families with a space at the school or district where families can go to find resources and materials related to special education and autism and that can be used to come together for meetings, support groups, or volunteer work
	• Provide a parent survey at the beginning of the school year with a variety of suggestions for volunteer opportunities, so that parents can determine where they most effectively fit in
	• Communicate frequently regarding volunteer opportunities (may be incorporated into a schedule of daily communication)
	• Recruit parent volunteers to assist in the implementation of classroom procedures and instruction (e.g., under guidance of the teacher, a parent may work with one or two students on particular skills or activities)
	• Provide a calendar or sign-up sheet for parent assistance in providing supplies, snacks, or other materials that may be used for classroom activities or instruction
	• Whenever possible, encourage families to participate in decision making regarding programming, methodology, and techniques used in the school setting

(continued)

TABLE 8.2 *(continued)*

	• Encourage families to participate in planning field trips and other class activities • Encourage the formation of parent advocacy groups, councils, and committees that bring families together and bring information about autism into the community • Provide information to families about participating in school, district, and government level autism, special education, or education policy making or reform
Meeting the Needs of All Families	• Provide information to all families regarding ways to get involved in various volunteering and decision-making processes at the school and district levels, not just parents who show an initial interest • Consider possible time and resource restrictions of families and be ready to plan activities conducive to these restrictions • Incorporate a variety of activities so that various time availabilities, talents, and resources are utilized • Provide training for parents on all volunteer activities, especially in working directly with students • Maintain confidentiality of sensitive student or family information • Consider that some students with autism have difficulty seeing and interacting with their parents at school • Consider the family's view of what their role in their child's education should be (i.e., different views for different families or cultures) • Make available volunteer opportunities that take into consideration cultural differences • Provide opportunities for parents who may not speak English • Consider any language barriers and determine ways to help parents overcome these barriers and get involved

FAMILY INVOLVEMENT IN THE COMMUNITY

Community involvement and social acceptance can alter a life for better or worse, and it is integral to the success of individuals with autism. Individuals with autism should be actively involved in their communities at every possible opportunity, just as nondisabled individuals would be. Parents should not be afraid to access their communities for fear that their children will not fit in. Epstein (2001) suggests sample practices for community collaboration, including providing families and students with information on various programs and services (e.g., cultural, recreational, social support, etc.) as well as information on community activities in relation to learning skills; devising plans for service integration through school–community partnerships; generating community service programs involving students, parents, and schools; and recruiting alumni to participate in school programs for students.

Active involvement in the community on the part of both parents and students can promote awareness, acceptance, and partnerships in advocacy, each of which can ultimately benefit students in both their home and school lives. Social and communication skills are also enhanced when children with autism move outside the walls of their home or school and learn by interacting with others and participating in new activities. Families of children with autism should be viewed as part of the community, rather than outsiders. Various types of social networking can help people get by, cope, get ahead, and change their opportunity (Briggs, 1998). Table 8.3 outlines the ways in which professionals can assist families in becoming involved with the community.

Family involvement is most successful when professionals communicate diligently with families and are willing to teach families as well as learn from them. If professionals and families take time to look at the "big picture" when it comes to educating their students and children with autism, they may be more likely to initiate and stick to plans for regular collaboration, which can ultimately affect not only the child's education for a school year, but for the rest of his or her life.

BUILDING COLLABORATIVE RELATIONSHIPS

Collaborative relationships can be difficult to develop when professionals do not understand what a child's autism means to a family, (NRC, 2001). Parents see their children in ways that teachers do not and can provide essential information that could not be acquired by reading a report or through discussion with another professional (Kluth, 2003). Stoner et al. (2005) identified three themes in their study of the interaction between parents and professionals in the field of education:

1. Influences on parent perception
2. Experiences that either encouraged or discouraged parental trust
3. Roles that parents took on as they interacted with professionals

These researchers focused in on the first and second themes because they are ones that help in the development of parent friendly strategies. Their findings suggest that parents have repeatedly experienced negative interactions with professionals, leaving them feeling "skeptical and cautious" (Stoner et al. 2005, p. 48). They also suggest that trust was built when parents and professionals clearly communicated and met expectations and when parents felt professionals genuinely cared about their child's education and well-being (Stoner et al. 2005). Strong communication and

TABLE 8.3

Family Involvement in the Community

Suggestions for Helping Families	• Provide families with information about community activities for children with autism or special needs • Provide families with information about community support programs or services for children with autism or special needs • Encourage school–community collaboration to promote autism awareness and support • Encourage community participation in Special Olympics or other activities for children with special needs • Plan class, school, or district events to promote autism awareness and support in the community
Meeting the Needs of All Families	• Consider the possibility that parents may not want other people in the school, district, or community to know that their child has a diagnosed disability • Consider the social, behavioral, and communicative needs of students and the effect these have on successful participation in the community • Consider community awareness of autism and receptiveness to children with autism and related challenges and needs • Consider family's financial constraints preventing participation in the community (i.e., many families pay a great deal for home programs, therapy, special equipment, etc.) • Consider any language barriers and determine ways to help parents overcome these barriers in the community • Be aware of community resources for families of various cultural backgrounds

collaboration between parents and professionals that focuses on the best interests of the child can positively influence parent perceptions and build trust.

For children with autism, home–school communication is crucial to the success of the student, the classroom, and the home environment. A bad morning at home could result in an even worse day at school if the teacher is not made aware of underlying issues the child may be experiencing. When the teacher is made aware of a situation, he or she can do everything possible to help that child turn his day around, whether it means presenting a less-demanding task first thing in the morning or reading a social story with the child about a similar situation. Parents and teachers can also keep one another informed of any progress or regression the student has made academically, behaviorally, socially, or in the area of communication.

Maintaining Home and School Communication

"Parents (or other responsible family members) and schools should communicate regularly and clearly about information important to student success," (National Coalition for Parent Involvement in Education, n.d., ¶ 2). Schools can communicate with parents in a variety of ways including (Hornby, 2000):

➤ informal contacts,
➤ social events,
➤ phone calls,
➤ written communication,
➤ meetings, or
➤ conferences and home visits.

For children with an autism spectrum disorder, it is especially vital that both parents and teachers be kept in the loop about events in the child's life. Many children with autism cannot communicate this themselves, and because of their special needs, communication patterns between home and school can make or break a day or even an entire school year for a child with autism. In this section, we explore the various forms of home–school communication and methods for developing effective communication routines. Table 8.4 provides an overview of various forms of communication, the best usage of each form, and advantages and disadvantages of each.

Agreeing on a Communication Method

Professionals and parents must come to an agreement as to what type of communication format would best meet the needs of both parties, to maximize the opportunity for a flourishing relationship. Home–school communication is only effective when it is conducted in the most beneficial format for everyone (Medlen, 2000). Depending on the needs of the family, communication methods may be highly individualized. Parent preferences may be based on many factors including convenience, cultural patterns, socioeconomic realities, or variations in ability. Whenever possible, teachers need to adjust their communication strategies to mesh with those of the parent in relation to these factors (Salend, 2005). Email, for example, may be the preferred mode of communication for parents who check their email regularly at work. Another parent may not have access to email or even a phone. One parent may feel she can express herself more effectively through writing, while another parent feels his handwriting is illegible and can articulate his thoughts more accurately by verbalizing them. Still other parents may not speak English as their primary language and do not feel comfortable communicating directly but may recruit one of their children to translate written communication at home. For children with autism, detailed communication usually happens on a daily basis. However, for some parents this may be too much, and they may prefer a system of once a week communication, unless an emergency arises. Whatever the case may be, the communication method should work for both parties, but especially for the parent.

TABLE 8.4

Home–School Communication

Mode of Communication	When to Use	Advantages	Disadvantages
Home–School Notebook	Less formal communications A variable amount of information to be relayed through narrative communications	Effective for daily communication Situational (allows parent and teacher to write more or less depending on situation) Lots of room to write All communications are kept in one place and teacher and parent can readily look back at previous communications Student is responsible for bringing notebook to and from school (opportunity for teaching skills in responsibility) Embedded documentation of communication	May be time consuming depending on the content of agreed upon communications Parents, teacher, or student may forget to send notebook home or to school Care must be taken to write neatly so information can be easily read Parents may not have the ability to read or write (in English or otherwise) Meaning can be misinterpreted by reader
Premade Checklist	Formal or informal communications (depending on checklist) Fixed amount of information and fixed content Daily communication (or other agreed upon schedule)	Can be tailored to fit individual needs of parents and students Teacher and parent can quickly gauge what information they should relay (checklist provides prompts) Less time consuming than narrative communication	Parents may feel that too little information is provided (not comprehensive) Information can get monotonous (teacher and parent are checking the same boxes over and over) Space may be limited for narrative portions from parent or teacher

(continued)

TABLE 8.4   Home–School Communication

Mode of Communication	When to Use	Advantages	Disadvantages
Premade Checklist (continued)		Narrative component may be coupled with checklist if parents and teacher wish	Certain thoughts or ideas may not be expressed due to limited nature of checklist components
		Student is responsible for bringing checklist to and from school (opportunity for teaching skills in responsibility)	Parents, teacher, or student may forget to send checklist home or to school
		Embedded documentation of communication (checklists must be saved by teacher)	Parents may not have the ability to read or write (in English or otherwise)
			Meaning can be misinterpreted by reader
Email	Informal Communications	Quick method of communication	Parents may not have access to email
	Student cannot be responsible for taking written communication to and from school	Several people can be included in one email	Parents or teachers may not receive email immediately
	Teacher or parent has something additional to add that was not included in the notebook or checklist	Immediate delivery	Meaning can be misinterpreted by reader
		Embedded documentation of communication	Can be accidentally deleted
	Communication must be made immediately	Situational (allows parent and teacher to write more or less depending on situation)	Parents may not have the ability to read or write (in English or otherwise)
	Contacting several parents at once		
	Others are being included in communication	Student may be able to participate in communication while increasing skills in technology	
	Students are involved in communications		

(continued)

TABLE 8.4

Home–School Communication

Mode of Communication	When to Use	Advantages	Disadvantages
Brief Note	Informal communication supplementary to regular communication To convey a timely message	Allows teacher or parent to communicate quickly or at the last minute Student is responsible for bringing note to and/or from school (opportunity for teaching skills in responsibility)	Hurried writing-can cause loss of comprehensibility or clarity Student may forget to give the note to teacher or parent Parents may not have the ability to read or write (in English or otherwise)
Student Agenda	Informal, brief communications To relay homework assignments Higher-functioning students	Student is responsible for bringing agenda to and/or from school (opportunity for teaching skills in responsibility) Agendas are often used in general education, promoting generalization of and efficiency in use Students usually carry agenda with them and all teachers have access to it Student may participate in keeping track of homework or notes	Limited space to write Student may not keep agenda neat, making it difficult to find conducive space Student may forget to give the agenda to teacher or parent Parents may not have the ability to read or write (in English or otherwise)
Newsletter	Formal communications To communicate to all parents about many important details	Keeps parents informed of happenings outside of those involving their own children	Not individualized to particular child If student names are included, must be aware of confidentiality issues

(continued)

TABLE 8.1

Home–School Communication

Mode of Communication	When to Use	Advantages	Disadvantages
Newsletter (continued)	To relay school, classroom or community information as opposed to individualized information	Students may help put the newsletter together	May be time consuming to create
			No room for parents to respond
	Supplementary to regular communication about individual student	Pictures or other graphics can be added	Too much information may be overwhelming for parents
		Teacher can communicate with many parents at once	Languages and abilities of all parents must be considered in any mass communication
		Student is responsible for bringing newsletter home (opportunity for teaching skills in responsibility)	Student may forget to give the newsletter to the parent
		Only has to be created a specified number of times per year (monthly, quarterly, etc.)	
Blog	To relay school, classroom or community information, as opposed to individualized information	Teacher can quickly add information to blog	If student names are included, must be aware of confidentiality issues
		Students can help with blog	Parents may not be able to respond (depending on type of blog)
	Supplementary to regular communication about individual student	Pictures or graphics may be added	Cannot provide individualized information
	To relay interesting, funny, or timely stories about classroom events	Parents can access at their leisure	Languages and abilities of all parents must be considered in any mass communication

(continued)

TABLE 8.4   Home–School Communication

Mode of Communication	When to Use	Advantages	Disadvantages
Website	To relay school, classroom, or community information, as opposed to individualized information	Parents are readily informed of homework or activities for week, month, or other predetermined time period	May be difficult to create or update depending on teacher knowledge
	Supplementary to regular communication about individual student	Useful links can be provided for parents	Parents cannot respond
			Cannot provide individualized information
	To post homework assignments, teacher biographies, and other class or school events and activities	Pictures or graphics may be added	Languages and abilities of all parents must be considered in any mass communication
		Parents can access at their leisure	
Phone Call (Consistent)	Formal communication	Two-way, synchronous communication can occur	Documentation of communication is not readily available (teachers must document conversations)
	In-depth, two-way communication		
	Parents request this as the regular method of communication	A great deal of information can be relayed and may not be misinterpreted as easily as written communication	When discussing confidential information, phone call must be made in private
	Student cannot be responsible for taking written communication to and from school		Can be difficult to stop conversation and may take up more time than expected
			Only parent and teacher can communicate at one time
			Parents may not have access to a phone

(continued)

TABLE 8.4

Home–School Communication

Mode of Communication	When to Use	Advantages	Disadvantages
Phone Call (Situational)	Informal communication	Two-way, synchronous communication can occur	Documentation of communication is not readily available (teachers must document conversations)
	When in-depth, situational information must be relayed	A great deal of information can be relayed and may not be misinterpreted as easily as written communication	When discussing confidential information, phone call must be made in private
	Emergencies		
	To discuss timely positive or negative information with parent	Best way to relay emergency information	Can be difficult to stop conversation and may take up more time than expected
	When issue of importance was not relayed in written communication		Only parent and teacher can communicate at one time
			Parents may not have access to a phone
Face-to-Face Meeting (Informal)	Informal communication (e.g., when parents pick students up from school)	Can quickly relay important information	When discussing confidential information, talking must be done in private
	To briefly relay information	Student may be directly involved (practicing communication skills)	Can be difficult to stop conversation and may take up more time than expected
	Supplementary to regular communication	Two-way, synchronous communication can occur	Documentation of communication is not readily available (teachers must document conversations)

(continued)

TABLE 8.4 Home–School Communication

Mode of Communication	When to Use	Advantages	Disadvantages
Face-to-Face Meeting (Formal)	Formal communications IEP and related meetings Parent/Teacher conferences When addressing formal issues (e.g., extreme behavioral issues, transitions) When many people are to be included in communication (e.g., therapists, administrators) Supplementary to regular communication	Student may be directly involved (practicing communication skills) Synchronous discussion can be done by many people at once	When discussing confidential information, talking must be done in private Can be difficult to stop conversation and may take up more time than expected Documentation of communication is not readily available (teachers must document conversations) May be difficult to determine agreed upon time depending the schedules of parents and professionals
Home Visit	At least once per year if possible To create a feeling for parents that you are interested in learning about their "whole" child When required by your school district as part of the reevaluation process or other process When assessing environments in a behavior assessment situation or other situation involving direct knowledge of the home environment	Student has opportunity to see home–school connection Teacher gets to know student in more depth than just the classroom environment and may be able to better understand student Gives teachers the opportunity to more easily take parents' or students' perspective	Parents or student may feel uncomfortable with a home visit Student may be confused about boundaries between home and school May be difficult to schedule an agreed upon time Documentation of communication is not readily available (teachers must document conversations and may wish to document relevant information about the home environment)

(continued)

TABLE 8.4

Home–School Communication

Mode of Communication	When to Use	Advantages	Disadvantages
Audio or Video Tape Exchange (Kluth, 2003)	If this method of communication is most effective for parents and teacher	May be beneficial for parents who do not have the ability to read	Both parent and teacher must have access to devices to record and play agreed upon audio or video
	Informal, asynchronous verbal communication	Audio may be played while parent or teacher completes another task (multitasking)	May be time consuming or cumbersome to record or listen to/watch
	Parents do not have the ability to read or do not have access to a phone	Many people can listen at once (e.g., an entire family)	Audio or video device or equipment may be expensive
		Verbal communication is readily documented	
		Student may be directly involved	
		Student is responsible for bringing audio or video to and from school (opportunity for teaching skills in responsibility)	
Progress Reports	Formal communication regarding progress made during a scheduled time period (e.g., quarterly)	Entire school usually uses same form of communication	May not be sent home frequently enough for parents
	To communicate information regarding grades, missing homework assignments, test scores, and other progress	Allow parents to see exactly why their child did or did not make progress (via accurately conveyed data)	May be difficult to understand, especially if teachers use abbreviations or jargon
	To communicate formal progress on IEP goals	Student is responsible for bringing report to and from school (opportunity for teaching skills in responsibility)	Students may be reluctant to bring progress reports home if they convey negative information
			Student may forget to give progress report to parent

Written Communication

The most widely preferred mode of home–school communication appears to be written communication (Epstein, Munk, Bursuck, Polloway, & Jayanthi, 1999). In a study by Turnbull and Turnbull (2001), results indicated that parents tend to prefer informal forms of regular communication, especially written communication, because they generate consistent contacts that align learning across all settings. The home–school notebook is the most common form of communication, but the needs and desires of families vary greatly, and not all families will find the home–school notebook to be effective (Hall, Wolfe, & Bollig, 2003). The home–school notebook is a narrative form of communication in which parents and teachers write back and forth to each other about daily events including all important and relevant information pertaining to the child. Because the home–school notebook has no set format, parents and teachers can limit their communication to the information they find it most imperative to share and may also include anecdotes or other bits of information that make the communication feel more personalized. Because all communication is kept together in one notebook, the use of a home–school notebook allows both parents and professionals to review data and any patterns found in the data and to use this information to guide instruction (Hall et al., 2003). Hall et al. (2003) describe three ways in which a home–school notebook can be used:

1. To provide general information
2. To provide specific instruction that is useful both at home and at school
3. To promote active collaboration on instructional activities that are shared between home and school

Alternative methods of communicating with parents via writing include notes or email, premade sheets with a checklist, premade sheets with fill in the blank or short answers that outline a student's day, newsletters, informal notes, student agendas, class blogs and websites. Figure 8.1 provides one example of a pre-made checksheet sent from school to home.

Advantages to using written communication are numerous but can be summed up by two main benefits: 1) Written communication produces a permanent product assisting in accurate record keeping, and 2) many people feel more comfortable expressing themselves through writing (Williams & Cartledge, 1997). Time constraints on the part of both the teacher and parent as well as the ability of more than one party to participate in communication without meeting face-to-face may also lend to the convenience and effectiveness of this form of communication. Lastly, written communication has the potential to be an effective instructional tool for students (Medlen, 2000). Students can be held responsible for bringing the written communication tool back and forth between home and school, including giving it to the parent or teacher. Information included in written communication may also serve as a catalyst for parents or teachers to ask children about their day or have them describe their day, using the written information as a cross-reference. Higher functioning students might also participate in the writing process, in turn working on a

My Day at School

Date _____

Person filling out form _____

Morning Activities

_____ Circle Time Comments _____

_____ Reading Group Comments _____

_____ Daily Exercise Comments _____

_____ Free Time Comments _____

_____ One-on-one Academics Comments _____

Lunch

I ate: _____

Behavior: _____ ☺ _____ ☹

Afternoon Activities

_____ Recess Comments _____

_____ One-on-One Academics Comments _____

_____ Special: Music Art PE Comments _____

_____ Snack Time Comments _____

_____ Group Play Comments _____

Therapies

Today I had: Speech   OT   PT   APE   Other

Comments _____

Overall

Behavior: ☺ ☹ Comments _____

Health: ☺ ☹ Comments _____

Communication: ☺ ☹ Comments _____

Social Skills: ☺ ☹ Comments _____

FIGURE 8.1

Example of a School-to-Home Communication Checklist Incorporating Comments Sections

variety of skills including communication, event recall, and various skills related to handwriting, word processing, or the writing process.

Verbal Communication

The National Coalition for Parent Involvement in Education recommends that personal contact via telephone or face-to-face interaction is the most effective method for promoting two-way communication (n.d., ¶ 2). While many parents may prefer written communication, others may find verbal interactions to be more conducive to their needs, or they may feel as if written communication is less reciprocal. Through verbal interactions, parents and teachers can give immediate feedback and use social cues like facial expressions, intonations, or body postures to more successfully interpret the messages.

Sometimes, the parent or teacher may not have the opportunity to communicate in writing. If a situation occurs at the end of the school day, for example, it may be too late for the teacher to write to the parent, and a phone call is warranted. It is also wise to communicate via phone calls or face-to-face meetings when a more severe or important situation arises, so that parents and teachers can discuss the situation with immediacy and work together in the moment to make necessary decisions. When verbal communication is used, written notes should be taken by both parties on what is communicated, so they always have a formal record if a parent or teacher finds a need to refer back to it.

While written communication produces an embedded permanent record of communications, verbal interactions do not. Both teachers and parents should maintain detailed records of their verbal interactions for future reference in planning, instruction and decision-making. As is the case in any human communication, disagreements may arise. Well-maintained documentation is key to preventing miscommunications, and in special education, this is imperative, although even meticulous documentation cannot prevent all miscommunications. When they do arise, however, it may produce tensions in parent–teacher relationships. Medlen (2000) stresses the importance of continued, open communication even when problems arise, as any tensions or lack of communication between the parent and teacher can negatively affect the child.

Communicating about Homework

Most teachers send or suggest work to be done at home to promote maintenance and generalization of skills. For higher functioning students, especially in general education, the responsibility for communicating homework assignments to parents is often placed on the child. In one focus group, parents, special educators, and general educators reported five relevant factors in relation to communication problems surrounding assigned homework (Jayanthi, Nelson, Sawyer, Bursuck, & Epstein, 1995):

1. Initiation of communication
2. Timeliness of communication

3. Frequency and consistency of communication
4. Follow through
5. Clarity and usefulness of information.

Contributing to these factors were (Jayanthi et al., 1995)

> ➤ time constraints in communication,
> ➤ lack of knowledge about homework or homework procedures by one or more communicators,
> ➤ lack of understanding between special and general educators about curriculum and expectations,
> ➤ parents' lack of awareness of whom to contact with questions or concerns about homework,
> ➤ divergent approaches toward improving student homework performance, and
> ➤ differing belief systems regarding the importance of homework.

Consistent communication patterns surrounding homework may assist in preventing misunderstandings of expectations. Teachers and parents should communicate clearly and effectively with one another about homework requirements, policies and practices, the expectations of all parties involved, student performance, difficulties that arise, and any other concerns related to homework (Warger, 2001).

Involving Other Parties

Though parents and teachers are often the primary communicators, they need not be the only parties communicating. Many children with autism work with a variety of professionals in both their home and school programs including paraprofessionals, tutors, therapists, consultants, and administrators. When away from school, they might be involved with siblings or extended family members. If agreed upon by the parent and teacher, other professionals or family members can contribute to the communication process. A grandparent might have a child for the weekend and wish to share the events of the weekend with the teacher, or a paraprofessional might deem it important to discuss an event that occurred in music class, when the teacher was not there. Therapists may work on goals completely different from those of the teacher and may wish to communicate progress to the parents more frequently than just the required progress report. In planning the communication process, the teacher and parents should come to an agreement about whom the parents wish to participate in the communication, and perhaps whom they do not wish to participate. For example, based on personal preference or confidentiality issues, a parent might not want a paraprofessional to know about a particular situation but might be okay letting the teacher know. As is always the case when planning communication techniques, it is important that both parent and teacher come to a consensus and then include other parties as necessary. Before other parties join in the communication process, it is wise for both teacher and parents to discuss with them the preferred communication methods and the "rules" behind the particular communication being used (e.g., confidentiality issues). If other professionals are not directly involved in the communication process, they can be recruited to work with students for a set period of time so that the teacher has enough time to produce meaningful communications.

For the Teacher: A Note on Contents and Etiquette

It is up to the parents and teacher to decide what contents to include in communication. Components of comprehensive communication might include

> ➤ progress on the day's activities (e.g., IEP goals, special classes, or a behavior being worked on in the lunchroom),
> ➤ any observed physical or medical issues (e.g., groggy from medication, wouldn't eat lunch, went to the nurse with a headache),
> ➤ behavioral concerns or successes,
> ➤ major events,
> ➤ homework assignments,
> ➤ suggestions for work to be completed at home,
> ➤ ideas for parents to aid in the success of their child at home and in the community, and
> ➤ any other relevant information.

Some parents may want to know exactly what goals their child worked on each day and his or her progress on each. Others may find this too burdensome, and may just want a report on any behavioral concerns. When creating a premade checklist, include information that is relevant to the agreed upon aspects to be communicated. If using a system of regular verbal communication, have an idea of what the parents want to be informed of and be responsive to what they wish to inform you. Not every communication exchange must follow a set format if the parent prefers informal communications, but having at least a general idea of parent preferences is helpful.

Teachers must remember that the students they work with are someone's children. No parent wants to hear negative comments about their child, but sometimes relaying this type of information is necessary. As is the case with any interaction with parents, always begin with one or more positive statements about the child. Even if something seemingly negative must be reported, maintaining a positive tone and receptive attitude can make all the difference in a parent's reaction to comments. Answer the parents' questions, consider any suggestions, follow through with what you say you will do, and make them feel that they are being listened to at every juncture. Be sure confidentiality is maintained as required by the state or school district, for both the family with whom you are communicating, and other children and their families. When in doubt about contents, etiquette, or any aspect of your communication methods, seek advice from an administrator or special education director. Simply following the Golden Rule in communications can facilitate a collaborative, successful relationship: treat parents the way you would want to be treated.

EDUCATING OUTSIDE OF THE SCHOOL DAY: STRUCTURED ACTIVITIES AND TEACHABLE MOMENTS

In their quest to increase the skills of their students with ASD, teachers (including therapists and other professionals who are involved in the teaching of a child with ASD) frequently elicit the help of parents to carry over instruction into the home and community settings. The importance of parent participation in their child with autism's education has been well researched and documented (Benson, Karlof, & Siperstein, 2008). But just like professionals, parents of children with autism can only provide an appropriate education for their child when they have access to specialized knowledge and skills in conjunction with scientifically based information (NRC, 2001). Furthermore, even the most well-intentioned parents may find it difficult to schedule enough time in the day to provide their child with ASD with the interventions or instructional activities requested by the teacher, even when they are knowledgeable about these activities and certainly believe the activities will help.

Daily stress surrounding families who deal with maladaptive behaviors may also cause parents to shut down and feel the need to take a break from their child with ASD. Family life can be strained and the education process can be difficult for many families of children with disabilities (Munn-Joseph & Gavin-Evans, 2008). Parents may feel as if bringing instructional activities to the home setting is just too much to handle. However, reports on studies done by Koegel, Bimbela, and Schreibman (1996) and Bristol, Gallagher, and Holt (1993) found that parents were less stressed when they were taught specific methods for working with their children with autism (NRC, 2001).

Research on the benefits of parental involvement in the educational program of a child with ASD is plentiful. Generalizing learning concepts from one environment to the next is an important issue in the education of a child with ASD. This issue must be anticipated and supported, and as a result, parents of children with ASD must be more intensely involved in their child's education when compared with parents of children with other disabilities (NRC, 2001). But the disconnect between what may be beneficial for children and the reality of the home environment needs to be addressed if families are to truly be able to take action. Teaching at home does not have to be in the form of preplanned activities, but can occur spontaneously at any time and place in the form of teachable moments, especially when a framework is in place that meets the needs of the family. Creating that framework in the home environment is the key to gaining easy access to instructional opportunities and in effect, helping to increase the skills of a child with ASD. Once the major components of a conducive framework are in place, instructional activities can be executed more efficiently, theories can be put into practice, and the disconnect can disappear, creating reduced stress on parents and the overall home environment. Following are 8 steps teachers (or other professionals) can recommend to parents that may simplify the implementation of instructional activities at home.

Step 1: Assess the Home Environment

Finances do not need to be readjusted in order for instruction to occur at home. With suggestions from the teacher, parents should assess the home environment and determine what they currently have access to that can be used to help put instructional activities into place. Examples of items that may be conducive to instructional activities include computers, toys, games, or other household objects that children may wish to gain access to. For example, Dana uses the pieces in a checkers game to help teach her daughter addition and subtraction concepts, and Max works on communication skills with his brother by having him request items he wants rather than making them readily available. Items of high interest to the child that are already at home might be the most important items a parent can employ as reinforcers when attempting to accomplish at-home tasks. Using special interests may motivate children with ASD to participate in activities that may not be intrinsically rewarding for them, and they may have not only interests, but obsessive interests, that can be used as reinforcers for particular behaviors (Aspy & Grossman, 2007). Additionally, incidental teaching, a naturalistic intervention procedure to elicit an individual's initiation of communication, may also occur when an environment is arranged to include materials that are attractive to the individual (Cowan & Allen, 2007).

Step 2: Structure the Home Environment

Most children with ASD thrive in a very structured, organized environment that is predictable for them, and they often have an intense desire to make sense of what is going on around them (Aspy & Grossman, 2007). However, too much structure may not be conducive to the needs of a family, or the family may not know where to begin to structure their home. Teachers should work with parents to determine what materials are already present in the home that would be favorable in structuring an environment for their child. For example, a tray table can be converted into a small desk for a child to be used for homework completion, or a folding screen may be used to separate a child from visual distractions or to create boundaries while working at home. Depending on the needs of the child, objects found in the home may be used to represent activities that the child is supposed to complete (an object-schedule), or pictures can be taken with the family camera to create a picture schedule.

Not all instructional activities have to be completed in a structured environment. Within the home environment, teachable moments, or moments of unplanned opportunities for teaching, will occur frequently and may even be more beneficial than planned instruction because of their naturalistic quality. After learning about potential fire hazards in school, Alan frequently got upset when his dad cooked on the grill. Each time this happened, Alan's dad would use the opportunity to read Alan a social story about overreacting. Alan's dad could have used the situation to develop a teachable moment without a social story in place, but with the social story readily available, he was able to facilitate an immediate teachable moment that was effective for Alan's needs. Even when instructional activities are not being overtly implemented, a structured and predictable environment can help teachable moments to occur with less frustration and can allow for an overall better quality of life.

Step 3: Get Educated with the Help of Professionals

In home-based educational involvement, teachers instruct parents in effective methods to manage and interact with their child (Benson et al., 2008). If a teacher or other professional is not available to help a parent get educated about teaching at home, parents should do all they can to educate themselves through collaboration with other families of children with autism, researching and accessing community resources, reading trusted books or magazines, searching trusted internet sites, and simply getting to know the needs of their child as intimately as possible.

Teachers cannot expect parents to implement instructional activities that they are not educated about. To reduce stress on parents, teachers should educate parents about the importance and effective execution of activities they request that the parents implement, from structured activities to activities that are highly unstructured (Benson et al., 2008). This can be done by providing informal or formal information through daily communication. Teachers might also provide parents with books, websites to peruse, information on conferences to attend, any extra materials they might have, or even video or audiotapes that explain instructional activities or demonstrate the activity taking place. Parents may be asked to observe instructional activities in the classroom, or conversely, a home visit from the teacher may allow the teacher the opportunity to show the entire family how an instructional activity might take place. Of course, it is necessary to assess the needs of the child with ASD before either of these situations occurs to determine how the child will handle seeing his teacher at home or his parents at school. When Carlos' parents began to come into his classroom to observe his educational activities (with the goal of generalizing them to the home environment), it did more harm than good in the beginning. Carlos was so confused each time his parents were at school that he would hide in the reading area and would only come out with much coercion. His parents and teacher found that simple verbal and visual explanations prior to his parents' arrival allowed Carlos to prepare himself for the situation.

Step 4: Determine Priorities

It may seem ideal for teachers to have parents reinforce all skills worked on in the classroom setting. However, teachers must realize that there are family activities that must take place while the child is at home, and that these are healthy for the child to engage in. The child should be a part of these activities and should not be excluded in favor of doing work. In reality, much instruction can take place through activities that are embedded into family time, such as social and communication activities and learning through community outings. In a study conducted by Benson et al. (2008), it was found that mothers frequently helped their children to practice communication, social, self-help, and other skills through normal daily events such as meals, car rides, and trips to the playground. A normal daily event for Kellen's family, for example, was to set aside an hour for family game time each evening after dinner. His family engaged in this activity long before Kellen was ever diagnosed with ASD, and they did not want to give it up. The family now uses this time to bond and be together (which was the original purpose), while at the same time working together to teach Kellen valuable turn taking and communication skills. Teachers and parents should collaborate to determine priorities for children at home whether they are as complex as one-on-one instruction in the area of reading comprehension, or as seemingly simple as facilitating hand-washing procedures. If parents determine that they have time to help with only one activity per night, they should decide what one activity is most important to the development of the child. Too many instructional activities can cause burnout for both parent and child. Individuals with ASD may already be more susceptible to and less able to cope with stress (Groden, Baron, & Groden, 2006; Groden, Cautela, Prince, & Berryman, 1994), calling for extremely mindful planning.

Step 5: Save Time by Interweaving Activities

The major deficits exhibited by individuals with ASD tend to be in the areas of communication, social skills, adaptive behavior, and oftentimes academics, especially when an MR component is present. Each of these, however, does not have to be a category separate from the next. Areas prioritized for skill improvement can be combined to create a holistic, timesaving learning experience. Collaboration can help parents and teachers determine what interventions and activities can be combined to work toward multiple goals at one time. Two examples of interweaving include the following:

Interweaving Behavior Management and Communication

Children with ASD often exhibit challenging behaviors when their receptive and expressive communication abilities are inhibited (Holden & Gitlesen, 2004). A tantrum was triggered every time Evelyn was asked to put on her gym shoes to go somewhere. With help from the teacher, her parents finally determined that the reason Evelyn threw these tantrums was because she was overwhelmed by the sensory input on her feet when her gym shoes were put on. Evelyn's teacher had been working on providing Evelyn with visual choices at school to increase her communication skills. For example, Evelyn was asked to communicate what she wanted or did not want during lunch, recess, and other class activities. After collaborating with the teacher, Evelyn's parents decided to incorporate visual choices when it was time for Evelyn to put on her gym shoes. Using materials they had at home, they drew pictures of gym shoes with socks, gym shoes without socks, sandals, sandals with socks, and a "Wait" card. The drawings worked for Evelyn. When it was time to put on her gym shoes, Evelyn was able to choose a different pair of shoes or combination of shoes and socks, or make the choice to wait to put on her shoes until she felt more ready. This increased Evelyn's ability to communicate with her family about her needs, while at the same time decreasing her tantrums. This is just one way that skills in communication and behavior management can be interwoven.

Interweaving Social Development and Academics

Jaime loved to use his talking calculator to complete math problems at home. Since the day his grandma bought it for him, he did his math homework consistently every single day. Jaime no longer had difficulty being motivated to do his math homework. However, he did have difficulty sharing his calculator with his sister and brother when they asked to use it. In fact, Jaime had difficulty sharing any of his possessions, until his sister Leticia came up with a way to work on sharing and math homework simultaneously. Leticia decided that she would do her math homework at the same time as Jamie and would ask to use his calculator to check her answers. At first, Jamie was his usual, very upset self when Leticia asked to use his calculator, as she knew he would be. Leticia then created a turn-taking schedule that included 5 minutes for Leticia to complete her homework while Jamie had the calculator, and 1 minute for Jamie to complete his homework while Leticia had the calculator. With the help of praise and stickers (which were of high interest to Jamie), he was eventually able to allow Leticia to use the calculator for up to 10 minutes, while he completed some of his math problems without it, as his teacher had requested. The turn-taking schedule was then carried over into other areas of Jamie's life such as sharing his toys and video games. Jaime's goals of increasing social skills and completing math problems without a calculator were interwoven into one all-encompassing activity.

Of course, skill areas can be interwoven to work toward multiple goals at one time in countless ways. Other examples include interweaving communication and social skills, which often go hand in hand, and addressing maladaptive behaviors due to frustration with academics by addressing both of these issues simultaneously. Teachers and parents can brainstorm and collaborate through daily communication to work toward a common goal of saving time for the family while working on multiple skill deficits.

Step 6: Recruit Family Members

With the help of family members, parents may not have to face the overwhelming task of implementing instructional activities on their own. Many parents work, have household chores and activities to tend to, and have other children to take care of. Studies indicate that parents of children with autism may adapt more healthfully with support from extended family (Siklos & Kerns, 2006). Siblings, grandparents, aunts, uncles, and cousins of a child with autism can be integral in the implementation of instructional activities at home. Children similar in age (such as siblings and cousins) can especially provide much needed opportunities for increasing social skills. These social interactions may then be carried over into the school environment, as the child interacts with his or her classmates. Teachers and parents can help family members to learn about the roles they might play in helping the child with ASD and any related methods or techniques they might use.

Step 7: Implement Activities and Be Open to Teachable Moments

Once materials are gathered, the home environment is set up as necessary, families are educated, and priorities are determined, instructional activities can take place. Families should determine the most advantageous conditions for the implementation of activities. If specific time must be set aside for instructional activities, the family must work together to be certain the time works for everyone. If instructional activities will take place in a specific location, family members should be certain the location is practical and is reserved specifically for the instructional activities if this is necessary. If several family members are participating in instructional activities, progress should be discussed and family members should collaborate whenever possible, to be certain the framework in place is working for everyone, including the child with ASD. Consistency is key in any instructional program for children with ASD, and each family member who has a role should be certain to reliably enact it.

If formal instructional activities were determined to not be conducive to the lifestyle of the family, teachable moments are readily available at all times, and can turn out to be some of the most successful learning situations for children with ASD. Even when more formal instructional activities do take place at home, it should not be forgotten that teaching can take place anytime, and anywhere. However, family members may not want to always feel that they have to be "on" and ready to teach the child with ASD some life changing new skill. The child with ASD needs to relax and have time to his- or herself just as much as the rest of the family does. Though implementing programs at home may be beneficial, they may also place high levels of demand on family resources, causing stress (Trudgeon & Carr, 2007). Family members may want to take turns teaching the child with ASD, whether formally or informally. In Ingrid's family, her sisters and brothers take turns working with her when they go out into the community. Her older sister may be "on duty" for a grocery store trip, helping Ingrid and teaching her whenever possible, while her younger brother is "on duty" for a trip to the movie theater the next day. All interactions can be conceived of as a teachable moments and are embedded in the activities of everyday life. Being open to and aware of the needs of the child with ASD, coupled with a desire to help the child increase their quality of life, may be all a family needs to be a part of their child's success.

Step 8: Assess for Effectiveness

As in any form of instruction, the environment and related interventions and activities must be assessed for effectiveness. It is not the job of the parent to give the child formal evaluations to determine whether learning at home is helping the child to make gains in progress (unless this is something the parents wish to do). With input from family members, parents can assess the effectiveness of the home learning environment by being keenly aware of the actions and emotions of the child with ASD as well as those of other family members. If the child appears unhappy or family members are stressed, it is time to reassess priorities and look for ways to make changes that better align with the needs of the family. Increases or decreases in skill acquisition may also be gauged through observation and communication with teacher. Adaptations to the process of learning at home will be easier to make, when all preceding components are in place, and parents, teacher, or other family members are on board.

REFERENCES

Aspy, R., & Grossman, B. G. (2007). *The Ziggurat model: A framework for designing comprehensive interventions for individuals with high-functioning autism and asperger syndrome.* Shawnee Mission, KS: Autism Asperger.

Benson, P., Karlof, K. L., & Siperstein, G. N. (2008). Maternal involvement in the education of young children with autism spectrum disorders. *SAGE Publications and The National Autistic Society, 12*(1), 47–63.

Bristol, M. M., Gallagher, J. J., & Holt, K. D. (1993). Maternal depressive symptoms in autism: Response to psychoeducational intervention. *Rehabilitation Psychology, 38,* 3–9.

Briggs, X. (1998). Brown kids in white suburbs: Housing mobility and the many faces of social capital. *Housing Policy Debate, 9,* 177–221.

Cowan, R. J., & Allen, K. D. (2007). Using naturalistic procedures to enhance learning in individuals with autism: A focus on generalized teaching within the school setting. *Psychology in the Schools, 44*(7), 701–715.

Epstein, J. L. (2001). *School, family and community partnerships: Preparing educators and improving schools.* Boulder, CO: Westview Press.

Epstein, M. H., Munk, D. D., Bursuck, W. D., Polloway, E. A., & Jayanthi, M. (1999). Strategies for improving home–school communication about homework for students with disabilities. *The Journal of Special Education, 33*(3), 166–176.

Groden, J., Baron, M. G., & Groden, G. (2006). Stress and autism: Assessment and coping strategies. In M. G. Baron, J. Groden, G. Groden, & L. P. Lipsitt (Eds.), *Stress and coping in autism* (pp. 15–51). New York: Oxford University Press.

Groden, J., Cautela, J., Prince, S., & Berryman, J., (1994). The impact of stress and anxiety on individuals with autism and developmental disabilities. In E. Scholpler, & G. B. Mesibov (Eds.), *Behavioral issues in autism* (pp. 177–194). New York: Plenum Press.

Hall, T., Wolfe, P., & Bollig, A. (2003). Home-to-school notebook: An effective communication strategy for students with severe disabilities. *Teaching Exceptional Children, 36*(2), 68–73.

Holden, B., & Gitlesen, J. P. (2004). Psychotropic medication in adults with mental retardation: prevalence and prescription practices. *Research in Developmental Disabilities 25*(6), 509–521.

Hoover-Dempsey, K. V., Walker, J. M. T., Sandler, H. M., Whetsel, D., Green, C. L., Wilkins, A. S., et al. (2005). Why do parents become involved? Research findings and implications. *The Elementary School Journal, 106,* 105–130.

Hornby, G. (2000). *Improving parental involvement*. London: Casswell Education.

Jayanthi, M., Nelson, J. S., Sawyer, V., Bursuck, W. D., & Epstien, M. H. (1995). Homework-communication problems among parents, classroom teachers, and special education teachers. *Remedial and Special Education, 16*, 102–116.

Kluth, P. (2003). *You're going to love this kid: Teaching students with autism in the inclusive classroom*. Baltimore: Brookes.

Koegel, R. L, Bimbela, A., & Schreibman, L. (1996). Collateral effects of parent training on family interactions. *Journal of Autism and Related Developmental Disorders, 26*, 347–359.

Medlen, J. E. (2000). Home-to-school communication. *Disability Solutions, 4*(2), 1–15.

Munn-Joseph, M. S., & Gavin-Evans, K. (2008). Urban parents of children with special needs: Advocating for their children through social networks. *Urban Education, 43*(3), 378–393.

Murray, M. M., Christensen, K. A., Umbarger, G. T., Rade, K. C., Aldridge, K., & Niemeyer, J. A. (2007). Supporting Family Choice. *Early Childhood Education Journal, 35*, 111–117.

National Coalition for Parent Involvement in Education. (n.d.). *Parent involvement: A framework for family involvement*. Retrieved June 5, 2009, from http://www.ncpie.org/DevelopingPartnerships/

National Research Council (NRC). (2001). *Educating children with autism*. Washington, DC: National Academy Press.

Salend, S. (2005). *Creating inclusive classrooms: Effective and reflective practices for all students* (5th ed.). Columbus, OH: Merrill.

Siklos, S., & Kerns, K. A. (2006). Assessing need for social support in parents of chidlren with autism and Down Syndrome. *Journal of Autism and Developmental Disorders, 36*, 921–933.

Stoner, J. B., Bock, S. J., Thompson, J. R., Angell, M. E., Heyl, B., & Crowley, E. P. (2005). Welcome to our world: Parent perceptions of the interactions between parents of young children with Autism Spectrum Disorder (ASD) and education professionals. *Focus on Autism and Other Developmental Disabilities, 20*, 39–51.

Trudgeon, C., & Carr, D. (2007). The impacts of home-based early behavioural intervention programmes on families of children with autism. *Journal of Applied Research in Intellectual Disabilities, 20*, 285–296.

Turnbull, A. P., & Turnbull, H. R. (2001). *Families, professionals and exceptionality: Collaborating for empowerment* (4th ed.). Columbus, OH: Merrrill.

Warger, C. (2001). Five homework strategies for teaching students with disabilities. *Autism Society of Greater Cleveland*. Washington, DC: ERIC Clearinghouse on Disabilities and Gifted Education.

Williams, V. I., & Cartlede, G. (1997). Passing notes to parents. *Teaching Exceptional Children, 30*(1), 30–34.

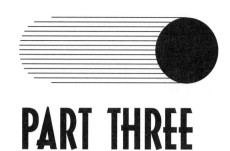

PART THREE

Interventions from Early Childhood through Adulthood

Early Childhood Education for Children with ASD: An Overview

Michele R. Bishop and Amy L. Kenzer

Early intensive behavioral intervention (EIBI) is an empirically supported treatment for ASDs that is based on the principles of applied behavior analysis (ABA). Researchers have demonstrated that EIBI can be used to improve skill deficits and eliminate behavior excesses (i.e., problem behaviors; Eikeseth, 2009; Eldevik et al., 2009; see Frea & McNerney, 2008, & Granpeesheh, Tarbox, & Dixon, 2009, for reviews). In fact, researchers have published data indicating that some children no longer meet the criteria for an ASD following participation in an EIBI program (Butter, Mulick, & Metz, 2006; Granpeesheh, Tarbox, Dixon, Carr, & Herbert, 2009). This chapter provides an overview of the essential features of an EIBI program including basic characteristics, composition of the treatment team, methods of instruction, format of service delivery, and curriculum. This chapter should not be viewed as a comprehensive review of the literature on any single component. Efforts have been made to include several references that readers can refer to for more information.

CHARACTERISTICS OF AN EIBI PROGRAM

Three features of EIBI programs investigated by researchers are

1. the age when treatment begins,
2. the number of treatment hours per week, and
3. the number of years that treatment is implemented.

Each of these characteristics contributes to the effectiveness of an EIBI program.

Early

Early refers to when a child begins treatment. Most families aggressively pursue treatment shortly after receiving a diagnosis of an ASD, which is frequently between the ages of 2 and 3 years. However, the age of diagnosis is decreasing as awareness increases and screening and assessment tools become more advanced (Rapin & Tuchman, 2008). After a child has been diagnosed with an ASD and the family has completed their research on effective interventions, treatment may be delayed, however, because of funding difficulties and agency wait lists (See Williamson, 1996, for a discussion of funding issues).

It is commonly believed that children with ASDs should begin an EIBI program as young as possible (Eikeseth, 2009; Fenske, Zalenski, Krantz, & McClannahan, 1985; Green, 1996; Harris & Handleman, 2000). Many children with ASDs begin treatment between the ages of 2 and 3 years old; however, EIBI programs have been successfully implemented with children as young as 1 year 2 months (Green, Brennen, & Fein, 2002) and older than 4 years of age (Eikeseth, Smith, Jahr, & Eldevik, 2002). For instance, Fenske et al. (1985) found that children with ASDs who began an EIBI program prior to 60 months of age were more likely to reside at home with their parents and attend public school classrooms than children with ASDs who began an EIBI program after 60 months. Similarly, Harris and Handleman (2000) reported a correlation between the age when children began an EIBI program and placement in a typical education classroom, with younger ages at intake most frequently correlated with placement in a typical education classroom.

Additionally, Granpeesheh, Dixon, Tarbox, Kaplan, and Wilke (2009) presented data describing the relationship between the child's age, the intensity of the treatment (see section on intensity of EIBI), and the number skills learned. These data revealed that younger children receiving more intense treatment learned more skills. Even though progress can be made regardless of the age when treatment begins, published research suggests that maximum gains are most likely when treatment is initiated early. Furthermore, after a child receives a diagnosis of an ASD, no persuasive evidence supports waiting to begin an EIBI program.

Intensive

Intensive refers to the number of treatment hours a child receives per week. An ongoing debate about the ideal number of treatment hours has resulted in several empirical studies examining the relationship between intensity of treatment and child progress. This research has revealed that high-intensity programs (i.e., 30 to 40 hours per week) are associated with significant child progress (e.g., Cohen, Amerine-Dickens, & Smith, 2006; Granpeesheh, Tarbox, & Dixon, 2009; Green, 1996; Lovaas, 1987; Reed, Osborne, & Corness, 2007; Sallows & Graupner, 2005). A study published in 1987 by O. Ivar Lovaas compared 40 hours treatment per week to 10 hours of treatment per week. Findings revealed that children who received 40 hours of treatment per week made significantly more progress than children who received 10 hours. In addition, Lovaas reported that some children were successfully integrated into a typical classroom and no longer met the criteria for an ASD.

Researchers examining lower intensity EIBI programs (i.e., fewer than 30 hours per week) have also documented significant child progress (Eikeseth et al., 2007; Eldevik, Eikeseth, Jahr, & Smith, 2006; Remington et al., 2007; Sheinkopf & Siegel, 1998; Smith, Groen & Wynn, 2000). For instance, Remington et al. (2007) found that children who participated in an EIBI program for 2 years with approximately 25 hours of therapy per week made significantly more progress than a comparison group (see Remington et al., 2007, for a description of the treatments received by the comparison group). However, Granpeesheh, Tarbox, and Dixon (2009) noted that even though significant progress has been achieved with lower intensity EIBI, these improvements are less than the improvements reported following high-intensity EIBI. Given these data, the authors concluded that for maximum progress to be achieved, an EIBI program must be implemented at a high intensity (i.e., 30 to 40 hours per week).

Duration

The duration of treatment refers to the number of months or years that the treatment is provided. Many researchers have suggested that a minimum of 2 years is necessary for children to achieve an optimal outcome (e.g., Cohen et al., 2006; Eikeseth, Smith, Jahr, & Eldevik, 2007; Granpeesheh, Tarbox, & Dixon, 2009; Green, 1996; Lovaas, 1987; Sallows & Graupner, 2005). In a study by Sallows and Graupner (2005), an EIBI program was implemented for 4 years. The authors reported that the children continued to progress throughout the 4-year duration.

Researchers have also documented significant progress in less than 2 years (e.g., Eikeseth et al., 2002; Howard, Sparkman, Cohen, Green, & Stanislaw, 2005; Reed et al., 2007; Sheinkopf & Siegel, 1998). For instance, Eikeseth et al. (2002) assessed progress following 1 year and found that children participating in an EIBI program made greater gains than children receiving eclectic treatment (see Eikeseth et al., 2002, for a description of eclectic treatment). Follow-up data, collected approximately 2.5 years after treatment began, indicated that significant progress continued for the children participating in the EIBI program (Eikeseth et al., 2007).

Granpeesheh, Tarbox, and Dixon (2009) compared the results of studies that implemented EIBI for less than and greater than 2 years and found a greater percentage of children made significant progress when EIBI was implemented for at least 2 years. Based on the previous findings, it appears that children with ASDs who are participating in an EIBI program may continue to make significant progress for several years. Furthermore, the likelihood of achieving an optimal outcome increases when EIBI is implemented for a minimum of 2 years.

Three components of an EIBI program that have been associated with the best treatment outcomes are:

1. implementation early in a child's development,
2. participation in EIBI programs for several hours each week, and
3. duration of several years.

With an idea of what it is like for a family and child with autism to participate in an EIBI program, the next section will discuss the team of individuals who provide EIBI services.

COMPOSITION OF A TEAM

An EIBI program is implemented by a team people with specialized training in ABA and teaching children with ASDs. The team members include the parents, a clinical supervisor, and therapists. Specific responsibilities are assigned to each team member depending on his or her position.

Therapists

The majority of the treatment hours are provided by therapists (sometimes referred to as tutors), home-based teachers (e.g., Green et al., 2002), or instructional assistants (e.g., Howard et al., 2005), depending on the specific EIBI program. The minimum requirements to work as a therapist are a high school diploma and satisfactory completion of a training course provided by the EIBI agency. However, some service agencies may have more stringent educational requirements.

Therapist training courses focus on an overview of ABA and how to implement instructional procedures and behavior-reduction protocols. New therapist training commonly includes a combination of oral and written instruction, demonstrations of the correct use of instructional procedures, and an opportunity to practice skills and receive immediate feedback from a senior therapist or clinical supervisor (e.g., Bolton & Mayer, 2008; Leblanc, Ricciardi, & Luiselli, 2005; Sallows & Graupner, 2005; Sarokoff & Sturmey, 2004; Schepis, Reid, Ownbey, & Parsons, 2001; Thomson, Martin, Arnal, Fazzio, & Yu, 2009). In addition, it is very common for EIBI agencies to require attendance at regular follow-up trainings to ensure that the therapist's skills maintain over time (Love, Carr, Almason, & Petursdottir, 2009; Perry et al., 2008). It is necessary for therapists to have extensive training and supervision (see section describing the role of clinical supervisors) to maintain high quality EIBI services.

Clinical Supervisors

Each child's individual program is supervised by someone with specialized training in behavior analysis and the application of behavioral principles to the treatment of children with autism. Clinical supervisors design curriculum, provide clinical oversight, conduct parent training, examine data, and consult with other service providers (e.g., speech and language pathologists, occupational therapists, and classroom teachers). The most commonly accepted measure of adequate training in behavior analysis for clinical supervisors is certification as a Board Certified Behavior Analyst by the Behavior Analysis Certification Board (www.bacb.com; Eikeseth, Hayward, Gale, Gitlesen, & Eldevik, 2009; Howard et al., 2005; Love et al., 2009; Perry et al., 2008).

In addition, Eikeseth et al. (2009) highlighted the importance of supervised clinical experience (i.e., cosupervision with a well-trained clinical supervisor) prior to independently supervising a child's EIBI program. Supervised clinical experience provides aspiring supervisors with on-the-job training in curriculum design and implementation for a variety of skill deficits, behavior excesses (i.e., inappropriate behaviors), and learning styles, along with training in consultation and treatment team management.

The intensity of clinical supervision refers to the number of hours a clinical supervisor spends monitoring a child's EIBI program. This includes time spent in meetings with the parents, therapists, and teachers; in-home observations during therapy sessions; consultation with other service providers; and curriculum development. Currently, no standard practice dictates the intensity of clinical supervision. Researchers have reported lower intensity clinical supervision (e.g., every 3 months; Bibby, Eikeseth, Martin, Mudford, & Reeves, 2001; Magiati, Charman, & Howlin, 2007) and higher intensity clinical supervision (e.g., 5 to 10 hours per week; Eikeseth et al., 2002; Hayward, Gale, & Eikeseth, 2009). Eikeseth et al. (2009) examined the relationship between the intensity of clinical supervision and child progress. Results indicated that higher intensity clinical supervision was correlated with greater gains in IQ scores. Given these data, it appears that increasing the intensity of clinical supervision may contribute to an optimal treatment outcome.

Parents

Parents are an important part of the treatment team. They participate in the curriculum development process by sharing information about which skills may be most functional for their child and which behavior excesses are most problematic (Moes & Frea, 2000, 2002). Parents also play an integral role in the reduction of problem behavior and the maintenance and generalization of skills throughout their child's day. For instance, Lovaas, Koegel, Simmons, and Long (1973) noted that children whose parents were trained in ABA procedures continued to progress after more formal treatment was discontinued.

While it is important for a child to be able to display skills with a therapist during therapy sessions, it is equally, if not more, important for a child to be able to display these skills in a variety of settings and with a variety of people. Therapists work on skills during scheduled therapy sessions, and even though efforts are made to practice skills in relevant environmental conditions (e.g., learning to wash your hands when they are dirty or learning to turn a light on when it is dark), in certain circumstances it is convenient for parents to work on skills. This is because parents spend a substantial number of hours with their child in a variety of different settings (e.g., on the playground, in a restaurant, in the car).

Additionally, many parents experience stress while raising a child with autism. This stress may stem from an inability to communicate with their child, difficulty managing problem behaviors, or a lack of knowledge about how to teach their child basic skills (e.g., dressing, toileting, self-feeding; Hastings & Brown, 2002; Hastings et al., 2005; Plant & Sanders, 2007). Researchers have found that parent education programs result in increases in parents' ability to reduce problem behaviors and teach new skills in addition to decreases in parental stress (Brookman-Frazee, 2004; Crockett, Fleming, Doepke, & Stevens, 2007; Frea & Hepburn, 1999; Koegel, Bimbela, & Schreibman, 1996; Koegel, Glahn, & Nieminen, 1978). For instance, Crockett et al. (2007) found that a combination of lecture, demonstration, role playing with feedback from the trainer, and practice with the child with feedback from the trainer was sufficient to educate parents on how to successfully use discrete-trials teaching. In light of the benefits of parent training, many EIBI service agencies offer a parent training component. Parent training may be offered as a separate service or in conjunction with a child's regularly scheduled therapy hours.

An EIBI program is implemented by a well-trained team of people including therapists, clinical supervisors, and parents. Other service professionals, such as speech and language pathologists, occupational therapists, and classroom teachers, may also participate as team members, depending on the particular needs of the child. It is essential for all team members to develop a trusting and collaborative relationship to ensure that the child receives the best treatment possible. The next section will review two common methods of instruction used by the treatment team.

METHODS OF INSTRUCTION

It is typical for several behavior analytic procedures to be incorporated into a comprehensive EIBI program including, but not limited to,

> ➤ discrete trials teaching (DTT),
> ➤ prompting and fading,
> ➤ shaping,
> ➤ chaining, and
> ➤ natural environment teaching.

See Cooper, Heron, and Heward (2007) and Miltenberger (2007) for comprehensive descriptions of ABA procedures. It is also vital for team members to learn how to use the child's motivation to maximize teaching opportunities. That is, therapists will observe which toys the child prefers to play with, which foods the child prefers to eat, and which activities the child prefers to engage in (see Chapter 5 for a description of preference assessments). Then, access to these preferred things will be contingent on the child engaging in a correct or appropriate behavior. A review of two commonly used teaching methods is presented below.

Discrete Trials Teaching

DTT is frequently used to teach children with ASDs *discrimination,* or how to receptively identify objects, vocally label objects, and perform actions. For instance, a child is presented with a picture of a ball, a truck, and a piano. A therapist says, "Touch ball," and the child touches the picture of the ball. This is an example of discrimination because the child has learned to touch the ball and not the truck or piano. Children learn to make vocal discriminations as well. In this case, when a child is shown a picture of his mother, he says, "Mommy." The child does not say "Mommy" when shown a picture of a different person. In other words the child will display an appropriate response in the presence of certain pictures, objects, or words and not others.

It is interesting to note that DTT was not originally developed as a method of instruction for children with ASDs. It began as a procedure used in basic laboratory research (see Mazur, 2002, & Pear, 2001 for a discussion of basic laboratory research). Its use with children with ASDs did not become widespread until after the influential work by O. Ivar Lovaas et al. was published in the 1970s and 1980s (Lovaas, 1977; Lovaas, 1987; Lovaas et al., 1981). Today some use the term DTT synonymously with treatment for children with ASDs; however, in reality this is only one application of a more general technique (See Ghezzi, 2007, & Tarbox & Najdowski, 2008, for reviews of DTT).

In DTT complex skills are broken down into simple skills and taught in a series of trials. For example, multiple-step instructions are initially divided into simpler one-step instructions. Then, as the child's ability to follow one-step instructions improves, two-step instructions are introduced. The skills taught will continue to become more complex until the desired goal is achieved.

Each trial has a clear beginning that is signaled by an instruction. Next, the child has an opportunity to respond, usually within 3 to 5 seconds. Prompts may be used to assist a child with the response (e.g., modeling the correct response, pointing to the correct response, physically guiding the child to engage in the correct response; see Demchak, 1990; Morse & Schuster, 2004; Schoen, 1986; & Wolery & Gast, 1984, for reviews of prompting procedures). Then, an immediate consequence is delivered for the response. The purpose of the consequence is to provide the child with feedback about whether the response was correct or incorrect. Preferred items, such as toys, edibles, activities, or praise, are delivered following a correct response. Following an incorrect response the therapist may say, "No" or "Try again" or look away to signal the absence of attention. The consequence signals the end of the trial. Additionally, a period of a couple of seconds, referred to as an *intertrial interval*, separates each trial.

DTT has become a popular method of instruction for children with ASDs because it is easily used in a one-on-one format and allows for numerous teaching opportunities (i.e., trials). It is a therapist-led procedure. A clinical supervisor identifies skills to teach, then therapists lead the instruction. Therapists will continue teaching a response until a mastery criterion is met (e.g., 80% to 100% correct over a predetermined number of trial blocks). Also, it is relatively easy to train therapists, parents, teachers, and classroom assistants to use DTT (Bolton & Mayer, 2008; Dib & Sturmey, 2007; Downs, Downs, & Rau, 2008).

Researchers have also highlighted some potential disadvantages (Sundberg & Partington, 1999). For instance, DTT has been criticized because the consequences used may not be functionally related to the responses, additional procedures may be needed to ensure generalization of responses, and responses taught may be become rote. Despite these criticisms, researchers have documented that this method of instruction can be effectively used to teach children with autism (e.g., Eikeseth et al., 2002; Howard et al., 2005; Lovaas, 1987; Perry et al., 2008).

Naturalistic Teaching

Naturalistic teaching is commonly used to teach children with ASDs language skills (Charlop-Christy & Carpenter, 2000; Charlop-Christy & LeBlanc, 1999; Koegel, Camarata, Koegel, Ben-Tall, & Smith, 1998), social skills (Harper, Symon, & Frea, 2008; Kaiser, Hancock, & Nietfeld, 2000; Kohler, Anthony, Steighner, & Hoyson, 2001; Krantz & McClannahan, 1998) and play skills (Stahmer, 1995; Stahmer, Ingersoll, & Carter, 2003; Thorpe, Stahmer, & Schreibman, 1995). Several instruction methods can be classified as naturalistic teaching including, but not limited to

- ➤ incidental teaching (Hart & Risley, 1975),
- ➤ mand-model procedure (Rogers-Warren & Warren, 1980),
- ➤ natural language paradigm (Koegel, O'Dell, & Koegel, 1987),
- ➤ milieu teaching (Kaiser et al., 2000), and
- ➤ pivotal response training (Koegel & Koegel, 2006).

See Allen and Cowan (2008) and Cowan and Allen (2007), for reviews of naturalistic teaching procedures.

In naturalistic teaching, therapists take advantage of teaching opportunities as they arise during the child's therapy session. In other words, as the child moves around and interacts with his or her environment, the therapist identifies responses that are relevant to the child's current activity. For example, if a child is playing with a puzzle, the therapist may have the child practice asking for puzzle pieces. Then, if the child stops playing with the puzzle and walks to the train table, the therapist may have the child practice asking for pieces of the train track. The consequence for correctly asking for a puzzle piece or section of train track is the actual object requested (i.e., natural consequences). The less structured teaching format that is characteristic of natural environment teaching encourages generalization of skills. The need for specific procedures to assist with generalization is less likely because teaching is conducted during naturally occurring activities.

Even though naturalistic teaching methods have effectively been used to teach children with ASDs, researchers have noted some potential disadvantages (Sundberg & Partington, 1999). Since naturalistic teaching methods follow the child's lead, it provides no scripted curriculum. This can lead to some confusion about what skills to target during therapy sessions, and it is even possible that some important skills are never targeted based on the activities that the child selects. Also, a child may receive fewer opportunities to practice a response (i.e., fewer teaching trials). For example, a child may choose to play with blocks on Monday and then not play with blocks again for a week. When using naturalistic teaching, skills related to block play would not be practiced for that week.

Both DTT and naturalistic teaching are effective methods that are frequently used to teach children with ASDs. It is sometimes thought that one method of instruction is better than another. However, it may be argued that a comprehensive EIBI program uses a balance of both DTT and naturalistic teaching with the proportion of time spent using each instructional method tailored to the individual needs of the child (Allen & Cowan, 2008; Sundberg & Partington, 1999). The following section provides a description of the primary settings where EIBI services may be implemented.

FORMAT OF SERVICE DELIVERY

EIBI programs may be home-based, center-based, or school-based, with some EIBI agencies providing therapy in more than one setting. Researchers have evaluated EIBI programs that are based in all three settings, but current findings do not suggest that one format is superior to another. Unique features are associated with each service delivery model, many of which are discussed in this section (see Harris & Weiss, 2007, for a review).

Home-Based

In a home-based EIBI program, therapy sessions are conducted in the child's home. This means that the child's therapists come to the home at regularly scheduled times to conduct therapy sessions. It is typical for the family to identify a specific location where, at least initially, the majority of the sessions will take place. This room should be free from distractions and include materials that are essential for therapy sessions (e.g., table, chairs, instructional materials).

One of the benefits of being home-based is increased access to the child's home environment and family, so the family should expect the therapists to conduct sessions throughout the home. As such, it is essential that the family be comfortable with a team of therapists working in their home several hours a week. Home-based sessions also allow increased access to the child's toys, daily living materials, and family routines, all of which provide excellent teaching opportunities. A limitation of a home-based program is reduced access to typically developing same-aged peers, with the exception of siblings, providing fewer opportunities to work on peer interactions and peer play. In addition, it may be difficult to minimize distractions that are commonplace in a home environment.

Center-Based

In a center-based EIBI program, therapy sessions are conducted at a clinic or center. This means that the child is brought to the center several times each week for therapy. At the center it is common for each child to be assigned a designated area for therapy sessions. Children at the center may also participate in group activities. It may seem as though center-based programs are similar to public school–based programs, and in some ways they are. The section on school-based programs will differentiate the two service delivery formats.

A benefit of being center based is increased control over environmental variables and sometimes increased access to upper level supervision. For this reason it is common for children with severe problem behavior to be treated in a center-based program. Some limitations of being center-based are the lack of access to the child's daily living environment and reduced access to the child's toys, daily living materials, and family routines. Additionally, there is no access to typically developing same-aged peers, unless the center has designed a special program to incorporate them into the curriculum.

School-Based

In a public school–based EIBI program, therapy sessions are conducted in a classroom at the child's school. This means that therapy sessions take place during the child's regular school day. A public school–based program is unique because it delivers a continuum of services. Therapy may be provided in the general or special education classroom. A benefit of public school–based programs is increased access to typically developing peers and social activities, making this an ideal setting for therapy focused on the development of social interactions and peer relationships. The school environment also provides exposure to typical classroom instruction and routines. Children with ASDs have an opportunity to participate in regular classroom activities with typically developing peers. However, classrooms are often noisy and contain numerous visual distractions. Even when efforts are made to reduce the noise level and minimize visual clutter, some children with ASDs may be distracted.

When a child begins EIBI treatment in a home- or center-based program, it is common for the child to eventually transition to school. In an effort to assist the child with the transition to a school environment, one of the child's therapists may accompany him or her in the classroom or a different classroom assistant may be assigned. This additional assistance may be valuable for the child at first; however, efforts should be made to minimize the child's need for a classroom assistant with the ultimate goal that the child becomes an independent and active learner in the classroom.

When selecting a service delivery model, families must consider the goal of treatment, the quality of EIBI services available, and cost. It is also common for a child to receive services in more than one setting (e.g., a child participates in a home-based program and attends preschool). This is done to maximize the benefits of different service delivery models. Ultimately, it is the family who must decide which format is most compatible with their lifestyle and treatment goals for their child.

CURRICULUM

In an EIBI program, the curriculum includes programs designed to address skill deficits and behavior excesses (Green, 1996). A *skill deficit* is a skill that the child does not display, and a *behavior excess* is a behavior that happens too frequently (i.e., problem behaviors). The curriculum is comprised of acquisition programs to remediate the skill deficits, behavior reduction protocols to eliminate any behavior excesses, and maintenance and generalization programs to ensure the child continues to display the newly learned skills under a variety of conditions.

Skill Acquisition

Many researchers have written about what to teach children with ASDs (e.g., Harris & Weiss, 2007; Lovaas et al., 1981; Maurice, Green, & Luce, 1996; Scheuermann & Webber, 2002). In a comprehensive EIBI program, lessons are designed to teach a child every skill that he or she does not already display but should. The clinical supervisor, in collaboration with the treatment team, uses a detailed skills assessment to identify the child's skill deficits (see Chapter 5 for a description of skill assessments). Then specific skills are targeted based on whether the skill is functional for the child and age appropriate. The treatment team teaches the child the targeted skills during therapy sessions. It is necessary for the clinical supervisor to closely monitor the child's progress to determine whether changes need to be made to the instructional procedures and to know when to begin teaching new skills.

Many children with autism display deficits in the areas of language (e.g., articulation, naming objects, requesting, conversation skills), play (e.g., pretend play, independent play), social skills (e.g., peer interactions, perspective taking), motor skills (e.g., jumping, running, handwriting), adaptive behavior (e.g., dressing, toileting, meal preparation), academic readiness skills (e.g., letter identification, counting), and classroom behavior (e.g., lining up, following whole class instructions, choral responding). Improvements in these skill deficits contribute to the child's overall development. Each area is listed separately; however, many times skills in one area influence skills in another area. For instance, language skills are associated with social interaction, play skills, and many academic behaviors. Also, basic motor skills are needed before a child can learn more complex motor skills related to play and adaptive behavior. The clinical supervisor will determine whether the child needs to display prerequisite skills before introducing a more advanced acquisition program or whether the child will benefit from learning many interrelated skills simultaneously.

Reduction of Inappropriate Behaviors

In a comprehensive EIBI program, a protocol will be developed to address any behavior excesses the child displays (e.g., repetitive behaviors, aggression, noncompliance). The clinical supervisor, in collaboration with the treatment team, will conduct a functional assessment to determine the conditions under which the behavior occurs (i.e., the function of the behavior; see Chapter 5 for a description of a functional assessment). Then results of the functional assessment are used to develop an individualized behavior intervention plan. This protocol is implemented during therapy sessions and at other times when the inappropriate behavior tends to occur. The clinical supervisor closely monitors the frequency of the inappropriate behaviors targeted to determine whether modifications to the protocol are necessary.

The reduction of behavior excesses is equally important as the improvement of skill deficits. Behavior excesses may interfere with the acquisition new skills, cause disruption in a home and classroom, or hinder social relationships with siblings and peers. Sometimes a problem behavior is directly related to a skill deficit. For example, a child may engage in problem behavior as a means of communication when appropriate language skills are lacking (see Durand & Merges, 2001, & Mancil, 2006, for reviews of functional communication training). Other times a problem behavior may serve a different function, such as escape from a demand, access to attention, or self-stimulation. Different behavior protocols are needed depending on the function of the problem behavior, and the child's clinical supervisor will ensure that the behavior protocol is appropriate (see Filter & Horner, 2009, & Ingram, Lewis-Palmer, & Sugai, 2005, for a discussion of function-based interventions). It is necessary for the treatment team to implement the protocol consistently across environments. While these protocols can be a demanding at times, it is through the treatment team's dedication that behavior excesses are eventually eliminated.

Maintenance and Generalization

Maintenance and generalization of skills and abilities are important components of a comprehensive EIBI program (see Brown & Odom, 1994; Ghezzi & Bishop, 2008; Stokes & Baer, 1977; and Stokes & Osnes, 1989 for reviews). Maintenance refers to a child's ability to continue to perform a skill or engage in a behavior with minimal errors over time. For example, during therapy sessions, the therapists frequently practice the skill of sitting down when a therapist says, "Sit down." Maintenance of this skill is demonstrated when, after a period of no practice, a therapist says, "Sit down," and the child sits down. Generalization refers to the likelihood that a new skill or behavior will occur under naturally occurring conditions (i.e., in various settings, with various people, and when various instructions are used). Using the same example, generalization would be demonstrated if the child responds correctly when a teacher at school says, "Okay class, everyone needs to take a seat."

Maintenance and generalization do not just happen automatically, although some methods of instructions (i.e., naturalistic teaching) are associated with increased generalization. The child's clinical supervisor will develop a maintenance and generalization plan and then closely monitor the plan to ensure that the child continues to display newly learned skills and abilities over time in the natural environment. The maintenance of skills is enhanced by manipulating the frequency with which preferred objects, toys, or edibles are delivered for correct responses. In other words, the child is not able to predict when a preferred item will be delivered. When preferred things are delivered less frequently, it allows the child to experience the naturally occurring consequences for the behavior. Some techniques that can be used to enhance generalization include varying the teaching materials, using natural consequences, and encouraging a variety of appropriate forms of the response (e.g., teach the child to say "Hi," "Hey there," and "Hello"). It is important to note that no one technique will be effective for every child. The treatment team should frequently test for generalization, and, if generalization is not observed, it may be necessary for the clinical supervisor to modify the protocol.

The primary components of an EIBI curriculum are

➤ skill acquisition programs,
➤ behavior reduction protocols, and
➤ maintenance and generalization procedures.

While each component is essential, it could be argued that maintenance and generalization are the cornerstones of a curriculum for children with ASDs. In the end, mastery of skills and abilities is determined when maintenance and generalization are observed.

SUMMARY

ASDs are characterized by repetitive and stereotyped movements and broad deficits in many areas, including language, play, social interactions, adaptive behavior, and motor skills. EIBI is an empirically supported treatment that has resulted dramatic improvements and even recovery for some children with ASDs (e.g., Butter et al., 2006, Eikeseth, 2009; Eldevik et al., 2009; & Granpeesheh, Tarbox, Dixon, Carr, & Herbert, 2009). The five essential features of an EIBI program are

1. basic characteristics,
2. composition of the treatment team,
3. methods of instruction,
4. format of service delivery, and
5. curriculum.

Each section highlighted important factors that must be considered during its implementation. To review,

1. Treatment effectiveness is influenced by the age when EIBI treatment begins, the number of hours provided, and the number of years that treatment is implemented.
2. An EIBI treatment program is implemented by a trained team that includes therapists, clinical supervisors, and parents.

3. Behavior analytic teaching procedures, such as DTT and naturalistic teaching, are used during treatment sessions.
4. An EIBI treatment program may be home-based, center-based, or school-based, depending on the specific needs of the child and family.
5. The curriculum is designed to remediate skill deficits, eliminate behavior excesses, and ensure maintenance and generalization of newly learned skills.

Ultimately, an EIBI program must be individualized to meet the needs of each child, giving each child the opportunity to achieve his or her educational and behavioral goals.

REFERENCES

Allen, K. D., & Cowan, R. J. (2008). Naturalistic teaching procedures. In J. K. Luiselli, D. C. Russo, W. P. Christian, & S. M. Wilczynski (Eds.), *Effective practices for children with autism: Educational and behavioral support interventions that work* (pp. 213–240). New York: Oxford University Press.

American Psychiatric Association (APA). (1994). *Diagnostic and statistical manual of mental disorders* (4th ed.). Washington DC: Author.

Bibby, P., Eikeseth, S., Martin, N. T., Mudford, O. C., & Reeves, D. (2001). Progress and outcomes for children with autism receiving parent-managed intensive interventions. *Research in Developmental Disabilities, 22,* 425–447.

Bolton, J., & Mayer, M. D. (2008). Promoting the generalization of paraprofessional discrete trial teaching skills. *Focus on Autism and Other Developmental Disabilities, 23,* 103–111.

Brookman-Frazee, L. (2004). Using parent/clinician partnerships in parent education programs for children with autism. *Journal of Positive Behavior Interventions, 6,* 195–213.

Brown, W. H., & Odom, S. L. (1994). Strategies and tactics for promoting generalization and maintenance of young children's social behaviors. *Research in Developmental Disabilities, 15,* 99–118.

Butter, E. M., Mulick, J. A., & Metz, B. (2006). Eight case reports of learning recovery in children with pervasive developmental disorders after early intervention. *Behavioral Interventions, 21,* 227–243.

Charlop-Christy, M. H., & Carpenter, M. H. (2000). Modified incidental teaching sessions: A procedure for parents to increase spontaneous speech in their children with autism. *Journal of Positive Behavior Interventions, 2,* 98–112.

Charlop-Christy, M. H., & LeBlanc, L. A. (1999). Naturalistic teaching strategies foracquisition, generalization, and maintenance of speech in children with autism. In P. M. Ghezzi, W. L. Williams, & J. E. Carr (Eds.), *Autism: Behavior analytic perspectives* (pp. 167–184). Reno, NV: Context Press.

Cohen, H., Amerine-Dickens, M., & Smith, T. (2006). Early intensive behavioral treatment: Replication of the UCLA model in a community setting. *Developmental and Behavioral Pediatrics, 27,* 145–155.

Cooper, J. O., Heron, T. E., & Heward, W. L. (2007). *Applied behavior analysis* (2nd ed.). Columbus, OH: Prentice-Hall.

Cowan, R. J., & Allen, K. D. (2007). Using naturalistic procedures to enhance learning in individuals with autism: A focus on generalized teaching within the school setting. *Psychology in the Schools, 44,* 701–715.

Crockett, J. L., Fleming, R. K., Doepke, K. J., & Stevens, J. S. (2007). Parent training: Acquisition and generalization of discrete trials teaching skills with parents of children with autism. *Research in Developmental Disabilities, 28,* 23–26.

Demchak, M. (1990). Response prompting and fading methods: A review. *American Journal on Mental Retardation, 94,* 603–615.

Dib, N., & Sturmey, P. (2007). Reducing student stereotypy by improving terachers' implementation of discrete-trial teaching. *Journal of Applied Behavior Analysis, 40,* 339–343.

Downs, A., Downs, R. C., & Rau, K. (2008). Effects if training and feedback on discrete trial teaching and student performance. *Research in Developmental Disabilities, 29,* 235–246.

Durand, V. M., & Merges, E. (2001). Functional communication training: A contemporary behavior analytic intervention for problem behaviors. *Focus on Autism and Other Developmental Disabilities, 16,* 110–119.

Eikeseth, S. (2009). Outcome of comprehensive psycho-educational interventions for young children with autism. *Research in Developmental Disabilities, 30,* 158–178.

Eikeseth, S., Hayward, D., Gale, C., Gitlesen, J., & Eldevik, S. (2009). Intensity of supervision and outcome for preschool aged children receiving early and intensive behavioral interventions: A preliminary study. *Research in Autism Spectrum Disorders, 3,* 67–73.

Eikeseth, S., Smith, T., Jahr, E., & Eldevik, S. (2002). Intensive behavioral treatment at school for 4- to 7-year-old children with autism: A 1-year comparison controlled study. *Behavior Modification, 26,* 49–68.

Eikeseth, S., Smith, T., Jahr, E., & Eldevik, S. (2007). Outcome for children with autism who began intensive behavioral treatment between ages 4 and 7: A comparison controlled study. *Behavior Modification, 31,* 264–278.

Eldevik, S., Eikeseth, S., Jahr, E., & Smith, T. (2006). Effects of low-intensity behavioral treatment for children with autism and mental retardation. *Journal of Autism and Developmental Disorders, 36,* 211–224.

Eldevik, S., Hastings, R. P., Hughes, J. C., Jahr, E., Eikeseth, S., & Cross, S. (2009). Meta analysis of early intensive behavioral intervention for children with autism. *Journal of clinical Child & Adolescent Psychology, 38,* 439–450.

Fenske, E. C., Zalenski, S., Krantz, P. J., & McClannahan, P. E. (1985). Age at intervention and treatment outcome for autistic children in a comprehensive intervention program. *Analysis and Intervention in Developmental Disabilities, 5,* 49–58.

Filter, K. J., & Horner, R. H. (2009). Function-based interventions for problem behavior. *Education and Treatment of Children, 32,* 1–19

Frea, W. D., & Hepburn, S. L. (1999). Teaching parents of children with autism to perform functional assessments to plan interventions for extremely disruptive behaviors. *Journal of Positive Behavior Interventions, 1,* 112–116, 122.

Frea, W. D., & McNerney, E. K. (2008). Early intensive applied behavior analysis intervention for autism. In J. K. Luiselli, D. C. Russo, W. P. Christian, & S. M. Wilczynski (Eds.), *Effective practices for children with autism: Educational and behavioral support interventions that work* (pp. 83–110). New York: Oxford University Press.

Ghezzi, P. M. (2007). Discrete trials teaching. *Psychology in the Schools, 44,* 667–679.

Ghezzi, P. M., & Bishop, M. R. (2008). Generalized behavior change in young children with autism. In J. K. Luiselli, D. C. Russo, W. P. Christian, & S. M. Wilczynski (Eds.), *Effective practices for children with autism: Educational and behavioral support interventions that work* (pp. 137–158). New York: Oxford University Press.

Granpeesheh, D., Dixon, D. R., Tarbox, J., Kaplan, A. M., & Wilke, A. E. (2009). The effects of age and treatment intensity on behavioral intervention outcomes for children with autism spectrum disorders. *Research in Autism Spectrum Disorders, 3,* 1014–1022.

Granpeesheh, D., Tarbox, J., & Dixon, D. (2009). Applied behavior analytic interventions for children with autism: A description and review of treatment research. *Annals of Clinical Psychiatry, 21,* 162–173.

Granpeesheh, D., Tarbox, J., Dixon, D. R., Carr, E., & Herbert, M. (2009). Retrospective analysis of clinical records in 38 cases of recovery from autism. *Annals of Clinical Psychiatry, 21,* 195–204.

Green, G. (1996). Early behavioral intervention for autism: What does research tell us? In C. Maurice, G. Green, & S. C. Luce (Eds.), *Behavioral intervention for young children with autism: A manual for parents and professionals* (pp. 29–44). Austin, TX: Pro-Ed.

Green, G., Brennan, L. C., & Fein, D. (2002). Intensive behavioral treatment for a toddler at high risk for autism. *Behavior Modification, 26,* 69–102.

Harper, C. B., Symon, J. B. G., & Frea, W. D. (2008). Recess is time-in: Using peers to improve social skills of children with autism. *Journal of Autism and Developmental Disorders, 38,* 815–826.

Harris, S. L., & Handleman, J. S. (2000). Age and IQ at intake as predictors of placement for young children with autism: A four- to six-year follow-up. *Journal of Autism and Developmental Disorders, 30,* 137–143.

Harris, A. L., & Weiss, M. J. (2007). *Right from the start: Behavioral interventions for young children with autism* (2nd ed.). Bethesda, MD: Woodbine House.

Hart, B. M., & Risley, T. R. (1975). Incidental teaching of language in the preschool. *Journal of Applied Behavior Analysis, 8,* 411–420.

Hastings, R. P., & Brown, T. (2002). Behavior problems of children with autism, parental self efficacy, and mental health. *American Journal on Mental Retardation, 107,* 222–232.

Hastings, R. P., Kovshoff, H., Ward, N. J., degli Espinosa, F., Brown, T., & Remington, B. (2005). Systems analysis of stress and positive perceptions in mothers and fathers of preschool children with autism. *Journal of Autism and Developmental Disorders, 35,* 635–644.

Hayward, D. W., Gale, C. M., & Eikeseth, S. (2009). Intensive behavioral intervention for young children with autism: A research-based service model. *Research in Autism Spectrum Disorders, 3,* 571–580.

Howard, J. S., Sparkman, C. R., Cohen, H. G., Green, G., & Stanislaw, H. (2005). A comparison of intensive behavior analytic and eclectic treatments for young children with autism. *Research in Developmental Disabilities, 26,* 359–383.

Ingram, K., Lewis-Palmer, T., & Sugai, G. (2005). Function-based intervention planning: Comparing the effectiveness of FBA function-based and non-function-based intervention plans. *Journal of Positive Behavior Interventions, 7,* 224–236.

Kaiser, A. P., Hancock, T. B., & Nietfeld, J. P. (2000). The effects of parent-implemented enhanced milieu teaching on the social communication of children who have autism. *Journal of Early Education and Development, 11,* 423–446.

Koegel, R. L., Bimbela, A., & Schreibman, L. (1996). Collateral effects of parent training on family interactions. *Journal of Autism and Developmental Disorders, 26,* 347–359.

Koegel, R. L., Camarata, S., Koegel, L. K., Ben-Tall, A., & Smith, A. (1998). Increasing speech intelligibility in children with autism. *Journal of Autism and Developmental Disorders, 28,* 241–251.

Koegel, R. L., Glahn, T. J., & Nieminen, G. S. (1978). Generalization of parent-training results. *Journal of Applied Behavior Analysis, 11,* 95–109.

Koegel, R. L., & Koegel, L. K. (2006). *Pivotal response treatments for autism: Communication, social, & academic development.* Baltimore, MD: Brookes.

Koegel, R. L., O'Dell, M. C., & Koegel, L. K. (1987). A natural language paradigm for teaching nonverbal autistic children. *Journal of Autism and Developmental Disorders, 17,* 187–199.

Kohler, F. W., Anthony, L. J., Steighner, S. A., & Hoyson, M. (2001). Teaching social interaction skills in the integrated preschool: An examination of naturalistic tactics. *Topics in Early Childhood Special Education, 21,* 93–103.

Krantz, P. J., & McClannahan, L. E. (1998). Social interaction skills for children with autism: A script fading procedure for beginning readers. *Journal of Applied Behavior Analysis, 31,* 191–202.

Leblanc, M. P., Ricciardi, J. N., & Luiselli, J. K. (2005). Improving discrete trial instruction by paraprofessional stadd through an abbreviated performance feedback intervention. *Education and Treatment of Children, 28,* 76–82.

Lovaas, O. I. (1977). *The autistic child: Language training through behavior modification.* New York: Irvington.

Lovaas, I. O. (1987). Behavioral treatment and normal educational and intellectual functioning in young autistic children. *Journal of Consulting Psychology, 55,* 3–9.

Lovaas, O. I., Ackerman, A. B., Alexander, D., Firestone, P., Perkins, J., & Younf, D. (1981). *Teaching developmentally disabled children: The ME book.* Austin, TX: Pro-Ed.

Lovaas, I. O., Koegel, R., Simmons, J. Q., & Long, J. S. (1973). Some generalization and follow-up measures on autistic children in behavior therapy. *Journal of Applied Behavior Analysis, 6,* 131–166.

Love, J. R., Carr, J. E., Almason, S. M., & Petursdottir, A. I. (2009). Early and intensive behavioral intervention for autism: A survey of clinical practices. *Research in Autism Spectrum Disorders, 3,* 421–428.

Magiati, I., Charman, T., & Howlin, P. (2007). A two-year prospective follow-up study of community-based early intensive behavioral intervention and specialist nursery provision for children with autism spectrum disorders. *Journal of Child Psychology and Psychiatry, 48,* 803–812.

Mancil, G. R. (2006). Functional communication training: A review of the literature related to children with autism. *Education and Training in Developmental Disabilities, 41,* 213–224.

Maurice, C., Green, G., & Luce, S. C. (1996). *Behavioral interventions for young children with autism: A manual for parents and professionals.* Austin, TX: Pro-Ed.

Mazur, J. E. (2002). *Learning and behavior* (5th ed.). Upper Saddle River, NJ: Prentice Hall.

Miltenberger, R. G. (2007). *Behavior modification: Principles and procedures* (4th ed.). Belmont, CA: Wadsworth/Thomson Learning.

Moes, D. R., & Frea, W. D. (2000). Using family context to inform intervention planning for the treatment of a child with autism. *Journal of Positive Behavior Interventions, 2,* 40–46.

Moes, D. R., & Frea, W. D. (2002). Contextualized behavioral support in early intervention for children with autism and their families. *Journal of Autism and Developmental Disorders, 32,* 519–533.

Morse, T. E., & Schuster, J. W. (2004). Simultaneous prompting: A review of the literature. *Education and Training in Developmental Disabilities, 39,* 153–168.

Page, J., & Boucher, J. (1998). Motor impairments in children with autistic disorder. *Child Language Teaching & Therapy, 14,* 233–259.

Pear, J. J. (2001). *The science of learning.* Philadelphia, PA: Psychology Press.

Perry, A., Cummings, A., Geier, J. D., Freeman, N. L., Hughes, S., LaRose, L., et al. (2008). Effectiveness of intensive behavioral intervention in a large, community-based program. *Research in Autism Spectrum Disorders, 2,* 621–642

Plant, K. M., & Sanders, M. R. (2007). Predictors of care-giver stress in families of preschool aged children with developmental disabilities. *Journal of intellectual Disability Research, 51,* 109–124.

Rapin, I., & Tuchman, R. F. (2008). Autism: Definition, neurobiology, screening, diagnosis. *Pediatric Clinics of North America, 55,* 1129–1146.

Reed, P., Osborne, L. A., & Corness, M. (2007). Brief report: Relative effectiveness of different home-based behavioral approaches to early teaching intervention. *Journal of Autism and Developmental Disorders, 37,* 1815–1821.

Remington, B., Hastings, R. P., Kovshoff, H., degli Espinosa, F., Jahr, E., Brown, T., et al. (2007). Early intensive behavioral intervention: Outcomes for children with autism and their parents after two years. *American Journal on Mental Retardation, 112,* 418–438.

Rogers-Warren, A., & Warren, S. (1980). Facilitating the display of newly trained language in children. *Behavior Modification, 4,* 361–382.

Sallows, G. O., & Graupner, T. D. (2005). Intensive behavioral treatment for children with autism: Four-year outcome and predictors. *American Journal on Mental Retardation, 110,* 417–438.

Sarokoff, R. A., & Sturmey, P. (2004). The effects of behavioral skills training on staff implementation of discrete-trial teaching. *Journal of Applied Behavior Analysis, 37,* 535–538.

Schepis, M. M., Reid, D. H., Ownbey, J. & Parsons, M. B. (2001). Training support staff to embed teaching within natural routines of young children with disabilities in an inclusive preschool. *Journal of Applied Behavior Analysis, 34,* 131–327.

Scheuermann, B., & Webber, J. (2002). *Autism: Teaching does make a difference.* Belmont, CA: Wadsworth/Thomson Learning.

Schoen, S. F. (1986). Assistance procedure to facilitate the transfer of stimulus control: Review and analysis. *Education and Training of the Mentally Retarded, 21,* 62–74.

Sheinkopf, S. J., & Siegel, B. (1998). Home-based behavioral treatment of young children with autism. *Journal of Autism and Developmental Disorders, 28,* 15–23.

Smith, T., Groen, A. D., & Wynn, J. W. (2000). Randomized trial of intensive early intervention for children with pervasive developmental disorder. *American Journal on Mental Retardation, 105,* 269–258.

Stahmer, A. C. (1995). Teaching symbolic play skills to children with autism using pivotal response training. *Journal of Autism and Developmental Disorders, 25,* 123–141.

Stahmer, A. C., Ingersoll, B., & Carter, C. (2003). Behavioral approaches to promoting play. *Autism, 7,* 401–413.

Stokes, T. F., & Baer, D. M. (1977). An implicit technology of generalization. *Journal of Applied Behavior Analysis, 10,* 349–367.

Stokes, T. F., & Osnes, P. G. (1989). An operant pursuit of generalization. *Behavior Therapy, 20,* 337–355.

Sundberg, M. L., & Partington, J. W. (1999). The need for both discrete trial and natural environment language training for children with autism. In P. M. Ghezzi, W. L. Williams, & J. E. Carr (Eds.), *Autism: Behavior analytic perspectives* (pp. 139–156). Reno, NV: Context Press.

Tarbox, R. S. F., & Najdowski, A. C. (2008). Discrete trial training as a teaching paradigm. In J. K. Luiselli, D. C. Russo, W. P. Christian, & S. M. Wilczynski (Eds.), *Effective practices for children with autism: Educational and behavioral support interventions that work* (pp. 181–194). New York: Oxford University Press.

Thomson, K., Martin, G. L., Arnal, L., Fazzio, D., & Yu, C. T. (2009). Instructing individuals to deliver discrete-trials teaching to children with autism spectrum disorders: A review. *Research in Autism Spectrum Disorders, 3,* 590–606.

Thorpe, D. M., Stahmer, A. C., & Schreibman, L. (1995). Effects of sociodramatic play training on children with autism. *Journal of Autism and Developmental Disorders, 25,* 265–281.

Williamson, M. (1996). Funding the behavioral program: Legal strategies for parents. In C. Maurice, G. Green, & S. C. Luce (Eds.), *Behavioral intervention for young children with autism: A manual for parents and professionals* (pp. 267–293). Austin, TX: Pro-Ed.

Wolery, M., & Gast, D. L. (1984). Effective and efficient procedures for the transfer of stimulus control. *Topics in Early Childhood Special Education, 4,* 52–77.

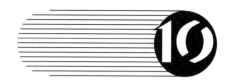

ABCs in ASD: Reading Strategies

Jennifer Laurence and Catherine Orsak

For the last two decades, educators have placed strong emphasis on teaching students to read using scientifically based interventions, implemented through the federal government's Reading First initiative and defined in research synthesis reports (Adams, 1990; Browder, 2008; National Institute of Child Health and Human Development, 2000a). The National Reading Panel (NICHD, 2000a) reports the essential components of reading (i.e., phonemic awareness, phonics, fluency, vocabulary, and comprehension) be taught using a balanced approach to reading instruction. A balanced reading program should include instruction that takes into consideration

> ➤ each child's background, strengths, and needs;
> ➤ early training in phonemic awareness, sound–letter correspondence, and decoding skills;
> ➤ the study of word-recognition skills;
> ➤ integration of writing instruction;
> ➤ vocabulary study in the context of meaningful print;
> ➤ an emphasis in reading instruction across the curriculum; and
> ➤ an integration of guided instruction and independent work.

Learning to read requires the integration of many skills. Many children with autism have impairments in language processing, analytic processing, semantic memory, social knowledge and learning through language (Brizant, 2000). Difficulties with integration of information, abstract reasoning, and cognitive flexibility will make teaching the five essential components of reading challenging for the teacher and the student.

LITERACY AND AUTISM:
REVIEW OF THE RESEARCH

Background knowledge or *prior knowledge* is what someone already knows about a subject or past experiences in regard to a subject. Prior knowledge has a large influence on student performance and a correlation between prior knowledge and reading comprehension is well established (Strangeman & Hall, 2004). Many students with autism experience the world differently as a result of sensory, social, cognitive, and communication impairments. Many will have limited experiences because of repetitive or inappropriate behaviors and need for routine. Mary, for example, is 15 and her only community outings are family trips to the zoo. Her interests and experiences are limited to movies, TV, and music. John is 10 years old and his parents have never taken him to a restaurant because of his auditory sensitivities, lack of communication, and inability to sit in a chair for more than 10 minutes. Mary and John have limited experiences, which in turn affect building a knowledge base.

Phonemic awareness, sound–letter correspondence, and decoding skills require attention, language processing, and integration of information. These skills also present a challenge for many individuals with autism as a result of difficulties with auditory processing, abstract reasoning, gestalt processing, and overselectivity, which make it difficult to attend to the multiple features at once. *Gestalt processing* is when information is processed and remembered as a whole and generally reflects a decreased understanding of the meaning of the parts (Quill, 2000). Individuals with autism are suspected of not being able to integrate parts to the whole; that is, they focus on a part but do not seem able to understand how the parts are related. Learning these skills can be challenging for many people with autism, given that learning requires attending to multiple features at once. Jack is 7 and has autism. He is working with his teacher on matching letter–sound correspondence. Every time the teacher asks him what sound /t/ makes, he says the letter name. He may not understand the directions or understand what the word "sound" really means. The teacher models the correct answer three times before he understands. For others these skills can come very early on.

Some children with autism also have hyperlexia. *Hyperlexia* is the ability to read words far above what would be expected at the child's chronological age or an intense fascination with letters or numbers. These individuals also have significant difficulty understanding verbal language and have abnormal social skills. Students with hyperlexia have difficulty comprehending what they are reading, even though oral reading sounds perfectly normal. Nation (1999) describes those students whose word reading skills are exceedingly advanced compared to their text comprehension and chronological age as having hyperlexia. While hyperlexia is reported in clinical populations other than those with ASD, the incidence may be elevated among those on the spectrum. Some studies have indicated that as a result of the higher incidences, researchers become tempted to conclude that many children with autism are hyperlexic, especially given the observation that many children with hyperlexia are autistic, or show features of autism. However, the research community has neither accepted nor refused this protocol yet (Grigorenko et al., 2002; Nation, 1999).

Despite the wide range of impairments in ASD, best practices in reading instruction include using a balanced program that teaches all five essential components every day. In Mrs. Smith's first grade class, the students are introduced to a book. She looks through the pages with them, talks about the story, and asks them to make predictions. She asks the students about experiences that might be similar to those in the story. She discusses the meanings of words that might be new to the students. She identifies sight words and puts them on the word wall. She plays phonemic awareness games, such as segmentation, with the students.

A comprehensive review of the research on reading instruction for students with significant developmental disabilities found that the majority of studies for this population focused on sight word acquisition. Only a small portion targeted comprehension of sight words, and only 6% of the participants in the studies reviewed were individuals with autism (Browder, Wakeman, Spooner, Ahlgrim-Delzell, & Algozzine, 2006). These findings substantiate that reading instruction for students with autism has been underemphasized and has gained very little research attention (O'Connor & Klein, 2004).

When students with autism and coexisting conditions that seriously affect cognition have access to literacy instruction, content has most often focused on the acquisition of high-frequency sight words needed for basic communication or functional skills such as reading survival signs (e.g., restroom, stop, go, walk, don't walk, etc.). Historically, reading instruction for students with significant cognitive disabilities has been underemphasized. Instead educators have focused on functional skills reflected in daily living activities. Although students do need functional skill instruction, reading is more than word identification, and instruction in other reading skills also should be available to children with autism. Educators limit future opportunities if they make a prior assumption not to teach reading to some students because of the nature or severity of disability (Browder et al., 2006).

In contrast to the example given earlier about Mrs. Smith's first grade class and their reading instruction, reading instruction in the self-contained autism program is very different. Many students will receive reading instruction with accommodations in resource rooms or general education settings. The type of reading instruction will be based on the needs of the student and the skill sets of the teachers.

FOUNDATIONS OF LEARNING TO READ

Recent legislation and focus on research-based instruction has lead to a more unified drive to teach students with significant cognitive disabilities how to identify more than simple words and phrases. Research results have demonstrated that many students with and without significant cognitive disabilities can learn how to read through intensive instruction using a variety of different strategies to teach the essential components of reading (Browder et al., 2006). Research on effective reading programs that focus on teaching the five essential components of reading for individuals with autism is needed.

Components of reading for ALL students

Since autism is a spectrum disorder, the individual needs of the student will guide instruction. The National Reading Panel (NICHD, 2000a) reports the essential components of reading are:

1. phonemic awareness,
2. phonics,
3. fluency,
4. vocabulary, and
5. comprehension.

The National Reading Panel (2000) further recommends that they be taught using a balanced approach to reading instruction. The ability to read is a critical skill that sets the foundation for learning.

Language and communication impairments are a core characteristic in autism. Some are very verbal, yet have difficulty processing auditory information, some are nonverbal and will be more proficient at language processing, and some will be verbal and have little auditory processing impairments. Steven is 7 years old and verbal. He can carry on a brief conversation, ask questions, and make comments relevant to topics being discussed. However, he has difficulty processing auditory information, reflected in difficulty following directions, attending to tasks, answering questions, and retelling the events of a story he has read. Nicky is 8 years old and is nonverbal. He uses a speech-generating device that produces synthesized or digitized speech to communicate. Nicky is able to use his device to request, comment, and answer questions. He is able to attend to activities and follows most verbal directions. Willie is 10 and has impairments in both categories. He uses picture symbols to communicate, has many stereotypical behaviors, and has difficulty following one step directions. Teaching the components of reading to individuals with autism will vary depending upon the nature and severity of these core characteristics, with communication impairments playing a major role.

Phonemic Awareness

Phonological awareness (PA) is the knowledge that spoken words are made up of tiny segments of sounds referred to as *phonemes*. PA is the ability to hear and manipulate sounds in words and does not involve recognition of whole words or print. PA allows students to notice, think about, and work with individual sounds in a given word. PA is a critical building block for success in reading. Children who have language impairments very often have poor PA, which will lead to continued reading struggles (McCauley & Fey, 2006). The degree to which disorders in auditory processing are present will impact phonemic awareness. Many individuals with autism appear to have difficulty processing auditory information.

Assessing phonemic awareness skills includes measuring the ability to blend the sounds in nonsense or unfamiliar words. Blending nonsense words is more predictive of later reading achievement because these are words that have not been rote memorized. The most important skill is the ability to decode and blend the sounds in a new word, because students cannot become successful readers if they can only read words they previously memorized.

Teaching these phonemic awareness skills to students with autism is challenging because of their gestalt processing. Because individuals with gestalt issues process information as an integrated whole, they usually cannot or have difficulty with assimilating parts to create a whole concept. John is 5 years old and found on the ASD. He appears to be able to read the story *Brown Bear Brown Bear* word for word. He reads each word and turns the page at the correct time, yet he is unable to read words from the story in isolation. John can produce sounds for the letters /c/, /a/, and /t/, but he cannot blend the sounds to create the word *cat*. Some children with autism will be minimally successful developing PA.

For children with disabilities who are at risk for reading failure, phonological awareness instruction must be taught explicitly. In order for most children to begin reading print, they must have an understanding of the sounds that make up the words (NICHD, 2000a). PA skills include

> *blending*, the combining or blending separate sounds in a word to say the word (e.g., blending sounds /m/, /a/, /t/ to say "mat");
> *segmenting* a word into its separate sounds (e.g., saying the word "Sam" slowly so that each sound can be heard, e.g., "Sssssaaaammmm"); and
> isolating and saying the first or last sound in a word (e.g., the beginning sound in "man" is "mmm").

Development of phonological awareness cannot be left to chance for most children with disabilities because their disabilities put them at risk for reading problems. However, with repetitive systematic instruction and the use of visual supports, assistive technology, motivating and fun activities, these skills can be taught to and demonstrated by most. However, the ability to truly demonstrate an understanding that the sound structure of language is different from its meaning is an abstract concept and might be difficult for some with autism to truly comprehend.

Children with autism may be able to develop and demonstrate phonological awareness skills; however, they may learn these skills more through rote memory as a result of gestalt processing. For example, some learn language as whole units but do not understand the individual words that make up sentences or phrases. Some will be able to demonstrate these skills through repeated activities and modeling such as songs, letter tiles, or visual supports, yet they may have difficulty generalizing these skills to new sounds and words. The use of visual supports and simple language can help improve comprehension of these tasks.

Phonics

Phonics refers to a method of teaching speakers of English to read and write that language. Phonics involves teaching how to connect the sounds of spoken English with letters (e.g., that the sound /k/ can be represented by /c/, /k/, or /ck/ or /ch/ spellings) and to blend the sounds of letters together to produce approximate pronunciations of unknown words.

Phonics is a widely used method of teaching to read and decode words. Children begin learning to read using phonics usually around the age of 5 or 6. Teaching reading using phonics requires students to learn the connections between letter patterns and the sounds they represent. Phonics instruction requires the teacher to provide students with a core body of information about phonics rules or patterns (Kluth & Chandler-Olcott, 2008). Memorizing phonetic sounds and some phonics rules may be an area of strength for many children with autism because they frequently exhibit gestalt processing and strong visual memory abilities. Applying and integrating these foundations in phonics may be challenging, however. Learning sound–letter correspondence can be accomplished through repetitive activities that teach to the strength of rote memory. The integration and application of these skills may be hindered by impairments in communication and language comprehension. Max is able to demonstrate the skills of sound–letter correspondence for many letters. He knows when he sees the letter /t/ what sound it makes and is able to demonstrate this skill with many letters. Max is able to read many sight words in isolation and in context, yet he is unable to decode unfamiliar words that contain letter–sound correspondences he knows. He has difficulty integrating the core phonics skills he has mastered and applying them to decode unfamiliar words.

Individuals with autism have problems learning abstract concepts that cannot be thought about in pictures (Grandin, 1995. Nouns are easy to remember because a concrete picture can be associated with it. Words such as *to, the, a, from,* as well as grammatical markers such as *-ing* are more challenging for many to understand and use because it is difficult to attach a picture to create meaning. Thomas is five years old and learning to read. When he speaks he does not use the present progressive *-ing* to describe actions and omits *-ing* when reading.

When teaching phonics to children with autism, most teachers use visual strategies such as picture symbols and active engagement. Temple Grandin, author of *Thinking in Pictures*, a successful woman who has autism and a PhD, stated that she was able to remember the approximately fifty phonetic sounds and a few rules. Lower functioning children often learn better by association, with the aid of word labels attached to objects in their environment (i.e., putting labels on doors, windows, tables, etc.; see Figure 10.1), and others learn better with words that are spelled out with plastic letters they can feel.

Phonics instruction that includes systematic and explicit instruction is more effective than nonsystematic. The hallmark of systematic instruction is the direct teaching of a set of letter–sound relationships in a clearly defined sequence. The set includes the major sound/spelling relationships of both consonants and vowel. When

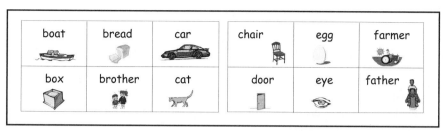

| boat | bread | car | | chair | egg | farmer |
| box | brother | cat | | door | eye | father |

FIGURE 10.1
Word Labels

teaching phonics to children with autism, use clear and easily understandable directions paired with visual cues

Phonics instruction should be included in any balanced reading program and should be incorporated and adapted for students with autism. Knowledge of phonics is one of the resources that learners use for *word recognition,* which is the immediate, accurate, and effortless ability to read words in context and isolation (Kluth, 2008, p.107). Students who were taught phonics were better able to spell and decode, as well as comprehend text according to the report by the National Reading Panel (NICHD, 2000a). *Decoding* is using knowledge of letter–sound relationships to pronounce unfamiliar words vocally (McCauley & Fey, 2006, p. 556).

Phonics instruction for some children who use speech generating devices will include preprogramming letters into the devices as along with the sounds those letters make. Some newer speech generating devices have this information already programmed. When the teacher asks Nicky, "What sound does the letter /a/ make," he pushes /a/ on his device and it says the phonetic sound /aa/. He is also able to go to the letter page when the teacher asks him what letter makes the /aa/ sound.

Many individuals with autism are motivated when using computers. Computer based phonics programs such as Click N Read Phonics, Earobics, and Starfall may be useful in motivating some of these students. Matching tasks where students need to match the sounds to spellings (i.e., phonics lotto) or write the spelling when given the sound may be more concrete for some. Instruction can be adapted in a variety of ways to actively engage and motivate students with autism depending upon their learning strengths and needs.

Fluency

Reading fluency encompasses the speed or rate of reading as well as the ability to read materials with expression. Verbal production in autism can be characterized by poor pitch modulation and monotonous tempo. These characteristics can impact reading fluency. Jason is hyperlexic and is a fluent reader, however he does not acknowledge punctuation marks or read with expression. Intervention with Jason needs to focus on his understanding of punctuation marks in order to improve comprehension. Jenny has difficulty decoding new words and reads very slowly. Instruction for Jenny needs to focus on improving decoding skills. Fluency can be affected by different impairments in other areas of literacy development or communication. Some individuals with autism have difficulty with attention, and attending to the lines and being able to visual track may affect fluency. Scott is a good reader yet is always losing his place and reading the same line over or skipping lines. He uses a place marker to assist him in keeping track of where he is. Reading too fast or too slowly as well as not understanding exclamation points, question marks, and the like are prevalent in autism. Reading fluency also impacts comprehension; therefore, it is important to measure and teach fluent reading. The best way to ensure fluency is through rapid decoding.

Vocabulary

Vocabulary development is critical to comprehension. Vocabulary development can also be referred to as *semantics*. Words are the tools we use to access our background knowledge, express ideas, and learn about new concepts. Students' word knowledge is strongly linked to academic success. True comprehension is far more than recognizing words and remembering their meanings. The impairments in social interaction, communication, and limited interests will significantly impact vocabulary development. Typical children learn new vocabulary and develop language through experiences and social interaction: They just pick up new words. They do not need to be explicitly taught that a dog is an animal, it has four legs, it barks, it is a pet. Typical children just learn this type of information through experience.

Many children with autism prefer to play by themselves and have limited interests. For many, vocabulary development takes place sitting at a table with pictures being systematically taught, for example, the features of a dog. Learning new words without being specifically taught their meaning requires abstract and analytical thinking along with the integration of old and new information. Angel is reading a book about apples and all the pictures of apples in the story are red, however is the book mentions that some apples are green. After reading the book, the teacher shows her a picture of a green apple and asks her, "What is this?" and she responds, "Green." Because of the range of abilities in ASD, some individuals will have rich vocabularies and be able to talk about a wide range of topics without explicit instruction. Some will have a rich vocabulary in a topic of interest, yet have difficulty learning new vocabulary. Julian is 6 years old and loves dinosaurs. His vocabulary on this topic far exceeds his age, yet when he is reading about other first grade topics, he needs to be taught new vocabulary words through numerous explanations paired with drawings and application of the new words. Many children with autism have strengths in visual learning. By modifying a reading program to focus on visual learning styles, many children with autism can experience success.

Attention and information processing can be impaired in some children with autism. Difficulties with the integration of information, abstract reasoning, and cognitive flexibility have been reported (Minshew, Goldstein, Muenz & Payton, 1992; Quill, 2000). These characteristics will significantly impact the ability to learn new vocabulary. Most children learn new vocabulary words by extracting meaning from other information such as pictures in the text. Many children with autism need to be explicitly taught how to extract meaning.

Overselectivity means difficulty attending to the multiple features inherent in all stimuli. Many individuals with autism have difficulty determining the most meaningful feature of a given stimulus (Frith & Baron-Cohen, 1987; Quill, 2000). Many children with autism focus on features or less relevant cues rather than on the meaningfulness of the image as a whole. Many individuals with autism learn through rote memory and have great difficulty making inferences and obtaining meaning found in parts of the text. Riley reads a story and has difficulty understanding the meaning of a few words. He is told to look at the pictures; however, she cannot extract meaning to determine the meaning of the word "tease" even though tease is made clear from an inference in the pictures. The teacher explains what the word means and then attempts to give an example that would be meaningful to Riley. When you tease your sister you are being mean to her. After reading the story, the teacher asks Riley to use the word "tease" in a sentence and she is unable to do so. She will need repeated exposure to this word and other vocabulary words in order to truly understand their meaning. When teaching an abstract concept, the use of visual supports is important, for example, writing sentences (if student can read) or drawing pictures, using the concept within different contexts, making a video that the student can watch. Breaking the abstract concept down into words and language that the student can comprehend and practicing what the word means in different contexts can be helpful in teaching more abstract concepts.

Margaret is 7 years old and has a younger brother whom she likes to push down, saying that pushing him was an accident. She does not understand the meaning of the word accident. To explain this abstract concept to her, the teacher writes down the word accident and breaks down the word into a word she is familiar with: "mistake," like when she is writing and needs to erase, that is a mistake. The teacher creates opportunities in the classroom to use the word accident in context as well as read stories about accidents or mistakes. At snack time, she gives Margaret two cups instead of one and then says " Oh, that was a mistake or an accident." Once Margaret starts to label some of the actions around the classroom correctly as an accident, she will then apply this concept to the interaction with her brother. Much of the vocabulary that students encounter when reading will need to be explained in a more concrete and detailed way to ensure comprehension and generalization of the word.

Comprehension

The National Reading Panel tied vocabulary development to reading comprehension. Many children with autism have delays in their receptive and expressive vocabulary development, which will impact their overall understanding of the text. Reading comprehension has been considered "the most important academic skill learned in school" (Chiang & Lin, 2007, p. 259). The deficits in reading comprehension reported for children with autism may be attributable to impairments in communication and unique cognitive abilities. Jesse is in first grade and reads at a high fourth grade level. Although Jesse is reading at fourth grade level, he comprehends very little of what he is reading. This is often the case with children with autism who are proficient decoders or hyperlexic. Impairments in communication (i.e., auditory processing, semantic memory) and gestalt processing can affect comprehension. The ability to understand what the words mean is lacking and the ability to look for context clues is absent. Jason reads the sentence "Mary went to the store because she needed some lemons to make lemonade for her friends." Jason is then asked a series of questions to examine comprehension. He is able to answer the simple questions such as "Who went to the store?" and "What did she buy?" because those words are visually available in the sentence and those questions would be considered more concrete. He is unable to answer the questions "What kind of store does Mary need to go to buy lemons?" "What are they going to do with the Lemonade?" and "Was she making Lemonade for only one person or more than one?" These types of comprehension questions require more abstract thinking and inferencing. Many individuals with autism have difficulty drawing conclusions from information that is not explicitly stated. Therefore, comprehension of concrete information may be easier than information that needs to be inferred from the text. In order to truly comprehend text the integration of both skills is necessary.

Many individuals with autism show impairments in comprehension of text, vocabulary, and oral language (Kluth & Chandler-Olcott, 2008). However, few reading programs systematically teach reading comprehension to individuals with autism. Comprehension is teaching children to understand what they read and is typically taught once a child has learned to use the mechanical skills associated with word recognition and decoding. Most middle school and high school students continued to struggle with comprehension, although teaching specific comprehension skills is initiated in kindergarten and continues through the early elementary grades (Carrier, 2006).

In order to improve comprehension, fluent readers use their background knowledge to help them make sense of text. Children with autism have difficulty integrating information and may have difficulty recalling and applying past experiences to the present. To increase motivation, use subjects of interest for children with autism. They will be more likely to recall and apply information they can relate to. Mark, for example, loves to go to Disneyland, so his teacher uses stories about Disneyland to engage Mark. Mark's reading comprehension is excellent when it is about a topic he enjoys. If the teacher assesses him on story about a topic he is not interested in, Mark appears to have trouble comprehending information. He does not have difficulty in his ability to comprehend material for which he has a prior knowledge base. Without this knowledge base, and in Mark's case the knowledge base is selective, he does not appear able to comprehend information. Without a knowledge base, most learners cannot comprehend well. The difference between Mark's comprehension skills and those of his more typical peers is that the typical learner has a wider range of interests and can also relate information from one knowledge base to another. Mark cannot relate information. For Mark every piece of information is a separate piece, for example, Mark knows who Mickey Mouse is and he knows who Minnie Mouse is, but he doesn't know that Minnie and Mickey are best friends. He also does not realize that the little live mouse that is kept as a pet in his classroom is also a mouse like Minnie and Mickey.

The Need for Print-Rich Learning Environments

Language- and print-rich learning environments that focus on building interaction, communication, and language skills are critical to literacy skills. Many students with autism are not exposed to this type of learning environment. Books are used only during certain times of the day. Reading instruction takes place individually at a table for short intervals maybe once a day. Many self-contained autism classrooms may not even address literacy at all because of the severity of the students' impairments.

Although the need for language- and print-rich learning environments is recognized most readily for young, typically developing children, it is no less critical to any student who has yet to be provided sufficient opportunities to develop foundational emergent literacy skills. Emergent literacy skills include (McCauley& Fey, 2006):

1. concepts about print (e.g., knowledge about book orientation, one-to-one correspondence between the written and spoken word),
2. letter identification,
3. word generation (i.e., numbers of words student can spell in 10 minutes),
4. phonological and phonemic awareness (i.e., ability to hear and manipulate words and individual phonemes within words), and
5. receptive language (i.e., background knowledge and experiences).

Although the evidence regarding the development of these emergent literacy understandings for individuals who use augmentative and alternative communication (AAC) is limited and mixed, it does suggest that this same foundation is important (Dahlgren & Hjelmquist, 1996; Vandervelden & Siegal, 1999).

Most individuals who have autism and use AAC can be taught to read and write. These skills can be taught using effective instructional strategies based on best practices in general education, with accommodations that make these practices accessible, interactive, and intensive (Cousin, Weekly, & Gerard, 1993; Mike, 1995; Worthy & Invernizzi, 1995).

As a teacher, if you identify and relate to a student who uses AAC as his or her primary mode of communication in the same manner as a student who uses speech, then you will realize the importance of using and incorporating these systems in all teaching practices, especially literacy. It sometimes requires more preplanning and an understanding of how to access the vocabulary on the device so it can be modeled for the student. These students are just as capable of learning to read as those who are verbal.

The use of visuals had been found to be highly successful when teaching children with disabilities, especially those with autism, as they tend to be visual learners. Pictures or other symbols used along with print are important in the early stages of phonemic awareness, but an emphasis needs to be placed early on print recognition as well. As McCauley and Fey (2006) stated, "Many children fail to learn to read because they are predominately visual thinkers, whereas reading and the methods used to teach reading are based predominately on an auditory mode of thought" (p. 347).

The National Reading Panel reports the combination of teaching phonics and word sounds and giving feedback on oral reading is the most effective way to teach reading. The best reading program has a balance between the skills-based and the meaning-based approach to reading instruction. A balanced literacy program has students partake in many aspects of reading. A balanced reading program should include:

> ➤ thoughtful instruction that takes into consideration each child's background, strengths, and needs;
> ➤ early training in phonemic awareness, sound–letter correspondence, and decoding skills;
> ➤ the study of word-recognition skills;
> ➤ integration of writing instruction;
> ➤ vocabulary study in the context of meaningful print;
> ➤ an emphasis in reading instruction across the curriculum; and
> ➤ an integration of guided instruction and independent work.

Whole word recognition has been used with developmentally disabled students in many successful interventions. Sight word games, word walls, and personal dictionaries are some ways to help facilitate word recognition (Freeman & Dake, 1997). "Many children with Autism Spectrum Disorder (or other developmental disabilities in which auditory processing is compromised) will find it easier and more efficient to learn to read by recognizing *whole words*" (Broun, 2004, p. 37). To teach sight words, a teacher may use pictures to aid in the learning and to increase success. Furthermore, it is important to teach words that are in high usage, are meaningful to the student, and are functional in everyday life (e.g., girl, boy, mom, dad).

Teaching Initial Reading

All children deserve the most balanced instruction possible to develop their ability to read at their highest level possible. Developing solid reading skills will enable participation in other academic areas in a meaningful way (Broun, 2004). The National Reading Panel recommends a balanced approach to literacy instruction for all students, including those with autism. For individuals with autism, instruction starts with words, not letters or sounds, and begins with words that have meaning and motivation for the student. Instruction and materials are individualized for each student, games are incorporated into instruction, and lots of practice is provided when working with words. Kevin is in first grade and loves Thomas the Train. Kevin's teacher asks him to find a list of specific sight words from a Thomas the Train book. The teacher is working on /t/ for this week phonics lesson, so he also asks Kevin find words that start with /t/ and end with /t/ in the story and in the classroom. He then introduces Kevin to rhyming words and word families beginning with the word "train." They then put these words on a word wall and match them to pictures of these objects to increase vocabulary. These skills are practiced every day, as they would difficult to learn without the repetition.

Many children with autism who cannot rely on speech as their primary means of communication may use AAC. AAC are communication modes used to supplement or used as an alternative to oral language, including gestures, sign language, picture symbols, the alphabet, and speech generating devices. See Figure 10.2 for examples. One of the more popular AAC systems used with some individuals with autism is the Picture Exchange Communication System (PECS). PECS was developed in 1985 as an augmentative and alternative training package that teaches children and adults with autism and other communication deficits to initiate communication (Bondy, 2001).

Literacy skills are important for children with AAC, as an estimated 70%–90% lag behind their typically developing peers in literacy. Children who use AAC begin to experience reading-related activity and participation restrictions when they are very young. They are less likely to engage in writing and drawing activities than peers without disabilities, less likely to be read to daily, and more likely to be relatively passive participants in story book interactions (e.g., answering yes/no question or pointing in response to "Show me" directives, rather than engaging in open-ended or child-initiated conversations) (McCauley & Fey, 2006).

READING INTERVENTIONS

The importance of literacy for persons with autism who have complex communication needs has been addressed in the literature for more than a decade (Sturm &

FIGURE 10.2

Speech Generating Device   Picture Exchange
                                           Communication System

Koppenhaver, 2000; Koppenhaver & Yoder, 1992). Combined with successful augmentative and alternative communication, literacy can affect access to education, employment, and the community. High levels of literacy affect the transition from school to work and overall independence.

Literacy has been addressed consistently over the years and efforts to identify instructional approaches that address the unique learning needs of students with autism have been sparse. Few published studies have provided empirical evidence regarding the effectiveness of literacy interventions, and most of those studies have modified instructional programs designed for students without autism or communication impairments.

No single reading program addresses the needs of all readers, particularly those as individually different as children with ASD. Instead, successful reading intervention carefully considers the student's instructional needs, skills, and experiences.

Whole-to-Part Model

One balanced approach to reading is the whole-to-part model of silent reading comprehension (Cunningham, 1993). The whole-to-part model is a method used with students who have speech impairments or use AAC. This model is being discussed because many individuals with autism have speech and communication impairments and use AAC as their primary mode of communication. Nicky is 7 years old, has autism, and is nonverbal. He has been participating in a balanced early literacy program for 6 months. He reads simple stories with sight word vocabulary and performs specific phonemic awareness activities as well as auditory comprehension activities. He is able to clap out syllables, point to words as they are read, identify the first and last sound in words, and answer comprehension questions. Students like Nicky are typically excluded from a balanced reading curriculum. Most programs for these students are designed to promote functional sight word recognition.

Whole-to-part reading instruction is a balanced intervention that is aligned with the best practices in general education. The intervention is balanced in three ways (McCauley & Fey, 2006):

1. By combining four distinct approaches to reading instruction emphasizing instruction in (a) phonics and sight words, (b) reading comprehension, (c) writing, and (d) self-direction in reading
2. In addressing all of the principle cognitive processes necessary for successful silent reading with comprehension
3. In being both teacher and student centered (teachers control selection of materials and activities to support student learning of phonics, words, and reading with comprehension; students control selection of writing topics, content, and forms as well as materials in self-directed reading)

The theoretical basis of the whole-to-part model underlying silent reading comprehension begins with the assertion that reading comprehension requires:

Word Identification

Automatic: The ability to read a printed word without conscious thought or effort

Mediated: The ability to read a word not known automatically

Language Comprehension

Knowledge of Text Structures: The ability to understand the form of written language in both narrative and expository text

Knowledge of the World: The ability to understand the meaning of spoken words

Print Processing

Eye Movements: The ability to move one's eye from left to right and top to bottom

Print to Meaning Links: Direct access to word meaning without phonological decoding

Use of Inner Speech: Word identification during silent reading takes place as inner speech

Integration: The ability to do all of these things at the same time

Reading comprehension is the goal of any reading intervention. Some or all of these components in the whole to part model will be more challenging to teach to individuals with autism. One of the core characteristics, impairment in communication, may affect word identification and language comprehension for some. Understanding new vocabulary words and the different genres, without specific and repeated explanations, may be challenging. These types of skills require abstract thinking and integration of information, skills that for many individuals with autism may be seriously limited or difficult to apply.

Simply asking comprehension questions only assesses how well a student understands what they read but does not teach comprehension. To teach comprehension, intervention needs to include instructional supports before, during, and after students read texts. Nancy is a teacher of a self-contained autism classroom, and she is going to be reading a story about eating out at a restaurant. She shows the students a book about behaviors expected when eating out and talks briefly about vocabulary and the purpose for reading this story. To ensure prior knowledge, she creates social stories about going to a restaurant for all of the students. She also introduces vocabulary, such as order, menu, restroom, cashier, pay, and so on, and engages the students with the new vocabulary. She does all of this before reading activities. She understands that because of their social, communication, and behavioral differences, some of her students may have never been to a restaurant. Then she takes the class to a restaurant and takes photos while they are there to be used for later discussions.

During reading activities, she refers back to the experience of going to the restaurant, has the students look at the pictures, and asks questions. After reading activities, such as asking simple questions about where they went, what they ate, and who they went with, need to be effective in teaching the student how to integrate all the information from the story and remember only what is important. Some individuals with autism will have little difficulty recalling all the information from what they previously read, but many will have difficulty recalling the important information they were supposed to remember. This inability to differentiate what is important from what is not is caused by gestalt processing and overselectivity. Nancy uses graphic organizers to help the students construct meaning from what they read and focus on important information. The students are then asked to write about what they ate, what they like about the restaurant, and what they did not.

Before Reading Activities to Enhance Comprehension

Before reading about a specific topic, it is important to activate background knowledge on that subject. This can be accomplished through generating ideas about the topic, creating a word list associated with the topic, and asking students to express their experiences in regards to the topic.

Activate Background Knowledge for Individuals Who Are Verbal and Nonverbal. Before reading teachers should build or activate student's background knowledge and discuss what type of material is going to be read. Building background knowledge and knowledge of text structures as well as setting a clear purpose for reading are important before-reading intervention activities. This vague referent gives students with autism an idea of what to expect so they can begin to create thoughts about the topic. Many individuals with autism can absorb more information when they know what is coming next, what is going to be discussed, and the like because of their stereotyped patterns of activities, interests, and behaviors. Many like routine, so activating background knowledge through similar activities may be helpful as part of the routine so the student can begin to think about the subject prior to reading. Explain the sequence of events when introducing new stories. For example a written schedule may look like this:

1. Talk about what we know
2. Write new vocabulary words
3. Read the story and look for new words
4. Answer questions about story
5. Write about the story.

Figure 10.3 is an example of a schedule with picture symbols.

The teacher reviews the outline of what to expect before reading a new story. She lets her students know step by step what they will be doing and what is expected. She writes a schedule or uses picture symbols for a schedule or sequence of events. This will assist the students in organizing their thoughts and ideas so they can participate more within the activities.

Recalling and expressing past events and integrating them with new ones is challenging for individuals with autism. For all students, it may be important to start with

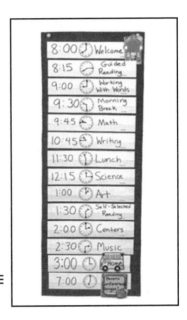

FIGURE 10.3
Schedule with Picture Symbols

topics they have an interest in when activating background knowledge. Brainstorming a list of vocabulary words associated with the text as well as taking students on field trips or watching videos related to the topic to ensure that experiential limitations are not the cause of a student's difficulty.

For students who use AAC, the time to navigate through the device or pictures can limit participation. Most AAC systems are not programmed with the intent of supporting students in accessing their memories and experiences. Attention to programming and access to these past events is important to ensure active participation. Talk to parents and ask them about trips they took or places they went so that vocabulary can be programmed into the device. Sally and her family went to the zoo over the weekend, and the theme for the week's reading was zoo animals. Vocabulary that was programmed into the device so Sally could talk about her experience at the zoo included family members who went, food she ate, and animals she saw. Also included was anything else that the parents said she experienced, such as riding on the train, and phrases, such as "I like that" and "I don't like that" as well as "yes" and "no." Without this type of intervention, students who use AAC will become passive and may not become cognitively engaged in the instruction, and teachers lose a valuable means of assessing student's understandings of the text.

AAC systems can be organized to support access to memories and background experiences. Phillip is nonverbal and got a dog over the weekend. Mom programmed in a picture of the dog with the dog's name and where they got the dog. When Phillip came to school with a note from his mom saying, "Phillip got a new dog this weekend and information is in the device," he was able to share this with the teacher or peers. Programmed calendars or categories of events can stay in the device and be supplemented. Photos of trips or activities can be downloaded onto many of these devices so the student can talk about them. Tyler went to the lake over the weekend, and his mom downloaded pictures into his speech-generating device of him on the beach, playing in the water, and eating lunch. The teacher was able to engage with him about his trip.

Vocabulary learning plays an important role in before-reading activities. For AAC users, it is common to find text-specific vocabulary programmed for these activities. However, it is important to select vocabulary that is going to be able to be used outside of the instructional activities. Using vocabulary that is already in many of these devices that has similar meaning to the vocabulary in the text can be beneficial for the student.

Knowledge of Text Structures.   Before reading, help students to recall and discuss other texts they have read that were like the one they are about to read. Previewing the text and searching for text features that are the same can focus the reader's attention by enabling him or her to anticipate text events or content. This is important for individuals who have autism who will be more successful when they know what to expect since new activities can be stressful.

Setting Purposes.   Clearly stating a purpose as to why something is being read is important because (1) this will assist the students in knowing what needs to be remembered and helps them identify what is important, and (2) this will help the student construct inferences or main ideas. Setting a purpose for reading is important for students with autism, since many attend to irrelevant details due to overselectivity and have difficulty drawing inferences.

During Reading Activities to Enhance Comprehension

During reading activities should support the student's background knowledge and focus students' attention. Comprehension can be improved whether students read the text themselves or whether they listen to others read. Students can identify a set of predetermined vocabulary words or phrases and describe why the author included them in the story.

Students should read material that is at their lowest level of ability across word identification, listening comprehension, and silent reading comprehension, (i.e., levels at which the students are making two or fewer errors per 100 words). For example, a student who can read words at the fourth-grade level, understand through listening at second grade level, and read silently with comprehension at the third grade level should have second-grade-level texts or easier during reading comprehension instruction.

After Reading Activities

After students have read a text successfully for a given purpose, they need to demonstrate their comprehension through different tasks. Verbal students can answer comprehension questions, retell the main events of the story, and write a summary of the story in order to demonstrate comprehension.

Developing ways to assess comprehension in students who use AAC can be challenging. The following are some examples of combinations of background knowledge, purposes, and tasks that can be completed even if a student does not use a complex communication system:

➤ The teacher writes the events on sentence strips, and the student then puts them in order (see Figure 10.4).
➤ The student uses an AAC device or picture symbols to answer questions about the story or to fill in Graphic Organizers about main idea, setting, and the like (see Figure 10.5).
➤ The teacher gives the student a definition of a word, and the student has to find the word in the story.

Whole to part instruction can also be applied to teaching phonics. When readers encounter an unfamiliar word in print, they may sound it out letter by letter— the strategy most often associated with phonics in school—or they may use picture cues or logos to make informed guesses or structural analysis to identify "chunks" of the

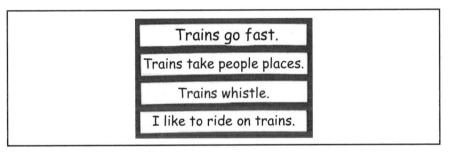

FIGURE 10.4
Sentence Strips

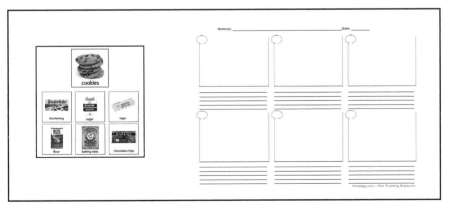

FIGURE 10.5
Using an AAC Device

word they know (e.g., suffixes such as -tion in the word reaction or parts of a compound word such as cow- in cowboy) (Kluth, 2008). Phonics instruction can be initiated once children begin to recognize many print words. Early readers read better in context, and the most effective way to help children recognize a lot of print words is to help them read stories with familiar language on topics in which they are interested. Max is in kindergarten and loves animals. He reads Brown Bear Brown Bear every day. This story has repetitive phrases so Max can become familiar with common words within the context of the text.

Shared reading is one way to engage children in stories. In shared reading, the teacher reads a story first to the child and then with the child while pointing to the text. Once the child has memorized the language of the story through repeated readings, the child then reads the story. This predictable and repeated use of stories is effective with children who have autism because it suits their learning style.

During the first story that children read, the teacher needs to check that each child can match spoken words to print words and teach one-to-one matching if needed. After they can read the story with one-to-one matching of spoken and print words, the teacher then shows the children the parts of the whole printed words. Children are more competent at analyzing spoken syllables into onsets and rimes than into phonemes. The onset is the beginning sound of a word (i.e., /c/ in cat), and the rime is the vowel plus the following consonant or consonants (i.e., at). Breaking words up by onset and rime allows for children to create new words with familiar endings, or word families. Ms. Izard has a pocket chart of onsets and a pocket chart of rimes. She breaks the class up into two groups. Some students have cards with onsets (single letters) and the other group has rimes. One student from each group goes to the onset chart and the other to the rime. The teacher writes the word that the onset and rime together created on the board so the class can read it. Jason has autism and is verbal and does not understand onset and rime after numerous demonstrations due to language impairments. Ms. Izard then tells him that the onset is the first letter in a word and writes the number 1 above the onset chart and the rime is everything after the onset and writes a number 2 above the rime chart, and then he understands.

Instruction in letters and letter-strings which represent onsets, rimes, and syllables (a unit of spoken language consisting of a single uninterrupted sound) will be more comprehensible to children than instruction in letters and letter strings that represent phonemes when onsets and rimes consist of more than one phoneme. This makes the process of decoding words faster, which increases comprehension. Frank is able to analyze the one syllable word "smiles" by breaking the word into the onset /sm/ and the rime /ilz/. But he may find it more challenging to break the word down into the individual sounds. A useful exercise is to have the students write down a sentence from a favorite part of the story draw a line between the onset and rime for each word in the sentence.

If a child has difficulty writing, the teacher could write the words and highlights letters representing an onset (e.g., sm-), a rime (-iles), or a syllable (e.g., un in unlock) in each word. The teacher could also have the child point to the onset, rime, or syllable as he or she reads them. Jeffery's teacher shows him an index card with the letter /b/ and another index card with /ag/ /at/ and /ank/. The teacher puts the cards together to make the words, and Jeffery points to the onset and rime when asked, or the teacher asks Jeffery to make a word using the onset and rime.

For a child with autism, words such as "onset," "rime," and "syllable" may be too abstract. If this is the case, the teacher can use words such as "beginning," "end," "first," "last," "consonant," and "vowel." The teacher than makes the sounds of the letters and puts the parts of the word in a pocket chart or tapes them on a plastic surface to make a moveable word wall (see Figure 10.6). Ms. Orwell is teaching the concept of onset and rime to her kindergarten class, which includes Mike, who has autism. He is having difficulty understanding and identifying an onset from the rime. He just points to various letters. Ms. Orwell has two pocket charts, one for the onset and one for the rime. Above the onset she puts a number 1 and above the rime she puts a 2. The teacher explains to him, using one index card with a single letter and another index card with different word family rimes that the onset is first and shows him a 1 and the rime is after that and shows him a 2.

He is then able to put onsets with onsets and rimes with rimes on the word wall. Then the teacher and children group words with similar letters or letter strings. This helps children make phonics generalities based on words they have learned to recognize in context. When multiple pronunciations of given letters or letter strings come up, the teacher uses a different color for each pronunciation of the identical letters (e.g., the g- in *girl* and *go* would be highlighted in red and g- in *giant* and *George* would be highlighted in blue). As more and more stories are read *to, with,* and *by* children, they learn more and more parts of words as well as multiple ways to pronounce given letters and letter strings.

Whole to part phonics instruction differs from traditional phonics instruction in that (1) it teaches the parts of the words *after* a story has been read *to, with,* and *by* children rather than before the story is read by children and (2) it teaches

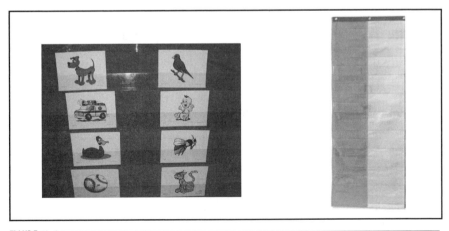

FIGURE 10.6

Pocket chart

letter–onset, letter–rime, and letter–syllable correspondences, rather than letter–phoneme correspondences (Moustafa, 2009). Gestalt processing and difficulty integrating information may render this approach less beneficial for some. When using this approach, it may be difficult for some individuals to break apart the word after learning the word as a whole as a result of repetitive behaviors and the need for routine. Once something is learned in a particular way, changing to a different way of using the same words may present a challenge for some students. It is important when teaching these skills to change instruction, use different materials, such as different books with the same words, different color cards with the same words, and the like. Using letter–onset and rime over phoneme may be more beneficial because the grouping of letters instead of each phoneme or individual sound, and for others this may be difficult. Learning just letter–sound/sound–letter correspondence may be more concrete for some. Both skills are important in the reading process. Teaching students how to decode words by breaking them into onset and rime as well as understanding letter–sound/sound–letter correspondence is critical. These skills can be taught using visual supports and tactile approaches (i.e., writing letters in shaving cream, feeling letters cut from sandpaper, making letters with playdoh) in conjunction with systematic instruction.

This type of instruction can also be used with students who use AAC. Students who use speech generating devices have phonics pages that can be adapted so they can participate in these activities through activating buttons that will say each sound or syllable. Alex is 6 and uses a speech generating device to communicate. He is unable to read aloud but when asked to find words he likes in the story, he points to them and the teacher writes them on the paper for him. She then says the onset and asks him to point to the corresponding letters in his device. Then he points to the letters for the rime and then puts them together to create the word. He is able to participate in putting similar sounds together on the word wall and putting new onsets and rimes together.

The whole to part model provides a framework for implementing successful balanced reading programs for individuals with autism. The whole to part model assumes that the cognitive processes involved in reading successfully with comprehension is the same for all readers but not that the instructional, assistive technology, or method of teaching literacy will be the same for all individuals.

Four Blocks Literacy Model

The Four Blocks literacy model is a multilevel, balanced literacy framework that incorporates four different approaches each day to teach children how to become better readers, writers, and spellers (Cunningham, 1993). Instruction is divided into equal segments of time devoted to four distinct approaches to reading instruction:

1. Guided reading
2. Working with words
3. Self-selected reading
4. Writing

Doing all four blocks acknowledges that children do not all learn in the same way and provides substantial instruction to support any student's learning style.

The Four Blocks framework was developed by a teacher who believed that to be successful in teaching *all* children to read and write, including children with autism, the subjects need to be addressed every day. In a report of 8 years of evidence gathered from schools, the authors report on the success of the balanced approach for children with a broad range of socioeconomic backgrounds and literacy levels (Cunningham, Hall, & Defee, 1998). At the end of first grade, 58–64% of children read above grade level (third grade or above); 22–28% read on grade level (preprimer or primer). On average one child every year was unable to meet the instructional level criteria. At the end of second grade, the number at grade level is 14–25%; the number above grade level (fourth grade level or above) increases to 68–76%; the number reading below grade level drops 2–9%, half of what it was in first grade (Cunningham et al., 1998, p.659).

A great deal of research supports the effectiveness of balanced literacy programs for students from diverse linguistic and ethnic backgrounds (Fitzgerald & Noblit, 2000) and low socioeconomic status. However, there is limited research on balanced literacy programs for students with autism or other developmental disabilities. One study that supports the effectiveness of the balanced reading approach with students who have developmental disabilities Hendrick, Katims, and Carr (1999) conducted a descriptive study of the effectiveness of a Four Blocks program on the reading achievement of nine elementary school students with mild to moderate mental retardation (Mean IQ = 58; range 40–76). The results indicate that a balanced approach to reading intervention led to improved student achievement across two formal measures, the Brigance Diagnostic Comprehensive Inventory of Basic Skills (Brigance, 1993) and the Test of Early Reading Ability–2 (TERA–2; Reid, Hresko, & Hammill, 1989) and five informal measures, concepts about print, story retelling, writing, word decoding, and the Analytical Reading Inventory (ARI; Woods & Moe, 1995). The students received four 45-minute reading segments that included a guided reading block, a literature/self-selected reading block, a working with words block, and a writing block. Time spent in reading instruction in most self-contained autism programs is much less per day than in general education classrooms. For individuals with autism and developmental disabilities, the more time and repetition spent on literacy instruction using a balanced approach, the better the outcomes, as reported by Hendrick et al., 1999.

The Early Literacy Skills Builder

The Early Literacy Skills Builder (ELSB) is a balanced early literacy program for students with moderate to significant developmental disabilities who have not acquired print and phonemic awareness and is designed to be used with verbal or nonverbal responses. Nonverbal students can use AAC, eye gaze, or pointing to make responses. It is similar to the Four Blocks approach to reading in that it is a multimethod, multilevel program that involves systematic instruction through a predetermined sequence of early literacy skills. The Early Literacy Skills Builder shows many similarities to Oelwein's methodology (Oelwein, 1995). Oelwein's methodology includes whole word sight recognition, using personal and meaningful vocabulary, and readiness skills such as matching. Oelwein's method of learning include the following (Broun, 2004, p. 38):

➤ *Acquisition*—the child is learning to recognize words.
➤ *Fluency*—the student recognizes the word with some degree of consistency.
➤ *Transfer*—the student recognizes the word printed on different surfaces, in different contexts, and with different fonts.
➤ *Generalization*—the child recognizes the word in any context.

Both Oelwein's methodology and the Early Literacy Skills Builder place emphasis on visual learning, whole word recognition, and phonemic awareness to teach reading and comprehension to students with autism and other developmental disabilities.

Edmark Reading Program

The Edmark Reading Program teaches basic reading skills to the most struggling readers and nonreaders. Through short instructional steps, students are taught recognition and comprehension of words. The words are then used to promote sentence structure and then language development. The program consists of two levels. Level 1 teaches 150 words from the Dolch Word List and basal readers as well as "-s", "-ed" and "-ing" endings, capitalization and punctuation. Students learn to recognize sight words, word meanings, and word context. Level 2 is an extension of Level 1 and teaches 200 words including compound words. This program is used frequently with students with autism (Edmark, 2009). This method might be chosen in conjunction with a balanced reading curriculum to teach word recognition of common high frequency words.

Lindamood–Bell Learning Processes

This program focuses on the integration of visual, auditory, and language processes to be a proficient learner. The ability to process language is a prerequisite to learning content. Specifically, the ability to decode, comprehend written language, comprehend oral language, spell, and think critically are necessary for success (Lindamood-Bell, 2009). Five different programs within the Lindamood–Bell learning program focus on different content areas:

1. Seeing Stars addresses phonemic awareness, sight words, and spelling.
2. Visualizing and Verbalizing covers language comprehension and thinking. Visualizing and verbalizing is a sequential program of instruction to develop mental imagery as a base for language comprehension and thinking (Lindamood-Bell, 2009).
3. The Lindamood Phoneme Sequencing Program (LiPS) addresses reading, spelling, and speech.

4. Talkies is a primer to the Visualizing and Verbalizing program with the goal of using mental imagery as a base for language comprehension and expression.
5. On Cloud Nine addresses Math.

No research is available on any of these programs for individuals with autism, but many parents are using these programs outside of school as an additional intervention.

TEACHING READING IN THE CONTENT AREAS

As we see an increase in students with ASD participating in the general education curriculum, teachers are being required to assess their students' unique needs and adapt their curriculum accordingly. Because reading is a skill that is common across all disciplines, teachers must have an understanding of how to best serve students with a diagnosis of ASD. Students may fail to receive literacy instruction because teachers (Kluth, & Darmody-Latham, 2003)

1. are unsure how to include them,
2. don't see all students as capable of benefiting from literacy development, or
3. simply don't know how to differentiate instruction for diverse learners.

Reading instruction commonly is thought of as the teaching of phonics to beginning readers, and after fluency has been reached, little formal reading instruction is necessary. Not true. Deficits in reading comprehension and vocabulary development of children with ASD are becoming increasingly noted in literature (Hale & Tager-Flusberg, 2005; Nation, Clarke, Wright, & Williams, 2006; O'Connor & Klein, 2004; Wahlberg, 2001). Although some evidence shows that some individuals with autism can read accurately and even well, levels of reading comprehension amongst these children are generally poor.

Children with ASD are challenged to integrate language, social understanding, and the emotional intent of messages to understand their social world (Quill, 2000). Their deficits in interpreting and labeling emotions and in incorporating them in social situations somewhat parallels their deficits in reading comprehension skills. Children with ASD are often so focused on the factual details of a text that they do not and cannot integrate and synthesize the narrative text, resulting in high frustration and low comprehension. Albert is 17 years old with HFA. He loves to read and share what he learns. However, those who work with him have noted that when he shares his newfound information, it is in the form of facts. He is unable to step back and synthesize all elements of a text to comprehend it in a wider sense. Understanding and interpreting various cues is necessary for effective comprehension of narrative texts. While reading, students must understand the author's vocabulary, style of writing, and story structure as well as characters' social experiences and how these contribute to the development of motivations, goals, and actions within a story setting. Developing sensitivity to the emotions of characters and the way these emotions play a role in characters' choices is vital in truly understanding text. Interpreting the motivation of characters and appreciating their intent are higher level comprehension skills, which may be difficult for children with ASD (Gately, 2008).

Setting the Stage

The majority of the following sections will cover vocabulary and comprehension development, their importance, and strategies to aide in building these skills. Identifying why children are struggling in their classes is imperative. Are the foundational phonics skills missing? Do they enjoy reading but have a false sense of how much they accurately understand? Did they have a bad experience that has them set up to hate reading? Getting started in the process will be very difficult without an idea of how to approach the situation.

Setting the stage for learners with autism in reading can be a challenge. Although classrooms are full of students with assorted likes and dislikes, learning styles, and multiple intelligences, the underlying rule is, while the reading assignment might not be liked, the work still needs to be done in order to earn a grade, pass the class and get credit, eventually leading to graduation as the long-term goal. On the contrary, the individual with ASD is often more likely to react impulsively when something is happening that "doesn't feel right."

Kelly sits in a government class where the students are asked to spend just a few minutes quietly reading an article and be prepared to identify two facts. Within just a minute or two, Kelly screams out, "I can't do this!" On the surface, Kelly's yelling appears to be a result of frustration at the work being too hard. However, academically she has no problems reading. Those who are familiar with her are able to see that the challenge of the work is not what's getting to her, but that the silence is what frustrates her the most.

Not only must academic needs be considered, but social issues need to be addressed as well. Individuals with ASD have some unique social skills, and not all are widely accepted by peers. When given an assignment to read on their own, typical children are aware of the unwritten rule that to stay quiet out of respect for those around trying to read.

Donner spends much of his quiet reading time upset because he says he needs to hear the words, and saying them in his head is not loud enough. Most children would read more quietly or silently with a snicker at the most. Not Donner. When he is asked to read silently because he is distracting those around him, he shouts out, "How do you expect me to get this assignment done if I can't read out loud?!?"

Individuals with autism frequently see being asked to follow socially acceptable requests as a personal attack on them. Working with these students to find replacement behaviors is generally successful if approached cautiously. For example, Donner needs to read aloud in order to understand the text. His neighbors need the room quiet so they can read. Simply moving him to a corner by himself during reading time only will allow him to read without disturbing others. Another option might be to have a form of technology, such as book on tape or CD, or text-to-speech software read aloud to him.

Choosing something to read

To help build their reading skills, Monique's teacher has the class participate in DEAR (Drop Everything and Read) time for 20 minutes daily. Each day, Monique complains she does not have any good books and all available books are too difficult. She says she hates reading, yet she has the decoding and basic comprehension skills to be an independent reader. After observing her trying to find something to read, her inability to choose a book that is right for her becomes clear. She simply picks something up and starts reading, not employing the strategies that her typical peers may have learned, such as skimming the summaries and reviews and talking about the books with peers. One strategy that would help alleviate some of Monique's frustrations is known by a couple of names: the five finger rule or just right books. This is one strategy available to help students to get a quick idea whether or not a book is about right for their independent reading level.

Just Right Books
Look at the cover.
Read the title and the author.
Read the blurb in the back.
Flip through the book.
Read the first page.

Use the 5 Finger Rule
Choose a book.
Open and find a page anywhere.
Make a fist.
Start to read the page.
Put up a finger for each hard word.
0-1 Finger – Too Easy
2-3 Fingers – Just Right
4-5 Fingers – Too Hard

In using this method, not only are the readers identifying whether a book is "just right," but they are interacting with them, getting comfortable with the relationships between cover, title, chapter headings, and even any illustrations. All that is needed is something to catch their attention or spark their interest and get them hooked. Once they learn how to use this method for recreational reading, they will become adept at using the method for choosing reading materials for content classes as well. Gerardo was given an assignment in Biology to construct a model of a plant or animal cell. He was more comfortable finding a book of interest that was "just right" for helping to complete the task since he had practiced the method several times previously looking for recreational reading. Gerardo was able to browse textbooks of varying levels and topics such as General Biology, Cellular Biology, Evolutionary Biology, and Microbiology, and even able to discern that the General Biology and Cellular Biology textbooks would provide him with the information needed to complete the assignment.

Vocabulary Development

During the school years children learn between 2,000 and 3,600 words annually (Nagy & Herman, 1984). Of these words, researchers believe that 25%–50% is acquired through incidental learning. *Incidental learning* is the learning that takes place without any specifically targeted or formal instruction. An example would be a student who learns compounds on the periodic table, not because she's being taught each one individually, but because her class is referring to it during an experiment. Another example would be a child who learns how to spell new words through reading them repeatedly.

Vocabulary constitutes information students should know to function within the subject and therefore plays an important role in content classes. While reading vocabulary is highly related to the amount a student reads, explicit instruction also contributes to vocabulary development. The National Reading Panel (NICHD, 2000a) recommends preteaching vocabulary by discussing words prior to reading. Preteaching helps students become familiar with concepts and words before they encounter them in print. The following are ways that can be beneficial to students learning new words:

➤ Preview the passage and select specific words to preteach before reading. Do not rely on the publisher of a series to do this. Classes are different and teachers should choose the words most relevant to their students.

➤ List the words that your students will find challenging. Many students get bored if they feel they are not learning anything new. The words may or may not be related to each other.

➤ Limit the list to the most important words. A list that is too long will not promote a deeper understanding.

➤ In choosing which words to pre-teach, ask two questions: First, is the word going to appear over and over in the reading selection, and, second, how important is the word to the overall understanding of the story?

➤ Identifying word parts (uni = one) and cognate relationships (police = policia) in words can be helpful for many students. For some students, this relationship is not always obvious.

➤ Actively involve students.

Using Visuals

Use a range of visual supports. While students with autism may benefit from verbal instruction, many also require an additional avenue of input as they learn. Students with autism may profit from the use of graphic or visual organizers such as flow charts, concept maps, Venn diagrams, clustering, or series of events chains. Temple Grandin (1995), a woman with autism, shared that those with autism may struggle to learn things that cannot be thought about in pictures (Kluth, & Darmody-Latham, 2003).

Graphic Organizers

A *graphic organizer* is a visual representation of knowledge. It is a way of structuring information and arranging essential features of an idea or topic to illustrate a pattern using labels (Bromley, Irwin-DeVitis, & Modlo, 1995). Flood and Lapp (1988) elaborate by using the term *mapping* generally to describe any material that helps the reader learn from the text using illustrations. These include but are not limited to maps, graphs, charts, and flowcharts. They use the terms graphic organizer and mapping interchangeably to describe similar instructional activities.

Graphic organizers come in many designs. A wide assortment of teaching books as well as websites provide ample models (multi-column comparison charts, vocabulary charts, 5Ws, cause and effect charts, and character charts), ready to be used. One key component in finding, designing, and implementing graphic organizers is that it must be visually appealing and user friendly.

Organizers can be as simple as a *Venn Diagram* (Figure 10.7) with two or more circles used to identify similarities and differences between two characters, objects, events, or anything else using comparisons.

K-W-L charts, (Figure 10.8), are commonly used at the beginning of a unit in order to help guide the instruction. KWL is a teaching technique intended to help students activate prior knowledge. Developed by Donna Ogle (1986) as a group instruction activity, the three-column chart serves as a model for active thinking during reading.

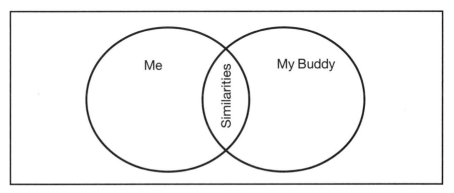

FIGURE 10.7
Venn Diagram

Know	Want	Learned	How
(What I know about _____)	(What I want to know about _____)	(What I learned about _____)	(How I can find out about _____)

FIGURE 10.8
K-W-L-H

K – what the students are able to recall; what they already **KNOW**
W – what the students determine what they **WANT** to learn
L – what students **LEARNED** throughout the unit as they read

The K-W-L-H chart is a variation of the K-W-L. The H is added to form a four-column table.

H – HOW more information can be obtained

While the K, W, and H columns are filled in as much as possible at the beginning of the unit, the L column is left to complete at the conclusion. Reflecting on the questions the students had and which answers were found can be an eye-opening lesson in asking good questions from the start. Question asking and answering will improve the more this method is used.

The K-W-L-H chart benefits students on the spectrum by helping them keep their ideas and thoughts organized. Organization is difficult for this population, and having everything on one sheet encourages them to be successful. A drawback is that some thought must be put into the way information will be added to the individual's chart. By the end of the brainstorming session, a lot of details may be cluttering one sheet. For the student who has a difficult time writing clearly, this can be a cause of contention for the student who likes his or her work to look a certain way.

Semantic mapping is a strategy for vocabulary expansion by extending knowledge displayed in categories. The teacher begins by introducing the concept. The students, in small groups or whole group discussion, brainstorm as many words as possible for a determined time. Words are recorded on the board. The students categorize the words to show how they are related to one another. While this method draws on prior knowledge, the relationships and the importance among the components are recognized. Included in the diagram are the concept word, two category examples, and other examples. This is a very interactive process and should be modeled by the teacher first.

Just two of the benefits in using semantic mapping with students with autism are the strong visuals and minimal writing to avoid overwhelm. Clear, simple, straightforward lines and boxes may be embellished with more detailed drawings for those who find colors, shapes, and the like more helpful (Figure 10.9). However, for those needing more text or written descriptions, these maps may become more elaborate and in-depth.

The Frayer Model (Figure 10.10) is another graphical organizer used for word analysis and vocabulary building. This four-square model prompts students to think about and describe the meaning of a word or concept in four ways: by defining the term, describing the fundamental characteristics, providing examples of the idea, and offering non examples of the idea.

This strategy stresses understanding words within the larger context of a reading selection. Students are required first to analyze the definition and characteristics of the item and second to synthesize and apply this information by thinking of examples and non examples.

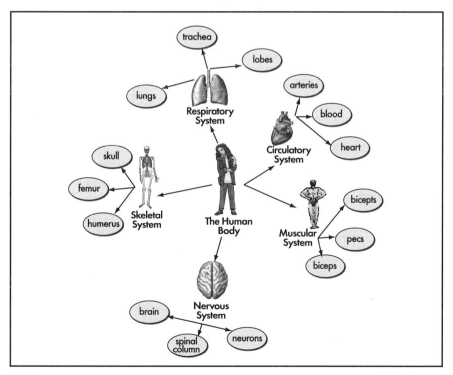

FIGURE 10.9

Semantic Mapping

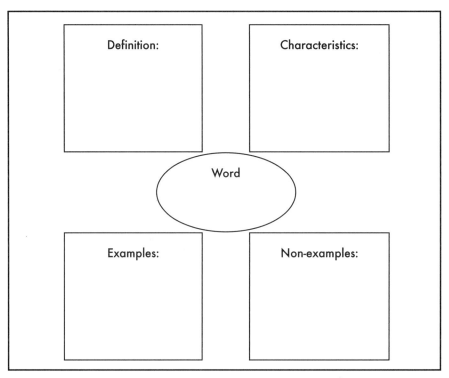

FIGURE 10.10
Frayer Model

Foldables

A Foldable is a 3-D, student-made, interactive graphic organizer based upon a skill. Much like a graphic organizer in that information is clearly and easily presented, foldables also allow students a fast, kinesthetic activity that helps them retain information. A popular example of this is the childhood "cootie catcher" (Figure 10.11). The foldable can now be turned into a way for a student to summarize text or identify required components from a selection.

The benefits of using foldables are numerous. Foldables can be modified easily depending on the student's needs and abilities. For those with more dexterity and fine more control, cutting, folding, gluing or taping, and coloring can all be incorporated. For students who have a harder time with fine motor skills, they can take over filling in the required areas and using colors to emphasize key points. Books by Dinah Zike are available with many ideas on how to incorporate foldables into content classes.

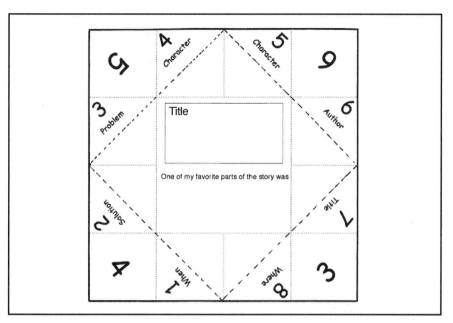

FIGURE 10.11

Foldables

Picture or Cartoon Vocabulary

Vocabulary Cartoons work on the principle of mnemonics as a visual cue. A *mnemonic device* is a pattern of letters, ideas, or associations that assists in remembering something. A mnemonic device could be in many different forms such as rhymes, songs, and pictures to name a few. Vocabulary cartoons can be used in two different ways. The first is to purchase those already drawn out, including a series by New Monic Books, available at http://www.vocabularycartoons.com/.

Another way to incorporate vocabulary cartoons or pictures is to have the students draw their own using assigned vocabulary words (Figure 10.12). The benefits of using this method with individuals with autism is that their interpretation could look any way they want. With no right or wrong way to interpret, pressure is minimized to look like everyone else's drawing. Color, details, and prior knowledge can all be incorporated as much or little as the individual needs. Following the mnemonic principle of association, Vocabulary Cartoons link together an auditory (rhyming) word association and a visual association in the form of a humorous cartoon. These powerful mnemonics help students retain the meanings of words longer and with less effort than trying to memorize definitions straight out of a dictionary.

FIGURE 10.12

Picture or Cartoon Vocabulary

Teaching Comprehension

Those with autism often have difficulty understanding narrative text found in stories because they tend to focus on details and interpret information in fragmented chunks, often getting "stuck" in one mode of understanding (Gately, 2008). One speculation as to why this interpretation of narrative text is so difficult is the concept of *theory of mind,* discussed in Chapter 3, which suggests that the ability to infer the full range of mental states of others and to reflect on one's own and other's actions is a key deficit of ASD (Baron-Cohen, 2001). Many individuals with ASD have a difficult time understanding what others are thinking or understanding. Many individuals with autism do not understand deception, certain types of metaphors, sarcasm, jokes, and irony. As a result many individuals with autism are challenged to develop the imagination that is so often needed to posses higher order understanding of narratives.

Based on proficient reader research, Gately (2008) suggests several strategies to help those with ASD develop higher order comprehension skills.

Priming background knowledge is important to help develop a mental set for an activity. Using tools, maps, and pictures sets the stage to help ensure the student is prepared to understand the text. This is especially helpful for those students on the spectrum who may not have the same prior knowledge as a typical peer.

Using illustrations from the story, the students make, and then confirm, the predictions. This is an effective method for struggling readers because it helps the students develop positive expectations regarding their experiences with the book. Students with ASD are particularly engaged because it addresses their need to be visually stimulated.

Think-alouds model how to think about text. Used mostly in reciprocal teaching, think alouds help struggling readers build four strategies: predicting, questioning, clarifying, and summarizing. The modeling process begins with the teacher reading a passage aloud. The reading is stopped often to share thoughts, explicitly using vocabulary that triggers feelings and explaining why. This can be a difficult concept for those with cognitive delays because those with poor comprehension skills have a harder time building mental models and relating text.

One of the most overlooked ways to encourage reading among students, especially those on the spectrum, is to capitalize on their interests. Students with autism often have interests that occupy periods of time and may be thought of as obsessive or not age-appropriate. However, using the interests is the ideal way to get them reading.

Given a selection on a U.S. president, Ray's English class is to diagram the subject's life in a timeline. Ray has no interest in this assignment and complains that what the teaching is asking is too hard. As a teacher, the importance of knowing your students and your instructional goal is illustrated here. In one classroom, Ray might get a zero for not completing the assignment. In another, he might be given a word search as an alternative assignment. Neither provides Ray with comparable practice for the desired goal nor does it tap into his interests. Ray has an uncanny way of following professional wrestling. He can state who the champions were and in what year, what area they were challenged in, and even who their trainers were. Knowing that the instructional goal is to diagram, which falls under "analysis" in Bloom's Taxonomy (levels of intellectual behavior; *remembering, understanding, applying, analyzing, evaluating creating*), a more appropriate alternate assignment would be to have Ray read an article on a wrestler and have him diagram the wrestler's life.

Overgeneralization is the overuse of a newly acquired skill in inappropriate situations. For example, when using the word "hot" to teach children not to touch something, they may in turn overgeneralize "hot" to mean anything they should not touch, because it is sharp or breakable, regardless of the temperature. While typical children exhibit similar behaviors, they are able to work through the stage without special planning or behavior modifications. Abbey was excited because she learned to read the word "comb." Shortly afterwards, she discovered the words tomb, bomb, Lomb, somber, and continued to use the –omb rule for each rule. It was not until her classmates laughed at her and her teacher showed her the differences among the –omb sounds.

Reading involves connecting new text to prior knowledge. Before, during, and after exercises are used to get students to activate existing knowledge, thereby creating a mental framework to which new text, terms, ideas, and the like can be connected. This mental framework begins before reading even begins, strengthened as students interact with the text during the reading, and reinforced after reading as students incorporate what they have just read into their core knowledge. The following are strategies that build connections.

Before Reading

Activating background knowledge (K-W-L) Chart
Investigating text structure
Setting a purpose for reading
Predicting text content (Book Bits)
Reviewing and clarifying vocabulary

During Reading

Establishing the purpose for each part of the reading
Self-monitoring
Visualizing
Summarizing
Confirming or rejecting predictions
Identifying and clarifying key ideas (think about what is read)
Questioning self

After Reading

Assessing whether the purpose for reading was met
Paraphrasing important information
Identifying the main idea and details
Making comparisons
Connecting
Drawing conclusions
Summarizing (Book Bits)
Analyzing (Students make judgments and form opinions using explicit information
    from the reading)
Anticipation guide

ASSISTIVE TECHNOLOGY AND READING

A wide range of assistive technology (AT) tools is available to help individuals with autism and others who struggle with reading. These tools help facilitate decoding, reading fluency, and comprehension and are implemented according to the student's needs. AT is allowing students access to curriculum that would not have been able to be utilized in recent years.

AT encompasses the needs of all students, from lower functioning nonverbal to those with AS. For some, AT may be as low-tech as color overlays to as high-tech as communication devices and text-to-speech readers.

Some children with autism are nonverbal, but with assistive technology, many nonverbal students can benefit from instruction in Phonemic Awareness. Bryan, who is nonverbal, is reading the word "cat" and is asked what the first sound is. He goes to his phonics page on his speech generating device and pushes /c/. He is then asked what word does /c/ /a/ /t/ make? He pushes the word cat on his device. (See Figure 10.2 under Teaching Beginning Reading)

On the other end of the spectrum is Eric. Eric is verbal, participates in the general education curriculum, and is on the road to attending a local university upon graduation. However, his limited fine motor skills make writing physically difficult for him. While he can read and comprehend his grade level reading materials, he needs assistance getting his words on paper. For him, a portable word processor, or Alpha Smart 3000 (Figure 10.13), allows him to respond to his reading selections and remain academically competitive among his nondisabled peers.

AT is broken down into three categories, low-tech, mid-tech, and high-tech. Low-tech constitutes visual support strategies which do not involve any type of electronic or battery operated device—typically low cost, easy to use equipment. Dry erase boards, clipboards, 3-ring binders, manila file folders, photo albums, laminated PCS/photographs, and highlight tape, are some examples.

FIGURE 10.13

Alpha Smart 3000

Mid-tech items are battery-operated devices or simple electronic devices requiring limited advancements in technology. Some examples are tape recorders, Language Master, overhead projector, timers, calculators, and simple voice output devices.

High-tech items encompass the complex technological support strategies—typically high cost equipment. Some examples are video cameras, computers and adaptive hardware, and complex voice output devices. They include the following:

> *Audible books and publications:* Recorded books, journals, or other publications that allow users to listen to text and are available in a variety of formats, such as audiocassettes, CDs, and MP3 downloads. These audio files assist individuals with autism by allowing them to use their auditory skills, which may be more in tune with their academic abilities. Some popular sources for audio files are Audible.com, Book Courier, Bookshare.org, and PlayAway.org.

> *Optical Character Recognition:* This technology allows a user to scan printed material into a computer or handheld unit. The scanned text is then read aloud via a speech synthesis/screen reading system. Optical Character Recognition (OCR) is available as stand-alone units, computer software, and as portable, pocket-sized devices. OCR is beneficial to individuals with autism because the programs allow information to be made more accessible without having to be completely dependent on others or risk getting only part of the information. WYNN Literacy Software Solutions, Kurzweil 3000, and The Quicktionary Reading Pen are three popular examples currently on the market.

> *Paper-Based Computer Pen:* This technology records and links audio to what a person writes using the pen and special paper. It enables the user to take notes while simultaneously recording the speaker. The user can later listen to any section of their notes by touching the pen to the corresponding handwriting or diagrams. One benefit of the paper-based computer pen is that it uses both auditory and visual learning styles to review notes. Another advantage is that the user is not solely dependent upon how organized or how clearly notes were written in order to review a presentation.

> *Speech Synthesizers/Screen Readers:* These are systems displays that read aloud text on a computer screen, including text that has been typed by the user, scanned in from printed pages (e.g., books, letters), or text appearing on the internet. Screen readers, also known as text-to-speech readers, allow those with ASD an additional way to stay focused on what is being read rather than getting easily distracted. Several screen readers highlight the words as they read, helping increase reading fluency and word recognition. AspireReader, Classmate Reader, Read and Write Gold, and Write: OutLoud are all popular programs currently being used (Stanberry & Raskind, 2009).

Different modes of technology have been used to improve the quality of life of people who have various developmental disabilities. However, the varied use of technology for children with autism continues to receive limited attention, despite the fact that technology tends to be a high interest area for many of these children (Stokes, 2009). The use of assistive technology can improve motivation, comprehension, and attention for a child with autism.

SUMMARY

This chapter attempts to provide a comprehensive, although not complete, guide to the reading process as well as reading interventions and accommodations for individuals with ASD. It is clear that autism is a complex disorder that manifests in diverse ways. In order to provide more effective interventions in all academic areas it is important to gain a clear understanding of the learning strengths of individuals with ASD.

There is limited research on effective reading programs for individuals with autism. Many teachers use a combination of programs when teaching these students to read. Sight word acquisition and vocabulary based programs are common; however based on the National Reading Panels report (NICHD, 2000a) it is recommended that all students receive reading instruction that includes Phonemic Awareness, Phonics, Fluency, Vocabulary, and Comprehension. Students with autism should also receive reading instruction that includes these components every day and be exposed to print-rich learning environments. Research results have demonstrated that many students with and without significant cognitive disabilities can learn to read through intensive instruction using a variety of different strategies to teach these essential components.

Different reading programs and instructional strategies are discussed in this chapter. The strategies and programs can be used with students who are verbal or nonverbal and use AAC. Computer based programs, using materials that are motivating to the student, systematic teaching, visual supports, and enhancing mental imagery are some of the strategies used with individuals with ASD. The Whole-to-Part Model and the Four Blocks Literacy Model when used in conjunction with some of the mentioned strategies are two balanced interventions that may be successful in teaching reading to individuals with autism. It is important to remember that no single reading program or intervention addresses the needs of all readers, particularly those as individually different as children with ASD. Instead, successful reading intervention carefully considers the student's instructional needs, skills, and experiences.

Teaching reading across content areas is discussed because of the increase in students with ASD participating in the general education setting. General education teachers are being required to assess their students' unique needs and adapt their curriculum accordingly. Reading to acquire information is a critical skill. Struggling readers will struggle in all academic subjects. Teachers need to be able to assess these skills while also using strategies to build vocabulary and improve comprehension. Graphic organizers, semantic mapping, foldables, and picture or cartoon vocabulary are visual supports that can improve vocabulary and comprehension.

Assistive Technology is a valuable tool to help individuals with autism and others who struggle with reading. These tools help facilitate decoding, reading fluency, and comprehension and are implemented according to the students' needs. Audible books, optical character recognition, paper-based computer pen, and speech synthesizers or screen readers are AT tools that can improve motivation, comprehension, and attention for a student with ASD.

Although more research is needed on how to best teach reading to individuals with ASD, this chapter discusses many programs and strategies that are used for those with ASD. The diverse learning and complexities involved with reading instruction and the lack of evidence based research on reading instruction for individuals with ASD makes teaching these students more of an art than a science. Future research is needed so educators can more effectively teach to the diverse needs of these students and those with ASD can learn the critical skills needed to be successful in school and life.

REFERENCES

Adams, M. J. (1990). *Beginning to read: Thinking and learning about print.* Cambridge, MA: MIT Press.

Baron-Cohen, S. (2001). Theory of mind and autism: A review. [Special issue]. *International Review of Mental Retardation, 23.*

Bondy, A. (2001). PECS: Potential benefit and risks. *The Behavior Analyst Today, 2,* 127–132.

Brigance, A. (1983). *BRIGANCE Diagnostic Comprehensive Inventory of Basic Skills.* North Billerica, MA: Curriculum Associates.

Bromley, K., Irwin-DeVitis, L., & Modlo, M. (1995). *Graphic organizers: Visual activities for active learning.* New York: Scholastic.

Broun, L. T. (2004). Teaching students with autistic spectrum disorders to read: A visual approach. *Teaching Exceptional Children, 36* (4), 36–40.

Browder, D. M., Wakeman, S. Y., Spooner, F., Ahlgrim-Delzell, L., & Algozzine, B. (2006). Research on reading instruction for individuals with significant cognitive disabilities. *Exceptional Children, 72,* 392–408

Browder, D., Gibbs, S., Ahlgrim-Delzell, L., Courtade, G., & Lee, A. (2007). *Early Literacy Skills Builder Implementation Guide.* Verona, WI: Attainment.

Browder, D. (2008) Evaluation of the effectiveness of an early literacy program for students with significant developmental disabilities. *Exceptional Children, 75,* 33–52.

Carrier, G. (2006). *Comprehension* (article). Retrieved October, 2008, from http://www.readinerockets.com

Chiang, H., & Lin, Y. (2007). Reading comprehension instruction for students with autism spectrum disorders: a review of the literature. *Focus on Autism and Other Developmental Disabilities, 22,* 259–267.

Cunningham, J. W. (1993). Whole-to-part reading diagnosis. *Reading and Writing Quarterly: Overcoming Learning Difficulties, 9,* 31–49.

Cunningham, P. M., Hall, D. P., & Defee, M. (1998). Nonability grouped, multilevel instruction: Eight years later. *The Reading Teacher, 51,* 652–664.

Dahlgren, S., & Hjelmquist, E. (1996). Phonological awareness and literacy in nonvocal children with cerebral palsy. *Augmentative and Alternative Communication, 12,* 138–153.

Edmark Reading Program (2009). Retrieved July 6, 2009, from http://www.donjohnston.com/products/edmark

Fitzgerald, J., & Noblit, G. (2000). Balance in the making: Learning to read in an ethnically diverse first grade classroom. *Journal of Educational Psychology, 92*(1), 3–22.

Flood, J., & Lapp, D. (1988). Conceptual mapping strategies for understanding information texts. *The Reading Teacher, 4,* 780–783.

Frith, U., & Baron-Cohen, S. (1987). Perception in autistic children. In D. J. Cohen & A. M. Donnellan (Eds.), *Handbook of autism and pervasive developmental disorders.* New York: Wiley.

Freeman, S., & Dake, L. (1997). *Teach me language: A language manual for children with autism, Asperger's Syndrome, and related developmental disorders.* Langley, B.C.: SKF Books.

Gately, S. (2008). Facilitating reading comprehension for students on the autism spectrum. *Teaching Exceptional Children, 40*(3), 40–5.

Grandin, T. (1995). *Thinking in pictures.* New York: Vintage Books.

Grigorenko, E. L., Klin, A., Pauls, D. L., Senft R., Hooper C., & Volkmar F. (2002). A descriptive study of hyperlexia in a clinically referred sample of children with developmental delays. *Journal of Autism and Developmental Disorders, 32*(1), 3–12.

Hale, C. M., & Tager-Flusberg, H. (2005). Social communication in children with autism: The relationship between theory of mind and discourse development. *Autism: The International Journal of Research and Practice, 9*(2), 157–178.

Hendrick,W., Katims, D. S., & Carr, N. (1999). Implementing a multimethod, multilevel literacy program for students with mental retardation. *Focus on Autism and Developmental Disabilities, 14,* 231–239.

Kluth, P., & Darmody-Latham, J. (2003). Beyond sight words: Literacy opportunities for students with autism. *The Reading Teacher, 56*(6), 532.

Kluth, P., & Chandler-Olcott, K. (2008). *"A land we can share": Teaching literacy to students with autism.* Baltimore: Brookes.

Koppenhaver, D. A., & Yoder, D. E. (1992). Literacy issues in persons with severe speech and physical impairments. In R. Gaylord-Ross (Ed.), *Issues and research in special education* (Vol. 2, pp.156–201). New York: Teachers College Press.

Lindamood-Bell (2009). *The Lindamood-Bell Learning Processes.* Retrieved July 6, 2009, from http://www.lindamoodbell.com/programs

McCauley R. J., & Fey, M. E. (2006). *Treatment of language disorders in children.* Baltimore: Brookes.

Minshew, N., Goldstein, G., Muenz, L., & Payton, J. (1992). Neuropsychological functioning of nonmentally retarded autistic individuals. *Journal of Clinical and Experimental Neuropsychology, 14,* 749–761.

Moustafa, M. (2009). *Whole to part phonics instruction.* Retrieved July 4, 2009, from http://www.instructional.calstatela.edu

Nation, K. (1999). Reading skills in hyperlexia: A developmental perspective. *Psychological Bulletin, 125*(3), 338–355.

Nagy, W. E., & Herman, P. A. (1984). *Limitations of vocabulary instruction.* (Technical Report No. 326). Champaign: University of Illinois Center for the Study of Reading.

Nation, K., Clarke, P., Wright, B., & Williams, C. (2006). Patterns of reading ability in children with autism spectrum disorder. *Journal of Autism & Developmental Disorders, 36,* 911.

National Institute of Child Health and Human Development. (2000a). *Report of the National Reading Panel. Teaching children to read: An evidence-based assessment of the scientific research literature on reading and its implications for reading instruction* (NIH Publication No. 00-4754). Washington, D.C: U.S. Department of Health and Human Services.

O'Connor, I., & Klein, P. (2004). Exploration of strategies for facilitating the reading comprehension of high-functioning students with autism spectrum disorders. *Journal of Autism & Developmental Disorders, 34*(2), 115–127.

Oelwein, P. L. (1995). *Teaching Reading to Children with Down Syndrome: A guide for parents and teachers.* Bethesda, MD: Woodbine House.

Ogle, D. S. (1986). K-W-L group instructional strategy. In A. S. Palincsar, D. S. Ogle, B. F. Jones, & E. G. Carr (Eds.), *Teaching reading as thinking* (Teleconference Resource Guide, pp. 11–17). Alexandria, VA: Association for Supervision and Curriculum Development.

Quill, K. A. (2000). *Do-Watch-Listen-Say.* Baltimore: PHB.

Reid, D. K., Hresko, W. P., & Hammill, D. D. (1989). *Test of Early Reading Ability–2.* Austin, TX: Pro-Ed.

Stanberry, K., & Raskind, M. (2009). *Assistive Technology Tools: Reading.* Retrieved July 6, 2009, from www.greatschools.org/LD/assistive-technology/reading-tools.gs?Content=948& page=all

Stokes, S. (2009) *Assistive Technology for children with autism.* Retrieved July 4, 2009, from http://www.specialed.us/autism

Strangeman, N., & Hall, T. (2004). National Center on Accessing the General Curriculum. *Background Knowledge.* Retrieved July 6, 2009, from www.cast.org/publications/ncac.ncac_backgroundknowledge.html

Sturm, J. (2006). What happens to reading between first and third grade? Implications for students who use AAC. *Augmentative and Alternative Communication, 22,* 21–36.

Vandervelden, M., & Siegal, L. (1999). Phonological processing and literacy in AAC users and students with motor speech impairments. *Augmentative and Alternative Communication, 15,* 191–209.

Wahlberg, T. J. (2001). *The ability to comprehend written text in high functional individuals with autism.* Unpublished doctoral dissertation, Northern Illinois University, DeKalb, IL.

Woods, M. L., & Moe, A. (1995). *Analytical Reading Inventory* (5th ed.). Upper Saddle River, NJ: Prentice Hall.

Written Expression: Why It Is Difficult and What Can Be Done

Juliane Hillock

Strong writing and communication skills are essential to an individual's quality of life. The ability to process, organize, and select the appropriate words to express thoughts, concerns, and needs is critical to a happy, successful, and fulfilling life. The report from the National Commission on Writing (2003) outlined that writing is an essential skill that throughout history has had the power to stir revolutions, record historical information for posterity, convey feelings, and propel changes in culture for future generations. For all its power and importance, the skill is actually nationally neglected in the classroom. This may be because writing is a subjective activity, which is approached by individuals differently and is difficult to assess. The task of teaching or learning writing skills is particularly difficult in the case of students with autism.

Jose is a third grade boy in a self-contained autism classroom. He does participate in some regular education math and spelling classes. Although he has functional language, he rarely initiates conversation. One of his favorite activities is to draw the titles of his favorite Disney movies on white boards. His drawings display the titles, exactly as they appear on the movie covers with their elaborate script, elegant borders, and varying fonts. No detail escapes his notice. He takes very little time to create one and often erases it and writes another within 5 minutes. However, when Jose writes his name, spells words, or responds to questions, his handwriting is barely legible.

Jose's teacher may think that since Jose can write the titles of movies, which contain a variety of different words, Jose should be able to write those words and others with equal control and legibility on demand and in other settings. For Jose, though, functional writing is much different than the writing in his drawings. Although the drawings contain words, Jose is not trying to communicate with written words; he is recreating a picture in his mind. Children with autism consistently have difficulty with written expression, and they may not develop writing skills in a typical manner. A teacher cannot assume that if a student can perform one task that he or she should therefore have mastered others. As in the case of Jose, assessment of the students' writing abilities and difficulties may be complex.

WHY IS WRITING DIFFICULT?

The National Assessment of Educational Progress (NAEP; Loomis & Borque, 2001), published results of assessments in writing for fourth, eighth, and twelfth grade students given over the period of 1992 to 1998. According to the results, between 56% and 61% of the students performed in the basic or minimal range. Only 1% in each grade level tested performed at an advanced level. These results indicate that even for students without disabilities, the process of writing is difficult to do well.

The National Commission on Writing, in its report "The Neglected "R,"" established that writing is effectively a skill that requires students to take unorganized information and ideas and "rework raw information and dimly understood concepts into language they can communicate to someone else" (2003, p. 9). According to the *DSM-IV-TR* (APA, 2000), to qualify for the diagnosis of autism spectrum disorder, language impairments must be exhibited; therefore, a student's diagnosis of autism indicates the individual has difficulty with language. The language impairments are typically pervasive and are present not only in oral language but also in all forms of communication, verbal and nonverbal (Landa & Goldberg, 2005). This communication impairment may vary drastically among individuals. However, even those individuals who have stronger communication skills may still lack the processing and organizational skills necessary to maintain discourse through multiple exchanges or to produce a piece of writing which connects with an audience and demonstrates an awareness of the reader's interest and comprehension level.

Students with autism have difficulty in the oral and written pragmatics of language because of deficits in "organizing written material" (Diehl, Bennetto, & Young, 2006). In addition, students with ASD tend to be very literal and have difficulty making inferences and deductions. A primary language deficit in students with autism equates to an inability to comprehend abstract and figurative language (Cascella & Colella, 2004) and a tendency to "interpret messages literally" (Landa & Goldberg, 2005). Jimmy's teacher points to his paper and says, "Let's go," and Jimmy stands up, puts on his coat, and waits at the door. For these reasons, students with autism have difficulties not only understanding language but using it in practical ways. They tend to exhibit "immature syntax [and] pronoun reversal" (Cascella & Colella, 2004, p. 245).

The difficulties are not confined to the lower grades but actually become more obvious at the intermediate level. As the student progresses through the grades, writing tasks are more difficult and require higher level processing skills, and few language intervention plans are available to meet those needs (Sigman & McGovern, 2005). Even if students with ASD develop simple written expression techniques, they may exhibit a difficulty with the formation of complex sentences (Landa & Goldberg, 2005). Expanding the written or spoken language into relevant, functional, and effective communication is such a complex activity that it rarely develops without targeted intervention.

The NAEP also determined a framework for assessment by outlining objectives that students with good writing skills have mastered. Each objective has its unique skill requirements, and each, in turn, poses particular difficulties to students with autism.

Writing to the Audience and Theory of Mind

To be an effective writer, the NAEP has determined that an individual should be able to write for a variety of audiences. A writer should be able to draft, for example, a letter to a friend or relative and use a certain familiar style and speak of more personal occurrences. The student should also be able to draft a letter to a principal, a business, or a government official with a more formal approach. The writer should further be able to alter the information for a known, as opposed to an unknown, audience or adjust the format according to the prompt. A student must be able to vary the format to produce a persuasive or narrative essay or a story. The writer needs to be able to ascertain which format applies to a given context. Determining the appropriate tone and format are very difficult tasks for a writer with autism because the disorder is characterized by a deficiency in the theory of mind (TOM), the ability to understand the feelings and perspectives of others.

An individual with autism may find it difficult or be unable to take the perspective of another's mental state or make predictions about another individual's likely feelings or opinions. This difficulty with TOM in children with autism was demonstrated in a 1985 study by Baron-Cohen, Leslie, and Frith. Since that time, a number of studies have attempted to determine whether this difficulty is cognitive or perceptual, but whatever the source, it impedes the ability of the child with ASD to respond appropriately to another's feelings. John makes a card for the principal's birthday. The front design is a picture of the Titanic sinking, and on the inside of the card it says, "On your birthday, think of those who lost their lives on the Titanic. Happy birthday." John's favorite subject is the Titanic, and he cannot understand why a tragedy may not be the best subject matter for a birthday card. He would enjoy receiving such a card.

When writing a response to a prompt, a student may need to consider how another individual may have felt and describe a range of emotions that are foreign to the student. Students with autism may have difficulty identifying, understanding, and empathizing with the emotions of others. When Sam was asked how he would have felt if Sue had walked away when he was talking, Sam indicated he would be glad because he does not like girls. Additionally, students with ASD do not always alter the tone or content of the communication, because they are unaware or unconcerned with the communication partner's perspective or level of knowledge (Rehfeldt, Dillen, Ziomek, & Kowalchuk, 2007). This impacts the students' ability to change the approach according to the audience. Children with autism have been characterized as "little professors" because of the formality of their speech. They often seem unaware that they are speaking in a more formal manner, in full sentences, as if giving a lecture on the topic as opposed to a friendly conversation. If students with autism cannot acknowledge the difference in audiences when speaking, they will no doubt have similar difficulties in the written expression as well.

Writing as Reflection and Rigidity/Repetitive Interests

Another objective of an effective writer determined by the NAEP is the ability to respond to a variety of writing prompts, including poetry, art, or information contained in charts. This requires a flexibility of mind and a willingness to contemplate and reflect on topics that are not necessarily of particular interest to the writer. The successful writer must be able to put aside personal preferences and develop ideas and examples based on the prompt's demand. Students with autism have a tendency to perseverate on one particular concept or a small range of interests. Despite the topic presented by the communication partner, an individual with autism may continue to speak off topic. Students tend to use language that is "ritualistic and perseverative with a focus on special topics, elaborated with the use of odd phrases and word choice" (Szelag, Kowalska, Galkowski, & Poppel, 2004, p. 270).

Students with autism simply may not want to reflect on, think about, write about, or respond to a topic outside of their realm of interests. They may not have the social connectedness to peers or the desire to perform to teacher expectations. If students attempt to write to an assigned topic, they may drift back to a topic of interest without an organized or purposeful transition.

The Labor of Writing

Students with autism tend to be reluctant to revise, edit, and rewrite their essays, which is another objective of the NAEP's framework to assess successful writers. The physical process of producing words on a page through the use of a writing utensil is often difficult for the child with autism. Fine motor difficulties are often prevalent (Berkeley, Zittal, Pitney, & Nichols, 2001). If the student overcomes objections or difficulties to produce one piece of writing, the direction to rewrite could very likely be met with resistance. In addition to fine motor difficulties, children with autism may have low muscle tone and poor trunk strength. The task of sitting for long periods of time may be difficult, and the child cannot explain why. Also, children with autism have perceptual difficulties and require greater sensory input. Typically developing children and adults can determine where their bodies are in space without additional feedback. Children with autism or sensory integration abnormalities may need extra motor input or more frequent proprioceptive sensory breaks in order to sit for long periods of time. Compound the inability to sit for long periods of time with a fine motor activity demand, and the task may seem overwhelming to a child with autism. It may be that a child with autism will never develop functional handwriting skills (Braun, 2009).

Developed Details and Weak Central Coherence

Finally, the NAEP indicated that an effective writer uses clear choices and strategies when delivering the response. Ideas should be organized in an effective manner with sufficient examples and details to support them. Students with autism may exhibit a *weak central coherence* (Frith, 1989), causing them difficulty distinguishing relevant details, separating general from specific information, and organizing or classifying data. All details seem to have equal importance, and none connect to any overall theme. When individuals without disabilities see, hear, or read information, they assimilate, classify, and organize it. They take data from all of the clues and determine an overall picture. In a game, Trevor needs to describe an object on a card for his partner to guess. It is a picture of a zebra. Trevor's clues are that it is part black and part white. He lists other attributes but never tells his partner that it is an animal. For individuals with autism, the details may not present an overall picture and seemingly have no connection to each other. Because of this, students with autism find it difficult to write on a topic, organize details effectively, and stick to the topic.

Lack of Intrinsic Motivation

Because students with autism have social difficulties, they do not respond to a teacher's demand in a typical fashion. They may be disconnected from any desire to please or to take pride in their work. Madeline is a first grade student who was moved to third grade because her academic skills were extraordinary. Her teachers felt her lack of interest in the class was due to boredom. Once in a higher grade, Madeline continued to take out books and read while the teacher was giving instruction. If asked to stop reading, she put her head down or sat under her desk. Her avoidance behaviors grew more extreme. She was eventually placed in a self-contained classroom for students with autism. Students like Madeline may be more motivated to escape writing than to produce a piece of work even if they are capable. Often nonpreferred tasks must be incorporated into a system of extrinsic rewards.

CONCRETE, VISUAL LEARNING STYLE

Individuals with autism tend to be very concrete learners. Vague directions that call for subjective judgments are difficult for them to follow. This is why writing is as difficult for students with ASD to learn as it is for their teachers to teach. Directions to develop ideas and demonstrate good voice cannot be measured by a concrete learner and are confusing to self-assess. In order for the student to be successful, it will be important for the student to have clear, measurable, and quantifiable expectations to obtain the greatest growth.

Even students who use alternative communication devices instead of conventional language can develop high levels of literacy when the appropriate methods or accommodations are implemented (Erickson, Koppenhaver, & Cunningham, 2006). A key factor is a relevant and effective visual component. Students with autism require visual instruction because of auditory processing difficulties (Agocs, Burns, De Ley, Miller, & Calhoun, 2006; Carnahan, Mutsi-Rao, & Bailey, 2009). Visual intervention methods are particularly important for these students to interpret abstract concepts (Hoffman & Norris, 2006). Students need to see step by step what the expectations are and what the final product should look like.

In addition to visual strategies, the student with autism needs a concrete and measurable assessment method based on quantifiable and clear criteria (Nelson & Van Meter, 2006). Even though the NEAP gave guidelines for what constitutes good writing, actually quantifying writing with a score is elusive and subjective. How does a teacher score for effective details or organized thoughts? Students with autism need visual representations for feedback to be effective. The Writing Lab (Nelson & Van Meter, 2006) offered a rubric that could meet this need. In the Writing Lab, students use a worksheet to determine the quality of their writing by calculating the total words used, the number of sentences, type of sentences (simple, complex), use of quotations, and correct conventions, among other categories. Teachers and students can use the worksheet to set goals, direct instruction, and assess development. District rubrics can be modified and language changed to reflect the needs of concrete learners. The writing process is broken down on a chart into smaller, more manageable areas to target. Students can even select what area they would prefer to work on and set goals for what they feel they can accomplish. Whatever the method used, the student needs to know clearly and precisely the expectations. If the goal is to work on vocabulary, for example, the student may need to know how many words to target for how many points.

Adam is a fourth grader diagnosed with ASD. He was on grade level for reading skills; however, he had significant delays in other academic areas as well as in adaptive functioning. He is a generally good-natured child with a tendency toward silliness, from which he has a difficult time self-regulating. He has an unusually slow processing time both expressively and receptively. He has delayed gross motor skills to the point where he often forgets to let go of a ball when he is trying to throw it. He has reduced oral motor control and, despite therapy, continues to drool and needs prompting to wipe his mouth. He drools on papers, his desk, and the desks of his classmates. He needs assistance when eating to keep clean. His perceptual skills are reduced, and he cannot transfer information from multiple planes (e.g., from board to paper). His handwriting is barely legible, even to him. When given an assignment to write three sentences on a topic and draw a picture, Adam was agitated after a few minutes and produced three short, illegible sentences and an unidentifiable picture. After a few weeks, his teacher recognized Adam's verbal language strengths and interest in the computer. Quickly his skills increased. He wrote a series of sentences on a topic, then, by the end of the school year, Adam was able to write multi-paragraph essays on the computer independently. Adam was able to improve his writing with the use of assistive technology, daily practice, and familiar, concrete directions. Adam was able to focus on idea development and not on handwriting. Additionally, word processing gives immediate visual feedback. Adam was able to check for spelling and punctuation errors with greater ease.

CHALLENGES WITH ASSESSMENT

The most critical, and perhaps most difficult, part of developing writing skills in students with autism is making accurate assessments of abilities. In examining the work of Adam and of the previous student, Jose, some incorrect assumptions might be made. In the case of Jose, his handwriting abilities may have been overestimated. The process of writing is obviously more than just handwriting in itself. However, in the case of Adam, a teacher assessing his work product might assume that the process of writing was difficult. Adam uses simple sentences and demonstrates little evidence of idea development. However, the handwriting itself is difficult and serves as a barrier to idea development. If this barrier were eased or eliminated, could Adam in time produce grade level written expression?

Examining Adam in other settings may give additional information. Adam reads a great deal and has a solid oral vocabulary. Although he has significant processing delays, when participating in class discussions, if he is given extra wait time to process questions, he readily shares his ideas, and these ideas are novel and thoughtful. He has had some keyboarding experience and is able to reproduce work on the computer with relative ease. Flexibility is important when assessing abilities and determining ways to approach development.

The key factor in assessments is to be clear and precise about what is being assessed. Often language lessons require extensive writing. Students are asked to rewrite sentences correctly; to write new, creative sentences demonstrating the use of a new vocabulary word; or to change tense in a sentence. If a language lesson, for example, on plural nouns requires the student to identify the nouns in a sentence and rewrite the sentence with plural nouns, the lesson should be assessed on identification of nouns and changing nouns to plural, not on handwriting. Making an accommodation so that the student with autism does not have to rewrite each example to demonstrate knowledge of plural nouns would reduce the stress and increase the focus on the intended objective.

Preacademic Resistance/Defensiveness

Typically, students are introduced to writing through the mechanics of handwriting and orienting writing utensils and paper. Students learn to hold a pencil or crayon and begin making marks on paper. This process for a young child with autism may be met with indifference or even resistance (Fuentes, Mostofsky, & Bastian, 2009).

A student with autism who lacks preacademic writing skills and resists writing, drawing, or coloring activities may be encouraged and given extrinsic rewards for successful markings on paper within a boundary. Another approach may be to extend the time on task writing functionally. Attentiveness must be shown and accommodations made to ease the effort of the writing process. Using slanted desks or easels will reduce pressure in the wrists. Using sandpaper or other textured materials will provide greater input and feedback to the student. Offering a choice of materials such as thicker pencils, magic markers, or paintbrushes as opposed to thin pencils may be helpful. Sometimes finger strengthening activities can be conducted prior to writing, such as squeezing clay or doing finger push-ups, to prepare the fingers for fine motor demands.

A teacher must be aware of any sensory defensiveness (Reynolds & Lane, 2008). Bobby refuses to participate in a table activity assigned by his teacher. He has run off and is hiding in the corner shouting that he will not do it. The teacher initially feels Bobby is being difficult until she notices he is sitting on his hands. She asks him if he will watch the other students at the table if he does not have to touch the paint or glue. He agrees and joins the group with no further difficulty. Bobby's language impairment prevents him from communicating the actual problem. His tactile defensiveness put him in a state of alarm. Bobby's teacher, within a month, is able to get Bobby to paint if he uses an extra long brush and gloves. In addition to tactile defensiveness, another difficulty may be that the student is too attracted to the medium and wants to play in the materials instead of use them functionally. Paul cannot help himself when finger painting and, instead of making a picture, dumps all of his paint and swishes it around until the paper crumbles or the teacher takes it away.

Some students may not find coloring or prewriting skills reinforcing enough to participate, and they may want to escape this activity. Or, the request to use certain materials may have the effect of a setting event. Children with autism tend to respond differently to environmental factors, often beyond the notice of the teacher. A child may react differently when hungry or tired than when full and well rested. Children with autism may have an aversion to light, texture, and other environmental conditions. These often unseen or undetected conditions, which potentially change the behavioral responses of the student, are called *setting events* (Bijou & Baer, 1961). Once a setting event is in place for a child with autism, a problem behavior may ensue (Horner, Vaughn, Day, & Ard, 1996). Some students with tactile defensiveness will resist the use of a particular writing instrument but work fine with another. Insisting that a student use a pencil for every task may be counterproductive, unless use of the pencil is the only objective. If the objective is to have the student write letters, the student may be more engaged if he or she has some choice in the instrument. Self-determination through choice can be used to obtain commitment to complete the task (Lytle & Todd, 2009). A simple sentence such as "We are going to write the letter A. Do you want to write it with a crayon or marker?" may increase compliance. Allowing the student choose an instrument will also gain the child's the commitment to complete the task and reduce the stress associated with the task (Lytle & Todd, 2009). Choice could also be given as to the letter to be written or the medium on which to write. A student may be motivated to write on an erasable board or a chalkboard. Perhaps the student could be allowed to use a stick in the sand or rice table. Computers are often very motivating media for children with autism.

If the objective is to increase paper and pencil use, then it may be necessary to offer choice in the item to be written. If the objective is to use a pencil, then an additional requirement to write a specific letter may meet with resistance. A statement such as "I want you to write with this pencil. Do you want to make letters or pictures?" may increase compliance (Lytle & Todd, 2009). A student with autism who refuses all attempts to write on paper may gladly do letter identification receptively by pointing to letters rather than writing them. Again, whether the lesson's objective is letter identification or writing must be clear. Also, having a clear schedule of the day's events (either written, interactive, or computer generated) and a preferred activity to follow a less preferred will be motivating (Stromer, Kimball, Kinney, & Taylor, 2006). If a student looks forward to computer time, a teacher could say, "Do you want computer time?" Wait for an affirmative response then add "First writing, then computer." Using a variety of materials, being flexible in the medium, and being very clear about the intended objective will increase student compliance and success. Or, in the alternative, establishing a momentum of compliance may be beneficial, depending on the student. Asking the student to do a number of tasks that would normally be met with ease and compliance may increase the likelihood that the student will comply with a less tolerated instruction (Mace et al., 1988). A teacher can say, "Take out your paper," wait for compliance, give praise, and add, "Take out something to write with," wait for compliance, give praise, then add, "Write your name at the top," wait for compliance and give praise. Then the teacher proceeds with the direction for the first step in the writing process, waits for compliance and gives praise, moving through the directions.

Hyperlexia and Perseveration

In some cases, letters and numbers are very attractive to young children with autism, and they may even perseverate on them. This is because letters and numbers, alone or arranged in charts, are "predictable, organized, repetitive, visual, and concrete" in nature (Quill, 2000, p. 28). They may write and rewrite them or ask adults to write and rewrite them repeatedly. Children with autism may fixate on letters and numbers and demonstrate stereotypical or self-stimulating behaviors while observing them. Joe's teacher knows when they are walking to the restroom, she needs to remind Joe to keep walking, as he likes to stop at the bulletin board covered with letters. He puts his nose right on the bulletin board at times while waving his hands up and down.

A very young child with autism may be able to receptively point to or even expressively write both upper case and lower case letters. The child may be hyperlexic and able to read words at a much higher level than expected at the child's age. Jonathan's parents had never heard him read anything before. No street signs, no menus, no books. One day, at age 4, he picked up a book and read the entire book aloud without pausing. His parents were stunned and handed him another. He read that one aloud as well. When he finished the second book, he set it down, walked off and played. Although this may happen, a child with hyperlexia does not have a higher cognitive awareness (Grigorenko, Klin, & Volkmar, 2003). As in the case of Jose's drawings, the letters may not represent a means of functional communication. However, interest and motivation may be factors. Writing letters may be a motivating activity after a less preferred activity.

Sometimes, children with limited verbal skills may demonstrate resistance to writing and keen observation may be necessary to determine the exact cause. Ruben is a nonverbal, 6-year-old boy with autism. His lesson was to use markers to color in the boundary of certain shapes. The first day, he was given hand over hand help with sensory input on his legs (weighted bean bags). He was tolerant of the activity. The second day, with the same sensory input, he was given the same page and a selection of markers. He demonstrated independence as he pushed the teacher's hand away and colored some of the shapes on his own. When the teacher attempted to hand over hand color the remaining shapes, Ruben threw his head back, screamed, and refused to finish the assignment. The following day, the same paper was given to Ruben, and he had the entire box of markers to choose from. Without sensory input, he quietly took out a marker and colored each shape without incident. The teacher noticed he was skipping around and seemed intentional in his color choice. She went over to the bin of finished work and pulled out the first copy she had done with Ruben. He had selected the same colors for the same shapes as the first day. Looking at the second day's work, the shapes Ruben independently colored were the ones he had the same color markers for. The shapes he had refused to color and had become so upset over were the shapes the teacher had tried to use different colored markers to color. Through the power of observation, Ruben's teacher identified the problem. Ruben was not resistant to the task if he was allowed to color in the shapes with the same colors. The teacher then chose to vary the shapes and forms each day so that Ruben would be able to focus on the coloring and not the insistence of using the same colors each day.

Sentence Formation: Structure and Conventions

Jeremy is a fifth grade student who works at grade level in most subjects. However, he is often unable to write a complete, intelligible sentence. He has a receptive processing deficiency, and what he hears is somehow scrambled from what is actually said. He puts sounds in where there were none and changes the sounds that are there. When he writes, which he is able to do on the computer, he may omit or add sounds or write words the way he hears them. It would seem, upon initial assessment, that his instruction needs to focus on basic skills for him to accomplish successful writing. However, Jeremy is highly creative and develops imaginative stories with intricate plots and unusual details that more sophisticated writers could only hope to achieve. When forced to focus on writing correctly, his imagination falters, and his sentences become short and repetitive with no creative detail.

Although sentence structure and basic conventions such as punctuation make writing readable and without proper conventions writing is difficult to assess, it may be necessary to find strengths in the writing of a student with autism beyond these typical conventions. Focusing on the structure or requiring the student to focus on the conventions and presentation may cause the student to reduce idea development and weaken the content.

On the other hand, conventions such as punctuation and capitalization are one of the aspects of writing that are clear, visual, and concrete. Teaching a student to capitalize the first letter of a sentence or put a period at the end of a sentence is easier than to improve than voice, organization, or other less tangible concepts of writing. Concrete, visual areas in writing are good places to make measurable improvements. Starting the process of implementing these changes may be better in the revision stage or in a separate lesson so that the focus in creative writing does not shift from creativity to rigidity.

On Topic Idea Development

The difficulty individuals with autism have ascertaining or maintaining the topic in conversation because of their weak central coherence may cause these students to struggle to distinguish the details from the main idea. Details may seem to them unlinked to an overall picture. Additionally, children with autism tend to perseverate on their own particular interests, unaware of the interest level of their communication partner. Children with autism often need to be taught to watch for nonverbal cues to check for interest. This significant communication difference in speech naturally this carries over to writing (Lewis, O'Donnell, Freebairn, & Taylor, 1998). Writing to an assigned topic is a more difficult task than responding to a general topic of choice. When assessing a student's ability to develop ideas and write on a topic, it may be necessary to have both assigned and free choice topics. Amy and Cindy are sixth grade students with autism. When given topics to write on, they are compliant and try to give their best effort. Despite this, they tend to write in a stream of consciousness and often derail from the topic, getting distracted by elaborating on the details and never getting back to the original topic. When asked to go back, read each sentence, and cross it off if it is not on the topic, they can do it accurately each time, but they cannot develop ideas on the original topic without assistance. When assessing Amy's and Cindy's abilities, it might seem as though they are completely unaware of the topic. They are aware and are able to correct their mistake, but they have trouble developing ideas on a topic with a very specific direction. They know what is it is not, but not how to tackle the assigned topic.

During a standardized test, a student with good writing skills wrote completely off topic. When asked later what had happened, the student replied that he did not feel like writing about that topic and thought his topic on his favorite video game would be more interesting and would gain more points. Students with autism often miss the point of an assignment. During a writing test, the student wanted to demonstrate his talents by showcasing them in an interesting topic despite being told that if he wrote off topic, he would lose all points. He felt his paper was all on one topic, his favorite video game, and was very well written. Additionally, he was unaffected by the loss of points. He lacked the interest in social praise for a good job. Often the student's ability to stay on topic must be evaluated not only on topics of choice but also on assigned topics.

It may be important for students with weak writing skills to improve their confidence initially by writing on topics of interest. The students develop ideas more fully on topics that interest them. Over time, they will come to understand the level of idea development required to meet the teacher's expectations on topics that interest them, and they will not be surprised when the same level of expectation is required on teacher-assigned topics. Occasionally, with warnings to predict change, a teacher may introduce a class topic. The teacher might say, "Write on a topic you choose today, but remember, next week, we will all be writing on a topic of my choice." The teacher's topic may be two choices if resistance to change is expected. Eventually, the teacher is able to introduce one topic to which all of the students are expected to respond. The single topic may eventually become a weekly exercise or even progress to a daily activity. Often, state departments of education will post sample responses to past testing prompts online. Students may benefit from reading and assessing the responses of other anonymous students to a topic either before or after writing to the same topic.

Trouble with Generalization

Learning a new skill is difficult for a student with autism, but even more difficult is generalizing these skills (Quill, 2000). Students with autism may overgeneralize or undergeneralize (Koegel & Wilhelm, 1973) because of their weak central coherence. A typically developing child makes connections and associations that a child with autism simply may not be able to make independently. What a student learns in one setting or in one format may not transfer automatically in another. In written expression, the same applies. A teacher worked on written expression every day by having the students write in their journal on a topic written on the board. She was pleased with their progress and looked forward to the state assessment where they could demonstrate their new skills. The state assessment was passed out to the students, and they could not even determine what the topic was. The directions were read and reread. The students began crying and putting their heads down saying they did not know what to do. Because the topic was in a packet and not on the board and because the students were to write in the packet and not in their journal, they simply could not comprehend what to do. In the future, the teacher used the state assessment format by having the topic and the writing to be done in a packet. The students were confident and knew exactly what to do on the next state assessment.

Often, a student with autism does not understand what is expected by reading or hearing directions. Although the students may have perfect hearing, a variety of processing difficulties may be present (Freeman & Drake, 1996). If students with autism are to be successful, they need to be familiar with the format. Then the writing skills can be generalized to other formats. In a typical classroom, the teacher varies the assignments to engage students and create interest. Utilizing the same format may seem boring and repetitive. However, many students with autism need to be familiar with the format to be able to produce effectively. Sometimes, the formats are unfamiliar because students with autism have trouble seeing the big picture through the details because of a weak central coherence. It takes longer to explain the directions and demonstrate how to meet the expectations than it would for the student to do the same assignment in a familiar format. If students are not successful in their writing assignments, it could very well be that they were confused over the directions. Providing instructions, or even a model, may be helpful but may not overcome the barrier of unfamiliarity. Whenever possible, use repetitive formats or a smaller selection of formats to obtain the best results initially. As the student develops skills and becomes more accomplished, introduce additional formats to test generalization of these skills.

ASSISTIVE TECHNOLOGY

Fine motor skills are often difficult for a student with autism (Berkeley et al., 2001). Tactile defensiveness, reduced muscle control, developmental delays, and lack of social connectedness, among other issues, cause children with autism to have difficulty with the task of handwriting. Penmanship is often a barrier to work product. Because handwriting is difficult, students avoid writing or write as little as possible. If the student shows any indication that handwriting is laborious, invariably this is limiting work product, and when assessing the student's work, this must be factored as a possible impediment. When this seems to be the case, consider the benefits of assistive technology (Braun, 2009).

Use of the computer is an integral part of developing writing skills. Computer time can often be motivating in itself, in addition to the added benefit of fine motor accommodation (Heimann, Nelson, Tjus, & Gillberg, 1995). Computers can be used to develop both language and academic skills (Agocs et al., 2006). In the case of Adam, assistive technology made all the difference in his ability to develop writing skills. Still, after several years, if Adam is given paper and pencil and asked to write a sentence, he will write a simple sentence and it will be barely legible. The task of handwriting is in itself so difficult that, despite his written expression abilities, they are still not evident in his handwritten responses.

Fine Motor Difficulties

The use of assistive technology is intended to ease the difficulties students may have as a result of their disabilities. Typically, students with handwriting difficulties use word processors, portable keyboards such as AlphaSmarts, laptops, or classroom computers. Students who have use of their hands and sufficient motor skills but who have difficulty writing may find computerized writing more efficient and effective (Braun, 2009). Typically, though, students do not have sufficient keyboarding skills to immediately see improvement or ease in assignments. Time must be spent in developing keyboarding skills. Students with developmental delays may still find traditional keyboarding difficult. Motor skills and finger strength may need time to develop. Students will invariably find ways to increase their keyboarding skills by finding comfortable ways to achieve faster keyboarding speeds (Braun, 2009).

Some students have more significant disabilities and may need to use voice activated typing programs or keyboards responsive to air. However, the same principles apply. Removing barriers will allow the student to work independently. Use of technology still keeps the work of the student dependent on the student.

Compulsive Tendencies

Alana is a fifth grade girl with autism and compulsive tendencies. When she writes, she takes an unusually long time to form each letter. If she is not satisfied with how the work looks, she will erase whole sentences and rewrite the exact sentence over again. After a class period, she has only a few sentences produced to her satisfaction. Her teacher introduced the use of assistive technology, and her work showed immediate and measurable improvement. Students with autism may have obsessive or compulsive tendencies. They may also demonstrate repetitive behaviors (APA, 2000; Quill, 2000). As in the case of Alana, these tendencies may interfere with the student's ability to write, and the use of assistive technology aides in eliminating the barrier while still keeping the student independent. With the use of a computer, the letters are of equal and conformed size. The spacing is controlled and the presentation is uniform.

Motivation

Students with autism are often not motivated by social praise of the teacher or intrinsic rewards such as pride in their work performance. They may not respond to competitive techniques to improve writing through social praise from peers. Often, students with autism need extrinsic motivators. Students with autism often respond to behavioral interventions through the use of token economies or other tangible reinforcers (Baldwin & Balwin, 2001); Cooper, Heron, & Heward, 2007; Schoen, 2003). For many students, use of the computer is very motivating and therefore may be the reward to the token system. It may be that computers have predictable and consistent responses. Interaction with others is difficult for individuals with autism, because people can be unpredictable. Conditions and situations vary responsiveness, but computers are nonemotional and very predictable. Whatever the reasons, if a student shows interest in computers, and assignments are given that can be completed on the computer, the student may be inclined to work longer or more efficiently. Use of a variety of programs such as PowerPoint can be motivating as well. John does not like to work on his writing projects. He had difficulty understanding paragraph organization. Through the use of PowerPoint, he was able to understand beginning his slideshow with an introduction and organizing separate thoughts on slides. Additionally, he was highly motivated to look for pictures on the internet that he could add to each slide. He liked to add animation schemes and even sound, which he discovered without assistance from his teacher. Finding the motivating format will allow the student to make exciting and creative pieces of writing.

Revising and Rewriting

Students who have difficulty with handwriting and are unmotivated to work may willingly accede to complete a task but will not submit to revising or rewriting their work. Melanie is a third grader who was taking a state assessment for the first time. After writing her story, which was clever and imaginative, the direction was to rewrite it with her revisions on another page. The test evaluators never see the rough draft, just what is turned in on the final copy sheet. She did not want to rewrite the page so she abbreviated and eliminated details so the final copy was a shortened, pale comparison to her rough draft work. Using assistive technology allows the student to see punctuation errors clearly. Additionally, with the touch of a key, space can be added between lines so that teacher comments can be made or students can add words or thoughts. With the saved work, the student can make a few changes without having to rewrite the entire piece. This will undoubtedly be an additional skill that a student will have to learn. Looking at corrections and changes on one pane (the printed paper), finding their place on the other plane (the computer screen), and making the changes without making additional errors is a definite challenge initially. Practicing on sample paragraphs not written by the student with simple changes may be a good place to start.

Access to the Regular Education Classroom

Students who use assistive technology may be in self-contained situations or may be in inclusion settings. Typically, at some point, all students will need to access some regular education classrooms. More and more school districts are requiring writing to be done across the curriculum, so that students who may only participate in art or physical education but have their core learning in a self-contained or resource setting will still be required to write in the regular education classes. Often the writing is confined to one-word or one-line responses, but at times students may need to write examples, list a number of points, or write a short essay.

Given this need, the special education teacher must work closely with the general education teacher. If possible, the special education teacher may request advanced notice of the assignment and review the format. If the student is to write short answers or an essay, the special education teacher can advise either the student or the general education teacher how the student can best respond with the use of technology. The special education teacher can check for understanding with the student to make sure the directions are clear. A teacher-made test or worksheet could even be emailed to the student so he or she could pull it up, fill in the blanks, and email it back to the teacher, all from the student's desk. Otherwise, arrangements need to be made for printing the assignment. Students will need to be taught how to save and organize files so that they can be easily retrieved. Reviewing the format and how the student will respond and produce the assignment is essential information for the student as well as the grading teacher.

DETERMINING GREATEST STRENGTH AND WEAKNESS

As discussed in other chapters, a student with autism may be in a variety of settings based on, among other things, student abilities, limitations, school or district population, and available resources. The student may be in a self-contained classroom, a resource pull out, or full or partial inclusion. Depending on the setting, the approach to writing may also vary. Accommodations will have to be made for schedules, instructional time, technology, teacher or paraprofessional availability, and the availability of other resources. The special education teacher, general education teachers, and administration may need to be involved to ensure that the student receives the time and assistance necessary to meet individual goals.

No matter what the setting, the student's writing abilities and deficiencies will be evident. Other critical observations will need to be made. Observing the student's work habits will provide the necessary information to begin moving the student forward. The student may demonstrate a willingness to work or an eagerness to produce a quality piece of work. It may be that the student will work an entire class period without having to be redirected to task. Despite the actual quality of the work produced, this willingness to comply and give a good effort may be that student's greatest strength in the writing process. Perhaps the student has adequate attention and seems to have a propensity to follow rules and may be very familiar with the rules of punctuation, grammar, and other conventions. Some students may have a unique imagination, even if centered on one particular interest. Adam, the student mentioned previously, loves dog and rabbits. Every story he wrote was clever and imaginative, but in most cases, the main character was a boy who had a talking dog.

In addition to the strengths, the impediments to successful writing may be equally clear. In many cases, the student will be a reluctant writer. People do not like to do something that they do not do well. Students with autism are no exception, and, in fact, they may have a greater obstacle because the desire to please a teacher or gain social rewards may be completely absent. If the student is reluctant, it will be important to know what is causing the reluctance. Does the student seem to struggle with handwriting? Does the student refuse particular topics? Does the student work well in a particular setting or with a particular teacher but act differently in a different setting? These circumstances impact writing even though they have nothing to do with the writing process. In order for the writing to improve, these impediments need to be addressed.

Minimize the Impact of Weakness

Often the greatest impediment will not be a technical or traditional writing delay, but more likely an environmental, motor control, or motivational issue. Once the greatest impediment is discovered, attempts need to be made to overcome or minimize the impact of the problem.

Students with motivational difficulties can be helped through extrinsic reward systems. Approaching instruction as a behavior change intervention through the use of token economies or other reinforcement of desired behaviors may be the catalyst to gaining the student's cooperation (see Chapter 5). Having charts on the wall or individual charts on desks can help students earn time doing more preferred activities. Setting a reasonable behavioral goal and gaining the student's commitment is vital (Baldwin & Baldwin, 2001; Cooper et al., 2007). If the student will only work for 10 minutes without having behavioral issues, have the student work for 10 or 11 minutes, offer a short break, and reward the time on the chart. Then advise the student it is time to return to work for another 10 minutes and continue this procedure. If a student is refusing to work, offering a reward to gain compliance will lessen the impediment. As the student spends more time on writing with targeted, measurable goals, the student's confidence will increase along with the voluntary time on task. As the student demonstrates more willingness to work, slowly increase the time required before marking the chart. In some cases, a student may have a real aversion to writing and may refuse all attempts to encourage improvement. Whenever behavior seems to be the direct impediment to writing, conducting a functional behavior assessment (see Chapter 5) may be necessary to determine the true function of the behavior so that it may be addressed effectively.

Naturally, if the impediment is a fine motor control problem, assistive technology will have to be investigated as a potential resource. The student may not show immediate benefits, as it will take time for the keyboarding skills to become more efficient. Over time, the student will develop proficiency, even if the keyboarding skills are not traditional. Many computer programs are available for downloading graphic organizers (see Chapter 10) and other helpful resources for providing writing tips and tools.

Sometimes, it may be that the student has a receptive language delay, and it impacts the ability to hear, process, and reproduce sounds both in speech and writing. Working with a speech therapist to collaborate on effective, small steps to improve phonemic awareness will be an important endeavor.

Goal Selection

Each student will present with a particular and natural strength based on a myriad of skills. In whatever way the skills present, a plan should be made to move the student forward in incremental, scaffolded steps. For example, if the student has imaginative ideas, the focus should be on idea or plot development. Developing confidence is vital. Starting the writing development with a focus on strength will more likely engage the student. Joseph is a student with autism in the fifth grade. He has difficulty with handwriting but was able to develop some basic keyboarding skills. At first, he practiced writing sentences on a topic. These were just lists of sentences and were often repetitive. He was asked to refrain from pressing the "enter" key after each sentence. He was then given a list of transitional words, which he used to connect thoughts. Slowly, as he mastered each step, he writing improved. He was able to develop multiple paragraphs within a few months.

Whether in the IEP or in a less formal goal setting procedure, the writing goals need to be challenging but incremental and measurable (Edelen-Smith, 1995). Focus on the next step that the student could achieve as opposed to focusing on the overall final outcome. In order to determine the best course of action, some experimentation may be necessary. A teacher and student may approach the writing process in many different ways, but the student may be more inclined to participate in some methods over others. The student's willingness and compliance if not total commitment will produce a greater success. Some methods are more concrete and measurable, and setting small, incremental goals will encourage both teacher and student when those goals are reached. Choosing to tackle vocabulary or transition words may both be concrete, measurable areas to develop goals, but the student may have a preference between these approaches, and the student's willingness to participate in the goal will impact the success rate.

Districts and individual schools or special education departments may have formal assessments, rubrics, or other standards in place to determine a student's overall writing score. This score, along with informal assessments of the student's areas of strengths, weaknesses, and interest, will direct the development of IEP or informal writing goals. Establish a goal by determining quarterly benchmarks. It may be necessary to consider the school's schedule when determining these quarterly goals. For example, if the third quarterly benchmark is after summer or winter vacation, determining a history of regression will be important. A student may make progress overall but need time to recoup lost skills after a long break, and maintaining a current performance level may be the most that can be expected for that benchmark period. The goal should clearly outline the progress to be made and the likely benchmarks if the student is progressing toward meeting that overall goal.

For example, selecting word choice and vocabulary development is a concrete approach. Perhaps the student could improve word choice by independently choosing three or four words in his or her writing to change to more descriptive or colorful words. The goal would state this performance expectation clearly (the student will change four words in a written response to a prompt), the conditions to change (through the use of a supplied resource such as a word bank or thesaurus), the rate of measurement (to be measured daily/weekly/quarterly), and the tool or method of measurement (teacher checklist, district rubric, other informal or formal assessment).

When selecting the goal, the benchmarks may be used to determine the yearly progress expected. Perhaps the first benchmark would be that the student would select and change one word, then the second benchmark may be for two words, and so on. Perhaps, given the needs of the student, the first benchmark may be four words with at least one to be used grammatically correctly. It may be that the student is willing to change four words but needs assistance selecting these words. If this is the case, the teacher may assist though highlighting the four words in the first quarter, highlighting only three by the second quarter with the student selecting one word independently, and being completely independent by the fourth marking period.

The student's writing may have multiple areas that need targeted interventions. Typically, writing is not the only area that will need an individualized goal. For this reason, the student will likely only have one or at the most two writing goals. However, by selecting one area in the student's writing to improve, it by no means eliminates the need to assess student writing in other areas. Informal assessments and the use of student portfolios help the teacher to see student progress on many levels and provide information on areas that will require targeted goals in the future.

Whenever possible, the student should be involved in the goal process. Having the student working to achieve the same goal that the IEP team has selected will increase the likelihood that it is eventually achieved, perhaps earlier than projected. This does not mean the student is simply aware of the goal and the steps being taken. This is important, but more than likely it will not be enough to motivate the student. The student with autism may need a visual reminder and motivator. The goal information and progress could be monitored interactively by the student on a wall or desk chart. As the student makes incremental progress, a sticker or a point on a graph is added or an object is moved toward a finish line. The student will enjoy the progress and is more likely to achieve the goal. If this is not enough, an extrinsic motivator may need to be used at the finish line or for movement on the writing goal chart.

BASICS OF WRITING

The writing process is difficult to break down into concrete elements or universal standards that if followed will produce great writing. No formula or consensus exists to outline what makes writing effective. Varying opinions based on preferences and subjective tastes may dictate the parameters. Different styles for different types of writing may be used for different purposes and varying audiences. In general, good writing must be organized, purposeful, informative or entertaining enough to hold interest. Writing should convey thoughts and feelings and allow others to share in those emotions. This all presents a challenge to the student with autism.

Within the writing process, a few elements are more concrete and easier to teach than others. As mentioned previously, vocabulary, word choice, punctuation, and other visual conventions that follow rules are more concrete areas to improve the mechanics of writing. The other, less concrete and more subjective elements of writing such as organization, sentence fluency, and style are more difficult to quantify and develop measurable goals around. These elements may not be the primary focus until other, more concrete methods have improved. However, in order to improve writing through these concrete methods, the student must have material with which to work. One of the biggest stumbling blocks in the writing process is the development of ideas.

Many students with autism seem to lack the ability to develop imaginative ideas. Imaginative play is often a goal for small children with autism in early intervention settings. Imagination involves social awareness and perspective taking. In order for a child to pretend to be, for example, an animal or astronaut, the child must be able to acknowledge the strengths, limitations, sights, sounds, and interactions of the character in order to extrapolate the character's possible activities and actions. Also, imagination involves thinking beyond the bounds of reality. Based on the *DSM-IV* criteria for diagnosis, children with autism are often preoccupied with rules, routines, and rituals (APA, 2000). They tend to prefer things to follow order and be in a regular and perceived proper place. Asking a student with autism to consider what it would be like to fly or talk to animals is asking the student to consider breaking the rules of nature, and this may be met with resistance. The student is not only being asked to use imagination to consider what things may happen but also to surrender the safety of rules.

Brainstorming

Typically, brainstorming or warming up of writing prompts is done in a whole class setting. Most regular education teachers may present a topic, have some class discussion about it, and put ideas on the board in front of the class as the teacher or assigned student writes the ideas into a graphic organizer. This is an efficient and fairly common way to have the whole class engaged in the activity and benefiting from the ideas. Students who have attention difficulties are able to stay engaged with the fast paced brainstorming. However, children with autism may have different difficulties with attention. Beyond the typical distractions of children with attention difficulties, a student with autism may display attention difficulties at the level of a child with ADD or ADHD (Leyfer et al., 2006). Also, oversensitivity to stimuli in the environment may lead to hypervigilance in children with sensory issues. The clock ticking, a paper clip on the floor, an itchy sweater, the change in schedule all impact the students' ability to concentrate, even if they are interested in the topic. Additionally, the student with autism is not necessarily motivated by the approval of peers or teachers. In a whole class setting, the attention difficulties of a student with autism are most noticeable.

If possible, close proximity of the student to the teacher or paraprofessional will help (Young & Simpson, 1997). The student may be given the job of writing on the board or perhaps typing the information into a computer to be projected on the board or printed and passed out to the class. Perhaps the students could work initially as partners to come up with a number of ideas that are later shared with the whole group. Any of these methods will more than likely enable a greater participation from the student with autism in a whole class setting.

Minimize the Number of Formats

Often a teacher will want to engage the students in writing and demonstrate the many ways to produce a piece of writing. By having many different formats for writing, the teacher is providing new and interesting ideas and stirring creativity. Students may work on class newspapers, journals, brochures, posters, and other creative formats. Most students would prefer the variety and find novel formats interesting and engaging. Students with autism have difficulty distinguishing between important and less important details. This weak central coherence causes them to flounder at times in assembling an overall picture, even when the overall picture is clear to everyone else. James is a fourth grade student with autism. He was helping his teacher move a desk into the hall. When they reached the doorway, it was clear to the teacher that the desk was wider than the door's opening and was not going to fit. The teacher told James they would have to turn the desk. James proceeded to turn the desk completely around in a circle until he was back in his original spot.

James, like many students with autism, did not think about the details in terms of an overall picture. He did not understand a simple direction that would have been clear to a typical fourth grader because he did not associate the direction with the overall task. This disconnect is present in classwork as well. If a teacher changes the writing format frequently, the student with autism will be concentrating on each individual direction and may need step-by-step assistance to connect the individual directions to the overall assignment.

It may seem to be more exciting for students to write in newspapers or journals with prompts written on worksheets one time, on the board other times. Students may find it interesting to write responses to art or poetry. However, if the format switches or the teacher changes how the writing is to be presented each time, the student will be focused on the format with equal emphasis as the writing. If the student with autism utilizes the same format such as a daily journal or a writing pamphlet, the student will be able to focus the attention and energy on the writing process itself. As the writing improves, then the writing could be generalized to other formats. Perhaps offering choice of formats may offer variety to some students and consistency to others.

Topic of Choice

In a standardized exam, the students must demonstrate their mastery of writing skills. In order to make this a fair assessment statewide, the prompts are closely guarded secrets. Since no one can know the topic ahead of time, typically, students are expected to respond to an assigned topic and not given choices. Although this is an important skill, many topics will be met with resistance. The student with autism may not have the desire to respond to the assigned writing topic if it is asking for an imaginative or reflective response or asking for an opinion on a topic that does not interest the student. Eventually, the student will need to practice responding to non-preferred topics; however, while developing the basic writing skills, having a topic of interest to the student may be helpful so that the idea development process is less labored or less stressful (Lytle & Todd, 2009).

Individuals with autism often have particular interests. They may perseverate by discussing their favorite topic at length. By tailoring the writing topic to the interest of the student, the student will have a wealth of information on which to draw to develop his or her writing. By developing a piece of writing with greater ease, the student can then have a feeling for how the writing process should flow on all topics, not just favored ones. The student may have less resistance to the revision process if the topic is of interest or if given a choice of topics. Also, if the length of the writing is greater because the topic was of interest to the student, the longer piece will give more opportunities to discuss vocabulary, grammar, punctuation, sentence lengths, style, and other writing elements.

Use of Drawings or Pictures

Another method that can be used to elicit idea development is the use of drawings. Students with autism are often visual learners. They may not even be aware that they have omitted details as a result of their communication or language impairments. Visually cued instruction is beneficial because it is clear and concrete (Quill, 2000). When the student has finished developing an idea or has reached a block, he or she can continue the development of ideas by drawing a picture associated with the writing. The teacher or a peer may look at the picture and start a discussion with the student to elicit further details. Tom is a fifth grade student in a regular education classroom. Writing is his most difficult subject. When given the assignment to write about his vacation, he produced only three of four sentences about a camping trip. When asked to draw a picture, he added details about fishing and boating that he had not mentioned in his writing. By looking at his picture, he and his teacher were able to point out details to add to his writing.

Students with autism may have difficulty with attention and working memory (Nakahachi et al., 2006). They tend to be distracted by many elements in their environment. If they do get an idea to write about, it may slip their mind before they are able to write it down, especially if they are dealing with fine motor difficulties in addition to attention and communication impairments. The use of a drawing will also hold a thought. This technique may be used on state assessments as well, because in most cases, only the final copy of the writing is submitted. The draft pages are for student idea development.

Dictation

As stated previously, many students with autism also have difficulty with attention and working memory. In addition to drawing, dictation is an effective method of holding ideas. Allowing a student with attention, memory, and fine motor difficulties to use a scribe is tempting. A student easily states ideas to a peer, paraprofessional, or teacher who records these sentences on paper. Dictation enables the student to concentrate on ideas and eliminates the fine motor pressure. This process may not be beneficial in the long term, however, for a number or reasons. In most cases, scribes or the use of dictation is not allowed as a standard accommodation on a state assessment. Unless the student will be allowed to use this technique, it may need to be avoided, because when the time comes to take the assessment, the student needs to have the tools to demonstrate skills independently. Whatever choices are used to accommodate the student, the accommodations need to make the student more independent, not more dependent on others. Dictation requires the assistance of another person.

Furthermore, the student would need to practice the format of delivering dictation and editing for details. The student needs to be making decisions about capitalization and punctuation. The person taking the dictation may be tempted to punctuate and add omitted words or spell words that the student may not have spelled correctly if left to his or her own skills. However, teaching the student to spell each word and indicate case and punctuation may slow down the idea processes that it is meant to assist.

Word Banks

A student with autism has difficulty seeing the connection of details to an overall picture. Each detail seems to be fragmented and disconnected to an individual with autism. In much the same way, a student with autism may not be able to determine a relationship among a group of words. A teacher can try to improve this skill through the use of word banks.

A seventh grade boy who performs near grade level in all areas, Derek, was asked to design a t-shirt on a cut out piece of paper taken from one of the many clubs and classes offered at his new school. The teacher held up visuals of shirts designed by other students in the past. When given his t-shirt, Derek indicated he had no idea what to do. The teacher pointed to all of the words on the board, which were the names of classes, clubs, and sports offered at the school. She asked him what the words had in common. He had no idea. He could not find the overall connection between the details of the list of words. In order to help him try to make a connection, as opposed to just telling him what the overall theme was, she wrote several words on a piece of paper such as cookie, soda, pizza, chips. She asked him what those words had in common, thinking that these words would be more familiar to him and he would be able to make the connection. He did not know. He was given another list of words such as giraffe, monkey, elephant, and zebra. Instead of the teacher asking Derek what this list had in common, she asked him what was different between the two separate lists. He was able to understand that one list was animals, another food. By helping Derek look for patterns, the teacher was helping Derek expand his ability to look for similarities and differences and categorize items accordingly. Once he practiced with a couple of lists, he was then asked to look at the group of words on the board. He was then finally able to determine that the words on the board were the clubs and classes of the school.

Even though Derek attends regular education classes, he needs support in areas that are second nature to students who do not have autism. After Derek understood what was being asked of him, he could demonstrate the knowledge. If given a list of words associated with a topic, Derek would be able to identify the relationship and possible add a few more words to the list. The list could then be used to write sentences associated with the overall topic. Eventually, this could be expanded to find more sophisticated words or to use two banks and compare and contrast topics.

Computer Graphic Organizers

Once the student is able to develop a few ideas, the next step would be to assist the student to organize those ideas. Graphic organizers are effective ways to not only to organize information but also to visualize it. The difficulty for a student with autism may be that the organizers are often circles with undefined inner space. Typically the spaces are small and have no lines to write on. In some cases, even in large circles, students may only place one or two words, as the boundaries are confusing. Also, children with autism have handwriting difficulties caused by fine motor deficits and tend to write large and often illegibly. They may be able to fit only a couple of words within the boundaries of the graphic organizer and then write outside the lines, making their attempt at organization a difficult mess to sort out visually. Many graphic organizers can be found online that allow the student to type the information directly. However, in some cases, the information cannot be saved, only printed, and this may cause an inconvenience. A teacher or the student him- or herself may create text boxes or tables in a basic word processing program and save it for future use. Whichever organizers are used, the student must become familiar with the format so that the writing process is the focus and not the details of the graphic organizer.

Modeled Practice

Even though students with autism may have difficulty attending to a whole class setting, modeled practice in a whole class setting may still be beneficial if the student is kept on task. Students, with or without autism, need to be shown the writing process even after idea development is complete. Moving the ideas on a graphic organizer to sentences and paragraphs on a rough draft is a process that may need to be modeled repeatedly. Ideally, the student with autism would either assist in the writing process on the board or on a computer word processing program projected on the board. If possible, the student with autism could choose the topic, or one could be prepared in advance tailored to his or her interests. The process of taking an idea, making a meaningful sentence, and grouping it with other sentences on the same idea is a difficult task for any student, but especially so for one with a language difficulty.

If possible, the class could be divided into groups, perhaps each one taking one circle on the graphic organizer to develop sentences. The smaller the group, the more likely the student with autism will be engaged in the activity. Then, when all groups have completed their sentences, the whole work is assembled. Eventually, the process could be done individually, and the variety of the finished product could be discussed. Whichever method is chosen, ideally, it should become a familiar format and varied as little as possible until the student has learned the expectations.

Group Inspiration

A group of 10 fifth grade students with autism were given the topic: what it would be like if they could be teacher for the day. Each student agonized over the assignment until they each had a few sentences. Most simply outlined what subject they would teach first, second, and so on. The teacher, in a whole class setting, asked if any students had taken a field trip. Since none had, she had the think for a moment about where they could have gone. Students began answering typical places such as museums. One student, in an effort to gain attention said, "to the moon." The teacher encouraged this response. Before long, the students were suggesting they could have gone back in time or into the future. The ideas developed and the assignment was given again. The students were anxious to share their final drafts after adding their new creative details. With help from peers and the right topic, students can have fun with the writing process. Sharing ideas may help the student discover his or her own creativity.

Another teacher gave a group of 20 students a scenario and asked how that individual might respond. She asked if someone liked sports and was very active, what might he or she say. As the teacher went around the room, one student said, "Hey, let's go have fun." Another said, "Running is awesome." One student said, "Let's go play basketball." The three students with autism were next. They all responded with the same sentence but changed the sport. Once a pattern is created, it may be difficult for students with autism to think of their own creative response. They may simply copy the format. Although group work may seem to inspire new responses, it may in some cases limit creativity.

Tackling Cold Prompts

In a formal testing situation, students are expected to respond to a cold writing prompt independently. They may not seek help analyzing the question or developing ideas. They are expected to demonstrate all aspects of the writing process, deliver an age appropriate response, and do so in the allotted time period. The time factor is often an issue for students with autism. For some of these students, effective writing takes time. Some writing assignments may be developed over the course of several days. Typically, the whole process of assessment is allotted 1 to 3 hours. Some higher level tests such as college entrance exams may require two or three responses in the same amount of time. It will definitely take practice to develop the ability to complete the entire writing process effectively in a short amount of time. Daily practice, such as responding to a journal topic first thing in the morning or at the start of class, will help students get used to some idea development on a daily basis. Then, perhaps once a week, the students may choose from journal responses one idea to develop more fully in one class period. For students with autism, having some extrinsic reward system for timeliness may be necessary to motivate the extra effort.

Another difficult aspect of the cold writing prompt is the analysis of the language in the prompt itself. If students do not write on the exact topic or address the points explicitly, some or all of the points will be lost. Sometimes, a practice prompt done recently will even confuse the student. Key words in the prompt may be ignored and the wrong idea may become the focus.

Mary is a sixth grade student whose writing abilities are on grade level. She is a thoughtful and careful writer. She had recently written an essay in which she discussed the steps she took to clean her room. She had done well on this assignment and had been pleased to share it with the class. On a standardized test, she was asked to write about why it was important to clean your room. She proceeded to write about all of the steps involved in cleaning a room. The teacher was not allowed to discuss the difference between how to clean a room (what she was writing) and why to clean a room (what she was asked to write about) in the prompt. Her score reflected a below grade level performance.

The writing prompts may be as much as a paragraph long. When giving directions to students with autism, short, concise, clear directions are best (Quill, 2000). It would not be effective to stop a child from running in the hall and explain the reasons why this behavior is unacceptable. The direction would simply be "Walk" or "Stop, use walking feet." Ideally, the directions for a writing prompt should be equally clear and concise, but this is not generally the case, nor is it within the teacher's control. Taking time to read prompts aloud in class and ask students to formulate a response on topic and offering "what if" scenarios to discuss may be helpful. Even just reading responses to determine whether they are on or off topic will help the student tune into what is actually being asked. For example, if the prompt requests that students write a letter to the principal about changes in the lunch menu, some questions that could be asked include: "What if the writer did not write a letter, would that be following the direction? What if the writer wrote a letter to the principal but on a different subject, would that be following directions?" Then allowing the students to review responses to determine how well the writers actually followed the directions will assist students in analyzing the prompt itself.

Warming Up Prompts

Students with autism sometimes have limited or particular interests that are not generally considered typical interests for children. Sometimes interests are not age appropriate. Mark, a seventh grade boy, brought his character backpack and lunch box to school. His teacher and mother worked to persuade Mark that Thomas the Tank was not age appropriate for a junior high school boy. Not caring for social conventions, it was not easy to convince Mark of this. Additionally, Mark would change every conversation back to his train topic. Everything seemed to remind him of a character or episode that he needed to share. These immature interests may surface in writing.

In many cases, the writing will also switch back to the topic of interest. Despite the topic assigned, the response will always come back to that one particular topic. However, in a standardized testing situation, the individual scoring the test will have no prior knowledge of the student or the fixation. In some cases, using the topic of interest is a clever tool to develop good writing, as long as the writing is still on topic. Trevor is a junior high school student. He participates in the regular education classes for most of his work. His writing prompt was to compare and contrast two animals. He has an interest in Godzilla and dinosaurs. He has a wealth of knowledge on these subjects. He was able to write an excellent essay that listed the many ways in which a tyrannosaurus rex and Godzilla are similar and different.

This essay, which probably would have been discouraged by his teacher because of its topic, turned out to be an excellent way to warm up and address the cold prompt. The key factor is that the essay cannot drift to the topic of interest aimlessly; it must appear to be used to address the topic intentionally. This can be practiced by having students clearly state and demonstrate understanding of the topic's directions.

Format

Once again, familiarity with the format is critical. The student with autism must have practice on the cold prompt format exactly as it will be presented on testing day. Ideally, the practice should be throughout the year so that the practice of the prompt is not resisted in that particular format or that format becomes associated with the standardized assessment. Having the prompt presented in the same way and the writing pamphlet assembled similarly will make the format familiar so that the student can focus on the writing.

Each state uses a particular test which may have information available on the state's Department of Education website. In some cases, sample tests may be available with graded results. Teachers can used these tools to have students write to a prompt, read other responses to a prompt, critique a response that is not their own or one of a classmate, and compare the responses and grades to their own response.

Accommodations

The same Department of Education website may also have a list of accommodations available to assist students with disabilities in having equal access to the test. The accommodations will not alter the expectations or change the format. The students are given accommodations to make the testing more comfortable, such as modifying the location or administrator. The accommodations may allow the student to type as opposed to handwrite the test. In most cases, the use of a scribe will not be allowed. The student will be expected to respond to the prompt and be subject to the same grading assessments. However, any accommodation that will be necessary for the student to perform to the best of his or her ability, such as a quieter space or assistive technology, needs to be clearly listed in the appropriate section of the student's IEP. These accommodations will need to be clearly defined, allowable, and utilized throughout the student's school year.

GRADE LEVEL EXPECTATIONS

As the student moves through the grade levels, differences in expectations for writing emerge and therefore the interventions will change as well. As discussed earlier in the chapter, in the preprimary and primary grades, students diagnosed with autism will be evaluated for fine motor difficulties. Strengthening exercises will be used and may need carryover in the classroom. Common classroom items may be utilized such as clay for squeezing prior to a hand writing activity. The occupational therapist may recommend the student use a variety of materials to write in and on. Drawing in sand or on sand paper will provide more feedback. Sometimes, the therapists will encourage the student to write on a slanted surface such as a wedge or the side of a binder to reduce the use of the wrist. Using thicker utensils such as markers instead of thin pencils will increase the students' performance. Although the student may have difficulties with handwriting, he or she may be accommodated with oral responses or the use of a receptive format (asking the student to point or circle the correct answer). The student may be introduced to keyboarding and the use of other forms of technology to explore accommodation options in the higher grades.

As the student progresses from about fourth through sixth grade, the demand for written responses increases. Student who are able to work at or near grade level will be expected to produce writing assignments in most subjects. Students will be expected to write multiparagraphed essays with organized and developed ideas and to demonstrate a solid use of most conventions. If fine motor problems are still impacting the student's abilities, the use of assistive technology will need to be emphasized and developed. Steps should be taken to determine the best means of independently in submitting written answers to questions as well as to respond to essay topics. By this age, some occupational therapists may not suggest continuing with handwriting as a goal, given that the nervous system is at or nearing maturity. Many of the students with handwriting difficulties can trace or copy words with adequate legibility; however, they cannot think of ideas, organize sentences, stay on topic, and make this functional writing legible. For this reason, the student may need to find a method that is the most convenient and legible. If keyboarding is the answer, assistive technology may be assigned to the student, and it will be the special education teacher's job to develop a plan of independence with the technology. Also, the special education teacher will need to work with general education teachers to make sure the technology is being utilized efficiently and that the assignments are being addressed.

By junior or senior high school, students will most likely not be working on fine motor or specifically handwriting goals. Hopefully, by this stage, the student has developed a method or system for responding to written questions. Writing will be expected in nearly every class and setting and will need to demonstrate mastery of audience awareness and persuasive reasoning. Writing will be expected to be of varying lengths and show maturity in organization and vocabulary. At this point, students will be expected to demonstrate these skills as opposed to being taught the skills.

PARAPROFESSIONAL

One of the greatest resources for students with autism and their teachers is the paraprofessional. The role of this individual will vary depending on the setting and needs of the student. A self-contained setting may have several instructional assistants providing varying levels of support to students. In such a setting, it may be easier for the teacher to give direction and monitor the paraprofessionals to make sure the individual goals are being met. Most often, the paraprofessional assists the student in a general education setting.

The paraprofessional can be a perfect liaison between the special education teacher, the general education teacher, and the student or small group of students. This instructional assistant can be available to make sure the student is accessing the curriculum, following directions, and interacting appropriately with teachers and peers. The paraprofessional can be available to convey student progress to the special education teacher and work with the general education teacher to make sure the student's goals are being addressed. In some cases, students are assigned a personal assistant, and the paraprofessional and teacher have minimal contact. The case manager for the student may not provide or be able to provide daily feedback or any consistent support to the assistant.

In the best case scenario, the paraprofessional works to develop student independence and social interactions. The role should reflect the individual needs of the student outlined by the IEP team and be clearly defined to the paraprofessional. Often, paraprofessionals may have the notion or may even be told that they are the assistant to the student and are there to help because the student is not capable of performing all of the tasks required. With this idea that the student is not able to meet the demands, the paraprofessional will write the work for the student or work on the project by researching the information and taking the notes for a report, because it would take too long for the student to do it. Before long, and with good intentions, the paraprofessional is doing the entire project while the student sits in proximity. If the paraprofessional is not available for a simple assignment, the student may refuse to work, saying he or she cannot work without his or her aide. The student may regard the assistant as a necessary mother figure, caregiver, or protector (Young & Simpson, 1997) and depend upon his or her presence to work. The paraprofessionals may even be told that they are needed and valuable because when present, the student's work is complete and when not present, the student does not complete assignments. This reinforces the behaviors of both the student and the paraprofessional.

However, the goal is student development and student independence. Unfortunately, a good paraprofessional works to eliminate his or her own position. With writing being one of the most difficult tasks for a majority of students with autism, the development of dependency in this area is likely.

A teacher in a self-contained autistic classroom assigned a project to the students. They were to write a paragraph or two about an animal and make a poster and model of the animal. The two assistants in the classroom, who had worked there for over a year, initially went around to the students and helped them select an animal and then went to the library to get books. The assistants brought back the books and began looking up information. When the students did not start writing right away, the assistants began taking notes and having the students copy the notes. The students looked engaged, but the teacher asked the assistants to let the students look up the information and write their own sentences. The assistants felt there was not enough time for this and that the students were taking too long. The teacher indicated the point was for the students to do as much as they could independently, even if it was not perfect. When the posters needed to be made, the assistants began cutting out all of the pictures. The teacher asked the assistants to let the students do that job. The assistants indicated that the students had difficulty cutting straight lines. The teacher again said that the project was for student work and for students to practice. If they make mistakes, they should reprint the picture and try again. The assistants felt the process was taking too long.

This scenario is very common, and, unfortunately, in some cases, the assistants are not asked to refrain from doing the work. The paraprofessionals are believed to be helping the student because the teacher, the paraprofessional, and maybe even the student have little faith in the student's abilities to perform at the level of his or her peers. Sometimes pressure of a deadline may also cause the paraprofessional to do more than necessary. Simply doing the work for the student and periodically consulting the student for input is easier than directing the student and being patient during the process. The student's work may not be perfect, but it should be as close to an independent effort as possible. Often there is little oversight of a paraprofessional in a regular education classroom setting, and this, coupled with the need to provide training and appropriate feedback, is an ever-growing problem (Giangreco, Smith & Pinckney, 2006).

The teacher and paraprofessional should have a plan for the student's independence. Expectations about the student's performance on assignments should be clear. If the student uses assistive technology, the paraprofessional's job is to make sure the student is using the technology to access the curriculum. If the student is having difficulty and perhaps even refusing to do the work, the paraprofessional should have clear directions from the teacher to manage the behavioral response, as opposed to being overly helpful with the writing assignment itself. The assistant should be helping the student to self-advocate. If the student seems unsure of the directions, rather than jumping in to give suggestions, the paraprofessional should be teaching the student to raise his or her hand and seek clarification. The paraprofessional is a facilitator for the student to develop independence in the classroom.

SUMMARY

Writing is an essential life skill that all students must master in order to communicate thoughts effectively. Even students without developmental difficulties find the writing process difficult. Students with autism are at a greater disadvantage because of their communication, organization, and processing impairments. Students with autism have difficulty with a weak central coherence and cannot always make connections and associations between thoughts. They have TOM issues, which make it difficult for them to take the perspective of another or change tone or vocabulary based on audience. Physically, gross and fine motor problems cause handwriting difficulties.

However, in many circumstances these difficulties may be overcome. Teachers need to make sure assessments are accurate and truly reflect the strengths and weaknesses of the student. Students with autism may not present with typical skill development. Assumptions should not be made about the student's abilities based on performance in one particular area. A whole language and skill assessment will give more information about the student's abilities and limitations.

Students with autism may not be intrinsically motivated to write and may respond to directions with refusals or reluctance. Behavioral interventions with extrinsic rewards may motivate the students to participate. Refusals to write or draw may be sensory based and interventions could be necessary to accommodate tactile defensiveness.

Fine motor problems can be overcome with the use of assistive technology. Concrete and clear directions and assessments must be emphasized. Teachers must determine the impediments to writing as well as the strengths the student exhibits and scaffold the student's skills. Children with autism may not generalize information or techniques. Students can be taught incrementally through the use of familiar formats, choice of topic, clear self assessments, and technology. All interventions and accommodations, including the use of paraprofessionals, should be frequently evaluated for effectiveness. Interventions should be moving the student to independence.

REFERENCES

Agocs, M. M., Burns, M. S., De Ley, L. E., Miller, S. L., & Calhoun, B. M. (2006). FastFor Word language. In R. J. McCauley & M. E. Fey (Eds.), *Treatment of Language Disorders in Children*. Baltimore, MD: Brookes.

American Psychiatric Association (APA). (2000). *Diagnostic and statistical manual of mental disorders* (4th ed., text rev.). Washington, DC: Author.

Baldwin, J. D., & Baldwin, J. I., (2001). *Behavior principles in everyday life.* New Jersey: Prentice-Hall.

Baron-Cohen, S., Leslie, A. M., & Frith, U. (1985). Does the autistic child have a theory of mind? *Cognition, 21,* 37–46.

Berkeley, S. L., Zittel, L. L., Pitney, L. V., & Nichols, S. E. (2001) Locomotor and object control skills of children diagnosed with autism. *Adapted Physical Activity Quarterly, 18,* 405–416.

Braun, L. (2009) Take the pencil out of the process. *Teaching Exceptional Children, 42,* 14–21.

Cascella, P. W., & Colella, C. S. (2004). Knowledge of autism spectrum disorders among Connecticut school speech–language pathologists. *Focus on Autism and Other Developmental Disabilities, 19*(4), 245–253.

Carnahan, C., Mutsi-Rao, S., & Bailey, J. (2009). Promoting active engagement in small group learning: Experiences of students with autism and significant learning needs. *Education and Treatment of Children, 1,* 37–61.

Cooper, J. O., Heron, T. E., Heward, W. L. (2007). *Applied Behavior Analysis.* New Jersey: Pearson.

Diehl, J. J., Bennetto, L., & Young, E. C. (2006). Story recall and narrative coherence of high functioning children with autism spectrum disorders. *Journal of Abnormal Psychology, 34*(1) 87–103.

Edelen-Smith, P. (1995). Eight elements to guide goal determination for IEPs. *Intervention in School & Clinic, 30*(5), 297–302.

Erickson, K. A., Koppenhaver, D. A., & Cunningham, J. W. (2006). Balanced reading intervention and assessment in augmentative communication. In R. J. McCauley & M. E. Fey (Eds.), *Treatment of Language Disorders in Children.* Baltimore, MD: Brookes.

Freeman, S., & Drake, L. (1996). *Teach me language: A manual for children with autism, Asperger's syndrome and related developmental disorders.* Langley, B.C.: SKF Books.

Frith, U. (1989). *Autism: Explaining the enigma.* Oxford: Basil Blackwell.

Fuentes, C. T., Mostofsky, S. H., Bastian, A. J. (2009), Children with autism show specific handwriting impairments. *Neurology, 73,* 1532–1537.

Giangreco, M. F., Smith, C. S., & Pinckney, E. (2006) Addressing the paraprofessional dilemma in an inclusive school: A program description. *Research & Practice for Persons with Severe Disabilities, 31*(3), 215–229.

Grigorenko, E. L., Klin, A., & Volkmar, F. (2003) Hyperlexia: disability or superability? *Journal of Child Pyschology & Psychiatry & Allied Disciplines, 44*(8), 1079–1091.

Heimann, M., Nelson, K. E., Tjus, T., & Gillberg, C. (1995). Increasing reading and communication skills in children with autism through an interactive multimedia computer program. *Journal of Autism and Developmental Disorders, 25*(5), 459–480.

Hoffman, P. R., & Norris, J. A. (2006). Visual strategies to facilitate written language development. In R. J. McCauley & M. E. Fey (Eds.), *Treatment of Language Disorders in Children.* Baltimore, MD: Brookes.

Horner, R. H., Vaughn, B. J., Day, H. M., & Ard, W. R. (1996). The relationship between setting events and problem behavior: Expanding our understanding of behavioral support. In L. K. Koegel, R. L. Koegel, & G. Dunlap (Eds.), *Positive behavioral support: Including people with difficult behavior in the community* (pp. 381–402). Baltimore: Brookes.

Koegel, R. L., & Wilhelm, H. (1973). Selective responding to the components of multiple visual cues. *Journal of Experimental Child Psychology, 15,* 442–453.

Landa, R. J., & Goldberg, M. C. (2005). Language social and executive function in high functioning autism; a continuum of performance. *Journal of Autism and Developmental Disorders, 35*(5), 557–574.

Lewis, B. A., O'Donnell, B., Freebairn, L. A., & Taylor, H. G. (1998). Spoken language and written expression: Interplays of delays. *America Journal of Speech and Language Pathology 7*(3), 77–84.

Leyfer, O. T., Folstein, S. E., Bacalman, S., Davis, N. O., Dinh, E., Morgan, J., et al. (2006). Comorbid psychiatric disorders in children with autism: Interview development and rates of disorders. *Journal of Autism and Developmental Disorders, 36,* 849–861.

Loomis, S. C., & Bourque, M. L. (Eds.). (2001). *National Assessment of Educational Progress Achievement Levels 1992–1998 for Writing.* Washington D.C.: National Assessment Governing Board.

Lytle, R., & Todd, T. (2009) Stress and the student with autism spectrum disorders: Strategies for stress reduction and enhanced learning. *Teaching Exceptional Children, 41*(4), 36–42.

Mace, F. C., Hock, M. L., Lalli, J. S., West, B. J., Belfiore, P., Pinter, E., et al. (1988). Behavioral momentum in the treatment of noncompliance. *Journal of Applied Behavioral Analysis, 21,* 123–141.

Nakahachi, T., Iwase, M., Takahashi, H., Honaga, E., Sekiyama, R., Ukai, S., et al. (2006). Discrepancy of performance among working memory–related tasks in autism spectrum disorders was caused by task characteristics, apart from working memory, which could interfere with task execution. *Psychiatry & Clinical Neurosciences, 60*(3), 312–318.

National Commission on Writing. (2003). *The Neglected "R."* New York: The College Board.

Nelson, N. W., & Van Meter, A. M. (2006). The writing lab approach for building language literacy and communication abilities. In R. J. McCauley & M. E. Fey (Eds.), *Treatment of Language Disorders in Children.* Baltimore, MD: Brookes.

Quill, K. (2000). *Do-watch-listen-say: Social and communication intervention for children with autism.* Baltimore: Brookes.

Rehfeldt, R. A., Dillen, J. E., Ziomek, M. M., & Kowalchuk, R. L. (2007) Assessing relational learning deficits in perspective taking in children with high functioning autism spectrum disorders, *The Psychologcal Record, 57*(1), 23–25.

Reynolds, S., & Lane, S. J. (2008). Diagnostic validity of sensory over-responsivity: A review of the literature and case reports. *Journal of Autism and Developmental Disorders, 38,* 516–529.

Schoen, A. A. (2003). What potential does the applied behavior analysis approach have for the treatment of children with autism. *Journal of Instructional Psychology, 30*(2), 125–131.

Sigman, M., & McGovern, C. W. (2005). Improvement in cognitive and language skills from pre-school to adolescence in autism. *Journal of Autism and Developmental Disorders, 35*(1), 15–24.

Stromer, R., Kimball, J. W., Kinney, E. M., & Taylor, B. A. (2006) Activity schedules, computer technology and teaching children with autism spectrum disorders. *Focus on Autism and Other Developmental Disorders, 21,* 14–24.

Szelag, E., Kowalska, J., Galkowski, T., & Poppel, E. (2004). Temporal processing deficits in high functioning autism. *British Journal of Psychology, 95*(3), 269–285.

Young, B., & Simpson, R. L. (1997). An examination of paraprofessional involvement in supporting inclusion of students with autism. *Focus on Autism and Other Developmental Disabilities, 12*(1), 31–40.

Mathematics: Instructional Considerations and Interventions

K. M. McCoy

Learning styles and behavioral issues characteristic of many individuals with autism present challenges for teaching mathematics. Mathematics is the investigation of quantity, space, relation, structure, and various aspects of pattern and form. Individuals who study math look for patterns and other quantitative dimensions by dealing with numbers or spaces (Devlin, 1996; Steen, 1988). Intact central executive function of the brain, that is, the ability of the brain to organize new information with previously learned knowledge, plays a major factor in understanding mathematics. When developing instructional strategies and interventions for mathematics, core behaviors associated with ASD must enter into the instructional equation.

MATHEMATICS, LEARNING STYLES, AND CORE CHARACTERISTICS

The central executive function of the brain influences math performance through the mechanism of at least three types of memory:

1. Semantic
2. Procedural
3. Visuospatial

Many theories of autism are supported by research suggesting abnormal development of the central executive function of the brain. To the degree that one form of

355

memory is atypical, the other two forms of memory are also impacted. More than one type of math disability can be attributed to problems with memory. Presley, for example, was able to do double digit multiplication with at least 95% accuracy. On his final assessment, his teachers had listed the problems horizontally. Presley got every question incorrect. He did not understand that 25×36 was the same as

$$\begin{array}{r} 25 \\ \times\,36 \\ \hline \end{array}$$

Presley did not understand that to solve the problem, he needed to change the horizontal form to a vertical one; to him, these problems were entirely different. Presley demonstrated problems with visuospatial and procedural memory. *Dyscalculia* is the technical term for neurologically based disabilities affecting learning mathematics for children like Presley. Dyscalculia is associated with

> ➤ trouble reading and writing numbers,
> ➤ problems aligning numbers in order to do calculations,
> ➤ problems performing calculations, and
> ➤ inability to comprehend story problems.

Dyscalculia or learning disabilities in math can be viewed from the perspective of problems with semantic memory, procedural memory and visuospatial memory (Geary, 2000).

Semantic Memory

Semantic memory issues refer to problems retrieving or recalling simple arithmetic facts. Simple arithmetic problems include all problems with correct answers up to 20 (e.g., $4 + 8$, $13 + 6$), in contrast to complex arithmetic problems, which cover more multidigit problems (e.g., $36 + 72$, $125 + 46$). A well-functioning working memory for number facts requires the central executive function of the brain to solve simple arithmetic problems (Deschuyteneer, Vandierendonck, & Muyllaert, 2006; DeStefano & LeFevre, 2004)

Many individuals with autism appear to have problems with executive functions (Frith, 2003) and not surprisingly also have difficulty with accessing and searching long-term memory for simple facts or calculating a correct answer. Problems with semantic memory, for some children with autism, can be accommodated by allowing the use of calculators, fact charts, computers, and counters. By freeing the student from recalling facts, higher level mathematics can be approached.

Procedural Memory

Procedural memory problems are reflected in difficulty understanding or applying mathematical rules. The central executive function of the brain also plays a part in activating procedural and conceptual memory. The executive function of the brain has a part in directing attention to various processes, such as controlling, planning, sequencing, and switching activities. Math processes beyond simple arithmetic are affected, and again many individuals with autism will have processing difficulties in math beyond calculating simple arithmetic problems. Visual prompts or diagrams may assist such students when attempting to calculate complex problems. Figure 12.1 provides an example of a visual diagram or visual support that could be helpful for some students with autism when attempting to solve for prime numbers.

Some individuals with autism may have difficulty linking two previously learned math concepts (Bulgren, Lenz, Deshler, & Schumaker, 1995; Goldman et al., 1997). Lucas, for example, may understand that addition means combining two groups of numerals to get a larger numeral. Lucas may also comprehend that subtraction means taking away, that is, starting with a big group of numerals that becomes smaller as numerals are subtracted. What Lucas does not understand is that a relationship exists between addition and subtraction. Lucas cannot comprehend that if he borrows 7 dollars from his 20 dollar savings account to pay for a movie, he is going to have to add 7 dollars to his 13 dollar base to get back to his original savings, that is, $20 - 7 = 13$ and $13 + 7 = 20$. Lucas does not see the relationship between spending, which reduces his funds, and returning money to his savings, which increases his funds.

Students like Lucas, whose procedural/conceptual knowledge is impaired in some way will have great difficulty dealing with new mathematical problems across a variety of settings (Hudson & Miller, 2006). Their capacity to generalize math information from one situation to another may mean that every time a new problem or math based situation is introduced, they have no connection to their knowledge base and must begin instruction from scratch. Many individuals with autism have

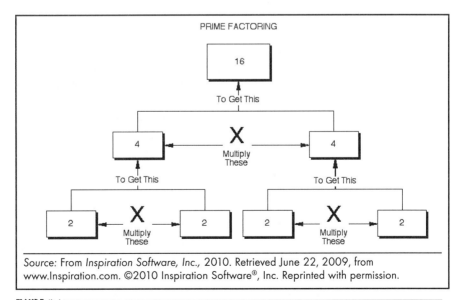

Source: From *Inspiration Software, Inc.,* 2010. Retrieved June 22, 2009, from www.Inspiration.com. ©2010 Inspiration Software®, Inc. Reprinted with permission.

FIGURE 12.1

An example of a visual support for prime factoring.

been characterized as having difficulty applying mathematical concepts to new situations or concepts.

Visuospatial Memory

Visuospatial memory refers to understanding spatially represented numerical information. Diagrams and geometric figures are obvious examples of visuospatial material. Other mathematical symbols which carry meaning also affected by visuospatial memory include operations such as +, &, x, or math symbols like >, <, or %. Numerals too, have visual properties related to shape and length. For example, a three digit numeral has a very different meaning than a four digit number, and the order of numbers also can be affected by visuospatial memory, that is, a 2 in the ones column has much different meaning when located in the hundreds column (Ashcraft, 1996). Problems with visuospatial memory can result in misalignment of columns, place value errors, or issues with geometry. Albert has visuospatial issues. He has serious trouble organizing his work. Problems that should be in nice straight column look like miniature leaning Towers of Pisa that have been randomly placed across the page. Alignment is unknown and unseen in Albert's papers. The ones column might be in the hundreds place or not. Giving students like Albert a blank piece of paper without supports takes away from the content they need to learn. Assistance for Albert's alignment problem arrived in the form of premade grids or tables that organize space for him and subsequently allowed him to concentrate on math concepts.

The relationship between visuospatial skills and poor math performance may be found in a basic inability to imagine a mental number line (Bachot, Gevers, Fias, & Roeyers, 2005). Closely related to visuospatial memory is *spatial–temporal reasoning,* that is, the ability to mentally visualize and manipulate patterns, an important skill necessary for generating and conceptualizing solutions to multistep problems found in engineering, art, games, and everyday life.

Many individuals with autism have issues with the mathematical concepts associated with visuospatial memory. Common classroom activities, such as putting together a jigsaw puzzle, matching numerals to objects, and comparing visual similarities and differences could be problematic. Other issues related to poor visuospatial memory may be related to difficulty keeping columns aligned or visually recognizing place value.

Balance between Inductive and Deductive Thinking

Inductive reasoning is making a conclusion based on a set of observations. When Jeremy observes something that is true many times and then concludes that these observations will always be true in all occurrences, then he is using inductive reasoning. Jeremy, for example, has observed that all numbers that he has seen that end in an even number can be divided by 2. Therefore, he concludes that all even numbers must be devisable by two. Inductive reasoning is very powerful and based on "discovery" which can be inferred, but not always proven.

Deductive reasoning, in contrast, begins with a rule or premise that has already been proven or accepted to be true. Based on that rule, conclusions are made about specific observations. Jeremy's friend Nathan knows the rule that all even numbers can be divided by 2. He discovered the even number 4826 and concludes that 4826 is an even number.

Inductive and deductive reasoning have direct application to how a person learns. With deductive learning, the individual collects a lot of observations and then creates a rule. With deductive learning, the individual learns a rule and matches observations to that rule.

Many individuals with autism who are highly systematic usually learn math concepts best through deductive, sequential, step-by-step approaches. Math learning also requires inductive thinking, visual–spatial, and pattern identification skills. Mathematics for most individuals requires integrating both the deductive and inductive reasoning (Sharma, 1990).

For many individuals with autism, the integration of inductive and deductive reasoning either does not appear to exist or is often not functional. Individuals with autism who tend to be inductive thinkers are most likely going to excel in concepts found in subtraction and division, estimation, fractions accompanied by visual models, and manipulation of spatial relationships and geometric shapes. Instructional methods found to be successful for inductive thinkers are often based in inductive, visual–spatial, and pattern strategies. Individuals with autism who are more deductive in thinking are often successful with lessons that are presented in a direct and step-by-step manner (Marolda & Davidson, 2000).

Jeffery appears to be an inductive thinker. He is frustrated when required to remember details associated with multistep problems. Word problems make little to no sense to Jeffery. In fact using exact mathematical language or being forced to use a single, specified approach when working with mathematics are true challenges for Jeffery. Jeffery's math understanding seems to work best when he is provided visual representations of concepts and is allowed to find his own solutions to problems. Frank, his older brother, is a seriously deductive thinker. Frank becomes extremely agitated if the instruction is not step-by-step and very articulate. Frank needs precision, rules, and order. Frank prefers being told exactly how to compute, calculate, or problem-solve in any math situation.

The imbalance between deductive and inductive reasoning sometimes results in highly honed splinter skills. Some students can independently solve high-level math problems. Jason, for example, can add and subtract mixed numbers with unlike denominators in his head. He can solve linear equations in a similar manner, but Jason cannot subtract ten minus one without writing this simple computation. Jason has not developed a big picture of the relationships that exist in various aspects of mathematics.

Characteristics

The highly structured rule-based parameters of mathematics often appeal to individuals who are themselves highly structured or systematic. Many individuals with

ASD have been noted both for academic strengths in mathematics and need for systematization. Other individuals have displayed impressive abilities for identifying mathematical patterns.

Taking into account the complex nature of mathematics, instruction for individuals with autism must include the level and degree of involvement associated with the three core characteristics of

1. disorders in social behavior,
2. abnormal verbal and nonverbal communication, and
3. limited interests and in some instances repetitive behaviors.

Because autism falls on a spectrum, teachers will need to be highly flexible in their thinking and ability to design math lessons based on the individual characteristics of the student. Characteristics vary widely by degree and are also influenced by coexisting disabilities.

The notion of a group lessons, for example, may not be feasible for some children and youth with autism, whereas for other individuals who fall on the spectrum, group lessons will be perfectly appropriate. Modifying instructional environments and mathematics curricula can be highly complex and creative for some students and require little to no instructional changes for other students found on the autism spectrum.

In planning mathematics instruction for students with autism, the developmental age and expected instructional level must be considered in relationship to characteristics particular to the individual. Three factors that should be considered when designing math instruction for individuals with autism are the student's particular responses to

1. the instructional setting,
2. social context, and
3. activities.

INSTRUCTIONAL SETTING

The instructional setting takes into account how the child's needs interface with variables in the classroom or home. Some important factors to consider for each child when designing a math lesson are (Quill, 2000)

➤ sensory sensitivities,
➤ anxiety,
➤ challenging behaviors,
➤ attention, and
➤ organization.

Sensory Sensitivities

Many children with autism are hypersensitive to sensory input (e.g., a loud classroom, the ticking of a clock, the sounds from the playground, or the quiet buzz of a fluorescent light). To provide a setting in which the child is relaxed, teachers must eliminate or reduce as much as possible distracters for the particular child. If Damian, for example, becomes upset every time he hears the school furnace turn on, a good time for math instruction would be between furnace start-ups. This accommodation seems obvious, but such sensitivities can be masked by other more dramatic behaviors. What if each time a math lesson is presented, Damian has a complete meltdown? The most immediate, and incorrect, assumption might be that Damian does not like math. For some learners the "I don't like math!" assumption could be correct, but for children like Damian, the teacher must look beyond the obvious to determine whether other mitigating factors are present in the environment that could be contributing to the inappropriate behavior which coincidentally happens to be during math time. Children with autism teach teachers to analyze instructional situations in ways that are usually not necessary for instruction of typical learners.

Anxiety

An anxious child is typically one who blocks new learning. Physical symptoms of anxiety (e. g., sweating, trembling, shaking, difficulty breathing or swallowing) signals that the child is feeling apprehension and fear. The source of the anxiety needs to be identified and reduced or eliminated before math or any other kind of positive learning can occur. Manipulatives (e.g., geoboards, Base 10 Blocks, Cuisenaire rods, geometric blocks, counters), the staples of math instruction for making abstract concepts concrete could be sources of anxiety for some children with autism.

If certain colors, odors, or shapes create apprehension, situations involving these events should be avoided during math (and other) instructional times. Donald, for example, cannot tolerate green cubes. Using green cubes as manipulatives would be counterproductive during a math lesson. Donald will break out in a cold sweat whenever he hears the clicking or clattering sounds like those often made when dice are tossed or plastic counting tiles or chips are placed on a desk. His breathing becomes labored and his eyes begin to blink rapidly. Sounds created when using many of the common hard plastic manipulatives found in math instruction raise Donald's anxiety to such a level that delivering a math lesson with these manipulatives would be futile.

A better choice of manipulatives for Donald would be relatively soundless, perhaps created from materials made from rubber, sponge, or foam avoiding any material that clicks, is cubed shaped, or green. Teachers need not throw out the favorite hard plastic manipulatives but instead reduce the offending *clicking* and *clacking* by providing a soft surface, like a sheet of felt, on the student's desktop or table when using tried and true favorites. The problem was not in the manipulative, but rather in the sensation created through use and the sensitivity of the student.

Challenging behaviors

Challenging behaviors are described in terms of frequency, intensity, and/or duration of a behavior that could result in physical harm to self or others and can seriously limit or delay social interactions. Challenging behaviors can include, but are not limited to verbal and physical aggression, self-injurious behavior, and noninjurious stereotyped behaviors. Under certain circumstances, Neil has been shown to exhibit challenging behaviors. Neil is almost always ready to go on the attack without obvious provocation, slapping the person next to him, spitting, or using rude language.

Neil, on the other hand, becomes the picture of decorum when using a computer for just about any activity. For Neil, challenging behaviors can be reduced when instructional conditions that are incompatible with his challenging behaviors are introduced. When Neil is working on the computer, his opportunities for slapping, spitting, and using rude language are significantly reduced. Math instruction for Neil is best presented via a computer, which does not provoke unruly behaviors and permits him to concentrate on the computer generated lessons.

Selective Attention

Selective attention is the cognitive process of selectively concentrating on one aspect of the environment while ignoring other persons, places, or events in that same environment. Selective attention involves focusing on a particular awareness either by sight, sound, or mind while simultaneously blocking out or ignoring other available information. Many children with autism have been characterized as being overselective in attention to details while ignoring important or critical information.

John Elder Robinson, a self-proclaimed Aspergian and noted author, described how, when looking at a person, his attention was drawn to the reflection in the person's eyes. This overselectivty to the reflection was so great that Robinson could not concentrate on the words the person was speaking. Language was incomprehensible until he turned away or looked beyond the person's face (2007).

Selective attention can also interfere with the ability to problem-solve in multiple ways. Some children with autism are "fixed" on the attention to routine. If a routine is interrupted, some learners cannot function and may either act out or withdraw. Until William hit third grade, he was always considered a model student, especially in the area of math. He was faster and more accurate than any of his classmates in solving any algorithm related to whole numbers. William's mathematical world came crashing down on the day his teacher showed him an alternate method for computing long division.

William became noticeably upset with this new process. He absolutely refused to try this different approach and became very angry and frustrated to the point of tears. This lack of fluidity in thinking prompted his teacher to ask William to solve a story problem unrelated to long division. William could produce the words of the story problem verbatim and solve the problem. When the words for the same problem were ordered in another way, William was at a loss. When William was asked to restate the problem in his own words, he continued to use a verbatim explanation. William could not alter his way of viewing the problem.

Math lessons for William would end abruptly if his routine or his way of solving a problem was interrupted. For children like William, math teachers would be wise to allow them to find their own systems rather than to impose a more or less elegant algorithm as an alternative.

Organization

Many articles and research support the idea that most learners acquire a great deal of information through a Gestalt process. That is, learners tend to organize and store information as a whole. For example, many individuals with autism focus on facial features but cannot find these same features when matching them on another face (de Gelder, Teunisse, & Benson, 1997; Ellis & Leafhead, 1996). In other words and wildly oversimplified, the whole is greater than the sum of its parts for typical learners, but for many individuals with autism no whole face exists, only the parts.

The overselectivity principle can be seen with Rich and his ability to work with the physical shapes of numbers. Rich, appears to focus only on the upper right hand corner single digit numbers. For the most part, this highly selective visual approach does not interfere with number manipulation, as long as the numbers shapes are distinctive in the upper right hand corners. When typical type fonts are used to create numbers, Rich has serious problems with 0, 3, 8, and 9. These numerals are identical in the upper right hand corner. He has no identification issues with 4, 5, and 6 and usually can distinguish between 1 and 7. The numeral identification accommodation for Rich is found in color-coding the numerals. His code is blue for 0, green for 3, red for 8, and purple for 9. As long as the color-coded numerals are used, Rich's visual overselectivity is no longer and issue during math time.

For some individuals with autism, a fixation with a part of the pattern in the big picture leads the learner away from understanding the whole piece; learning is fragmented (Bosnan, Scott, Fox, & Pye, 2004). Consider the case of Greg. Greg, a high school sophomore, has memorized every theorem in his geometry text, but he is unable to calculate the area of a triangle or the perimeter of a square. Seven-year-old Dennis becomes so absorbed in physically lining up counting sticks that he cannot verbally count past 3. Math instruction for Dennis must take into account his obsession with lining up objects and see this behavior as an opportunity to create a positive learning experience.

Another type of overselectivity can be associated with place. Nine-year-old Paul had linked regrouping with the location of the piano. Paul appeared to have a firm grasp of regrouping until the day the janitor moved the piano from the left side of the room to the right side. Paul mysteriously could no longer regroup. Paul had learned that he should regroup his numbers toward the direction of the piano. Once the piano was moved, Paul continued to use the piano position as a prompt, but unfortunately the prompt was now in the wrong position for regrouping. Paul had seemingly "forgotten" how to regroup.

INSTRUCTIONAL SOCIAL CONTEXT

"To work in a group setting or not to work in a group setting?" that is the question. The answer is determined, in part, by the objectives for the student. If the objective is to have the student learn math, then the value of group work must be weighed against the need for learning math. Darius is not a team player. As is fairly typical of many individuals with autism, Darius prefers the company of an adult. He finds his peers to be annoying at best and threatening at worst. Darius works well with his math teacher and is currently a solid B student in his advanced calculus class.

When Darius first entered the class, he received instruction in a small group setting. Initially, Darius appeared very passive and did not engage in any social interactions with his peers. In fact, Darius did not engage in any interaction with his math lessons either. Within 3 weeks of class attendance, Darius began displaying panic responses through ritualized rocking and gaze avoidance.

Time for a change in social context. Darius remained in the class, but now his instruction was delivered one-on-one by his math teacher. Darius no longer was required to work in the social context of a group. His math skills soared, and his panic attacks disappeared.

Brad, in contrast to Darius, loved being in a group setting. His hand was always the first one raised; he blurted out answers over those of his peers and was constantly attempting to be a "one man math show." Brad's math skills were very good, but his presence was truly disruptive to the learning of his peers. Brad's ability to learn math needed no particular intervention. Brad's autism did not affect his ability to learn math; he needed no accommodations to learn math. Brad did need intervention for learning how to participate in a group.

The decision to learn math in a group setting or one-on-one format should also be made in consideration of the learner's language skills. Many individuals with autism are quite literal. The more literal the learner, the greater the need for the student to work closely with a teacher who can rephrase information in case of a language glitch. John, for example, a fifth grade student, was learning standard versus expanded form in math. The example was to covert the standard number 247 to 200 + 40 + 7. John, who is at grade level in math, was not clear about the directions. After a number of examples and probing, his teacher was confident he was ready to try the conversion. She gave John the number 654 and asked him to write this number in expanded form. Instead of the expected response 600 + 50 + 4, John wrote the phrase "this number in expanded form."

INSTRUCTIONAL FACTORS

Instruction is composed of many interrelated factors, most of which revolve around the learner's receptivity to learning. The learner has to want to learn, that is, become engaged enough with the concept to remember and relate the new information to previously learned knowledge. Many children with autism have their own learning agenda, which may or may not coincide with the curriculum. The teacher's role is to create situations in which the new knowledge has personal relevance to the learner. How the teacher builds on the student's interests to a large degree will determine the success of the instruction. Many factors, such as teacher skill in adapting to the students personal learning preferences, ability to take into account the learner's involvement with autism, as well as the teacher's understanding of content are complex and interrelated instructional factors.

Motivation

Motivational factors for many individuals with autism will not be the same as those found for more typically developing learners. Acquisition and retention of math skills will require positive use of the learner's interests and skills. What constitutes an "M & M" for a student with autism could be very different from the reinforcers typically used with children who are normal. A smile, a positive phrase, sticker, or good grade is highly motivating for most children. For some children with autism, these common motivators are applicable. For other children and youth with autism, the smile, positive phrase, sticker, or good grade has no personal meaning and therefore will not be motivating. In addition, for some individuals with autism, what is motivating may change overtime to reflect changes in interests experienced by most typically developing students. Between preschool and fifth grade, Dan's universe was filled with dinosaurs. Somewhere in mid-sixth grade, dinosaurs became extinct in Dan's world and were replaced by a fascination with the Beatles. Counting with dinosaurs gave way to problem solving algorithms involving the interests of the Fab Four. Treading sensitively into the world of the individual with autism is the first instructional step in learning how to provide instructional motivation.

The nature of mathematics can either be very motivational or extremely discouraging for most individuals with autism. The systematic nature of math is appealing to many individuals with autism, but rigidity of thinking can stifle mathematical growth, which in turn can complicate the student's life. Two representative areas of mathematics that are impacted in individuals with autism are time and money.

Time and Money

Mastery of practical aspects of math related to time and money is important in raising the quality of life and developing independence. Time and money management skills are lifelong (e.g., using a calendar to remember important dates, balancing a checking account, figuring percentages on interest for credit cards). The systematic and mechanical aspects of money and time can be highly motivating to some individuals with autism, for other individuals with autism the very same mechanics can be frustrating. *Elapsed time* and *how much time is needed* are difficult concepts for many children with autism to understand, much less calculate.

The elegance of the monetary system can be very appealing to those individuals who are highly systematic and enjoy identifying and creating patterns. Money equivalents, however, can be problematic if the learner has difficulty with multiple combinations of coins being comparable. Jack loves to manipulate nickels and quarters. When Jack is asked to make change, his responses are perfect until he needs to use pennies or dimes. Without his nickels and quarters, Jack simply cannot conceive that any issue related to money can be solved. No amount of cajoling has been able to convince Jack that two nickels are equivalent to one dime or that a quarter can be the same as two dimes and five pennies.

Similar equivalency issues can be found with time telling. The same time can be expressed in different ways (e.g., 2:45 is the same as 15 minutes to 3:00 or a quarter to 3:00). For those learners who have focused on only one way to express time, social issues can arise. Carter is never late for appointments on the hour or half hour, but for any other stated time, like 2:25 or 9:15, his promptness is highly variable.

Initially simple judgments might suggest that Carter is looking for attention, does not care, is resistant to authority, and so on. Upon closer inspection, the problem is based in the language of the sender and the understanding of the receiver. If the principal asks Carter to report to his teacher at *twenty to ten*, Carter would have no idea what specific time *twenty to ten* means, although he may have a global notion that the message has to do with 10 o'clock. On the other hand, had the principal phrased the time as 10:20, Carter would have made his appearance promptly. Carter can only comprehend one way to tell time.

Although the concepts involved in time and money are both systematic, they can also involve the need for experiences based on social connections. Most children and youth with autism are characterized as having disorders in social behavior and communication: they do not make social connections very well. Concepts of time and money, when involving social situations, can be very difficult for individuals with autism.

Money, technically, is a social medium, as is time. No one would need to think about time or money if isolated on an island, but this Robinson Caruso experience is fiction. The fact is that individuals with autism, although in many cases socially isolated, must deal with others when applying concepts associated with money and time. Money usually requires a social exchange; for example, when shopping at the store, buying clothes at the mall, or purchasing food at a restaurant. When an individual with autism prefers avoiding social contacts, the motivational factors usually associated with spending power are highly diminished.

Comprehending time can also be problematic for many individuals with autism. Time is an abstract concept and is often quantified by social conventions, like hurrying to be on time to meet expectations or approval of others or awareness of time passing while waiting for social engagements. If social engagements are not motivating, then developing an awareness of time may not be motivating either.

Intense interests

Intense interests can be used as opportunities to motivate students with autism. Motivational factors for many individuals with autism will not be the same as those found for more typically developing learners. Acquisition of skills will require positive use of the learner's interests. For those students whose BFF is the computer, many opportunities are available for teaching practical math skills. Amazon.com and online banking and bill payments, among other activities, are tailor made for teaching math life skills to some individuals with autism.

Technology also can play a major role in motivating a student to learn to tell time. Many children will learn to tell time if that skill is linked to finding the time for a favorite television show. Garth discovered the value in learning to tell time when he was making a transition from leaving the classroom to entering the computer center. Garth preferred being in the computer center to spending time in his classroom. He was motivated to learn to tell the time when he was given the responsibility of making the transition. This first step for Garth was the beginning of his ability and motivation to find value in learning to tell time.

Math Games

Math games can be highly motivating or can be a great source of discomfort to many children with autism. Math games, especially those that incorporate a student's intense interests, work very well for some children with autism. Kei is fascinated by cars. He especially loves Mazdas. Kei is not particularly fond of probability. When information using probability related content is incorporated into math games involving Mazdas, Kei is ready to engage in learning. Last week he calculated the mean, median, and mode for finding the number of miles to the gallon a Mazda must use when traveling to Phoenix from Las Vegas. The objective of his "game" was to determine whether the Mazda was more cost effective than his parent's Buick LaSabre. In order to play this game, Kei was also required to learn how to read a map. Normally Kei would have resisted visualizing the imaginary trip and would have missed out on some important spatial thinking opportunities, but the game format motivated him to go in math spaces where he had never gone before.

If Kei's Mazda themed game had involved more than a passing interaction with his classmates, the power of the Mazda may not have been strong enough. Kei, unlike most children his age, does not care for much social interaction. Although Kei was "playing" his game with another student, for all practical purposes, he had very little communication with his peer. For children like Kei, math games requiring a lot of social interaction, cooperation, and communication in small or large groups would not be beneficial for learning.

MATHEMATICS AND LANGUAGE

"I have heard many People say, 'Give me the Ideas. It is no matter what Words you put them into.'"
[To this he replies,] "Ideas cannot be given but in their minutely Appropriate Words."

William Blake

As so eloquently stated by William Blake, thoughts are inextricably connected to language. Language is considered to be a systematic communication process through which ideas or feelings are communicated through meaningful signs, sounds, gestures, or symbols. Languages vary from culture to culture and for specific fields of knowledge.

Terminology

Mathematics, for example, has specific vernacular and specialized word usage, which in many instances is much different from daily language (Adams, 2003; Donoghue, 2001; Hersh, 1997). Definitions and terms often have meanings that are different from or overlapping with language used in day-to-day communication. For example, consider the word "point." In everyday usage, this word has numerous meanings although in geometry *point* refers to a specific location in space. The language of math is also filled with homonyms; for example, *plane* as a surface and *plane* as a flying machine and *plain* as in unadorned, or *sum* as a group and *some* as an indicator of number. To understand the language of mathematics, students have to constantly consider context, acknowledge the necessity of general language terms, and accurately apply the specific mathematics vocabulary (Adams & Lowery, 2007).

The language of mathematics can be incredibly vague in some instances, for example, *a number of puppies had white tails*. How many puppies does a number represent? On the other hand, mathematics language can be highly precise to the point of creating discomfort because of a literal rigor that can be exasperatingly annoying for nonmathematicians. Consider the meaning of *equal* and *equivalent*. Equal means *exactly the same* and equivalent means *has the same value*. Teachers often let students say "7 + 3 equal 10, but for mathematical correctness, teachers should be teaching "7 + 3 is equivalent to 10."

For most teachers and students the difference between *equal* and *equivalent* would not make much difference when computing or comprehending the concept of a problem. For some mathematicians and some individuals with autism, the incorrect usage of *equal* and *equivalent* could be the equivalent of a mathematical tsunami. Teachers need to help their students navigate between the extremes of precision and vagueness and must check all definitions and descriptions to be certain of their student's understanding of the vocabulary.

Formulas

Formulas are double edged mathematical swords for many individuals with autism. Some students will be thrilled with the precise expression of thoughts or concepts, clearly stated with straightforward elegance, squelching any possibility for interpretation. In solving for the unknown integer X in an equation like $4x^2 + 3x = 10$, the formula for some individuals with autism can be likened to following a recipe for baking chocolate cookies. The formula, just like the recipe, provides exact steps and rules. Follow the formula and the unknown quantity is revealed. Follow the formula, solve the problem.

The other edge of the sword, however, is that mathematical formulas can present a series of traps associated with core issues characteristic of autism. For some students with autism, changing the order of the formula will result in a seriously burned cookie. The formula $10 = 4x^2 + 3x$ could be viewed as an entirely different problem with a completely dissimilar set of rules because of the the slightest modification in format. Even the least change in format could throw off some students with autism in their ability to use the formula; for example, employing letters other than X, using upper case rather than lower case letters, or varying where the squared quantity appears in the order of the mathematical phrase.

Differences in deductive and inductive learning styles would also impact how the delivery of the lesson would need to be modified. For students whose style is predominantly deductive, the focus on formulas as a step-by-step process may be quite effective in a teacher led presentation. For learners whose style is predominantly inductive, opportunities to create a formula might be a more effective approach in a student centered format. In addition, teachers of students with autism must also account for the student's ability to use everyday language and the language of mathematics. In order to develop appropriate mathematical lessons, teachers need to account for the degree and types of language skills the student with autism utilizes.

Expressive and Receptive language

Expressive and receptive language skills impact how a math lesson can be delivered. See Chapter 2 for a detailed discussion of expressive and receptive language skills among children with autism. Expressive language refers to how a student demonstrates knowledge to others, either verbally, in writing, or any by other means of conveying information. Many individuals with autism who are nonverbal use computers or visual support systems involving pictures or symbols to convey their thoughts to others. Keith could never use his voice to recite his times tables, but he can point to the correct responses. Jamey uses voice output software to speak for him when participating in discussions during math class.

Receptive language refers to how a person receives or understands the message others are sending. Presenting information primarily through lecture format is not likely to result in successful instruction for students with receptive language impairments. For many individuals with autism, the spoken word moves too quickly to be processed. Zack cannot follow even the simplest directions. For Zack, words are streams of sounds that can come and go too quickly for him to process and understand. For children like Zack, visual supports are important tools to help them understand the math concepts in any given lesson.

Many children with ASD have strong visual skills. Visual strengths can be capitalized on during math lessons by using visual supports. Visual supports are images or representations that are visual and permanent in nature. A number card with object correspondence is a good example of a visual support in math. Figure 12.2 is a visual support for the vocabulary term *decimal*. Other forms of visual supports include real objects, picture symbols, and photographs. Blackboards, whiteboards, and overhead

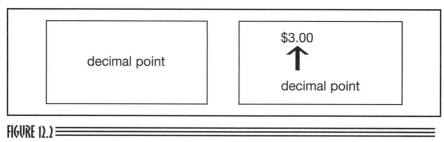

FIGURE 12.2
Visual support for vocabulary term

projectors can be use to provide visual supports, but the information conveyed typically is not permanent and can also be affected by how long the information is posted or available to the student.

Visual supports need not be complex or difficult to create. Ms. Horvath used the science boards for science fairs to make visuals for the students when she taught pre-algebra. When the class would learn a new concept, Ms. Horvath would put the rule or example on the science board so the students could use it to help them throughout the year.

One visual support that can be helpful in teaching individuals with autism math problems that have multiple steps is literally a step-by-step listing modeling a particular class of problems to be solved. For other students with autism, illustrating story problems prior to attempting associated calculations can be very helpful. Whenever feasible, the student should be the creator of the illustration, but for some children with autism, the teacher may need to provide the visual image.

Story Problems and Language

Story problems or word problems are any mathematics exercise presented as a real or imagined situation explained in words. Four cognitive skills associated with analyzing story problems are the ability to

1. establish main ideas and important details,
2. utilize mathematical words and phrases,
3. problem solve, and
4. look for meaning.

The extent to which students can use these strategies is a direct reflection of their ability to work through story problems. Story problems hold many pitfalls for most math learners but even deeper and more challenging issues for individuals with autism.

Contextualization and Imagination

Story problems require contextualization and imagination, two skills that are often atypical for individuals with autism. Context and imagination are strongly influenced by language skills. Not only is the context of the word meaningful but so also is the perspective of the child's world.

Story problems require the solver to analyze and relate to the context of the situation, that is, to apply and integrate real-world knowledge to the solution (Chapman, 2006; National Council of Teachers of Mathematics [NCTM], 2000). The "real world" for some individuals with autism may not translate to the same "real world" experienced by learners who are typical. To utilize the real life experiences of any student, but particularly a child with autism, is to identify experiences to which the student relates and whenever possible personalize the situation (Barwell, 2003).

Literal Comprehension

A second serious and related issue faced by individuals with autism is the tendency to be highly literal. Arthur, for example, was involved in a game focusing on probability. He was given a problem about the likelihood of a spinner landing on a certain color unevenly distributed around the spinner. The question showed a table of previous spins and the number of time each color came up. Blue had the most, then red, green, and last yellow. The question was, "If you were to play the game, which color are you more likely to choose?" Arthur said, "Green,. It's my favorite color."

Stephen also came from his own literal perspective when dealing with a word problem involving fractions. Ms. Soto, Stephen's teacher, knew that he loved pizza and she could get his attention if pizza was mentioned. One day, Stephen was working on fractions in a small group. Ms Soto asked him, "If someone brought in a pizza to share with the group and divided the pizza evenly among the students at the table, how many pieces would he need? Stephen replied, that depends if it is pepperoni or not. As the Red Queen from *Through the Looking Glass* would say, "Sometimes it takes all the running you can do to stay in the same place!"

Many individuals like Arthur and Stephen tend to interpret language based information, like story problems, literally, suggesting a disability in flexibility of thought (Happe & Frith, 2006; Osonoff & Miller, 1996). Planning and flexibility are necessary when using models to plan and devise alternative ways to achieve solutions to problems. The ability to plan and be flexible in thinking is often minimal, if it exists at all, for some individuals with autism. Table 12.1 presents two frameworks for general problem-solving with word problems that have been used successfully with children at risk for mathematics failure, but if used with children with autism must take into account the individual language needs and particular behavioral idiosyncrasies of each individual with autism.

Solving mathematical word problems requires the learner to translate linguistic and numerical information into a reasoned, integrated description (Montague, 2002). To develop understanding, teachers will need to help students with autism put the word problem in their own words whenever possible. If the student is nonverbal or does not have verbal language skills sufficient for paraphrasing, other representational forms can be used. In place of or in addition to verbal paraphrasing, students with autism may be able to use three dimensional manipulatives or draw a schematic

TABLE 12.1

General Problem-Solving Steps Employed in the SBI and GSI Conditions

Schema-based instruction (SBI)	General strategy instruction (GSI)
➤ Read to understand	➤ Read to understand
➤ Identify the problem type and use the schema	➤ Draw a picture to represent the problem diagram to represent the problem
➤ Transform the diagram to a math sentence and solve the problem	➤ Solve the problem
➤ Look back to check	➤ Look back to check

Source: from "Effects of Mathematical Word Problem–Solving Instruction on Middle School Students with Learning Problems," by Y. P. Xin, A.K. Jitendra, & A. Deatline-Buchman, 2007, The Journal of Special Education, 39, p. 184). Reprinted with permission.

representation on paper, computer, or whatever medium is preferred to demonstrate their understanding of the story problem (Jitendra, DiPipi, & Perron-Jones, 2002). Problem solving routines typically incorporate (Montague, 2002)

➤ reading the problem for insight and comprehension,
➤ paraphrasing and visualizing the problem or representing the problem,
➤ developing a premise or solution plan,
➤ guesstimating the answer, and
➤ computing and checking the problem for correctness.

Word problems involve constructing mental models of the problems to be answered. The creation of some sort of concrete image may compensate or assist in utilizing a mental model related to verbal problems. (Kyttälä & Lehto, 2008).

Synonymous phrases

When solving story problems, students are also faced with the challenge of understanding vocabulary and phrases that are synonymous. Phrases that are used interchangeably could create serious confusion for some children with autism, for example, *how much do they have together, how many do they have in all, what is the total cost.* Jaime simply cannot mentally shift from one synonymous phrase to another. His teacher made a visual supports math dictionary for describing these phrases. Jaime's format was simplified in format. Each phrase was listed horizontally and linked by an equal sign. The implied operation was also visually presented with the mathematical symbol. An entry in Jaime's dictionary looks like this:

Addition (+) *how much do they have together =*
how many do they have in all = what is the total cost

Jaime's math dictionary had entries for the four basic operations of addition, subtraction, multiplication, and division.

Billy also has problems with synonyms, but he needs more direction than a visual supports math dictionary for describing phrases that have the same meaning. To ensure that Billy understands his assigned word problems, his teacher reads the problem and simultaneously presents the information on the overhead. If that visual does not work, his teacher then goes to a more intense accommodation. She reads the problems with Billy and uses the whiteboard; inserts pictures from Google.com using Billy's favorite topic, the planets, to create a picture sentence; and asks him to explain which computation needs to be done.

INTERVENTIONS

Decision-making policies for determining the "best" instructional interventions for all children with autism do not exist (National Research Council [NRC], 2001). Given that autism is a spectrum disorder, this finding should neither be alarming, surprising, nor unanticipated. Additionally, no single approach is more effective than another, although a lot of research evidence supports a variety of approaches for individual students (Dunlap & Fox, 2002; Prizant & Wetherby, 1998).

The match between students with particular issues in autism and a definitive instructional approach in mathematics or any other area has yet to emerge, and improvement in one challenging area does not necessarily improve any coexisting problems (NRC, 2001). Ruben responds very well to math instruction when he is provided lessons through a video model. Ruben returns to portions of the lesson over and over again until he is satisfied that he can move on in the lesson. Video modeling works for Ruben in the area of mathematics, especially geometry, but this same approach is an utter failure with Tony. Tony learns math best with hands-on material, such as counting sticks and bead frames. The fact that effective instructional techniques for Ruben and Tony have been discovered for math instruction has in no way altered the occurrence of Ruben's lip smacking and mouth popping or Tony's hypersensitivity to loud high pitched sounds, acrid odors, and florescent lights.

The search for the one definitive holy grail of instructional interventions for individuals with autism is about as real as Camelot. No one definitive person with autism exists, and accordingly no one approach is ever likely to meet the mathematics needs all individuals who fall under ASD. Regardless of the intervention, learning differences more likely are more intense in younger children or lower functioning individuals.

The good news, however, is that several essential components of effective practices for individuals with autism have emerged to guide instructional decision making for most content areas (Iovannone, Dunlap, Huber, & Kincaid, 2003). Although not all practices will be effective with all students and some practices may be more appropriate with students of different developmental ages, teachers can design instruction within three suggested parameters:

1. Individualization
2. Structured and systematic teaching plans
3. Well thought-out and methodical classroom organization

Adjustments are made according to individual needs. The three practices listed in Table 12.1 are as applicable to mathematics as any other content area and are focused on instructional delivery of academic material.

Teachers, interventionists, and other service providers should appreciate the opportunity to incorporate a variety of instructional strategies within the suggested parameters of individualization, structured and systematic teaching plans, and classroom organization. Through constant monitoring, the effectiveness of the intervention or strategy can be evaluated and data-based decisions can drive instructional design.

Many strategies have been developed to help children with typical development learn mathematics. Mathematics instruction in school is most often presented in verbal, pictorial, or mathematical symbolic forms or some arrangement of the three formats (Chapman, 2006).

Most math strategies have focused on approaches that are applicable to normally developing learners. Few strategies for instructing mathematics have been specifically designed for children with autism. With a little experimentation, consideration of the core deficits associated with autism, and a lot of data collection, the value of most math strategies can be evaluated for effectiveness and efficiency for individual children with autism. Three commonly used interventions to facilitate students' ability to remember mathematics concepts are

1. mnemonics,
2. exemplars and nonexemplars, and
3. drill and practice.

Mnemonics

Mnemonics are mental or visual supports or codes, like formulas or rhymes, that help learners remember facts, steps involved in a complex concept, or exceptions to rules. Three examples of math mnemonics (Math Mnemonics, n.d.) that use a code, a rule, and a rhyme, respectively, are the following:

How to SOLVE a Word Problem

➤ Study the problem.
➤ Organize the facts.

➤ Line up the plan.
➤ Verify the plan with computation.
➤ Examine the answer.

When Multiplying by 9...
the digits of the answers always add up to nine.
For example, $2 \times 9 = 18$ $(1 + 8 = 9)$; $3 \times 9 = 27$ $(2 + 7 = 9)$ and so on.

Find the Area and Circumference of a Circle.
Tweedle-dee-dum and Tweedle-dee-dee,
Around the circle is pi times d,
But if the area is declared,
Think of the formula pi r squared.

One of the most celebrated of the entire math mnemonics in pre-algebra used to help students recall the order of operations is PEMDAS

1. **Parentheses** (and other symbols of inclusion)
2. **Exponents**
3. **Multiplication** and **Division**, in order from left to right
4. **Addition** and **Subtraction**, in order from left to right

The first letters of these operations, PEMDAS, creates the famous mathematical mnemonic: Please Excuse My Dear Aunt Sally.

Use of mnemonics must always be considered in relation to the impact of the core deficits characterizing individuals with autism. Mnemonics can be very helpful for some individuals with autism but create unnecessary stress or distraction for other learners with autism. How disorders in social behavior, abnormal verbal and nonverbal communication, and limited interests interact with a particular mnemonic may be very different for one student with autism than for another. Librado, for example, engages in repetitive verbal behaviors. He knows every jingle heard on TV related to the sales of breakfast cereal. On first thought, Librado seems like a good candidate for using rhyming mnemonics. On second thought, Librado just likes to rhyme. He does not appear to attach meaning to his rhymes, and he only likes rhymes dealing with cereal. Could Librado's behaviors be used to create a rhyming mnemonic related to cereal that he will then apply to solving a mathematics problem?

Another case in point is Dale. Dale seems to enjoy following mathematical formulas. His basic problem is that he cannot remember any of the formulas. What strategy would be best for Dale, the use of a formula like PEMDAS or a visual model? Would the memorization of PEMDAS serve as a prompt for Dale, or would PEMDAS be one more stressor for his already inefficient memory skills? The decision to use a mnemonic is partly decided through teacher observation and the learner's idiosyncrasies. The decision to continue using a particular mnemonic or to try a different type of mnemonic is based on the documented progress of the student.

Exemplars and Nonexemplars

Exemplars and nonexemplars are a more sophisticated way to say examples and nonexamples. An exemplar is a model to be imitated and the reverse is true of nonexemplar, the example is not to be used. Examples are used to show the learner what the expected processes and outcome should be. When teaching the concept of a triangle, for example, plastic shapes or pictures can be shown. The model of the triangle is shown as the teacher simultaneously says the word "triangle." Students can repeat the word each time the triangle shape appears. A nonexample of a triangle would be any other shape, like a square, circle, silhouette of a pear, and the like. Exemplars and nonexemplars can be used for any level of mathematics instruction, from the very basic number–object correspondence to advance calculus and beyond. Using strategies involving exemplars and nonexemplars is considered an excellent inductive learning approach (Miller & Hudson, 2006).

Use of exemplars and nonexemplars requires categorization. Categorization reduces memory demands, permitting individuals to focus on relevant details to the exclusion of irrelevant features. Problems with categorization can result in poor organizational skills, resulting in inappropriate behaviors or fatigue, overtaxing the ability to learn (Gastgeb, Strauss, & Minshew, 2006). Even very early in life, many learners with autism appear to differ from learners who develop typically in their ability to categorize.

Individuals with autism seem able to categorize simple or rule based tasks but experience difficulty with abstract or complex categorization (Klinger & Dawson, 2001; Minshew, Meyer, & Goldstein, 2002; Plaisted, 2000). In addition, many individuals with autism are slower at processing atypical exemplars, possibly because of semantic and perceptual differences from individuals without autism (Gastgeb, Strauss, & Minshew, 2006; Jolicoeur, Gluck, & Kosslyn, 1984; Piatt & Tanaka, 2005). The implications for mathematics teachers who use exemplars and nonexemplars with students with autism are significant. To increase the chance that the student with autism can actually use the exemplars and nonexemplars for categorization purposes,

> ➤ use simple, uncomplicated exemplars,
> ➤ be careful with the semantic demands of the language of instruction, and
> ➤ allow for time to process the exemplar and nonexemplar.

Complicated models or exemplars may be confusing to some individuals with autism as a result of perceptual differences. Attention to detail can become confusing if multiple and overlapping details are present in the model. Keeping the exemplar simple and highlighting the critical features could be helpful to many children with perceptual issues related to their condition. On the other hand, if the learner is too detail oriented, then even the slightest change in detail can collapse understanding. Lee, for example, got used to viewing models that had the critical features highlighted in red. Once the red color was removed, Lee had no idea what to look for. His perceptions focused on the color rather than the concept.

Underlying the notion of using exemplars and nonexemplars is the relative strength of semantic processing. Because many individuals with autism have difficulty with understanding language, they may not have sufficient skills to categorize the information. Keeping verbal explanations to a minimum and asking the student to paraphrase a description of the model may support the learner's semantic vocabulary.

Perceptual differences in processing time may also be a factor in using exemplars and nonexemplars. Many individuals with autism categorize more slowly from models than would be expected. Robby, for example, did not seem to understand how to visualize relationships of objects in space. Spatial visualization skills, the heart of geometry, are important in everyday life for tasks like following diagrams and illustrations for putting together toys, playing certain types of video games, and reading maps.

Robby's teacher felt that visual models might need to be presented initially in concrete experiences. Accordingly, when introducing the concept of simple symmetry, Robby's teacher embarked on the objective of teaching bilateral symmetry through showing that the same pattern can be arranged symmetrically on two sides of a center line. by using the tried and true "paint blob" approach. Robby dropped a blob of paint in the middle of a piece of paper, folded the paper in half and squished the folded paper. Upon opening the paper, a perfectly symmetrical bilateral shape appeared. Within five minutes, Robby had created 3 more perfectly symmetrical bilateral shapes but appeared to have no better understanding of the concept before his foray into paint blob symmetry. The next day in math class, however, Robby seemed to be a mathematically changed person. He had grasped the concept of bilateral symmetry. Robby, apparently, had needed additional processing time to draw the relationship between symmetry and the math lesson. Perhaps, if Robby's teacher had provided more time for processing the images in class, Robby would have come to understand bilateral symmetry more quickly.

Drill and Practice

Drill and practice techniques are repetitive and structured review techniques used to maintain or raise concepts to a predetermined level of mastery. Drill and practice strategies are often associated with retention, that is, the automatic recall of information previously learned after some time has passed without opportunity to practice. Teaching basic skills through drills usually leads to increased retention, which in turn provides the basis for increased performance on more advanced skills (Burns, 2004; Dehaene & Akhavein, 1995; McCurdy, Skinner, Grantham, Watson & Hindman, 2001). Accuracy as well as fluency are considered necessary when learning number facts.

Fluency refers to accuracy that is automatic and effortless and often when considering math facts includes the rate of speed at which facts are produced (Mercer & Mercer, 2001). As students become more accurate, attain fluency, or both, they demonstrate excellent retention (Berens, Boyce, Berens, Doney, & Kenzer, 2003; Bucklin, Dickinson, & Brethower, 2000; Peladeau, Forget, & Gagne, 2003).

Observations and data collection easily and objectively can distinguish the fluent from the dysfluent student. Ralph quickly and errorlessly produces responses to his 9 times tables. Ralph can correctly produce 68 number facts per minute with fewer than two errors. His classmate Smitty presents an entirely different picture with the 9 times tables. Smitty's responses, although accurate, are halting and slow. He can barely produce 15 responses within a minute. Convincing research suggests that children with a rate of 40 to 50 basic math facts per minute can use these facts fluently with advanced skills, such as complex addition or multiple digit problems with regrouping (Haughton, 1972).

Fluency, that is, accuracy and speed, must be reached if a student is ever to have a chance to maintain the concepts for use in later generalizations (Kubina, & Wolfe, 2005). To date very little information is available describing how fluency is achieved with individuals with autism.

Teaching components

A possible approach to teaching fluency with math facts, generalized from a reading study, suggests teaching component parts to fluency first and then putting the parts together to become fluent with the larger more complex behavior (Kubina, Young, & Kilwein, 2004). Recall Smitty, who is not fluent with his 9 times tables. Smitty struggles to produce an answer to 9×5. His intervention would focus on building fluency with the discrete behaviors associated with this fact. The component skill includes hearing the name of the numbers and multiplication and equal symbols; then he would write the corresponding number or symbol and segment the whole number facts $9 \times 5 = 45$. Each part of the fact is learned fluently before all the parts are put together. That is, once Smitty can say and write the number 9, he can then practice saying and writing the symbol x for multiplication and = for equals. As Smitty becomes fluent with each of the component skills in 9, ×, 5, and =, theoretically he should become fluent with the larger or composite skill of $9 \times 5 = 45$ (Berens et al., 2003; Kubina et al., 2004; McDowell & Keenan, 2002; Smyth & Keenan, 2002).

Incremental Rehearsal

Another type of drill and practice found effective for teaching children math is called the incremental rehearsal technique or drill ratio procedure (Burns, 2005; Skinner, Hurst, Teeple, & Meadows, 2002). A drill ratio procedure with number facts would intersperse a ratio of unknown number facts with known number facts (Joseph, 2006). The ratio of known to unknown content is up to the instructor's discretion and the student's learning curve. Allan has a very low tolerance for error or ambiguity. His drill ratio procedure is very low 90% known to 10% unknown. His classmate Jorge has a much more challenging drill ratio of 60% known to 40% unknown. In most drill ratio procedures, in spite of of the ratio, the same fact, known or unknown, is banned from being accessible multiple times. The following are steps in implementing a drill ratio procedure with math facts (Joseph, 2006):

1. Present the first unknown fact, orally read the fact to the student, and then have the student read the same fact orally.

2. Present the first known fact and have the student read this fact orally.
3. Present the first unknown fact, have the student read this fact orally and then have the student read the first known and the second known facts orally.
4. Present the first unknown fact; have the student read this fact orally; and then have the student read the first, second, and third known facts orally.
5. When the first unknown fact becomes a known fact, it remains in the stack and the known fact is removed.
6. Continue the procedure until all unknown facts have been introduced.

Use of drill and practice, regardless of type, must always be considered in relation to the impact of the core deficits characterizing individuals with autism. Abnormal executive function of the brain, suspected in the case of individuals with autism, affects the individual's ability to actively rehearse information subvocally or store certain aspects of language (Imbo & Vandierendonck, 2007). Incremental rehearsal can be used as a support to accommodate language issues that affect basic math facts (Joseph, 2006).

Teaching components and drill ratio procedures, like all other math approaches to retention and fluency, must be evaluated in light of how disorders in social behavior, abnormal verbal and nonverbal communication, and limited interests interact with the approach.

Antecedent-based Interventions

An *antecedent-based intervention* is the technical term for using environmental or instructional conditions to improve the odds that the student will learn. Antecedent-based interventions include providing the learner with choices, integrating a student's interests, and modifying the curricula prior to beginning a behavioral change (Hinton & Kern, 1999; Lee, Sugai, & Horner, 1999; Umbreit & Blair, 1996). Reggie likes to be able to pick which of the math problems he will do. He likes to create patterns on his math worksheet by completing every third problem. Reggie's need for creating patterns does not interfere with completing work samples.

Reggie's friend Duke loves basketball. All of Duke's math work is set in the context of basketball (e.g., graph the number of times, Steve Nash, a guard for the Phoenix Suns, has made free shots in the latest game against the Lakers). Jay, on the other hand, has lots of missing math skills. As a result, his math curriculum is taken from many grade levels in an attempt to provide him with a more complete math skill set. Antecedent-based interventions are commonly used classroom practices, which, when the core characteristics of autism are taken into account, can be useful for teaching mathematics to students with autism.

Antecedent-based strategies increase the odds that the learner will be open to learning when provided with an activity or event that is pleasing. The value of the antecedent-based intervention will be based on how well the teacher or interventionist understands the student's preferences (i.e., likes and dislikes). To quote G.K. Chesterton, "When giving treats to friends or children, give them what they like, emphatically not what is good for them." Antecedent-based approaches are motivators to jump start willingness to learn, but development of skill level or accuracy rests squarely in the hands of the teacher or interventionist by designing adaptations through informal data collection.

Two additional types of antecedent-based interventions not typically found in classrooms are interspersed-request intervention and high-probability request sequences (high-*p*; Banda, McAfee, Lee, & Kubina, 2007). The *interspersed-request intervention* approach entails mixing simple problems with more complex ones and typically results in an increase in completing problems (Cates & Skinner, 2000). Julian thrives when his teachers use the interspersed-request approach with him by mixing problems that are easy for Julian with problems that are more difficult. When given simple fractions with the same denominator and no carrying, a task in which Julian always gets a perfect score, he is then more willing and more successful at completing more complex fractions involving mixed numbers or unequal denominators. Initially, when Julian began learning with this approach, he needed a simple problem first and then a difficult one. As Julian became more confident with his fractions, the proportion of simple to complex became smaller. Julian now needs only one simple problem and will happily complete the three complex ones that follow. His ratio for needing the simple problem to encourage him to complete more difficult ones has gotten larger.

High-p request sequences use the learner's preferred academic tasks as an incentive to increase willingness to work on a task that is usually avoided with the expectation of an increase in finishing problems, quicker starting of a task, and more overall cooperation (Belfiore, Lee, Scheeler, & Klein, 2002; Belfiore, Lee, Vargas, & Skinner, 1997; Lee & Laspe, 2003). Ted, for example, loves to solve geometric problems, especially when they involve puzzles, but he is very reluctant to begin any work involving money. If asked to complete a problem involving shopping at the store or buying clothes at the mall, he typically stalls and only with the greatest reluctance will attempt the problem. If Ted, however, is given a sequence where he first gets to solve a short puzzle, his willingness to "go shopping" increases. No one can say for sure, but being able to do his favorite activity seems to put Ted in a "good mood" which in turn influences his willingness to try material that he would otherwise find distasteful.

Interventions for Deductive and Inductive Learning Style

Deductive and inductive reasoning have a very different "feel" to them. Deductive reasoning is narrower in nature and is concerned with testing or confirming hypotheses. Inductive reasoning is more open-ended and exploratory, especially at the beginning. Both deductive and inductive reasoning are important aspects in comprehending mathematics, but some individuals tend to learn more efficiently with an emphasis on either deductive or inductive instructional strategies.

Deductive Strategies

Having taken into account the many idiosyncrasies found in an individual with autism, some general instructional recommendations can be made for individuals who appear to use predominantly deductive learning. Explicit instruction in mathematics in combination with a specifically well-organized sequence, in most cases, will improve the odds of successful learning (Kroesbergen and Van Luit, 2003; Rosenshine, 1995). Explicit instructional practices include presentation of new information in sequentially and conceptually small steps, incorporation of examples and nonexamples, and ordered and continuous monitoring for acquisition and maintenance.

A well-structured lesson sequence begins with a review of prerequisite knowledge and sets the purpose and rationale of the lesson. The lesson is demonstrated and supported practice is provided followed by guided practice, creating a gradual shift of responsibility from supported practice to independent practice for solving the math problem. During the guided practice portion of the lesson, a high level of questioning provides insight into the student's conceptualization. Incorrect or faulty conceptualizations must be corrected quickly to prevent habitual incorrect thinking, which could impact future mathematical operations or processes.

An explicit lesson in math for most learners would have a teacher leading, demonstrating, and guiding. The degree of direct teacher involvement with individuals with autism varies from one individual to another. For many individuals with autism, a teacher led lesson would be appropriate. For some individuals with communication and social skills issues, the less interaction with a human teacher, the more likely learning can take place. Once again, the characteristics of the particular learner will shape the lesson.

Delivery of a well-structured explicit lesson can be designed with literally no direct human interaction. Steve finds interactions with any person, adult or child, very distracting. Steve appears to prefer to be alone in a classroom. Steve really enjoys working with measurement. Steve engages willingly in any hands-on experience with measurement as long as he does not need to interact with anyone for over 2 to 3 minutes. Given Steve's emotional needs, his teacher provides him with measurement experiences in well-structured lessons that make minimal use of teacher interaction in favor of using visual supports, most often in the form of a step-by-step pictorial guide. The visual guide presents the advanced organizer and the purpose of the lesson pictorially with an accompanying narrative. An advance organizer is any information presented that can be used by the learner to organize and interpret new incoming information, that is, prepare the learner to learn new content (Mayer, 2003).Demonstration of the expected product is found in the form of a model. A picture model of the expected produce is presented. Steve is given supported practice through provision of extremely simple to more complex problems with feedback. The pictorial guides have feedback embedded within, which provides immediate feedback in terms of the expected response for each step. Steve matches his response with the expected answer.

If Steve's response is correct, his answer will match the response provided in the lesson. The correct answer is coded with a happy face. The happy face is his signal to proceed to the next step. If Steve's response is incorrect, then he sees a number that is coded to the previous step in the lesson. The number is linked to another example of the expected product for that particular step. If after completing the response incorrectly a second time, a picture of his teacher is shown. The picture is Steve's signal to contact his teacher.

Steve's materials gradually shift from supported practice consisting of the feedback cycle for correct and incorrect response to independent practice for solving the measurement problem. During the guided practice portion of the lesson, a high level of feedback provides insight into Steve's conceptualization of a particular measurement lesson. Steve's incorrect or faulty conceptualizations are corrected quickly to prevent habitual incorrect thinking.

For some students with autism who have lesser problems in communication and socialization than Steve, some commercial programs that provide well-structured lessons may hold promise for math instruction. Saxon Math and SRA Corrective Mathematics are examples of two common basic math programs that provide highly structured material. Both approaches utilize very focused programs in which instruction is incremental and explicit. Prior mastered concepts are reviewed and frequent cumulative assessment is built into these programs. Programs such as Saxon Math and SRA Corrective Mathematics present mathematics rules and strategies focusing on specific skills. Although many mathematics would cringe at the direct instruction teacher-led approach to mathematics, because direct instruction often is interpreted as emphasizing procedures rather than developing conceptualization, the explicit nature of these and similar no frills math programs would be appealing to some individuals with autism who prefer deductive instruction and precision.

Inductive Strategies

Inductive reasoning moves from specific observations to broader generalizations and theories. In inductive reasoning, the learner begins to solve problems through specific observations and measures. The observations prompt the learner to look for and, with perseverance, discover patterns and regularities that in turn help to put together some tentative hypotheses about how to solve the problem. Once the theory is tested, the learner can develop a general conclusion or premise about how to solve a particular problem. Individuals who primarily use inductive thinking project information from what they know to what they do not know. Using inductive reasoning based on personal experiences, some students with autism are able to problem-solve in unique ways. Several of Ms. Witt's students were most happy solving problems when left to their own thinking. Ms. Witt would often let her students go to the board and explain their answers. Ms. Witt always let them use the method that made sense to them and was constantly amazed at how they could get from point A to point B in so many different ways.

When presented with new situations or experiences, some individuals with autism become highly anxious until and unless the new situation can be altered to a personal level of comfort. Feelings associated with the presentation of new or unfamiliar circumstances create anxiety for many individuals with autism, and adaptation to the new situation often does not occur, even if that situation is only the introduction of a new concept in math. Exposing many learners with autism to new experiences, even when supported, can be highly stressful, resulting in inappropriate behaviors (Cashin, & Waters, 2006). Presenting a step-by-step language-based explanation of how to solve a math problem also could be overwhelming to some learners with autism as a result of problems with language and communication.

Mathematics is filled with new and often unfamiliar routines, theorems, shapes, and explanations that to some children with autism seem confusing and anxiety-producing. If, however, the learner is allowed to use known experiences to bridge the unknown, then anxiety levels may be significantly reduced. One approach to help learners make sense out of a potentially senseless chaotic mathematical world is to utilize metaphors that are based on personal experiences of the student.

Using metaphors, similes, and personifications can often be effective with children who predominantly use inductive reasoning. A *metaphor* is a figure of speech in which an implied comparison is made between two dissimilar concepts that in fact have commonalities. Similes and personifications are special types of metaphors. A metaphor creates opportunity for comparing the unfamiliar in relation to the familiar. Metaphors can make use of familiar experiences.

David, for example, is highly focused on all aspects of solar power. He can recite facts, figures, and projections with a precision worthy of a dedicated and skilled researcher. David, however, could not multiply with regrouping. When initially presented with a multiplication problem requiring regrouping, David had a meltdown. His eyes glazed over, and he began rocking to his personal rhythm. David was not going to learn how to do multiplication with regrouping without an intervention. Enter David's personalized simile. A solar cell reorganizes energy like a multiplication problem with regrouping reorganizes numbers. Not only did the simile utilize David's interest in all aspects of solar power, but it also created a situation where David's prior knowledge of solar power could be extended to regrouping in multiplication. David could use the known, which to him was concrete, and extend this information to the abstract and heretofore uncharted territory of regrouping with multiplication.

Metaphors can also promote categorization, grouping, and quantification of experience. For children whose world may be fragmented, metaphors can structure experience into logical wholes based on personal experience and interests. Metaphors are inductive inferences or generalizations that exceed experience. Inductive inferences usually entail inferring a general pattern from experience with a few examples (Pillow & Pearson, 2009).

Metaphors can also be visual. A familiar example of a visual metaphor is the strategy of juxtaposing one image with another in the attempt to imply that both have similar qualities. In advertising, for example, an image of a motorcycle might occur with a picture of a cheetah, suggesting that the motorcycle has comparable qualities of swiftness, power, and stamina as the cheetah. A visual metaphor for Alonzo would entail his favorite food, the apple. Apples produce positive feelings in Alonzo. For Alonzo the juxtaposition of a picture of a whole number and the number broken into component parts next to an image of an apple split in half could help him associate the whole to part concept related to equivalencies plus conjure the same positive feelings as his favorite fruit. Just as the whole apple can be cut into two equivalent pieces so can the number 4 be seen as 2 + 2. Visual metaphors for many individuals with autism must be customized to tap into the learner's past experiences and current interests.

Personification, a variation of the metaphor, may be a helpful strategy for some individuals with autism when engaging in math learning. In *personification* an inanimate object or concept assumes human qualities of abilities. Because personification involves comparisons between known and unknown, either directly or indirectly, the same considerations for using metaphors apply (i.e., involvement of past experiences and current interests).

Personification is often a hook for new learning. Most children have a tendency to view the world in human terms, but this generalization must be reassessed when working with some individuals with autism who may not be able to relate to others. The personification approach must take into account to what or whom the child relates. Harold is thrilled with Thomas the Tank Engine. Personifications for Harold would not be with a real person, but rather with the train. The "personification" of moving through a multistep math problem could be introduced using the setting, "like Thomas the Tank Engine, the journey took him through many different lands." The journey was the process for the multistep problem, and the different lands each represent a step toward the end of the trip or the solution to the multistep problem. Thomas the Tank Engine could personify one type of mathematical problem, and his other train companions could each represent a different type of math problem.

Developing Generalization: Beyond Manipulatives

Many teachers of mathematics are strongly committed to the use of manipulatives in teaching. Although manipulatives have proven to be successful for teaching math concepts for many students, the overriding concern for individuals with autism is the ability to generalize concepts. One of the most highly revered instructional approaches to facilitate the development of generalization has been the concrete-representation-abstract teaching sequence (CRA; Miller & Hudson, 2007).

The CRA follows three distinctive and hierarchical steps. First the concept is explained using a concrete manipulative. Once the concept is mastered with the manipulative prompt, the next step is to introduce an abstract representation of the concept. The concrete prompt is dropped. The representation of the concept most often consists of line drawings, although any one-dimensional pictorial illustration of the concept is acceptable. Once the student has demonstrated understanding of the math concept using a representational image, instruction proceeds without any concrete or representational prompts to a purely abstract format.

Typically a minimum of 20 problems using manipulatives over three lessons and three lessons using representations is adequate for most students to understand the concept being taught (Butler, Miller, Crehan, Babbitt, & Pierce, 2003; Harris, Miller, & Mercer, 1995). Using CRA with individuals with autism, however, may or may not follow the traditional practice. For some students with autism, the CRA approach may be highly beneficial, especially if the manipulatives and representations are linked to a favorite interest. For other students with autism, however, skipping the C and the R might be a better approach.

Evan never could get past the concrete stage when trying to learn multi-step multiplication. In desperation his teacher showed Evan the steps using a white board and verbal explanation, and within five problems, Evan had the process down. Could Evan's success be a result of the earlier work with concrete objects? To test this question, Evan's teacher presented a lesson in mutli-step long division going directly to a white board and verbal explanation. Within four problems, Evan could successfully complete multi-step long division.

For those students like Evan who truly do not generalize from concrete to representational to abstract, the CRA method may be teaching three different and unrelated lessons, as far as the student is concerned. As with all interventions, in math or any other area, data need to be taken to determine the value of the intervention in time and efficiency.

GENETICS, MATHEMATICS AND CLASSICAL AUTISM: WHAT ARE THE ODDS?

Although mathematicians are typically held in high regard, many stories about eccentric math professors exist. Descriptions like aloof, strange, and a little peculiar are frequently mentioned in the same sentence as mathematicians, engineers, musicians, scientists, and even librarians. Individuals drawn to these fields are often characterized as having a strong need to systematize, as if they are almost compelled to analyze or create systems of any kind based on input and output rules (Baron-Cohen, Wheelwright, Burtenshaw, & Hobson, 2007). Some of these highly organized thinkers also seem to be a little short on understanding the needs of others, lacking in empathy, and in some cases slightly robotic in communication skills.

The odd couple of poor empathy and superior systematizing are suspected of being part of autism. An empathizing–systemizing theory holds that impaired empathy and well-developed or superior systemizing are two core features of classic autism (Baron-Cohen, 2002). Even though caution must be taken and conclusions lightly drawn, some evidence actually exists that, in the case of mathematicians, the chance of finding a mathematician with an autism classification is three times higher than for a nonmathematician (Baron-Cohen et al., 2007). Mathematical talent and a number of autistic traits have been linked (Baron-Cohen, Wheelwright, Skinner, Martin, & Clubley, 2001).

No theory about autism would be complete without climbing around in the family tree. A short trip up the genetic trunk finds a higher rate of autism in siblings of mathematicians compared to the siblings of individuals in other disciplines. Fortunately for all mathematicians, the numbers involved are quite small, with 0.5% of the siblings of the math students officially diagnosed with classical autism, HFA, or AS, as compared to 0.1% of siblings of controls. Although a fivefold greater chance seems impressive, the information is based primarily on the work of one set of researchers headed by Simon Baron-Cohen (Baron-Cohen et al., 1998). Nonetheless, future research may add more substance to the finding that relatives of individuals who are low in empathy and high in system building are at risk for being autistic.

Much more research evidence must be compiled before mathematicians and their siblings should feel compelled to enroll in courses in group dynamics or sit around campfires singing Kumbaya. Very few mathematicians suffer from full-scale autism although some might suspect that a little smidgen of autism could be essential for becoming a mathematics "superstar."

SAVANT SYNDROME

Who cannot be fascinated by witnessing the extraordinary skills of an individual who has the ability to name the day of the week on which a particular date, past, present, or future, has fallen or will fall, has lightning fast mental calculation, or who can beat the house in a Las Vegas casino? Even more captivating is the paradox of the person who in many other ways could be labeled mentally challenged but is considered brilliant in one or more areas. Hollywood has been smitten with savants and placed permanent images of Dustin Hoffman in *Rainman,* a card counting individual with autism, and more recently Jon Nash, a schizophrenic mathematician played touchingly by Russel Crowe in the film *A Beautiful Mind.*

All savants are intriguing, but can fact and fiction be separated? A striking characteristic of some individuals with ASD is the strange mix of cognitive strengths and weaknesses. The juxtapositions of severe mental handicap and prodigious mental ability is known as the Savant Syndrome and has been well documented in the psychological and medical research literature for over 100 years (Tredgold, 1914; Wallace, 2008).

Although much literature has been written about Savant Syndrome being associated with individuals categorized as mentally retarded, in actuality this rare condition is significantly more common in individuals with autism (Rimland, 1978; Nettelbeck & Young, 1999). Many theories, as of yet unproven, suggest that the obsessive and restricted interests and weak central coherence, that is, a limited ability to comprehend context or to "see the big picture," solidly implies that Savant Syndrome is closely associated with ASD (Heaton & Wallace, 2004).

Rule based knowledge

Individuals displaying Savant Syndrome rely heavily on rule-based knowledge and can break down information into basic components that can then be reassembled to form meaningful wholes (Cowan, Stainthorp, Kapnogianni, & Anastasiou, 2004; Heavey, Pring & Hermelin, 1999; Hermelin & O'Connor. 1999). Twelve-year-old DiVon, for example, is a calendar savant. His skills go beyond rote memory. DiVon has knowledge of calendar regularities that he can use to complete calendar calculations for specific dates and days in both the past and the future. In contrast to his calendaring skills, DiVon has very limited verbal skills and apparently does not need higher level linguistics to apply his calendaring skills to past, present, or future.

Rapid Processing

Savants like DiVon also show rapid processing rate in those areas of their excessive talent that often far exceeds their expected intelligence level. In the area of calendaring, DiVon demonstrates a superior processing speed as well as attention to detail. Processing which focuses on details and mental arithmetic have been linked to savant calendar skills (Anderson, 2001; Happé and Frith, 2006; Heavey, 2003). For DiVon dates can be perceived as fragments of the calendar, and his rapid processing time for mental math may be able to explain the paradox of the coexistence of his brilliance and disability.

Segmentation

A predisposition toward segmentation is common among mathematical savants. Many savants have a propensity to proceed by breaking down any quantity or function that can have a mathematical operation performed into their respective factors or smaller units (Wallace, 2008). Five-year-old Harry is the king of disassembling and reassembling three dimensional math puzzle games. One of his favorite games is Cubes in Line. In this game Harry and his challenger have to try to create a horizontal, vertical, or diagonal line of the same color by placing cubes one by one in any of the holes provided in a larger frame. (See Figure 12.3). Harry has competed with other much older students in the school and even several of the math teachers. Harry, who is always the winner, makes more "3 in line" rows than any of his opponents.

Savant skills in math and other areas are exceptional and used to be seen a little more that circus tricks. Many stories in the past dwelt on the sensationalism of such amazing feats. In the 21st century, however, neuroscientists are beginning to study savant skills as a means to understand ASD as well as giftedness. Mathematics, with its rule-governed discipline, is beginning to provide an excellent forum for understanding many aspects of ASD.

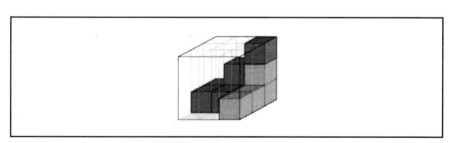

FIGURE 12.3

Example of Cubes in Line

SUMMARY

Many aspects of math instruction seem tailor-made for individuals with autism who thrive on systems and predictability. The core traits of autism, however, complicate learning mathematics in many significant ways. Learning styles and behavioral issues characteristic of many individuals with autism present challenges for teaching mathematics. Instructional strategies and interventions for individuals with autism must take into account the role of central executive function of the brain and subsequent influences on math performance through semantic, procedural, and visuospatial memory. Predominant learning styles of deductive and inductive reasoning influence the design and delivery of mathematics lesson to individuals with autism. The environmental and social setting plays key roles in how math lessons can be formatted. The language of mathematics, when interfaced with the linguistics skills of individuals with autism, must also be considered in the development of instructional events. Although much is still left to be learned about how mathematics can be taught to individuals with autism, some specific guidelines have been created for lesson presentation. Many interventions have been reported which are successful for an individual with autism, but to date, no one intervention will or can fill the instructional needs of all individuals with autism.

REFERENCES

Adams, T. L. (2003). Reading mathematics: More than words can say. *Reading Teacher, 56*(8), 786–795.

Adams, T. L., & Lowery, R. M. (2007). An analysis of children's strategies for reading mathematics. *Reading & Writing Quarterly, 23,* 161–177.

Anderson, M. (2001). Annotation: conceptions of intelligence. *Journal of Child Psychology and Psychiatry, 42,* 287–298.

Ashcraft, M. H. (1996). Cognitive psychology and simple arithmetic: A review and summary of new directions. In B. Bulterworth (Ed.), *Mathematical cognition I* (pp. 3–34). Hove, UK: Psychology Press.

Bachot J., Gevers, W., Fias, W., & Roeyers, H. (2005). Number sense in children with visuospatial disabilities: Orientation of the mental number line. *Psychology Science, 47,* 172–183.

Banda, D. R., McAfee, J. K., Lee, D. L., & Kubina, R. M., Jr. (2007). Math preferences and mastery relationship in middle school students with autism spectrum disorders. *Journal of Behavioral Education, 16,* 207–223.

Baron-Cohen, S. (2002). The extreme male brain theory of autism. *Trends in Cognitive Science, 6,* 248–254.

Baron-Cohen, S., Wheelwright, S., Burtenshaw, A., & Hobson, E. (2007). Mathematical talent is linked to autism. *Hum Nat, 18,* 125–131.

Baron-Cohen, S., Wheelwright, S., Skinner, R., Martin, J., & Clubley, E. (2001). The autism spectrum quotient (AQ): Evidence from Asperger syndrome/high functioning autism, males and females, scientists and mathematicians. *Journal of Autism and Developmental Disorders, 31,* 5–17.

Baron-Cohen, S., Bolton, P., Wheelwright, S., Short, L., Mead, G., Smith, A., et al. (1998). Does autism occur more often in families of physicists, engineers, and mathematicians? *Autism, 2,* 296–301.

Barwell, R. (2003). Patterns of attention in interaction of a primary school mathematics student with English as an additional language. *Educational Studies in Mathematics, 53,* 35–59.

Belfiore, P. J., Lee, D. L., Scheeler, M. C., & Klein, D. (2002). Implications of behavioral momentum and academic achievement for students with behavior disorders: Theory, application, and practice. *Psychology in the Schools, 39,* 171–179.

Belfiore, P. J., Lee, D. L., Vargas, A. U., & Skinner, C. H. (1997). Effects of high-preference single digit mathematics problem completion on multiple digit mathematics problem performance. *Journal of Applied Behavior Analysis, 30,* 327–330.

Berens, K., Boyce, T. E., Berens, N. M., Doney, J. K., & Kenzer, A. L. (2003). A technology for evaluation relations between response frequency and academic performance outcomes. *Journal of Precision Teaching and Celeration, 19,* 20–34.

Brosnan, M. J., Scott, F. J., Fox, S., & Pye, J. (2004). Gestalt processing in autism: Failure to process perceptual relationships and the implications for contextual understanding. *Journal of Child Psychology and Psychiatry, 45,* 459–469.

Bucklin, B. R., Dickinson, A. M., & Brethower, D. M. (2000). A comparison of the effects of fluency training and accuracy training on application and retention. *Performance Improvement Quarterly, 13,* 141–163.

Bulgren, J. A., Lenz, B. K., Deshler, D. D., & Schumaker, J. B. (1995). *The Concept Comparison Routine.* Lawrence, KS: Edge Enterprises.

Burns, M. K. (2005). Using incremental rehearsal to increase fluency of single-digit multiplication facts with children identified as learning disabled in mathematics computation. *Education and Treatment of Children, 28,* 237–249.

Burns, M. K. (2004). Empirical analysis of drill ratio research: Refining the instructional level for drill tasks. *Remedial and Special Education, 25,* 167–175,

Butler, F. M., Miller, S. P., Crehan, K., Babbitt, B., & Pierce, T. (2003). Fraction instruction for students with mathematics disabilities: Comparing two teaching sequences. *Learning Disabilities Research & Practice, 18,* 99–111.

Cashin, A., & Waters, C. (2006). Autism: Chaos theory as a metaphor and beyond. *Adolescent Psychiatric Nursing, 19,* 224–230.

Cates, G. L., & Skinner, C. H. (2000). Getting remedial mathematics students to prefer homework with 20% and 40% more problems: An investigation of the strength of the interspersing procedure. *Psychology in the Schools, 37,* 339–347.

Chapman, O. (2006). Classroom practices for context of mathematics word problems. *Educational Studies in Mathematics, 62,* 211–230.

Cowan, R., Stainthorp, R., Kapnogianni S., & Anastasiou, M. (2004). The development of calendrical skills. *Cognitive Development, 19,* 169–178.

de Gelder, B., Teunisse, J-P., & Benson, P. J. (1997). Categorical perception of facial expressions: Categories and their internal structure. *Cognition and Emotion, 11,* 1–23.

Dehaene, S., & Akhavein, R. (1995). Attention, automaticity, and levels of representation in number processing. *Journal of Experimental Psychology: Learning, Memory, and Cognition, 21,* 314–326.

Deschuyteneer, M., Vandierendonck, A., & Muyllaert, I. (2006). Does solution of mental arithmetic problems such as 2 - 6 and 3 - 8 rely on the process of "memory updating"? *Experimental Psychology, 53,* 198–208.

DeStefano, D., & LeFevre, J.-A. (2004). The role of working memory in mental arithmetic. *European Journal of Cognitive Psychology, 16,* 353–386.

Devlin, K. (1996). *Mathematics: The science of patterns: The search for order in life, mind and the universe.* (Scientific American Paperback Library). Boston, MA: Freeman.

Fox, L., Vaughn, B. J., & Dunlap, G. (2002). Research partnership: One family's experience with the process of positive behavior support. In J. Lucyshyn, G. Dunlap, & R. Albin (Eds.), *Families and positive behavioral support: Addressing the challenge of problem behavior in family contexts* (pp. 417–438). Baltimore: Brookes.

Donoghue, M. R. (2001). *Using literature activities to teach content areas to emergent readers.* Boston: Allyn and Bacon.

Ellis, H. D., & Leafhead, K. M. (1996). Raymond: A study of an adult with Asperger syndrome. In P. W. Halligan & J. C. Marshall (Eds.), *Methods in madness: Case studies in Cognitive Neuropsychiatry* (pp. 79–92). Hove, UK: Psychology Press.

Frith, U. (2003). *Autism: Explaining the Enigma* (2nd ed.). Oxford: Blackwell.

Gastgeb, H. Z., Strauss, M. S., & Minshew, N. J. (2006). Do individuals with autism process categories differently? The effect of typicality and development. *Child Development, 77*(6), 1717–1729.

Geary, D. C. (2000). From infancy to adulthood: The development of numerical abilities. *European Child and Adolescent Psychiatry, 9,* II11-II16.

Goldman, S., Hasselbring, & the Cognition and Technology Group at Vanderbilt (1997). Achieving meaningful mathematics literacy for students with learning disabilities. *Journal of Learning Disabilities, 30,* 198–208.

Happé, F. G. E., & Frith, U. (2006). The weak coherence account: Detail focused cognitive style in autism spectrum disorders. *Journal of Autism and Developmental Disorders, 36,* 1–21.

Harris, C. A., Miller, S. P., & Mercer, C. D. (1995). Teaching initial multiplication skills to students with disabilities in general education classrooms. *Learning Disabilities Research & Practice, 10,* 180–195.

Haughton, E. C. (1972). Aims: Growing and sharing. In J. B. Jordan & L. S. Robbins (Eds.), *Let's try doing something else kind of thing* (pp. 20–39). Arlington, VA: Council for Exceptional Children.

Heaton, P., & Wallace, G. L. (2004). The savant syndrome. *Journal of Child Psychology and Psychiatry, 45,* 899–911.

Heavey, L. (2003). Arithmetical savants. In A. Baroody & A. Dowker (Eds.), *The development of arithmetic concepts and skills: Recent research and theory* (pp. 409–432). Oxford: Oxford University Press.

Heavey, L., Pring, L., & Hermelin, B. (1999). A date to remember: The nature of memory in savant calendrical calculators. *Psychological Medicine, 29,* 145–160.

Hermelin, B., & O'Connor, N. (1999). Art and accuracy: The drawing ability of idiot-savants. *Journal of Child Psychology and Psychiatry, 31,* 217–228.

Hersh, R. (1997). Math lingo vs. plain English: Double entendre. *The American Math Monthly, 104,* 48–51.

Hinton, L. M., & Kern, L. M. (1999). Increasing homework completion by incorporating student interests. *Journal of Positive Behavior Interventions, 1,* 231–234.

Hudson, P., & Miller, S. P. (2006). *Designing and implementing mathematics instruction for students with diverse learning needs.* Boston: Allyn & Bacon.

Hurth, J., Shaw, E., Izeman, S. G., Whaley, K., & Rogers, S. J. (1999). Areas of agreement about effective practices among programs serving young children with autism spectrum disorders. *Infants and Young Children, 12,* 17–26.

Imbo, I., & Vandierendonck, A. (2007). The role of phonological and executive working memory resources in simple arithmetic strategies. *European Journal of Cognitive Psychology, 19,* 910–933.

Inspiration Software, Inc. (2010). Retrieved June 22, 2009, from www.Inspiration.com

Iovannone, R., Dunlap, G., Huber, H., & Kincaid, D. (2003). Effective educational practices for students with autism spectrum disorders. *Focus on Autism and Other Developmental Disabilities, 18,* 150–165.

Jitendra, A., DiPipi, C. M., & Perron-Jones, N. (2002). An exploratory study of schema-based word-problem solving instruction for middle school students with LD: An emphasis on conceptual and procedural understanding. *The Journal of Special Education, 36,* 23–38.

Jolicoeur, P., Gluck, M. A., & Kosslyn, S. M. (1984). Pictures and names: Making the connection. *Cognitive Psychology, 16,* 243–275.

Joseph, L. M. (2006). Incremental rehearsal: A flashcard drill technique for increasing retention of reading words. *The Reading Teacher, 59,* 803–807.

Klinger, L. G., & Dawson, G. (2001). Prototype formation in autism. *Development and Psychology, 13,* 111–124.

Kroesbergen, E. H., & van Luit, J. E. H. (2003). Mathematics interventions for children with special educational needs: A meta-analysis. *Remedial and Special Education, 24,* 97–114.

Kubina, R. M., & Wolfe, P. W. (2005). Potential applications of behavioral fluency for students with autism. *Exceptionality, 13,* 35–44.

Kubina, R. M., Young, A. E., & Kilwein, M. (2004). Examining an effect of fluency: Application of oral word segmentation and letters sounds for spelling. *Learning Disabilities: A Multidisciplinary Journal, 13,* 17–23.

Kyttälä, M., & Lehto, J. E. (2008). Some factors underlying mathematical performance: The role of visuospatial working memory and non-verbal intelligence. *European Journal of Psychology of Education, 23,* 77–94.

Lee, D. L., & Laspe, A. K. (2003). Using high-probability request sequences to increase journal writing. *Journal of Behavioral Education, 12,* 261–273.

Lee, Y. Y., Sugai, G., & Horner, R. H. (1999). Using an instructional intervention to reduce problem and off-task behaviors. *Journal of Positive Behavior Interventions, 1,* 195–204.

Marolda M., & Davidson, P. (2000). Mathematical learning profiles and differentiated teaching strategies. *Perspectives, 26,* 10–15.

Math Mnemonics. (n.d.). *Education World.* Retrieved June 27, 2009, from http://www.education-world.com/a_curr/archives/mnemonics.shtml

Mayer, R. (2003) *Learning and Instruction.* Boston, MA: Pearson.

McCurdy, M., Skinner, G. H., Grantham, K., Watson, T. S., & Hindman, P. M. (2001). Increasing on-task behavior in an elementary student during mathematics seatwork by interspersing additional brief problems. *School Psychology Review, 30,* 25–32.

McDowell, C., & Keenan, M. (2002). Comparison of two teaching structures examining the effects of component fluency on the performance of related skills. *Journal of Precision Teaching and Celeration, 18,* 16–29.

Mercer, C. D., & Mercer, A. R. (2001). *Teaching students with learning problems* (6th ed.). Upper Saddle River, NJ: Prentice Hall/Merrill.

Miller, S. P., & Hudson, P. J. (2007). Using evidence-based practices to build mathematics competence related to conceptual, procedural, and declarative knowledge. *Learning Disabilities Research & Practice, 22,* 47–57.

Minshew, N. J., Meyer, J., & Goldstein, G. (2002). Abstract reasoning in autism: A dissociation between concept formation and concept identification. *Neuropsychology, 16,* 327–224.

Montague, M. (2002). *Solve It! A practical approach for teaching mathematical problem solving.* Reston, VA: Exceptional Innovations.

National Council of Teachers of Mathematics (NCTM). (2000). *Principles and standards for school mathematics.* Reston, VA: Author.

National Research Council (NRC). (2001). *Educating children with autism. Committee on Educational Interventions for Children with Autism. Division of Behavioral and Social Sciences and Autism.* Washington, DC: National Academy Press.

Nettelbeck, T., & Young, R. (1999). Savant syndrome. In C.M. Glidden (Ed.), *International review of research in mental retardation* (pp. 137–173). New York: Academic Press.

Ozonoff, S., & Miller, J. N. (1996). An exploration of right hemisphere contributions to the pragmatic impairments of autism. *Brain and Language, 52,* 411–434.

Peladeau, N., Forget, J., & Gagne, F. (2003). Effect of paced and unpaced practice on skill application and retention: How much is enough? *American Educational Research Journal, 40,* 769–801.

Piatt, C. G., & Tanaka, J. (2005, April). *The electrophysiology of categorizing typical and atypical objects.* Paper presented at the PEN X workshop, Pittsburgh, PA.

Pillow, B. H., & Pearson, R. M. (2009). Children's and adults' evaluation of their own inductive inferences, deductive inferences and guesses. *Merrill-Palmer Quarterly, 55,* 135–156.

Plaisted, K. C. (2000). Aspects of autism that theory of mind cannot explain. In S. Baron-Cohen, H. Tager-Flusberg, & D. J. Cohen (Eds.), *Understanding other minds: Perspectives from developmental cognitive neuroscience.* New York: Oxford University Press.

Prizant, B. M. & Wetherby, A. M. (1998). Understanding the continuum of discrete trial traditional behavioral to social-pragmatic, developmental approaches in communication enhancement for young children with ASD. *Seminars in Speech and Language, 19,* 329–353.

Quill, K. (2000). *Do-Watch-Listen-Say.* Baltimore: Brookes.

Rimland, B. (1978). Savant capabilities of autistic children and their cognitive implications. In G. Serban (Ed.), *Cognitive defects in the development of mental illness* (pp. 43–65). New York: Brunner-Mazel.

Robison, J. E. (2007). *Look me in the eye: My life with Asperger's.* New York: Crown.

Sharma, M. (1990). *NCTM student math notes.* Reston, VA: National Council of Teachers of Mathematics. (ERIC Document Reproduction Service No. ED328413).

Rosenshine, B. (1995). Advances in Research on Instruction. In J. W. Lloyd, E. J. Kameanui, & D. Chard (Eds.) (pp. 197–221). *Issues in educating students with disabilities.* Mahwah, NJ: Erlbaum.

Skinner, C.H., Hurst, K.L., Teeple, D.F., & Meadows, S.O. (2002). Increasing on-task behavior during mathematics independent seat-work in students with emotional disturbance by interspersing additional brief problems. *Psychology in the Schools, 39,* 647–659.

Smyth, P., & Keenan, M. (2002). Compound performance: The role of free and controlled operant components. *Journal of Precision Teaching and Celeration, 18,* 3–15.

Steen, L. A. (1988). The science of patterns. *Science, 240,* 611–616.

Tredgold, A. (1914). *Mental Deficiency.* Baltimore: Williams & Wilkins.

Umbreit, J., & Blair, K. S. (1996). The effects of preference, choice, and attention on problem behavior at school. *Education and Training in Mental Retardation and Developmental Disabilities, 31,* 151–161.

Wallace, G. L. (2008). Neuropsychological studies of savant skills: Can they inform the neuroscience of giftedness? *Roeper Review, 30,* 229–246.

Xin, Y. P., Jitendra, A. K., & Deatline-Buchman, A. (2007). Effects of mathematical word problem–solving instruction on middle school students with learning problems. *The Journal of Special Education, 39,* 181–192.

Young, R., & Nettelbeck, T. (1995). The abilities of a musical savant and his family. *Journal of Autism and Developmental Disorders, 25,* 229–245.

Transitioning and Postsecondary Life

Angie Caruso and Simon Crawford

"What will happen after I am gone? Can I live that one day longer than my child?" These are the tormenting thoughts that face the parents of individuals with autism spectrum disorder (ASD). J. Randolph Lewis, a Vice President of Distribution and Logistics for the company Walgreen's and the father of a child with ASD, shared those questions during an interview on NBC news (Brzezinski, 2007). While Walgreen's has made great strides in helping individuals with disabilities transition into the workplace, few other companies have made such efforts, and national statistics on transition are alarming. A 2008 Easter Seals study found that 80% of adults with autism between the ages of 19 and 30 were still living at home and that about 25% of children with autism over the age of 16 are employed, compared to 75% of people that age without developmental disabilities (Huppke, 2008). The study went on to say that children with ASD have more difficulty making use of basic conveniences like cell phones and credit cards. As increasing numbers of individuals are diagnosed with autism, the need for effective transition planning and services will also grow exponentially. Researching and utilizing effective strategies and techniques to help individuals with ASD transition to adulthood is a crucial responsibility for teachers. This chapter will introduce the fundamentals of transition planning and implementation for students with ASD.

WHAT DOES TRANSITION MEAN?

Within the field of education, numerous transitions occur as students move from one school to another or one grade to the next. Change, by nature, can be a great challenge for students with ASD. The Individuals with Disabilities Education Act (IDEA) has outlined and defined transition with regard to special education classified students. In particular, the updated version of IDEA in 2004 is very specific when describing *transition,* which is

> designed to be a results-oriented process, that is focused on improv-ing the academic and functional achievement of the child with a dis-ability to facilitate the child's movement from school to post-school activities, including postsecondary education, vocational education, integrated employment (including supported employment), continu-ing and adult education, adult services, independent living, or com-munity participation (Whitney, 2009).

Essentially, transition services involve a plan for what the student will do after grad-uating from high school. Effective planning should facilitate a smooth transition from high school to postgraduate experiences (e.g., college, workplace). Transition planning should prepare the student for the day after graduation, and can be success-fully assessed in the weeks and months immediately after that date rather than 10 years in the future.

Another section of importance from IDEA explains the student's role in the transition process. The law states that transition services should be "based on the individual child's needs, taking into account the child's strengths, preferences, and interests" (Whitney, 2009). The field of transition is a relatively new one, but it is clearly of great importance to students with ASD. The National Secondary Transition Technical Assistance Center (NSTTAC, n.d.) creatively describes the per-ception versus the reality of transition for individuals with autism. They explain that transition services are

> a coordinated set of activities for a child with a disability that (a) is designed to be within a results oriented process, that is focused on improving the *academic and functional achievement* of the child with a disability to facilitate the child's movement from school to post-school activities, including postsecondary education, vocational education, integrated employment (including supported employment), continuing and adult education, adult services, independent living, or community participation; and (b) is based on the individual child's *needs, taking into account the child's strength's, preferences and interests;* and includes instruction, related services, community experiences, devel-opment of employment and other post-school adult living objectives, and, if appropriate, acquisition of daily living skills and provision of a functional vocational evaluation. (Test, 2009, emphasis mine)

While this comprehensive description explains what transition services should be, the NSTTAC acknowledges that the reality is quite different when they describe the present state of secondary transition for students with ASD as "a period of *flounder-ing* that occurs for at least the first several years after leaving school as adolescents attempt to assume a variety of adult roles in their communities" (Test, 2009). The hope of those who work in the field of transition is to bridge the chasm between these two realities.

TRANSITION FROM IDEA TO SECTION 504 AND THE ADA

As students transition from school to postsecondary life, the laws which give them protection transition as well. IDEA is replaced by multiple civil rights laws such as Section 504 of the Vocational Rehabilitation Act (Section 504) and the Americans with Disabilities Act (ADA). The mandates under IDEA entitle students to certain services where Section 504 and the ADA transition to qualification of eligibility. Danya International, Inc. (2006) stated in order for students to be eligible, they must have (p. 4):

1. a physical or mental impairment that limits at least one major life activity (e.g., functions such as caring for oneself, performing manual tasks, walking, seeing, hearing, speaking, breathing, learning, and working), and
2. a history of this impairment in a major life area.

Because of this, the supports and services the student previously received may be reduced if not completely eliminated (Graetz & Spampinato, 2008). The change in protection under the laws is arguably the most confusing but significant concept for parents and the individual to comprehend.

IDEA protects individuals from the age of 3 until they either receive their high school diploma or until their 22nd birthday, whichever comes first. Under this law, the student is entitled to a Free and Appropriate Public Education (FAPE). FAPE mandates that students receive an Individual Education Plan (IEP) that guarantees the appropriateness of the individual's education. The parents can play a major role in the IEP process, as they are asked for consent and input during the development of the plan. Often, the parents are the main advocates for the student while he or she is covered under IDEA.

Once individuals no longer fall under IDEA, they must meet the criteria mentioned above (e.g., they must have a physical or mental impairment that limits at least one major life activity) to become eligible for Section 504 and the ADA, both of which protect individuals from disability-related discrimination. Under these laws, individuals with disabilities cannot be denied access to services that would be available to individuals without disabilities, though they do not guarantee the appropriateness of those services (Danya International, Inc., 2006). For example, a person with autism cannot be denied entrance to a postsecondary educational institution. However, the educational institution is not required to provide specialized services, such as one-on-one aides or curriculum modification.

Section 504 and the ADA differ from one another. Specifically, Section 504 protects individuals attending federally funded institutions such as postsecondary education, whereas the ADA is more expansive. It covers local and state funded services as well, such as Vocational Rehabilitation or the Division of Developmental Disabilities, described later in this section. The ADA's ultimate goal is to provide access for all while removing barriers to guarantee reasonable accommodations so that persons with disabilities can participate alongside their nondisabled peers (Think College!, 2009a).

This fundamental change in the mechanism of the law impacts the individual and his or her parents in a variety of ways. Upon graduating high school, the known expectations based on FAPE and the IEP no longer exist. The parents' role changes from being the primary advocate to the individual being the primary advocate (unless the individual transfers his or her rights back to the parents). The protections of Section 504 and the ADA are only obtained after the student advocates for what she or he is eligible. Specifically, in the areas of postsecondary education and employment, the student is responsible for obtaining any accommodations necessary to succeed at school or in a job setting. Although accommodations may be granted by higher education institutions or an employer, neither are mandated by Section 504 or the ADA to provide special programs or modifications, as is the case under IDEA (Danya International, Inc., 2006).

THE TEACHER'S ROLE

IDEA outlines the transition requirements for schools with regard to special education students. The law states that, by the time students are 16, their IEP should contain a transition component (Bateman, 2009). Many professional organizations, however, are encouraging parents of children with autism to begin the transition process even earlier, because this intensive planning process requires extensive research and organization (Test, 2009). Each state and even each district may have its own layout for the transition component, but it must address the following areas:

➤ Living arrangements
➤ Postsecondary educational plans, including vocational training
➤ Work experience and possible job placements

Many transition forms also describe future community involvement. IDEA is also specific when it states that a transition form for an IEP must include transition goals (U.S. Department of Education, 2007). These goals are similar to measurable IEP goals and objectives, but they connect to the transition plan. Whenever possible, the curriculum should be aligned to these transition goals in order to better prepare the student for the future.

Teachers can and should take an active role in the transition process. Educators can do this in a number of ways. First of all, they can provide information. By attending in-services, conferences, and staying abreast of changes in legislation, teachers can provide valuable transition information to both parents and students. By including the student in the process, teachers can help students build critical self-advocacy skills. In addition, teachers can help students better understand their own disability in an effort to build the independent skills necessary for higher education and the workplace. Educators can help students complete career assessments, which can help students narrow their focus as they consider options for the future. Additionally, teachers need to be sure that they are providing accommodations and modifications and also explaining their importance to students and parents who will need to take advantage of similar support after graduation. Additionally, special education and general education faculty will help to oversee the process and ensure that the transition IEP is in accordance with IDEA and state guidelines. It is important that teachers explain they are part of a team working with parents and students to accomplish transition goals. Through collaboration, the parents, the student, and the teachers are able to plan and implement a transition IEP that will guide the student with ASD through school and prepare him or her for the all important day after graduation.

POSTSECONDARY OUTCOMES

One size fits all solutions can rarely be used for individuals with ASD as they transition to postsecondary life.

> No single pattern of development and adult outcome characterizes the autistic condition. There are many possible patterns, and many factors—some controllable, some not—shape those patterns. Parents need to know this. So too do the physicians and others—professionals and nonprofessionals—who interact with children who have autism and their families. (Cohen, 2006, p. 41)

One family with two boys exemplifies this disparity of potential postsecondary outcomes. The brothers, Cole and Denny, were both diagnosed with ASD within the first 3 years of their lives, and both currently attend high school. Cole was diagnosed with AS, and Denny with autism.

Throughout his academic career, Cole has always been fully included in the general education setting with the support of a one-on-one assistant and has not participated in a special education class to date. He is very articulate and maintains above average grades. Cole's favorite classes are in the area of science, and he hopes to pursue a career in that field. His own postsecondary plan is to live at home and attend a local community college before transferring to a 4-year university. Cole has no desire to drive a car but plans on either riding his bike to the community college or taking public transit (even though he has no experience with the latter). Cole's parents are pleased with his academic progress but often wonder if he has received adequate schooling specifically in socialization.

Two years younger than Cole, Denny, on the other hand, has participated in self-contained special education programs since his introduction to school. He began communicating verbally when he was in the fourth grade and speaks in simple sentences. Academically, Denny has consistently been one of the better readers in the self-contained program, with a high aptitude for spelling words due, in part, to his assumed photographic memory. In elementary school, Denny's class utilized public transit (city bus) to take field trips throughout the community, and he became proficient and comfortable using public transit. Now in high school, Denny's self-contained program primarily focuses on independent living skills while providing a vocational element. However, his program is flexible enough to allow him to seek areas of interest. After being introduced to Spanish during elementary school, Denny was not given the opportunity to further explore foreign languages during middle school. Even after a multi-year hiatus, the time away has not deterred Denny from planning to take his first formal Spanish class in high school. Denny's other passion is dancing. In elementary school, Denny would randomly break out into dance moves, so his parents enrolled him in a dance program. Through the years, Denny has performed multiple genres of dance during various recitals and has continued to follow his passion by joining the high school dance troupe.

The boys' parents are outstanding advocates for their sons, being consistently involved in the IEP process for both. The parents admit they have projected separate postsecondary outcomes for each of their sons. They envision Cole being totally self-sufficient: attending postsecondary education, finding full-time employment, and living with a family of his own. Equally rewarding for them would be to see Denny entering the workforce upon completion of high school and living in a group home.

As mentioned at the beginning of this section, postsecondary outcomes are unlimited. However, two of the primary outcome categories are discussed in the following sections: postsecondary education and employment. Elemental to both are the range of possible living situation outcomes as well. Each category involves a process and contains numerous outcomes respectively, and each is explained through either Cole's or Denny's projected outcome.

PREPARATION FOR POSTSECONDARY EDUCATION

At least by the time Cole is a junior in high school, he can begin a number of proactive steps to ensure a successful transition to postsecondary education. In the same way, Denny can also take proactive steps to during high school to obtain postsecondary employment.

1. Both Cole and Denny can seek federal and state services such as Vocational Rehabilitation (VR) eligibility, described in detail later in this section.
2. Cole can start visiting the Disability Resource Center at the postsecondary school of interest (if there is one). Note that if students are unsure of which school they would like to attend, this is a good time to explore and look for a

"goodness of fit" between the individual and the campus environment based on the size of the school, average class size, or the services provided (VanBergeijk, Klin, & Volkmar, 2008).

3. For the first time, the reauthorization of the 2008 Higher Education Opportunity Act (HEOA) has made a variety of grants available specifically for individuals with intellectual disabilities who lacked a regular high school diploma or GED equivalency (Lee, 2009). Therefore individuals with ASD who meet this criterion may be able to obtain financial assistance and broaden the list of potential postsecondary institutions of interest.

Division of Vocational Rehabilitation (DVR)

Nationally, the U.S. Department of Education created the Rehabilitation Services Administration (RSA) within the Office of Special Education and Rehabilitative Services (OSERS) as a federally mandated and funded program to assist people with disabilities to prepare for, obtain, and maintain employment.

Denny's goal of directly entering the workforce after high school fits well within the VR framework. Although Cole has aspirations for postsecondary education, VR may still be able to assist him with counseling while still in high school and possibly even support him with his postsecondary education's tuition.

Even though each state must have a DVR, where the program fits in a state's governmental structure, as well as the services provided, vary by state. For example, Arizona currently combines VR with Independent Living Rehabilitation Services under the state's RSA, which, in turn, is part of the Arizona Department of Economic Security. In contrast, in Indiana, VR is a program through the Bureau of Rehabilitation Services under the Division of Disabilities and Rehabilitative Services.

If a person is eligible for VR, he or she may receive the following depending on the specific services included by the state:

➤ Diagnostic services
➤ Vocational evaluation
➤ Counseling
➤ Training
➤ Medical services and equipment
➤ Placement assistance
➤ Assistive technology
➤ Support services (e.g., Danya International, Inc., 2006)

To be eligible, a person must require VR services because of the barrier her or his disability creates in preparing for (e.g., participating in job readiness training), obtaining, and maintaining employment. More importantly, in some states it is also required for the individual to want to be employed (Arizona Department of Economic Security–VR, 2009).

Three steps in the VR process can begin during the student's last 2 years of high school:

1. A student, family member, agency or school makes a referral.
2. The VR counselor sets up an interview and provides the application.
3. The VR counselor determines eligibility.

An Individual Plan of Employment (IPE) from VR is developed once eligibility is determined. During high school, the following services are generally available: vocational counseling; coordination of IEP and IPE; and a "Job Club" that includes career exploration, individual information about the individual's disability and job accommodations, and job development and coaching (Arizona Department of Economic Security–VR, 2009).

Unfortunately, certain circumstances beyond the students' control impact the availability of VR services. If and when federal or state funds are not available, a priority system called Order of Selection is implemented based on the severity of related service needs. Upon eligibility, individuals are placed into three priority levels based on need. Individuals with the most significant disability related service needs are placed in the First Priority category. At the other end of the spectrum, some individuals may meet some of the eligibility requirements but do not have disability related service needs. These individuals might not receive VR and may not even be placed in the Third Priority category. Typically, when Order of Selection is in effect, only individuals from the first and perhaps the second category are served, and all other students are placed on a waitlist.

Cole may be eligible for the Priority Three category because of his organization and socialization needs, while Denny would likely be in the First Priority category. Even if Cole and his family are proactive by initiating services while he is a junior in high school, if Order of Selection is in effect, he is unlikely to receive services prior to graduation. Because of the waitlist, Cole should initiate services as early as possible.

Administration on Developmental Disabilities (ADD)

"The ultimate goal of ADD is to support the independence, growth, and productivity of people with developmental disabilities"(Danya International, Inc., 2006, p. 6). Mandated by the Developmental Disabilities Act, the name of ADD agencies varies from state to state. Division of Disability and Rehabilitative Services is the name of the ADD in Indiana. In California, the ADD is referred to as Department of Developmental Services. In Arizona, the Department of Economic Security oversees the ADD called Division of Developmental Disabilities (DDD) which offers support to those with disabilities and their families with the eventual goal of self-sufficiency (Arizona Department of Economic Security–DDD, 2009). Often when a person is determined eligible for VR, the VR counselor can recommend the individual to also pursue DDD services. Cole did not qualify for DDD services, as his diagnosis of AS deemed him ineligible because his case was insufficiently severe.

However after years of trying and reapplying, Denny finally became eligible under the category of autism.

Disability Resource Center

Another proactive step Cole can take is to visit the Disability Resource Center (DRC) on the campus of the school he is interested in attending (each school may have a different name for its DRC). This will begin to prepare Cole for the differences in expectations between high school and college and the changes he will need to make in response. For example, advocacy for Cole will become solely his responsibility, whereas his parents may have been equally sharing or even taking the lead in this role up to this point. In addition to being introduced to the campus, he will also receive a packet of information to help them navigate through the college system: necessary documentation to apply and register, available supports (e.g., preferential seating, note takers, tape recorded lectures, taking exams in quiet and less distracting environments, and extra time for exams; Adreon & Durocher, 2007), student rights and responsibilities (including how the law affects them), and other tips and suggestions.

Higher Education Opportunity Act

The 2008 HEOA is a reauthorization of the Higher Education Act of 1965. This act provides students with intellectual disabilities who receive a modified high school diploma or GED equivalency eligibility for Pell Grants, Educational Opportunity Grants, and Federal Work–Study Programs (Lee, 2009). Since Cole will likely receive a regular high school diploma, these new provisions may pertain more to Denny if he decides to pursue a degree, certificate, or nondegree program from a qualifying institution. Nevertheless, Cole has numerous opportunities for receiving scholarships and grants as qualifications for each become more and more specific. And, like his non-ASD peers, the earlier potential sources of funding are tapped the better.

POSTSECONDARY PROGRAMS

Students with ASD interested in postsecondary education have the same options as their non-ASD peers:

> ➤ Community college
> ➤ Four-year college or university
> ➤ Vocational training institute

Community College

After assessing the goodness of fit between postsecondary programs, Cole may choose to attend a community college before enrolling in a 4-year university for several reasons (VanBergeijk et al., 2008). If a large university or college is too imposing or the transition is too extreme, the community college may a better alternative, as the campus is generally easier to navigate (Adreon & Durocher, 2007). In addition, community colleges tend to have smaller classes and commuter-style campuses (no dormitories) and are often closer to the home. As stated previously, Cole intends to live with his parents and commute to the community college via bicycle.

Community colleges, like their 4-year counterparts, also provide services through a DRC. As an alternative for some individuals with ASD who find large groups and group work aversive, many community colleges provide online class offerings as well. Dr. Dawn Prince-Hughes, an anthropologist with ASD and author of *Gorilla Nation* (2004), completed much of her postsecondary and graduate work online. She stated that once she found a university that supported her learning needs, she continued on to graduate school, and her dissertation was "a fairly easy experience" (Prince-Hughes, 2004, p. 181).

Four-Year College or University

Although it seemed impossible a decade ago, the numbers of students with autism attending 4-year colleges is on the rise (Trachtenberg, 2008). The goal of universities is for students to fully engage in the college experience by developing skills for adulthood, forming lifelong relationships, identifying a vocational pathway, and participating in extracurricular activities (VanBergeijk et al., 2008).

While Cole may bypass entrance exam requirements by attending a community college before transferring to a university, others with ASD who select a 4-year university may need to take the standardized entrance exams with accommodations.

The services and support provided for individuals with ASD vary greatly at 4-year universities. Some universities offer specialized programs for individuals with ASD and other developmental disabilities. The following are examples:

➤ Marshall University created an Autism Training Center in response to a group of parents who lobbied state legislatures to develop more intensive support and programs for their sons and daughters (Marshall University College of Education and Human Services, 2001). The center offers weekly meetings for students and connects graduate students to undergraduates to help them navigate both the academic and social challenges on campus (Trachtenberg, 2008).

➤ The University of Iowa recently created a program called Realizing Educational and Career Hope (REACH). The program is offered to students with multiple learning and cognitive disabilities. REACH supports students by offering classes that emphasize life and social skills for independent living, specific course work in academic enrichment, and career development (University of Iowa College of Education, 2009).

➤ The University of Arizona offers a variety of services through their Strategic Alternative Learning Techniques Center (SALT). Learning strategies instruction; individualized education planning; academic, leadership, and social programs; and tutoring are a few of the services provided to students with special learning needs (University of Arizona, 2009).

Regrettably, these programs are rare. Yet, more and more colleges are attempting to find innovative ways to accommodate students with ASD. Further information regarding these programs is available in the "Future Trends" section of this chapter.

Potential Challenges

Differences in the college structure, independent living, and socialization may be the biggest obstacles for individuals with ASD attending college. Students who may already struggle with relationships go from living with the comfort of their family to living with strangers. Independent living skills such as budgeting, shopping, hygiene, and getting up to an alarm may pose a challenge (Adrean & Durocher, 2007; VanBergeijk et al., 2008). Relationship issues may arise as the student learns to get along with a roommate or ventures into the dating world. To top that off, the most common comorbid conditions for students with AS are anxiety and depression (VanBergeijk et al., 2008). For Cole or any student with an ASD receiving one-on-one assistance, the biggest challenge he may face is participating in class without an assistant.

Despite these difficulties, the DRC is available to help students with these challenges. As long as students with ASD utilize self-advocacy skills, remedies are available for the challenges they face. Cole would be able to receive tutoring. Students with anxiety or depression may benefit from counseling provided by the school. Lastly, depending on the program, social and organizational help can also be embedded into the program through the use of peer mentors. Because of new technology, federal laws, and increased awareness, colleges are becoming better prepared to help students with ASD (Stout, 2009).

Vocational Training Institute

An alternative to a traditional community college or a 4-year university setting, a Vocational Training Institute (VTI) may be a good choice for some students with ASD. Since Cole has a general interest in science, a VTI may not be the most appropriate choice for him. However, it may be appropriate for Denny, depending on his skills and preferences. VTIs are typically coed institutions offering a variety of specializations such as cosmetology, computer design, and film technology, to name a few. Cole and Denny could have the opportunity to attend a VTI part-time as juniors in high school and eventually receive all classes at the institute. VTI is an excellent choice for some individuals with ASD, as they are able to take classes specifically in their area of interest. However, generally VTIs do not have special education classes, DRCs may not be available, teachers may be overwhelmed by students with more severe support needs, and students with more severe needs may become overwhelmed with the instruction or class size.

JOB READINESS

Just as Cole could take a number of steps during high school for successful transition to postsecondary education, generally, multiple types of job readiness opportunities are also available to students like Denny during high school. In Denny's self-contained program, students' duties range from performing job tasks on campus (from reshelving books in the library to wiping down tables in the cafeteria) to participating in job enclaves off campus and potentially even extend to obtaining part-time employment (e.g., working at a nursing home, folding silverware into napkins at a local restaurant, cleaning video games at an arcade). Students benefit greatly from achieving competitive employment before they graduate high school (Wehman, 2002).

Because Denny may choose to remain in high school until his 22nd birthday, his special education teacher has ample time to assess Denny's "needs, preferences, and interests as they relate to the demands of current and future work" (NSTTAC, n.d.). The teacher could assist Denny with finding the most appropriate employment match by facilitating multiple diverse opportunities and environments for Denny to explore based on his skills, preferences, and needs.

Three areas to consider when analyzing potential job matches are (Grossi, personal communication, July, 2007)

1. environmental conditions,
2. physical demands, and
3. attributes.

Environmental conditions at potential work sites must be considered in light of any sensory sensitivities individuals may have. For example, Denny may be aversive to flashing lights; therefore, working in a bowling alley during Rock'n'Bowl or in an arcade may not be the most appropriate fit, whereas working outdoors on a farm or garden or landscaping may be a good choice. Considering a job's physical demands in relation to the student is significant, as it directly relates successful performance of the job functions required. Although Denny has a great amount of endurance while dancing, he does not perform job tasks with great speed. Therefore, working at the snack bar of the movie theatre may not be the best fit. However, translating documents from English to Spanish may suit his needs, as the time demands may not be as severe. Lastly, matching the student's attributes to the requirements of the position increases the possibility of maintaining that position. Denny is able to verbally communicate using one-word answers or simple sentences, yet he does not currently initiate conversations or ask questions without being prompted. Working in a position requiring Denny to verbally communicate may not be the most appropriate fit, whereas putting library books back on the shelves may be a good fit due to his strong visual memory.

Like Cole, Denny will also need to begin the referral process for VR when he is a junior in high school. Because Denny receives DDD services, his DDD coordinator may initiate contact with VR. Coordinating the VR services with DDD services to assist Denny with his postsecondary life is optimal. However, because of waitlists, funding constraints, and high workloads of the DDD coordinators, the reality is that the process, uninitiated by the student or parents, might not start until closer to 6 months prior to exiting high school, if at all. Therefore teachers and parents should not wait for the process to come to them; rather, they should begin looking into programs as early as possible. Many postsecondary vocational training facilities have coordinators who specialize in giving teachers and parents information about their programs. Often, the student, teachers, and parents can take facility tours to help discern which program is the best fit.

Well before Denny graduates high school, the IEP team should have a good idea of what type of postsecondary employment setting best suits Denny's needs. This may range from placement in Day Treatment for Adults to receiving or maintaining competitive employment straight away. The following sections give a brief summary of the general postsecondary employment outcomes for high school individuals more severely affected by autism. The programs are listed ranging from most supported to most independent.

Training Programs for Competitive Employment

A few noteworthy items include the debate over the effectiveness of certain programs. Research suggests programs solely focusing on prevocational skills may actually limit the individuals' opportunity of eventually achieving competitive employment. According to Steele, Burrows, Kiburz, and Sitlington (1990),

> The facility should never be viewed or utilized as a training vehicle to teach work skills and behaviors ... because usually the opposite occurs in that individuals acquire undesirable behavior and develop few work skills that are applicable to community employment (28). (cited in Nuehring & Sitlington, 2003, p. 25)

Individuals must have the opportunity to learn skills in the genuine work setting. Not only will they acquire the problem solving skills required to perform the job function, they will also benefit from the modeling aspect of working alongside their nondisabled peers.

In addition, the program each provider offers differs greatly as along with the competency of staff, the quality of the facility, and its overall mission. Therefore the importance of researching each program prior to graduation becomes paramount.

Day Treatment for Adults

Day Treatment for Adults (DTA), also known as Day Programs for Adults, is one of the main outcomes for individuals more severely affected by autism. The individuals who attend these programs usually exhibit behaviors severe enough to inhibit them from performing basic job tasks in supported employment (see Challenges).

Although the individual may be capable with appropriate assistance, many programs do not have the funding available to permit one-on-one guidance.

Individuals often attend DTAs 5 days a week for 6 hours a day. As long as individuals qualify for DTA services, they may attend day programs for the rest of their lives. DTAs include activities to enhance independent living and usually have a prevocational element. Some of the programs include excursions for leisure as well as for volunteering opportunities to create hands-on training. Certain sites incorporate a transition program within the day program to help individuals achieve the skills necessary to advance to supported employment.

Supported Employment

Different from VTIs, which provide a diploma upon completion of the curriculum, a Vocational Training Center (VTC) includes different types of supported work programs for adults upon exiting high school. Like DTA, those who are eligible may attend VTC for their entire life. Some VTCs encompass a tiered hierarchy of program options depending on strengths and behaviors for individuals with ASD. The participants are able to advance from one of the four supported employment programs to the next based on their job performance. Unlike DTA, individuals participating in a VTC have the opportunity to receive payment for the jobs performed.

The first type of supported employment was once referred to as a *sheltered workshop* and may now go by titles like *vocational training center* or *vocational training academy*.

The work takes place in a central location and is typically performed in a warehouse setting. The VTC is contracted by businesses to perform repetitive job tasks. Based on the size of the program, up to 100 individuals may sit and perform the task under supervision and are provided with assistance when necessary. The individuals may work at their own pace and are paid based on their level of production. Their workday typically includes two 15 minute breaks and a lunch break.

The second level of supported work is *job enclaves* with job coaches. Individuals perform work at different job sites and have the opportunity to receive higher pay, although it is still sub–minimum wage. The job coaches learn the necessary job tasks and help individuals in the enclave execute the job function. Individuals who need continual support may remain at this level. Those who show readiness and willingness may advance to the next level of employment, semi-independent employment.

With the agreement of an establishment, *semi-independent employment* involves nearly continual supervision from trained employees of the establishment rather than a VTC job coach. The individual may receive support from the VTC on a weekly basis or as needed. An example of semi-independent employment would be working as a receptionist alongside a trained employee.

Independent competitive employment is the final level of employment, where the individual performs job tasks without continuous supervision by an employee with only periodic VTC support. Some individuals have achieved this level through the support of a VTC.

A few VTCs have created a process specifically designed for individuals with autism to obtain competitive employment. First, the VTC initiates partnerships with local businesses. Second, the staff from the VTC train the employees of the businesses on ASD. Third, job coaches learn the job duties and create the accommodations (e.g., visual supports) necessary to support the individual in performing the job function. After the individual starts the job, the final element is to eventually fade the direct job coach support so that the individual is performing the job function independently. One parent whose son participated in the VTC described had tears of joy in her eyes when she discussed how her son was working independently at a local steakhouse, something she never thought would be possible.

Challenges

The main employment opportunities available for individuals with developmental disabilities have been referred to as the "Five Fs": filth, flowers, fun, food, and filing. Instead of focusing on the individuals' interests, preferences, and needs, the main focus is often productivity, whether in performing repetitive tasks or data entry. Performing these job tasks for some individuals is greatly rewarding and meets their needs perfectly. Considering the number of individuals with ASD who are unemployed, this may be one of the only alternatives. Yet for others, their interests, capabilities, and preferences may be better utilized elsewhere. Unfortunately not all businesses, more specifically the people operating the businesses, are open to accommodating individuals with ASD in the workforce, thereby leaving a limited amount of options available. At times, professionals who do not have ASD are the biggest barrier for people with ASD to obtain employment, primarily because of low expectations or lack of awareness (Duran, 2001). Efforts have been and continue to be underway to change those attitudes through education. "You don't need to change [employers'] minds about people's disabilities, you need to change their minds about themselves" (Sawalich, 2006).

The Employed!

As mentioned previously, many people with ASDs successfully maintain full-time employment.

> Eileen holds a position as a receptionist. She types 120 words per minute and has memorized hundreds of zip codes. The challenge Eileen's boss consistently has with her is keeping her busy because she is so efficient. (Eder, 2001)
>
> Another woman severely affected by autism was able to obtain employment through a community integrated approach. She started by working part-time for a trial period with a job coach with nearly continual physical prompting and support. After 4 months, the job coach's support was minimal and the employees eventually took the job coach's place. (Wehman, Gibson, Brooke, & Unger, 1999)
>
> Nancy was described as exhibiting severe and often dangerous behaviors. After successfully completing each of the steps previously outlined, she currently

maintains a 40-hour per week position with benefits. With her training and natural ability, Nancy is capable of performing microfilming tasks two and a half times faster than her nondisabled colleagues. (Henn & Henn, 2005)

Getting Creative

Some parents have been very creative in developing opportunities for their child with ASD. One parent created a position at the furniture store he owned for his son who is nonverbal and severely affected by autism. Another parent who was dissatisfied with the job outcomes available for her daughter was able to secure state funding to create her own supported work program, after obtaining the necessary licensure needed to start a DTA. Other parents who owned a ranch developed a program for their son called Rusty's Morningstar Ranch. This program provides adults with ASD the opportunity to work and live on the working ranch (Rusty's Morningstar Ranch, 2004).

Microenterprises are another great option for individuals with ASD (Koegel & LaZebnik, 2009). In most cases, the individual creates her or his own business based on an interest such as a computer-related business (i.e., data entry, web design, graphic design), dog grooming, car detailing, or accounting (Koegel & LaZebnik, 2009, p. 267–268).

A number of lists are available for possible job options specific to individuals with ASD as well as marketable strengths. Koegel and LaZebnik's *Growing Up on the Spectrum* gives ideas. The local library has books one could find information on this topic. In *The Gifts of Asperger*, John M. Ortiz outlines numerous ways individuals on the spectrum have utilized their unique talents to suit a particular vocation (2006). Yet since every individual's strengths and interests are different, the possibility for jobs is limitless.

So what about Denny? What will his outcome be? Only time will tell. Hopefully through person-centered transition planning and careful job analysis, he will be guided to obtain competitive employment based on his strengths, skills, preferences, needs, and interests.

MILITARY

Some individuals with ASD may be interested in a career in the military. Typically, individuals with ASD are not recruited into the United States military because of the arduous screening process and possible need for medical interventions. Psychotropic medication, such as antidepressants, antipsychotics, and stimulants (Aspy & Grossman, 2007), automatically disqualifies these individuals from being accepted. However, individuals less affected by autism who do not require medical interventions may enlist if they pass the physical and mental capability tests.

Teachers need to be aware that military recruiters may have contact with students and be prepared to answer questions about military service. Rather than influencing the student's decision, the teacher should work with parents in order to provide information. Parents must be aware of the fact that rights transfer to the student at the age of 18 and take necessary precautions if they need to retain responsibility of their child. In 2006, an 18-year-old young man with autism passed army examinations and enlisted to become a cavalry scout, a combat role. Only after his parents voiced their concerns did the army release the young man from his commitment. His parent's reported that "'he'd play with one toy for days. Loud noises bothered him. He was scared to death of the toilet flushing, the lawn mower'" (Klatell, 2006). Ultimately, the military may be a possibility for some individuals with ASD, but teachers and parents should help that individual make an informed and reasonable decision.

LIVING

A pivotal transition decision for individuals with ASD involves living accommodations. One possibility is for parents to have their children live at home with them. This approach offers a number of advantages for worried parents. People with ASD can be sheltered from the pressures and dangers they may face living independently. Additionally, parents can control the home environment for their child and ostensibly teach independent living skills while keeping him or her in a supportive and safe environment. Ultimately, safety and protection are the main reasons that some parents choose to have their child with ASD live with them. The disadvantages to this approach include potential stress for a family who must monitor and supervise their child and the inevitable worry about how their child will survive once they are gone. Lyn Kyneson, a 59-year-old woman, was interviewed about their 28-year-old son who still lived with them. She reported that "he remains with us—probably until one of us dies or we're in crisis. We have limited time to ourselves and never any time away. We worry constantly about what will happen to him when we're gone" (Baskin, 2008).

Parents who are wary of their child living at home for the aforementioned reasons have other options. One possibility is *respite service,* which involves an agency providing support to the family of an individual with ASD. This support could involve a certain amount of supervised time or perhaps weekend housing to provide parents with a break. Two other possible options are group homes and assisted living facilities. *Group homes* are a supervised residence where a group of individuals with disabilities live together and their work and leisure are constantly monitored. For an individual with increased independent living skills, an *assisted living facility* places individuals with autism in a dwelling and provides some supervision, though not as intensive or constant as a group home. The decision to place someone in a group home or assisted living facility is largely dependent on that individual's functional independent living skills. Other options include having two or more people with ASD living in apartment with supervision provided. Another possibility is to have an individual with ASD live with a nondisabled peer who can provide a level of support and supervision. Some parents have even taken the extraordinary measure of creating a living environment for their children, such as a home or even a self-contained village in which housing and all basic needs are provided in order to ensure their safety and well-being.

FUTURE TRENDS

Societal trends are changing. Innovative programs that focus on social or prevocational skills, collegiate level programs for students with and without ASD alike, and transition specialist development are working to create a more inclusive society.

Online Portfolios

Over 15 states are taking advantage of Career Information System (CIS), a program developed by *intoCareers*, based at the University of Oregon. CIS is an online program designed to help middle and high school students with and without ASD explore postsecondary opportunities, as well as to assist students to design pathways for reaching their career goals. CIS includes an online portfolio for students to develop and plan their future as early as middle school, which can be updated through high school and beyond. Some states are mandating CIS be in place so that the graduating class of 2012 will all have an online portfolio. This type of backward planning can be used by students with ASD to supplement the transition process and can create lasting benefits by placing them squarely in charge of developing and creating their own life plan. (University of Oregon, 2009)

Inclusive Society

Autism awareness and building an inclusive society has become an integral component of today's programming. The focus is not only to help the individual with ASD to adapt to the environment but also to educate those who will be working with the individual about ASD. The old African proverb that it takes the village to educate the child, in this case, can be restated: It takes an individual with an ASD to educate the community. The Community Coaching Center (CCC) and Community*Works* exemplify this philosophy.

The CCC is an after-school and weekend social skills program in San Diego, CA, for children and young adults with ASD between the ages of 6 and 22. The CCC program has two main components.

The first is to build appropriate social and behavior skills in students with ASD by participating with neuro-typical peers in community outings and activities. Four groups of five to seven students go out into the community with peer "pals" and volunteers to partake in activities such as taking a dance class, going to the mall, exploring the botanical gardens, taking a yoga class, or visiting a farmers market, to name a few.

The other mission of the program is to increase autism awareness and promote inclusion in the community by handing out cards containing basic facts on autism to people with whom the students come in contact while on their outing.

Although CCC does not tout itself a vocational or transitioning program, the students indirectly learn essential skills for future employment through the activities, volunteering experiences, and friendships created by participating in the program. Increasing the awareness in the community may also contribute to additional future employment opportunities.

Conversely, the Community*Works* program has a prevocational, community-based job training focus, while simultaneously developing social skills through social relationships obtained within the program. Community*Works,* based out of Southwest Autism Research and Resource Center in Phoenix, AZ, is a program for adolescents and young adults with and without ASD between the ages of 13 and 18. The young adults participate in numerous volunteering activities such as volunteering at the zoo, working at the botanical gardens, assisting at a public library, and donating service at a local food bank. Through this program, all students are able to explore potential job avenues and attain a set of skills necessary for future employment. Similar to the CCC, it has a major emphasis on educating the community to create a more inclusive society.

College-Based Inclusion Programs

The Institute for Community Inclusion at the University of Massachusetts at Boston created a website dedicated to postsecondary education options for individuals with intellectual disabilities called *Think College!* The website is an outstanding resource for students, parents, and educators, as a major component is to disseminate information that promotes ideas for improving postsecondary outcomes for individuals with intellectual disabilities. Think College! discusses three models for postsecondary education alternatives, all of which include a dual enrollment aspect that allows students to participate in higher education at the age of 18, at least on a part-time basis, instead of solely remaining in high school until their 22nd birthday (Hart, Grigal, Sax, Martinex, & Will, 2006).

By using funds through IDEA or the local district, collaborative partnerships are created between the school district and 2- or 4-year colleges and universities to implement the program for individuals who, in the past, were thought to not have the capability to achieve higher education. However, once the students reach their 22nd birthday, the local education agency is not required to continue providing support. Nevertheless, by having this opportunity, the students are truly in their least restrictive environment as they receive their education with their age-appropriate peers (Alpern & Zager, 2007).

The three models outlined by the Institute for Community Inclusion are mixed/hybrid, substantially separate, and inclusive individual support. When a student participates in a *mixed/hybrid* program model, the students take classes and participate in social activities with their typical peers as well as take classes such as "life skills" with peers who also have special needs. The *substantially separate* program model includes classes only taken by individuals with special needs. The students have the opportunity to participate in social activities on the campus and may be involved with vocational programs. Lastly, in the *inclusive individual support* students receive individualized services, including an educational coach. The students participate in the college courses offered for credit or audit, and the program of study is centered on the students' career goals.

An example of a program offering a hybrid college and vocational experience is a pilot program at Eastern New Mexico University in Roswell, NM. The program offers students the residential life experience of college, albeit in a closely supervised environment, and the program offers vocational training in areas like auto mechanics, animal care, and fashion merchandise (Eastern New Mexico University, 2008). The program offers on-campus classes in the mornings and work–study opportunities in the community in the afternoons. Another college campus used a transdisciplinary collaborative approach as a pilot program to make the college setting an appropriate place for four individuals with ASD aged 19 to 21. Formed by a partnership between a school district and a local university, the campus utilized the different departments to supply the services necessary to support the students with ASD. Specifically, undergraduate students majoring in the communication sciences program provided speech and language services to the students with autism in the area of pragmatics, perspective-taking tasks, and conversation skills to build social competence (Alpern & Zager, 2007).

Currently, there are 110 of these postsecondary education programs in approximately 34 states across the country, and the number is trending upwards.

Dormitory Life

Given that postsecondary education has become a more feasible outcome for individuals with ASD, the question of living arrangements comes to the forefront. With the exception of core classes (which are difficult because students on the spectrum have trouble understanding why they should be required to take courses that are not in their area of interest), college may be an ideal postsecondary outcome, as the students have choice and are able to complete a program of study in their area of interest. However, going to college is a major transition for all students, especially those with ASD. The comfort of home and familiar structure of school cease, and a daunting new independence and different living arrangements such as living in college dormitories take its place. A few programs have been specifically designed as an answer to the potential obstacle students with ASD may face while attending college. For example, Spectrum College Transition Program (SCTP), founded in 2009, supports the emotional, social, and academic needs of individuals with ASD as they transition to the postsecondary setting. SCTP is the first Residential Transition Program in the state of Arizona (Spectrum Transition Program, 2010).

Living with Peers

Living with peers without ASD is not a new scenario, yet this innovative living arrangement unfortunately does not often occur. Through state programs or from families utilizing state, federal, private money, or a combination, the individual without an ASD is given a stipend along with room and board to live with a person with an ASD.

Living with peers who also have ASD is another option. Lizzie Gottlieb, the filmmaker who created the documentary *Today's Man* about her brother with AS, described the ideal living situation for her brother as follows:

> We are hoping to find a way for him to live on his own. We would like to create a home for young adults with Asperger Syndrome, where they could live independently, but with some supervision. And maybe Heather Locklear could stop by. (Gottlieb, 2009)

One mother stated the ideal living situation for her son who is more severely affected by autism would be for him to live with one other person who also has an ASD with 24-hour supervision. Unfortunately, states do not currently finance living situations such as these, and most families do not have the financial means to create this arrangement.

Professional Development

Some research suggests teachers who participate in transition planning need further professional development in the area of transition. One journal article reveals teachers not being well trained specifically to give transition assessments (Thoma, Saddler & Held, 2002). Along with assessments, other professional competencies helpful for facilitating transition plans are

> collaborative consultation; behavior management and programming; crisis intervention; creative problem solving; family coordination; social, communication, job and employability skills training and coaching; sexuality advising; and coordination of community services. (Clark, 1999, cited in deFur & Patton, 1999, p. 188)

Generally, no degrees or special licensing is required to facilitate transition plans or to be a transition specialist. Because of the impact transition plans have on postsecondary outcomes for students, the University of Kansas at Lawrence recently created courses to support transition professionals. A few examples of the courses offered are Transition Assessment, Preparing Students for Employment/Postsecondary Education, and Family Involvement and Student Involvement in Transition. (University of Kansas, 2009). Hopefully this trend will continue at other institutions to achieve more consistent results.

IMPLICATIONS FOR TEACHERS

To date, there is very little research on current postsecondary outcomes, and unfortunately the majority of research available portrays negative postsecondary outcomes for those with ASD. Dunlop, MacKay, and Knott (2007) noted that adults with ASD do not have the same outcomes as their typical peers, as they are less likely to complete college, move away from home, obtain friendships, marry, or work independently. In the 2006 *Newsweek* article "What happens when they grow up?" the CEO of the Autism Society of America stated that once students with ASD "lose the educational entitlement and become adults, it's like they fall off the face of the earth" (Kantrowitz & Scelfo, 2006).

Yet with the surge of accurate diagnoses in the 1990s, autism awareness abounded. Because of this awareness, students with ASD were more accurately placed and started receiving services necessary to achieve a free and, most importantly, appropriate public education. Parents started getting answers to some if not all of their questions and, with this knowledge, became powerful advocates for their children as they rallied together to build outstanding organizations dedicated to research. A huge emphasis on the importance of early intervention came to the forefront, successful models specific for students with ASD were implemented, and opportunities for teacher training emerged. The students with ASD who received early intervention over the past two decades are now becoming adolescents and adults (Koegel and LaZebnik, 2009). What will future research reveal?

The true test of our combined efforts is how prepared the student is for life the day after graduating high school (or turning 22 years old). A recent study conducted by the Easter Seals listed the top five concerns parents have for their children with ASDs upon exiting high school in order of importance (2009):

1. Independence
2. Financial well-being
3. Quality of life
4. Employment
5. Independent living

For teachers, this should reinforce the imperative to keep the big picture in mind: School prepares students for life. Is any one year a student with autism spends in school more important than any other? Early intervention is indeed essential, but it should not minimize the significance of the years that culminate with the completion of high school, as each year is a stepping stone for postsecondary life.

The following seven implications,

1. self-determination,
2. start transitioning skills early,
3. know your students,
4. focus on ability versus disability,
5. maintain high expectations,

6. parent connection, and

7. social competence: the power of peers

are dedicated to teachers, regardless of grade level, who work with individuals with autism. These implications were created through a compilation of interviews conducted with transition specialists, exceptional educators, and adults and students with ASD to give advice to teachers. Keep in mind that although the areas are presented separately, they are truly all interconnected. With more understanding and awareness, we can better reach our goal as educators: to help our students achieve the quality of life about which they dream upon exiting high school.

Self-Determination

What is self-determination?

> Self-determination refers to an individual's ability to express preferences and desires, make decisions, and initiate actions based on those decisions. Simply, self-determination refers to choice. It stresses goal setting and active follow through to achieve the goals. (Wilson, 1998, p. 247)

Why is self-determination important? First of all, a direct correlation has been established between self-determination and better adult outcomes (Thoma et al., 2002). Secondly, IDEA mandates a transition plan be based on a student's interests and desires. Lastly, the overall quality of life is defined as the individual's ability to exercise self-determination, choice, and control (Wilson, 1998). By definition, self-determination encompasses an individual's desire, choice, and control by extension.

What does self-determination look like? A teacher implements self-determination instruction by promoting choice making, encouraging exploration of possibilities and reasonable risk taking, fostering problem solving, promoting self-advocacy, facilitating the development of self-esteem, developing goal setting and planning, and helping individuals to understand their disabilities (Bremer, Kachgal, & Schoeller, 2003).

A variety of strategies foster self-determination: facilitating person-centered planning, encouraging student-led IEPs, role playing before conducting student-led IEPs, and utilizing student created portfolios to share at meetings (Thoma, Saddler, & Held, 2002). The most difficult aspect for teachers in implementing these strategies is giving up control. Especially in transitioning, students with ASD should have as much autonomy as possible (LaCava, 2005). Self-determination is central to all aspects of transition discussed in the following sections.

Start Transition Skills Early

Four primary areas of transitioning are (Halpern, Herr, Doren, & Wolf , 2000)

1. personal life,

2. jobs,

3. education and training, and
4. independent living.

Any 16-year-old, regardless of ability, benefits from skills taught in these areas. Most 16-year-olds who do not have ASD acquire the skills needed in these four areas, for the most part, without explicit education by learning from example, learning through experience, and observing peers. Students with ASD do not have the same luxury. Although IDEA mandates transition must start by the age of 16, a number of transition skills can be attained prior to the mandate. In other words, the high school teachers are not the only ones responsible for the student's transition; all teachers play a role in the process.

The first area of transitioning, personal life, includes family, culture, friends, and leisure activities, in a nutshell, what makes getting up in the morning worthwhile. Certain activities used throughout all grade levels support this area. In elementary school, the celebration of cultures helps give students definition to who they are while respecting other student's differences. Building a portfolio of autobiographies of their lives, written or story mapped, even at an early age, assists students by building self-advocacy and self-determination skills essential for their future. Middle school is a time students start to really look into themselves. By this age, the students are aware of who their friends are, what their strengths and weaknesses are, what activities they enjoy, and what possible career avenues they may be interested in pursuing. By high school, students should be on their way to exploring the career interests they have already identified, have a strong sense of the leisure activities they enjoy, and hopefully have established and maintained friendships. The ability to articulate wants and needs and to know when and how to disclose information on their disability is an essential skill students should grasp after they have completed high school.

How the student is supported in the area of employment, the second category outlined by Halpern et al. (2000), may depend on the students' program placement. Middle school and high school self-contained programs often have an intense vocational focus where students have the opportunity to receive on-the-job training. However, a certain set of skills referred to as the *hidden curriculum* or *soft skills* need to be explicitly taught to students in the self-contained programs as well as their to higher skilled peers in full inclusion (M. Greenberg, personal communication, May 2009). Soft skills are described as dressing appropriately in different social contexts, using proper hygiene, being punctual, being able to work in groups, participating in active listening, having a work ethic, and understanding the concept of sharing, just to name a few. These soft skills are not typically taught directly and are usually not the skills evaluated to earn a diploma or degree. However, soft skills are required to obtain and maintain employment. An example of directly teaching a soft skill is to have the students create their own checklist on personal hygiene to aid them with self-care as a visual cue to use at home and in school. Using a simulated "time card" at a young age by having the students obtain teachers' initials upon on-time arrival to their class supports punctuality and instills the soft skill needed for a vocation. A soft skill such as work ethic could be explicitly taught during the early elementary years by teaching the students to continue working when the teacher is not in the students' proximity. Often, students with ASD need to be explicitly taught how to ask for more work when they are finished or how to ask for help when they do not understand an assignment. Teaching communication and social skills such as the difference between what is said to the teacher versus to their peers sets students up for success once they are employed, as they have a better understanding of how to communicate with their supervisors versus their colleagues. These and other soft skills can be taught and reiterated throughout the academic life of the student with ASD.

The third category of transition is education and training. Allowing students to be in charge of their IEP, also known as a student-led IEP, gives students a great deal of awareness in the area of goal setting, whether it be for college, vocational or technical college, or the workforce. Once students graduate high school, they must continue goal setting on their own to achieve their postsecondary education or career goals. By this time, the students should have an extensive portfolio as well as the skills to be strong advocates for themselves. Students will need to know the type of accommodations they will need to be successful in their future endeavors, like going to the Disability Resource Center in postsecondary education or to a job coach in the workforce. Assisting students to create a letter to a future faculty member or employer explaining their learning needs is an excellent strategy that supports self-advocacy (Think College!, 2009a). Another issue individuals with ASD may face upon graduation from high school is proper time management skills. Helping students to use day planners and calendars will support their postsecondary life as the familiar structure of elementary, middle, and high school ceases. At any grade level, utilizing field trips to local businesses, community colleges, vocational schools, and 4-year universities may encourage students to create long range goals while completing the short range goals they have year to year as they complete their program of study.

Independent living is the final area of transition for the student. Again, some self-contained programs focus on daily living skills such as money management, cooking, laundry, or utilizing public transit to familiarize students with their possible future modes of transportation. Asking a question such as, "Will the student be able to function as an adult if he or she does not learn the skill being taught?" helps keep things in perspective as well as assess priorities (Carothers & Taylor, 2004, p. 102). Often, educators focus on goals such as shoe tying, money skills, and knowing certain facts such as the names of colors in a box of crayons (Dr. P. Gerhardt, personal communication, May 21, 2009). If a student has spent years with shoe tying as a goal on her or his IEP, likely the student is disheartened from not mastering the task year after year, and the time spent on the goal could have been better spent elsewhere. Jaime Burke, a university student diagnosed with autism articulated his frustration with the emphasis everyone had put on him to succeed with shoe tying versus trying to help him verbally communicate. He stated "Isn't tying the speech from my mouth to my brain more critical to life than making a piece of cotton secure?" (Biklen & Burke, 2006, p. 171). If by high school students can identify every coin with proficiency but are unable to make change or understand the difference between expensive and inexpensive, do they really grasp the concept of money? For example, Sasha was able to combine coins and even make change, yet to her a 50-cent soda was the same as buying a $100 pair of jeans. Lastly, how will knowing the difference between Indigo and Magenta help the student who does not know the difference between male and female symbols used for the public restrooms (Dr. P. Gerhardt, personal communication, May 21, 2009)?

One of the most important skills to teach for independent living is how to enable the student to be resourceful. When a problem does occur, does the student know whom to call or how to find the right resource for assistance? Does the student know how to ask for help? While teaching independent living skills, Gerhardt (personal communication, 2009) recommends teachers create problem-solving opportunities. For example, taking students to the grocery store while they purchase items next to the teacher is not as effective a strategy as a teacher setting up opportunities for the students themselves to purchase the items with the teacher observing from a distance. Many times, cashiers look to the teacher or assistant instead of communicating directly with the student. Taking it a step further, Gerhardt recommends that teachers build relationships with the store and train the cashiers to work with the students (personal communication, May 21, 2009). Throwing kinks in the scenario during instruction creates authentic opportunities to solve problems while support is readily available.

People with ASD often become stressed and overwhelmed by even minor life events. Helping students learn strategies to cope with stress and anxiety at an early age may positively impact their ability to deal with future major life demands. Students can build their own "bag of tricks" of techniques they find useful for relaxation. A young woman with an ASD was highlighted in a Discovery Health Channel documentary on autism. To alleviate stress while on the job, she would sing "stress, stress, go away, come again another day" (Eder, 2001).

As mentioned previously, the following are specific examples of the hidden curriculum, or soft skills, that teachers either assume students are capable of performing or have or will develop automatically like individuals without ASD. Think about the skills required for a conversation, which teachers do not typically tend to think about. However, these skills often prove to be problematic for individuals with ASD in their adult life. The following anecdote is from a teacher explaining how she had to teach a soft skill on cleanliness:

> My student would come to school every day in the same clothing. When I tried to explain why we need to change clothes I realized I needed to make it more concrete. I told the student items such as socks, underwear shirts, basically anything that came in contact with the skin should be changed daily. (S. McClure, personal communication, April 15, 2009)

Areas of this student's life such as making friends or one day obtaining employment may be positively affected from learning that skill.

Although not under the four topics listed, collaboration among teachers across the various grade levels is invaluable for creating smooth transitions from one educational setting to the next. Often, teachers become extremely focused on the area and grade level that they teach. Think of how powerful the students' education track would become if the elementary school teachers collaborated with middle school and high school teachers to know and understand what will be expected or to solicit feedback about areas of improvement. Are high school teachers aware of the postsecondary options for their students? Involvement of the school with the postsecondary programs depends upon the district. A vocational director of a habilitation program stated that the school districts involved in transition by visiting vocational placements while corresponding with the transition specialist and involving parents in the process had the most successful transitions as a result (F. Siegel, personal communication, April 23, 2009). This type of true backward planning will have powerful effects on the students' postsecondary outcomes. Again, keeping the big picture in mind is the key.

Know and Advocate for Your Students

Not focusing on the disability and understanding a diagnosis such as an ASD are divided by a fine line. Without comprehending the underlying characteristics of autism, such as differences in communication and socialization, repetitive behaviors, and restricted interests, students with ASD are often misunderstood, misplaced, and subjected to lowered expectations. The gifts and abilities of these students are overshadowed by the negative effects of autism. A student with an ASD described his school's environment metaphorically, comparing himself to a saltwater fish being forced to live in fresh water. The student explained that when there is a "match" between students with ASD and the environment, the problems go away and people with ASD thrive (Humphrey, 2008). It is our job as educators to create the correct environment to allow students to flourish.

A variety of software and assistive technology is available today that can help students to read, write, and communicate in multiple ways. The earlier students become familiar with utilizing the alternative modes necessary to access their education, the more the assistive technologies will enhance the students' future potential to attain employment. Augmentative and alternative modes of communicating are especially vital to students who are unable to express their ideas fully if they have limited speech or no functional speech whatsoever. Teachers who take passive roles regarding the need for augmentative and alternative communication allow the students to become even more isolated and dependent upon others (Cohen, 2006). Being an advocate for students truly impacts the quality of their postsecondary lives.

Knowing your students is critical when creating goals and objectives for the students' IEP. With online IEP programs, teachers are able to choose general goals and objectives from a dropdown box. Doing so at times takes the "individualized" out of the IEP. One parent relayed her frustration on this subject as follows:

> Work on functional living skills that are specific to the individual.
> There is a tendency to be too broad when working on functional

> living skills. For example: IEP goal: Appropriate change to buy a
> soda in a vending machine. My son does not drink soda, only water,
> so he would need to know the appropriate amount of money to buy
> water out of a vending machine. Teach a child how to pop popcorn
> if that is what they eat or make a bologna sandwich not PB&J if they
> don't eat PB&J. Take them to the grocery store and show them where
> the items they need are, they will remember! It is very tough, I know,
> but it has to really mean something to these kids. (J. Ciraolo, personal
> communication, April 25, 2009)

Developing goals based on students' natural motivators increases the likelihood of
mastery for students and supports generalization of the skills into their postsecondary lives as a result.

Focus on Strengths and Abilities

Focusing on students' strengths and capabilities is essential, as the lack thereof may
be a detriment to the students' postsecondary outcome. John Elder Robison, the
author of *Look Me In The Eye: My Life With Aspergers* (2007), elaborated on this
topic in the following email:

> Teachers often see kids when their lives are ruled by failure. The
> focus is always on what they can't do, not what they can do. It's a
> never-ending stream of "Johnny can read at grade level," "Bob won't
> talk and has no friends," and "Ann can't get basic algebra no matter
> what I do."
>
> Kids with neurological differences live their early lives with a ter-
> rible burden of failure. Life can be one disappointment after another
> as they see what sets them apart from other kids.
>
> However, things often change for the better as they get older, as
> unique strengths and abilities start to emerge. The adult result can be
> seen in people like Daniel Tammet, Temple Grandin, and myself. All
> of us were looked upon as failures as children and all of us went on
> to achieve considerable success as grownups.
>
> If teachers were to take one vital lesson away from that, it would
> be this: You can never predict the future success of a child from
> today's classroom failures. Some of the most successful people in the
> world struggled terribly in school, and some even dropped out. It's
> vital for teachers to have that perspective and be aware of each
> child's hidden potential. (J. E. Robison, personal communication,
> April 7, 2009)

When teachers are aware of students' strengths and abilities, they may discover the
students' hidden potential and foster this potential appropriately, leading to positive
postsecondary outcomes. In her memoir, *Songs of a Gorilla Nation: My Journey*

Through Autism (2004), Dawn Prince-Hughes described the one and only teacher with whom she was able to connect during her primary and secondary education:

> I was amazed when I started fifth grade and my teacher, Kay Eckiss, seemed to understand my problems. She let me complete the scholastic reading achievement tests at my own pace. When I finished them, she let me choose my own reading material and write book reports. She never criticized my bad penmanship. She allowed me to help start and edit a class poetry journal called "writers on the wing." She allowed me to do minimal math, and if my problems resurfaced in one area, she would let me try another area altogether. Best of all she did not make me go outside for recess and play with the other children. We would have long talks. She didn't laugh at me. She took me seriously ... when she disagreed with me she gave me reasons, logical well-thought-out ones. This separated her from almost everyone else I had ever known. She made me want to understand. I started to feel like there might be a chance for me not to be alone. (p. 47)

This is an excellent example of a teacher focusing on student's abilities rather than disabilities or deficits. As a teacher, focusing on the disability may come more naturally, as the teacher's role is to assist and prepare the student for life in the mainstream world. When working with students with ASD, discerning a natural ability that may be a potential career avenue from a possible barrier to succeeding can be incredibly challenging. Natural gifts and talents that students exhibit may clash with the academic objectives for the day. Linus, a high school student with an incredible gift for drawing and inventing characters for comic books, was often reprimanded by his general education teachers for drawing during their lectures. In this scenario, the teachers feared Linus's habit for doodling was interfering with his academics. However, often, Linus's doodling enhanced his comprehension of the lectures as a personal way of taking notes.

One of Temple Grandin's many talents is drawing. Her ability to draw developed into one of her current careers as a designer of humane cattle handling systems. In an article on giving advice to parents of children with autism, Grandin discussed the importance of developing children's talents and using their talents as motivation for learning skills (Adams, Edelson, Grandin, & Rimland, 2004). Jack, a high school student diagnosed with HFA loved to do surveys. In the morning, Jack would pick the topic of his survey. His survey topics were wide ranging but often revolved around sports, for example, polling which NFL team would win the Monday night football game. Every day during the multiple 7-minute bell transitions between classes, he asked for students' prediction. Sometimes, he would survey over 200 students in a single day. Jack's math teacher would utilize the polls in her lessons to teach him percentages, averages, probabilities, and the like. "Some of the most successful people on the autism spectrum who have good jobs have developed expertise in a specialized skill that often people value" (Adams et al., 2004).

Maintain High Expectations

Keeping high expectations of the performance of a student with ASD can help foster lasting positive impacts for years to come.

> Nadia graduated high school with straight As. She attributed her success to family, good teachers, and friends. Nadia just completed her first year in a community college, taking an academic load of 15 hours each semester, including courses such as English 101, computers, college algebra, sociology, and psychology.
>
> Nadia intends to transfer to the 4-year university after she completes her associate's degree at the community college. Although Nadia would love to become a teacher, she has chosen to pursue a program of study geared toward information systems and technology, as there are many opportunities for employment and to make a higher salary. Nadia has the diagnoses of ASD and visual impairment. She stated, "I thought a lot of things might not ever happen to me, but with help and support, anyone can succeed." (N. Gonzalez, personal communication, April 10, 2009)

Teachers have an influential role in the outcomes for the students they teach.

"When teachers tell students they will succeed and then create a context to help them do so, students so often become successful" (Kluth, 2003, p. 152). Yet, having high expectations and the same expectations for every student are not synonymous. Knowing the student paired with focusing on the student's abilities creates the formula for maintaining high expectations.

Parent Connection

The greatest advocates, before students are capable of advocating for themselves, are their parents. Parents are the ultimate teacher's resource for learning how autism affects their child. In many cases they already have strategies to help support their child in the home environment that may be easily replicated in an inclusive setting (Fredlander, 2009). Many times, parents are the teachers' greatest allies. Often, parents are willing to take the lead and expend a great deal of energy on the teachers' behalf. Some of the most effective programs and organizations were started by parents recognizing a need and collaborating with the teacher to fulfill that need. One of many examples is a mother of twins with ASD who launched a lunch-recess program that is now implemented in her daughters' school district called The FRIEND Playground Club (The FRIEND Playground Club, 2009). Although her daughters were progressing academically, she was concerned about their social progress after observing them isolated from their peers during recess. By collaborating with the Southwest Autism Research and Resource Center (SARRC) and her daughters' school district, the successful program was put into place.

Conversely, if parents do not have the information they need, especially if their child was recently diagnosed, teachers can take the lead and become a resource by disseminating information to parents. Helping parents understand services available for their son or daughter is crucial. It is not uncommon to hear stories of elderly parents waiting until they are on their deathbeds before pursuing state help for their 50- or 60-year-old son or daughter because they were not aware of services available. The earlier parents are informed of available services and programs for their son or daughter, the more likely they will benefit and not be denied access to those services because of waiting lists.

Social Competence: The Power of Peers

Some people with ASD have difficulties with job retention because of lack of social competency rather than inability to complete job tasks (Alpern & Zager, 2007). Social competency begins at an early age when friendships are formed and maintained. Because of differences in socialization and communication, making friends and maintaining friendships is challenging for some students with ASD (Dunlop et al., 2007). Although certain students with ASD often appear to be disinterested in developing friendships, their limitations in the social skills required for friendships may make them merely appear aloof. Unfortunately, bullying can be a consequence. If students cannot develop friendships in school, they may have difficulties with getting along with others in the future, which could lead to job loss, loneliness, depression, and low self-esteem.

A large amount of research has established the importance of utilizing peers to increase social competence in students with ASD (Dunlop et al., 2007; Legler, 2007). This information has great significance, as peers have been used in powerful ways, providing opportunities for students with ASD to practice socialization and communication in natural contexts (Legler, 2007).

Successful programs have a dual purpose. One is to increase the social competence of students with ASD through natural contexts. The other more subtle purpose is to develop awareness in peers without ASD. Programs such as The FRIEND Playground Club not only increase the self-esteem and social competence of students with ASD, they also simultaneously instill a sense of acceptance and compassion in their peers without ASD. As stated by Donmoyer, these students will one day be the neighbors, colleagues, bosses, and even employees of their peers with ASD (The FRIEND Playground Club, 2009).

Utilizing peers is not just about placing students with ASD in a group of students without ASD. More importantly, peers can be instructed in a variety of ways to take active role. As social role models, peers can model certain functional tasks in the community, such as how to cross the street, how to select a library book, or how to purchase an item from the bookstore (Carothers & Taylor, 2004). Individuals with ASD need to learn how to "socially engage with others in accordance with standard societal practices, at home, school, and within the community" to learn the skills necessary to get their needs met in all types of community settings (Stichter,

Randolph, Gage, & Schmidt, 2007, p. 228). Peers can facilitate social skills lessons. One high school teacher of students with ASD handed over her social skills lesson plans once a week to the peer tutors who came into her classroom. The peers without ASD found creative ways of delivering the social skills lesson targeted for the day. In most cases, the students with ASD were much more interested in learning from their peers than from their teacher.

Implementing peer programs in elementary and high school potentially creates individuals like the one discussed in the following case study about a college student with ASD who was fortunately placed with a compassionate roommate:

> The roommate acted as a life skills coach for Mike. This person helped him navigate the social complexities of dorm life and taught him independent living skills. They ate meals together. The roommate even invited him on social outings like camping trips with friends. This 'intervention' happened through serendipity—not through design. The roommate took a genuine interest in helping Mike decode the social world. A key function the roommate provided Mike with was a list of rules of how to behave and under what circumstances. Mike did well in situations where rules were defined. (VanBergeijk et al., 2008, p. 1366)

Research suggests that students profit from peer training and support models in college, because many times the students with ASD are more able to benefit from the full college experience (Adreon & Durocher, 2007; VanBergeijk et al., 2008). Yet many college campuses may not have programs geared toward peer mentoring specifically for students with ASD. In college or the workforce, the initiation from others without ASD plays a role in supporting their peers or colleagues with ASD. "A truly inclusive world will depend on the efforts and courage of those who are not disabled—in a word, society at large" (Hockenberry, 2005, as cited in Byrnes, 2008, p. 5).

SUMMARY

Many schools are not prioritizing properly when preparing individuals with ASD for transition. School personnel create an IEP for a student, which dictates and controls the student's educational plan, and the transition plan is included as somewhat of an afterthought. This philosophy requires a paradigmatic shift: The IEP and the transition plan should be given equal weight and consideration when educationally planning for students. Classes chosen should be appropriate to IEP goals and should also prepare students for their transition. This change will help schools address academic needs while still preparing students for the future and improving the likelihood of successful transition outcomes for individuals with ASD. Another concern originates from the teachers themselves. If asked what their most valuable resource is, it is safe to say that many teachers would mention time. If they were asked what resource would help them do their job more effectively, many would likely respond the same way. Teachers are constrained by their need to plan lessons, grade papers, meet with parents, attend in-services, and the list goes on. With all of those time demands, a logical question for a teacher to ask is, "How will I have time to work on transition skills with my students?" Even those who do not feel they have a free second during the day can find ways to ensure that transition skills are part of each and every day. The simple answer to the question posed above is, "Make transition skills part of the lessons you are already teaching." This could include everything from fractions being represented as food items to geography lessons that have students read a map and plan a vacation. The opportunities are limitless. State standards and educational objectives should still be the guiding forces, but in order to better serve the transition needs of their students, teachers need to be asking themselves this vital question during every lesson of every class period of every school day: "How will this help my student transition and be successful in the future?"

REFERENCES

Adams, J. B., Edelson, S. M., Grandin, T., & Rimland, B. (2004). Advice for parents of young autistic children. *Autism Research Institute*. Retrieved June 29, 2009, from http://www.autism.com/autism/first/adviceforparents.htm

Adreon, D. & Durocher, J. S. (2007). Evaluating the college transition needs of individuals with high-functioning autism spectrum disorders. *Intervention in School and Clinic, 42*(5), 271–279.

Alpern, C. S., & Zager, D. (2007). Addressing communication needs of young adults with autism in a college-based inclusion program. *Education and Training in Developmental Disabilities, 42*(4), 428–436.

Arizona Department of Economic Security–DDD. (2009). *The Division of Developmental Disabilities*. Retrieved March 9, 2009, from https://egov.azdes.gov/cmsinternet/main.aspx?menu=96&id=2454

Arizona Department of Economic Security–VR. (2009). *Vocational Rehabilitation (VR)*. Retrieved March 9, 2009, from https://egov.azdes.gov/CMSInternet/main.aspx?menu=32&id=1300

Aspy, R., & Grossman, B. G. (2007). *The Ziggurat Model: A framework for designing comprehensive interventions for individuals with high-funtioning autism and Asperger Syndrome*. Shawnee Mission, KS: Autism Asperger.

Bateman, B. (2009). *Legal Requirements for Transition Components of the IEP*. Retrieved March 11, 2010, from http://wrightslaw.com/info/trans.legal.bateman.htm

Baskin, A. (2008). Empty Nest Envy. *More.ca*. Retrieved February 22, 2009, from http://www.more.ca/relationships/family-and-friends/empty-nest-envy/a/18861

Biklen, D. & Burke, J. (2006). Presuming Competence. *Equity & Excellence in Education, 39,* 166–175.

Bremer, C. D., Kachgal, M., & Schoeller, K. (2003) Self-determination: Supporting successful transition. Research to practice brief: improving secondary education and transition services through research. *The National Center of Secondary Education and Transition, 2*(1). Retreived July 4, 2009, from http://www.ncset.org/publications/viewdesc.asp?id=962

Brzezinski, M. (2007). Walgreens program puts the 'able' in disabled. *Msnbc.com*. Retrieved January 23, 2009, from http://www.msnbc.msn.com/id/19417759#storyContinued

Byrnes, M. (2008). *Taking sides: Clashing views in special education*. Dubuque, IA: McGaw-Hill Contemporary Learning Series.

Carothers, D. E. & Taylor, R. L. (2004). How teachers and parents can work together to teach daily living skills to children with autism. *Focus on Autism and Other Developmental Disabilties, 19*(2), 102–104.

Cohen, S. (2006). *Targeting Autism: What we know, don't know, and can do to help young children with autism spectrum disorders*. Berkeley and Los Angeles: University of California Press.

Danya International, Inc. (2006). *Life journey through autism: a guide for transition to adulthood*. Arlington, VA: Organizaton for Autism Research.

Dunlop, A., MacKay, T., & Knott, F. (2007) Developing social interaction and understanding in individuals with autism spectrum disorder: A group-work intervention. *Journal of Intellectual & Developmental Disability, 32*(4), 279–290.

Duran, E. (2001). Overcoming people barriers in placing severely aberrant autistic students in work sites and community. *Education, 107*(3), 333–337.

deFur, S. H. & Patton, J. R. (1999). Transition and school-based services: Interdisciplinary perspectives for enhancing the transition process. *Focus on Autism and Other Developmental Disabilities, 5*(3), 188–189.

Easter Seals. (2009). *Living with autism study*. Retrieved July 5, 2009, from http://www.easterseals.com/site/PageServer?pagename=ntlc8_living_with_autism_study_thankyou

Eastern New Mexico University. (2008). *Special Services—Occupational Training Program*. Retrieved February 17, 2009, from http://www.roswell.enmu.edu/special_services/occupational_training_program.php

Eder, S. (2001). The Invisible Wall: Autism [Documentary]. *The Discovery Health Channel*. Terra Nova Production.

Fredlander, D. (2009). Sam comes to school: Including students with autism in your classroom. *The Clearing House, 82*,(3), 141–144.

The FRIEND Playground Club. (2009). *COX Studios, Level Image and Lyndsey Waugh*. Retrieved June 29, 2009, from http://www.youtube.com/watch?v=ZFxDjKokQWA

Gottlieb, L. (2007). Today's Man. *Independent Lens*. Retrieved May 20, 2009, http://www.pbs.org/independentlens/todaysman/

Graetz, J. E., & Spampinato, K. (2008). Asperger's Syndrome and the voyage through high school: Not the final frontier. *Journal of College Admission, 198* (Winter), 19–24.

Grossi, T.A. (2007). I'm on my way…, but I don't know where I'm going: preparing for life after high school [pp handout]. *Indiana's Center for Excellence*. Indiana University.

Halpern, A., Herr, C. M., Doren, B., & Wolf, N. H. (2000). *Next S.T.E.P.: Student Transition and Educational Planning*. Austin, TX: Pro-Ed.

Henn, J. & Henn, M. (2005). Defying the odds: you can't put a square peg in a round hole no matter how hard you try. *Journal of Vocational Rehabilitation, 22,* 120–130.

Hart, D., Grigal, M., Sax, C., Martinez, D., & Will, M. (2006). Research to Practice: Postsecondary Education Options for Students with Intellectual Disabilities. *Institute for Community Inclusion*. Retrieved June 19, 2009, from http://www.thinkcollege.net/for-professionals/pathways-to-postsecondary-education

Humphrey, N. (2008). Autistic spectrum and inclusion: Including pupils with autistic spectrum disorders in mainstream schools. *Support for Learning, 23*(1), 41–47.

Huppke, R. W. (2008). Autism Study: Fears for the future. *Chicagotribune.com*. Retrieved July 1, 2009, from http://archives.chicagotribune.com/2008/dec/16/local/chi-autism-study

Kantrowitz, B., & Scelfo, J. (2006, November 27). What happens when they grow up: Teenagers and young adults are the emerging face of autism as the disorder continues to challenge science and unite determined families. *Newsweek*. Retrieved July 5, 2009, from http://www.newsweek.com/id/44634

Klatell, J. M. (2006). Army Releases Autistic Teen. *CBSNews.com*. Retrieved March 11, 2009, from http://www.cbsnews.com/stories/2006/05/12/national/main1613987.shtml

Kluth, P. (2003). Seeing students with autism as literate: Beyond sight words. In *You're going to love this kid: Teaching students with autism in the inclusive classroom* (pp. 135–152). Baltimore: Brookes.

Koegel, L. K., & LaZebnik, C. (2009). *Growing up on the spectrum: A guide to life, love, and learning for teens and young adults with autism and Asperger's*. NY: Penguin.

LaCava, P. G. (2005). 20 ways to facilitate transition. *Intervention in School and Clinic, 41*(1), 46–48.

Lee, S. S. (2009). Policy brief: Overview of the federal Higher Education Opportunities Act Reauthorization. *Institute for Community Inclusion, 1*. Retrieved June 19, 2009, from http://www.thinkcollege.net/for-professionals/higher-education-opportunity-act-of-2008

Legler, L. (2007). Social fitness for students with Asperger's Syndrome: A classroom-based program for secondary schools. *The ASHA Leader, 12*(17), 12–13.

Marshall University College of Education and Human Services. (2001). *The West Virginia Autism Training Center*. Retrieved March 3, 2009, from http://www.marshall.edu/coe/atc/about.htm

National Secondary Transition Technical Assistance Center (NSTTAC). (n.d.). *Age appropriate transition assessment guide*. Retrieved July 4, 2009, from http://www.nsttac.org/products_and_resources/tag.aspx

Nuehring, M. L., & Sitlington, P. L. (2003). Transition as a vehicle: Moving from high school to an adult vocational service provider. *Journal of Disability Policy Studies, 14*(1), 22–35.

Ortiz, J. M. (2006). *The Gifts of Asperger*. Pennsylvania: The Apsperger's Syndrome Institute.

Prince-Hughes, D. (2004). *Songs of the Gorilla Nation: My Journey Through Autism*. NY: Harmony Books.

Robison, J. E. (2007). *Look Me in the Eye*. New York: Crown.

Rusty's Morningstar Ranch. (2004). Retrieved July 4, 2009, from http://www.rmr.org/index.html.

Sawalich, S. (2006). *Music Within* [Motion Picture]. United States: Metro Goldwyn Mayer.

Spectrum Transition Program. (2010). *Spectrum College Transition Program*. Retrieved March 14, 2010, from http://www.spectrumcollegetransition.org/Home_Page.html

Stichter, J. P., Randolph, J., Gage, N., & Schmidt, C. (2007). A review of recommended social competency programs for students with autism spectrum disorders. *Exceptionality, 15*(4), 219–232.

Stout, C. (2009, June 7). Students with disabilities finding that higher education is within their grasp. *Memphis Commercial Appeal*. Retrieved June 29, 2009, from http://www.commercialappeal.com/news/2009/jun/07/college-bound/

Test, D. W. (2009). Evidence-based practices for helping secondary students with autism transition successfully to adulthood. *National Secondary Transition Technical Assistance Center*. Retrieved January 23, 2009, from www.nsttac.org/nsttac_presentations/autism2407.ppt

Think College! (2009a). *Differences between high school and college.* Retrieved June 19, 2009, from http://www.thinkcollege.net/for-families/high-school-v-college?

Think College! (2009b). *Transition Checklist.* Retrieved June 19, 2009, from http://www.thinkcollege.net/for-families/transition-checklist

Thoma, C. A., Saddler, S., & Held, M. F., (2002). Transition assessment practices in Nevada and Arizona: Are they tied to best practices? *Focus on Autism and Other Developmental Disabilities, 17*(4), 242–250.

Trachtenberg, T. (2008, April 2). More students with Asperger Syndrome going to college. *ABC News.* Retrieved January 22, 2009, from http://abcnews.go.com/GMA/Turning Points/Story?id=4568471&page=

Trudeau, M. (2008). An autistic student's journey to college. *National Public Radio.* Retrieved July 4, 2009, from http://www.npr.org/templates/story/story.php?storyId=94429083&ft=1&f=1007

University of Arizona. (2009). *Strategic Alternative Learning Techniques Center.* Retrieved July 5, 2009, from www.salt.arizona.edu

University of Iowa College of Education. (2009). *Realizing Educational and Career Hopes.* Retrieved July 5, 2009, from http://www.education.uiowa.edu/reach/

University of Kansas. (2009). *Transition Coalition.* Retrieved July 5, 2009, from http://www.transitioncoalition.org/transition/tcfiles/files/docs/Transition_Short_Courses_flyer_summer09-spring101237996553.pdf/Transition_Short_Courses_flyer_summer09-spring10.pdf

University of Massachusetts Boston. (2009). Institute for Community Inclusion. *Think College!* Retrieved July 5, 2009, from www.thinkcollege.net

University of Oregon. (2009). *Intocareers.* Retrieved July 5, 2009, from http://oregoncis.uoregon.edu/home/AboutCIS/CISFacts/tabid/125/Default.aspx

U.S. Department of Education. (2007). *Secondary Transition.* Retrieved January 23, 2009, from http://www.ideapartnership.org/oseppage.cfm?pageid=53

VanBergeijk, E., Klin, A., & Volkmar, F. (2008). Supporting more able students on the autism spectrum: College and beyond. *Journal Autism Developmental Disorders, 38,* 1359–1370.

Wehman, P. (2002). A new era: Revitalizing special education for children and their families. *Focus on Autism and Other Developmental Disabilities, 17*(4), 194–197.

Wehman, P., Gibson, K., Brooke, V., & Unger, D. (1999). Transition from school to competitive employment: Illustrations of competence for two young women with severe mental retardation. *Focus On Autism and Other Developmental Disabilities, 13*(3), 130–143.

Whitney, S. (2009). Doing your homework: Making the transition from school to work & future education. *Wrightslaw.* Retrieved February 17, 2009, from http://www.wrightslaw.com/heath/transition.work.htm

Wilson, K. E. (1998). Centers for independent living in support of transition. *Focus on Autism and Other Developmental Disabilities, 13*(4), 246–252.

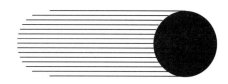

Name Index

Subject Index